P9-DXZ-740

Widespread acclaim for IDEOLOGY OF DEATH...

"Compelling....Weiss convincingly reminds us that ideas are no mere playthings; they develop a certain logic and have consequences, often dreadful ones."—Michael Sherry, *New York Times Book Review*

"A magnificent achievement...superbly written, analytically penetrating, and supported by a wealth of knowledge, this fascinating study makes abundantly clear that the Holocaust had widespread roots in German culture." —Robert J. Soucy, Oberlin College

"Deeply disturbing...*Ideology of Death* irrefutably lays bare the black thread of anti-Semitism woven into the very fabric of German history."—*Philadelphia Inquirer*

"In this important book, Weiss convincingly argues that the plan to murder Europe's Jews was implicit from the start in Nazi rhetoric." —*Choice*

"Scrupulously done history and the best explanation I've seen to date for the question in the subtitle."—Alan W. Bock, *Orange County Register*

"A valuable history of German anti-Semitism."—*American Historical Review*

"The Holocaust happened in Germany, Weiss argues, because 'the special nature of German and Austrian history' gave an utterly racist form of anti-Semitism 'immense power.'...An effective overview of an essential subject."—Mary Carroll, *Booklist* (starred review)

"Undeservedly neglected....The book is a narrative history of ideas, tracing the influence of anti-Jewish stereotypes on German and Austrian society from the early 19th century to their gory climax in the Third Reich."—Robert S. Wistrich, *Commentary*

"A convincing portrait of the ways in which discoverable historical forces and developments prepared the way over the course of hundreds of years for the explosive carnage and cruelty of our own century....Weiss carefully interweaves the history of anti-Semitism and German history."—Allen J. Share, *Louisville Courier-Journal*

IDEOLOGY OF DEATH

IDEOLOGY
OF DEATH

Why the Holocaust
Happened in Germany

JOHN WEISS

ELEPHANT PAPERBACKS
Ivan R. Dee, Publisher, Chicago

IDEOLOGY OF DEATH. Copyright © 1996 by John Weiss. All rights reserved, including the right to reproduce this book or portions thereof in any form. For information, address: Ivan R. Dee, Inc., 1332 North Halsted Street, Chicago 60622. First Elephant Paperback edition published 1997. Manufactured in the United States of America and printed on acid-free paper.

Library of Congress Cataloging-in-Publication Data:
Weiss, John, 1927–
    Ideology of death : why the Holocaust happened in Germany / John Weiss.
        p.   cm.
    Includes bibliographical references and index.
    ISBN 1-56663-174-2
    1. Antisemitism—Germany—History.   2. Antisemitism—Austria—History.
    3. Christianity and antisemitism.   4. Holocaust, Jewish (1939–1945)—Germany—
    Causes.   I. Title.
    DS146.G4W43   1997
    305.892'4043—dc20   95-22792

For the victims

PREFACE

DESPITE a vast literature about anti-Semitism and the Holocaust, we do not yet understand why the destruction of the Jews was conceived and implemented by the Germans. In many nations, of course, the Jews have been reviled and persecuted as a people whose religion or innate racial traits supposedly make them cunning heretics and destructive social parasites. But only among the Germans did racist stereotypes evolve into a popular mandated ideology of such lethal force as to end in the horror of the death camps. To understand this, the most important and difficult historical question of our time, it is necessary to explore the special nature of German and Austrian history, for therein lies the key to the immense power of anti-Semitism among millions of Germans and the reasons why, long before the Nazis, the historical basis of their success was built.

In 1945 the widespread revelations of the horror of the Holocaust caused some to seek its origins in the full sweep of modern German history. These efforts were unconvincing. The necessary evidence was unavailable, and one could not tell which social classes and groups did or did not adopt political anti-Semitism and why. In a counterreaction, today most historians believe that the Nazis had no deep roots in German history, that anti-Semitism in Germany was not essentially different from that of some other nations—notably France and Eastern Europe—and that therefore no long-range historical connections should be drawn. Moreover, most historians have come to believe that anti-Semitism was not the major cause of the rise of the Nazis to power, and that the Holocaust was the result of decisions taken by only a handful of obsessed Nazi leaders. Some have even claimed, "No Hitler, no Holocaust."

I believe these views to be incorrect. It seems evident to me that historians have vastly underrated the Nazis' adroit use of anti-Semitism in political campaigns, the resounding echo their hatred of the Jews found among large sections of the German public, and above all the long decades of historical preparation that made that echo deafening. We have also failed to recognize the decades-long power of anti-Semitism among those groups and classes decisive for Nazi votes and Hitler's appointment as German chancellor. I have interwoven the history of the political uses of anti-Semitism among the Germans with major political and economic events to reveal how anti-Semitism and German history were related to the rise of the Nazis and the Holocaust. Even as anti-Semitism began to wane in Western Europe in the 1800s, in Germany and Austria it grew rapidly during the Napoleonic era, became a forceful popular ideology in the 1870s, and in the 1890s gained lasting and intense support among the generation that eventually brought Hitler to power.

Few doubt that traditional Christian enmity toward Judaism reinforced modern racism. But I hope to demonstrate why Christian anti-Judaism was much more intense among German Lutherans and Austro-German Catholics than among Christian clergy elsewhere in the West, such that in the nineteenth century the first powerful anti-Semitic mass movements were founded by prestigious German and Austrian clergy and Christian rightists. Although the liberal and secular ideas of the French and British Enlightenment created a cultural counterforce to racism, they failed to do so in Germany and Austria. The majority of churchmen in the West, though usually anti-Judaic and sometimes racist, were less willing or able than their German counterparts to join with powerful groups capable of harming the Jewish community.

But Christianity alone could not produce a Holocaust. It was the singular path of modern German history that ultimately gave anti-Semites the power to destroy the Jewish community. Racism was increasingly used by upper-class reactionaries, middle-class nationalists, and lower-class populists as a weapon against the growing influence of democratic liberalism, economic modernization, and calls for social reform. Long before the Nazis, millions of Germans and Austrians denounced Jews and "international Jewry" as both symbol and cause of challenges to their power, interests, status, and values. Caught up in a conflict they were far too weak to influence, German Jews became the victims of a uniquely powerful culture of racism. Without this historical base, anti-Semitism would not have exploded with such fury after 1918, producing, as it did, hundreds of groups with hundreds of thousands of followers whose ideas were no different from those of the Nazis.

The secret of Nazi success was their ability to focus a preexisting anti-Semitism against the Weimar Republic in order to exploit the rage aroused by the many threats to the old order that burst upon a defeated Germany and a dismembered Austrian Empire in 1918. Racism was the cement that enabled the Nazis to hold together a variety of disparate constituencies which, though racist long before Hitler, were otherwise separated by contradictory interests. Fusing historical anti-Semitism with the many traumas plaguing specific groups, the Nazis broke traditional party allegiances to gain the highest percentage of votes ever recorded by any political party in German history. This could not have occurred if Hitler's hatreds were unique. In fact, Hitler's racism was typical of millions of lower-middle-class Germans and Austro-Germans of his generation. These common attitudes explain why "racial purification"—or "ethnic cleansing," as we would call it today—had the voluntary support of so many public and private institutions and the vast personnel necessary for the unprecedented task of isolating, oppressing, and murdering millions. The Nazi drive to conquer a racial empire in the east entailed the destruction of Jews and millions of Slavs as an essential component of Nazi social and economic policies, and was not, as is claimed, the arbitrary decision of Hitler and a few leaders. The fascist parties of Eastern Europe, though equally virulent, could not draw upon the industrial power of a Germany to conquer the lands containing millions of Jews.

But I do not wish to revive bankrupt theories of collective responsibility. Even at the height of Hitler's popularity about half of all Germans, mainly but not solely progressives or leftists, rejected the racist violence of the Nazis, though they could not halt it. Consequently I discuss the earlier political and intellectual allegiances that made them oppose the persecution of the Jews. I conclude by showing how the German bureaucratic, academic, and military elites in place at the end of the war, though heavily implicated in Nazi terror, nevertheless avoided punishment and, conditioned by a century of racism, were unencumbered by any sense of personal guilt. Shocked by the Western reaction to their voluntary complicity, they had little desire to uncover the historical roots of anti-Semitism among the Germans, even as they absolved themselves and their peers.

The Holocaust is unique, but it is not unintelligible. Like all historical traumas, it is subject to a rational analysis of cause and effect. We are too ready to believe that the causes of racial hatred are located chiefly in the deep recesses of deviant psyches. We remain relatively unaware of the particular historical situations and social traumas that, in times of crisis, release and sanction the almost universal need to punish racial or religious outsiders. Sadly, as it recedes into the past the Holocaust takes on the aura of a sacred event, an abstraction closed to human understanding, incomprehensible to the intellect. One is left with a sense of despair and frustration; what we cannot explain we cannot prevent. "Never again" becomes a pious hope, for we are rendered incapable of distinguishing between the ever-present but transient obscenities of thousands of anti-Semitic incidents reported each year, and a full-blown ideology of hate which points to deeply rooted social tensions and presages mass violence. Unexplained, the horror is mourned, memorialized, and given over to the ruminations of moralists, psychologists, and theologians. They have much of value to say, but they cannot tell us what we most need to know: how it was that in one of the most advanced nations of the West, millions of innocent civilians were sacrificed in the service of an ancient and barbarous mythology.

The conditions that create genocidal violence are not unique. As German history demonstrates, racist myths repeated over decades and manipulated to "explain" the sufferings of dominant groups can generate overwhelming support for a powerful and murderous ideology. In today's post–cold war environment, as minorities struggle to redefine borders drawn without regard to religious rivalries or ethnic integrity, the world witnesses a resurgence of ethnic and religious conflict. Given the intensification of global economic traumas and the competition for decreasing resources among expanding populations, a clear understanding of the underlying social, political, and economic causes that feed racial hatreds and nationalist passions becomes imperative. The study of the origins of genocidal hate in Germany may serve as an example of the ways in which words and deeds, when reinforced by profound social tensions, can foster powerful ideologies that threaten mass violence. By understanding mankind's darkest moment, we may enter the twenty-first century better prepared to defuse racial unrest before it erupts into the conflagrations of tomorrow.

More than any of the catastrophes of history, the Holocaust raises agonizing questions of moral culpability about highly charged matters of ethnicity and religion. I believe, therefore, that the reader should know the ethnic and religious backgrounds of those who write about it, if only to be alerted to possible intellectual manipulation in the service of a hidden agenda. This applies to me more than most, I think, because I stress the strong influence of Christian anti-Judaism on modern secular racism, and because my name will lead many to assume I am Jewish and thus may harbor a distorting antagonism toward Christianity.

I am neither Jewish nor of Jewish origin, although in the United States the name Weiss indicates the opposite. My father was a Catholic born in Austria, where Weiss is often a Christian name indicating neither Jewish origins nor past family conversion. Indeed, a few well-known Nazis bore what Americans assume to be Jewish names: Alfred Rosenberg was the chief Nazi ideologist, Wilhelm Weiss was an editor of the official Nazi paper, Martin Weiss was one of the commandants of Dachau. As for me, my father was a Catholic follower of the popular Detroit radio priest and anti-Semite, Father Charles Coughlin; my mother was a Protestant of English peasant stock; and I was raised as a member of the Presbyterian church. I grew up in a Protestant (Slavic-German) working-class neighborhood where there were no Jewish families and where anti-Semitism was more or less taken for granted. Finally, I was a student at Henry Ford

Trade School from 1941 to 1944. This was long after Ford had been forced to mute his famous anti-Semitism, of course, but Jewish boys were not welcome in his school.

I am bothered by the assumption of many scholars that an interest in anti-Semitism indicates Jewish origins, and the companion idea that it is somehow not a "normal" historical topic for mainstream historians of Europe, Jewish or not. Anti-Semitism was far too powerful and successful to be, as it is, only briefly noted in general accounts of European history before the Nazis. As for me, if I have gained anything from the misperceptions of others, it is some slight awareness of the ambivalent position of Jewish intellectuals among a Christian majority. Even with the best of intentions, others often do not take one's views at face value and regard them as conditioned by ethnic or religious considerations. Be that as it may, I hope I have not bent over backward or forward to compensate. I do not believe I have exaggerated the role of German and Austrian Christianity in modern anti-Semitism. If I have, it is not because I am Jewish and bitter, it is because I am wrong.

I am grateful to Otto Feinstein and Hayden White who first started me on this subject. Professor Allon Gal of the Ben-Gurion University of the Negev deserves special thanks for his wisdom and our many conversations about related topics. I thank my older students, especially those who lived through the terrible years in Germany. They have encouraged my views and often modified them with their own. I also learned much from those Austrians and Germans with whom I had long discussions about fascism during my student years there in the 1950s. Because most of them were ex-Nazis, they would not approve of this book. Thanks are also due to Professor Jack Judd for helping me find time for the book and to Professor Ruth Zerner for her extensive knowledge of the Holocaust. The writings of Professor Franklin Littell have been very helpful indeed. No one named, of course, is in the least responsible for my conclusions.

A book like this depends heavily on the research of many scholars, and the reader will find some of them listed in the notes. I should add that I am especially indebted to the work of Omer Bartov, Thomas Childers, Christopher R. Browning, Istvan Deak, Martin Gilbert, Arthur Hertzberg, Raul Hilberg, Robert Gellately, Jacob Katz, Richard S. Levy, Walter Laqueur, Arno Mayer, George L. Mosse, Ingo Mueller, Detlev Peukert, Robert Proctor, and Peter D. Stachura. Their studies are invaluable to historians concerned with Germany, anti-Semitism and the Holocaust.

None of the people named above, of course, is in any way responsible for my conclusions.

The help of my wife, Barbara Hart, cannot possibly be overestimated.

She has worked her way through many lengthy drafts, and her invaluable and extensive comments have helped me write clearly, succinctly, and always with the needs of the reader in mind. Finally, there is nothing so valuable as a fine editor, and in Ivan Dee I have been blessed.

J. W.

June 1995
Nyack, New York

CONTENTS

IDEOLOGY OF DEATH

1: THE CHRISTIAN LEGACY

It is a marvelous thing to observe the Jewish people existing for so many years and always in misery; for it is necessary as proof of Jesus Christ both that they should continue to exist, and that they should be miserable because they crucified him.

—Pascal, 1670

IN 1633 plague ravaged the village of Oberammergau in Bavaria. Believing they were being punished for displeasing God, the villagers vowed to show repentance by performing a Passion Play every ten years to honor the resurrection of Jesus. The play is still presented and, though rewritten after World War II, remains a distorted version of the New Testament. Its perversions of Gospel arise from a compulsion to vilify the Jews as willing tools of Satan, collectively responsible for the death of Christ. Hitler himself praised the play: "It is vital that the Passion Play be continued at Oberammergau, for never has the menace of Jewry been so convincingly portrayed."[1] The Nazis honored the play as a racially vital event of folk culture. In 1934, on its three hundredth anniversary, Nazi dignitaries attended the performance to watch as Jesus and his disciples were transformed into heroic Aryans beset by viciously stereotyped Semitic demons.

The tragic history of hostility between Christianity and Judaism is well known. When Christianity dominated Europe, Jewish communities were slaughtered, driven out, or forced into ghettos and restricted to demeaning petty trades. But in Germany and Austria the force of Christian anti-Judaism was more powerful than elsewhere, lasted longer, and more strongly reinforced the secular racism of the modern era—the belief that the inborn, unchangeable nature of the Jews—their blood—as well as their religion make them mortal enemies of society. In Catholic Austria in the 1890s, for example, the most powerful politician after the emperor, Mayor Karl Lueger of Vienna, an idol of the young Hitler, gained millions of Austro-German votes for his anti-Semitic Christian Social party, a party founded and inspired by Catholic intellectuals and priests. In Germany the first modern political anti-Semitic movement began in Berlin

3

in 1879 and was led by no less a figure than a royal chaplain to the court of the kaisers, Pastor Adolf Stoecker, known as the "King of Berlin." At the turn of the century, Georg von Schoenerer, leader of the Austrian pan-German movement, attracted 200,000 zealous, virulently racist followers, including young Hitler. A Nazi in all but name, Schoenerer urged the Austrians to break with Rome and convert to Lutheranism, to him and hundreds of thousands of German racists the only true Germanic religion. His conversion efforts were aided by Lutheran ministers from Germany, who openly declared their desire to continue the ancient struggle against the killers of Christ.

Even during the days of the Weimar Republic in the 1920s, constant harangues against the "Jewish" republic were preached from the pulpits of Evangelical Lutheran ministers, and many local pastors allowed the SA (the Sturmabteilung), Hitler's private army, to decorate their churches with swastikas for Sunday services. Protestant Prussia was the home of the first reactionary elites to sanction and support the Nazis, and it was among the fundamentalist Protestant peasants of Prussia that late-nineteenth-century anti-Semitic political parties made their not inconsiderable gains. The same peasants were also the first Germans to vote for the Nazis in significant numbers. In France, by contrast, though the Catholic church supported political anti-Semitic movements, as during the Dreyfus Affair, a powerful secular and republican tradition was a countervailing force; anti-Semites were never politically strong enough to harm the Jewish community until the Nazi conquest gave them free reign. Even then, numerous Catholic and Protestant leaders protested and even tried to prevent the Nazis' deportation of the Jews, something that the overwhelming majority of German and Austrian clergy never did.

Accompanied by pogrom and massacre, the cry that "the Jews" killed Christ has rung down through centuries. Until recently, Christian theologians and the Christian masses have held all Jews, and for all time, responsible for the events of two thousand years ago in Palestine. In the powerful documentary film of Claude Lanzmann, Shoah, a Polish peasant woman emerges from a Catholic church to tell how, during World War II, she witnessed Jews being gassed by Germans, adding with great sincerity how she "remembers" them crying out to Jesus and Mary for mercy as they died. Another Pole declares he heard of a rabbi in a village who, allowed to speak to his people during an SS roundup, instructed them to obey, saying, "Did we not kill Christ, and did we ourselves not cry out, Let the blood be on our heads?"

The past lives in memory and belief; early Christianity is a state of mind, not a closed time in history. Because Christ and Christianity stemmed from Judaism, the relationship between the two religions has always been complex, subtle, and explosive. Before Christianity there were conflicts between Jews and others. Although often fierce, such conflicts cannot be compared with the profound hostility so deadly during the height of the Christian medieval era, nor with the systematic, popular, and intense anti-Semitism so prevalent in Central and Eastern Europe in modern times. While we now invoke with ecumenical approval the Judeo-Christian tradition as though it spoke with one moral voice of humane concern and mutual toleration, until very recently this tradition has been one of unremitting conflict, and the Jews have been its victims.

To the early followers of Christ, of course, Judaism and Christianity were not separate religions; Christ was the Messiah of the Hebrew Scriptures sent to fulfill the prophecies of Judaism. Without official status within the Jewish community, Christ nevertheless claimed that he could interpret the Law and Torah. When opposed by the established religious authorities of the Jewish community, he denounced them as hypocrites and betrayers of the faith. When his disciples justified Christ's claim to be the Messiah by invoking the authority of the God of Abraham, the religious authorities of Jerusalem could scarcely be expected to surrender their sacred guardianship to one who not only violated Torah but declared that he possessed the divine power to distinguish between the spirit and the letter of the Law. Yet Jesus could not deny the intense religious passions surging within him: he had heard the voice of God. Such disputes cannot be compromised; conflict was inevitable. Nor could Christ's miracles persuade his enemies: Christ might change water into wine, heal the sick, or even raise the dead, but others claimed to do these things and were believed, though they and he were accused of gaining their powers from demons, not from God. The century referred to as the "Age of the Messiahs" was a time when many spoke with God and many more believed them.

In accord with Jewish law, Christ was found guilty of heresy and turned over to the Romans. Pontius Pilate, assumed to be unwilling to resist the will of a rapacious Jewish mob, was in fact a brutal oppressor, later punished by Rome itself for his atrocities as provincial governor. Pilate did not need to be persuaded to execute a potential revolutionary against Roman rule. To convert these events into the accusation that "the Jews" killed Christ is neither the historical nor the Gospel truth. The New Testament tells us that crowds of welcoming Jews greeted Christ when he appeared; moreover, the vast majority of Jews, scattered about the empire, never even heard of Jesus. Nor did the disciples, including Paul, accuse "the Jews" of killing Christ. Themselves Jews, they lived before the separation of the two religions. Then as now, Christ's followers believed themselves loyal to the Messiah promised by the covenant of the God of Abraham with the Jewish people.

The accusation of Jewish deicide contradicts Christian theology itself.

If God gave his only begotten son to atone for sinning mankind, then mankind is responsible for his crucifixion, and by accepting Christ one acknowledges his sacrifice as necessary for the salvation of one's guilty soul. If collective guilt means anything, then all mankind is guilty of the death of Christ. For Christians, Christ's death and resurrection were divinely ordained, the ultimate miracles they hoped would convince their fellow Jews that he was indeed the promised Messiah. There is no place in Christian sacred mythology for mere human crime. Yet nothing reveals the anxieties of the Christian psyche more than the need to believe in the guilt of the Jews. Unable to deny the divine basis of their own faith in the parent religion, Christians attempted to resolve their anxiety with the intricacies of theology and constantly renewed hostility against those who remained loyal to Judaism. Biblical scholars have found the charge of deicide false, but no amount of scholarship can change the minds of those driven by intense psychological need. Hence for centuries Christians have demanded that Jews testify to the truth of Christianity by conversion. Even today the myth lives on: some 60 percent of religiously conservative white Protestants in the United States, polled in 1987, agreed: "The Jews can never be forgiven for what they did to Jesus until they accept him as the true savior."[2]

After the Hebrew Scriptures became the Christian Old Testament, for Christians the sacred scriptures of the Hebrews *must* prove that Christ was the Messiah. A vast array of subtle interpretation by way of allegory, metaphor, and arcane symbolism was and is used to do so. In the early centuries the Old Testament became a "vast quarry with no other function than to provide, by any exegesis however farfetched, arguments for his claims."[3] Because Judaism was held to validate the central Christian truth, Jewish refusal to accept Christ was soon viewed as nothing less than resistance to the will of the one God of Judaism and Christ. The persistence of Judaism inevitably created profound doubts. Ultimately the Jewish denial of Christ's divinity became the true deicide, an act which every Jew commits simply by remaining faithful to Judaism. No pagan or heathen ever held such power over Christianity—indeed, this is the psychological source of the legend of the occult powers of the Jews, for what other people has had the power to deny for millennia their own God? Loving concern for the salvation of one's former coreligionists easily turns into righteous anger at their "arrogant" refusal to acknowledge the "truth" of their own sacred works. Much of the New Testament is meant to prove that Christianity is the divine fulfillment of Judaism. In the different versions of the passion of Christ, responsibility for his death is gradually shifted away from some Jews in Palestine to a collective entity called "the Jews." By the Fourth Gospel, John, the Jews are regarded as the bitter enemies of Christianity, the two religions distinct and separate.

For Christians, a Jew could be true to Judaism only if he or she became a Christian, the new chosen people; yet the vast majority of Jews remained within the faith of their fathers. In a time drenched with religion, compromise was impossible. If Christianity is true, Judaism is false; if not, then Christianity is blasphemy. Even today the Vatican and Protestant Fundamentalists cannot recognize Judaism as a separate and valid religion, for that would be tantamount to announcing that Jesus was not prophesied by the Hebrew Scriptures. In the early centuries, passions were at their most intense, for the identity of Christianity was being formed, and it could only be done at the expense of the parent religion. Mythology, as yet untempered by secularism or science, made it inevitable that Christians would turn against the Jews, the one people among them whose faith denied Christ and whose religious credentials could hardly be ignored.

The first followers and missionaries of Christ were, in their own minds, Jews who obeyed Jewish law and felt themselves part of the Jewish community, persuading their people of the truth of Christ. Paul and Peter expected that the Jews of the Diaspora would accept Christ, and they never argued that "the Jews" killed Christ. At first Paul held that in all things one must obey Jewish law. But the failure to convert significant numbers of Jews and the successful conversion of Gentiles inevitably brought Paul to absolve Gentiles from obedience: "No man is ever justified by doing what the Law demands, but only through faith in Jesus Christ." To this he added the revealing phrase: "For if righteousness comes by Law, then Christ died for nothing."

When personal faith in Christ overrode Jewish law, Christianity ceased to be a Jewish sect, and yet no one, least of all Christ, had set out to found a new religion. Accepting Christ became the central belief and also the greatest obstacle to compromise with Judaism. By the second century C.E., Gentiles dominated the church and drew little meaning from Jewish laws and customs. They were condemned, falsely, as a collection of rituals without moral meaning, because they denied the believer a personal relationship with God through Christ. In the early centuries, deicide was fixed in Christian consciousness as a Jewish crime, and Christianity was constantly validated by denunciations of Judaism and Jews as bereft of deeply felt personal moral precepts. From Luther through Pastor Stoecker and the numerous anti-Semitic movements of the nineteenth century, the Jewish denial of their own God would be the "explanation" for their alleged immoral influence on society.

Still, there were Jews loyal to Judaism who also believed Christ was the Messiah, and Christians who saw no contradiction in observing the religious practices of Judaism. In the minds of the early Christian church fathers, therefore, was always the fear that Christians might return to

Judaism; the separation must be made absolute to avoid risking the salvation of Christians. Thus not only ignorant or ill-willed Christians reviled the Jews but some of the most respected and saintly representatives of the church, for those whose faith in Christ was most intense were all the more likely to believe that the Jews deliberately and maliciously denied him. By the fourth century, for Christian theologians the Jew was "a monster, a theological abstraction of superhuman cunning and malice."[4] Saint Jerome accused the Jews of deliberately falsifying their own Scriptures in order to hide the prophecies of Christ. Saint John of Chrysostom—beloved by the people, one of the greatest of the Greek fathers, and a rigorous opponent of immorality whose homilies are still studied in the seminaries of the church—in 1909 was named the patron saint of priests by Pope Pius X; yet Saint John found no insult too vile to hurl at the Jews: wild beasts, devil worshipers, murderers of children: "God hates them, and so also should all good Christians." Christians must cease consorting with Jews during Passover and Easter, Saint John advised, at the time when the Jews had crucified Christ. On Judgment Day, he thundered, the Lord would say, "Depart from me, for you have had intercourse with my murderers."[5]

Saint Ambrose, adviser to the emperor Gratian, defended the burning of synagogues because they were places "of unbelief which God Himself has condemned."[6] Saint Gregory of Nyssa, the champion of orthodox theology, called the Jews "murderers of the Lord, assassins of the prophets, rebels and detesters of God; they outrage the law, resist grace, and repudiate the faith of their fathers." They were "companions of the devil, a race of vipers, informers, calumniators... demons, accursed, detested... enemies of all that is beautiful."[7] Saint Simeon Stylites, who punished his flesh by living for thirty years on a pillar in the Syrian desert, was famed for his hatred of the Jews. Their denial of Christ seemed to mock his agonies, and perhaps their very existence helped create doubts that he could only suppress by self-punishment. Saint Augustine, second only to Saint Paul in theological brilliance, declared the Jews the instrument of Satan. In Renaissance Italy, Savonarola, briefly the spiritual ruler of Florence, pursued by visions of the devil, drove the Jews from the city. For him too the Jews were the tools of Satan. As Saint John Chrysostom wrote: If your love of Christ is unlimited, so too there can be no limits to your "battle with those who hate Him."[8] Luther would outdo them all.

To the truly religious, history is a scenario written by God; all great events have a divine cause and purpose. In the famed witness theory, as it is called, Saint Paul explained why the Jews failed to accept Christ, and why the Second Coming—then expected almost momentarily—had not yet occurred. Saint Paul held his failure to convert the Jews as divinely ordained: God himself had made the Jews disobedient by "hardening their hearts" against Christ, and he had done so in order to allow time for the conversion of the Gentiles, who would be witness to his wrath upon the Jews. In the end he would redeem the Jews, but not until all the Gentiles had been brought into the church. Then, just before the Day of Judgment, "the whole of Israel will be saved"; proof that Christ was mankind's savior would be irrefutable, and all mankind would be united in Christ. Until then Jewish suffering, preordained, would demonstrate the fate of any who sought righteousness without Christ. Paradoxically, the rejection of Christ by his own people was thus converted into a sign of his and their sacred mission. Anxious to still murderous antagonisms, the leaders of Catholic Christianity thus insisted that the punishment of the Jews be left to the Lord, and the Vatican chastised those who attacked Jews with murderous intent.

But the witness theory made the failure of Jewish belief in Christ seem an obstacle to the salvation of mankind. At first the reaction was benign. Early Christian mythology is filled with tales of the miraculous conversion of individual Jews through the intervention of the Lord. A Jew stabs the Host, symbol of the body of Christ, blood flows, and the blasphemer falls to his knees trembling in fear, converted by the power of Christ. Now truly the Lord's anointed, he gives far more cause to rejoice than the conversion of any number of pagans. But over time, hatred for the unconverted became the counterpart of the joy experienced through their conversion. And even if the punishment of the Jews was supposed to be left to God, those who harmed them could claim they were "doing the work of the Lord." How else does God work except through human instruments? The dangerous symbolic power of Jewry over Christians remained, and unlike Saint Paul, Gentiles were not interested in reconciliation through compromise. It is no surprise that those saints who preached the imminent coming of the Final Days also preached most violently against the Jews. Persuasion yielded to righteous demands and finally violent anger with a people so satanic as deliberately to thwart their own God's plan for the salvation of mankind. For the Jews of Europe, as the Crusades would show, it was a terrible burden to bear.

During the early Christian centuries the myth of the Jews as an avaricious race of parasites added force to that of the Jews as deicides. As Roman influence waned and Christian clergy gained power, they successfully restricted the activities of Jews, creating the basis for endless calumnies about the alleged Jewish attraction to dishonest practices in petty commerce, secondhand trade, and moneylending, as well as complaints that the Jews refused to assimilate and preferred parasitic and nonproductive commercial activities in order to dominate local and international trade and harm honest Christians. Leaving aside the question of whether or not small-scale commerce, lending money, and international trade are parasitical activities, and if so to whom and by what criteria, the attack against the Jews for their supposed unwillingness to do productive work became one of the first of many self-fulfilling prophecies common in the history of Christian attitudes. For the accumulated hostility of Christians in the early centuries restricted Jews to such activities, keeping them, with rare exceptions, in the lowest, least profitable, and most despised branches of commerce until the late eighteenth century. In pagan antiquity and the advanced civilizations of the East, no such accusations were made, for there Jews were found in almost all vocations, and banking and trade were occupations of high status, even as they are today.

Jewish settlers first came to Europe as international merchants bringing the much desired products of the advanced civilizations of the Middle East, China, India, and Spain. Small and flourishing communities of Jews were soon established along the great European trade routes and in urban centers. By the ninth century the Jews of Europe enjoyed their greatest success as international merchants and traders; the words Jew and merchant were virtually synonymous. Along with Greeks, Syrians, and Italians—Christians all—Jews were the advance agents of a society yet to come. Their knowledge of and connections with the culture, products, customs, and languages of the East gave them a powerful advantage over competing Europeans.

Increasingly, however, clerical influence isolated the Jews from Christians. Where they could, the clergy forbade intermarriage, prevented the participation—still common—of Christians in Jewish holidays and services, nullified evidence given by a Jew in court, and made it a crime to convert to Judaism. But the activities of the Jews were valuable to the secular authorities of Europe. Trade brought luxury goods, stimulated production, opened new markets, and increased general well-being. Emperors, princes, and regional rulers often encouraged and welcomed Jewish settlers and protected them with special rights. In medieval society each social group had different privileges and duties, and local rulers who desired economic growth and were not excessively pious willingly granted special protection to Jewish merchants. Some towns competed to offer better terms. Though the clergy opposed it, princes and even some bishops put secular interests first. One German bishop invited Jews to his domains, granted them a generous charter, and exclaimed to his emperor: "They should enjoy the most favorable legal treatment accorded the Jewish people in any city of the German Empire."[9]

Like all merchants, Jews wanted their property, persons, and freedom to trade protected from extortion and arbitrary regulation. They also needed to give credit and change or transfer currency. Tiny Jewish communities needed protection in a crude and hostile environment as well as the freedoms we associate with the unhindered laws of the modern marketplace and the sanctity of contracts. These were revolutionary demands. In medieval society free enterprise was not even a subject of theoretical speculation. Serfs were not free wage earners; land conferred status and power and was not simply real estate to be bought and sold as the market determined; prices and markets for local products were regulated by guilds. Moreover, traditional practices created a bewildering variety of local limits on commercial activities. Thus demands for economic freedom were often viewed as "Jewish" and subversive of the old ways— as ninteenth-century reactionaries would insist. But there was of course nothing ethnic or religious about the needs of Jewish merchants. In the Muslim East, foreign Christian merchants from a variety of nations requested and received these same rights. Long before Adam Smith argued for economic freedom so that the "invisible hand" might generate wealth, Caliph Omar II, petitioned to limit the price of staples, replied, "This is not our business; only Allah can set prices."

In Europe the cooperation between Jewish communities and secular rulers was challenged by clerical authorities. Were not the Jews the connecting link with the worldly luxuries of the East, encouraged by princes who scorned Christian asceticism? In the ninth century, during the relative enlightenment of the Carolingian Renaissance, Saint Agobard, archbishop and learned reformer, was outraged by the special status conferred upon the enemies of Christ. He claimed that Jewish success would confuse the simple and gullible, who would see the Jews as devout, prosperous, and favored by princes. The archbishop noted bitterly that Jews had even converted some of their Christian employees. To the son of the great Charlemagne, Agobard complained: "The Jews, abusing the naiveté of Christians, deceitfully pride themselves on being dear to your heart . . . "[10] Agobard angrily demanded that the special rights of Jews be revoked, their intermingling with Christians forbidden, and the building of their synagogues ended. The Jewish merchant communities contradicted the Christian prophecy that the wrath of God would make them a despised and wretched people, condemned to suffer until their conversion. Down to our own time, the wealth of some highly visible members of the Jewish community has generated a righteous anger not directed at rich Christian merchants.

Over generations, ethnic minorities tend to assimilate if the majority population is not extremely hostile, but in medieval society, movement between classes and occupations was extremely limited. The individual was closely identified with his social group, and each group was seen as a fixed part of a divinely established and static social order. Jews nevertheless began to move into other vocations. Gradually acquiring land by purchase and as payment for debts, they cultivated it and became well known as vintners. But land was the primary source of power and status. Through a chain of mutual obligations sanctioned by religion and stretching from village and peasant to prince and pope, the landowner was the vital link in a society with little commerce and no industry. The large landowner, with his power over serfs and free peasants, was the patron of the church, empowered to appoint the local priest. Jewish landowners became a contradiction in terms. By 1200 church councils feared that Jewish landowners would refuse to pay church tithes and might convert their serfs or even demand a voice in the appointment of priests.

For Jews, landowning became dangerous. Life in the countryside put one at the mercy of the most primitive and hostile Christians. Wealth in land, easily seized, made one vulnerable. The countryside also lacked the protection offered by the communal strength of an urban Jewish quarter as well as proximity to secular rulers with an economic interest in protecting the Jewish community. Christian clergy pressured their coreligionists to refuse to sell land to Jews, warning that in a Christian society Jews should not be allowed to purchase land or receive it as debt payment. Christians who traded with Jews who had not paid tithes to the church were threatened with excommunication. Ironically, as they became less and less evident on the land, Jews were denounced as they would be by modern racists: Peter the Venerable, abbot of Cluny, accused them of being an urban people content to live from the labor of others rather than by toil in the fields. The abbot did not complain, of course, that the aristocracy and clergy also avoided the pleasures of such work, preferring to live from the tithes, dues, and labor of the peasantry.

So the common myth of modern anti-Semites was born. Jews avoid manual labor for the easier life of commerce. Yet Jews were famous artisans in the Eastern civilizations and were especially noted in early medieval Europe for their skills in glassblowing, cloth dyeing, and metal and gold work. Here too, Jewish participation was gradually ended by Christian restrictions. Free choice of work was not a medieval value. Guildmasters determined who would be allowed entrance into the guilds, and thus who might eventually become a master or worker in a small business. The guilds were Christian guilds, with Christian ceremonies, rituals, and holidays, their patrons usually churchmen. Consequently, guildsmen and clergy pressed secular authorities to exclude Jews from the guilds and permit Christians to take over guilds originally started by Jews. Gradually Jews were excluded from the crafts. As greed and faith forced the Jews out of the working class, they also turned many Jewish craftsmen into supporters of free enterprise before the fact, for some petitioned secular authorities for permission to practice their trades without restriction. Because it offered economic opportunities to all, free enterprise aided persecuted minorities. Thus, already in the medieval centuries, guildsmen and clergy adopted the notion popular among European anti-Semites in the late nineteenth century: free enterprise is not only a threat to a traditional and stable economic order, it is a Jewish threat. Whatever their personal preference, increasingly the Jews found relative safety only in towns and commerce. Forced to operate on the margins, they looked to find their way in pioneering enterprises not already occupied by Christian masters. New techniques were needed for survival—door-to-door selling, new products, trading in secondhand goods, and, much later, of course, low markups combined with high turnover. Well into our own time, these business activities would become associated with "being Jewish." And so the old accusation was born: the Jews, innately immoral, deal in shoddy and secondhand goods; they haggle, peddle, cut prices, force out honest businessmen, and cheat the customer as well. Accused of violating the ethical norms of the staid and respectable Christian guilds, the Jews could not safely respond that guildsmen were protecting their own monopolies at the expense of their customers, as some princes pointed out. When, in the nineteenth century, the petty monopolies and inherited regulations of the guilds gradually succumbed to the onslaught of free enterprise, German and Austrian guildsmen held the Jews responsible and denounced them in the most vicious terms. In a tradition that would continue to the Nazis, small businessmen and artisans, fearing the harsh imperatives of free competition, were famous for their overwhelming support of anti-Semitic politicians.

Through the ages the Jews have been denounced as cowards, a trading people fearing physical confrontation, and this in spite of their well-deserved reputation as ferocious soldiers in the ancient East. In medieval Europe, Jews had the right to bear arms because they needed to protect themselves against bandits, and they often served as soldiers in militias raised to defend besieged cities. Gradually, however, they were excluded from the military, not because of a lack of fighting qualities but because military service conferred high status and the right to command Christians. The officer class was the prerogative of the nobility. For a short time in the early centuries there had been Jewish nobles and officers, but Jews could not be expected to give up commerce to become ordinary peasant-soldiers, fighting for a society that denied them ordinary freedoms. Except for those who were useful as economic advisers to princes, Jews were excluded from state service. The civil service conferred status and power over Christians, and the faithful regarded it as inconceivable that Jews should have such power. Anti-Semites in later times would argue that Jews were too unpatriotic or too intent on lucrative business occupations to serve the state, that their loyalties lay with international Jewry. In modern Germany,

Jews were routinely refused entry into the officer class and the civil service. As usual in the mythology of anti-Semites, the reasoning was circular: excluded, the Jews' absence became evidence of their innate unfitness for such tasks.

In the repetitive iconography of racism, Jews are condemned because of their alleged propensity to exploit others' misery by lending money at extortionate interest rates. The three universal religions originated in agrarian or nomadic cultures where borrowing was a desperate means of avoiding the consequences of crop failure, livestock disease, or natural disaster. Then, as now, high risk meant high interest, but the lender was also seen as profiting from others' misery. Judaism, Christianity, and Islam all condemned moneylending as a sin. But progress in commerce meant that money was lent for mutually profitable ventures, and the moneylender became a respected contributor to economic growth, a prestigious banker legitimately entitled to share in the profits his money helped generate.

Theologians adjust sacred traditions to new experience by drawing subtle distinctions and redefining sin. Thus ways were found to sanction the taking of interest. In Muslim civilizations contemporaneous with medieval Europe, Christian, Jewish, and foreign merchants were excepted from the Koran's injunctions against interest, otherwise the extensive international trade of Muslim countries would have been impossible. Muslims themselves benefited from a variety of theological subtleties. Today, Shi'a theologians in Iran find ways to sanction interest without violating the faith. Moneylending was never seen as "Jewish" in Muslim lands; indeed, Christians dominated the activity. Today, of course, even Protestant Fundamentalists and the Vatican are adept at moneylending, now called investing.

Anti-Judaism was weakest in Italy and the Netherlands, where commerce and trade were extensive and prized activities. But in underdeveloped and agrarian Central Europe, moneylending remained a sin, denounced by clergy as the un-Christian behavior of parasites. In pious rural societies, buying and selling have always been viewed as suspicious and nonproductive. Banned from other professions, Jewish merchants in Europe remained in commerce, and for them as for other merchants, moneylending was convenient because they possessed liquid capital. Jews never dominated moneylending, their tiny numbers alone prevented that; but they did predominate in some areas, especially where loans to peasants were refused by Christian businessmen with more profitable options. Interest rates to desperate peasants are always higher, regardless of religion or ethnicity. Moreover, Jewish merchants were more accustomed than Christian traders to taking and giving merchandise on consignment, using credit, and dealing in foreign currencies. Even so, the bulk of moneylending in Europe was in fact carried on by wealthy clerical and monastic institutions along with secular officials and groups such as the Lombards, Venetians, Syrians, and Greeks—Christians all. The Vatican itself was well known for its sophisticated credit practices. In 1430 the rulers of Florence requested Jews to be moneylenders to prevent Christians from imposing outrageous rates on the poor.

The accumulated hatreds and fears resulting from charges of deicide and usury exploded in the Crusades. In the eleventh century, Christian pilgrims to Jerusalem were persecuted by the ruling Muslims, who also defiled the most sacred of Christian churches, the Church of the Holy Sepulcher, site of the Resurrection and the tomb of Jesus. Spurred by the preaching of Pope Urban II and scores of Christian clergy, in 1095 crusading nobles set out under the sign of the cross to free the Holy Land from the infidel. Crop failure, famine, and plague created a surge of religious passion; in a prescientific age natural disasters were seen as the wrath of the Lord. To appease God, the holy places must be redeemed. The pope promised salvation to those who would slay the offending Muslims. Local priests reminded the faithful that the most terrible enemies of Christ were permitted to live and prosper in the very midst of Christian civilization. "First avenge the crucified," a monk wrote, "then go off to fight the Turks."[11] As a contemporary noted, the Crusaders "exterminated by many massacres the Jews of almost all Gaul, with the exception of those who accepted conversion," deeming it "unjust to permit the enemies of Christ to remain alive in their own country, when they had taken up arms to drive out the infidels abroad."[12] The abbot of Cluny asked why Christians should travel to "the ends of the world to fight the Saracens, when we permit among us other infidels a thousand times more guilty toward Christ than the Mohammedans?"[13] Religious passion, greed, and the vulnerability of the Jews led to the rise of violent mobs who murdered thousands to the cry of conversion or death. It seemed just that the wealth of blasphemers should fall to those who did the work of the Lord.

After victory in Jerusalem, the Crusaders hacked and burned to death thousands of Muslim and Jewish civilians regardless of sex or age, and waded in blood as they liberated the Church of the Holy Sepulcher. In Europe, offered conversion or death, few Jews converted. Mass suicides were common; it was an age of faith for Jews as well. Amidst carnage and horror, the Crusades devastated the Jewish communities of Europe. Many civil authorities and important religious leaders opposed the massacres, and some, not wanting their domains thrust into turmoil, protected "their" Jews, punished some murderers, and begged Jews to convert and return to Judaism when the storm passed. Even as they preached the Crusades, some popes denounced the murderers in the name of the witness theory. Innocent III, patron of the fourth Crusade (1198–1216), announced in a papal bull that it was wrong to kill the Jews, for they must survive to remind the Christians of divine law, though they must live in shame as outcasts until they "seek the name of Jesus Christ the Lord."[14]

The most important churchman of the twelfth century, Saint Bernard of Clairvaux, friend and counselor to popes, a mystic famed for miraculous cures and extreme devotion to the cult of the infant Jesus and the Virgin Mary, was the most illustrious preacher of the second Crusade of 1146. It is said that he saved some Jewish communities from destruction by the very people he had inspired. Leave the punishment of the Jews to God, he thundered, until the time when God's infinite mercy through Christ would be revealed to them by the Lord himself. But even Saint Bernard could not resolve the contradictions of the witness theory, for he could not foretell if the Day of Judgment was at hand, nor could he deny that men were the instruments of God's will. Was not the murder of the Jews proof of God's wrath, and were they not offered the chance to accept Christ? As violent mobs killed and robbed, even the saintly Bernard declared, following the witness theory, that though one must not kill the Jews, it might be permitted to plunder their property and cancel debts owed to them.

Abelard, a teacher and theologian famed for applying reason to the mysteries of faith, concluded that Jews were not collectively responsible for the death of Christ. Saint Bernard, furious, had Abelard and his views condemned. By virtue of his intense mystic passion, Bernard overrode contradictions between faith and reason sanctioning violence precisely because he was truly a man of faith, his uncertainties resolved and invulnerable to earthly logic. In any event, mere theology could hardly restrain the passions and greed of the killers; the very violence that contradicts the witness theory can also be seen to fulfill it. Out of theological necessity, the church hierarchy had made antagonism toward the Jews a central doctrine; having done so, it could not control the terrible consequences. Through spiritual devotion to Christian faith, humane and brilliant men became accomplices of murderers. It would not be the last time.

Nothing reveals the need for Jewish witness and the resulting contradictions more than the debate about forced conversions. As the Crusades waned, should those Jews who had been forced to convert be allowed to return to the faith of their fathers? Some princes thought they should. After all, forced conversions had been forbidden by the church hierarchy for centuries. But the popes could not cancel forced conversions without denying the divine power of the sacrament of baptism, and with it the justification of the divine origins of the institutionalized grace of the church altogether. In 828 Gregory IV wrote: "Jews are not to be forced to accept the faith, but if they accept it, however unwillingly, they ought to be forced to adhere to it." In 1201 Pope Innocent III insisted that those receiving the sacrament of baptism, even if only to avoid "violence . . . or torture," could be "forced to abide by the faith."[15] For baptism, however received, transformed the soul by the grace of God, reaffirming the sacred inheritance through Saint Peter to the bishop of Rome. The popes themselves, try as they might, could not avoid being an accomplice to the cry of "convert or die." The highest Christian authorities could escape complicity only by breaking with Christian dependency on Jewish witness, and this they could not do.

Jews' refusal to accept Christ aroused a belief that they were agents of Satan himself. Early churchmen did not believe in the corporeal manifestation of Satan or the demonic power of the Jews, and thus could more easily expect their swift conversion and the Second Coming. By the later Middle Ages, however, belief in Satan was commonplace; Augustine and Aquinas even described his earthly attributes. Pre-Christian ideas never died out among the masses or the parish priests who were selected from among them; the earth was peopled with demons, demons banished from heaven along with Satan for deliberately choosing evil. Rebels against God, they were the source of evil, for God Himself could not will it. In the age of the Crusades, it was no great leap to see the devil's surrogate in the Jewish Antichrist.

Increasingly the image of the satanic Jew appeared in the cathedral courtyards and town squares of Europe where "miracle" plays presented the life, death, and Resurrection of Christ. As at Oberammergau, popular dramas distorted the image of the Jew far beyond anything found in the New Testament. Jews were depicted as demons who knew full well that Christ was the son of God, gleefully plotting his death with sadistic violence. As Christ carries the cross, he is tortured by bloodthirsty, cursing devils with hooked noses, horns, and tails. Hanging from the cross, he is mutilated by Jews screeching obscenities. His life is presented as though tormented by Jews throughout his days and with no Jewish followers whatsoever. To pacify a wrathful God after plague or famine, miracle plays were held where all could participate in the primitive mix of hate, blood, and religious exaltation. The Jews were made to seem as evil as Jesus is divine. Massacres often followed hard upon the presentations.

The most famous anti-Semitic fantasy charged the Jews with murdering Christians because they needed Christian blood for their satanic rites—the charge of ritual murder. It was alleged that Jews, usually led by rabbis, kidnaped Christian children on Jewish holy days to bleed them to death for occult rituals, rituals which proved that the Jews knew Christ was divine and Christian blood unique. Race and racial contamination is not a modern idea, as so many contend. Medieval myths insisted that Jews believed only Christian blood could purge the diseases caused by their own corrupt blood or cure the wounds caused by circumcision. Christians believed that Jews mixed the blood with their ritual foods at Passover in order to sanctify them. Some believed that captive Christians were crucified to reenact Christ's murder. If a Christian child was murdered near Easter or Passover, there was a good chance that local Jews would be massacred. The Catholic church condemned these beliefs, but in this too it could not carry the flock with it. Even in the later nineteenth and early twentieth centuries, some two dozen ritual murder trials took place in Central and Eastern Europe. Public prosecutors were extremely skeptical, and the accused were often acquitted. But anti-Semites saw this as evidence that judicial authorities were in league with the Jews, as Julius Streicher later insisted. Famous and well-educated writers and politicians of the modern era, including Hitler's idols in Vienna, the pan-German Schoenerer and the mayor Lueger, still flung ritual murder charges.

The greatest natural disaster of history was the Black Death which killed more than a third of the population of Europe in the fourteenth century in an indescribably horrible manner. In art, literature, and popular culture, the century is famous for its obsession with death and the imminent coming of the "end of days," usually accompanied by religious imagery and depictions of divine ecstasy. For many the "time of troubles," the necessary prelude to the Last Judgment, had arrived. Now the Jews must convert if Christians were to be saved. Large groups of flagellants, preaching the coming of the End of Days, traveled from village to village, scourging themselves with whips. Summoning all to the village square or town center, the hooded flagellants called upon the fearful denizens to repent before it was too late, and demanded that Jews must finally accept Christ or die.

In those days, as one observer wrote, "All diseases of Christians are caused by demons." All knew who the demons were. Jews were said to have been caught in the act of poisoning the wells of Christians, and many, it was rumored, had gleefully confessed. Jews were massacred or expelled. As before, popes and archbishops warned against blaming the Jews, but again the hierarchy was necessarily ambivalent. Before the plague, two church councils had warned Christians not to purchase food from Jews because it might be poisoned; many churchmen believed famine and disease to be God's judgments upon the toleration of Christ's killers in Christendom. In the worst plague years some two hundred Jewish communities were laid waste and Jews were banished from England and France. Because there was no central authority in Germany, hundreds of tiny Jewish communities remained.

By the end of the fourteenth century the popular mind saw the Jews as a separate and literally diabolical race, unredeemable and determined to destroy Christians. Human beings could sin and might repent, but Satan's disciples preferred the dark. Earlier tales of their miraculous conversions were replaced by tales of their vindictiveness. A Jew stabs the Host, it bleeds; the Jew curses Christ and buries the mutilated Host to hide evidence of its divinity, whereupon a spring gushes forth. A Jew kills a Christian child, who is seen to ascend heavenward; the site is marked and remembered as a holy place. On the sides of cathedrals, Jews are depicted as scorpions or pigs. Witches, when tortured, confess they were inspired by Jews. Jews are overheard boasting that they killed Christ and destroyed their own prophets for predicting his coming. Should a Christian wish to sell his soul to the devil, he needs a Jewish intermediary. Jews are horned, wear goat beards, are demonically virile, have sex with demons. Vampire legends warn the unwary of the Jews' need for Christian blood; the vampire retreats snarling vile oaths when the cross is thrust in his face. There is even a Jewish odor, and it is not the odor of sanctity. In communities without Jews, when plague struck, mobs murdered Christians thought to have Jewish forebears. Race is not a modern invention.

So it was that in medieval Europe the iconography of modern anti-Semitism—the Jew as deicide and parasite—was perfected. A religious vision, it was invulnerable to rational criticism. In the midst of famine, plague, murder, and religious exaltation, the modern stereotype of the Jew was fixed in the popular imagination. Soon Luther would inherit and intensify the demonic image of the Jew. It was he who initiated that blend of German conservatism, nationalism, and anti-Semitism that was to be so deadly to the Jews of Central and Eastern Europe. With the Reformation came the Wars of Religion. The age of the ghetto had arrived.

2: LUTHER AND THE REFORMATION

I cannot convert the Jews. Our Lord Christ Himself did not succeed in doing so; but I can close their mouths so that there will be nothing for them to do but lie upon the ground.

—Martin Luther

MODERN Italy began with the flowering of humanist culture in the Renaissance, England with the creation of a constitutional monarchy in the seventeenth century, France with the Enlightenment and the Revolution of 1789. But modern Germany began its historical career with the sweeping religious revolution of Martin Luther, the German Reformation of the sixteenth century. Starting as a religious revolt against the Church of Rome, the Reformation culminated in the Wars of Religion of the sixteenth and seventeenth centuries, European civil wars in which religious and political opponents were massacred regardless of age, sex, or military involvement. From 1618 to 1648 the Germanies suffered most. Amid scenes of horror, whole communities were wiped out, and what the marauding soldiers of four nations did not destroy was laid waste by famine and plague. In the blood-soaked and plague-ridden lands of Central Europe, the population was reduced by more than one-third, and the tender shoots of commerce, trade, and humanist civilization were all but destroyed. Amidst such terrors, traditional Christian hatred for the Jews intensified manyfold.

Luther has often been credited with advancing religious freedom because he broke with the institutional power of the Vatican, establishing man's personal and unmediated relationship to God. This he did, but he also revived the passions and conflicts of the early church and the Crusades, reinforcing the hatreds of a generation. Unlike the Catholic hierarchy, Luther refused to heed the Christian limits to violence established by the witness theory. No pope ever uttered such vile attacks upon the Jews; Luther's anti-Semitism was more obscene than even Hitler's *Mein Kampf*. And his violent religiosity struck a powerful chord in the souls of

20

millions of peasants and artisans of northern Germany, a chord echoing down to the twentieth century. It inspired the racial nationalists and Christian anti-Semites of modern Germany, men who rejected Catholicism as a Latin "Black Internationale" that, along with the "Yellow Internationale" of Jewry, were considered mortal threats to the racial spirit of the Germanic peoples. Most tragic of all, Luther was Germany's first modern national hero.

Luther followed a psychological pattern similar to the early Christians and not uncommon among fundamentalist Protestants today. For Luther, the personal acceptance of Christ became the sole existential experience upon which faith was based. Such reductionism often brings frightening doubt and an intense need to be certain of divine grace. Through the centuries, in hymn and sermon, those who have believed unwavering and absolute faith in Christ to be the only means of fending off the death of the soul have left moving testimony to their struggles with doubt and guilt. To find Christ, to lose Christ, to be born again to eternal life through Christ—these are the powerful themes of the personal dramas of multitudes. But such deep anxieties all the more readily bring a dangerous need to validate the faith among non-Christians, most especially the Jews, the people of Christ. Even in the United States today, as various polls have shown, anti-Semitism is strongest among Fundamentalists, although it is frowned upon by the leadership and hardly comparable with the intense hatreds unleashed by the Reformation.

Young Luther's terrible doubts were fed by the passions of those violent centuries before religion was mitigated by secularism, and in a Central Europe where Renaissance humanism was powerless. Obsessed with the profound sense of sin that often marks the lives of saints, Luther, searingly aware of his own unworthiness, found no consolation in the rituals of a church that claimed to help the sinner find forgiveness and salvation through its power to dispense the grace of the Lord through divine sacraments. Training for the priesthood, Luther punished himself physically and mentally in a vain attempt to find the certainty of salvation. Tormented, unable to accept the advice of church elders who urged him to trust the church to lighten his burden, Luther, a throwback to the early Christians, could not accept the institutional traditions, bureaucratic compromises, and theological niceties that the established church had built over centuries to help the faithful.

Luther resolved his inner turmoil by concluding that nothing he or anyone could do would yield certainty of salvation. The vast distance between the infinite mercy of God's grace and the vile sins of man was not to be breached by any human act or institution. Ecstatic and liberated, he declared God alone through Jesus Christ could reach across that terrible abyss and grant salvation. Faith, not works, rituals, or the law, would bring salvation, a faith which must come from the divine grace of Christ and could not be earned by word or deed. In one leap of faith he rejected the compromises and contradictions of theology and those concessions to human frailty that calmed the anxieties of a society dominated by religious precepts in a way we can hardly grasp. Luther believed he had destroyed the justification for the existence of the Roman church, its hierarchy, sacraments, and priests. Man's personal relationship with God through Christ became the sole focus of faith; only those who accepted this could form the "invisible church" of true believers.

At first Luther reached out to the Jews. Having revealed the true and original meaning of Christianity and exposed the falsehoods of the Roman Church, he believed the Jews would rush to convert, finally seeing the light darkened by the bishops of Rome through centuries. The Jews, Luther argued, had rightly rejected the corrupt and degenerate teachings of the papal "antichrist" and his underlings—"imbeciles" and "ignorant louts." As he wrote, "If I were a Jew I would have preferred to be a pig before I became a Christian." Having failed to convert the Jews, established Christianity treated them "as if they were dogs and not men," falsely accusing them of ritual murder, the poisoning of Christians, and devil worship. As punishment for these alleged crimes, the church banned Jews from all honest professions so that they must live by usury, and condemned them for this as well![1]

Luther was convinced the Jews would swiftly convert, his vain hope revealing the blinding power of his own will to believe. For millennia Judaism had provided the Jews with their identity, their culture, and their guidance in daily life. Their faith had survived even the horrors of the Crusades. How could they be expected to surrender their own prior and complex religion to yet another upstart who claimed once again that Christ was their Messiah? Luther had not even been able to persuade the majority of Christians. Only awesome self-righteousness led him to expect that the Jews would reject their ancient culture and faith because of an internal and, to them, irrelevant conflict among their Christian oppressors. The immensely popular reformer made few converts among the people of the Book.

Once again the witness people failed to provide the necessary validation to those who had gained certainty at the cost of an intense psychic struggle. Luther, repeating the cycle of the early church fathers, swiftly became a far more brutal and virulent enemy of the Jews than Catholic leaders had ever been, for his psychic defense against the uncertainties of faith was more at risk. Exploding in violence and obscenity, he demanded to know how the Jews could possibly resist the pure love of Christ:

Cursed Goy that I am, I cannot understand how the Jews manage to be so skillful, unless I think that when Judas Iscariot hanged himself, his guts burst and emptied. Perhaps the Jews sent their servants with plates of silver and pots of gold to gather up Judas' piss with the other treasures, and then they ate and drank his offal, and thereby acquired eyes so piercing that they discovered in the Scriptures commentaries that neither Matthew nor Isaiah himself found there, not to mention the rest of us cursed goyim.[2]

The Catholic hierarchy counseled against the massacre of Jews, but Luther, the informal head of a new version of Christianity sweeping Germany, had no patience with centuries of doctrinal evasions in the interests of social peace. In letters and pamphlets he denounced the Jews with a violent gutter language previously limited to the demagogues who had slaughtered the Jews during the first Crusades: The devil is the God of the Jews. Christ has no enemy more "bitter, poisonous, virulent, than a real Jew who is sincerely Jewish." The Jews are literally the "spawn of the Devil," the most "poisonous, bitter, and desperate" enemies of Christ and Christians.[3] All the old myths spewed forth with a virlulence no Catholic leader had allowed himself since the fifth century. Allowed to live in our midst in peace, Luther wrote, the Jews repay us by usury, poisoning our wells, and murdering our children in their obscene satanic rituals. They even dare to revile Christ as the son of a whore and a Roman soldier. Luther's voice is that of the killers of the Crusades. He who claimed to base his faith on Gospel alone could never find in the Gospels justification for his scatological virulence, nor did he try.

Luther outdid even the murderous mobs; they at least had offered conversion or death. Luther declared that a Jew could never be converted anymore than one could convert the devil they so eagerly served. It was dangerous even to discuss religious matters with these satanic Jews, he insisted. It was enough to remind them of their historical fate since the destruction of the temple, for it proved well enough how the Lord hated their accursed race. Luther would not baptize a Jew even if asked, he wrote; instead he would drown him like a poisonous serpent. "I cannot convert the Jews. Our Lord Christ Himself did not succeed in doing so; but I can close their mouths so that there will be nothing for them to do but lie upon the ground."[4] He could hardly have spoken more plainly; death was his final solution to the "Jewish problem."

Luther's last sermon in 1546 was devoted to the "arrogance and obduracy" of the Jews, the Antichrist incarnate whose vicious economic dealings had made them the masters of Germany. In 1543 he published his famous and oft-cited "The Jews and Their Lies," a vicious tract accusing the Jews of planning to dominate the world. They were a "plague and a pestilence." The princes of Germany should ban Judaism, destroy Jewish property, execute rabbis who continued to teach, burn their schools, synagogues, and houses, seize their wealth, destroy their prayer books and Talmudic writings, and either "drive them like mad dogs out of the land" or place them all "under one roof"—in short, a concentration camp. Following his advice, the princes of three Prussian provinces drove out the Jews. Luther's rhetoric foreshadowed that of nineteenth-century racists who—if with fewer references to filth and excrement—held that Jewish blood prevented any regeneration by assimilation or conversion.

Luther was a racist, pure and simple, bothered not at all that his hatred of the Jews denied the power of Christ to redeem all humanity. To him the Jew was simply not human. As the Protestant "German-Christians" of the Nazi movement would later claim, the blood of a Jew was beyond redemption. For Luther, the devil walked on earth; he himself, he wrote, had seen Satan and often heard his vile voice. He once confessed that, plagued by inner torment, often he could hardly tell the difference between the power of God and that of Satan, especially when contemplating the activities of Satan's people. Luther's obsession with the devil has been interpreted by psychologists as a strange deviation from normality, but he shared it with millions in his own day. It was a belief still held down to World War II by millions of peasants in Central and Eastern Europe, peasants who also supported a variety of Christian fascist groups.

Luther's anti-Semitism was no personal idiosyncrasy. A flood of widely circulated pamphlets and posters accompanied the spread of Protestantism in Germany and elaborated upon his vile attacks. "Studies" described the obscene practices of the Jews in synagogues and ritual baths, their unholy lust to drink Christian blood, their ability to transform themselves into demons and serpents, their secret crimes and vices and their bizarre sexual and toilet practices. Significantly, the evil and demonic qualities of the Jews were often not attributed to their failure to adopt Christianity; they were presented as inherent and ineradicable qualities of Jewish blood. Luther may have provided the most famous model for these writings, but in fact he was expressing a deeply felt folk belief with no equivalent anywhere else in Europe. Luther spoke for those millions of peasants and rural artisans who, throughout modern German history, were the backbone of populist and racist social movements, culminating with the Nazis. Even before Luther's death, a host of popular writings and crude cartoons depicted Luther as a saint, a John the Baptist, a Moses leading his people out of the wilderness created by the Roman church and the evil machinations of the Jews.

In England and France, Jews were few in the sixteenth century. In

France the Calvinist Huguenots, who looked favorably upon the Jews, were the prime objects of Catholic antagonism. Because of their forced absence, the Jews were more of a symbol than a clear and present danger. The most popular French priest of the century, Claude de Montfort, though he attacked the Jews for their guilt in the death of Christ, also stressed the guilt of sinning Christians in the primal crime. In England, Switzerland, and Scotland, and among the colonials of what would become the United States, the spread of different varieties of Calvinism broke the tie between Christianity and the violent rhetoric of the Crusades. By Lutheran standards, Calvinists and Puritans were exceedingly well disposed toward Judaism and Jews.

Indeed, Martin Luther was the only important Protestant leader who believed in the irredeemable corruption of Jewry. John Calvin and Ulrich Zwingli, the most influential leaders of Calvinism, were not obsessed with the Jewish refusal of Christ. Their attitudes were favorable if patronizing. Calvin, an avid admirer of the Old Testament, was a student of Hebrew and a humanist man of letters before he became a theologian. Zwingli, who founded the Reformation in Switzerland, was a devotee of humanist literature. Neither experienced Luther's desperate psychic trauma about his personal salvation. When Calvin spoke of his conversion, he depicted it as an intellectual search for knowledge of God's will, and he seemed content to live without absolute certainty about his own salvation.

Both Calvin and Zwingli believed there could be no certainty of salvation through either faith or works. "Predestination [is] the eternal decree of God by which He has determined with Himself what He would have become of every man. For . . . eternal life is foreordained for some and eternal damnation for others."[5] By constantly inspecting one's impulses, thoughts, and acts, one might discover sufficient reason to hope one had been selected for the elect, but no more. God had decided which few would be saved, and they were few indeed. Nor was his decision tyrannical. Mankind was so corrupt that to save anyone was an act of infinite mercy. Such thinking allowed for no stark contrasts between God-fearing Christian and satanic Jew, the staple imagery of so many in the Germanies.

Predestination lessens hostility and mitigates the psychological need to have Christianity validated through Jewish conversion. It is surprising how little concern for the Jewish rejection of Christ is found in Calvin; for Calvinists, their conversion is truly left to the Lord, as is the salvation of all. Why blame the Jews for the death of Christ when one believes Christ's fate to be as divinely predetermined as was the divine selection of the elect? However harsh Calvin was on his enemies in Geneva, in this instance theology and intellect overrode passion. If the Jews had called for the crucifixion of Christ, were they not merely obeying the dictates of the Divine Will? Theodore Beza, chief aide to Calvin, did believe the Jews to be an ungrateful people justly punished by the Lord. But in a much published prayer he wrote, "Grant that we may not become for them [the Jews] instruments of Thy wrath."[6] Protestant generosity, persuasion, and moral probity, he believed, should set an example. God alone would bring the Jews back to the fold.

Calvin and Calvinists, strong admirers of the God and prophets of the Old Testament, were never driven single-mindedly to search scripture to find prophecies of the coming of Christ. Some Calvinist sects adopted Jewish laws, and a few converted to Judaism. Calvin's followers did not care to force Jews to convert, let alone drive them from Europe, preferring to let them live in peace where the Gospel was preached so the word of God might reach them. Cromwell, the Puritan revolutionary, attempted to lift the ban on Jews so they might return to England in the seventeenth century. Outraged, Cromwell's royalist antagonists circulated rumors that the Jews hailed Cromwell as their Messiah and planned to turn Saint Paul's Cathedral into a synagogue. Cromwell retreated, though unofficially Jews were allowed to return. Nor did the Puritans of New England hold a unique animus against Jews. Only in the religious revivalism of rural America in the late eighteenth century did finding Christ through an ecstatic religious experience become the essence of the Protestant faith, and then it sometimes caused hostility toward the Jews.

Unlike France and England in the sixteenth and seventeenth centuries, in the Germanies discussion of the "Jewish problem" was intense. Social ills were more likely to be blamed on the Jews, a tradition unbroken through the Nazis. Like anti-Semites after him, Luther believed commerce and city life to be morally suspect and "Jewish." True Germans led a simple rural life. Perhaps aware that Jews played but a minor role in their economy, it was common for Germans to denounce the "Christian-Jews" who, though not Jewish, practiced the allegedly harmful and "Jewish" professions. Already in the Reformation "international Jewry" was singled out as symbol and cause of German economic troubles, especially during the devastating Wars of Religion. The accusation was common among extreme conservative nationalists in all Europe through the centuries, but in Germany, as we shall see, liberal counterforces were too weak to prevent their success.

Calvin and his followers accepted the new entrepreneurial spirit in Europe, but Luther did not. Although Calvin did not believe worldly success to be a direct sign of God's favor, as did some of his followers, he welcomed capitalism, encouraged trade, and extolled the virtues of thrift, industry, and commerce. Calvinism spread swiftly in Switzerland, Scotland, England, and New England, all places where the entrepreneurial spirit was well advanced, while in France the Calvinist Huguenots, composed of disproportionate numbers of professional and commercial bourgeoisie, also supported the values of commerce. Throughout the modern era anti-Semitism has been most pronounced among the pious who, like Luther, dislike the city, fear commercial capitalism, and identify the Jews with both. Such ideas would come to dominate the prestigious German Conservative party of Prussia.

Nineteenth-century German anti-Semitic social movements came to idealize the simple agrarian life of the teutonic *Volk*, denouncing finance capitalism as unproductive, parasitical, and Jewish—ideas that found their most extreme expression in the Nazi ideology of blood and soil. But away from the backwaters of Central Europe and in the midst of a commercial revolution, Calvinists were less susceptible to the hostile economic stereotype of the Jews in Lutheran Prussia and Catholic Austria. Absence helped, of course. When Swiss Calvinists, for example, complained about usury, they did not mention Jews: there were few in Switzerland. But even had there been more, they could have taught the Swiss nothing about the ways of credit and commerce. Some historians have even equated the Calvinist ethic with the spirit of capitalism. The association is too simple, but it is certain that in the more economically advanced nations, Calvinists were not only among the first to welcome the new age of international commerce but to call for the toleration of Jews, as in Holland during its golden age of commerce in the seventeenth century.

Unlike other Protestant reformers, Luther detested the urban and humanistic culture of the Renaissance, a threat to the simple peasant piety he admired. As a young priest he visited the Rome of Pope Leo X and was appropriately shocked. Rome's worldly spirit had no place for a troubled religious idealist. The pope was a Medici; birth rather than piety had made him a cardinal when still a boy. It was Leo who triggered the Reformation by offering the sale of pardons (indulgences) for the remission of sin. His representatives traveled throughout the Germanies promising that sufficient money given to the church could release the souls of dead relatives from purgatory. "When the money in the coffer clings / Then the soul from purgatory springs," was the popular refrain of Tetzel, the papal delegate who raised money to build Saint Peter's Cathedral. Luther despised the crass salesman, and Tetzel's activities were the immediate cause of his violent attack against the church's power to dispense grace in any way whatsoever. It was also Leo X who excommunicated Luther, the momentous act that raised up the German masses, precipitated the religious revolution, and shook to the core the worldly, sophisticated, and uncomprehending Vatican.

Humanists welcomed Lutheranism at first, assuming that Luther's call

for the "inner freedom of the Christian man" meant freedom in general
and not simply a denial of the Vatican's claims to dispense grace and an
affirmation of the supremacy of the individual's relationship with Christ.
The most famous humanist, Erasmus, had long wanted church reform.
To him the Reformation seemed to presage a burst of freedom from institutional and cultural tyrannies. But Luther was never simply a church
reformer. Institutional corruption was less important to him than the divine pretensions of the Roman church. As Erasmus soon learned, the liberation of human thought and culture was no part of Luther's passionate
cry for salvation. Luther also rejected the humanist emphasis on virtue
as the result of virtuous acts; without faith in Christ, he held, virtuous
acts could not make a man truly righteous. As for anti-Semitism, as Erasmus once ironically noted: "If to be a good Christian is to hate the Jews,
then we are all good Christians." He broke with Luther, remaining
Catholic. Other humanists embraced Calvinism in the face of Luther's
increasingly virulent conservatism. Calvin himself, though stern and
tyrannical in Geneva, originally viewed the break with Rome as a new
burst of the spirit of freedom against the bonds of traditional idolatry and
ritual. Though he severely punished the "libertines" of Geneva for offending Christ by licentious behavior, Calvin never turned against humanist learning.

The German Lutheran tradition has always been one of subordination
to the state. Luther himself depended on the rulers of several German
territories to protect him from the Vatican, though none did so simply
out of a belief in religious freedom. Some were sincere Lutherans, but
most seized the chance to limit the power of Rome and confiscate the
considerable wealth of the church in their domains. Moreover, unlike
popes and Calvinists, Lutherans did not challenge political authority.
Their clergy were concerned only with the salvation of souls. At first many
of Luther's peasant and artisan followers assumed that the new movement
meant freedom not only from Rome but also from serfdom and the
tyranny of princes and nobles. In the great peasant revolts of 1524–1526,
many marched under banners bearing his name. Furious, Luther insisted
that the social order was divinely ordained; to attack it was blasphemy.
His rage thundered from the pulpit as he demanded that princes had a
sacred duty to destroy the revolutionists by fire and sword. They were
happy to oblige, and the carnage was immense.

Luther's unquestioning support of the state was not shared by other
Protestant leaders. Zwingli supported the peasant revolts, and other famous Calvinists harangued against the divine right of kings, urging their
overthrow. In the Puritan Revolution in England, Cromwell defeated the
monarchy and led those who demanded the beheading of the king. Some
Puritan sectarian groups even founded communitarian movements in

England—the Diggers and Levelers—hoping to end private property and social hierarchy: "When Adam delved and Eva span / Who was then the gentleman?" Although Calvin established a theocracy in Geneva, even he preferred a mixed government of aristocrats and elected representatives of the people. Reformers in England, France, Holland, and Scotland demanded religious freedom and toleration in order to organize voluntary theocratic communities, and this often caused them to recognize, if grudgingly, the demand for toleration by other sects. After the long and bitter French Wars of Religion in the late sixteenth century, the Calvinist Huguenots of France gained political autonomy and freedom of worship in some two hundred towns, though they would be driven from France by Louis XIV in 1685. The Huguenots (and the Calvinist Dutch Reformed church) supported freedom of worship even for Jews. Only Lutheranism in Prussia welcomed princely authoritarianism, and did so from the time of the reign of the kings of Prussia through the kaisers of the Second Reich and down to the appointment of Hitler as chancellor—an appointment welcomed by the vast majority of Evangelical clergy. The only German government they did not support was the liberal and democratic Weimar Republic.

Luther was the only religious reformer to identify himself narrowly with nationalism. In his most important work, an "Address to the Nobility of the German Nation," he announced that he spoke only to and for Germans, demanding that German princes control ecclesiastical matters and throw off the subversive influence of Rome. He would often be cited later by German philosophers, politicians, and theologians who interpreted the Reformation as the first great expression of the Germanic soul, rejecting Catholic Christianity as Latin, un-German, and cosmopolitan, a threat to the Teutonic peoples second only to international Jewry. After the French Revolution of 1789, German conservatives, appalled, held the German Reformation to be an alternative and superior creative force, an expression of a far more profound inner freedom of the spirit than the "superficial" spirit of 1789. Thus Luther's primitive and reactionary spirit was disguised. Some German historians continue to regard the Lutheran Reformation as an advance in human freedom, though Nietzsche believed it to be "the peasant revolt of the spirit."

As the Reformation swept Europe, the Catholic Counter-Reformation rose in response. As Christian slaughtered Christian, further misery was the lot of the remnants of the Jewish community. Now little more than vagabonds seeking sanctuary wherever they could, the Jews were driven into the ghettos, there to remain for almost two centuries. In the midst of the sixteenth century, Pope Paul IV reigned in Rome. A pious reformer and ascetic quite unlike the Renaissance popes, he was consequently far more hostile to the Jews. He even believed that the Reformation was a

Jewish-inspired plot to destroy the Vatican; for Paul, the Jews were the "fathers of iniquity and parents of protestantism." Revitalizing medieval legislation against them (legislation usually ignored by his predecessors), he proceeded to force the Jews of Italy to live almost as miserably as their coreligionists to the north. In the papal states and in Rome he banned them from many trades and professions, destroyed their synagogues, prevented them from owning land, and forced them to listen to sermons intended to convert them. They had to wear both the yellow Star of David and special head coverings designed to warn Christians of their presence. The pope banned the Talmud, forbade the celebration of the Jewish High Holidays, and prevented the purchase of kosher food. Reviving the Inquisition, he burned sixty converted Jews at the stake on suspicion of lack of sincerity. Following the demand once made by Innocent III and the Lateran Council of 1179, Paul IV confined the Jews of his states to ghettos, exhorting all Christian leaders to do the same. By such means he hoped, in his words, to use "Christian charity to bring the brothers of Christ back into his family." Paul IV was hardly alone; the scattered communities of Jews in Central Europe were all gradually forced into ghettos. Jews and Christians, he proclaimed, should neither mix nor intermarry, thus avoiding religious contamination. Many Jewish rabbinical leaders also wished to avoid assimilation, as they still do today. And the unleashed passions of the religious wars made it advantageous to live in guarded quarters that were locked by night, especially at Easter, as violent mobs roamed the streets seeking loot and vengance. But no rabbi welcomed the miserable conditions that prevailed in the Germanies, where ghetto life was the most repressive.

The ghettos of Central Europe were poor, unbelievably overcrowded, and periodically devastated by fire. By law, moneylending, pawnbroking, and dealing in secondhand wares were the only vocations open to their inhabitants. Forbidden to own shops outside the ghetto, the itinerant Jewish peddler became a fixture of the European town. Through the seventeenth and eighteenth centuries the Jews of Central Europe lived behind ghetto walls in penury, isolated and subject to all manner of special taxes. Forced to wear the yellow badge, locked behind walls at night, forbidden to mingle in groups in town, they dared not purchase ahead of Christians in markets, and were forced to pay a body tax and beg a safe-conduct pass in order to travel. To cut down on the number of Jews—for only those economically useful were desired—marriage, household, and business permits were restricted, and Jewish "estates" were heavily taxed upon death. Forbidden to own dwellings in the ghetto, Jews were at the mercy of Christian slumlords who never hesitated to dump them into the streets without notice should they fail to pay a suddenly announced raise in rent. They could hire no Christian servants or employ a "sabbath goy" to light their fires in winter; like cattle, they were subject to a special toll upon entering many towns. Humiliated by special oaths in the courts, they were excluded from many public places. In some localities, even the solace offered by the study of the Talmud was denied them.

The Jews of Central Europe were pauperized, repressed, cut off from European culture, devoid of contact with nature. Forced by heavy and arbitrarily imposed taxes to invent subterfuges in order to survive, they were then accused of chicanery and suffered still further restrictions. Special assessments bankrupted some ghettos. It is true that after 1648 many a prince had his favored and wealthy court Jew to handle his finances, but this only spread the image of the usurious Jew. Even when liberated, the ignorant could now maintain, the Jew was attracted to nothing but money. Should the prince's high taxes anger his citizens, this too could be blamed on the greed of his "Court Jew," and some rulers often punished publicly their former favorites in order to deflect discontent. In the ghetto the self-fulfilling prophecies of Christian anti-Judaism were fulfilled. Until the eighteenth century, lack of contact between Gentile and Jew made it impossible for ordinary citizens to gain even the slightest experience which might have enabled them to question religious and racial stereotypes.

The periodic expulsion and return of the Jews at the time of the Crusades led to the revival of the old myth of the "wandering Jew," Ahasuerus, condemned to wander homeless until the Second Coming of Christ. Published in Germany in 1602, it was extremely popular. Also in Germany, but not elsewhere, a growing number of Christian Hebrew scholars pored zealously over Hebrew literature, no longer searching, as in the early centuries, for prophecies of the coming of Christ, but looking for attacks against Christianity. In France and England, by contrast, Christian Hebrew scholars, often Calvinists, were more favorable to the Jews. The search to justify Christian hostility against the "pariah people" culminated, not surprisingly, in Prussia in 1711 with the publication of one of the most popular source books for anti-Semites in modern Europe, Johannes Eisenmenger's *Judaism Unmasked*. Ostensibly intended to convert the Jews by revealing to them their numerous errors, given its content it was far more likely to persuade Christians that Jews should disappear from the face of the earth.

Eisenmenger "demonstrated" through interpretations of Hebrew passages how the Talmud commanded the Jews to lie, cheat, and even murder non-Jews. Though faithfully translating his sources, by ignoring the historical context of ancient texts Eisenmenger was able to portray Jewish antagonisms toward their tribal rivals in ancient times as though they applied to Christians in his own. Confirming every Christian myth about the Jews, the book was also popular because it attacked the Talmud rather than the Old Testament which, of course, Christians claimed as their own. The Jews, Eisenmenger proclaimed, were ordered by their religious precepts to destroy Christianity, to attack all that Christians held sacred, and to destroy all races but their own. That was why, he insisted, Christians must destroy their synagogues, confine them to ghettos, degrade them in all possible ways, and avoid all unnecessary contacts—especially with their physicians, who were uniquely qualified to do harm. Once again we hear that the Jews must not be killed, however, for they were destined to bear witness to Christianity. In the nineteenth century many who were less devoted to Christian verities insisted that Eisenmenger would have been more consistent had he recognized that a people such as he described would find conversion itself the best means for destroying Christianity from within.

Eisenmenger's work was at first suppressed by the emperor of the Holy Roman Empire as a favor to his invaluable court Jew. But in 1711 the first king of Prussia, Frederick I, assured its publication. It was not just a gesture. Frederick I was an avid admirer of an idealized vision of the Middle Ages and, paradoxically, a pious believer in the principles of the Reformation. His intervention indicates how the reactionary influence of Lutheranism was intensified by its association with the history of Prussia throughout the modern era. The autocratic and military state that ultimately united Germany by force and largely determined its political fate was born out of the passionate religious idealism and hatreds of the time of the Crusades and the Reformation.

The formation of Prussia began in 1197, when, during the third Crusade, German nobles formed a monastic crusading order, the Teutonic Knights, taking vows of chastity, obedience, and poverty so they might better do battle to spread Christianity. The grand master of the Teutonic Knights placed himself and his monks under the sovereignty of Innocent III, the most famous and militant imperialist of the crusading popes, for whom the conquest of the Holy Land was to be but the beginning of Christian global dominance. The first pope to claim the title of Vicar of Christ (Christ's representative on earth), Innocent III sponsored a brutal and bloody crusade against the Albigensians of France, accused of heresy because they believed that Christ appeared on earth only in "semblance," i.e., in outward appearance, not in reality. Their enemies insisted that the Albigensians could only have learned this from pernicious Jews, for who else possessed the malice and the will to seduce the innocent believer into denying Christ's actuality? Consistent with his crusading imperialistic spirit, Innocent III was the first pope to demand that the Jews wear the yellow Star of David, and he persuaded the Fourth Lateran Council to make this church law. He also tried, unsuccessfully, to banish the Jews of Europe to ghettos.

Fortified with the blessings of the pope, in the thirteenth century the Order of Teutonic Knights crusaded against the Hungarians and the Prussians, a Baltic people. Roaming along the coast of the Baltic Sea amidst furious slaughters, the Knights seized Prussian lands and virtually exterminated the indigenous people. Building castles, forts, and towns, they converted the remaining natives to Christianity, reduced them to serfdom, and made themselves lords of the land, attracting colonists from the Germanies and constantly battling Russians and Poles to expand their domains. Henceforth Prussia would be German. In the sixteenth century the grand master of the Teutonic Knights, a member of the Hohenzollern family that eventually produced the kaisers of modern Germany, declared his territories a secular duchy and converted to Lutheranism. Swift to see the political and economic advantages of independence from Rome and the Catholic Hapsburgs, he understood that a Lutheran state church would be concerned solely with the spiritual salvation of its flock and would subordinate itself to the will of the prince.

In the seventeenth century the new duchy merged with Brandenburg to establish modern Prussia. East Prussia, forged out of the bloodied and Christianized territories of the Teutonic Knights, never lost its feudal ethos. The center of German reaction, its army, under Bismarck and William I, forged the greatest political achievement of modern German history when it united Germany in 1871, defeating first the Hapsburgs and then Napoleon III of France. With this, Prussian military and autocratic values were sanctified among the German elites and eventually the middle classes as well. Once again German history deviated from that of the liberal West. Understandably, Nazi intellectuals, great admirers of the Teutonic Knights, also believed it to be Germany's destiny to seize Eastern Europe from the inferior Slavs and resettle it with Germans—not for Christianity, of course, but in pursuit of Germany's sacred racial mission to assure the permanent dominance of the Aryan peoples.

During the Wars of Religion, however, such ambitions were far beyond Prussia's capacities. When in 1640 the great elector ascended the throne of Prussia, his lands were unbelievably devastated. Foreign armies roamed the countryside unchecked, laying waste to what remained of his ruined territories. To rebuild, the great elector created a disciplined army and an obedient and loyal bureaucratic and officer class out of the once independent and feudal-minded nobility. To compensate them for yielding to him absolute sovereignty, he gave them the right to dominate provincial affairs, monopolize high office, and oppress their peasants, and at a time when serfdom and feudalism were rapidly declining in Western Europe. In 1648 the settlement of the Wars of Religion gave each prince the right to enforce his own religion in his domains. In Prussia the Lutheran clergy became practically a branch of the state, their task spiritually to buttress the power and values of prince, aristocracy, and army. It was the only church west of tsarist Russia to be so subordinated.

It is a common belief that the Evangelical clergy in Germany failed to resist the Nazis because they were politically passive, but in fact they had always been active political propagandists for the Prussian aristocracy and military and welcomed Hitler to power as well. In countless sermons and writings, the clergy bestowed religious sanction on the autocratic ideals of the Hohenzollerns and the Prussian aristocracy, preaching obedience as a sacred duty. In Prussia, as the famous phrase has it, the Evangelical Lutheran church was the "spiritual army of the Hohenzollerns." The kings of Prussia and the kaisers of a united Germany were de facto heads of the Evangelical church, demanding and receiving strict obedience to conservative mandates on the part of "their clergy," and insisting it their duty to transmit Prussian ideals in their sermons. The least sign of enlightened attitudes toward religious dogma was crushed, Frederick the Great being the one exception to this policy.

When elections commenced in the 1870s, the Evangelical clergy, convinced of the need for the unity of throne and altar against all democratic institutions, could be counted on to support the German Conservative party, the party of the military and aristocratic elites of Prussia. During the Weimar Republic of the 1920s the overwhelming majority of the clergy remained monarchists, often denouncing from the pulpit parliamentary sovereignty, Western liberalism, and democratic socialism as un-German, anti-Christian, and "Jewish." Prominent Lutheran clerics played important roles in the Conservative party, which sought to reverse the civil rights Bismarck had granted the Jews when Germany was unified. The party embraced anti-Semitism in its platform in the 1890s. In the inner circles of the Evangelical church, retired generals, high Prussian civil servants, and conservative politicians always had the decisive voice. It was not only a question of the leadership. By 1931–1932 the elected lay councils of the Evangelical church regularly returned large Nazi majorities. In turn, during their campaigns the Nazis gleefully published Luther's anti-Semitic obscenities, including his well-known admonitions to outlaw Judaism, seize Jewish property, burn the synagogues, and drive the Jews from the land—all accompanied by dark hints of slaughter. Luther's document "The Jews and Their Lies" was exhibited in a glass case in Nuremberg during Nazi party rallies. Significantly, the few Protestant clerics who opposed Nazi anti-Semitism, men like Dietrich Bonhoeffer, Martin Niemoeller, and Martin Dibelius, came from the Calvinist wing of the German Evangelicals, who had been commanded by the king to merge with the Lutherans in the Evangelical Protestant Union of 1817.

With the Reformation, Germany started down an historical path that combined reactionary nationalism with anti-Semitism. During the centuries when the spirit of commercial capitalism and relative tolerance forged ahead in the West, the Germanies were cut off and torn apart by war and religious strife. Certainly modern anti-Semitism in France also derived much of its force from its alliance with powerful reactionary classes, and by itself Christian anti-Semitism could scarcely have led to the Holocaust. And little that led to the Nazis was unique to Germany, even the racism of blood and soil. But there was a crucial difference. In the West in the seventeenth and eighteenth centuries, powerful intellectual and political forces were at work which would counter the influence of reactionary and racist nationalism: constitutional monarchy in England, the rise of a secular and numerous powerful commercial and entrepreneurial class, and above all the Enlightenment and the French Revolution of 1789.

In Scotland, England, and France, the prestige of the new science and the demands of an increasingly powerful commercial and professional bourgeoisie—and even some nobles and clergy—combined to create a secular culture eroding the power of the old Christian mythology. From this mix emerged the secular liberalism of the Enlightenment. Challenging Christian fundamentalism in all areas of thought, it created cultural and social alternatives to traditional Christian values and institutions. For the first time in centuries, the Jews of Europe would have a chance to assimilate and prosper, a way out of the ghetto and—it was hoped—the constant threat of destruction. It is one of the great tragedies of modern history that the new ideology would have relatively little impact on German thought and culture, and most especially on those upper- and lower-class conservatives who, one way or another, would have the greatest impact on modern Germany.

3: THE ENLIGHTENMENT

Theology is the philosophy of the world's childhood; it is time it gave
way to its age of reason.
—Destutt de Tracy

The universe will only be happy when it is atheist.
—La Mettrie

DURING the 1670s the Frenchman Richard Simon, a Christian Hebrew
scholar, began the study of the Bible as a secular historical document.
His studies led him to praise the piety and charity of the Jews and to defend them from charges of satanism and ritual murder. Outraged, the
powerful Bishop Bossuet of France, counselor to monarchs, forced Simon
out of the Oratory, an association of secular priests, and harassed him for
the rest of his life. But the force that would sustain Simon's views was
growing among the educated: the scientific worldview of Isaac Newton
and John Locke. In the greatest revolutions in the history of ideas, the
new science would inspire the ideas of the Enlightenment and the Revolution of 1789, and lead as well to the liberation of the Jews.

In the medieval mind, the Christian drama of salvation was blended
with Ptolemaic astronomy and Aristotle's physics into one universal vision. The earth was the center of the universe not only because man's
senses told him so, but because it was farthest from God's grace, hence
the natural place for sin, lust, base matter, and mankind—all that was
imperfect and decays. Flesh was bound to earth, but the soul of man was
pure spiritual substance striving upward for release from the corruptions
of earthly desires, seeking the heavens where crystalline spheres revolved
in perfect circles powered by the divine force of angels, and the Lord
dwelled in the final realm. For medieval man, science elucidated the
Christian drama of salvation as revealed in the material world.

But the new physics created a counterculture challenging the Christian worldview, a counterculture encouraging secularism and ultimately
modern liberalism. Mathematical reasoning led Copernicus to believe
the earth was not the center of the universe. Galileo's telescope revealed

that the supposed divine and crystalline spheres of the heavens were in fact rough, coarse, and imperfect, like the earth. For Descartes the cosmos was a vast, soulless construction built according to the laws of mechanics. From Newton came the most compelling vision of all: the universe was a vast harmonious machine, its motions governed by a few basic mathematical laws of mass, force, acceleration, attraction, and inertia. Matter was naturally attracted to matter, and the mathematical relationship between mass and distance explained the movement of the whole. As seventeenth-century physics progressed, it eroded the notion that the earth was the central stage for the Christian teleology of sin, redemption, and salvation. As Bertrand Russell once observed, the earth was just a fifth-rate ball of mud revolving around a seventh-rate star, a mere speck in the infinite and indifferent heavens, themselves without spiritual significance.

The Newtonian system did not encourage atheism, as Newton himself insisted. Such a vast and complex mechanism, self-regulating, governed by the laws of matter in motion, and intelligible only through the arcane intricacies of the laws of mathematics, could not be merely the fortuitous result of accidental forces. The creation must have sprung full-blown from the mind of a Great Mathematician or a Great Engineer, as God now came to be labeled. Malebranche, Fontenelle, and Spinoza, to name only the famous, believed that a Supreme Being must have been the creator of the harmonious universal order revealed by science, the fount of the geometrical truths and mathematical harmonies that underlay the whole. God was to be found in the elegance and precision of natural laws, not in the anthropomorphic and primitive foundation myths of the great religions.

Spinoza regarded the biblical tales of God's miraculous interference in the natural order as merely the superstitions of the simple. God did not violate his own Perfect Being by interfering with his creation; the universe itself was the miracle. Scripture, Spinoza believed, was neither science nor philosophy, and the myths of the historical religions should not be taken literally, let alone fought over. The Bible presented merely edifying fictions meant to teach moral lessons to those millions incapable of comprehending mathematical and scientific truth. The Great Mathematician would not part the Red Sea or give his only begotten son to die for the sins of mankind. The God of Mathematical Harmony smote not, neither did he raise the dead or punish mankind with natural disasters. Above all, it was wrong to think that he visited his wrath on one part of mankind for not accepting the religious fictions of another.

Spinoza accused Jews and Christians alike of blasphemy for claiming that their particular myths came from the hand of God. Accordingly, Spinoza believed that religion was a private matter, and that religious freedom should be defended by the state. To those inspired by the vision of the new science, the violent rhetoric and bloody acts of the intolerant were battles over fictions. Thus for a multitude of educated in the eighteenth century, the religious oppression of the Jews by Christian Europe lost divine sanction and become a primitive conflict between competing superstitions. We are light years away from the Crusades, Luther, and the Wars of Religion.

In the 1660s John Locke wanted to know, given the new science, what certain knowledge men could have about the external world and the dogmas of Christianity? His conclusions laid the foundation for the Enlightenment's pluralism and tolerant skepticism. Science demonstrated, he held, that we cannot know the external world directly, only through the images it produces upon our senses through experiment and experience. But our senses are limited and our experience changes, hence knowledge is always probable, never absolute. Given the temper of the times, Locke modified his pragmatic doubt when it came to religion, but he believed that one day, like geometry, fundamental religious principles would be confirmed by "human reasoning operating on self-evident axioms."[1] In his famous *Letter on Toleration* he asserted that though it might be necessary to accept Christ in order to be saved, Jews and Muslims should never be persecuted. He did allow for political restrictions on Catholics, however, for under Spain they had become England's bitter enemies, plotting tyrannicide in the name of the Counter-Reformation. Locke also rejected toleration for atheists; without faith, he feared, men would have no incentive for moral behavior. Nevertheless, by basing faith on rational propositions, Locke undercut the passion that persecutes; one does not kill for a rational proposition or a merely probable truth.

The floodgates were open. A host of deists, as they were called, sought a religion in accord with the method of the new science: rational or natural religion. Just as Galileo and Newton had discovered the fundamental laws of motion by reducing specific examples to a few common principles, so too the deists scrutinized the inherited myths and dogmas of religions to derive the basic propositions common to all. These, they assumed, must be the primary and fundamental religious truths implanted in man by the Divine Being—self-evident and rational religious propositions whose warrant was the innate "universal consent" of all mankind. With slight variations they arrived at the following: There is a Supreme Being. He is the omnipotent Creator of the universe, man, and the moral order. He should be worshiped and obeyed, and for this there will be rewards and punishments, perhaps in the afterlife. The "perhaps" is significant.

The rituals, sacraments, and myths of the historical religions that deviated from these primary truths were unnecessary distortions. One need not abolish them, but they ought not be forced on others. Not the dogmas but the purpose of religion was the essential matter: to sanction moral behavior. The deists thus created modern liberal attitudes toward religion. Men of reason could wear the specifics of their faith lightly, without the impulse to force others to accept their particular religious views. To those passionately moved by faith, deism was cold, rational, and unworthy of the ecstatic intensity of true religious experience. But for those who suffered from the brutalities of religious persecution, it was a blessing.

In his *Historical and Critical Dictionary* of 1697, Pierre Bayle collected a vast list of the religious curiosities and contradictions men had believed through the ages. Reviewing them, he argued that the dogmas of faith did not conform to common sense and could not be demonstrated by reason. Bayle counseled his readers not to try to understand the absurdities of revelation. With tongue in cheek, he wrote that religious truths must be revealed, for they were beyond the power of reason to fathom. Unable to judge the truth of different revelations, man must opt for "universal tolerance" and freedom of worship. Bayle even dared suggest that, given the bloody history of religious strife and persecution, there was no evident correlation between religious faith and moral behavior. He reserved special scorn for the persecutors of the Jews, though he found the myths of Judaism, like those of their persecutors, hopelessly irrational.

In the middle of the eighteenth century, David Hume took the implications of the new science to the extreme. If all knowledge came from experience, then even science could make no claim to absolute truth. After all, the law of gravity was but a deduction from man's experience that what was dropped always fell; science could not demonstrate any absolute necessity to this. Similarly, the basic propositions of the deists, their "rational religion," assumed that human religious experience allowed man to deduce fundamental sacred truths, but nothing in his observation or experience allowed such a conclusion. There could be no rational proof for the existence of God. To argue, for example, that he was the necessary first cause of the universe was to assume that the universe must have been created; it was just as easy to assume that the universe had always existed. For all man knew, Hume dryly noted, God might or might not have created the world; there might have been many Gods; God might be a woman, he might even be evil. About such matters man might believe what he would. It was senseless to persecute others for not believing what man could not prove to be true. Nor did the miracles recorded in the Bible prove the divinity of Christ. Science told man that nature operated by constant and uniform laws, and a miracle must be a violation of those laws. Should someone claim to have witnessed a miracle, it was far easier to believe he was mistaken, mentally deranged, or simply fraudulent, than to believe that a miracle had actually occurred. For one or even several persons' testimony about personal experience could not be superior to the collective experience of scientists about the constant uniformity of the laws of nature. Choosing his example cautiously, Hume wrote that if someone reported that Queen Elizabeth had risen from the dead to return to the throne, he would be dismissed as either deluded, medically ignorant, blinded by faith, or simply insane. But even if he were believed, the queen's resurrection would not be grounds for founding a new religion. One could not demonstrate the occurrence of a miracle, for if man observed something in nature that had never been seen before, he could only assume there were laws of nature that had not yet been discovered. Taking the sage advice of his friend Adam Smith, Hume did not publish these remarks during his lifetime.

It followed that there could also be no miraculous conversions of Jews by the bleeding of the Host, and none of the sinister, occult, or satanic powers attributed to them by so many ordinary Christians. The vast majority of Europeans might still believe these things, but the educated must choose between them and the new scientific worldview. Increasingly, skeptics challenged the verities of particular faiths and the will to persecute in their name. Some argued that whatever revelations man needed for salvation must have been implanted in his instincts at the time of creation. A benevolent God could scarcely have limited his grace to an insignificant tribe in a remote corner of the globe, or condemn all those who died before the appearance of Jesus. Quarrels over myths created by the primitive mentality of thousands of years ago were pointless, for how could man take as literal truths the mutually contradictory accounts of the Crucifixion and Resurrection according to Matthew, Mark, Luke, and John—all born, moreover, far too late to witness these events? One author put the disciples on trial and found cause for reasonable doubt in their testimony. Voltaire found it unlikely that God would have chosen for divine enlightenment a people so miserable as the Jews; he also believed Jesus far too noble to have been a Christian. John Toland, in *Christianity Not Mysterious* (1686), asserted that Christians must stop persecuting Jews. If Christians wished to purify religion, let them start with their own distorted version of Christ's message. Many argued that a reasonable assessment of the evidence demonstrated that Christ fulfilled none of the prophecies of the Old Testament. Many Christian clerics, however, anxious to prove that Christianity was the true religion of reason, often expressed unambiguous anti-Judaic sentiments, denouncing Judaism as a dead religion of ritual. But this was quite different from seeing Judaism as the belief of an arrogant, Christ-killing, and satanic people whose race determined them to be evil. The rational norms of deism, even when used to buttress Christianity, could give no intellectual support to the blind faith that leads to hate.

The Anglican Church of England was a tame and passionless branch of the civil service, tolerant by the eighteenth century because of the power of Protestant sectarianism and the fears aroused by the Puritan Revolution of Cromwell. But the Catholic church in France, independent, extremely wealthy, and oppressive, was headed by a hierarchy enjoying many prerogatives and great political power. And the close connection of the church with the abuses of the old regime made the French philosophes, as they were called, more radical and anticlerical than the British, and more anxious to use the new ideas as weapons against the iniquities of king, noble, and church. Diderot, editor of the most famous and influential publication of the Enlightenment, the *Encyclopedia*, found both Judaism and Christianity absurd. Only the censors prevented him from calling Jesus an "obscure and fanatical Jew," forcing him instead to refer to the "Son of God." But if the article on the Messiah in the *Encyclopedia* appeased the censors by denouncing the Jews for rejecting Christ, it also repeated stories that Jesus was in fact the son of a prostitute and a Roman legionary and practiced black magic, and it praised those princes who protected the Jews. Diderot found Judaism absurd, but "The Christian religion is to my mind the most absurd and atrocious in its dogmas; the most unintelligible . . . the most mischievous for public tranquillity . . . the most dangerous to sovereigns . . . by its persecutions . . . the most puerile and unsociable in its morality . . . the most intolerant of all."[2]

Enlightened critics denounced the Old Testament as a collection of erotic and sinful tales about a vile people who waged endless wars, their primitive hatreds encouraged by a tribal warrior-God. But their denunciations were thereby also aimed at one of the sacred texts of Christianity. Jean d'Alembert, a typical philosophe, admired Christ as a moral teacher but ignored claims for his divinity. D'Alembert found Christian dogmas unbelievable and priests and persecution detestable. Montesquieu, perhaps the most pro-Jewish of the philosophes, wearied of the sterile debates about supposed rational proofs for the existence of God. Like Hume, he was far more interested in the reasons why different peoples had different sacred myths. Naturally, he supported the liberation of the Jews from Christian persecution. An extensive travel literature, the prelude to anthropology, was for others a convenient way to praise the allegedly sensible and reasonable religious practices of "noble savages," leaving the contrast with the bloody history of Christianity unspoken but obvious.

Countless writers enthused about the marvels of God's creations, describing, for example, how the intricately designed human eye was perfectly created for human vision. In this manner, science became the ultimate standard for religious faith, and scientifically derived evidence of the work of the Great Author of Nature, as he was often called, supported no particular religious mythology. Among the educated, traditional theologians were required to prove themselves in the light of secular rationality; there could be no passionate crusades for divine truth. For those accepting the new ideas, it was impossible to cling to the old absolutes, ridiculous to persecute in their name. Thus the eighteenth-century critics of religion helped forge the happy compromise that protects all religious faith in the name of liberal pluralism: Let each practice his or her faith in freedom.

The massacres of the Wars of Religion reinforced enlightened hostility toward the destructiveness of religious faith. Certainly economic and political motives helped cause the wars, but in the seventeenth century religion and politics were not separated—political motives were thus driven by deadly passions, and civilians often became the enemy. For the emerging bureaucratic, professional, and business classes, this was bloody and wasteful. More and more were convinced that religion must be separated from politics, a subversive idea at a time when the rights of kings, the duties of subjects, and the hierarchies of society were seen as divinely ordained. Deism provided the rationale, death and destruction the motive. "No more theological wars, no more soldiers of religion," cried La Mettrie, the French materialist. "The universe will only be happy when it is atheist."[3] Few were ready for that. Jean Bodin, lone disciple of tolerance during the French Wars of Religion, had argued for the separation of church and state and toleration for Judaism. Accused of atheism, he was fortunate to have powerful protectors. Thomas Hobbes wisely kept his atheism to himself, but he insisted that princes "stop the mouths of insolent priests." Born prematurely, as he tells us, the "twin son of fear," his mother gripped by terror as the Spanish Armada prepared to invade England in the name of the one true faith, Hobbes boasted he was the first to flee England when the Puritan civil wars broke out. But this only brought him to France in time for the assassination of Henry IV by a pious killer, who was furious that the king had sought peace through compromise between Protestants and Catholics, casually switching religions himself in pursuit of political goals. As Henry IV declared, "Paris is worth a Mass." Hobbes's famous phrase, mankind's life is "nasty, brutish, and short," is a distillation of his personal experience. Enamored of the new science, he held that religious revelation came through the testimony of men who could never prove they had spoken with God, hence all were free to doubt. The prince should destroy those who raised the sword for such fantasies.

Even Rousseau, the only philosophe with an emotional attachment to the mysteries of faith, believed that only a deist civic religion should be enforced, one including only those few precepts necessary to support social peace and encourage civic duty. Those who would not swear to these principles should be banished as antisocial; those who betrayed their oath might be put to death. But once having sworn to these civic principles to protect the peace, all ought to be free to follow their chosen religion, and none should be permitted to force their beliefs on others. Rousseau regretted that Jewish beliefs were known only through Christian distortions. He insisted that Jews should be free from persecution and allowed to present their side of the Christian-Jewish debate. Even today in the most liberal of nations, such truly free expression is far too strong for most, for Christians would be forced to confront powerful arguments against the idea that Jesus was the Messiah of the Jews, and this from a community well represented by learned biblical scholars who best know the original languages and texts. "Jews for Jesus" is one thing; Jews against Jesus would be quite another.

Voltaire, a violent antagonist of Christianity and Judaism, was famous for his defense of freedom of conscience and his outcries against the religious persecutions of his day. Yet he was also a vicious anti-Semite, his work peppered with tirades about usurious calculating cheats, thieving moneylenders, superstitious wretches, the "scum of the earth." And he believed these traits innate. Nevertheless, he demanded an end to the persecution of the Jews. Ironically, Voltaire was an anti-Semite because he failed to share the most revolutionary idea of his fellow philosophes: he did not believe that the characteristics of a people were the result of their historical experience and social conditioning. Consequently the most famous of the philosophes, like the defenders of the old regime, utterly failed to understand that it was the historical and social force of the degrading roles Christian persecution had forced upon Jews that distorted their behavior.

The vast majority of the enlightened, though they despised the petty moneylending and peddling of the ghetto Jews, believed that no people had fixed or innate traits, and that ethnic character was the result of social and historical experience. Intellectually pioneering, the philosophes' message is still not accepted by most ordinary citizens, even in the liberal nations of the West. Racial stereotyping is far easier than puzzling out the complex ways by which ethnic groups are channeled into different occupations by a variety of social pressures and opportunities, or lack of them. Rejecting the traditional belief in innate ideas and fixed traits, the philosophes asked the question: How then does the human mind get its contents? Locke declared the mind a clean slate at birth; experience gave it content. Starting from this, a generation of thinkers studied the interaction between mental experience, social attitudes, and moral values. All were fascinated by new studies aimed at understanding how an infant learned to perceive the world. The most radical insisted that all actions as well as beliefs were caused by external stimuli—the self was nothing but a collection of all the sensations it had experienced.

Such inquiries were literally revolutionary, for if human character was not the consequence of inborn traits, then there was no basis for the corresponding belief in the divine sanction of inherited institutions, customs, and class characteristics. These were dangerous ideas. Diderot was briefly imprisoned for simply publishing speculations about the heretical moral and religious ideas that a blind man might build from his unique sensory limitations. Condillac insisted that even the intellectual powers of the mind were nothing more than the product of experience and education. The philosophes, intent upon destroying the received ideas of the defenders of the old regime, claimed that all men were equal at birth. Peasants, merchants, aristocrats, kings, even Jews did not possess traits or abilities determined by divine or fixed characteristics. Condorcet recommended mass education in order gradually to perfect mankind; Beccaria argued that criminal behavior was a product of social conditions; Pinel suggested that the mentally ill were not possessed of the devil but curable by humane rehabilitation. In an extremely popular book, Helvétius insisted that man's character, abilities, and achievements were a product of his class, his social circumstances, his family upbringing, and his formal education. Let us transform society, he urged, so that all are given an equal chance to develop their abilities. The book was condemned by the pope, burnt by the clergy, and constantly harassed by state censors.

For philosophes, the task was to build a social and educational environment capable of forming a talented, virtuous, and flourishing people, and to do so by ending the artificial class and religious divisions of French society. Rousseau, as usual, took this to its logical conclusion. Education must create rational humans fit to live in a reasonable and just society. Because society was malformed, ideally one ought to isolate the child so that experience would not teach him it was just to reward the parasitic aristocrat and demean the honest toil of the manual laborer. Let the young learn that religious mythologies were just that, and teach them nothing about God until they were old enough to understand the difference between superstition and science, and wise enough to scorn the destructive irrationalities of religious persecution.

The new science of mind was a powerful intellectual force against the isolation and persecution of the Jews. The petty moneylending and commerce of the Jews, almost all philosophes believed, were a result of social conditioning through Christian oppression. Liberation from civic disabilities would bring the assimilation of the Jews into all occupations. Toland denied that Jews either had unique physical characteristics or were natural parasites. Christian clergy, hating and fearing the Jews, he wrote, limited their choice of occupation and isolated them in order to steal their property and curry favor with the ignorant masses. The allegedly unique Jewish antisocial behavior that Christians complained about, Toland insisted, was the result of Christian oppression. Liberate the Jews and you would see them in all professions, even that of warrior. Toland was one of the first to call for full citizenship and freedom for the Jews of Great Britain, demanding they be encouraged to return to the land from which they had been driven. In his famous work *The Spirit of the Laws*, Montesquieu argued that governments and people were formed by historical circumstances. He demanded an end to the civic disabilities of the Jews. Condorcet and Buffon, the great French naturalist, refused to believe Jews (or blacks) were innately inferior. Rousseau insisted the Jews could not possibly be a race, precisely because they were scattered among all peoples and had intermarried with them over the ages.

For the medieval Christian intellectual, each class had its proper and natural place in a divinely created social order. Social divisions and class rank were the consequences of a "final cause," the divine idea of the ordered Christian society in the mind of God. Consequently each group and class had the appropriate rights, duties, and innate qualities for its station and function. In medieval art, princes and priests were depicted at the apex of society followed by nobles; behind them trailed merchants, craftsmen, and peasants, then beggars, actors, and prostitutes, with Jews bringing up the rear.

Freed from divine determinism, the philosophes believed mankind capable of building a just social order. As in constructing a rational religion, the philosophes used what they assumed to be the method of Newtonian science. To decide what changes ought to be made, they imagined man as he might be in a "state of nature," that is, "natural man" before he was "malformed" by historical accident, religious myths, the vagaries of specific laws and customs, and the arbitrary rulings of princes. From this they hoped to deduce a few basic, rational, and self-evident propositions essential to human nature and guides for reform. This was subversion writ large, for at one stroke the established system and class relationships of the old regime became nothing but an irrelevant obstacle to man's similar and fundamental needs. The purpose of society and politics must be, as John Locke insisted, to protect the "natural and inalienable rights of man" as deduced from the state of nature and embodied in a bill of rights. Most agreed these should include the right to property, reasonable laws, and equal opportunity for the pursuit of happiness. Significantly, religious conformity was ignored, for in the state of nature there were no Christians, Jews, or Muslims, and no warrant for supporting or repressing any religion. The separation of church and state became liberal dogma, and there was no support among the enlightened, even Voltaire, for the persecution of the Jews.

Nothing helped to liberate the Jews of Europe more than the liberation of the entrepreneurial spirit from the restrictions of government and guild. By the eighteenth century the great spurt of trade and international commerce, led by the Italians, Dutch, English, and French—but notably not the Germans—brought admiration for commerce and impatience with traditional religious prejudices against lending at interest. Far more than just a new economic theory, free enterprise demanded a revolutionary transformation of society by liberating man's most basic social activity. For those who accepted its precepts, it necessarily lessened the scorn and limits that Christian society had aimed at the commercial activities of the Jews.

Adam Smith, an avid devotee of the Enlightenment, had also reached his conclusions by applying the Newtonian method to the science of economics. Writing before the age of specialization, Smith published works in ethics, astronomy, and physics before his famous *Wealth of Nations* in 1776. In all his works he wrote of the grand and beneficent design of the "Great Author of Nature" as revealed by the laws of the universe, society, and ethics. As with the laws governing the movements of the universe, Smith believed, so too with the millions of decisions made in the marketplace. Both were governed by general laws, in spite of the seemingly random choices of buyers and sellers and the arbitrary movements of prices, wages, and interest rates. Smith concluded that the "natural" laws of economics, set by an "invisible hand," controlled the whole, which, if men did not interfere, would bring well-being. Mankind should no more interfere with the laws of economics than he should attempt to tamper with the laws of the universe. As Smith wrote, "The administration of the great system of the universe . . . the cause of the universal happiness of all rational and sensible Beings, is the business of God and not of man."[4]

It followed that legislation should not restrict the legitimate economic activities of any group, least of all for religious reasons. The greatest good for all would be served if independent businessmen were allowed to search for profit unhampered by guild, princely, or feudal restrictions. Provided he did not engage in restrictive monopolistic practices (a big if, Smith knew), the entrepreneur was the unwitting benefactor of all. Wherever the new science of economics was accepted, prejudices against the economic activities of the Jews weakened. Even moneylending, thought for so many centuries to be a degrading "Jewish" activity, was praised in Diderot's influential *Encyclopedia*, and others agreed: moral disapproval of "usury" was damaging. Credit promoted economic growth; interest rates should be regulated only by the law of supply and demand. For the enlightened, economic freedom became the basic liberal freedom. Regardless of any personal animus he or she might have against the Jews, no liberal could support economic restrictions against them.

The philosophes also tried to separate ethical conduct from religious faith, using the cruelty of religious conflicts to make the point. How then was the undoubted fact of moral behavior to be explained? As before, many sought an innate moral sense or instinct originally implanted in man's nature by the Supreme Being, and hoped to reduce moral behavior to a few fundamental principles, creating thus a rational morality to fit a rational religion, both free from the superstitions of primitive taboos. Some agreed with Locke: one day there would be a rationally self-evident science of ethics as demonstrable as mathematics. Others held there were but two basic and inherent moral principles common to all mankind: calculating or self-regarding hedonism, modified by a humane regard for others. Both must be inherent and "natural" because both were necessary, for without them neither the individual nor society could survive. Once again it was impossible to single out any unique "Jewish" moral traits.

In his famous The Fable of the Bees, Bernard Mandeville wrote, "Private vices are public virtues." Greed was the powerful engine of economic growth and promoted the welfare of all. The ascetic Christian code was a fiction created by clergymen who manipulated the public by guilt. In all the moral writings of the Enlightenment, the notions of original sin, self-sacrifice, and spiritual redemption through self-sacrifice are notably lacking. A belief in a natural harmony of interests, if each were guided by his or her own rational self-interest, became the core of nineteenth-century liberalism. Those who believed this could hardly denounce the Jews for excelling in commerce and trade. It would be the reactionaries of nineteenth-century Europe—enemies of Enlightenment thought—who would endlessly denounce what they labeled as "Jewish" materialism, liberalism, greed, and free enterprise.

Historians call the eighteenth century in Europe the "Age of Enlightenment," but in truth the vast majority of Europeans were ignorant of or rejected the new ideas. But ideas gain force when they fit the experience and aspirations of large and influential groups, and the late eighteenth century witnessed a veritable explosion of commercial progress in France, Holland, and England. Merchants, manufacturers, bankers, and entrepreneurs ranged far afield in search of markets and products in the new empires overseas, and even some nobles engaged in commerce or manufactures. Germany possessed no colonies; her nobles avoided commerce. It was the commercial and professional classes who found the new attitudes most congenial. In Amsterdam, the most cosmopolitan and international trading center in Europe, diversity was tolerated, the middle classes flourished, and most of the classics of Enlightenment thought were published. It was a safe haven for those fleeing persecution. Bayle, born a Calvinist, had been converted to Catholicism by the Jesuits. When he recanted he fled to Amsterdam. Spinoza was the son of Orthodox Jews whose ancestors, forced to convert to Christianity by the Spanish Inquisition, retained their hidden Jewish identity. Although excommunicated and banished from the Jewish community of Amsterdam for heresy, and ostracized by Christians as well, Spinoza would otherwise live freely. John Locke, suspected of radicalism by the British government, lived in Amsterdam for some years as well. Voltaire wisely dwelt on the Swiss border.

By the end of the eighteenth century middle-class aspirations and interests, buttressed by the new science, seemed rooted in the very nature of the universe, society, and man, and this alliance forged a powerful confidence in those who opposed the old regime. Armed with such formidable weapons, their leaders increasingly attacked the tyranny of princes, the restrictions of guilds, and the privileges of aristocrats. With the significant exception of Prussia, government bureaucrats were recruited from the middle classes and supported secular rationalism against church, noble, and guild. More than one prominent bureaucrat in France, for example, dismissed the anti-Semitism of the guilds as the desperate cry of the inefficient who cynically used religion simply to restrict successful competitors.

The new classes, cosmopolitan and independent of mind, were in nothing extreme, least of all religion. Although they thought church attendance necessary for social respectability, they scorned the passionately religious as fanatics. When the middle classes meditated upon God, they did not dwell on Calvin's righteous tyrant, Luther's passionate need for salvation, or the grace offered by the sacraments of the Church of Rome; if they thought about such matters at all, they envisioned the Supreme Being, the natural laws of society, the rational nature of man, and the ethics of the harmony of enlightened self-interest and social well-being. Within this intellectual context there was no reason to continue the Christian oppression of the Jews.

The old regime in France was on the defensive. No philosophe favored revolution; it would be enough to have enlightened princes whose decrees would be influenced by their interests, not by the backward views of arrogant priests and idle aristocrats. But it was not to be, and soon the leaders of the enlightened in France would demand, not request, free trade, equality before the law, equal access to all offices, universal elementary education, toleration for all religions, freedom of conscience, and the separation of church and state. With this would come, naturally enough, demands for the liberation of the Jews, for the new worldview allowed for no exceptions because of race, religion, or birth. Just as the aristocracy should have no special rights, so also the Jews should have no special disabilities. Consequently the "Jewish question" was increasingly raised in the last decades of the eighteenth century in France. Allow the Jews to pursue all occupations freely and they would soon find respectable careers. With this went the patronizing expectation that, once liberated, the Jews would assimilate into the enlightened minority, drop their religious "superstitions," and be grateful for the chance. It would not be so simple. Nevertheless, the Enlightenment had created the cultural environment for liberation. Soon the revolutionists of 1789 would make good the promise. France would become the first nation in Europe to legislate an end to all legal civic disabilities leveled against the Jewish community.

4: THE LIBERATION OF THE JEWS IN FRANCE

All citizens, being equal before the law, are equally admissible to all public offices, positions, and employments, according to their capacity, and without other distinction than virtues and talents.
—*Declaration of the Rights of Man and the Citizen*, 1789

IN eighteenth-century France many occupations and regions were closed to Jews, who were also subject to special taxes and forbidden to own homes or marry without special permission. Royal administrators protected those who were deemed useful, such as traders in military supplies, but all rights were subject to arbitrary reversal. French monarchs could no more place the Jews on an equal footing with others than they could decree equality before the law or the separation of church and state, for their powers were held by divine right, an integral part of the Christian worldview sanctifying the power of the church, the rights of the aristocracy, and the oppression of the Jews. Jean Colbert, the famous finance minister of Louis XIV, for example, hoped to improve the economy by inviting "useful" Jews into the realm but reserving agriculture and the guilds for Christians, as medieval princes had done. Even for this he was accused of a lack of piety by court, guilds, and clergy. Louis XIV drove the Protestants out of France in 1685, and he and his clergy wished to throw out the Jews as well. Colbert objected, complaining that both groups were economically valuable to the realm. But given prevailing attitudes, he and other bureaucrats could only shrug their shoulders and hold their tongues.

One hundred years later, the power of the intervening Enlightenment was shown by another famous royal administrator, Robert Turgot. A philosophe who wrote for Diderot's *Encyclopedia*, he served under Louis XVI, the monarch destined to be the most famous victim of the revolution. Turgot administered the province of Limoges in the enlightened spirit, improving education and agriculture, introducing new industries, building roads and public works. Appointed finance minister in 1774, Turgot tried to tax wealthy landowners, end forced peasant labor, and abolish the guilds. He aided Jews who tried to break down guild barriers, and wrote that freedom of religion and free choice of occupation were rights, not privileges, to be enjoyed by all citizens. Hoping to liberate the Jews from all civic disabilities, Turgot advised the king to ignore his royal duty to destroy heretics. Incensed, the higher clergy, landowners, and the court aristocracy forced his resignation. Louis XVI repealed Turgot's edicts.

But the new attitudes abounded. In his excellent study *The French Enlightenment and the Jews*, Arthur Hertzberg tells of a group of French Jews who in 1775 petitioned for admission into a merchant guild. The lawyer representing the Jews, Lacretelle, agreed with guild spokesmen that the Jew "has a unique passion for money" and, "deprived of any resources other than deceit, the Jew has made a vocation of the art of lying." But these traits, he argued, were the result of society's restrictions. The courts, he pleaded, must help liberate the Jews, thereby encouraging their virtues and lessening their faults: "Reason has raised its radiant head in our century. . . . It is everywhere attacking laws it did not enact. . . . Let us open our cities to them and allow them to spread out in our countryside. . . ."[1]

In 1785 the academy at Metz, where anti-Semitism was particularly strong, offered a prize for an answer to the question: "Are there ways of making the Jews happier and more useful in France?" Most of the essays submitted "cite our prejudices against the Jews as the primary cause of their vices . . . ," and the academy agreed: "We make it impossible for them to be honest. . . . Let us be fair to them so that they can be fair to us."[2] Again and again the idea appears: liberate the Jews from Christian oppression and the despised traits would disappear. If the Jews were usurers, it was because Christians had driven them from honest occupations, forcing them to live thus or starve. As a prize winner wrote: "It is we who must stand accused of those crimes so unjustly blamed on the Jews; it is we who forced them to commit them," for "it is to our fathers' barbarous behavior toward them, it is to our own injustice that we must attribute it. . . ."[3]

The emancipation of the Jews was necessary if only because any exceptions to the demand for liberty and equality would contradict all progressive change. Henri Gregoire, a cleric and a supporter of the Enlightenment, fought the privileges of the higher clergy and nobility, demanded equality for all races, wanted slavery abolished, and advocated tolerance. He disapproved of Judaism, yet he played an important role in the emancipation of the Jews. The Jews were not innately and absolutely depraved, he wrote, "they are men like us . . . born with the same capacities as ourselves."[4] Moreover, Gregoire and thousands like him also believed that French Catholics should reject those Christian dogmas that did not square with reason. As he exclaimed: "A new century is about to begin. . . . The Jews are members of the universal family which is . . . creating fraternity among all peoples. . . . Children of the same father, cast off every pretext for hating your brothers."[5]

Until his death in 1791, Mirabeau, favorite of the Parisian crowds, led the revolution. In 1787 he published *On Moses Mendelssohn*, a German Jew who against great odds had been permitted to leave the ghetto. His fame was spread by Gotthold Lessing, Germany's most enlightened thinker, who in his popular play *Nathan the Wise* depicted Mendelssohn as one who had the courage to demonstrate that Judaism was as reasonable as Christianity. Mendelssohn inspired a generation of young Jews to break with the restrictions of ghetto life and join the mainstream of European culture. Inspired by him, Mirabeau and thousands of his supporters held it absurd to keep the Jews in the ghetto. Allow the Jews to liberate themselves from the tyranny of a ghetto religion and they would join in the fight against the real enemies of France—the aristocrats, tyrants, and Catholic leaders who held off reform.

On the eve of the revolution the works of the Enlightenment were diffused throughout France. They could be found in private diaries and libraries, in journals, the publications of academies, in works of lesser authors, in book collections, circulating libraries, pamphlets, songs, ballads, and poems, and even in staid publications of societies for the improvement of agriculture and commerce and lawyers pressing for legal reforms. Through them the abstract ideas of the Enlightenment were connected to the practical interests of millions. It is this unity of ideas and interests that gives ideas the force to change society. When, on the eve of the revolution, the king himself requested representative groups from all over France to express their grievances in the famous *cahiers*, their complaints, though practical, were derived from Enlightenment thought. In effect, the new ideas defined discontent, located its causes, suggested practical solutions, and offered radical new perspectives on sufferings once accepted fatalistically. The intellectual bases of the old society, with its extreme social distinctions, daily injustices, and unearned privileges, was eroding, and the travail, interests, and experience of millions of Frenchmen were seen in a new and radical light.

But hostility toward the Jews was embedded in the institutions and values of the old regime. To the majority, talk of liberating the Jews was sacrilegious, frightening, and deeply subversive. Hertzberg tells us of Liefman Calmer, a Jew who purchased a barony in 1744 and with it the right to appoint priests. A priest wrote that this "descendant of the killers of Christ," these "born and sworn enemies of all Christians," could not be permitted to appoint Christian priests. Calmer's purchase was a Jewish plot to destroy Christendom and prepare for the ultimate dominance of the Jews. The priest forged a letter to make it appear as though one rabbi had written to another to instruct Calmer to appoint only circumcised men as priests on his estate. Another forged letter, also pretending to be from one Jew to another, declared that Calmer was preparing the way for the destruction of all churches and the rule of the Jews "over Christians all over the world."[6] Angered by enlightened bureaucrats' attempts to limit the restrictions of the guilds in the name of free enterprise, Louis-Sebastien Mercier, a spokesman for the guilds, in 1770 wrote a novel predicting that the Jews, once freed, would enslave all Christians through the great wealth they would amass by their vile economic chicanery. A voice from the future talks to the enemies of the guilds: you allowed this to happen, and the Jews tried to destroy us, but we will take "decisive action" against them and "their ferocious superstition."[7]

Anti-Semitism was most powerful in the eastern province of Alsace, where more than half of all French Jews lived, some twenty thousand. An extremely high percentage were moneylenders. Alsace had been a French possession only for a few years, and Alsatian Jews lived more like the ghetto Jews of Central Europe than those of France. Yiddish-speaking, Orthodox, and from German, i.e., enemy, territory, they generated such forceful antagonisms that even most of the revolutionists from Alsace did not want them liberated. The accusation of usury, of course, was constantly hurled at the Jews of Alsace and Lorraine. But the phrase was loosely used; it means the charging of illegally high interest, not just high interest. In France the legal interest rate differed from province to province and depended on the relative risk involved. Christians as well as Jews were convicted of usury by the courts, and the proportion of Jewish defendants was roughly similar to their activity in petty commerce. The king himself allowed usury when his treasury received a percentage of the profits.

Anti-Semitism arose because Jews were often lenders of last resort to peasants; local governments allowed a higher rate of interest to anyone who would assume the high risk. When peasants attacked Jewish "usury" they were often really complaining about the refusal of anyone to lend to them at rates reserved for wealthier creditors. Some complaints accused Christians of charging higher rates than Jews, for usury was a problem even where no Jews lived. As Mirabeau remarked, having forced the Jews out of all honorable occupations, society refused to admit that many Christians with no such excuse charged extortionate interest. Usury, undefined, also became an excuse to expel Jewish business competitors and cancel debts. There were vastly more accusations of "Jewish usury" than ever came to court. As some Jewish writers complained, why are there not more court cases if we are really so guilty? But even the conviction of one Jew for usury brought an outcry against "the Jews." Subtle distinctions were rare among peasant anti-Semites, and their representatives in the revolution would attempt to prevent the liberation of the Jews.[8]

The aristocracy itself unwittingly started the revolution of 1789 by demanding its ancient right to approve new tax burdens through a meeting of the Estates General, the representative body of clergy, aristocracy, and the middle class. Easily dominated by the aristocracy when it had last met in 1614, now the body faced the middle class, fully conscious of its new power, productivity, and values. It demanded a full range of constitutional changes. The Third Estate resisted the king's attempt to dissolve it by force, and with self-confident audacity and the unexpected support of thousands of radical Parisians, it declared itself the National Assembly. Lawyers, former government officials, merchants, and some 200 clerics and 50 nobles led the 830 members. Even a few Jewish delegates had been elected, in itself revolutionary. The agenda of the Enlightenment proceeded apace; by late summer the feudal rights of the nobility were abolished and the principle established that no group should have special rights or disabilities. On August 27, 1789, "The Declaration of the Rights of Man and the Citizen" was promulgated. Some delegates held that it liberated both Jews and Protestants from all civic disabilities, but the document did not specifically say so, and further legislation was required. By December 1789 Protestants were declared eligible for military and civic office. Mirabeau and other delegates wanted Jews freed as well, but the clergy objected. Moving on, the delegates granted equal access to offices, equality before the law, equal taxation, and freedom of assembly and press and from arbitrary arrest. Property became a "sacred" right. Economic freedom was granted as guilds were abolished along with customs tolls and fiscal immunities favoring church and aristocrat. Males who paid the equivalent of three days' wages in taxes were given the vote, but, though the more radical leaders of the assembly protested, Protestants and Jews were not. The most radical called for women's suffrage as well.

As reform followed reform, denying Jewish rights became untenable, and radicals, including Robespierre and Danton, insisted that the next step must be the liberation of the Jews. Of the 45,000 Jews in France, some 8,000 were Sephardic. More affluent than the Ashkenazi Jews, Sephardic Jews were more likely to be found in enterprises thought respectable. Indeed, the Sephardim prided themselves on their "superiority" to the Ashkenazim, whom some Sephardic leaders believed had been degraded by a ghetto mentality. Many Sephardim were angered by the historical failure to distinguish between the two groups, but racists would not be racists if they made such distinctions. Many delegates were willing to grant civil rights to the Sephardim, and in January 1790 Mirabeau managed a quick vote when clerical delegates were temporarily absent.

The Sephardim were liberated. Mirabeau's opponents on the right angrily accused him of being in the pay of the Jews, an accusation flung at "righteous Gentiles" until the Nazis and after.

The most powerful opponent of the Jews, the Catholic church, was itself under siege. Owning one-third of the national wealth and wielding much secular authority, the church was denounced by the revolutionaries who hoped to end the political power of private corporations. In 1790, after heated debate, the assembly passed the most famous and divisive legislation of the revolution, the Civil Constitution of the Clergy. Deprived of most of their secular power, clerics became elected civil servants paid by the state. Parish priests were to receive higher salaries than before, bishops considerably less; church property was nationalized. The final blow fell when the clergy were required to swear an oath of allegiance to the revolutionary state and the Civil Constitution of the Clergy. Many clerics, including some sympathetic to reform, declared that the revolutionaries were attacking Christ and the faith. Revolutionaries replied that they had changed no divine dogma but only man-made administrative and legal arrangements, making the church more responsive to the will of the nation. Furious, many clergy responded that the church was responsible to the will of God, not the people. But revolutionary leaders declared that there could be no state within the state, and allowed the clergy only spiritual powers over their flock. Pope Pius VI was incensed. He anathematized the revolution in 1791, an act similar to excommunication, and condemned those bishops who took the oath. About half the clergy refused the oath, and many priests who replaced them in rural areas found their churches empty at Mass and their recalcitrant predecessors treated as heroes by their parishioners. Clergy, now on the run, became a focus of counterrevolution, and many began to blame the Jews for 1789. In 1790 even Edmund Burke condemned the revolution as in part the work of "usurious Jews"—another myth was being added to the armory of anti-Semitism.

Finding the votes to liberate the Ashkenazim was still difficult. Delegates from Alsace and Lorraine insisted that Jews could not be citizens of any nation, for "The Laws of Moses make the Jews a distinct nation among all the nations of the earth; they take the greatest precautions so that they will never be mixed or assimilated. . . ." Others held that Jews did not mix, marry, or even eat with Christians. If they were allowed to maintain their separate communal institutions and be liberated as well, they would use these advantages to harm the French. What the Jews gain from us, one monarchist wrote, they will keep for themselves, and Jews will descend upon France from everywhere to carry out a "legal conquest" of the French.[9]

François Hell, deputy from Alsace, led the fight against Jewish liberation, but his reputation was tarnished because he had organized a campaign to forge documents to cheat Jewish creditors out of the legal payment of debts, though the crime made him popular among peasants. A supporter of the king, Hell later died on the guillotine for promonarchist activities. In the assembly he demanded that Jews be expelled from France as unassimilable or forced into "honorable" professions. Some noted it was Hell and those like him who prevented Jews from entering the professions in the first place. In Alsace, Jews were forbidden to farm or join guilds. One delegate suggested that if laws were the same for all and enforced equally, no conclusions about the alleged corruption of any group need be made. If usury was a crime, enforce the law and leave it at that. A Parisian deputy remarked, "If they have any foundation, the moral and political objections against the Jews do not mean anything but that the Jews, like Christians, will have to regenerate themselves through the constitution."[10]

Many rabbinical leaders opposed the liberation of the Jews. A number of young Jews of Paris had already deserted Judaism, and, declaring their deism, ignored dietary laws and rabbinical authority, and publicly consorted with Gentile women. They too hoped to end the secular power of all religious authorities. But for most Jews matters were not so simple. A Gentile deist did not have to break with his family and community and become vulnerable in a world where only a tiny minority might welcome him. And if the revolution were defeated? It is no surprise that some Orthodox Jews fled France with the aristocratic reaction.

In general, the more radical the revolutionary, the less hostility toward the Jews. The delegate Anacharsis Cloots, who dragged a tiny replica of the guillotine behind him as a warning to the enemy, had demanded the emancipation of the Jews in 1783. Far from being a degraded nation, he declared, they made valuable contributions to the economic life of Europe. Their bad reputation was the slander of Christian theologians who feared the Hebrew knowledge of the texts they claimed as proof of the divine origins of Christ. Before the revolution, Robespierre favored unconditional liberation for all Jews. The Paris Commune, the revolutionary government of Paris and the most radical institution in all of France, supported liberation practically unanimously. Reporting to the National Assembly, it insisted that the Jews had given sufficient proof of their devotion to the revolution. As for their alleged crimes, were not all Frenchmen in need of regeneration? Persecution of the Jews, the Commune declared, was unworthy of the newly created revolutionary consciousness of the people of France. Most Jews supported the revolution, and many had joined the National Guard to defend it or had signed petitions of support. And so it was that, on September 27, 1791, the Ashkenazim were liberated. For the first time in a European state, all Jews were officially equal with their fellow citizens before the law.

Amidst foreign invasion, counterrevolution, a raging inflation, and mob violence, the barely established First Republic gave way in 1794 to the dictatorship by committee of Robespierre. He hoped to establish a Republic of Virtue where human nature could be perfected through a Cult of the Supreme Being and Nature, a civic religion dedicating the citizenry to the support of the common good, as Rousseau had wanted. In this utopian endeavor Jews could hardly be singled out; citizens of all religions needed moral transformation. Moreover, and with good reason, anti-Semites were regarded as enemies of the regime. But Robespierre had gone beyond the consensus of the educated public, and the ultimate outcome was Napoleon and the restoration of a more moderate consensus.

Excluding self-government and freedom of expression, Napoleon believed in the revolution's reforms, including the liberation of the Jews. He knew his power depended on supporting the early gains of the revolution, and he did so in his famous Napoleonic Code of 1804. Indifferent to religion, Napoleon nevertheless found it useful: Why would the starving poor accept their misery, he once asked, if they did not believe that God would reward them after death? Religion "prevents the massacre of the rich by the poor."[11] Consequently Napoleon ended Robespierre's attempt to de-Christianize France, regaining the loyalty of Catholic peasants who provided armed support for the counterrevolution. Compromising with the pope, Napoleon angered revolutionaries and disturbed his own generals, who knew their victories against the mercenary troops of Europe were partially based on the republican sentiments and nationalistic fervor of their own troops. To calm these fears, Napoleon demanded major concessions from the pope. Nationalized church property, if already purchased, was not returned; all bishops, whether or not they supported the revolution, were forced to resign. The pope, anxious to restore France to the fold, betrayed those bishops who had risked life and liberty to remain loyal to him, and allowed Napoleon the right to nominate new bishops, though the pontiff retained the right to consecrate them. The pope recognized the Republic, and in return Napoleon simply declared, "Catholicism is the religion of the great majority of Frenchmen." Clerical salaries were paid by the state, and the church ceased to denounce the new France. Indeed, the pulpits of France often seemed merely public relations fronts for the glories of the new regime. Most significant, the church lost secular powers and had to accept religious toleration. To symbolize his victory Napoleon appointed as bishop Gregoire, the idol of the revolutionaries who had done so much to liberate the Jews. Most dramatic of all, Judaism was declared equal to

Catholicism and Protestantism, with the sole exception that its governing religious bodies would not receive government subsidies.

Napoleon, like the philosophes, detested Jewish involvement in moneylending and petty commerce but supported their liberation. As he said, "If I were governing Jews, I would restore the temple of Solomon."[12] In 1806 he convoked a general assembly of rabbis and Jewish laymen to ask: Would they be loyal to France and defend it as their homeland? The assembly shouted unanimously, "Yes, to the Death!"[13] In 1807 Napoleon convoked a Great Sanhedrin in Paris, so named to invoke memories of ancient Israel. He hoped to establish a central Jewish governing body from all of Europe. Orthodox Jews denounced the Sanhedrin as a violation of Jewish law, which it was. Only French and Italian Jews participated. German leaders would not permit "their" Jews to attend, and many Germans insisted that Napoleon was creating an anti-Christian and prorevolutionary force out of world Jewry, a complaint that rang through the century. The Holy Synod of Moscow proclaimed that the killers of Christ had found their new Messiah in Napoleon; other devout Christians denounced Napoleon as the Antichrist incarnate, for was the Great Sanhedrin not the very court that had pronounced Christ guilty of heresy?

In the patronizing spirit of the enlightened, Napoleon assembled the Sanhedrin to gain Jewish support for assimilation. The delegates, mostly rabbis, were asked to support intermarriage. They refused. When asked to limit Jewish commercial activities, they correctly pointed out that Jewish participation in usury was greatly exaggerated, and again they refused. Nor would they agree to civil marriages or to end the practice of buying substitutes for service in the French army. After all, as the rabbis noted, many Jews already served in the revolutionary armies, and non-Jewish Frenchmen were allowed to purchase substitutes. Rebuffed by the rabbis, and disturbed by counterrevolutionary activities in Alsace, Napoleon restricted the economic rights of Jews through what have been rightly condemned as his "Infamous Decrees," restricting the movement and activities of Alsatian Jews, annulling debts to Jews incurred by minors and women, and authorizing the courts to cancel, reduce amounts, or extend the time of payments of debts owed to Jews. Unfairly singled out, many Jews were ruined.

Napoleon justified his decrees by indicating that they were meant to weaken counterrevolution and hasten assimilation. But such actions seemed to substantiate his opponents' claim that the Jews were indeed a menace to society. The decrees illustrated the fragility of Jewish rights even with a basically friendly regime committed to enlightened ideals. Napoleon, like many, was ignorant of the great inertia holding back social change. Liberation, he assumed, should swiftly be followed by assimilation, as though legislation could obliterate the consequences of centuries of oppression, social conditioning, and religious identity. Conservatives shared his illusions, demanding to know why, if Jews were innately similar to all, they did not rush to become artisans and farmers?

As foreign governments fell before his cannons, Napoleon sought to gain the loyalty and support of the peoples of the new French Empire by reforms calculated to consolidate his power. The synergy of power and ideas accounts for the dramatic transformations he brought about. His famous codes of law struck a powerful blow at discrimination, with one crucial exclusion: Napoleon deliberately ignored the rights of women. Otherwise, in the empire, Napoleon established equality before the law, abolished serfdom, secularized education, loosened guild restrictions, established unified customs, created efficient bureaucracies, and built the roads and canals necessary for trade and communication. Almost everywhere Napoleon favored the enlightened and educated upper middle classes at the expense of the wealth and power of the old aristocracy. He also curbed the powers of the church, secularized church property, dissolved monasteries and convents, and enforced religious toleration. As he said, once the most progressive groups tasted the freedoms of Frenchmen, they would never wish to return to the oppression of their old rulers.

To build a base for an empire beyond Europe and create a strongpoint for his wars with the British—who had cut the French off from overseas riches—in Egypt in 1799 the conqueror called upon the Jews to "rally under their flag" and restore the Jerusalem of old. "You are the rightful heirs" of Palestine, he proclaimed, inviting Jews of all nations to establish a Jewish state.[14] Counterrevolutionaries declared that Napoleon wished to recreate the Jewish nation in order to destroy Christianity, but Orthodox Jews opposed the emperor's attempt to preempt the return of the Messiah. It was even widely rumored that Napoleon abandoned his plan to create a Jewish nation when he realized he was thus hastening the end of the world.

The struggle for Jewish liberation and assimilation began with the Napoleonic era. In Italy and the Germanies, Napoleon's Jewish soldiers often led the way into the ghettos, there to destroy the walls and free the inhabitants. Wherever Napoleon's armies conquered and his rule was established, Jewish liberation and assimilation commenced. Even the Vatican ghetto was dissolved. Throughout Europe, Napoleon was hailed by Jewish communities. Backed by the French and local liberals, Jews participated in Napoleon's reforms and the liberalization of Europe. But the power of traditionalists would revive, and with it anti-Semitism. In Poland, Napoleon withdrew the rights he granted Jews after Catholic and aristocratic protests; Poland was his buffer against Russia. And wherever there was no sizable enlightened middle class, Napoleonic reforms failed to

hold. Spain and Russia, backward, peasant, and pious, started his downfall. Where his reforms succeeded, Napoleon was vilified by royalists and
reactionaries, and Jews were singled out as the true beneficiaries of the
revolution, the lackeys of a foreign tyrant and oppressor.

Even before Napoleon's fall, the ultraroyalists of France persuaded
themselves that the Jews, not the ills of French society, were responsible
for 1789. With Napoleon gone, the ultras returned with Louis XVIII. A
"white terror" raged. Often led by nobles, mobs murdered thousands of
Jacobins, Bonapartists, Protestants, and Jews. The most influential reactionary during the years of exile was the Comte Joseph de Maistre. For
him 1789 was an attack against a divinely created social order, in nothing so clearly revealed as the liberation of the Jews from the historical
punishment decreed by the Almighty. Man could not even create an in-
sect, he argued, let alone a new constitution. The social order was the
work of God. Indeed, man's puny intellect could not understand God's
work, let alone improve it. Reason said it was absurd to select a ruler by
birth, yet must man not admit he was better off when the choice came
by divine fiat rather than when men alone attempted to create an ideal
social order?

The ultimate Christian religious determinist, de Maistre insisted that
Napoleon and Robespierre were instruments of God's wrath. Altruistic
revolutionaries and the God-haters of the Enlightenment had destroyed
divine institutions and proclaimed that human reason alone should rule.
So be it, God declared, and gave men Robespierre and Napoleon so they
might know once and for all the brutal and bloody consequences of the
reign of reason and the Antichrist. De Maistre even declared that no one
should interfere with Napoleon's rule: Let "God's monsters," the Jacobins
and Napoleon, liberate "God's enemies," the Jews, let them violate his
divine arrangements and ravage Europe. Let the consequences of 1789
run their full course until Europe was purged of its blasphemy by blood.
Never allow the masses to believe that if the revolution had continued it
would have brought them untold delights. After God's demons had completed their work and destroyed themselves, like Danton and Robespierre,
the terrorized and bleeding masses would beg for the return of king,
church, and aristocrat. Princes would no longer toy with reform, nobles
would cease reading Voltaire, and the clergy themselves would be
cleansed of their worldly cynicism. The Jews would find themselves back
in the ghettos, suspended in time until they witnessed for Christ in the
Final Days.

The leader of the ultraroyalists, the Vicomte Louis de Bonald, was
elected to France's most reactionary Chamber of Deputies, that of 1815.
There he announced that the Jews, if not pushed back into the ghetto,
would reduce Frenchmen to slaves. Evidently unable to believe Chris-

tians capable of selfishness without role models, he held the Jews responsible for the "spirit of greed" that inundated Europe with free enterprise. Allow them equal rights, he warned, and they will destroy us. In the chamber he argued that France must become a Christian theocracy, and the right of Jews to marry and propagate must be limited. Praising the Germans for restricting the activities of the Jews, Bonald insisted that France was at risk. "Christians may be cheated by Jews, but they ought not be governed by them."[15] God had decided the destiny of the Jews, and society went against his will if it made them citizens. No government could really liberate them. Spiritually corrupt, their murder of their own Messiah was proof of degradation. They despised and hated Christians. Liberation could not change the Jews; only conversion could make them morally fit to be French citizens.

Bonald was one of the first of a long line of reactionaries to attack liberal capitalism as Jewish. Unchecked by moral regulations, capitalism was the product of "Jewish" materialism and greed, he insisted. Soaring economic growth would drive men into vast cities and factories, tearing them from their village roots; spiritually empty, they would become victors or victims in a struggle for gain through merciless competition in anonymous cities where no man knew his neighbor. Life would grow harsh and lonely, and man's moral relationship with God, the church, and his fellow man would be destroyed. Restrict the Jews, he declared; return to the balanced life of village and church, guild and peasant, a life which generated and reinforced the norms of Christian ethical behavior. Bonald and de Maistre initiated the use of anti-Semitism as an essential part of the Catholic counterrevolutionary attack on modern liberalism, an attack that would find its most powerful political representation among the Germans of the Austrian Empire.

With tragic consequences, European Christian reactionaries, unable or unwilling to accept secular explanations, continued to associate the Jews with threats to their interests and privileges down to the rise of Hitler. Bonald declared there was no need for a parliament whatsoever; let the king rule as before, for the new order was a Jewish order bereft of Christian moral principles. But, fearful of unleashing revolutionary forces yet again, Louis XVIII compromised: "Long live the King in spite of Himself!" became the rallying cry of the ultras. The ultras achieved some important successes, but the bulk of the legislation of 1789 remained in place. Within the church, however, piety was restored. As de Maistre predicted, worldly church dignitaries cast aside Voltaire, and, as church attendance rose dramatically, a host of ultraconservative Catholic lay organizations sprang up while hundreds of thousands of Frenchmen attended religious ceremonies in public squares to purge the sins of Jacobinism and swear allegiance to king and pope. But if the right in

France was now firmly associated with Christian anti-Semitism, the whole of France was divided, and the division would protect the gains of the Jews. In the Germanies and Austria, their situation was far more precarious and dangerous.

Even in France, though the Jews were liberated, they were not free. The costs and dangers of their new position were varied. They were expected to change vocations and dampen their enthusiasm for their religion, if not abandon it; if they could not become Christians, at least they ought to become deists. Jews were expected to be more patriotic and with less cause than others. Judged not as individuals or Frenchmen, they remained Jews who, in return for patronizing toleration, must be grateful. Subject to expectations that Christians could ignore, all Jews were judged as representatives of their people, as strangers are judged in foreign lands. It became high praise to be a "credit to one's race," but those Jews who behaved badly were also seen as a discredit to their people; the crimes of a Jew were seen as the crimes of "the" Jews.

Nor were Jews free to express political opinions without arousing special antagonisms. Their fate depended on the fate of liberalism in Europe, and, with few exceptions, they were not welcome among the parties of the right even if baptized. Regardless of the law, informal sanctions would always be used against them in social institutions dominated, as they often were, by conservatives. In Europe and down to our day, Jews could never relax and just *be*. There would always be a double consciousness, an awareness of their ambiguous and frail position and a frustrating sense that they were not judged as individuals, even by their non-Jewish friends. They were symbols of a race, evidence of a problem, the embodiment of someone else's exaggerated expectations, suspicions, or hatreds. Jewish intellectuals adapted by forming an ironic sense of the ambivalence and ambiguity of their position, painfully aware of the difference between theoretical acceptance and informal discrimination, official attitudes and actual practices, public voices and private meanings. For this awareness too there was a price. Critics of the failure of society to live up to the full meaning of liberation would be accused of "Jewish" skepticism, oversensitivity, and radicalism, especially by those who believed traditional society and its institutions just and had never wanted Jewish liberation in the first place.

Above all, Jews depended for their rights upon the permanent institutionalization of the liberal gains of the French Revolution. They became symbols of those changes, whatever the complexities of their individual attitudes. Enemies of liberalism tended to become enemies of the Jews. Although strong in France, the right was predominant in Germany, determined to cancel the reforms of Napoleon and restore the old restrictions. Jewish rights depended on the progress of enlightened liberalism, a fragile hope in Central Europe, and no hope at all farther east. The long and ultimately tragic history of the association of the Jews of Europe with modern liberal ideals had begun, and with it the counterattack of Germans and German-Austrians. Among them, unlike the French, there would be no powerful and lasting intellectual or revolutionary tradition to help consolidate the liberation of the Jews.

5: THE NATIONALIST REACTION: GERMANY, 1815–1848

> What people will want to retain arbitrary Prussian rule, once it has
> tasted the benefit of a wise and liberal administration?
> —Napoleon

NAPOLEON burst upon the Germanies like a hurricane. He dissolved the Holy Roman Empire, replacing hundreds of separate sovereignties with thirty-eight; outraging clergy, he abolished ecclesiastical states, church courts, tithes, monasteries, and convents and seized church property. Nobles fumed as he abolished their feudal states, feudal dues, and tax exemptions, broke up large estates, and cut their power over their peasants. Decreeing equality before the law, Napoleon opened public office to the middle class, guaranteed private property, established modern economic laws and institutions, and built public works, roads, canals, and bridges. He created secular public schools to spread the ideals of the revolution. Most shocking of all, he not only destroyed the ghettos, he gave Jews freedom of worship and the right to own land and practice trades. Frenchmen or liberal Germans replaced those bureaucrats who resisted these changes; supporters were rewarded with church and feudal lands. To his brother Jerome to whom he gave the throne of a province of Prussia, Napoleon wrote: "I want your subjects to enjoy a degree of liberty, equality, and prosperity hitherto unknown to the German people. . . . Even if reason and the enlightenment of the age were not sufficient cause, it would be good policy for one in your position; you will find that the backing of public opinion gives you a great natural advantage over the absolute kings who are your neighbors."[1]

Napoleon's cannons might blast open ghetto walls, but they could not conquer the German mind. German intellectuals, with some exceptions, rejected his tyranny and his Enlightenment ideals. Reaffirming the Christian worldview in philosophy, they retained Christian hostility toward Judaism and Jews. Immanuel Kant, Georg Wilhelm Hegel, and Johann

Gottlieb Fichte, the philosphers of German Idealism, accepted Newtonian principles as valid only for science; they rejected the philosophes' attempt to use them to transform man and society. The philosophes' vision was a cold, depressing, mechanistic image of man and society, they argued, denying the validity of the creative spirit of the artist, the insights of the mystic, the ideals of the moralist, and the creative powers of the human soul. Newtonian science, Kant reasoned, was a pragmatic means of comprehending a part of man's experience, but it could not reveal the ultimate nature of the universe, let alone exhaust the varieties of human experience. Mathematical rationality and empiricism were useful tools for investigating the material world, no more.

German intellectuals were appalled by the deists' use of the Newtonian method to shape a "religion of reason" out of a few rational propositions. Like Hume, Kant believed that no rational propositions could prove the existence of God, but he rejected Hume's skepticism, insisting that man found certain proof for the existence of God, immortality, and free will in his own innate moral precepts. Scientific theories were only probable truths about a universe man could not directly observe, but his inner moral perceptions he knew directly, and they explained why he behaved morally or thought he should. Friedrich Schleiermacher, the most influential Lutheran theologian of the century, denounced deism as the destroyer of the intensity of faith which was itself proof of its truth. Fichte would not subordinate the emotional experience of the truly religious and the mysteries of Christian theology to the irrelevant desire for proofs acceptable to physics. J. G. Hamann, the "mystic of the north," forgotten now but then extremely influential, hated the very notion of a rational religion: the visions of the mystic were valid, religious faith and moral ideals were absolute.

Such ideas were not necessarily hostile to Judaism, but they were accompanied by the desire to demonstrate the superiority of Lutheran Christianity. Thus they resulted in the persistent belief at the highest levels of German intellectual life that Judaism was morally inferior to all forms of Christianity. Hamann, Schleiermacher, Hegel, and Fichte believed that Christianity was the highest manifestation of the religious experience mankind had reached, and they all believed a truly moral life could come only by personal regeneration through Christ. Even Kant, who favored religious freedom, insisted that "Judaism is not really a religion," just a collection of "coercive laws" requiring no "moral disposition."[2] Judaism gave man the Commandments, but Jews obeyed them only because they feared God, not from moral rightness. Hence, Kant declared, their arrogant claim to be the chosen people made them enemies of all other peoples. Schleiermacher declared Judaism dead, its worshipers presiding in eternal lamentation beside an ancient mummy. Fichte hoped that Christianity might find a way to break altogether with the "primitive" tribal religion of the Old Testament.

German philosophers reinforced the insurmountable obstacles between Christian and Jew. For the German Idealists, Christianity was the revelation of the "Divine Absolute"; a belief in the unity of God and man in Christ was the fount of all moral idealism. Rejecting Judaism, Christ was the eternal antagonist of all obscurantism and ritualism; rejecting Christ, the Jews demonstrated moral bankruptcy. Hegel and his peers regarded the Jews' "antisocial" behavior and degrading occupations as symptoms of innate moral incapacity, not the result of centuries of Christian persecution. Both Hegel and Fichte had been seminary students at the famous theological school of Fulda, and behind all the difficult abstractions of German philosophy lurks the spirit of the early Christian fathers. In a burst of anger rare for the calm and magisterial observer of world history, Hegel wrote:

> Spirit alone recognizes spirit. They [the Jews] saw in Jesus only the man . . . for He was only one like themselves, and they felt themselves to be nothing. The Jewish multitude was bound to wreck His attempt to give them the consciousness of something divine, for faith in something divine, something great, cannot make its home in a dunghill.[3]

Hamann declared that the passion of Christ revealed the ecstasy of the soul's experience of the divine in the world, a revelation utterly opposed to the primitive ritualism of Israel. Furious when Moses Mendelssohn held Judaism to be as rational as Christianity, Hamann called him a liar, a hypocrite, and a satanic Antichrist, echoing Luther and presaging the verbal violence visited upon any Jew who attempted to defend Judaism against Christian distortions. Deists believed Judaism to be riddled with superstition, but they found Christianity no better, seeking common ground for toleration. German philosophers rejected citizenship for Jews; true Germans must be Christian, preferably Protestant. Through the nineteenth century, the moral emptiness of Judaism would be a constant theme of Christian anti-Semitic movements, and they would find their greatest welcome among German Protestants.

The anti-Judaism of German philosophy stemmed from a theological view of history. For the philosophes the past was of little interest except for locating individuals or epochs they deemed their forerunners. Otherwise, history was a bloody tale of princely tyranny and priestly obscurantism. Hence their critique of politics based on a "state of nature," arrived at by divesting man of the "distortions" of the past in order to see him as he "really was." But German Idealists believed that Western civilization showed a progressive and sacredly determined divine development. In

Hegel's famous phrase, "History is the march of the Absolute Spirit through time." Consequently there were no fixed and inalienable rights of man. Man's rights and duties were determined by the history and nature of his ethnic group as reflected in its institutions, customs, and moral values. Judaism was the product of an early and primitive morality and history, the earliest and least perfect manifestation of the divine spirit as it gradually revealed itself in time. No talk of the supposed equality of all men could make the Jews the moral equals of the Germanic peoples. Their historical choice against Christ had been determined by their nature. There could be no inalienable rights for all; it would be morally dangerous to liberate the Jews. As Christian anti-Semites would insist down to Hitler, the "baleful" influence of the Jews on society was the behavior of a people left behind by man's moral development in the Christian era.

The German Idealists rejected the philosophes' belief in the social causes of man's ideas and character. Christians were free to choose good or evil; they were not simply a *tabula rasa* on which experience wrote, as Locke would have it. No passive object shaped by external stimuli, man was free to follow or ignore the inner voice of moral judgment. His body must obey the laws of physics, but his soul was free. As a young seminary student, Fichte was deeply depressed by the cold reasoning of the Enlightenment, reducing man to an object denied moral choice and innate ethical idealism. Thus Fichte: Society does not form us; we create a spiritual order out of our own inner resources. This admirable belief in human moral freedom seemed to argue for mutual respect based on the demonstrated ability of the individual to make moral choices. But German Idealists, by claiming that each people expressed its innate spirit (*volksgeist*) in its history, concluded that the occupations of the ghetto Jews were the result of the inherent spirit of the Jewish people. Even the moderate Kant thought Jews by nature "sharp dealers" who were "bound together by superstition." Their "immoral and vile" behavior in commerce and trade showed they "do not aspire to civic virtue," for "the spirit of usury holds sway amongst them" . . . a "nation of swindlers" who benefited from deceiving their host's culture.[4] Their "Jewish consciousness" made them a nation of crass salesmen and moneylenders, constitutionally incapable of higher spiritual manifestations. Society might need their peculiar talents, Hegel wrote, but they could not really be assimilated, for they were driven by their materialism and greed to follow an "animal existence that can only be secured at someone else's expense."[5]

Napoleon's cosmopolitan claims were absurd, Hegel remarked. All peoples could not be given the same constitution, for it depended on their moral development. Fichte believed Germans to be ennobled by a spirit of sacrifice for the common good, as opposed to French individu-

alism and Jewish materialism. Jews could not change: "As for giving them
civil rights, I for one see no remedy but that their heads should all be
cut off in one night and replaced with others in which there would not
be one single Jewish idea."[6] Fichte found the Jewish spirit as destructive
and irreversible as later anti-Semites would find Jewish blood. Even Kant
wrote of their "innate, natural character" which had "its origins in the
composition of the human blood." The Jews should remain without civil
rights. Schopenhauer wanted Jews excluded from the civil service, for
they had no roots in the national spirit. Fichte wanted them driven out
of Germany altogether.

The German Idealist philosophers were not precursors of the Nazis,
for the fate of the Jews was no overriding concern to them. But their work
and their numerous disciples dominated the German academy, contributing to the rejection of secular liberalism and the hostility toward the
Jews so characteristic of German university life. Westerners too often assume progressive values to be the result of educated intelligence. But
throughout the modern era, highly educated German publicists invoked
the spiritual idealism of the Germanic soul when attacking the Jews and
harped on the "inevitable march of world history" when justifying German conquests. Academics and high school teachers, trained in German
Idealist philosophy, denounced Jews as carriers of a liberalism grossly car-
icatured as mere greed. In countless sermons, lectures, and writings, popularizers used their ideas to attack Jews far more often and bitterly than
anything written by Kant, Fichte, or Hegel.

It was not just a matter of the influence of ideas. The Enlightenment
shaped modern France and England because the educated, professional,
and business classes found its values appropriate to their experience and
interests. But Prussia did not possess a significant number of similarly dis-
contented and modernizing bourgeoisie, and Prussian experience proved
decisive for Germany's future. Unlike Holland, England, or France, Prussia had no overseas empire or cosmopolitan commercial class engaged in
colonial trade. Parochial in spirit and interests, the Prussian middle
classes were often lesser civil servants rarely critical of the government.
The Prussian merchant class, content with traditional limits to the entrepreneurial spirit, prided themselves on their respectability, status, and
loyalty to the established order, modeling themselves on the elites of the
civil service, the military, and the aristocracy.

Certainly many Germans welcomed reform, but they turned swiftly
against Napoleon when he allowed no self-government or free press, taxed
the wealth of Europeans to fill the coffers of France, and conscripted their
sons to die on the steppes of Russia. As always with imperialism, Napoleon
generated support for reform among those already so inclined, but his
tyranny turned them against him. And few were so inclined in the first

place. Prussia was not France. Until his death in 1786, Frederick the Great increased the wealth and territory of Prussia and ruled with the well-being of his people in mind. And if it was natural in France to demand an end to the parasitical special privileges and petty rituals of the aristocracts living at Versailles at taxpayers' expense, Prussian Junkers were admired as a hard-working civil service and military class. The Prussian peasantry, still serfs or close to it, were less free, less turbulent, and more tied to parochial self-sufficiency than those to the west. They absorbed little of the calculating market spirit that stimulates rural folk to look for new opportunities, lessens religious fatalism, and breaks with inherited customs. The guilds of France, bastions of traditionalism, had been abolished by the revolution; those of Gemany maintained some of their powers and all of their anti-Semitism until the Nazis gathered up their votes. Among German intellectuals and the middle classes, furthermore, there was little of the anticlericalism of the Enlightenment, for the Evangelical clergy of Prussia were neither powerful nor wealthy. Their business was strictly the salvation of souls. Governed by lay bodies composed of the governing elites, they parroted the autocratic values of the regime. The philosophes used ideas as weapons for social reform and found a resounding echo among the middle classes. German thinkers offered no alternatives to the given social order. Like early Christians, they viewed history as a divine, predetermined drama; the role of intellect was not to change the world but to interpret it, just as theologians interpret the word of God. The political activism of the philosophes seemed to German intellectuals superficial, naive, and subversive.

But reform had to be considered in 1807, for Napoleon routed the Prussian army and the king fled Berlin. Prussia, deprived of half its territory and treasure, existed only at Napoleon's pleasure. The shock forced the younger members of the Prussian establishment to ask why France was suddenly so powerful? General von Scharnhorst understood: "The French Revolution has released all the energies of the French people." Revolutionary reforms generated a surge of national loyalty enabling Robespierre and Napoleon to conscript large masses of ordinary citizens, collect huge sums in taxes, and field troops who fought with more independence of spirit than the apathetic mercenaries and commandeered peasants of the opposition. Prince von Hardenberg, new chief minister of Prussia, believed that 1789 created a powerful identity between government and people, while in Prussia and Austria war remained the affair of princes and nobles seeking only to increase their treasure and territory, neither asking for nor receiving the moral support of the middle classes, whose sons were not conscripted and whose cities were left unscathed after the Wars of Religion.

Led by Baron von Stein, Prince von Hardenberg, and Generals Gneisenau and Scharnhorst, younger civil servants and military leaders swiftly moved to "release the moral energies" of the Prussians. Serfs were freed, guild restrictions reduced, military and government offices thrown open to the middle class, education enhanced, and limited self-government granted to cities. Free peasants would be more productive, fewer guild restrictions would aid economic progress, and talented bourgeoisie would improve the civil service and officer corps. Even the Jews were given new rights; Napoleon demanded it, but also the government believed that the economic talents of liberated Jews would improve the economy. Hardenberg noted how important Jewish military suppliers had been to the French armies since Louis XIV. To cap the whole, a demoralized king even promised a constitution. Significantly, these reforms were not stimulated by the ideals that motivated the revolutionaries of France. They were pushed by soldiers and bureaucrats to increase Prussia's military strength. Demands for reforms from below had renewed France, but in Prussia reforms came through orders from above. They would not last. The dramatic changes of Napoleon had stimulated an even more powerful defense of tradition and custom by those who saw their interests, prestige, power, and values placed at risk.

The Prussian nobility responded to Hardenberg's reforms in a memorandum by Friedrich von der Marwitz, a Junker army officer. Defeat, he declared, was not brought on by lack of reform but because the government, always eager to adopt foreign ways, had destroyed the independent power of the nobility. Now it threatened the aristocratic monopoly of civil service and army; in the name of the alleged equality of man it ignored the talent responsible for past victories. Liberating serfs, Marwitz claimed, would free a justly conquered race, inherently stupid and lazy. To prate of their rights would simply render them unwilling to cultivate the land or serve in the army with the unquestioning obedience of old. Destroy the guilds and economic stability would be sacrificed to the "Jewish" principles of laissez-faire, eroding communal strength with economic adventurism. Marwitz denounced the reformers for even considering women's rights. Born domestics, women could not rise above the care of children and the pleasures of sex and gossip. Patriarchy in family and village was the core of Prussian greatness. Worst of all, the Junker manifesto concluded, Hardenberg's reforms meant the domination of the immoral, antiChristian "Jewish" spirit of destructive competition between individuals freed of all traditional limits to raw greed and the bonds of social duty. Shocked by the liberation of the Jews, Marwitz and his fellow nobles insisted, as the memorandum put it, that the Jews were a doomed race, fated by the Almighty to wander the earth nationless, miserable parasites devoted only to usury and petty trade. How was it possible in Christian Prussia to allow Jews to purchase land, join guilds, and enter the professions? If Hardenberg and his allies persisted, Marwitz wrote, they would deliver Prussian soil, economy, and values to those greedy "stock jobbers" and transform "old and honorable Prussia" into a "newfangled Jew state."[8]

Hardenberg scornfully dismissed the defenders of privilege, but without the power of an enlightened bourgeoisie, the reformers were vulnerable, charged with serving Napoleon's will to turn Prussia into a French satellite. Some reformers themselves were uneasy about the sweeping changes introduced by Hardenberg, especially the liberation of the Jews. Baron von Stein believed that liberation would not change their "bad character": it would be better to ship these "parasitic plants" to Africa. General Gneisenau believed that the new legislation would destroy the nobility and replace them with "Jews and speculators."[9] It was only the beginning. Down to the rise of the Nazis, the right accused liberals and socialists of being un-German and anti-Christian, traitorous allies of subversive Jews.

Yet neither aristocratic reaction nor enlightened reform appealed to most German intellectuals. Shattered by the Napoleonic experience, they sought a new nationalism, one derived from traits assumed to be uniquely Germanic. Humiliated, they found compensation in the presumed superiority of the Germanic peoples and their ancient institutions and beliefs. Imperialism often generates a will to reject it totally and return to the uncontaminated original spirit, religion, and ways of the *Volk*. Such conservative nationalism always threatens religious or ethnic minorities, for by definition they do not share the historic soul of the *Volk*. At such times, Jews have always suffered.

Fichte was the philosopher of the war of national liberation against Napoleon, the first to try to rouse the slumbering Germanic spirit to its "moral vocation" to create a new nation. In 1808, even as French troops occupied Berlin, he delivered a series of public *Addresses to the German Nation*. Denouncing old Prussia as a barracks state whose rulers preferred French culture and language, he insisted they could never inspire the moral energies of a new generation. Defeat must awaken Germans to build a united nation worthy of Germanic ideals. Legislation in the French manner was alien; it would destroy the "pure inwardness of the German spirit" that had stormed through Germany with Luther. With the Reformation, Luther had freed the moral message of Christ from Catholic ritualism, completing Christ's work against primitive Judaism. Fichte was one of the first of a long line of Germans who could not believe Jesus was Jewish; the founder of the greatest moral revolution in history could not possibly have come from such a miserable people. Like later racists, he thought that Saint Paul, fearing a break with Judaism, had distorted the pure message of Christ with Jewish "superstitions." The Reformation purged these remnants of ritualism, Fichte argued, because only the Germanic peoples could absorb the true meaning of Christianity. Even converted, Jews could never be Germans. They would always be all that was un-German: cosmopolitan, soulless traders, exploiters unable to participate in a moral social order. "A mighty state stretches across almost all the nations of Europe, hostile in intent and in constant strife with all others . . . this is Jewry." They could never be loyal to any other nation. "To protect ourselves against them I see no other way than to conquer for them their promised land and ship them all there."[10]

With the significant exception of Slavs and Jews, Fichte believed all Europeans to be related by blood. But the Germans were the only people who retained their ancient spirit undistorted by foreign influences. While the French adopted a Latin language, Germans kept their original tongue, retaining their spiritual qualities as "the original race." Still close to the ways of their tribal-warrior ancestors, they were free of Latin, French, and Jewish individualism, obsession with property, and the crass pursuit of material well-being. We alone, Fichte said, still feel as did the ancient Germanic tribes: duties and rights are derived from subordination to the common will. Only Germans were fit for the new era of social cooperation and collective moral idealism.

To protect the Germanic spirit, Fichte urged German leaders to control production and consumption so as to end the rapacious adventurism of international entrepreneurs and speculators obsessed with economic growth. Economic self-sufficiency would prevent these forces from flooding Germany with imports that would destroy the old craft guilds and awaken corroding desires for products foreign to the *volksgeist*. Similarly, German language, art, and culture, the fruits of centuries-old Teutonic consciousness, must be freed from foreign influences. Fichte rejected democratic representation in favor of what later conservatives (and Italian fascists) called the corporate state: political representation by craft, guild, and corporate organization, not by masses of anonymous voters. Above all, Fichte wanted a new educational system to protect the young from the moral contamination of alien ideas and nourish the Teutonic spirit. Once spiritually one, Germany must expand to her "natural frontiers" and include all Germans in a greater Germany. In the Germany Fichte envisaged, the Jews would have no place. Similar ideas led many rightist intellectuals to the Nazis in the 1920s.

Appointed the first head of the University of Berlin in 1809, Fichte helped to establish an institution designed to reveal cultural and historical traits that were uniquely German and to create a new national consciousness. With fiery speeches, Fichte and Schleiermacher, head of the faculty of theology, recruited students for voluntary units to serve against Napoleon. Tempered by battle, youth would be imbued with the sacrificial idealism essential to create a united Germany. In the lecture halls of

Berlin, Fichte and his colleagues stressed the ethnic and religious differences separating peoples and the superiority of the Germanic *Volk*-soul. Hostility toward the Jews thrived. In other lands, nationalists like Giuseppe Mazzini believed that each people had unique traits valuable to all humanity; but, like later German racial-nationalists, Fichte's claims were far more grandiose and aggressive: "It is you Germans who, of all peoples, possess most clearly the germ of human perfectability, and to whom belongs the leadership in the development of mankind. . . . There is no escape; if you sink, then mankind sinks with you, without any hope of resurrection."[11]

Appropriately, Fichte died from a disease contracted treating wounded student soldiers fresh from battle against Napoleon's troops. But neither Hardenberg's reforms nor Fichte's nationalism brought Napoleon to his knees. He fell before the troops of the regular armies of England, Prussia, Russia, and Austria, not idealistic volunteers or reformers. In 1815 the victorious allies, united in a Holy Alliance of Christian Europe, tried to create a Europe free of revolutionary liberalism and nationalism, backed by the might of the victorious allies. At the Congress of Vienna, all Christian sects were granted equal rights, but Jews were allowed to retain only those rights agreed to by their former princes, now restored to their domains and busily invalidating French reforms. But the ghettos were not restored, Jewish civil rights were curbed rather than canceled, and the guilds were able to end Jewish participation only in some trades.

In Prussia, Frederick William III returned to Berlin from exile hoping to banish the Jews or drive them back into ghettos. His advisers, finding Jewish economic skills useful, prevailed upon him to stay his hand. Serfs remained free but were forced to pay so much compensation to their former lords that they hardly benefited. The guilds regained most of their powers. Talk of liberating women ended, and membership in the civil service and officer corps was restricted once again to aristocrats and a few of "good family." The royal promise of a constitution was broken. Though Jews had fought against the French, they were no longer allowed to join the military or to be teachers, judges, or civil servants. These were crushing blows to assimilation, for the bureaucracy and officer corps were the most prestigious institutions of the state. Until 1914 Jews would be kept out of them, even when it became constitutionally illegal.

With the French defeat, racist literature became more vulgar and strident. Nationalism now meant the racial as well as the spiritual superiority of Germans, and the dangers of Jewish "blood" were stressed. In other European nations there was nothing comparable. Praise of the Germanic warrior race and anti-Semitism littered the textbooks used by Prussian schoolboys. Liberalism was scorned by the reaction as the ideology of diseased Frenchmen and Jews; treason was inherent in Jewish blood. Stu-

dent nationalist societies blossomed. Their hero, Professor Friedrich
Ruehs of the University of Berlin, was appointed royal historiographer of
Prussia, the highest honor the king could bestow on an historian. Ruehs
believed Jews to be racially inferior; conversion could not change them.
Germany's most famous legal scholar, Friedrich Carl von Savigny, tutor
to the crown prince who was himself an anti-Semite, wanted Jews back
in the ghetto. Hoping to restore Germanic communal laws of the pre-
Roman past, Savigny founded a famous school of legal history. Professor
Johann Fries of Heidelberg, prominent disciple of Fichte and a well-
known Jew-baiter, also enjoyed great influence among student societies;
to him the Jews were a "rotten" race of "worthless cheats" . . . "bloodsuckers," a "diseased people" who should be forced to wear special signs
to warn of their presence.[12] He even called for their "extermination."[13]
When told this was unseemly for a scholar, he lamely replied that he
meant only Judaism, not the Jews.

   One of the most influential of the new demagogues of race and blood
was Ernst Moritz Arndt, one of a few intellectuals listed officially by the
Nazis as honored predecessors. Poet, historian, and professor at the University of Bonn, he was forced to flee Germany during Napoleon's rule.
A deeply religious Lutheran and German Idealist, for Arndt the Reformation was a divine spark that leaped from the Germanic soul. Obsessed
with racial mixing, he imagined that if Germans maintained racial purity
they could revive the bloody idealism of the Teutonic Knights and the profound simplicity, power, and faith of Luther, the true voice of the German folk. Arndt's other great hero was Arminius, who, in defeating the
Romans in 9 C.E., saved the noble culture of Germanic barbarians. With
a host of later nationalists, Arndt idealized the nobility of this tribal chief,
the blond barbarian leader of warriors free of the Roman decadence that
had racially corrupted the "mongrelized" tribes of ancient France.

   Elated by the wars of liberation, Arndt thundered to the Germans to
rise up once more and destroy foreigners bent on weakening them. The
French were not the only enemies blocking national regeneration. The
Jews, "a rotten and degenerate race" with "evil and worthless drives and
desires," were enemies within the gates.[14] A separate species, this devious,
cunning, and cowardly race of merchants was inexorably opposed to the
Germans, the people of the light, frank and honest peasant-warriors,
God's own *Volk*, upon whose "powerful and vigorous wild stock" he
"grafted the divine shoot."[15] End racial mixing, he demanded, for the pure
of blood and spirit were destined to be masters of Europe. Bar Jews from
the universities, for there the elite was spiritually prepared for its future
tasks. Arndt was extremely popular among the exclusive and famous
dueling fraternities joined by the offspring of the aristocratic, military, and
civil service elites, students who believed they had inherited the glories

of the Teutonic past. The children of an elite so easily defeated, and lacking a Napoleon or Wellington, needed to establish their unique warrior qualities. Correspondingly, they made a cult of the duel and eventually refused to accept Jews.

Friedrich Ludwig Jahn was another student hero. A high school teacher, son of a Lutheran minister, coarse, violent, and charismatic, he was a rigid authoritarian whose courage in battle against the French made him a national hero. He too demanded that Germans revive their ancient traits and purge foreign influences. Wearing a costume modeled on the imagined dress of the ancient Germans, he revived ancient tribal rites to prepare the citizens of the future Germanic Reich. The idealism of a Fichte did not interest him; he was a racist of the barnyard: "mongrel peoples" could not survive as nations, he said, just as "hybrid animals have no capacity for reproduction."[16] Both men insisted that those who married foreigners should lose their citizenship.

Arndt and Jahn despised peace. War fostered nobility, curbing selfishness in the name of sacrifice for the community. Jahn created a unit of "storm troopers" to fight the French, and he pioneered the cult of physical fitness. (*Turnen* means gymnastics, hence *Turnvater* Jahn, as he is known.) Physical fitness was not meant simply for health and certainly not to glorify the competitive individualism of record-seekers, as today. It was needed to purify the national soul in preparation for mighty deeds. Thousands joined Jahn's gymnastic paramilitary societies. Imagining themselves the reincarnation of the Teutonic Knights, they marched, made camping trips and paramilitary excursions, and cultivated what they supposed were tribal instincts free from the corruptions of urban life. Such youth movements continued throughout the nineteenth century and became increasingly anti-Semitic.

In 1817 a huge festival was held to celebrate the four-hundredth anniversary of the Reformation; Turnvater Jahn and Professor Fries were honored guests. Student associations burned books, and calls rang out for a united Germany and war with the French. Metternich, chief minister of the Hapsburg Empire of Austria and the most powerful statesman in Central Europe, knew that German unity would reduce the Austrian Empire, one-third of whose citizens were German, to a second-rate power. Arndt, Jahn, and their followers were a new phenomenon—reactionary nationalists—and Metternich, though a reactionary, could hardly support nationalism if he wished to preserve the multinational domains of the Hapsburgs. He purged student associations and nationalist movements throughout the empire. German university authorities obliged, censored their students, and deprived Arndt of his professorship. Civil authorities threw him in jail.

The new emphasis on race and blood paralleled the swift rise of the

Jews. Freed from the ghetto, they moved rapidly out of peddling and petty trade, as the philosophes had predicted. By the 1830s the son of a secondhand clothes peddler might be a clothing salesman or a textile manufacturer, moneylenders might be bankers, and their sons might become professionals or journalists or publishers—all occupations less subject to discrimination. Moving into better neighborhoods, many broke with orthodoxy. In short, the modern, secular, and successful Jew was appearing. Anti-Semites who were convinced that Jews would never assimilate did not appreciate it when they did. As one academic wrote, "Educated Jews are a cosmopolitan rabble, who must be tracked down and expelled from everywhere."[17] In truth, anti-Semites always preferred the Orthodox ghetto Jew to those whose secularism and success contradicted both the myths of fundamentalist Christians and the superiority of Germanic blood. Antagonisms intensified when Jews, responding to new opportunities, emigrated from poverty-ridden Eastern Europe. From 1816 to 1848 Berlin's Jewish population more than tripled, though overall the Jewish population of Germany remained about 1 percent throughout the modern era. But the small numbers of Jews made the myths of the anti-Semites all the more extreme, for it was necessary to assume the Jews were powerful far beyond their numbers in order to explain their success if one refused to admit their abilities.

With assimilation, a rash of literature predicted that the Jews, with hoards of ready cash, would soon dominate Germany and Europe. In fact, emigrating Jews from the east were usually desperately poor. Anti-Semitic riots broke out in Germany in 1819, 1830, 1834, and 1848. More than thirty cities were involved, and some riots lasted weeks. Synagogues were burned; roving mobs beat Jews and destroyed their property. Rioters were often guild members or small businessmen who feared Jewish competition, joined by those who lived in neighborhoods where Jews, once forbidden, moved in after Napoleon destroyed the ghettos. Disturbances resulted when Jews bought Gentile businesses or land. Economic discontent fueled the riots, for the end of Napoleon's blockade of trade with Great Britain brought a flood of cheap goods. Small businessmen were unable to compete, peasant indebtedness soared, artisans lost customers. Because German liberals supported Jewish rights, by the 1830s comparatively large numbers of Jews were active liberals, and those Germans unable to adjust to free competition often struck out at them. Peasants blamed their indebtedness on Jewish cattle traders and rural middlemen, especially after an agrarian crisis in 1820. Authorities finally suppressed the riots, having let them continue because they were content to see the Jews and liberals taught a lesson.

Upon his coronation in 1840, the new king of Prussia, Frederick William IV, presented the Iron Cross to Jahn at his coronation in 1840, restoring his university post. The most reactionary of monarchs, Frederick William hated anything smacking of the Enlightenment. King and courtiers called for the return of the medieval social order and condemned 1789 as the work of Freemasons and Jews who had manipulated the citizens of France for profit and power. Like his predecessor, the king hoped to drive the Jews back into the ghettos or out of Prussia altogether. Confronted by liberal demands, he rejected them as attempts by a "contemptible Jewish clique" to destroy our good "German character."[18] He and his courtiers belonged to the mystical counterrevolutionary Order of the Rosicrucians, which prided itself on its occult learning, symbolized by the Cross of the Rose and the swastika. Devotees of intricate rituals alleged to release the supernatural powers of pre-Christian peoples, they also supported a literal belief in the Bible, including the usual arcane interpretation of obscure passages. Believing alchemy and astrology to be exact sciences, they dismissed Newtonian physics as a façade for revolutionary subversion. For amusement, king and advisers engaged in mystic rituals and speculated about raising the dead and the secret of perpetual youth. If educational reform was suggested, the king insisted the catechism was good enough for the masses, otherwise they need only know that one owed perfect obedience to superiors. It was a philosophy fit for a king.

Such beliefs are easy to ridicule, but the prestige of the king and his court—aristocrats, generals, high civil servants, and clergy—set the tone for the ambitious, the servile, the greedy, and the ignorant. In the court's immense patronage fiefdom, even the most mildly enlightened could find neither place nor favor. In 1817 the king's predecessor had united the Lutheran and Reformed branches of the Evangelical church to strengthen orthodoxy and reaction. Consequently, ordinary Prussian citizens were cut off from liberal ideas. Until the rise of a mass press, the pulpits of Prussia were their only source of ideas. Hence, after the Napoleonic era, anti-Semitism had a force and sanction in Prussia not found in other Western nations or, for that matter, in other German states.

In 1848 revolution swept through Europe. The king of Prussia, shocked, retreated from Berlin as riots broke out, convinced they were the work of Jewish agitators. Elsewhere frightened princes rushed to appoint progressive ministers who passed liberal legislation and called for a national parliament in Frankfurt, a prelude to a united and liberal Germany. Artisans and students manned barricades. In elections to the new parliament the liberals won. It seemed 1789 had arrived. But the triumph was short. Church and aristocrat were not as hated as in France in 1789; German liberals and princes both feared the masses more than each other. Liberals wanted only a stronger voice in government, some civil rights, and a market economy. The princes retained control over the military.

The revolution failed because those who fought for it really wanted traditional policies. Only the leaders—largely merchants and professionals—were liberals. Peasants and artisans had rioted mainly because terrible harvests had caused food shortages; both soon discovered their interests were not shared by the liberals. Liberals were willing to end feudal dues and forced labor but insisted that landlords receive due compensation. The rights of property, even feudal, were sacred. The introduction of free trade in commodities would harm peasants unable to adjust to growing outside competition. Soon, in some districts, peasants attacked Jews, carried anti-Semitic banners, and shouted the familiar slogans, for the Jews were symbols of the liberal market policies they feared, and Jewish moneylenders and middlemen were blamed for peasant debt and low prices for farm products. Still close to serfdom, peasants had little awareness of the complexities of a national economic system in fact dominated by Gentiles and controlled by capitalist rules, not ethnic character. The liberals of the Frankfurt Parliament could not satisfy what they saw as retrograde economic demands, nor did they try. By 1849 the peasants had retreated into sullen discontent.

Liberalism also offered no comfort to the guild masters. They wanted their traditional right to regulate markets, prices, wages, and entrance into the guilds. Liberals scoffed at such reactionary and selfish demands, and ignored calls that old skills and small businesses would be destroyed by the unfettered power of new technology and capital. The new parliament demanded free enterprise except in matters of public health, insisting on free entry into the trades as well. The liberals also declared the Jews liberated from all civic disabilities. In turn, guildsmen blamed their troubles on "Jewish," and "un-Christian" liberalism, alleged threats to the stable and just Christian economic and moral order. The guildsmen turned away from the revolution. Down to the Nazis, artisans in Germany and Austria would be among the strongest supporters of racist movements. By 1849 the liberals were reduced to asking Prussia to use force to unite Germany against the will of other German princes.

A delegation led by the parliamentary vice-president, Gabriel Riesser, an unconverted Jew, offered the imperial crown to the Prussian king. But Frederick William IV would accept no "offer from the gutter" or trample on the rights of his fellow princes at the behest of civilian upstarts led by a Jew. He also knew that Austria, Russia, and France would defeat any attempt to unite Germany. It was far simpler to reconquer Berlin. In the end the parliament asked the king to suppress its own left wing; Prussian soldiers obliged with sadistic pleasure. Even so the king, haunted by fear of revolution, reluctantly allowed a Prussian constitution. But it was scarcely liberal. Creating a three-class suffrage that allowed the wealthiest to dominate, it also gave the king an absolute veto and the power to rule without parliament in national emergencies declared by himself. The ministers of the Prussian government would not be responsible to the deputies, and the king's appointed chancellor could rule without parliamentary support. The king also selected the upper house. Because the crucial power of the budget was divided among the king and the two houses of parliament, he controlled state budgets. Aristocracy, army, and king ruled once more. The new constitution of Prussia lasted until the Weimar Republic of 1918, and with it the power of the reactionaries.

Prominent liberals were jailed, exiled, or shot. Reactionaries, among them Otto von Bismarck, who had urged violent counterrevolution from the start and hated the slightest constitutional limit on royal power, organized a force to fight liberalism. Aristocrats and retired military officers founded what became the voice of the reactionary wing of the Conservative party, a newspaper aptly dubbed the *Crusade* (*Kreuzzeitung*). It was extremely hostile toward "Jewish liberalism" and Jews throughout the century. Aristocrats founded a "Fatherland Society" to prevent attempts to tax them, regain their rights over "their" peasants, and support the guilds.

Increasingly, liberal reforms were associated with revolution and above all with Jewry, as they would be during the Weimar Republic. Now began the invidious device of selecting a few prominent Jewish names from the mass of Christian revolutionaries to prove that "the Jews" were collectively responsible. But traditional Christian myths now had to be supplemented by the racism of blood, for assimilated, secular, and progressive Jews were rarely religious and never Orthodox. The king, pious to a fault, had not only tried to keep Jews in the ghetto, he had also tried to keep them Orthodox by preventing the rise of Reform Judaism, founded in 1810 by those who wished to bring Judaism closer to Christian practices so as to facilitate assimilation. Anti-Semites always preferred the Orthodox ghetto Jew to those whose secularism and success contradicted both the myths of Christians and the superiority of Germanic blood. Now the issue was much confused. What was it that made the Jew dangerous? Indeed, what made him Jewish? Was it blood or religion? Both theories remained in play, reinforcing each other. Paradoxically, the progress of liberalism and assimilation made the status of the Jews more precarious. Their fragile and dangerous position became clearly evident in the 1870s when Germany experienced its first decade of liberal ascendancy, yet anti-Semitism became more intense than ever.

6: ANTI-SEMITISM IN THE BISMARCK ERA

All nations that reject the teachings of the New Testament are destined to disappear from the face of the earth.
— Pastor Adolf Stoecker, 1878

Anti-Semitism rises as the stock market falls.
— German saying

AMIDST the pomp and splendor of Versailles in 1871, the Second Reich was founded. German unification was achieved. With crushing victories over Austria and France, the Prussian army restored the glory of the autocracy Napoleon had humiliated. Countless pamphlets, speeches, and sermons invoked the God of Battles in praise of Prussia. Rightists declared race and autocracy the keys to victories over French republicanism and the "mongrels" of the Austrian Empire. The Franco-Prussian War, the first to be interpreted by Social Darwinists, was seen as an example of the success of "the most favored" races in the struggle for survival. In the famous words of Bismarck, the "Iron Chancellor," who led the struggle, "The great decisions of the day are not made by parliamentary majorities but by blood and iron."

Until 1861 the reaction ruled in Prussia, but in that year liberals shocked the right by electing 256 delegates and only 15 conservatives to the Prussian House of Deputies. Economic progress had produced large numbers of liberal-minded industrialists, merchants, and professionals with the wealth necessary to qualify and outvote the representatives of traditional Prussia. Conservatives had accepted elections only because the king had ordered them, and they had done much to sabotage them. With no secret ballot, estate owners withdrew their trade from liberals, and government funds and licensing powers were illegally used to punish opponents. But by the 1860s it was no longer enough, and the liberals demanded their constitutional right to a voice in the army budget. The king's adviser, General von Roon, insisted Bismarck be appointed minister president of Prussia to oppose the liberals. The king was reluctant. The "red reactionary," as he was known, had been a Junker representative in 1848, openly calling for counterrevolution and no concessions. But Roon insisted on Bismarck: "It is better to bleed to death than slowly rot away." In 1862 Bismarck was appointed, and he promptly violated the constitution by collecting taxes and insisting that no constitution could be allowed to threaten the state by cutting off funding.

Yet Bismarck hoped to win liberal support to strengthen his own position. With the time-honored attractions of an aggressive foreign policy, he maneuvered Austria and then France into war. His victories swayed liberal opinion, for German unification—though by negotiation, not war—had been the goal of hundreds of liberal organizations since the 1840s. Spurred by nationalist enthusiasm, the renamed National Liberal party, once adamantly opposed to Bismarck, overwhelmingly approved his foreign policy, declared his actions retroactively constitutional, and even voted him a stipend. Bismarck rewarded the liberals with concessions in the constitution for the new Germany, but he also pacified Prussian reactionaries who feared the addition of millions of liberals and Catholics to their nation. The king, himself uneasy, reassured them: a united Germany would be but an extension of old Prussia, an imperial possession more than an integrated nation-state. Out of these contradictory political pressures came the new constitution of Germany. The king of Prussia was declared William I, emperor (or kaiser) of Germany, Bismarck the minister president of Prussia and chancellor of Germany. An upper house for the new German Reichstag was composed of appointed delegates from the different German states, with sufficient Prussian delegates to prevent any constitutional changes.

Bismarck shocked the right by granting universal male suffrage for the lower house of the Reichstag, though retaining for the emperor sole power to make foreign policy and war. Above all, the chancellor of Germany was to serve at the pleasure of the emperor; he was not to be the elected representative of the people. If need be, legislation could be forced through regardless of majority will. Conservatives had a clear view of the way the new constitution ought to work. The emperor should declare his desires to his ministers, and they should instruct the parliament to carry out the royal will. If a minister disagreed, he should resign; if a Reichstag delegate questioned the word of a minister, a duel was appropriate. Protracted discussion was pointless, disobedience was treason. But the very existence of a democratically elected Reichstag frightened traditionalists, for in every Western nation parliament had gradually extended its powers at the expense of the old guard. A time might come when democratically elected civilians, representing nothing but the despised interests of commerce, would be able to overrule the aristocrats, military officers, and civil servants who believed they represented the true interests of the state. Among reactionaries, Bismarck was now called a traitor to his class.

The constitution also completed the liberation of the Jews. Excluded so long from traditional pursuits, many Jews had pioneered new enterprises and techniques, and had risen swiftly on the swelling tide of economic progress. Jewish youth poured into the universities, free to make careers in medicine, law, journalism, and culture where, as independent professionals, they were relatively free from restrictions. After the liberal defeat of 1848, leading Jewish observers noted that anti-Semitism seemed to be dying. But the liberal surge frightened conservatives, now isolated by the Iron Chancellor, and the reactionary wing, led by the *Kreuzzeitung*, which was now must reading for landowners, aristocrats, civil servants, and military officers, renewed its battle with "Jewish liberalism."

Ignoring the constitution, conservatives used informal means to keep Jews out of the military and civil service, declaring them unfit for such noble occupations. In the countryside, peasant superstitions and the power of the autocracy still prevented Jews from being anything but middlemen and moneylenders. And in a time of upward mobility bred by commercial expansion, few Jews indeed would adopt rural life, especially if made unwelcome. They were naturally attracted to urban centers where they could find anonymity and a measure of tolerance, as well as patients, clients, customers, and cultural allies among coreligionists. Their vocations naturally reinforced liberal attitudes, especially given their exclusion from the political establishment. But their vocations also validated the self-fulfilling prophecies of the racial nationalists: Jews could never be true Germans, for they were an urban and commercial people out of touch with the rural, warrior spirit of the Germanic-Christian soul. In France anti-Semitism was powerful among rightist Catholics, but there was always a haven to be found among those who supported 1789 and found in Napoleon's exploits military glory equal to that of the victors of the Franco-Prussian War. In Italy, committed to urban and commercial values since the Renaissance, Italians of Jewish descent were readily accepted and found important positions in the civil service and the army. In spite of talk of the assimilation of German Jewry, informal restrictions limited their social fate and made them vulnerable to racist stereotypes.

The liberal press of Berlin and Vienna infuriated German conservatives, and it was dominated by Jewish editors and journalists. Not so the German press as a whole, for the extensive rural and small-town press was conservative, and its owners hired no Jews. In big cities one could enter journalism more readily. Jewish journalists and editors, because of their ambivalent position, were quick to detect and expose the difference between public law and private behavior and often wrote of the hypocrisies disguising the private interests and privileges of the establishment. In turn, their skeptical criticism was taken by the right as proof that Jews, ungrateful for their liberation, were a race of subversives inherently incapable of appreciating German national values and institutions.

In 1874 the right suffered another profound shock when the two liberal parties, National Liberals and Progressives—scorned as the parties of the Jews—again were winners in the Reichstag elections. Conservatives gained 14 percent of the vote, liberals 40 percent, and the newly formed Social Democrats 7 percent. Bismarck, always the realist, cooperated with the liberals while the crown prince exhibited decidedly liberal tendencies. Suddenly it seemed as if Germany, in spite of Prussian victories, would be swept up by the tide that had made France a republic in 1876 and created a liberal and united Italy; even the decrepit Hapsburg Empire had adopted a liberal constitution. Bismarck seemed about to create that "newfangled Jewish state" the Junkers had feared since Napoleon.

Tensions mounted when two unconverted Jews, Edward Lasker and Ludwig Bamberger, the most prominent leaders of the Progressive forces, guided a series of liberal economic reforms through the Reichstag. Among these were laws which limited the liability of investors in enterprises to the amount invested rather than their total personal assets. Amassing capital for corporations became far easier, and a great speculative boom surged. Unaccompanied by regulation, the reforms encouraged unwise and often fraudulent ventures. In 1873 many new enterprises collapsed and thousands of small investors were ruined in the first economic crash not caused by crop failure. Pouncing, the right blamed the crash on Bismarck's liberal Jewish allies. The importance of Jews in the stock market, and their fund-raising for new enterprises, gave racists a chance to accuse "the Jews" of collective responsibility for the tragedies of trusting investors.

Bitter, frustrated, and unable to comprehend the complexities of economic change, the small investor was ready to blame his personal loss on Jewish speculators hoping to make a quick killing. That all investors, including themselves, hoped to do the same was an idea too upsetting to the victims. Nowadays speculative investment is not assumed to be immoral, and those who "make a killing" are admired, but then it was seen as gambling with other people's money. Moreover, the ordinary German investor had no access to the learned confusion of economists speaking arcanely of necessary cycles of boom and bust. It was easier for the victims to project their own greed and guilt onto those traditionally held to be immoral parasites.

But thousands of Jewish investors were also ruined by the collapse, and the new legislation had in fact originally been proposed by Bismarck and his cabinet, Christians all. Liberals, Jewish or not, had supported them in the name of free enterprise. Lasker himself was the first to expose fraud and propose legal remedies. But the hunt was on, and much was made of the highly visible presence of Jews in speculative enterprises, even though upper- and middle-class Germans were also heavily involved. Peasants, artisans, and the urban poor do not play the stock market. And for handsome fees, many of the nation's leading aristocrats lent their names to public relations brochures touting risky ventures. Indeed, the scandals reached to the court of the kaiser, implicating among others his privy councilor, Herman Wagener, a leading anti-Semite and former *Kreuzzeitung* editor, who was forced to resign. Even so, the crash brought blanket condemnations of the Jews. A writer insisted, "As long as Prince Bismarck remains the all powerful Idol of the German people, then the German nation will be sacrificed to the Empire, the Empire sacrificed to the Chancellor; and the Chancellor belongs to the Jews and speculators."[1] Calling for unity between aristocrats and peasants, pamphleteers demanded the overthrow of the legislation and "Jewish international finance" in general.

"Today the social question is essentially the Jewish question. All other explanations of our economic troubles are fraudulent cover-ups." With these famous words in 1876 Otto Glagau, organizer of anti-Semitic groups, created a slogan famous down through the Nazi era and launched a series of racist articles in the most widely circulated and respectable of bourgeois family magazines, the *Gardenhouse.* It had close to 400,000 subscribers—amazing for the time—and is a "gold mine" for understanding the "thoughts and feelings of the . . . middle class."[2] Since 1870 the popular magazine had reviled liberalism and praised the military, the aristocracy, and the court. Ignoring the distinction between honest promotion and fraud, Glagau used false statistics to claim that 90 percent of business promoters were Jews. He wasted no words on the thousands of ruined Jewish investors or aristocratic speculators. Concluding that liberalism threatened to destroy Christian ethics and deliver Germany to the Jews, he wrote: "Actually they already dominate us . . . an alien tribe rules a truly great nation. All of World History has no comparable example of a homeless people—a physically and psychically degenerate race—commanding the globe by means of mere cunning and slyness, usury and shoddy dealings."[3]

After its defeat in 1874, the right founded an anti-Bismarck league. Insisting the chancellor was a pawn of Jewish bankers and speculators, the *Kreuzzeitung* published a series of racist articles: "Modern Judaism denies its faith, flaunts its enlightenment and liberalism," and "dominates press, parliament, and politics." It was "a real misfortune for our people."[4] The source of conservative fears was obvious. Bismarck's alliance with liberals meant that mere civilians would vote on army budgets and the civil service and military would be opened to other than nobles. Germany would become a "red" republic like France or a nation of "vile shopkeepers" like England.

In 1874 Constantin Frantz published *National Liberalism and the Rule of the Jews*. (In the Nazi era, Frantz was the subject of Kurt Waldheim's Ph.D. thesis.) Extremely popular among German conservative intellectuals, Frantz stressed the symbolism of the Jew as liberal—nonsense when one considers the Enlightenment was a Gentile creation. Under Bismarck, Frantz declared, Germany was ruled by a Jewish nation which would destroy the Germany of village, guild, regional variations, and communal loyalties. Social equality and uniform rights would subject Germany to state tyranny by ending those autonomous powers of the elites who once stood between the people and a Robespierre or Napoleon. Only Jews benefited from a society designed for merchants and speculators, one that converted everything into commodities to be bought and sold. Jewish capitalists were free to purchase the nation itself—the land, so intimately tied to the responsibilities of the aristocracy and the traditions of the peasants. Lack of capital would bring these most Germanic of classes to the mercy of the Jew. Nationless, bereft of his own religion, the Jew had carved an existence outside the moral limits of German history and those communal restraints that curbed the drive for gain and pleasure. For the Jewish liberal, Frantz argued, individual rights were the sole reality; he would never sacrifice for the good of the community that he exploited to prosper.

German Catholicism added to the rising chorus. In 1870 Pius IX declared that in disputes with political leaders the pope was the final authority, and that his secular powers came from Christ himself. Bismarck struck back, beginning the *Kulturkampf*, or battle for culture, by proposing legislation to restrict the powers of the church over education, marriage, divorce, and even the training of priests. He found willing allies in the National Liberal party and press. Hoping to separate church and state, they also resented the pope's repeated condemnations of their views. The battle was joined, and clergy who opposed Bismarck's measures were fined, jailed, or exiled. To Catholics it seemed a replay of 1789.

Although the majority of liberals were not Jewish, in 1876 the official Catholic journal *Germania* accused "Jewish" liberals in the Reichstag of seeking to rob the church of its legitimate rights because of their ancient battle against Christ. For the first time in a respectable periodical, a boycott of Jewish businesses was called for, and in the phrase the Nazis were to make infamous: "Buy not from Jews!"[5] *Germania* also blamed Jews for the economic collapse of 1873, following the lead of Pope Pius IX, who declared them "The enemies of Jesus, they have no other God but their money."⁶ Some three hundred local Catholic newspapers in Germany were even more racist. The *Kulturkampf* aside, anti-Semitism was a means for Catholics to defend themselves as "good Germans" to those Prussian and Protestant rightists who, disturbed when unification brought millions of Catholics into the empire, often accused them of being more loyal to the Vatican than to Germany, and halfhearted in their support of the wars against their coreligionists in Catholic France and Austria.

Liberals saw the *Kulturkampf* as a legitimate response to the authoritarianism of Pius IX; Bismarck saw it as a contest with a political rival, preferring subservient Lutherans. Like Prussian rulers and the Protestant right, he believed the Vatican was a "Black International" demanding loyalties above the nation. With the pope's blessing, Catholic dignitaries organized the Center party to protect the church, and it immediately became a major force. By 1879 Bismarck, realizing he had created a political enemy he could not influence, compromised with the new pope, Leo XIII. Disavowing his liberal allies, who were now politically weak, Bismarck encouraged the press, including papers he illegally subsidized with secret funds, to blame the Jews in the Reichstag for the persecution of the church. By betraying his allies, Bismarck encouraged the Catholic press to claim that the *Kulturkampf* was orchestrated by Jews to cover up their frauds during the crash. They ignored the fact that many Jewish leaders, including Lasker himself, opposed the conflict.

In popular culture, Jews were also defamed. By the 1870s an extensive and cheap literature provided millions of Germans with stereotypes indistinguishable from anti-Semitic tracts, all the more powerful because the unsophisticated assumed that novels were based upon actual observations. In an enormously popular novel by Felix Dahn in 1867, the Jewish villain is cowardly and evil. His face reveals "all the calculating cunning of his race," contrasted with the blond and manly purity of the German protagonist.⁷ In Gustav Freytag's *Debit and Credit* (1855), the most popular novel of the century, Jewish businessmen form an "underworld prepared to exploit any weakness in the moral or economic structure of Gentile society."⁸ The Jews are depicted as out to destroy honest German businessmen through cunning, acquisitive instincts unmodified by honor or loyalty. Freytag believed Polish Jews to be "filth" existing at a "primitive moral level." "Jews are a "disease . . . which can be cured only by rigorous means."⁹ The novel was highly praised by critics for its realism.

Wilhelm Raabe's extremely popular *Der Hungerpastor* (1864) was required reading in many schools until 1914. In it the idealistic piety of a German cleric is contrasted with the destructive, cynical rationality of a Jewish intellectual. Raab's Christian pastor is respected for his modesty, the Jew despised because he has abused so many to gain his wealth.

He ends as an outcast. The image of the evil Jew penetrated even the nursery. The Grimm Brothers' immensely popular fairy tales were based on old German legends, but the brothers, reactionary nationalists, edited the tales to fit their hatred of republican cosmopolitanism and show the purity of the German racial soul. In "The Jew in the Thornbush" they replaced the original villain, a monk, with a vile Jewish thief who confesses and is hung.

Heinrich von Treitschke is the classic example of the prestige that anti-Semitism gained among many German academics. Treitschke's *History of Germany in the Nineteenth Century* (1879) was the most popular historical work ever published in Germany. A dogmatic paean to the Prussian elites, crudely Hegelian, the book holds the unification of Germany to be the culmination of the Will of the Absolute as embodied in German martial racial qualities, furthered by the necessary subordination of individual rights to the nation. Treitschke was the most popular lecturer at the University of Berlin, where he taught the future rulers and secondary school teachers of Germany. As racist furor grew in 1879, Jews were beaten in the streets. "Do not buy from Jews!" was scrawled on Jewish businesses, and demagogues led numerous small but vocal organizations that demanded harsh measures against Jews and those "Judeophiles" who, they insisted, controlled Bismarck's Reich. In a famous article in a prestigious journal, Trietschke noted that he disapproved of violence but understood the reasons for it. The "healthy volk sense" . . . "has correctly detected a strong danger directed against German life." Although the number of Jews was small, "over our eastern borders lies an inexhaustible Polish cradle, from it streams year after year a host of hustling second-hand pants peddlers whose children and grandchildren will one day rule Germany's stock market and newspapers."[10] Even honorable Jews were far too influenced by the cosmopolitan Enlightenment. To be accepted, they must think and behave like Germans. If they preferred their outmoded religion, so be it, but Christian faith was essential to German nationalism. Treitschke denounced the "arrogant" Jewish press for attacking German institutions and even Christianity. He ignored the constant Christian insults against Judaism, for he thought the criticisms correct, as pious Christians usually did. The "dangerously arrogant . . . Semites bear a great share of responsibility and guilt for the lies, betrayals, and arrogant greed which has animated the despicable speculative business practices and base materialism of our day. . . . In thousands of German villages sits the usurious Jew, selling out his neighbor for greed and gain."[11] Treitschke and many educated Germans hoped to end the emigration of Polish Jews and limit the civil rights of German Jews; extremists simply wanted them thrown out. Even educated Germans, Treitschke warned, "say today as if with one voice: *The Jews are our misfortune!*" The famous phrase rang through decades and in 1923 ended on the masthead of Julius Streicher's violently racist journal *Der Stuermer.*

In 1880 a mass meeting of racists led by Bernhard Foerster began an anti-Semitic petition campaign. Jewish usurers had gained control of the ancestral land won by German blood, the petition claimed, and "everywhere it is only the callused hand of the Christian that is active" while "the Jew harvests the fruits of this labor." An alien tribe "furthest removed" from the "thought and feeling" of the "Aryan" world conquered Germans with wealth and immorality. As teachers and lawyers they destroyed "Germanic ideals of honor, loyalty, piety." Circulated in Prussia, the petition urged the kaiser to end Jewish emigration and bar Jews from all positions of authority, including law and education, where they "corrupt" youth.[12] More than half the non-Jewish students of the University of Berlin signed the petition.

With a quarter-million signatures the petition was presented to Bismarck and the Prussian House of Deputies. Progressives spoke against it, confident Bismarck would reject it out of hand, for it violated the constitution he himself had crafted. Instead his ministers merely noted that "the government intends no action to deprive Jews of their rights." Immediately liberals submitted counterpetitions calling for an end to illegal discrimination in the civil service and the army, but anti-Semites took this as more proof that liberalism was Jewish. In 1881, stirred by the success of the petition, the German Students' League was founded. Hailing Treitschke as a source of inspiration, the students "consecrated themselves to the fight against materialism, liberalism, and the Jews."[13]

The Evangelical pastor Adolf Stoecker, cofounder of the Students' League, rose with the wave of anti-Semitism and organized the most successful of the anti-Semitic movements of the 1880s. No ordinary priest, he was elected royal chaplain to the court by Kaiser William I. Stoecker, the son of a sergeant, spent his childhood in a Prussian military compound. He enjoyed lining up his classmates in military formation and commanding them to crawl to the cross in penance for their sins. Later he became a tutor to a Prussian aristocratic family, joining them in long conversations about Prussian virtues and contemporary decadence. Like most Lutheran clergy, he saw himself as a spiritual servant of the Hohenzollerns. He was a true fundamentalist. When a seminarian expressed doubt about a church dogma, Stoecker curtly announced: "Doubts come from the devil. Some thoughts should simply be beaten to death."[14] Priesthood gave the son of a lowly soldier an otherwise unattainable status, confirming his belief in Prussian virtues. His rural flock approved his charismatic sermons on the sanctity of autocracy. Total acceptance of the established order and church dogma—these gave Stoecker's authoritarian personality the certainties he needed during the turmoil of unification, industrialism, and progressive challenges to his beloved Prussia.

In 1866 Stoecker was transferred to a parish in a mining town. His parishioners were miners who led a harsh, dangerous, and ill-paid life, with no room for illusions about the divine beneficence of the establishment. Like most proletarians, they voted socialist, scorned religion, and spent Sundays in the local beer garden. Stoecker was shocked when, during the Franco-Prussian War, they sympathized with Parisian radicals who resisted the Prussian army even after France had surrendered, formed a commune, terrorized priests, and shot an archbishop. Striking a blow at treason, Stoecker wrote essays for a church publication praising Prussian arms and the virtues that caused the God of Battles to favor them. Like his fellow pastors, he took charge of the local victory celebrations but was utterly humiliated when his preparations for a solemn religious ceremony were rejected by public officials in favor of a beer festival. The kaiser, the church, and the honored dead, he protested, were treated with treasonous contempt. His flock dwindling, his patriotism ridiculed, a discouraged Stoecker arranged for transfer to the army as a military chaplain.

Stoecker's division was stationed in Alsace-Lorraine, the territories Bismarck had seized from France. There, in 1871, the army had brutally driven out thousands of Jews. In his glory on the battlefields and in military cemeteries, Stoecker preached to soldiers, one of a vast chorus of German academics, clergy, journalists, and politicians idealizing the conflict. "In its war songs," he expounded, "the German *Volk* does not celebrate the modern God of doubt and criticism, but the old powerful God, the mighty Lord of armies who uses them to work his great miracles, and thus, with all his power, reigns over the history of peoples."[15] Stoecker's sermons gained him the accolade of the high command as a "true warrior-priest." He drew the attention of the kaiser, who in 1876 appointed him imperial chaplain to the court.

Stoecker's new parishioners were the aristocratic and military elites, the soul of Prussian greatness. Still, he hoped to persuade workers to discard atheistic socialism and return to throne and altar. As royal chaplain he ran the city mission, established to aid the destitute. Here Stoecker found more discontent among the many new arrivals from the countryside who, unemployed, succumbed to Berlin's temptations and seemed hopelessly lost to church and kaiser as their church attendance, marriages, and baptisms rapidly declined. Stoecker detested city life; "sinful Berlin" was a common phrase among conservatives, for whom the city was a haven for revolutionaries, emancipated women, homosexuals, prostitutes, and Jews. In Berlin's poor districts, anarchists heaped scorn on everything Stoecker held dear. Worst of all, the Progressive party of left-liberals dominated the

Berlin electorate, Conservative candidates were weak, and socialists were gaining.

To counter such "moral decay," Stoecker took a risky step for a royal chaplain: in 1877 he founded the Christian Social Workers party, hoping to win proletarian votes for the right. To the consternation of his superiors, Stoecker ran for election with a program to restore the guild system, outlaw usury and stock market speculation, forbid child, female, and Sunday labor, and offer social insurance for the poor, the orphaned, the disabled, and the widowed, measures to be paid for partly by inheritance and income taxes on the well-to-do. Stoecker did not mention the Jews. Campaigning in proletarian districts, he met tumultuous opposition led by Johann Most, a famous anarchist member of the Reichstag later expelled from Germany. Recognized for their ridicule of religion and patriotism, Most and his followers invaded Stoecker's meetings, shouted him down, pounded on tables with beer steins, and reviled, in Most's words, "the black army of spiritual oppressors" who had never helped workers and had the gall to offer petty reforms when the system itself had to be overthrown. They demanded to know from the flustered pastor how a member of the establishment could expect his masters to tax their wealth for the good of ordinary Germans. Stoecker's campaign failed miserably. In the national Reichstag elections in Berlin in 1878, the Progressives won 86,000 votes, the Social Democrats 56,000, and the Conservatives 12,000. Stoecker's Christian Social Workers party managed only 1,241. But during his campaign, Stoecker noted how his supporters had tried to drown out his opponents with crude racist slogans, urging him to speak about the "real cause" of German misery, the Jews.

Stoecker now saw his chance. Running for the Prussian Chamber of Deputies, in a famous speech of September 1879 he began his campaign with Glagau's phrase, "The social problem is the Jewish problem." His first public denunciation of the Jews, it was both opportunism and a sincere expression of his faith. Using familiar themes, Stoecker declared that the Jews rejected Christ and Luther because they were tied to an ossified religion of ritual. Many also broke with Judaism, and, bereft of moral restraints, prospered in an economic system they created, one based on greed and materialism. "Having forsaken the path of God, they now worship the idol of Gold . . . and reap where they have not sown." "Liberalism," an "emanation of the Jewish spirit," was pursued by assimilated, secular Jews, enemies of kaiser and God. Their call for toleration and the separation of church and state was but a continuation of their ancient "bitter battle with Christianity" and an attempt to remove the last barrier to their domination.

To curb the Jews, Stoecker demanded legislation restricting their use of capital and moneylending, and forbidding them to be judges or teachers. Landed property, the root of German ethical life, must be protected from Jewish speculators and cheap credit made available to protect small businesses from "Jewish" usury. Only thus could be ended the "encroachment of Jewry on Germanic life, the worst kind of usury." Stoecker proclaimed, "The German is a great idealist"—as if there were no German stockbrokers, bankers, or speculators, and no aristocrats living in ease from an inheritance supplemented by the labor of their peasants. Stoecker also conveniently forgot that he himself had profited from investments in a Jewish corporation.

Stoecker was even willing to deny, if indirectly, the power of Christ to transform all humanity through conversion. The Jews, he declared, were "a separate tribe [living] among a foreign race." Why else had "all immigrants but the Jews become Germans in every sense?" Stoecker warned that "Israel must renounce its ambition to become the master of Germany" and cease using its capital and press to bring "misfortune to the nation" and "ruin the German people who have offered it hospitality and civil rights." Otherwise they would face a violent reaction. If they were not stopped, the "cancer" would grow and Germans themselves would be Judaized, for the Jews were destroying all German traditions. "Return to Germanic rule in law and business, and . . . Christian faith. May every man do his duty, and God will help us all."[16]

Anti-Semitism won Stoecker the election. Sensing his newfound popularity, Conservative party candidates also denounced the Jews. In an amazing comeback from their humiliation of 1874, Conservatives doubled their seats as Liberal and Progressive candidates took heavy losses. For the first time a high-ranking member of the famed "apolitical" religious establishment was a force in politics, and the authorities, including Bismarck, were pleased at the new power of the right to hold off the left. Stoecker had attracted not proletarian socialist votes but failed peasants, unemployed artisans, shop clerks, and small businessmen, as well as rural migrants hoping to find respectable white-collar jobs in the civil service, banks, or shops. Their traditional loyalties made them hostile to proletarians; their Christian faith enhanced their belief that their economic difficulties had been caused by Jewish land speculators, moneylenders, and rural middlemen. Cut loose from village and small town, Stoecker's voters blamed their troubles on the mysterious financial power of the Jews. It was easier for them to blame the ancient enemy rather than face their own inability to compete in the new national market, a market in fact dominated by the elites they admired.

Berlin was a culture shock to those who had left old kinship ties behind and were confronted with a sensationalist press carrying daily revelations of rapes, murders, and financial scandals. Street-corner anarchists mocked all they respected. The ancient enemies of Christianity paraded their success in activities considered parasitic by rural folk, and published newspapers critical of established virtues and elites. Filled with temptations, Berlin unleashed powerful anger and painful frustration among newcomers freed from the intense scrutiny of village life, tempted yet repelled by Berlin's liberation from the limits of traditional behavior. This could not be Christian Germany.

Regardless of their failures and low rank, Stoecker and anti-Semites gave these rural migrants the solace of believing they belonged to the real Germany as no Jew ever could. Their village pastor writ large and a representative of the kaiser himself, Stoecker was a fiery champion of the values of the familiar world they had lost to new forces they could not grasp. Throughout the West, radical and racist movements to preserve traditional values have often attracted new arrivals to big cities, where, before the media explosion homogenized culture, deracinated farmers and rural artisans confronted what they could only view as "moral decay." Protest movements combining racism with attacks against moral decay have often been led by clergy, as with Father Charles Coughlin and the Reverend Gerald L. K. Smith in the United States, or Muslim extremists today. By casting social behavior in terms of guilt, sin, and religion, Stoecker enabled his followers to personalize their enemies and avoid analyzing the actual workings of society or supporting the left they feared.

Allied with conservatives, Stoecker dropped income and inheritance taxes from his party program and the threatening phrase "Workers" from the party title. Conservative nationalists, as they would with the Nazis, wanted anti-Semites to defend their interests but feared stirring up a populist radicalism they could not control. Racism became Stoecker's major theme. When his posters declared Jewry was his topic, attendance at his meetings soared—as with Hitler in the 1920s.

Stoecker's party did not have the required number of delegates to gain speaking rights in the Prussian chamber; it needed the cooperation of the Conservative party, which happily obliged. Stoecker used his first allotted time to threaten the Progressives for denouncing the anti-Semitic petition of 1881: "You will be destroyed," he warned, "if you continue to associate yourselves with the Jews."[17] In 1881 he won a seat in the national German Reichstag, supported by the Conservative party which also ran four other well-known anti-Semites as candidates. The party was overjoyed when it quadrupled its Berlin vote. Although still trailing the Progressives, Conservatives now passed the Social Democrats in numbers. The drop in the Social Democratic vote was partly a result of laws Bismarck passed against socialists. But racism seemed to promise Conservatives votes in cities where, traditionally dependent on rural constituencies, they had been in retreat. Popularly called the king of Berlin, Stoecker declared in the Reichstag (to "lively approval!"), "We challenge the Jews to battle . . . we will not rest until we have driven them from their high position in Berlin into the dust where they belong."[18]

Bismarck was not averse to racism; in the Prussian Diet of 1847 he had declared, "If I should imagine having before me as a representative of the King's sacred Majesty, a Jew whom I would have to obey, I must confess that I would be deeply depressed and humiliated."[19] But he was ambivalent, chastising anti-Semites for attacking Jews of wealth and standing when they should denounce Jewish radicals instead. Now he himself was attacked by conservatives intent upon breaking his alliance with the liberals, and the *Kreuzzeitung* infuriated him by reporting that his banker, lawyer, and physician were Jewish. Stoecker had important supporters at the court, including the kaiser's grandson, one day to be the last kaiser of Germany, who told an audience of ten thousand that Stoecker's ideas were vital to Germany's future. Soon Bismarck joined the chorus of those calling the liberal parties "Jewish" and demanding a return of the right to power. The chancellor used secret government funds to bribe the press to publish articles favorable to Stoecker, and he instructed his son, later a fan of Hitler's, to support Stoecker without involving the government. Bismarck's press secretary, Moritz Busch, helped provide anti-Semitic propaganda for elections and suggested it would be wise to organize an anti-Semitic party that did not flirt with reform as Stoecker did.

Bismarck and conservatives were all the more willing to use racism because of a new threat. Founded in 1875 by Marxists and more moderate socialists, the Social Democratic party was making swift gains. The rapidly growing industrial proletariat gave them half a million votes in 1877. Bismarck's immense prestige as the unifier of Germany tamed the National Liberals, but the internationalists of the left were unimpressed, denouncing his big military budgets and constant electoral cries of "The Fatherland in Danger." Worse, the Social Democrats also demanded an end to the three-class voting system in Prussia which favored the wealthy, and called for a chancellor responsible to parliamentary majorities. Bismarck decided to outlaw the Social Democrats. An attempt on the kaiser's life gave him pretext, though there was no socialist involvement. To conservative hurrahs and National Liberal support, Bismarck deprived socialists of their civil rights, jailed or exiled many, ordered police to break up their meetings, forbade or censored their speeches, and outlawed their publications. Some six hundred socialists were put behind bars, sent there by judges who often violated the law to do so. Treitschke demanded that all workers voting Social Democratic be fired. Although Bismarck could not get the votes to outlaw the party altogether, it was unable to campaign and lost a third of its votes in 1881.

Bismarck now sought to blunt socialism's appeal by adopting Stoecker's strategy. In 1881, the year of Stoecker's greatest success, Bismarck proposed legislation to insure workers against sickness, accident, or disability. By 1889 the measures had passed, but workers' contributions paid two-thirds of the costs. Such reforms could not appease Social Democrats. As their parliamentary leader declared, they would gladly help Bismarck draft the legislation necessary to put the whole burden on capitalists where it belonged. Neither Bismarck nor Stoecker could win over the workers. After their defeat of 1881, urged on by union leaders, the workers rallied in 1884, shocking Bismarck by winning 10 percent of the Reichstag vote. They more than doubled their vote in Berlin, outpolling Conservatives and nearly defeating the Progressives as well. Stoecker himself ran for the German Reichstag against the famous scientist Rudolf Virchow, a Jew and the most popular Progressive deputy in Berlin, and lost. The pastor retained his seat in the Prussian chamber, but he was no longer the King of Berlin. Conservatives, shocked by huge workers' demonstrations in support of the left, feared an electoral alliance between Progressives and socialists.

Socialism could not be dismissed—as it would be later in the United States—as a foreign ideology introduced by immigrants. Jews would have to take the blame. Stoecker shouted at leftists who disrupted his campaigns that the founders of German socialism, Ferdinand Lassalle and Karl Marx, were Jewish, though he knew from his own industrial parish that the vast majority of its voters were Gentile. With their theory of the racial conversatism of Germans at risk because of this uncomfortable fact, rightists sought to attract workers, as Hitler later would, by declaring they had been duped by traitorous Jewish "reds" into believing their enemies were Christian-Aryan industrialists when in fact they were Jewish international financiers. "Jewish socialism" was constantly denounced, though almost 90 percent of the Jewish electorate voted for the liberal parties. Neither Christian conservatives who flirted with racism nor Marxists who denounced capitalism could expect allegiance from the urban Jewish commercial and professional classes. But many independent intellectuals of Jewish origins were prominent among leftist publicists. Secular or atheist, they rejected ethnicity and religion, and, less cautious than their elders, exposed the difference between constitutional guarantees of equality and the realities of government and institutional discrimination. As usual, the right concentrated on a few prominent Jews, refusing to admit the support of radical dissent by millions of Gentiles. Racist conspiracy notions allowed them to avoid facing rising mass dissatisfaction with the Germany they had built and still dominated.

Fearing the power of Progressives and socialists, Bismarck declared, "If I do not make a *putsch*, I will not prevail." In the 1880s he purged "unreliable elements" from the civil service, mostly liberals. The minister of education increased the teaching of Christian dogma and rightist nationalism in the schools, and the army prepared its recruits for possible action against liberals and leftists. Bismarck tried to remove army budgets from parliamentary control in order to forge a reliable sword against democrats and socialists. He failed but made it more difficult for deputies to query military expenses. He also gave economic concessions to industrialists and tariffs to landowners at the expense of consumers in order to forge a conservative electoral majority. Consequently Germany now suffered the highest bread and meat prices in Europe. Bismarck paid for higher military budgets by increasing indirect taxes, further burdening those least able to pay. Even his officials complained that Junkers refused to increase their taxes to provide funds for the large military they demanded. To justify subsidies and tariffs to the well-off, the government insisted that German agriculture must not be sacrificed to international commodity traders; the racist subtext was obvious. Above all, they added, Junker landowners and peasants were the bulwark of defense, unlike the subversive proletariat and unreliable city masses who degenerated under the impact of urban life. The *Kreuzzeitung* insisted that if agriculture were harmed, Germany would become a nation of shopkeepers fit only for trade, ruled by the "Jewish" spirit of pacifism. Soon such thoughts would be commonplace.

In 1887 Bismarck exaggerated a minuscule threat of war to demand a higher army budget. He knew the Reichstag would refuse, but he wanted new elections. War drums pounded in his subsidized press while he demanded war loans and called up reserves. The cry of "The Fatherland in Danger" rang through the land. Bismarck formed a coalition of Conservatives and National Liberals, and in the elections of 1887 they gained almost 60 percent of all Reichstag seats; Progressives and Social Democrats lost more than half of theirs. The ultra right, however, lost seats as well, as did Stoecker's party. It was Bismarck's greatest electoral victory. No longer required to placate reactionaries or Progressives, and with his industrialist allies angry at Stoecker's interference, Bismarck muzzled him. Denouncing this "favor to the Jews," the *Kreuzzeitung* published Bismarck's numerous anti-Semitic statements over the years. Stoecker risked his post, asking, "Do the Bismarck people know how the Jews and the Social Democrats enjoy the attitude of the regime toward us?" The *Kreuzzeitung* recalled that Bismarck had said, "We Germans fear only God," and added, "Unfortunately" we now "fear the Jews as well. . . ."[20] Reactionaries braced for a liberal onslaught and intensified their anti-Semitism to near epidemic proportions.

In blaming the revolutions of 1848 on the Jews, conservatives had singled out the religious Jew, Gabriel Riesser, the former vice-president of the Frankfurt parliament who had led the committee offering the imperial crown to the king of Prussia. Angered by claims that the left was predominantly Jewish, Riesser did not apologize for his liberal views, but he insisted that only those faithful to Judaism could be considered Jews. Why should leftists of Jewish origin, but hostile to Judaism, be used to condemn Jewry in general? Riesser protested in vain. Political reactionaries could not allow Jews to stop being Jewish even if they deserted their religion. Attacking liberalism and socialism as "Jewish" allowed them to ignore the defects of society and unite all who feared change. But conservative constituencies were growing less religious; Christian mythology was beginning to wear thin. More and more it was reinforced with newer, more extreme, and more dangerous stereotypes of race and blood. A trap was being set. There had to be a subversive conspiracy. It had to be led by Jews. And their blood had to prevent them from ever being anything but Jews.

7: THE RISE OF POPULIST ANTI-SEMITISM

A Jew remains a Jew, in Germany or any other country. He can
never change his race, even by centuries of residence among other
people.
　　　　　　　　　　　　　—*Handbook for the Hitler Youth*, 1937

THE first popular book to declare that the "antisocial" traits of the Jews
were determined by blood was Wilhelm Marr's *The Victory of the Jews
Over the Germans*. Published during the racist agitation of 1879, it went
through twelve editions in one year. Marr invented the term "anti-Semitism" and exhorted his readers not to blame the destructive behavior of
the Jews on their religion or their refusal to assimilate. Corrupt by blood,
the Jews of necessity made war "on all ideals" and transformed "everything into merchandise."[1] For them, even conversion and assimilation
were merely ways to infiltrate and conquer Gentile society. Jews used the
ideas of the Enlightenment as vehicles for racial conquest, and in the
"new Palestine of Bismarck's Reich" they voted liberal because religious
toleration, equal rights, and free capitalism brought them power—as
when the National Liberals passed legislation enabling Jewish speculators
to exploit Germans in the crash of 1873. Already, said Marr, the Jews so
dominated Germany that one could hardly distinguish between commerce and crime. The Jewish press converted culture into commodities
touted by cheap sensationalism and fraudulent advertising, meanwhile
publishing pompous editorials about human rights as Jewish press lords
hastened the decomposition of traditional values. Social Democrats were
nothing but the "bodyguards of the Jewish stock exchange," and financiers the real enemies of the workers.[2]

Indeed, everything threatening Germans was the product of this "demonic" race that had conquered Germany "with its Jewish spirit."[3] Germans had lost because they lacked the will to sacrifice for their ideals and
the social vision to counter liberalism: "You elect the alien masters to
your parliaments. You make them legislators and judges. You make them

97

the dictators of the state finance system. You deliver up the press to them. . . . "⁴ Successfully resisting centuries of hatred, Marr declared, "No conquering hero of ancient or modern times could boast of greater spiritual, cultural, and historical success than the Jew peddler hawking shoelaces from a street-corner pushcart."⁵ Vanquished, Germans would end as slaves under a Jewish kaiser; at best they might establish a tiny community somewhere where idealism could survive. The German Reich was destined to become the first Jewish world power. Moral indignation was pointless: "No people can help its special nature."⁶ "To Jewry belongs the future and life, to Germandom the past and death." Judaism ruled the world, reconcile yourselves to the inevitable: "FINIS GERMANIA."⁷

But Marr did not resign himself to the inevitable, urging readers to boycott Jewish businesses, and, in the elections of 1879, with conservative backing, Marr founded an Anti-Semitic League and a journal, *German, On Guard!*, demanding restrictions on Jews and declaring "Elect No Jews!" Marr insisted he was above party politics, but the only parties nominating German Jews were Progressives and Social Democrats. In the elections Marr helped boycott Jewish stores and campaigned for Stoecker, even though as an atheist he thought Christian anti-Semitism far too moderate. As Hitler would complain, it offered the Jews a chance to escape our righteous wrath with a "mere splash of holy water." One day, Marr warned, the victims of the Jews, finally driven too far, would rise and exact a "terrible revenge."

Inherent in Marr's racism of blood was a potential for genocide. If the Jews were evil, unchangeable, and about to conquer, they must be dragged from their positions in society and rendered harmless; even a Jewish infant was a mortal threat. At least they must be driven out of the land. Marr's was the racism that led to the death camps

By the 1880s Marr was one of many intellectuals, government officials, army officers, and politicians who insisted that Germany's difficulties were caused not by class conflict or social change but by the fixed racial behavior of the Jews. In 1876 a pamphleteer wrote: "Even the most honorable Jew is under the inescapable influence of his blood, carrier of a Semitic morality totally opposed to Germanic values . . . aimed at the destruction and burial of German values and traditions. . . .Before you vote for anyone, first ask about his blood and worry later about his political opinions."⁸

Adolf Stoecker limited himself to organizing Berlin. The first significant rural anti-Semitic movements began under the leadership of Otto Boeckel, the "King of the Hessian Peasantry," as he became known, an agrarian populist who scorned Stoecker's close relationship to aristocracy and court. Born in rural Prussia in 1859, son of a successful artisan,

Boeckel loved to assume the guise of a simple peasant, though in fact he held a Ph.D. in languages and literature and was the assistant librarian to the University of Marburg. Marburg was a delightful medieval town, located in a pastoral district of villages where peasants and artisans were famed for Protestant piety—and anti-Semitism. Passionately interested in folk customs, songs, legends, and superstitions, Boeckel was one of many German intellectuals, Himmler included, who idealized the peasant as the backbone of the nation, the purest of the race. His rough, simple ways, closeness to the soil, and stubborn attachment to the values of his ancestors were the product of the "Germanic" virtues of work, loyalty, traditionalism, and strength of character. In wartime the best recruit, in peace his hard labors assured Germany's independence from foreign control. He was the Germanic life-force, free of cosmopolitanism, uncorrupted by the drive for endless gain.[9]

The peasants of Boeckel's Hesse, like those of Eastern Europe, lived with superstitions dating back to the medieval era and into the mists of pagan antiquity. For them, Satan still roamed the countryside, the local witch was shunned, and natural disasters were the work of demonic forces or the wrath of God. Jews were the blood enemies of Christ, a people whose occult powers enabled them to defy the will of the Almighty himself. Boeckel praised the blood and instincts of the peasant, glorified him in novel and poem, and lamented the intrusion of market forces and urban ways into the countryside. Unchecked, they would destroy the healthy racial instincts of the Volk. In the revolutions of 1848, the artisans of Hesse, Boeckel's father perhaps among them, were the most prominent in the struggle against the introduction of "Jewish" free enterprise. After Napoleon's defeat, the restored rulers of Hesse abolished most Jewish rights.

In mid-century, in their dark, primitive, and isolated villages, most Hessian peasants had little entrepreneurial spirit; unaware of the latest agrarian technology, they were slow to adapt to new opportunities. Guilds were still protected, not forced to compete for urban markets, adopt new techniques, or find the credit necessary for such investments. But in 1866 the rulers of Hesse fought on the Austrian side against Prussia. Defeated, Hesse was annexed and its semifeudal manorial system abolished. Suddenly it was thrust into the modern world. As Richard S. Levy has written, "The stagnant, patriarchal government of electoral Hesse had suddenly given way to the most efficient, rationally directed administration in Europe, that of the Prussian state. The Prussian financial, commercial, military, and railroad systems had an almost immediate effect on the old routine way of life."[10]

The conquest brought the liberal economic reforms of the Second Reich and equal rights to Jews. New opportunities opened to a Jewish community "among the poorest in Germany . . . squeezed into viciously competitive marginal businesses and trades."[11] Jews now became brewers, canners, sugar refiners, wholesalers, moneylenders, and land speculators. Local patriotism intensified old antagonisms, for many Jews welcomed Prussian rule because it offered them the chance to compete in activities once prohibited. Boeckel and others accused the Jews of collaborating with the enemy for economic advantage at the expense of the artisans and peasants of Hesse.

Many Jews were dynamic entrepreneurial newcomers, often with sufficient capital to establish small businesses. As before, they were seen as symbol and beneficiary of new forces upsetting the traditional order. Throughout Germany, small-holding peasants were victims of a long agrarian depression starting in the 1870s, most devastating to those who tried to remain self-sufficient or work as their ancestors had. Others adjusted, some even prospered, producing for markets free of the old tariff barriers and connected by the new railroad lines of a unified Germany. Nevertheless, from 1873 to the late 1890s, small peasants suffered a rapid fall in income and, increasingly dependent upon local moneylenders, often lost their lands. Anti-Semitism was especially bitter among those who lived in "underdeveloped areas where Jewish middlemen enjoyed a near monopoly of credit, the cattle and grain trade, and many times also the real estate business."[12] In backward Hesse, Jews accounted for "well over half" of those in retail business, Jewish moneylenders gave credit to peasants too poor to qualify for bank loans, and Jews held "a monopoly of middleman functions in agricultural goods."[13] Crop failures had been accepted with traditional fatalism, but the peasant was ill equipped to grasp the new reasons for the failure of the old ways. His interests, once protected by conservative governments, were now hostage to changes welcomed by liberals but since Napoleon associated with Jews.

In 1885 Boeckel published *The Jews: The Kings of Our Times*. By 1909 more than 1.5 million copies had been sold. He also published an anti-Semitic newspaper, cleverly placing attacks against Jews alongside weather reports, crop prospects, and price fluctuations. Repeating the complaints of numerous countrymen, Boeckel held Jewish moneylenders responsible for high interest rates, low prices for farm goods, and high prices for farm equipment, while Jewish speculators manipulated credit and mortgage rates to seize the land of the bankrupt farmer. Taken together, Jewish actions raised land values beyond the reach of even successful peasants. Boeckel agreed with Glagau: "All Jews and descendants of Jews are enemies of agriculture."

But peasants who switched from grain to dairy or livestock production, and artisans whose skills were useful in the new factories or whose products were not amenable to factory specialization, were less anti-Semitic.

So too were those who detected new needs, introduced new technology, and learned the arcane mysteries of credit, investment, and the market. But the losers, envious and resentful, were vulnerable to the fiery demagogues who denounced "Jewish liberalism," enabling them to blame the old enemy for their misery. It was difficult to blame themselves and impossible to accept the success of a people traditionally isolated and feared as the Antichrist. Fundamentalist peasants had little means of understanding complex factors governing interest rates, land values, price fluctuations, and the impact of distant markets. In a world they could neither understand nor control, no matter how hard they worked in field or small shop they could not change the factors determining the difference between profit or loss.

More was involved than economic incapacity. Ancestral farming methods shaped peasant identity; new ways were held in suspicion. In popular literature the ruined peasant, symbol of dying values, became a stock character, a solid man of the soil driven from his ancestral homestead by ruthless speculators, usually portrayed as urban Jews with no love for the soil or interest in working it. Rural artisans were depicted as skilled and honest cabinetmakers, bakers, or shoemakers, their traditional skills replaced by machinery and mass production in factories financed by foreign or Jewish capitalists, producers of shoddy goods sold to customers duped by false advertising. Boeckel gave voice to a populist anti-Semitism even more dangerous than Stoecker's. As with Marr, his mentor, Boeckel insisted that Jewish activities were the consequence of racial corruption. Where are the Jewish peasants, Jewish artisans, Jewish workers? Look at sinful Berlin for the answers, he declared—a city of Jewish anarchists, atheists, and financiers. In his political campaigns Boeckel anticipated the charges that Nazi campaigners hurled when Protestant peasants gave them their first major electoral success.

Complaining bitterly about the influx of Jews, Boeckel "proved" mathematically that in the future there would be more Jews than Germans in the cities. Throw them out, he demanded. "You must combat with all your power the machinations of the Jews. The people yearn for an Emancipator!"[14] Unlike Stoecker, Boeckel was no defender of the Prussian establishment. In conquered Hesse it would have been political suicide. Boeckel attacked Junker landowners for sympathizing with the victims of the Jews yet using their political influence to further only their own interests. Stoecker and his aristocratic allies were "Cohnservatives" who behaved "like Jews" in betraying the ordinary farmer. Early on, Boeckel's followers often rallied to his populist cry, "Against Junkers and Jews."

In rural societies, moneylending is seen as the power to take advantage of others' misery. If the lender is of another religious or ethnic group, racial tensions surge. In the Italian countryside, for example, moneylenders were Italian and Catholic, so ethnicity was irrelevant though violence was common. In the American Midwest, anti-Semitic populism spread rapidly during the agrarian depression of the 1890s. Although banks were Gentile-owned, many insisted that the Jews were "really" the force behind them. But American populists were recent immigrants, not isolated villagers working ancestral land, hostile to the modern world. The vanguard of the great movement westward, and more market oriented than the villagers of Central or Eastern Europe, they naturally sought new land and opportunities in an expanding frontier. They might be fundamentalist, but rural Americans had lost contact with the superstitious anti-Judaism of the Dark Ages, or they were Calvinists who had never held such stark views. And in America, secular deism and the ideas of the Enlightenment were associated, however weakly, with the Founding Fathers themselves, not with foreigner or Jews.

Boeckel had a far more fruitful region for organizing his anti-Semitic People's party, and, unlike other racists, his people did more than simply issue anti-Semitic proclamations. They organized boycotts and established producers' cooperatives, cattle markets, and credit institutions, all *Judenrein* (free of Jews). Boeckel campaigned like a professional in rural areas, something no German political party had ever done. Indeed, Boeckel's young organizers, some of whom would later support the Nazis, invented techniques that the Nazis used to great effect. With extensive knowledge of local dialects and customs, Boeckel moved from pub to pub and spoke at rural feast days, weddings, and county fair celebrations. Maintaining his pose as a simple peasant, he would arrive in full regalia on horseback surrounded by strong young peasants, budding stormtroopers. His studies and experience made him supremely able to discuss topics that peasants understood best—crops, weather, prices, costs, and the decline of the old skills and ways, and always and everywhere the machinations of the Jews. He organized torchlight processions featuring Lutheran hymns and fiery speeches laced with sayings from his collection of anti-Semitica. Lauded as a reincarnation of Luther, he won the enthusiastic support of the local clergy, usually but one generation removed from the land. No urban politician could match his appeal to a peasantry suspicious of outsiders and city folk.

In spite of his populism, Boeckel's party did not attack the Prussian establishment, declaring loyalty to Reich, kaiser, and Fatherland. The party called for free credit for the peasantry, reduced farm taxes, protection for agricultural goods, and an end to foreclosures, demanding as well support for guild monopolies. It even favored inheritance taxes and a progressive income tax, extremely radical proposals then. Above all, Boeckel's party demanded the repeal of Jewish emancipation: "Only Christian men (of non-Jewish extraction) are to be elected to legislative bodies and employed in state or municipal offices."[15]

Boeckel won a seat in the Reichstag in 1887, holding it until 1903. His victory inspired other anti-Semites to run in rural constituencies; by 1890 a network of small racist peasant and artisan organizations had been organized or inspired by Boeckel. In 1890 five candidates, four from Hesse, won Reichstag seats in rural districts previously held by aristocrats. The nobles took their voters for granted, thinking it beneath their dignity to campaign, usually depending on the support of the local clergy to put in a good word for them in their sermons. But as Boeckel charged, conservatives had done nothing for the small landholder, using their influence to gain high grain tariffs for themselves and harming those peasants who purchased grain to feed livestock. By 1893 eleven anti-Semites from Boeckel's organizations had been elected to the Reichstag. Four more were elected by other populist groups.

Boeckel was that most dangerous of racists, a true believer, but the equally prominent Herman Ahlwardt was a crook who used anti-Semitism strictly for personal advantage. One of many schoolteachers who supported racist movements in the 1880s, Ahlwardt, heavily in debt, embezzled large sums from a fund for poor students and was dismissed. An energetic organizer and powerful speaker in Stoecker's movement, Ahlwardt made his reputation spreading false tales of Jewish scandals. He blamed his own large debts on Jewish usurers, but in fact his creditors were Christian. He dismissed the embezzlement charge as a Jewish plot. Ahlwardt wrote a pamphlet accusing Bleichroeder, Bismarck's Jewish banker, of fathering an illegitimate child, claiming the government had saved him from a paternity suit. The pamphlet sold out. Accused of libel, while in jail he wrote another pamphlet, "Jewish Rifles," accusing a Jewish firm of selling defective munitions to the Prussian army to help the French win the 1870 war so that the principles of 1789 might triumph over Germany. The pamphlet caused a sensation, swiftly selling out, and Ahlwardt became a popular leader among tens of thousands of lower-middle-class Germans. But he had insulted the Prussian army with his trumped-up charges, and the government, now under Leo von Caprivi, not Bismarck, prepared to prosecute him. The maligned Jewish firm sued for libel. Ahlwardt's large and vocal following believed the government hoped to silence him in order to pacify wealthy Jews.

In 1892 Ahlwardt ran for a seat in the Reichstag, his political ambitions stimulated because parliamentary immunity would protect him from prosecution. He chose a seat previously safe for conservatives, in Saxony, a backward district where, as one local official put it, the "Protestant peasant's outlook was still that of the Thirty Years War."[16] There were few Jews in the Saxon countryside but many in Dresden and Leipzig, mainly in retail trades and thus, of course, blamed for high prices. Moreover, thousands of Jews fleeing Russian pogroms had moved into Saxony, though many were promptly expelled. The local press believed the tsar had good reason to hate the Jews. The Saxon government was the "chief agent of political anti-Semitism" in Saxony, having fought the assimilation and liberation of the Jews since the time of Napoleon.[17]

Rapid industrialization had created a powerful socialist movement in "red Saxony," and blaming Jews for socialism bore fruit among peasants and artisans, especially because industrial wages outstripped their incomes. Voters, tired of conservative passivity, welcomed Ahlwardt's charge that "red traitors" aided atheist Jewish revolutionaries while Jews bribed high officials. The government suit against Ahlwardt turned him into a martyr, and the local press compared him to Luther and Christ. Was he not trying to cast the money changers from the temple? Stoecker, still powerful in the Conservative party, was a close friend of Ahlwardt; he had confirmed his daughter and given his blessing to Ahlwardt's calumnies. But the reactionaries did not yet control the Conservative party, and after much hesitation it shrank from supporting a man in prison for defaming the army, its sacred icon. But to the surprise of the national leaders, the local branch of the party ignored them and cooperated with Ahlwardt. In 1892 elections, Ahlwardt defeated the Conservative candidate in a landslide, joining Boeckel and the small but growing number of "single-issue" anti-Semites in the Reichstag.

Worried Conservative leaders, their districts threatened, began to form alliances with racist demagogues, who were, after all, firm supporters of conservative causes and bitter enemies of Social Democrats and liberals. Even Ahlwardt's most extreme attacks did not repel the reactionaries. In 1899 the most important anti-Semitic party, the German Social Reform party, called for a "final solution" to the Jewish question through "complete isolation" or "annihilation."[18] In the Reichstag in 1895 Ahlwardt, who could speak only with permission of the Conservatives, shouted, "It does not matter if [a Jew] is born in Germany: A horse that is born in a cowshed is still no cow. [Laughter and approval on the right]."[19] He then demanded the extermination of the Jews. He was not disciplined; Conservatives were too anxious to gain votes among swiftly growing new constituencies.

In mid-century many observers, left and right, had predicted that the proletariat would expand so rapidly that socialism would overwhelm the old order. But the fastest-growing groups in the 1890s were in fact small retailers, sales personnel, bank clerks, educational functionaries, and clerical workers needed in the vast new bureaucracies of private corporations and the state. The German phrase for them is *Mittelstand*, implying respectable semiprofessional status and conservative views. Most identified with the propertied and elites of corporation and government. Striving for status, the *Mittelstand* dressed to indicate respectability, attended church to display piety, and if possible bought or rented housing in decent neighborhoods. Even their furniture was a cheap imitation of that of their betters. Saving to educate and keep their children in the middle class, anxious that they should not fall into the proletariat (even though many skilled workers earned more than the average white-collar clerk), the *Mittelstand* believed in hard work, saving and investing, and the efficacy of individual effort, scorning collectivism and leftist criticism. The lower-middle-class German symbolizes, incorrectly, the typical German: rigid, orderly, humble before superiors, contemptuous with inferiors, organized to a fault.

Above all, the *Mittelstand* admired the values of the aristocratic and military elites. The magazines popular among them, including the *Gardenhouse* for which Marr, Glagau, and other anti-Semites wrote, glorified imperialism and thundered against the "treason" of the left. From the ranks of clerks, shopkeepers, and teachers came the members of patriotic societies, fatherland leagues, and colonial associations that sprang up in the 1890s. Led by high-ranking members of society, teachers, or academics, the organizations allowed clerks and secretaries, still mostly male, to experience vicariously the glory of imperial warriors, powerful industrialists, and titled aristocrats. Shopkeepers and their clerks were always among the strongest supporters of anti-Semitic movements. Small businessmen, propertied but marginal, suffered high bankruptcy rates and were politically more extreme than those who were better off. Family-owned merchants were outcompeted by large retail outlets and department stores able to buy in bulk, set low prices per unit, and offer special sales with costly advertising. Moreover, the new department stores were pioneered by Jews, partly because the new techniques they had adopted when excluded from Christian merchant guilds fit well a new era of mass retailing. Small retailers who did not or could not adjust, condemned department stores as immoral disruptions of the traditional relationship between small merchant and loyal customer, blaming Jewish owners for their plight.

The most influential anti-Semite among the *Mittelstand* was Theodore Fritsch. From the 1880s through his death in 1933, his publications reached millions of Germans, and he was honored as "master teacher" by the Nazis, eulogized at his funeral by Hitler himself. A racist entrepreneur, Fritsch owned an anti-Semitic publishing house and newspaper and helped Marr organize the German Anti-Semitic League. Inspired by Fritsch, Alfred Ploetz, founder of the Society for Racial Hygiene, formed a *Deutschbund* demanding the "extirpation of the inferior elements of the population" and battle against those of "Jewish and Slavic blood."[20] In 1893 Fritsch published his famous *Anti-Semitic Catechism*, its title changed to *The Handbook of Anti-Semitism* in 1896. By 1914 it had gone through thirty-seven editions; another eleven followed. Fritsch warned his readers never to mix with Jews or read Jewish books or their liberal press. Above all, Germans must keep their blood pure. By 1913 his organization had more than a half-million members, one of many smaller groups rapidly recruiting from the swiftly expanding *Mittelstand* of Germany and Austria.

Belief in the superiority of German blood enabled men of lesser rank and status to maintain their pride as Jews rose rapidly in commerce and the professions. Sales clerks and bureaucratic menials, semiskilled and with a weak grip on the lower rungs of the middle-class ladder of success, clung to racism to confirm a supposed latent superiority reinforced by joining patriotic groups, egos buttressed in racial communion with elite leaders. Beneath the façade of the petty clerk there often lurked a frustrated romantic, whose boring routines and precarious life made him identify with aristocratic warriors and powerful industrialists. Shared anti-Semitism yielded shared identity; no matter how high a Jew rose, he could never be a true German.

The most prominent association of German white-collar workers, the German Nationalist Commercial Employees Federation (DNHGV), formed in 1894 as socialist votes soared. By 1912 one-quarter of all private salaried personnel had joined. Typically *Mittelstand*, DNHGV members avoided confrontational trade-union tactics, preferring to act as a dignified guild with traditional attitudes, not mere wage workers. Avoiding strikes, they preferred negotiation, though they sometimes struck when opposing a Jewish boss. The DNHGV worked closely with the Conservative party and Reichstag anti-Semites. Its official handbook declared Jews could not join due to "lack of courage, greed for profits, sultry sensuality, lack of honor, and cleanliness."[21] Here were servile clerks finding false comfort in an imagined courage, selflessness, and honor. The ridiculous reference to Jewish "sultry sensuality" reveals the repressed desires of the puritanical and authoritarian type, bolstering a fragile image with meager means.

The DNHGV owned its own bookstores, where the works of Marr, Fritsch, H. S. Chamberlain (favorite of the kaiser and Hitler), and other famous anti-Semites were prominently displayed. Here too could be found books on the Teutonic past of the *Volk*, the medieval pageantry of the guilds, and the Aryan art later to be labeled Nazi, with its blond Nordic warriors and peasants in heroic poses, symbolizing the virtues of the race. The retailers' association printed anti-Semitic books free of charge and sponsored lectures detailing the crimes and blood corruption of the Jews. It also condemned parliamentary democracy and universal suffrage, praising the ideal of the Christian corporate state where vocational groups such as theirs would be represented. In elections the DNHGV often helped anti-Semitic candidates with funds and literature. In 1896 it elected Wilhelm Schack president. Teacher in a commercial school and official in an anti-Semitic organization, even among racists Schack was noted for his extremism. The DNHGV grew swiftly under his guidance. Elected to the Reichstag in 1905, Schack was driven out of politics and the association in 1909 when, unable to resist "sultry sensuality," he placed an anonymous ad for a young woman, preferably bisexual, who would be willing to share the "joys of love." He also may have been siphoning DNHGV funds to his separate anti-Semitic movement.

The conservatism of the clerks is shown by the failure of the Social Democrats' rival Central Organization for Retail Clerks. Declaring clerks proletarians who ought not delude themselves, the socialists asked them to unite. To most clerks this was an insult, compounded when the socialists not only elected a Jewish bookkeeper as president of the organization but actively recruited women. Jewish and female rights were not separate issues to anti-Semites. From Stoecker through the Nazis, they saw women's liberation as a Jewish-socialist attempt to cut the patriarchal roots that made Christian Germanic *Kultur* and society great. August Bebel, a worker and the most prominent founder of the Social Democratic party, wrote *Women and Socialism* in 1879. With the approval of Friedrich Engels himself, Bebel supported a separate socialist movement for women with its own press, declaring that just as men were exploited by capitalism, so too men, including socialists, exploited women as "cleaning animals" and sex objects. But Ludwig Langemann, editor of an antifeminist journal and author of anti-Semitic pamphlets, insisted that both socialism and feminism were foreign movements, hostile to healthy Germanic life.[22] And many leading feminists were socialists of Jewish origin, educated, secular, and natural targets for conservative contempt. Feminism had to be yet another expression of subversive Jewry, even if it attracted many non-Jews. As the popular philosopher and virulent racist Eugen Duehring put it, "This deformed ephemeral phase of thought may be put down in the main to the discredit of Hebrew women."[23] White-collar workers were especially furious. To their chagrin, in the 1890s women competed for secretarial and clerical jobs. To be deprived of the subject of one's petty tyranny in the home frightened most men, but it was worse for clerks and shop personnel whose precarious status and manly confidence were confronted with women in their workplace, women who demonstrated the falsity of the stereotypes keeping them subordinate.

The contrast between the German and French lower middle classes is revealing. By the 1890s most French peasants and the lower middle class tended to identify with the Republic, not its enemies, right or left. In turn, the Republic protected them from aristocratic reaction and proletarian socialism. In France, moreover, military glory was associated with the victories of the First Republic and Napoleon, while for Germans victories occurred under autocratic rule. In the small towns of France, schoolteacher and civil servant, in stark contrast to their counterparts in Prussia, were likely to be radical republicans, supporters of the Enlightenment, often engaged in running disputes with local royalists, priests, and estate owners. The French Republic fought religion and royalism in the schools; imperial Germany reinforced both. When the Dreyfus case showed that royalists, church, and army hoped to use anti-Semitism to break the Republic, the left and center rallied to the Republic. German conservatives purged liberals from government and army; the French Republic purged rightists. The Dreyfus case showed the power of anti-Semitism in France, but the republican victory showed its inability to push the nation to the right.

Racist extremism is most strongly revealed by those nineteenth-century Germans and Austrians who formed the volkist movement, a term derived from *Volk*, or people, but indicating a tribal unity of blood, unmodified by ideas of a common humanity. Religious in the intensity of their beliefs, volkists had no real equivalent in other Western nations. Before 1914 Guido von List and Lanz von Liebenfels of Austria, a former monk whose *Ostara* Hitler read during his youth in Vienna, were the most important volkists, but Fritsch used many of their ideas, ideas that later became the core of Nazi ideology (though the Nazi leadership muted them during election campaigns for fear of alienating Christian voters). Volkists sought purity of doctrine, not election victories, rejecting Christianity as Jewish, the enemy of the healthy warrior instincts of the Nordic *Volk*. Animistic nature and sun-worshipers with a variety of rites, honoring gods such as Wotan and Thor, they scorned the transcendental monotheism of Judeo-Christians. A God removed from nature could not be a God of blood and soil. Fritsch even composed ten new commandments. The first read: "Thou shalt keep thy blood pure. Consider it a crime to soil the noble Aryan race of the *Volk* by mixing it with the Jewish race. For thou must know that Jewish blood is everlasting, putting the Jewish stamp on body and soul down to the furthest generation."[24] Consequently Fritsch and others believed the very existence of Jews to be a mortal threat to future generations: "Thou shalt avoid all contact ... with the Jew; thou shalt keep him away from thy family and especially thy daughters, lest they suffer injury of blood and soul."[25]

Volkists believed Semites were originally formed by the harsh and arid landscape of the desert, where sun and nature are enemies of man and nature encourages the belief in a single tyrannical and transcendent God, literally unnatural. Thus incapable of creative relationships with the land, Jews preferred artificial city life, where there was no awareness of the natural limits to greed instinctively absorbed by those who worked the soil. Given only to commerce and trade, contemptuous of rural values, cosmopolitan Semites were innately incapable of building a nation; they must live at the expense of a host culture. By contrast, the Germanic peoples came from the vast forests of the east or the plains of north India. A true *naturvolk*, their gods and goddesses personified a close bond with a fruitful environment. Tillers of the soil won by their blood, for them city and commerce were unnatural and soul-destroying. In the words of Liebenfels: "Only the man who is wedded to the soil, the peasant, is truly a man. . . . The Aryan race will prosper only in the culture of the countryside; the city is its grave."[26] Peasant blood was the fount of national greatness, the city a cancer of mongrel races and rootless revolutionary proletarians, egged on by Jews who hated all things Germanic. Like numerous fascist organizations in Central and Eastern Europe that sprang up after 1918, including the Nazis, volkist ideologists revered the warrior-peasant as the ideal type.

In the 1890s volkists founded a few small communal agrarian societies, models for a racially pure Germany, free from the corruptions of the modern world and infused with the spirit of the Germanic *Volk*. Turning away from the cities, Nordic youth would associate with its own and restore the long slumbering kinship with its pre-Christian forebears. Here the racially elect, their enemies destroyed, would live with nature, and, raising their arms to the sun, source of all energy, swear blood oaths of comradeship. Great runic rings of fire were lit in the mountains at summer solstice, and ancient rituals were performed amidst forest shrines filled by symbols of earth-mother cults. Rebirth and purification rites awakened and restored the collective racial soul, forging anew its mystic connection with the cosmos, liberating Aryans from the false Hebrew-Christian God. To purify the blood, tobacco, alcohol, and meat were forbidden. Like Hitler, Fritsch and volkist leaders were vegetarians who neither smoked nor drank in order to protect their vital racial body fluids. Fritsch held the Jews responsible for the alcohol trade. (In 1989 Cardinal Glemp of Poland, well known for his anti-Semitic statements, revived the charge.) The Aryan warrior would no longer submit to the sickness of guilt and humility taught by diseased priests and rabbis. The gods and goddesses of Valhalla would replace the bloody symbol of repentance and weakness who was nailed to the cross to fulfill the Hebrew Scriptures. As one Nazi leader put it: "What was Christ but a Jewish coward?"

Reactionaries in all European nations detested modern institutions.

But only Germans and Eastern Europeans created an alternative past of tribe, blood, and soil. Modern culture was of course overwhelmingly a consequence of Christian and Gentile behavior and beliefs, not the creation of a tiny, weak Jewish community. More than most anti-Semites, therefore, volkists had to exaggerate wildly the power, unity, and influence of international Jewry. If Gentiles had caused the hated social changes, a revival of the Aryan spirit would hardly reverse the course of history. Conspiracy theories were necessary. And as liberal and leftist ideas were taken up by millions of Germans, it was necessary to explain why they too had adopted enemy ways. In 1913 volkists, under the sign of the swastika, published a guide to the alleged semi-Jewish racial origins of the aristocracy. This infuriated those who were named, for given the centuries-old mixing of German and Jew, one could never disprove such charges. A Fritsch commandment read: "Beware of the Jew in Thyself"— in other words, detect and fight the "Jewish traits" that, through an erring ancestor, might infect even an Aryan with the temptation to behave in "Jewish ways." For volkists, all Jews, regardless of class or public stance, were part of a conspiracy of blood. Jewish leaders even planned to corrupt Nordic blood by seducing Aryan women, a theme later to fascinate Julius Streicher. For ordinary anti-Semites it might be enough to end Jewish rights; for volkists, Jews must be isolated or destroyed, for their fearful powers would remain with them wherever they were sent. What was caused by blood could only be cured by blood.

The volkists demanded *lebensraum* (living space) precisely as the Nazis would—the conquest and exploitation of the east in order to relocate Germanic stock in racially pure settlements, gathering in dispersed ethnic Germans. Slavic cities, razed, would be replaced by networks of communal Nordic peasant-warrior villages. There would be no place for the millions of Slavs and Jews already there. Guido von List yearned for a Germanic Fuehrer, who, resurrected in spirit from the ancient Teutonic gods, would lead Aryans in the bloody conquest and show no mercy to Jews or Slavs. The Nazis also derived rituals, symbols, and sacraments from volkist cults. Hitler would be the apex of a sacred personality cult, its saints the great heroes who had died in the race war, solemnly sanctified on holy days in vast sacred monuments. Himmler created marriage and baptismal ceremonies for the SS (*Schutzstafel*) from volkist models. Future rulers of the Reich trained in ancient castles, and the special killing units studied volkist racial "science" to prepare for ethnic cleansing. Himmler himself informed them that any guilt feelings they might have were remnants of a degenerate Judeo-Christian heritage meant to destroy Nordic peoples. Stern pioneers of what the Nazis called "racial hygiene," the Nordic people of the future would thank them, grateful to live in a world purged of the threat of Jewish blood. As Hitler said, "People accuse us of being barbarians; we are barbarians, and we are proud of it!"

The volkists were too opposed to mass democracy even to consider campaigning for votes. Moreover, Boeckel, Ahlwardt, and Fritsch were held at arm's length by upper-class anti-Semites; populist demagogues with strong lower-middle-class followings threatened established rights and privileges. And under Bismarck, all but the minority ultrareactionary wing of the Conservative party believed their interests well protected, with no need for rabble-rousers. But in the 1890s a sudden surge of liberal and socialist prospects caused great political changes and thrust Prussian autocracy on the defensive. Anti-Semitism seemed more essential than ever to defend their power and privileges. The fateful alliance of upper- and lower-class reactionaries that ultimately brought the Nazis to power began.

8: ANTI-SEMITISM AMONG THE ELITES, 1890–1914

Even if they did not personally vote for the Nazi Party, the economic and educated elites of the German Conservative Party between 1890 and 1914 had already produced the ideology that the National Socialists propagated as their own and translated into deeds of terror.
—Ernst Roloff, German historian

In 1890 German conservatives were stunned: Bismarck was forced to resign by an apparently reformist new kaiser; the Progressives doubled their Reichstag seats; and the Social Democrats gained the largest popular vote of any political party in the history of the Reich. Bismarck's conservative coalition collapsed, Stoecker's anti-Semites were all but wiped out, and for the first time the Berlin City Council showed a socialist majority. Industrial Germany had generated progressive forces that the Prussian elites could no longer control.

Before he was forced out, Bismarck contemplated a *putsch*, for he believed the socialist problem "will not be solved without a bloodbath."[1] But in 1888 William II, the last kaiser, ascended the throne, unwilling to inaugurate his rule with bloodshed. An admirer of Stoecker, he believed a few reforms might win the loyalty of the workers. Bismarck blocked his efforts, and after other disputes, Bismarck was out. The kaiser selected General Caprivi as new chancellor. Conservatives were not pleased. Though a Prussian, Caprivi opposed Bismarck's autocratic ways and divisive attempts to punish Catholics and outlaw socialists. In office he cooperated with parliament, including socialists, and cut the influence of Prussian elites. Suddenly radical change seemed poised to sweep the field. Conservatives had never held more than 25 percent of the German vote; liberals averaged over 35 percent. But the National Liberals had supported Bismarck, and the Prussian upper class had enjoyed unchallenged influence in army, court, and civil service, where the Reichstag counted for little. Now the liberals threatened. Bismarck kept Prussia preeminent by remaining its minister-president, even when he became chancellor of

Germany. Desiring to be the evenhanded chancellor of all Germans, Caprivi resigned as minister-president. Offering accommodations to Progressives and socialists, he remarked, "There must be more respect for public opinion than in Bismarck's time."[2] He refused to renew Bismarck's antisocialist laws and shocked the right by compromising to gain socialist votes for legislation.

Caprivi also collaborated with the Catholic Center party, which commanded the most Reichstag seats. He tried to end the remnants of anti-Catholic legislation and blocked an attempt to subject freethinkers to government censorship. Clergy decried such "great offenses against our Protestant kaiser!" Moreover, the proud descendants of the Teutonic Knights had to sit by as Caprivi granted concessions to the despised Poles of East Prussia. Bismarck had treated them as conquered peoples, but Caprivi, to furious *Kreuzzeitung* editorials, ended the subsidies that allowed Germans to take over Polish land, and approved the appointment of a Polish archbishop. He also offended the army by offering concessions to the Alsatians who, torn from France in 1871, had also been treated as an occupied people. Poles and Alsatians had votes in the Reichstag, and Caprivi wanted them. He even suggested that Prussia's three-class voting system, so favorable to the wealthy elites, be dropped, as socialists and Progressives demanded. Caprivi threatened both Prussian primacy in Germany and the power of the elites in Prussia itself. He struck at the estate owners of East Prussia by lowering tariffs on grain. Swift to denounce "Jewish" materialism, landowners defended the tariffs, angry that the chancellor would sacrifice them to "Jewish-English" free trade. To Caprivi this was mere greed, and he was supported by industrialists fearing trade wars, as well as liberal and socialist defenders of consumer interests. The cost of living in Germany was the highest in Europe, and the Social Democrats had gained votes when they sponsored mass consumer demonstrations in the 1890 campaign. Caprivi's attempt to rule as a German, not a Prussian, surprised even the kaiser.

Bismarck had protected the military from parliament, but now socialist votes gave the legislature the right to inspect military budgets once unassailable by civilians, let alone "reds." Caprivi forced the army to make cuts at the behest of elected civilians; worse, he refused to raise Bismarck's cry of "The Fatherland in Danger" during elections, and, seeking international reconciliation, he allowed Bismarck's alliance of Russia, Austria, and Germany to lapse, ending the conservative ideological front meant to weaken republican France. Appeasing Russia and France with concessions, Caprivi made peaceful gestures to Italy and Great Britain as well. Had he prevailed, Europe would not have been divided so disastrously into rival camps in 1914. Caprivi was one of the few military leaders aware of the destructive potential of the new weapons of war. He feared the next conflict would be far longer and deadlier than earlier ones. When generals close to the kaiser counseled "preventive" war against Russia, Caprivi opposed them, aware there was no significant threat from Russia. When the rightist press waxed hysterical about Russian troops marching on the border, Caprivi dryly remarked that such troops usually marched up and down the newspaper columns for a few weeks and then disappeared. They did indeed, but his observation did not endear him to the warmongers.

Caprivi opposed military adventures in pursuit of empire. Bismarck had backed German colonial demands to win votes against the Progressives and to put England on the defensive. The public appetite for the blood sport of imperialism, fed by the new yellow press, was enormous. But Caprivi showed more realism by trading Zanzibar to England for Helgoland, a strategic North Sea island. A storm of protest arose, led by Treitschke, other academics, and the Colonial Society, largely funded by banks and representatives of industry and commerce hoping to profit in Africa. Conservatives accused Progressives and socialists of doing the work of the Jews by opposing German imperial greatness. Caprivi decried their use of anti-Semitism. He also noted laconically that the worst thing that could happen to Germany would be for someone to give her half of Africa.

Caprivi was reviled as a traitor to his class and socially ostracized. His enemies demanded that the kaiser dump him. Now heroic legends of Bismarck's greatness began to circulate, for until Caprivi, Conservatives found the Iron Chancellor too "parliamentary," too liberal, and not sufficiently aggressive in foreign policy. Many had never forgiven Bismarck for introducing universal (male) suffrage. Most frightening, Conservative votes, at their lowest since 1877, trailed those of the Social Democrats. Caprivi refused to use his powers illegally to aid his party in elections. Unless Caprivi was repudiated, Conservatives would have to compete for the allegiance of an electorate they disdained in a democratic system they despised.

But Boeckel and Ahlwardt seemed to point to new constituencies that might be used against the moderate Caprivi wing of the Conservative party. When Ahlwardt's ridiculous "Jewish rifles" charges proved popular, Conservative delegates in the Prussian House voted 95 to 1 to put anti-Semitism in their platform. They drew back when the minister of war tried Ahlwardt for slandering the army; they could scarcely afford to offend the military, for they were the military. To Ahlwardt's followers the laws of libel were designed to protect Jews from justice, and the large number of Jewish lawyers proved the courts were manipulated to harm Germans. The populist press declared it no accident that Caprivi's government hounded anti-Semites as Bismarck never had.

Moderate Conservatives were ascendant in the party in 1890. When Ahlwardt, supported by local rightists, defeated his Conservative rival in a landslide in 1892, Stoecker told his ultraright colleagues that anti-Semitic demagogues could help them, and reactionaries moved to coopt racist votes—as they would in 1930 when the Nazis began to take their voters from them. In 1892 the *Kreuzzeitung* insisted that the party "take a leading role against the arrogant power of Jewry."[3] "Anti-Semitic ideas must be rooted in conservative soil, otherwise they will become more dangerous than useful."[4] Not dangerous for Jews, of course, but for the privileges of the elites. Conservatives and anti-Semites had already collaborated in the fight against Caprivi's grain treaties, when the *Kreuzzeitung* had written of the "certain doom which awaited Germany if it placed its trust in revolutionaries, liberals, and Jews."[5] Boeckel and anti-Semitic delegates needed Conservative party funds and support to join Reichstag committees and speak during sessions, and had willingly betrayed those peasants who needed to purchase grain for their livestock. Free trade in grain was a Jewish measure, Boeckel declared; if Caprivi's bill passed it would be a defeat as disastrous as Napoleon's conquests. Caprivi's measures, he added, were ordered by Jewish speculators in grain, and they, not tariffs, caused high bread prices.

Ahlwardt's landslide victory came as the Conservative party prepared for its first general meeting since 1876. Cooperation with the populists was the main item on the agenda. Many local Conservative caucuses selected anti-Semitic representatives; the ultraright rejoiced: "There is no denying that anti-Semitism's mighty powers of recruitment lead many back into the loyal camp who would otherwise have had to be considered irretrievably lost to liberalism or social democracy."[6] But party leaders still felt uneasy when the Conservative conference opened at the Tivoli Beer Garden in December 1892. The rabble once taken for granted were there in force, no longer passive before their betters. On the first day Caprivi and the moderate leader spoke against the racists, but Boeckel and Ahlwardt, vociferously aided by numerous anti-Semitic delegates, held the majority. The moderate leader was forced to resign, vitally weakening Caprivi. Boeckel and Ahlwardt, just three days after his victory, joined forces with Stoecker. Led by a new chairman, Otto von Manteuffel, the representatives introduced an anti-Semitic motion, though it included a reproach against the use of overly violent rhetoric in the battle against the Jews. Provinicial delegates, incensed, rose in turmoil and greeted Stoecker with "enthusiastic uproar" as he led the fight to rid the motion of its restraint. A moderate pointed out that Ahlwardt was a convicted criminal and self-confessed liar who boasted about his frauds. But another speaker noted that the Social Democrats had passed a motion condemning anti-Semitism. Then the man Ahlwardt had viciously defamed and defeated in 1892 nevertheless shouted out, "Better ten Ahlwardts, better ten anti-Semites, than one Progressive!"[7] All but seven members of the conference then voted to reject the attempt to moderate the violence of anti-Semitic rhetoric.

The motion, now in the party platform, read: "We will do battle against the many-sided aggressive, decomposing, and arrogant Jewish influence on the life of our people."[8] Moreover, no Jews should be allowed to teach or become civil servants or judges. Guilds and peasants must be protected against liberalism, and peddlers and financiers restrained. For, the program announced, "The Jews [are] the uncompromising opponents of Conservative principles."[9] Stoecker, Boeckel, and Ahlwardt were ecstatic; anti-Semitism had been endorsed by the party of the most prestigious and powerful classes in Germany. Hellmut von Gerlach, former Stoeckerite, observed that anti-Semitism "made the greatest possible gain in prestige when it was included in the Conservative program." Now it was "the legitimate possession of one of the greatest parties, of the party closest to the throne and holding the most important positions in the state."[10] In the Reichstag, Caprivi denounced the racist motion as reactionaries exulted. Ahlwardt declared that delegates who supported Caprivi were bribed by Jews who stood to make millions from his policies. The right wing of the party and anti-Semitic delegates now moved to abolish the Jewish Emancipation Law of 1869. Caprivi objected: "When the first legislative step is taken to this end—already a matter for anti-Semitic agitation outside this House—I shall use the means at my disposal to oppose it actively."[11] The proposal failed of the necessary votes.

In February 1892 the wealthiest and most powerful anti-Semitic organization in Europe, the Agrarian Bund, was formed to unite landowners against Caprivi, who was supported mainly by East Elbian aristocrats and politicians. Rural nostalgia and extreme anti-Semitism informed the Bundists, in effect the public relations arms of the Conservative party; many of the same men held high positions in both. Bund leaders believed that as landowners, high civil servants, and military officers of ancient lineage, they, not the masses, were the natural rulers of the nation. After all, they, not parliamentary politicians, had united Germany, and their army and institutions uniquely embodied the military and state-building qualities of the race. Protecting their privileges was a German national duty.

Berthold von Ploetz, a leader of the Agrarian Bund, dedicated it to "war against the destructive powers of left liberalism, Jewry, and social democracy."[12] Many professional anti-Semites became Bund advisers. The anti-Semitic Peasants Bund and a racist small businessman's organization, the Economic Union, also joined forces with the Agrarian Bund. Angered at Caprivi's scorn for imperialism, academics, businessmen, and teachers lobbied for an overseas empire and expansion to the east. One of their academic advisers greeted the Agrarian Bund as the "shock troops for a racially pure Germany."[13]

Aroused reactionaries persuaded the kaiser to refuse support for Caprivi's army bill, which would have forced the military to compromise its budget requests. When the measure failed, Caprivi's government went with it. In the elections of 1893 the issues were the agrarian depression, increasing strikes, and consumer complaints against the grain tariffs. Conservatives and populist anti-Semites joined to declare that striking workers and protesting consumers were victims of the manipulations of Caprivi and "Jewish" Progressives and Social Democrats, and began their endless denunciations of the socialists as the "shock troops of the Jews." The Agrarian Bund funded Conservative and anti-Semitic demonstrations against Caprivi, and the Conservative party gained nineteen additional seats in the Prussian parliament. But in the national elections, Progressives and Social Democrats organized hundreds of thousands of angry consumers, and Caprivi denounced racist attacks on his regime. Anti-Semites, he said, "persecute Jews back to the third or fourth generation. They begin to mix religious with racial anti-Semitism. . . . This is most dangerous."[14] Although the Conservative party made only slight gains in the Reichstag, Caprivi's wing was all but wiped out, and the Progressives lost more than half their seats. The most spectacular results were those of the anti-Semitic parties, whose votes rose from 56,900 in 1890 to about 400,000 in 1893—some 5 percent of the electorate; in 1895 they held sixteen Reichstag seats. More important, numerous Conservative candidates found that attacking Jews increased their votes, and the 20 percent of the electorate who voted for the Conservative party were in any event supporting an anti-Semitic program.

When Caprivi lost the kaiser's support and the party's, moderate reform was finished. "At a secret meeting of Conservative leaders" in 1894, Count Eulenberg, reactionary minister-president of Prussia, intimate of the kaiser, and virulent anti-Semite, declared his willingness to replace Caprivi should the upper house of the Reichstag "immediately suspend universal suffrage."[15] The kaiser and most of his leaders agreed. But the autocratic Eulenberg, contemptuous of those who gained power by majority vote, would be satisfied with no less than unanimity. Throughout the struggle, William sabotaged his chancellor. Fed up, isolated, and powerless, Caprivi resigned in the summer of 1894.

It is a necessary defect of the historian's profession to concentrate too much attention on victorious and powerful politicians like Bismarck. Caprivi strove for a truly united and parliamentary Germany as well as a policy of international reconciliation far more advantageous to Germans than Bismarck's divisive actions after unity. Although he was by no means free of the social prejudices of a Prussian general, Caprivi understood how dangerous anti-Semitism had become, to Jews and to reform. As he said in parliament, he could "perhaps comprehend" why one might be an anti-Semite, but "when anti-Semitism . . . is manipulated in this dema-gogic way, then it is impossible for the Reich government not to set it-self against it, and I cannot understand how patriotic men can go along with it."[16] By 1894 no chancellor could separate racism from German con-servatism; Caprivi was the last even to try. From 1893 until the rise of the Nazis, the reversal of the Jews' civil rights became an integral and ever-increasing demand of the Conservative party.

In 1894 thousands of landowners attended the first general meeting of the Agrarian Bund, greeted with an opening speech by Stoecker. Repeat-ing yet again that Caprivi was the tool of the Jews, he urged them to pro-tect the noble families of east Prussia. They and their posterity must remain on the land, the only proper environment for those whose tradi-tional sense of duty and sacrifice made them best fit to serve in the na-tion's highest offices. Otherwise, said the royal chaplain, "Kohn and Itzig, mortgage holders and land speculators, will take over and corrupt and ruin the Volk with their revolutionary and subversive beliefs."[17] In 1895 Georg von Hammerstein, Stoeckerite and editor of the Kreuzzeitung, led an attempt to halt all Jewish immigration into Germany after some 44,000 Jewish refugees fled tsarist oppression. Ahlwardt was the Conservatives' weapon of choice in the Reichstag, where he declared that even if a Jew had not yet done anything bad, sooner or later "his racial qualities [will] drive him to do it." In spite of their small numbers, the Jews were like "cholera germs." They must be kept separate and out of Germany, "a poi-son in the land; we must purify ourselves. . . ." The British in India had exterminated the assassination cult of the Thugge even though many of them had committed no murders, for they knew "in the proper moment every member of the sect would do such a thing." Ahlwardt ended by roaring, "Destroy these beasts of prey!"[18] These were the words of a Reichstag ally of the Conservative party, not an isolated fanatic.

As socialist-led workers' strikes increased, the kaiser told his courtiers it would soon be necessary to use force against the left. Determined to dom-inate the government, the kaiser appointed as chancellor the elderly Prince von Hohenlohe, a simpleminded nonentity whose main concern was his pension. Meanwhile the victorious hard-liners of the Conserva-tive party moved to tame the populism of their anti-Semitic allies, de-nouncing even Stoecker for still believing that reforms might move the workers away from socialism. Some populists, including Boeckel, feared that the Conservatives' drive for high grain tariffs and army budgets harmed populist constituencies. When industrialists lobbied for a bill to build a large fleet, a few populists demanded taxes on the wealthy to pay for it. Angered by this "subversion," one high-ranking Conservative wrote, "We in no way combat the kernel of good anti-Semitism . . . ," but the "attachment of many propertyless people to this movement conceals a possible danger" they may turn against property, and then "anti-Semitism will sink to a species of social democracy!"[19] In 1929 similar fears turned many industrialists against the Nazis until they received Hitler's assurance that their interests would not be harmed by his populist followers. In 1894 Conservatives demanded that anti-Semites search for votes only among the "shock troops of the Jews," that is, socialists and liberals. In the official *Handbook of the Conservative Party* of 1894, populists were warned against their sometimes "unconservative stand" that does not stop with "combating the harmful influences of Jewry" but attacks "leading classes of the Fatherland" and "discredits the anti-Semitic cause."[20] In 1907 anti-Semites won seventeen Reichstag seats, the most that "single-issue" racists held before 1914. To gain more votes they would have had to exploit populist discontent against the wealthy contributors of the Conservative party. With Caprivi gone, the Conservatives no longer needed to cater to peasants and the lower middle class. Only with the Weimar Republic did mass populist demagoguery become vital to combat democratic reforms.

Boeckel, harassed by libel suits, saw his paper fail because socialist printers refused to print it; his *Judenrein* banks and cattle markets also collapsed. Christians evidently followed the same market principles as Jews, and there were complaints that, free from Jewish competitors, they charged even more. Boeckel's crusade against "Jewish" moral decay foundered when he fathered an illegitimate child; denounced by local clergy, he lost his seat when anti-Semites refused to elect him to the leadership. Swallowing his pride, he took a humble job from the "Cohnservatives" he had once labeled the "Bund of Agrarian Windbags," and died poor and alone in 1923. The Nazis honored him with a monument and reprinted his slogans in a book for schoolchildren. Ahlwardt lost his seat and, a crook to the last, sold fraudulent shares to investors. Fleeing the law, he ended in New York City in 1896, now Pastor Ahlwardt, delivering public hell-fire anti-Semitic sermons. But he attracted numerous riotous hecklers, and police board chairman Teddy Roosevelt provided a guard of forty Jewish police to stand in front of Ahlwardt to "protect" him. He was laughed out of the pulpit; it could never have happened in Germany.

In 1890 Heinrich Class, associate of Boeckel and a future ally of Hitler, formed the Pan-German League. Dedicated to supporting German imperialism and eastward expansion, the league attracted civil servants, military officers, teachers, academics, and industrialists who stood to profit from large arms budgets. Among them was Alfred Hugenberg of the Prussian Ministry of Economics, who became director of the mighty Coal and

Steel Syndicate of the Rhineland and chairman of the board of Krupp Armaments. Most funds for the league came from industry and banking, and Hugenberg directed them to politicians and publicists who supported Germany's bid to become a global power.

Colonial associations existed in many nations, but the pan-Germans also demanded a renewal of the old German "drive to the east," to forge a land power equal to Great Britain and the United States at the expense of the Slavs. Their predecessor, the Colonial League, was organized in 1882 by Carl Peters, a vicious anti-Semite. Germany's "Cecil Rhodes," he negotiated fraudulent treaties with African tribal chiefs. All imperialism embodies racism; Rhodes preached the destiny of the Anglo-Saxon race to civilize the lesser breeds. In the United States the Reverend Josiah Strong's best-seller *Our Country* (1885) envisioned the Protestant Anglo-Saxon "race" spreading its power and faith worldwide. But German imperialism was more racist than imperialism elsewhere. The British wished to rule India, not populate it with racial brethren; the French hoped to convert the elite of their African subjects into Frenchmen; Americans were content to open the globe to American economic interests. But the pan-German did not aim to civilize, convert, or exploit "savages" in far-off lands. In Eastern Europe, ethnic German minorities and their lands were to be freed from Slavic inferiors and joined to the Reich, completing unification. Racial superiority justified the use of force against "unworthy" Slavs. German conquest in Eastern Europe was held to be a necessary counterbalance to the subversive decadence of the Latin races, the arrogance of the British ruling classes, and the international power of world Jewry. In the decade before 1914, pan-German publicists in Germany and Austria pushed for preventive war against Russia, the first step toward the completion of Germany's historic destiny.

Before 1907 some eastern-border chapters of pan-Germans included German Jews in order to buttress claims to areas with only a tiny number of ethnic Germans. But Jews were banned from the main branch in Berlin, and Ernst Haase, the first president, worked to forbid the migration of Jews into Germany. Ludwig Scheman, founder of a series of racist Gobineau societies, was a member of the board of directors. An elite lobby, not a mass organization, the Pan-German League had forty thousand members by 1900, and by 1914 anti-Semitism was the norm. Pan-German publications routinely called the Social Democrats puppets of an un-German "element of decomposition," a famous code phrase for Jews. Small businessmen were numerous among the pan-Germans, and one-third were secondary school teachers, who also chaired more than a third of the chapters. For teachers and lesser civil servants, to support the league was a declaration of solidarity with the upper classes. Unlike their French and British counterparts, they had been educated by academics who overwhelmingly supported autocracy. Indeed, the highest proportion of propagandists in the league were academics, instructors of future civil servants. Although it was a middle and upper-class organization, it was supported by the anti-Semitic parties, and 15 percent of their members joined the league, high when one considers the league said nothing about the problems of peasants and artisans.

During the 1890s anti-Semitism intensified in the imperial civil service. A bastion of reaction, the civil service was subject only to chancellor and kaiser. Progressives and Social Democrats tried to open office to merit alone, but the bureaucrats insisted its members hold conservative beliefs and must be simply tools of elected governments. After all, autocratic rule was associated with Germany's greatness in ways the Reichstag had never been. In contrast, the French Chamber of Deputies was part of a republican tradition going back to 1789, and the British parliament had been sovereign a century before that. But the Reichstag was not a generation old and had been created by the victories of the Prussian army. Among the elites, few thought civilians elected by semieducated masses should be permitted to decide great matters of state.

German chancellors were the last in Europe to appear before parliament in military uniform, and they did so down to 1914. Recruited from among aristocrats, the Prussian civil service was a quasi-military hierarchy complete with titles and medals. Unquestioning obedience to superiors and contempt for democracy were expected. In this self-selecting caste, preferment came from membership in the correct fraternities and the dueling corps, almost exclusively limited to sons of the military, aristocracy, or the civil service itself, who together composed some 75 percent of civil servants as late as 1910. Bourgeoisie allowed in had to be more royalist than the king. If this were not enough to keep the rabble out, during the first four years of a civil servant's career, his salary was too low for someone without independent means. In the provinces the landowning elite dominated government office, routinely and illegally influencing election results to protect the ancestral system so superior to the democratic confusion of liberal politics.

During the liberal ascendancy of the 1860s and 1870s, however, Progressives had been allowed into the civil service. Bismarck ended that in the 1880s when the "primary task of the official was now seen as the loyal and unquestioning defense of the status quo."[21] Civil servants sabotaged Caprivi's attempts to enforce the laws forbidding the consideration of religious or political qualifications in the selection of public officials. Even Catholics were informally excluded from the Prussian civil service. "Social Democrats and even the sons of Social Democrats were excluded . . . automatically."[22] One risked one's career by reading the liberal press; the *Kreuzzeitung* was required reading.

Anti-Semitism was taken for granted in the civil service. By 1914 Jews had been excluded from nearly all bureaucratic posts in every German state, except among the lowest of railroad and postal employees. Although Jews counted for 10 percent of positions in higher education, the figure was less than one-half of 1 percent in the civil service. It was possible to be selected if one came from a converted and wealthy family and married into a noble family down on its luck, for then "people were prepared to ignore his race as long as it was not too obvious in his facial features."[23] He would also have to tolerate anti-Semitism and break with family and friends if they seemed too obviously "Jewish." Even then the ethnic trap could not be avoided; a count was once accused by an imperial official of flaunting his Catholic principles so as to obscure his Jewish blood. The medieval principle still held. During the election campaign of 1893, a flyer distributed by the Conservative party maintained: "The officials of the government are nothing other than the Ministers of God. Can Jews, who do not acknowledge Jesus, the Son of God, be appointed officials of our government?"[24] So it was that in their daily contacts with government officials, ordinary citizens would never see Jews, reinforcing the old belief that they preferred the profits of commerce to service to the nation. Only the Weimar Republic brought Jews and leftists into state service, whereupon many civil servants turned to the Nazis, who promised to throw the Jews out.

Like the bureaucracy, the army was loyal only to the Hohenzollerns and represented the interests of ruling groups. In 1789 more than 90 percent of its officers were aristocrats. Retired officers were given government posts in the countryside in order to maintain a militarylike discipline among the population. The army was the bulwark against democracy, a sword ready to be raised against the left. Of all German institutions, the army most strongly welcomed Hitler. During the Napoleonic era Jews had been soldiers, but they were barred again until the liberals of 1848 briefly reigned. In the wars of unification, Jews were again allowed to die for Prussia. Afterward, officer candidates had to be from Aryan families, by now a familiar phrase. In the liberal 1860s, when more than half of newly commissioned officers came from outside the nobility, 80 percent were sons of the elite. Others had to show impeccable proof of loyalty to the autocracy. Army leaders demanded ideological correctness as well as military skills. Propaganda in lectures by army education officers and in military training manuals was common. One manual called the army a "rock in the sea of revolution that threatens us."[25] It was stated policy that officers must obey the king-emperor and him alone; even reserve officers who returned to civilian life were told that it was a matter of honor to resign their commissions if they supported any party opposing the government. Cultivating a famous and crude arrogance, officers remained isolated from dangerous ideas and lesser mortals. Openly consorting with Progressives, let alone Jews or socialists, was unthinkable.

In the 1860s William I and General von Roon sought to increase the army's size and budget. Parliamentary liberals would go along only if the civilian reserve militia, less subject to autocratic control, was also increased and compulsory military service cut from three years to two. Although he did not carry the day, von Roon insisted that civilians could only be properly indoctrinated in three years. Like all professional officers, he detested the citizen-soldiers of the militia. Middle-class in origin and not rigidly unfriendly to liberal ideas, in 1850 some militia had been reluctant to shoot down the unarmed radicals of the Frankfurt Parliament, to the horror of the high command. Furthermore, concessions to parliament meant that army budgets would need approval from mere elected civilians, even Jews. In the 1870s Bismarck, while he was unable to place the army budget beyond parliament's reach, could always force it through with little opposition. Later, Progressive and Social Democratic military experts, sometimes joined by the Catholic Center, challenged budgets to great effect, but Caprivi fell when he tried to force the army to compromise.

To augment the army for national emergencies, revolution included, Roon had created commissions in the Prussian officers' reserve for those found worthy by their fellow officers when returning to civilian life after regular service. The commissions were much prized; like dueling scars, they greatly aided a civilian career. The high command saw the commissions as insurance that Germans would fire on Germans to preserve the Reich from democracy and leftism. In addition, by 1900 more than 2.5 million ex-servicemen had joined army clubs and navy leagues where pan-Germanism and anti-Semitism were rife. Indeed, reserve officers were proud to be identified with the institution that had forged modern Germany. Progressives rarely received commissions, Jews almost never. Socialists did not apply. The last Jewish reserve commission was granted in 1885; of some 25,000 Jews who served over the next twenty-five years, not one received a Prussian army reserve commission. A few baptized Jews were given commissions, but only if they did not "look" or "act" Jewish, did not associate with Jews, and had Christian wives. Presumably they maintained a discreet silence when racist remarks were bandied about in the barracks. There would be no Dreyfus case in Germany because no Jew could conceivably have become, like him, an intern on the General Staff. Once again the trap of the self-fulfilling stereotype was closed: Jews cannot really be patriotic Germans, so they must not be allowed commissions even if, as conscripts, they had proven to be good soldiers.

Jewish groups, Progressives, and Social Democrats protested in the

Reichstag this flagrant violation of the constitution, but the military insisted it did not discriminate. The backgrounds and skills of Jewish citizens had simply turned out to be inadequate—for the average citizen, proof enough of the Jewish lack of valor and patriotism. In cartoons the racist press made much fun at the expense of drafted Jewish soldiers. Insisting the Jews' loyalty was only to international Jewry, the Conservative party and populist anti-Semites in the Reichstag supported the army. The Catholic Center kept a discreet silence, though aware of difficulties Catholics often faced in the army. In 1913 Progressives and Social Democrats had enough votes to adopt Reichstag resolutions to end discrimination, but the upper house, dominated by Prussia, rejected them. Even in 1914, when once again Jews were dying for Germany, there were objections to placing them in sensitive positions. Some suggested they be imprisoned in camps until the end of the war.

The kaiser had the final say in the selection of those who made policy. William II's influence is often ignored because of his bellicose fantasies and crude interventions in foreign policy, yet this made him popular in a nation literally schooled to admire such traits. He was scarcely unique. His views were shared by the ultraright wing of the Conservative party. Like them he wanted to imprison strikers, end universal suffrage, reverse Jewish rights, and ignore the Reichstag. As for the Social Democrats, un-German, antireligious enemies, they "must be destroyed." He hated the Reichstag, saying it "swings back and forth between the Socialists, who are driven on by the Jews, and the ultramontane Catholics. . . . Both parties will soon be ripe for hanging."[26] When Chancellor Hohenlohe, too timid for coups, was replaced in 1900 with Prince von Buelow, flatterer extraordinaire, the kaiser announced that he and Buelow "will clean up the filth of parliamentary democracy."[27]

William II needed to project the image of militarist and autocrat far more than his father and grandfather. Both had distinguished themselves in battle; he never did. Verbal aggression was all he could offer to show himself worthy of the Hohenzollern name. He remarked publicly that he hoped one day to see the German fleet sailing victoriously up the Thames, and he told the troops sent to fight the Chinese during the Boxer Rebellion in 1900 that they should behave so that the Chinese would forever tremble when they heard the name of Hun. Born with a withered arm and poor coordination, he was humiliated when, taught to ride, he fell repeatedly off his mount, to be forced back by his harsh tutor. A Hohenzollern must ride; the calvary officer was the very model of an aristocratic warrior.

William hated his father, and there was nothing subconscious about it.

His predecessor, Frederick III, who distinguished himself in battle against Austria, had been surprisingly liberal, popularly referred to as the Progressives' kaiser. Disliking Bismarck, he wanted to cooperate with the Reichstag and admired British parliamentary government. He announced he would fire Court Chaplain Stoecker when enthroned and publicly attended a synagogue service to demonstrate his concern for all Germans. Tragically, but to the relief of Bismarck and the right, in 1888 cancer cut his rule to three months of agony. Institutions and societies have their own powerful drives and inertia, but his death was a tragedy for Germany and Europe.

William II surrounded himself with the crudest of military men, trading vulgar jokes and righteous arrogance about Progressives, socialists, and Jews. To the chagrin of his army commanders, he insisted on conducting military maneuvers; appalled at the results, those interested in their careers nevertheless praised him. Famous for embarrassing his fellow princes with demands for medals, his vast collection of military uniforms was second only to that of Emperor Franz Josef of Austria-Hungary, but William shared none of Franz Josef's modesty, dignity, and common sense. Without the self-assurance of earned achievement, William allowed no one to contradict him. His ministers discreetly told foreign diplomats that his bombast did not reflect the opinion of the Foreign Office. None of his chancellors had any respect for his judgment, or so they indicated later, but they had every incentive to blame him for their mistakes when they learned, too late, what war is like in an industrial age.

In the kaiser, racists believed they had the leader who would punish the Jews. As crown prince he had publicly supported Stoecker and usually protected him at court. Rejoicing at the infamous pogrom of Kichenev, when Jewish refugees fled Russia into Germany, he wrote, "Throw the pigs out."[28] Told that Russian soldiers cooperated with the pogromists, he observed that all real Germans would approve.[29] When Theodore Herzl requested that he use his influence with the sultan of Turkey to create a Jewish state, the kaiser wrote on the petition how happy he would be to rid Germany of all "yids." He promised to end "Jewish influence in the army and government, and limit their activities in art and literature. . . ."[30] He often spoke of the coming racial war of Aryan against Jew, and, when told of the Russian Revolution of 1905, exclaimed. "Always the Jews," and "It will happen here someday."[31] More than once he remarked to his courtiers that when war broke out there would have to be a bloodbath of Jews and socialists.

In 1901 the kaiser was introduced to Europe's most famous racist intellectual, H. S. Chamberlain. Entranced, William began a lengthy personal correspondence, writing that Chamberlain's work released all the

126 IDEOLOGY OF DEATH

pent-up Aryan-Germanism in the royal soul and revealed the global importance of the battle of the Teutons against "Rome and Jerusalem" for the "salvation of Germans and all mankind!" Both men agreed that Christ must have been Aryan and intended a Germanic Christianity purged of all Jewish traces. The kaiser praised Chamberlain for revealing the divine destiny of the race to conquer the east. "You were chosen by Him to be my ally, and I shall thank Him through eternity." Chamberlain was "my comrade in arms and ally in the struggle for the Teutons against Rome, Jerusalem, etc. The feeling that we are fighting for an absolute holy cause guarantees our victory." Chamberlain replied that Germany must save "the moral order of mankind," for without the Hohenzollerns and the Teutonic race the world would belong to the "soulless materialism of the Jews." The Germans must unite, end mass democracy, and fulfill their destiny, for "God relies only on the Germans" to destroy the "caustic poison of Judaism" and redeem the world.[32]

But the kaiser could not even save Germany. When war came, his generals would not let him command so much as a platoon. Although the public was told he commanded the battle of Verdun, he was never consulted and rarely even informed. His generals made fun of him behind his back even as they pretended to clear momentous matters with him, or took him on elaborately staged tours to parade as the commander-in-chief, presumably to stiffen the morale of the troops and the home front. To his credit, after viewing the consequences of a particularly murderous engagement, he was dazed and speechless, horrified, perhaps, at the real meaning of his bellicose fantasies. In the end he found his vocation, a royal exile chopping wood in Holland. But he never changed. During the war he had called for the genocide of Russian prisoners of war; at its end he blamed the Jews for its loss and wanted them killed. He supported the Nazis and allowed his sons to campaign for Hitler during elections. Of the Jews he wrote in 1919, no German "should rest until these parasites have been destroyed and exterminated." He added that he thought the "best" method would be "gas." In 1941, just before his death, he exulted in Nazi anti-Semitic activities. Yet until recently most German historians have insisted he was no anti-Semite![33]

The kaiser symbolized a more pervasive phenomenon: by 1914 the Prussian establishment was riddled with anti-Semitism. Respected dignitaries and street demagogues combined with the increasing racism of peasants and artisans to make anti-Semitism essential to the definition of a patriotic German nationalist. Until the 1890s it still seemed likely this association would pass. After all, industrialism, urbanism, and liberal politics still advanced, Christian fundamentalism steadily weakened, the constituencies of the right waned, and democratic socialism waxed. But in the 1890s even those who, in Western nations, usually represent the most advanced thinking of society—intellectuals, academics, and university students—added more dangerous racial antagonisms to the thunder on the right.

9: ANTI-SEMITISM, ACADEMICS, AND INTELLECTUALS, 1890–1914

I am convinced that in the next century, people will slaughter each other by the millions because of the difference of a degree or two in the cephalic index [skull measurements]. It is by this sign . . . that men will be identified . . . and the last sentimentalist will be able to witness the most massive extermination of peoples.
—Vacher de Lapouge, "Revue d'Anthropologie," 1887

UNTIL the 1850s the major intellectual creations of the West, with the significant exception of German philosophy, sanctioned a belief that human character was largely formed by experience and education. But in the 1860s Social Darwinism seemed to show that inborn traits selected by the struggle for survival were dominant. By 1890 it was dogma. The president of the Anthropological Society of England, John Hunt, believed the new science revealed the falsity of "utopias of equality and fraternity."[1] Herbert Spencer gained immense fame denouncing aid to the poor as merely increasing the number of "unfit" losers in the struggle for survival; Andrew Carnegie insisted before the U.S. Congress that millionaires and corporations were the rightful victors in the struggle. In the West, Social Darwinism was adapted to buttress the competitive individualism of a forceful liberal tradition, and to argue against its competition on the left.

But on the Continent, especially in Germany, the struggle between nations and races for survival was of greater concern than the struggle between individuals. Today the terms "racism" and "racist" describe a wide range of subtle attitudes, but in the late nineteenth century there was little subtlety. Prominent academics declared that races were marked by the color of skin, eyes, and hair, and measurements of skull and body, differences indicating innate intelligence, moral character, and the capacity for civilized life. In the 1870s thousands of Germans and Jews had their skin and eye pigmentation recorded by those searching for differences between Semites and Aryans. Anthropologists and popularizers bombarded the public with equations between levels of civilization and race, solemnly declaring the superiority of Caucasians and the inferiority of yellow, black, and brown races. In the popular press and in magazines, Darwinism was the rage. Vacher de Lapouge, a prominent French anthropologist, insisted that republicanism in France, and the loss to Prussia in 1870, were the result of the defeat in 1789 of the fair-skinned, longheaded natural aristocracy by the roundheaded dark masses of racial inferiors. In 1859 the famed Paul Broca founded the Anthropological Society of Paris, collecting vast amounts of data about religion, social achievement, and behavior to "demonstrate" the correlations between them and the "cephalic index"—the breadth of the skull divided by its length, multiplied by one hundred. Professor Karl Vogt wrote numerous textbooks and popular treatises that charted the distance of each race from the apes.

In Western nations some intellectuals demanded an end to the reproduction of those with hereditary defects—the new science of eugenics. In Germany, ominously, eugenicists were more concerned with racial than individual defects. In 1900 the Krupp family sponsored a prestigious essay contest on "racial hygienics," asking what lessons the principle of heredity posed for politics and the state. Ernst Haeckel, Germany's leading Darwinist, led the judges, who concluded that the laws of heredity refuted the "old theories of equality" and threatened the "deterioration and degeneration of the natural qualities of mankind."[2] The winner held that "all legal systems, technical advances, morals, and even concepts of good and evil" must be judged by the "laws of the racial struggle for survival."[3] Most agreed that states should try to increase the Nordic-Germanic race.

The most famous entrant, Professor Ludwig Woltmann, later editor of a journal dedicated to Nordic racial supremacy, believed "the Germanic race has been selected to dominate the earth."[4] Others wanted selection used to preserve warlike qualities; some attacked the socialist doctrine of class struggle because it divided Germans and weakened the military power gained from racial unity. Socialism and humanitarianism were condemned because they empowered and protected the weak. Academic publicists issued dire warnings against the contamination of Nordic blood; societies were formed to educate the public against race mixing. Naturally, a chorus of voices was raised against the "Jewish" liberal economic system as "unnatural," for it gave the race to the cunning, not the swift.

In 1895 the famed German eugenicist Alfred Ploetz, editor of journals devoted to the social implications of race, founded a Society for Racial Hygiene, a phrase later used by the numerous medical personnel involved in the Nazi destruction of "racial inferiors." Scholars, research scientists, and industrialists joined Ploetz's society, the latter attracted by his attacks on the "race-weakening" social reform demands of the Social Democrats. Ploetz also joined a Bund dedicated to purifying the Aryan race by selection. Like the volkists, some in the Bund wanted racial agrarian colonies established for Aryans who would be able to begin a "crash-breeding program" through polygamy. A few suggested that labor camps be built for "undesirables," where they could not reproduce. Ploetz and Fritsch believed physicians should decide if infants should live or die. In 1936, Hitler appointed Ploetz a distinguished professor.

Forced euthanasia was so strongly advocated by Germans that it was known as the "Prussian science." The popular Ernst Haeckel demanded death for "incurables" and the mentally ill, including cancer victims, alcoholics, and "congenital" criminals. His books, vulgarized Darwinism, were highly popular. A dignitary in the Conservative party, Haeckel was one of many who believed that Jews carried hereditary diseases of blood and brain. Anthropologists of rank and standing popularized the belief in two separate races, Aryans and Semites, with opposed physical, mental, and moral traits. Aryans, fair-skinned, long-skulled, and light of eye, were an agricultural and warrior people, Semites a swarthy, roundheaded, dark-eyed trading race. Such images naturally found great resonance among the landowners and militarists of Prussia, for they gave scientific validity to their superiority and allowed them to ignore complex considerations of the ways in which groups are shaped by social and historical experience.

From secondary school texts to university lecturers, racial doctrines were transmitted to the future leaders of the nation. By 1900 teachers formed the greatest number of anti-Semitic writers, speakers, and organizers. As George Mosse has noted, volkist ideology "was to see its greatest triumph . . . where it mattered most: in the education of young and receptive minds."[5] There was nothing comparable in Western nations. From 1890 to 1914 the generation that would support the Nazis found the superiority of Germanic racial stock a textbook cliché. Countless memoirs of German and Austrian Jews tell of harassment received from public school teachers, petty classroom tyrants enforcing the discipline of the barracks, spiritual warriors for the Germanic soul. Although millions of Germans supported liberalism and socialism, their ideas were not to be found in the schools. Jewish teachers might have contradicted stereotypes, but of some eight thousand teaching appointments from 1875 to 1895, about forty went to Jews. Prussia never had more than twelve Jewish secondary school teachers.

In universities the Germanic "Volk soul" was contrasted with other peoples. In economics the laws of classical economics were subordinated to the study of the history of economic systems, systems depicted as springing from the inner spirit of the peoples concerned or their special economic interests. In the 1840s Germany's most influential economic theorist, Friedrich List, denounced international free trade as a creation of the English imperialist mentality, designed to keep less industrialized nations weak. He demanded tariff barriers and government railroad construction to make Germany united and strong. Adolf Wagner, scholar of the guild system and follower of Stoecker, blamed "Jewish" free enterprise for the destruction of the guilds he idealized. In *The Jews and Modern Capitalism*, Werner Sombart, famed German economist, lamented the passing of the traditional economy and the rise of "Jewish" commercial capitalism, propelled by racial traits. The Germans were peasants, engineers, inventors, and entrepreneurs; Jews were nomadic salesmen, who, having "unlocked all the secrets which lay hidden in money . . . recognized its incredible powers . . . became masters of money, and through money . . . became masters of the world."[6] Hence, Sombart claimed, it was they who pioneered modern commercial capitalism. Given the overwhelming role of the Italians, Portuguese, Dutch, English, and French in early commerce, this is an odd idea. That it was taken seriously indicates much about the use and abuse of racism among German scholars.

Literature, folk tales, music, and customs were studied in the academy as emanations of the German *volksgeist*. German philosophy, still Idealist and Christian, led many academics to find unbreachable spiritual barriers to Jewish participation in German culture. The most famous German military historian, Hans Delbrueck, insisted that Jews could not be historians because only Protestants could understand the German past. Many of his colleagues agreed, and young Jewish historians were well advised to forget about high academic posts. Even before the Nazis, some German physicists denounced the theory of relativity as a "Jewish" attempt to deny the objective truths of Aryan science. Academic halls resounded with denunciations of the industrial, urban, and liberal world, associating it with the Jews. Academics who were activists were usually racial nationalists, not liberals or leftists as in the West.

German medical students were famous for their anti-Semitism. Jewish youth were highly overrepresented in medical studies, because private practice enabled one to avoid institutional discrimination. But opportunities were scarce, and competition intensified racism. The Social Democrats supported health insurance societies limiting costs, and the number of Jewish member-physicians was high. Many private physicians attacked such "Jewish socialized medicine" and the alleged Jewish preference for large-scale care that destroyed the personal relationship between patient and physician. German medical associations routinely demanded restrictive quotas on the number of Jews in medicine. Most non-Jewish physicians supported the Conservative party, and it echoed their demands.

Later, German physicians were the single most overrepresented professional group in the Nazi party. Thousands cooperated with the euthanasia murders and racial selection programs leading to the death camps.
Careerism encouraged German academics to support the right. Lacking private endowments, universities were branches of the government,
thus the faculty were civil servants funded by the Ministry of Education.
The selection of faculty had to be cleared with the government, hence
progressive academics were rare indeed. Socialist tendencies could ruin
one's career. In 1898 a Prussian law declared social democratic principles
incompatible with teaching.

Heinrich von Treitschke's career mirrors the increasing racism and
reaction of the universities. The favorite of the Prussian establishment,
he was appointed royal historiographer of Prussia by the kaiser, and no
middle-class household was complete without his famous *History*. He was
even able to reproach the kaiser with impunity. In 1892, when Pastor
Stoecker was ordered by the kaiser to hold his tongue at a dinner honoring a liberal prince, Stoecker nevertheless attacked "Jewish liberalism,"
and the kaiser fired him. Treitschke complained that William had "disarmed the only party ... with a chance to break the pernicious rule of
the Progressives and the Social Democrats."' He was not disciplined.

Idol of the German Student Federation, Treitschke gave scholarly sanction to establishment prejudices. For two decades his public lectures at
the University of Berlin were attended by the highest-ranking members
of government and the military, his classes crammed with their sons and
future schoolteachers, who, while their opposite numbers in France
taught the virtues of republicanism, taught those of autocracy. His strident voice harshened by near deafness, Treitschke ranted like a demagogue, praised imperialism, denounced the Jews, and raged against
democracy and socialism. Civilians, he insisted, should have no say over
the sacred army budget; thank the God of Battles there had been no universal suffrage when Prussia unified Germany. Why give the vote to readers of a daily press that encouraged every ignoramus to utter opinions on
matters best left to a few? Universal elementary education created discontent. If it must be, appoint retired noncommissioned officers as teachers to instill the right values. For Treitschke, socialism was the treason of
the Jews, feminism the illegitimate offspring of Jewish socialism and Hebrew females. Violating nature, feminism also threatened the sources of
Prussian greatness, the patriarchal family and the warrior ethic. As the
Nazis would insist, woman's role was one of childbearer for the race,
nurse to the warrior, symbol of the gentler sentiments.

Treitschke even criticized Bismarck for not completing the holy task
of uniting all Germans in an imperial *Weltmacht* (world power). A people with the power to conquer and absorb weak states had a divine man-

date to do so. "Brave peoples expand, cowardly peoples perish." Treitschke looked forward to the day when a German fleet would sail up the Thames and a German army occupy London. Bismarck saw no reason why Slavs should rule themselves, but he would not prop up the dying Austrian Empire. To Treitschke and the leagues he inspired, it was inconceivable to allow the thinly scattered Germanic stock in the east to be overwhelmed by the vast flood of inferior Slavic peasants, then in the grip of nationalistic anti-German movements. If Austria and Russia fought, Germany must support Austria, for it was the racial destiny of Germans to rule over "inferior" Slavs. In politics, all was force. War united the race and fostered the heroic; peace mutilated the personality and brought the domination of vulgar commerce. Might did not make right; it *was* right. Treitschke said, as Hitler would, "History is nothing other than the eternal struggle of race against race." The glittering, uniformed elites and arrogant youth of the dueling fraternities received academic sanction for their power and interests from Treitschke, the crude voice of the barracks writ large.

Angered by the advance of democracy, socialism, and international pacification under Caprivi, Treitschke's racist vituperation intensified. With simpleminded abandon he assigned racial characteristics: orientals were effeminate, the French (or Latin "race") had a natural penchant for shallow-minded superficiality, blacks were natural servants, gifted only with athletic talent—as Hitler maintained when he explained away the victories of Jesse Owens in the 1936 Olympics. Treitschke noted that even the United States kept blacks and whites separate to avoid racial contamination. Once he had conceded that some Jews made valuable contributions to German society, but by the 1890s he made no exceptions. All Jews were driven by a "trading instinct developed into the wildest passion" combined with a "deadly hatred of Christianity," responsible for "national decomposition" and the "disintegration of nations." Their only virtue was to have kept their blood relatively pure, the secret of their ability to further their own interests at others' expense. They did not really assimilate; baptism changed nothing. "International Jewry" was responsible for the revolutions of 1848; had they succeeded, Germany would have become a decadent republic.

"Great states either expand or die," Treitschke wrote. Unable to build their own nation, the Jews weakened Germany's as well. With hysterical fervor, Germany's most famous academic insisted, like the Conservative party, that Jews be forbidden to serve in government, teaching, or the law. Warning Germans they must end their tragic tendency to assimilate foreign elements, Treitschke called for Germans to take greater pride in their unique national qualities, reject the "filth of Judaism," speak out against it, and "repel voluntarily everything which is foreign to the Germanic

nature."[8] The enormous popularity of Treitschke's harsh simplicities illustrates how racism enabled so many upper-class Germans to reduce social and moral complexities to racial differences and take seriously those
who later, in the midst of social trauma, preached racial revolution and
war. Treitschke's writings were revived by the radical right in the 1920s,
and he was one of the very few nineteenth-century writers to win a place
in the official Nazi pantheon of required reading. Quotations from
Treitschke were included in the small books of readings carried into battle by German soldiers during World War II.

Opportunism as well as nationalist fervor motivated the educated.
Higher civil service posts were reserved for university graduates with faculty recommendations; correct views were crucial. The majority of German undergraduates came from the conservative elites, and students with
liberal leanings had a doubtful future in the civil service and no hope of
joining the networking fraternities of Germany's future rulers. In lower
schools, teachers made it clear that children of peasants and workers
should be satisfied to remain in their class, and fewer than 1 percent of
undergraduates came from their ranks. Consequently there was no alternative authority to challenge the self-satisfied certainties of the future ruling classes, and few Jewish voices. The universities made every effort to
avoid hiring or promoting Jews, though it meant ignoring the brilliant
achievements of many. In 1900 some 2 percent of German academics
were of Jewish origin, but in lower ranks and with dim prospects. At
Berlin in 1910 there were no Jewish full professors. Precisely because Jews
were illegally excluded from the establishment and rarely raised in conservative families, they understood the hypocrisies of German life and society in ways insiders rarely could, and their scholarship tended to be
critical. As before, the circular reasoning of racists allowed them to believe that such criticism meant Jews could not understand the German
racial spirit—another reason to keep them from teaching undergraduates.

The proportion of Jewish undergraduates, however, was high. "For
every 100,000 males of each denomination in Prussia, 33 Catholics, 58
Protestants, and 519 Jews became university students."[9] In 1885 one student in every eight in Berlin was Jewish, though Jews comprised less than
1 percent of the population. The figures were even more lopsided in Vienna. In part it was a natural reaction to discrimination. Upper-class students had connections and lower-middle-class Germans could rise by
ability, but Jewish males had to cultivate professional skills if they were
to avoid discrimination: higher education meant liberation. Their success
increased envy among precisely those budding professionals who, in a liberal culture, are usually the most tolerant. Law and medicine were the
favorite studies of Jews because careers in these professions avoided institutional discrimination, but this meant competition with Germans un-

able to count on family connections, fearful of becoming an academic proletariat. Consequently they were among the most extreme racists in Austria as well as Germany, highly overrepresented in the Nazi elite. In Western societies university attendance tended to lessen racism and conservatism; in Germany emphasizing one's racial uniqueness and identifying with the ruling class advanced one's career.

The high number and success of Jewish students was much debated in the 1880s. Rightists would not admit the consequences of discrimination and insisted that Jews merely wished to avoid manual labor. Even intellectuals with liberal leanings often said—as some still do—that there was a "Jewish problem" because too many were in the professions. For those who do not believe Jews are a corrupting influence, this is a non sequitur. Some suggested that Jewish verbal talent resulted from centuries of Talmudic training in dialectical subtleties, something rare among Evangelicals, for whom a declaration of faith in Christ was enough. But as sons of the urban middle and professional classes, Jews were bound to be overrepresented among undergraduates. The children of peasants and workers did not attend universities; for them, college was irrelevant and verbal skills unimportant. Given class conditioning and traditional aspirations, and allowing for the protection that education offered Jewish youth, their high attendance at university is easily explained. Suddenly the mysterious inner traits are gone, and one is left with mere human beings responding to social experience and institutional discrimination. The racist's rationale for his own failure is destroyed. It was no accident that many who joined the Nazi party in the 1920s, including Hitler, were middle-class youth who failed to maintain their status through educational success.

Even among achieving youth, romantic nationalism and anti-Semitism were popular. Hundreds of thousands of males aged fourteen to eighteen were members of the famous Youth Movement, the *Wandervogel*. In their struggle for male identity and adolescent idealism, unaffected by the practical considerations of adult life, they were repelled by the bourgeois respectability and materialism of their elders. Seeking to return to nature through hiking, camping, and mountaineering, and finding male bonding in forest campsites, they sang the ancient folk songs, lit huge fires in the mountains, and celebrated Teutonic rites to mark the solstices. Class origin generated a nostalgia for an imagined past rather than leftist utopianism. For many, the battle of the German Idealists against Enlightenment ideas was revitalized by a quasi-religious striving for a spiritual reality beyond the mundane lives awaiting them in office and profession. They despised politicians as lying panderers for the votes of the ignorant. Thousands of these youthful romantics saw Jews as a race of city people incapable of appreciating the Nordic past; reflecting the views of their pan-German teachers, they projected the Jews as the cause of social ills. By 1904 most *Wandervogel* chapters excluded Jews from their ranks. The young Adolf Eichmann belonged to a branch of the Youth Movement, "The Hawks," in Austria, where the movement and university students were even more racist. But working-class youth had antidotes to racism in Social Democratic cultural institutions. Proletarian youth also saw traditionalist ideas and anti-Semitism as beliefs of their oppressors, and welcomed the advance of industrialism and democracy.

Members of the Youth Movement, university students, academics, and intellectuals were too sophisticated for the crude racism of peasant populists or Stoecker's Christian fundamentalism. Racist intellectuals such as H. S. Chamberlain were more to their taste. In Vienna, the most anti-Semitic large city in Europe, he published *The Foundations of the Nineteenth Century* in 1899, an instant best-seller and very well reviewed. The son of a British admiral, raised in France, Chamberlain became a German citizen because of his worship of all things Prussian. His origins no doubt helped convince him that race, not nationality, was the unifying spiritual force of a people. Convinced that all great creations stemmed from Teutonic blood, he believed the only flaw of the ancient tribes was their failure to destroy all peoples within their reach. We must correct this error, he insisted, and also breed for superior human types, as dictated by Darwinism. However stern the measures necessary, Aryan blood must be purified, liberating its martial spirit and creative power. The Jew was the most powerful foe. Other races were merely inferior, but Jews, the unnatural result of accidental crossbreeding in the ancient Middle East, through millennia of inbreeding had created a uniquely evil racial force. And Germany's unnatural tolerance for alien blood meant that "our government, our laws, our art . . . have become more or less willing slaves of the Jews. . . . Moved by mistaken but ideal motives, the Indo-European opened the gates of friendship, the Jews rushed in like the enemy, stormed all positions, and planted the flag of his alien nature."[10] The Jews knew Germany was the last obstacle; elsewhere they had subverted civilization through the intellectual Judaization of Enlightenment ideas, ideas denying the reality of race, preaching cosmopolitanism, and denying blood loyalties. If purged, however, the race of Luther could not fail in the struggle with the race of money changers. Chamberlain, darling of conservative intellectuals, envisioned the future as Hitler did, a racial battle to the death against Jewry.

In the 1890s most educated people in the West admired the liberalization of society. But German intellectuals, excluding Progressives and the left, rejected it. Between 1890 and 1914, and again during the Nazi era, Paul de Lagarde and Julius Langbehn, amazingly popular cultural critics, preached a revolt against modern society and identified it with

ANTI-SEMITISM, ACADEMICS, INTELLECTUALS 137

Jewry. Lagarde's *German Essays* (1886) was a best-seller; Langbehn's *Rembrandt as Educator*—a literary craze among the elites—saw forty editions in two years. In other Western nations these vicious anti-Semites would have been dismissed as cranks. But as Fritz Stern has noted in a brilliant study, only in Germany were they so astonishingly popular.[11] Huge commercial successes, the books were reviewed or commented upon in nearly every important journal or paper—and favorably, except, of course, in the liberal press. These cultural facts alone are enough to tell us about the power of racism in Germany at the turn of the century, a time when most scholars still persist in telling us that German anti-Semitism was on the wane.

The two prophets denounced the spiritual emptiness, money-grubbing careerism, and cynical *Realpolitik* of the "Jewish" Reich as institutionalized mediocrity bereft of higher ideals. They preached a racial resurrection of the Germans and a break with the cosmopolitan thought of the French and the Jews, who, they alleged, had long since destroyed their "folk soul" in the belief that man was nothing but a bundle of reflexes, his moral judgments, religious impulses, and ideal strivings no more than illusions. The Germanic soul was instinctively idealistic, if now contaminated by the cosmopolitanism of those who prated of international standards of truth and rights. For Germans there was only German justice and German truth. Educators must teach only Germanic culture and reject the degenerate naturalism of the French, the sordid depiction of the disease, prostitution, and squalor of lower-class life combined with leftist zeal found in the work of an Émile Zola. It was no coincidence that Zola had defended Dreyfus.

German educators, they insisted, must stimulate the heroic and aristocratic values inherent in the *Volk*. "Equality is death, hierarchy is life."[12] Liberal toleration was nihilistic, pandered to base instincts, and avoided all serious commitment to anything but greed. Commerce was the God that destroyed all Gods: "Money is dirt," Langbehn said to his startled publisher, refusing all royalties so that his work could reach a vast public—which it did.[13] He and Lagarde condemned the "Jewish" love of gain that had reduced culture to the lowest common denominator of taste; even the value of art, like cabbages, was set by market price. Mass culture destroyed the intellect and withered the soul. In Bismarck's Reich the talented strove for power and money, the timorous clung to security, and the spirit of Jewish commerce dominated the whole. Crush democracy, destroy the Reichstag. Eradicate this "miserable republic" calling itself an empire. Return to the old Germanic system of rule by the best.

Both intellectuals wrote for the Conservative party off and on, and, flattering their masters, declared that all political achievement, like art, was the result of the superior instincts of a few. They demanded that leaders be selected from among those who had served the nation well, as with the ancient German clans, and be led by a "Fuehrer" able to intuit the will of the Volk soul (as Hitler later claimed to do) and carry it out by force if need be. True politics was the politics of mystery, command, charisma, and unity of will. Annihilate modern society, Lagarde preached; return to Germanic primitivism, Langbehn demanded, extirpating root and branch the "abominable" consequences of 1789. During the Franco-Prussian War of 1870, Lagarde passionately hoped the Prussians would reduce Paris to rubble and wipe out the "Judaized" revolutionists.

Ignoring the complexities of Marxist ideas as simply Jewish intellectual trickery, Lagarde argued that socialism appealed only to those whose morality was destroyed by cheap gin and city life. Germans needed a "national socialism," wrote Langbehn, a society guided by a spirit of communal sacrifice, free of Jewish financiers and Marxists. Like Stoecker, Boeckel, the Prussian ultraright, and Hitler, for that matter, Lagarde and Langbehn hated all big cities, the enemies of all that was Germanic, rural, and unspoiled by industrial blight. They were not surprised that the deracinated masses and Jewish cultural "trashmongers" in Berlin voted for the left. Like Turnvater Jahn, both predicted that one day rural Germany would rise up, march on Berlin, and cleanse it by force—Hitler's goal in his putsch of 1923.

Both men called for lebensraum. Langbehn wrote of Germany's "calling to world domination," Lagarde wanted the lands of the Austrian Empire colonized by Germans, and Poland and France conquered.[14] Should Russia object, as it must, let it also experience the sacred force of the German sword. Surviving Slavs should be removed to some remote and worthless corner of the vast reaches of the east. In a manifesto written for the Prussian Conservative party, Lagarde wrote of the Slavs: "The sooner they perish the better it will be for us and them."[15] Lagarde called the Jews a "bacillus," the "carriers of decay" . . . [who] pollute every national culture . . . exploit the human and material resources of their hosts," and "destroy all faith with their materialistic liberalism."[16] Millions of Germans had already been Judaized, Langbehn declared, and the French, British, and Americans, obsessed with commerce, might as well be Jews. Already the German press has been "Palestinized," so too literature, medicine, law, and the economy. Their association between the Jews and the characteristics of a world they hated could scarcely be more deadly. Destroy these "usurious vermin" before it is too late, Lagarde demanded, "With trichinae and bacilli one does not negotiate" . . . they are exterminated as quickly and thoroughly as possible."[17] The Jews were deadly infectious parasites, a "poison . . . and must be treated as such. . . ." Langbehn preached a war of extermination against the Jews, and his and Lagarde's calls for genocide were republished in many versions by the

Nazis and distributed to soldiers at the front.[18] In short, the two most influential and popular intellectuals of late nineteenth-century Germany
were indistinguishable from Nazi ideologists. Given this cultural fact, it
is amazing how many still think that National Socialism had little intellectual connection with the German past. At the very least, the popularity of these two cultural critics also casts serious doubt on the received
idea that the elites disliked Nazi anti-Semitism.

The radical racism popular among the educated was often a blend of
religious fervor with racist "science." Anti-Semites did not so much
replace Christian anti-Judaism with secular racism, as many claim; they
adjusted Christianity to create a new racist faith. Racists who publicly
scorned Christianity had little success. Wilhelm Marr, avowed atheist,
ceased attacking Christianity when seeking campaign funds from wealthy
rightists. Hitler purged Nazis who called for a public break with Christianity. German conservatives were uncomfortable with a racism based
on Social Darwinism, not wanting to think of man as but a species of animal who had clawed his way out of primeval slime to dominance merely
because of a superior capacity in a brute struggle for survival. Christian
and conservative, they preferred to believe man had been formed in a
unique act of divine creation. Many anti-Semites, including Nazis, did
not believe the superior race was simply the product of the struggle for
survival through the selection of accidental variations. Aryans were superior at the creation, and the continuation of this superiority depended on
will, not brute biological accident. Thus Nazis were rarely atheists. Even
Himmler saw in race the foundation for a new religion. And most radical anti-Semites hoped to unite racism with a Christianity purged of its
"Jewish" elements. A Germanic Christianity, not just racist science, would
preserve Nordic idealism.

Christ was the obstacle. During the Dreyfus affair a famous French
anti-Semite was known, when drunk, to seize any hapless priest he came
across and demand, "How is it possible that Christ was a Jew?" Fichte
and Fritsch believed he was not. Chamberlain, wanting Christianity *Judenrein*, spent a hundred pages "proving" Christ the offspring of a Roman
soldier and a Gentile woman. Christ's blood was Aryan blood, his victory
over Judaism the victory of Aryan idealism over Jewish ritualism. For
Chamberlain, Christ was not the culmination but the conqueror of Judaism. Lagarde, like many, insisted that Saint Paul had contaminated
Christ's message with Jewish ideas. "Diseased priests," Jewish influenced,
made Christ's death degrading and humiliating because they feared the
heroic vitalism surging in the Germans of old. Lagarde and Langbehn
called for a "Germanic Christianity." Son of a minister, Lagarde considered Luther the greatest German hero, who had erred only by preserving much that was Jewish and rotten in Christianity. Many writers

rejected the Christian idealization of the meek and the passive, the rabbinical "guilty conscience" that repressed violent instincts and caused
Aryans to allow inferior races to live among them on equal terms. Create a religion of race, Chamberlain declared, and a Jew would be as unable to convert as he was to change his skull measurements. Jewish
infiltration into German society would be forever barred. The popular
philosopher Eugen Duehring insisted that the critic Gotthold Lessing was
Jewish because he admired the Enlightenment. In blood and spirit, progressives *had* to be Jewish: by their works shall ye know them. Chamberlain and Fritsch both planned to write a new gospel, in which religion
would be a matter of blood as much as faith.

No less a giant than Richard Wagner provided the sacred music for the
religion of race. To the German bourgeoisie, Wagner was not only the
greatest composer of the century, he was also the supreme cultural
prophet of the German soul, his music inspiring the awesome feelings of
religious cultists for their leaders. Wagner's soaring unresolved chords expressed the longing of the Germanic peoples to restore their heroic *volk-
seele*, a mystical nostalgia for the Teutonic gods destroyed by a mundane
civilization built on greed, bereft of ideals, and a stranger to sacrifice. The
anti-Semitic petition of 1881 was drawn up at Bayreuth and approved by
the master, who heartily endorsed the anti-Semitic movement, pleased to
think he was responsible for its rapid increase in the 1870s. As a disciple
wrote, Bayreuth, Wagner's wife Cosima presiding, was a shrine, a new
Jerusalem for mystic racists. Wagner societies proliferated, and Chamberlain became another of their heroes.

Wagner's Ring cycle, first performed in 1876 at Bayreuth, abounds with
Teutonic mythology. Today its narrative seems absurd to most, forcing directors to create exotic sets and costumes in order to prod our unwilling
suspension of disbelief. But in Wagner's tales of the doomed warrior heroes and heroines of the *Volk*, the German bourgeoisie found an ecstatic
lament for the erosion of "Germanic" idealism in a world of commercial
values. In the concert hall they could vicariously participate in Germanic
spirituality. For Marr, the acolytes of Bayreuth, and for Chamberlain, who
married Wagner's daughter, the Ring dramatized the liturgical passion of
the gods at the beginning of Aryan history. (Wagner himself hoped to
write a history of the Aryans.) Wagner's *Goetterdämmerung* was a
metaphor for the destruction of the Nordic animism of forest and nature
by Jewish monotheism. As Wagner wrote, "the Jewish race, born enemy
of humanity," was responsible for the urban, industrial, and liberal order.
Like "vermin in a corpse," he declared, Jews polluted Germanic culture
through their domination of criticism. Restless, nervous, sterile, the Jewish *Volk* soul had withered by assimilation. True art was rooted in racial
loyalty; in the Diaspora the Jews had adopted sterile cosmopolitan cul-

tural ideals. Soulless critics, they had "infected" many Germans with the standards of racial mongrels, destroyers of all ideal forms. Wagner too insisted that Christ was Nordic and that no German should marry even a converted Jew, for their blood polluted through generations. In her diaries, as undoubtedly in her conversations with "the master," Cosima constantly reviled Jews as vermin, lice, insects, and bacillus, the terrible metaphors reeking of death so popular among the Nazis.

But context is all. Theodore Herzl wrote his famous demand for a Jewish state in one fervid session immediately after attending the performance of Wagner in Paris. Wagner's racist subtext resonates only with an audience for whom anti-Semitism is commonplace; we do not sense it now. But after all they had read and heard, his German audience then could hardly miss the message. Wagner himself called for the destruction of the Jews. Today his defenders, incapable of such hatred, insist he did not mean it literally. But we cannot know, nor is it relevant. It is enough for such an influential genius to have said it repeatedly, as the immense homage given him by anti-Semites shows.

Next to his grandiose architectural fantasies, young Hitler's most intense passion was for Wagner. Adolescents, sensing inner power but with little to show for it, found release in the striving tensions of Wagner's music and the mystic powers of his gods and goddesses. The Wagner cult held sway among nationalist students at Berlin and Vienna. When the Jewish Gustav Mahler was hired to conduct Wagner in Vienna, riots ensued. The Wagners, contributors to Hitler from 1922 on, treated Hitler at Bayreuth as the potential savior of the racial soul. The master's music reinforced Hitler's faith that destiny had selected him to be the messiah of a regenerated *Volk*.

In 1927 the circle of influence was completed in the holy precincts of Bayreuth; there Chamberlain was greeted by Hitler and declared the prophet of the National Socialist movement. In parade, pageant, film, newsreel, and solemn ceremonial, the Nazis used Wagner's music in architectural settings built on a scale transcending the merely human. Its soaring foreboding tones destroyed the emotional distance needed for critical thought, stirring many to idealize the power of the folk unleashed in racial war in the east. Even when the war was going badly, Hitler left his "Wolf's Lair" in Prussia to renew his spirit at the fount at Bayreuth. In Berlin in 1945, amidst the smoking ruins of Allied bombs, Albert Speer organized a last concert to play the *Goetterdämmerung*.

Among the millions of avid readers of all the racist cultural prophets, including Lagarde and Langbehn, were the kaiser, Bismarck, aristocrats, and military officers, countless academics and schoolteachers, the Youth Movement, the Federation of German Students, and the Pan-German League. The popularity of racism and antimodernism among the middle and upper classes of Germany belies the notion that fervid political anti-Semitism was largely confined to the ignorant, the uneducated, and the unsophisticated, as it was outside Germany, Austria, and France. Political anti-Semitism attracted millions in the United States but was never decisive because it was not adopted by dominant elites. In liberal nations university students, if politicized, move to the left; German and Austrian undergraduates, inspired by racist intellectuals and reactionary professors, moved to the right. Extremely active in anti-Semitic groups, undergraduates in many German and Austrian universities greeted classroom references to Jewish scholars with hoots of scorn. They ostracized and sometimes physically attacked Jewish students. In 1892 Caprivi's government, forced to intervene, urged the faculty to halt these depredations in the name of "Christian tolerance," threatening to cut off university subsidies. Stiff with righteous indignation, academics upheld the sacred principles of academic freedom. The oldest German student organizations excluded Jews by 1896; by 1904 Jews were banned from all German fraternities. Austrian undergraduates beat them to it by a decade. By 1930 German student organizations were Nazi dominated. As one scholar writes, "An entire generation of Germans had absorbed generous doses of anti-Semitism at the gymnasium and the university."[19] The future leaders of Germany and their supporters were created long before 1914. It was never just Hitler and a few Nazis.

10: OPPOSING ANTI-SEMITISM

> Of all the vulgar modes of escaping from consideration of the effect
> of social and moral influences upon the human mind, the most vul-
> gar is that of attributing the diversities of conduct and character to
> inherent natural differences.
>
> —J. S. Mill

WHEN the Conservative party adopted anti-Semitism, it became difficult
to believe, as most Jews and liberals did, that racism was a fading holdover
of primitive Christianity, confined to the uneducated and the powerless.
Political opposition was organized by the Jewish community, the Progressives, and the Social Democrats. The National Liberals, labeled the
"Party of the Jews" in 1870, had moved swiftly to the right. Although they
did not sanction racism, they took no stand against government discrimination, nominated no Jewish candidates, and on occasion cooperated
with anti-Semites in elections. Like the clergy and most Germans, they
believed one could not be a true German without being Christian.

Most Jews wished to assimilate without converting, hoping that one day
Jews would be viewed as Germans of Jewish faith. After all, they had
made enormous progress since Napoleon: from the ghetto to equal constitutional rights, from peddlers to businessmen and professionals with
university educations. But the renewed onslaught against them in the
Caprivi years led them to fight back in 1893 by founding the Central
League for German Citizens of Jewish Faith. Its 100,000 members supported a variety of liberal causes, not wanting to seem to fight only for
themselves; they also knew that successful liberal reforms would ultimately protect them. Some 13,000 Gentiles joined an Association for Defense Against Anti-Semitism in the 1890s, and the Progressive party
cooperated in the fight. As secular professionals likely to have professional
contacts with Jewish colleagues, racist hatreds had little currency among
them. As a group, however, the German elites were of no help. At the
height of anti-Semitism in the 1890s in the United States, for example, a
number of important non-Jewish political and religious leaders publicly
opposed anti-Semitism. Even in France half of all Frenchmen favored

Dreyfus. Although often violated in practice, civic disabilities against religious minorities in England and the United States were regarded as violations of civilized norms, however much personal hostility there might be toward Jews. But in Germany and Austria, millions on the right saw the Jewish struggle not as a demand for the right of common citizenship but as the attempt of a foreign race to impose its values on a culture not its own.

Liberals had difficulty understanding the causes of anti-Semitism. The famous liberal German historian, Theodore Mommsen, called anti-Semitism "a horrible epidemic like cholera, which can neither be explained nor cured. One must patiently wait until the poison consumes itself and loses its virulence." This admission of helplessness did not prevent Jewish organizations and Progressives from suing racists for libel, pressuring governments to end discrimination, denouncing the use of anti-Semitism in politics, and publishing literature refuting racist charges. But success depended on a liberal consensus among German leaders, something not seen until our own day. As ever, the progressive-minded hoped that education would weaken racism, but the German educational system was itself dominated by anti-Semites. And if racists were convicted of libel, the verdicts were taken as evidence of Jewry's power, and the many dignified refutations of racist literature had little effect. The high visibility of Jews in commerce, cities, and liberal politics, and as rural middlemen, was enough for those who needed to personalize their fears about modern society. As for those sophisticated rightists who knew better, the issue was too useful to drop.

Many Jews took comfort in the knowledge that, after all, Germany was not Russia or a primitive eastern peasant culture. Moreover, by 1900 the Social Democrats were the most popular party in Germany, opposed to racism and committed to peaceful democratic change. The Central League, once strongly antisocialist, informed the Jewish community it was better to vote for a Social Democrat than allow an anti-Semite to gain office. Many young Jews supported democratic socialism outright, but no more than 20 percent of all Jewish voters ever did, though those who read conservative propaganda must have thought all Jews were leftists. From Stoecker through the Weimar Republic, German and Austrian socialists opposed anti-Semitism. But Karl Marx, son of a Jewish father who had converted, made strong anti-Semitic statements in his early writings. In 1844 he called the Jews a nation of commercial traders, the "embodiment of materialistic egoism," dominated by money and trade. Marx also made extremely racist remarks in his private correspondence, but he never called for discrimination against the Jews or believed in innate racial traits. Indeed, like other young leftists (and Zionists later), he believed the victory of socialism would end the "distortion" of the Jewish character under capitalism. Most important, anti-Semitism had no place in the Marxist system he and Engels created.

For Marxists, race was irrelevant, class was all. Marx died in 1883, before anti-Semitism was politically effective. In 1890 his cofounder, Friedrich Engels, gave the Marxist position: "Anti-Semitism is nothing but a reactionary movement of decaying, medieval social groups against modern society, which is essentially composed of capitalists and workers. . . . Anti-Semitism serves only reactionary purposes. . . ."[1] Engels, son of a Christian textile manufacturer, ironically noted that he himself had been called Jewish by the popular middle-class magazine *Gardenhouse*. It was a persistent tradition; leftists had to be Jewish lest the racist stereotype fail.

As George Mosse has noted, "Millions of Germans, mostly of the left, were never captives of the voelkisch ideology."[2] To socialists, anti-Semitism seemed a Christian throwback until 1890, and only then did they fight for the right of Jews to be army officers or civil servants, though some still thought it an irrelevant conflict among the bourgeoisie. Similarly, in the early stages of the Dreyfus case, French socialists kept aloof. What did a struggle to keep a Jewish officer in the French army have to do with them? But when they realized that church, army, and aristocracy were using anti-Semitism to shore up reaction, they swiftly joined the fray. In Germany it was the rise of populist and conservative racism against Caprivi that roused the left to see anti-Semitism as a tool against democratic reform and them. In 1892 the Social Democrats issued their official position: "The exploitation of man by man is not a specifically Jewish form of livelihood but one peculiar to bourgeois society, which will end only with the decline of bourgeois society." It was a "reactionary" movement supported by "Junkers and clerics." Unlike all other parties, Social Democratic leaders refused all offers to combine with anti-Semites in election runoffs, even though in the few cases where the offer was made, it would have helped them.

For ordinary workers the capitalist was the enemy, Jewish or not; for sophisticated Marxists there were no "enemies"—the system created both exploiters and exploited. For the consistent Marxist the fight against capitalism was a battle against a necessary, exploitative, but ultimately doomed system, having nothing to do with ethnicity. As Karl Kautsky, the leader of Marxist orthodoxy, wrote in *Race and Jewry*, there were no fixed racial traits. Class experience determined social attitudes and behavior. Moreover, international finance, Jewish or not, was of secondary importance; industrialists and the owners of the means of production were primary. Anti-Semitism would end, Marxists believed, when the inevitable contradictions of capitalism and the consciousness of the workers brought its collapse. With capitalism gone, moneylenders, speculators, industrialists, and international financiers would also go, of whatever race or religion. This was a mistaken prediction, of course, a failure the Marxists shared with liberals—underrating the potential political power of anti-Semitism. Socialists assumed that racism was simply a means to distract the attention of ordinary citizens from social injustice and exploitation. Industrialization, they were convinced, would destroy the influence of the feudal elites and force peasants, artisans, and the Mittelstand to become part of the capitalist system. As the Social Democratic party wrote: artisans and peasants would one day see that the "capitalist class in general is their enemy and that only the realization of socialism can free them from their misery."[3] Underestimating the racism of the lower middle classes and their admiration of the establishment, socialists only increased the fears of these classes, as did socialist atheism and internationalism. Nevertheless, as Peter Pulzer has written, "The anti-Semites and the Social Democrats were at the opposite ends of the political world, and their mutual enmity was deep and lasting."[4]

Paul Singer, a Jewish socialist, was twice elected to the Reichstag from Berlin in spite of Pastor Stoecker's attempts to defeat him. A hero to his working-class constituents, he received an unprecedented mass demonstration at his funeral in Berlin in 1909, outraging and frightening the establishment. The knowledge that millions of Aryan proletarians rejected the alleged superiority of the power elite and blood of the Volk raised self-doubts that had to be assuaged. From Stoecker to Hitler, rightists rarely attempted to refute socialism, preferring to cite the high percentage of intellectuals of Jewish origin among socialist publicists as proof of its subversion, ignoring the low percentage of Jewish socialist voters. For non-racists, of course, Jewish participation or lack of it in leftist politics was irrelevant. When questioned in 1878 by a reporter for a Jewish newspaper seeking biographical details for a directory of Jewish members of the Reichstag, the first German Jew to enter the legislative body as a socialist said he did not wish to appear in the directory; he had been elected as a Socialist, not as a Jew.

German liberals and leftists believed, correctly, that their battle for a democratic and secular Germany was also a struggle against racism. But it was difficult to fight a future one could not predict with weapons one did not have. Only after the Nazis were defeated did a general awareness of modern genetics render racism a crude myth for the ignorant. Before then, anthropologists and their popularizers simply assumed that those with similar physical traits belonged to separate races with different mental and moral capacities. We know now that the physical traits then used to define the Aryan or Germanic "race" are possessed by many other groups, including Jews. Moreover, the wide range of skills, capacities, and intelligence within each ethnic group is vast, while the differences between groups are minimal and far more consistent with environmental and cultural factors than with the mythical construct of race. Many experiments and observations show that, as the Enlightenment thought, education and social environment, not race, are decisive. Children of a verbal and professional family will do better when tested. Artisans, peasants, and proletarians do not find verbal communication vital to their occupations as do salesmen, lawyers, physicians, and bankers. Early anthropologists simply assumed that the cultural level of an ethnic group revealed innately different intellectual and moral capacities. But it is now agreed to be impossible to disentangle environmental from hereditary factors—a simple fact that destroys the basis for all racist dogma.

Even if there were separate races with fixed traits, the Jews, scattered by the Diaspora, have experienced a constant influx of new genetic material by assimilation, intermarriage, and conversion. During the early centuries of Christianity the rate of conversion between Judaism and Christianity was high, and by the 1890s the rate of intermarriage was between 15 and 20 percent in Europe. As for professional choices, as the Jews of the nineteenth century knew, scientific achievement and higher education protected against discrimination, as did diamond cutting, tailoring, international trade, or any portable skill. Jews have been overrepresented in pioneering ventures because there talent is rewarded regardless of ethnic credentials, and one is less likely to be excluded by entrenched non-Jews. (In the early days of the movie industry in Hollywood, Jews pioneered because it was a new and expanding business. In return, anti-Semites like Henry Ford, Gerald L. K. Smith, and the Ku Klux Klan insisted the new cultural values presented on the silver screen—drinking, smoking, liberated women, idealized gangsters—were Jewish attempts to destroy the values of small-town Protestant America. Ironically, these were the people who made such movies popular.)

The nineteenth-century anti-Semitic stereotype is not based on "the Jews," it is a caricature of the features of some Ashkenazi Jews and is just as applicable to Arabs or many Germans, for that matter. To end racial stereotyping, one need only consider the yellow Jews of China, the brown Jews of India, or the black Jews of Ethiopia. As for the idea of Jewish blood, blood type is inherited, and wherever Jews have lived for centuries, their type resembles the local population more than it does Jews elsewhere. Moreover, the "genetic distance" between peoples can be measured, and it shows that Jews are closer to the people they live among than to Jews in other lands. Indeed, there is no better place to observe the vast range of human physical types than modern Israel. As for the "Aryan" type—tall, blond, light-eyed, and long-skulled—it too was a stereotype found more often among Poles than Prussians, to the chagrin of the Nazis. In the 1930s party officials instructed enthusiasts to stop idealizing the type, and special "Aryan" categories were created for Hitler and Goebbels. In spite of all their talk, in the end the Nazis could only decide who was a Jew by their or their ancestors' allegiance to Judaism as revealed by parish records and baptismal certificates. To speak of fixed racial traits is to speak nonsense; there is no Semitic race.

Many German Jews, liberated just as Germany was swept by the commercial and industrial revolutions, gained significant advantages from the skills they had needed to survive in the ghetto. By the 1880s about 60 percent of German Jews were in middle- or higher-income brackets. Sociology tells us how minorities are tracked into different vocations. But most German academics detested sociology. Treitschke, of course, led the battle to keep sociology out of the university curriculum, decrying it as un-German and a threat to patriotic unity because it explained poverty and crime as results of the inequities of the social system rather than of innate character. The establishment preferred racial explanations for social ills. Many uneducated people still do, of course, but they are politically ineffective wherever there are serious educational standards.

By 1900 it seemed that those opposing political anti-Semitism would prevail. A new generation gave less prestige to Germany's unifiers, conservative rural constituencies waned, and the right was challenged by the most successful electoral force in German history, the Social Democrats. With the blessings of the retired Bismarck and the kaiser, Buelow, chancellor from 1900 to 1909, counterattacked. He forged an alliance between industrialists and large estate owners, groups previously at odds over Bismarck's grain tariffs. Industrialists who exported feared a tariff war, and trade unions demanded higher wages to compensate for what was already the highest cost of living in Western Europe. Buelow hoped to distract and unite the people behind him with a global politics of imperialism. Industrialists received lucrative contracts for a huge naval buildup; landowners were bought off by increased tariff protection. The alliance was supported by anti-Semitic populists. Conservatives and pan-Germans joined the campaign for a German navy to equal or surpass the British fleet. Historians rightly call Buelow's alliance a "cartel of fear" against the left: "Junker landowners, bureaucrats, and officers were joined by a significant number of bankers, industrialists, and professors. Knitted together by common fears and interests, these forces and the institutions they dominated formed an almost irresistible barrier to substantial social and political reform."[5]

Industrialists now demanded tougher government action against workers. Newspapers were banned for supporting strikes, and workers who attended Social Democratic meetings were fired. Landowners, once indifferent to the level of workers' wages, now supported men like Kardorff and Krupp, who regarded the least rise as anathema. In the Reichstag,

Stoecker, still a force, protested that such measures would only drive more workers to the left. Greeted with cold anger by his former allies, he was stripped of his leadership positions and labeled a "revolutionary" when he protested a bill making it a crime to speak against the monarch, religion, or private property. Industrialists demanded he be silenced, and the church hierarchy happily obliged. Ironically, Stoecker now echoed the complaints once hurled against him by anarchists: "The Evangelical Church is more and more an institution which exists solely for the rich and wealthy." Stoecker's pietistic fundamentalism failed to comprehend a world where Christians were as greedy as his mythical Jews, and now the Evangelical hierarchy itself contradicted the presumed moral superiority of Christianity, the central conviction of his racist crusade. By the time of his death in 1909, bereft of all influence, rejected by church and kaiser, Stoecker despaired. His church was "shameless and without honor."[6]

In 1896 the kaiser deliberately offended the British, suggesting that Germany ought to send troops to help the Afrikaners as the Boer War approached. Arms were sent, and with them the kaiser's famous telegram to Ohm Kruger, hero of the Afrikaners, congratulating him for repelling a British raid. The British were outraged, but the reaction of the German public was extremely favorable, and much of it was racist. The Pan-German League, other rightist organizations, and large segments of the middle classes regarded the Dutch Boers as racial brothers fighting for national liberation against British imperial greed. When war broke out in 1899, publicists and newspapers called it a racial struggle of the Germanic *Volk*. Anti-Semitic leaders declared the British a "Judaized" collection of merchants out to destroy Germanic farmers for the gold and diamonds of the Transvaal. Bernhard Foerster, originator of the anti-Semitic petition of 1881, insisted that England was ruled by the Jews, offering prime ministers Benjamin Disraeli and "William Glattstein" (alias Gladstone) as evidence. After all, had not the Jew Disraeli declared race the key to history, praising the Jews as the most clever race of all? Disraeli's remarks were often quoted by anti-Semites as certain evidence of the ambitions of "international Jewry."

When the Boers won the first battles, the rightist press crowed over the superior military virtues of their Teutonic blood brothers. Pan-Germans and anti-Semites sponsored demonstrations and stressed the prominence of Jewish names in British South African financial circles. When the British drove the women and children of the Boer guerrilla movement into camps, where they were brutally treated and many died of disease, many Germans were persuaded it was a racial war—genocide, as we would say today. Long after the war, accounts of the inhumane treatment of Boer civilians were published in Germany. After 1945 many Germans even cited the British camps as precedents for the Nazi death camps, as if the Jews had died only from disease and wartime lack of food, as current "revisionists" still claim.

In the 1903 elections the Social Democrats appealed to consumers to reject the expensive and dangerous expansion of the navy, and they gained a surprising twenty-five seats while the Conservatives suffered yet more losses. Buelow was desperate. Under the aegis of the Conservative party, the Agrarian Bund, and the Pan-German League, he tried to see if constitutional restrictions on universal suffrage could be made to give more votes to the elites. In 1905 the kaiser almost provoked war with a dramatic visit to French Morocco, offering German protection to the sultan. General Alfred von Schlieffen, chief of the general staff, called war with France an urgent necessity and hoped a pretext could be found before 1907 when the French planned a huge ceremony to celebrate the anniversary of Napoleon's victory over Prussia. To the consternation of England, German naval bills were passed in 1898, 1900, and 1906. The British insisted that a navy second to none was essential not only to the empire but to the home islands as well, for imported food was a necessity; a large German navy would be a mortal threat. Russia was angered by German protection against its grain exports. England, Russia, and France discussed possible alliances against the Germans. For the first time the German government supported Austrian attempts to curb Serbia and Russia and extend German dominion over Slavs. The cartel of fear had exposed Germany to a two-front war it claimed it wanted to prevent. Even so, and in spite of high profits and the doubling of the German national debt after 1900, the ruling classes refused to be taxed for their dangerous new toys. Buelow, unable to face down his own allies, decided instead to raise taxes on consumers, with much smaller contributions from inheritance and property taxes. To silence the opposition, patriotism, imperialism, and anti-Semitism were used to rally the masses to a new election.

The central issue of the "Hottentot" election of 1907 was funds for the colonization of southwest Africa. Unfortunately the Herero peoples were already there, and they suffered massacres by the German army brutal even by imperialist standards. In 1905 the Social Democrats infuriated the right by forming a parliamentary alliance with Progressives to fight proposed army budget increases. To the rage of imperialists, socialists and Progressives exposed the brutality of the German colonial administration and the government's corrupt collusion with colonial commercial companies. The Catholic Center, thought to be part of Buelow's coalition, also voted against the funds needed for conquest. High Evangelical clerics and court circles bitterly objected to this Catholic "treason."

Buelow ignored domestic problems. Imperialism was his single campaign issue. Instructing his government press to call the election a life-

or-death struggle against international rivals trying to reduce Germany to a second-rate power, he mounted a massive campaign of vilification, hammering with unprecedented fury at the "treason" of socialists and Catholics. Conservatives, pan-Germans, Navy Leaguers, the anti-Semitic parties, and assorted patriotic leagues joined in the fight against the "Red and Black International," aided by huge electoral funds from business leaders. Buelow harped about the "enemy within the gates," and the bourgeois press trumpeted incessantly about German destiny, the perfidy of France and England, and the treason of Catholics and socialists. Anti-Semitism was also used in the campaign; the Pan-German League, the Agrarian Bund, the Navy League, and the Conservative party took the initiative, and also gave financial aid to the anti-Semitic parties, as did the government itself, illegally. In 1904 an Imperial League Against Social Democracy had been formed, its board of directors including landowners, industrialists, bankers, bureaucrats, and military officers. Now they too mounted a drive against the "Black and Red traitors." A few anti-Semites insisted that many cardinals and popes were of Jewish origin. Surprisingly, the Progressives joined the patriotic wave, throwing their support to four anti-Semitic candidates in election runoffs against Social Democrats.

Buelow's campaign succeeded far beyond his expectations. The Social Democrats lost almost half their seats, sinking to forty-three. The conservative parties rose to a startling eighty-four; populist anti-Semites held at sixteen; and a newly formed Economic Union, an anti-Semitic small businessman's party, gained thirteen seats. Stoecker and two of his Christian anti-Semites also won. But the Catholic Center remained strong, and its leaders, frightened by Buelow's vicious attacks, never again opposed imperialism. The lesson seemed clear. An aggressive foreign policy combined with the libeling of socialists, Catholics, and Jews raised conservatives to new heights and savaged the socialists. The Pan-German League immediately elected as president one of Germany's most prominent and vicious anti-Semites, Heinrich Class, later a partner of Hitler.

Buelow's victory was short-lived. Conservative leaders blocked his attempts to tax them. The kaiser, interviewed by an English newspaper, made wildly aggressive anti-British statements. Buelow failed to support him and continued his efforts to tax the wealthy to meet army budget increases. Angered, conservative leaders deserted him; the kaiser happily dumped him and ultimately appointed Bethmann-Hollweg chancellor. The man who presided over foreign affairs during the perilous years before 1914 was a well-meaning bureaucrat, no more, inexperienced in international politics. Confident of their formula for success, conservatives attacked Bethmann for his lack of an aggressive foreign policy and his renewed efforts to tax them. Rather than rally the Reichstag as Caprivi would have, Bethmann gave in. Erich Ludendorff, later head of the armies on the western front and a fanatic anti-Semite, led the army's public campaign for more funds. Bethmann's minister of finance, though a conservative, resigned in frustration at the amounts demanded and the refusal to be taxed, finding the military simply irresponsible. But Bethmann did gain a tax on inherited land, the first tax won over conservative objections.

Food prices rose even higher because of crop failures and high consumer taxes. By 1908 the army had practically wiped out the Herero peoples, and there was no other convenient "Hottentot" issue. The right was disunited, angry at Bethmann's tax and his failure to challenge France forcefully during yet another Moroccan crisis. An election was scheduled for 1912. Social Democrats and Progressives agreed to support each other in runoffs, and both campaigned against militarization and its burden on consumers. The National Liberals, now liberal in name only, joined the right. The Social Democrats, who had ceased acting like a revolutionary party in 1880, stopped talking like one by 1900. Now they strove for more votes and practical reforms for workers. The swift increase in socialist votes and the failure of Marx's predictions about the collapse of capitalism (real wages had risen dramatically since 1870) persuaded the new leadership—mostly trade unionists and Reichstag delegates—to work within the system. Paradoxically, their new pragmatism made them even more threatening to the right, for it attracted more voters. Social Democrats were now the major force for liberal progress and peaceful social reform.

The elections of 1912 were a disaster for the right. Conservatives lost 27 of their 84 seats; anti-Semites dropped from 17 to 9, National Liberals from 54 to 45. But the Social Democrats, in spite of heavy gerrymandering, soared from 43 seats to a spectacular 110. One-third of German voters had given the Social Democrats one-fourth of the Reichstag's seats, and more votes than the conservative parties and the National Liberals combined. The Reichstag resounded with demands for democratic constitutional changes. On the right there was panic. In a parliamentary system the Social Democrats, Progressives, and Catholic Center would have been asked to form a government, but this was unthinkable to the kaiser and the military. Bethmann, desperate and unwilling to work with such a majority, was forced to rely on nonparliamentary forces—the army, the aristocracy, the bureaucracy, and the court. Consequently he had to choose suppression of democracy at home and more aggression abroad. The cartel of fear was still alive.

Shocked at the electorate's leap toward "red revolution," proposals to restrict suffrage or organize a *putsch* circulated among government bureaucrats, pan-Germans, Agrarian Bundists, veterans' groups, and anti-

Semites. As Bertolt Brecht once said about the East German Communists: "The people is dissatisfied with the government; therefore the government must elect itself a new people." From now on the Conservative party referred to the 1912 Reichstag, the last until 1918, as the "Jewish Reichstag." It made no difference that only seven Jews by religion and eleven by "race" were elected. (Of three thousand delegates to the Reichstag from 1867 through 1916, only fifty-two were Jewish or of Jewish origin.) Labeling the Reichstag "Jewish" allowed the right to believe that their overwhelming repudiation was the consequence of Jewish manipulation and socialist treason, not the people's rejection of autocracy. Prussian conservatives would have to admit that they no longer represented the true Germany; this they never did.

Consequently 1912 marks the start of the most vicious of all anti-Semitic campaigns before 1919. The head of the Agrarian Bund, a Conservative party leader, announced to the Bund's general assembly that the "powerful, provocative, and destructive influence of Jewish money and the Jewish spirit" was so "manifest in campaign money and the press, that I believe in the future we will see the resurrection" of "an even more powerful anti-Semitism."[7] The anti-Semitic parties called for a dictator, angry because "the masses blindly go along with the stupidities of their Jewish or Jewified leaders."[8] The kaiser, shocked, could not believe the 1912 elections reflected the honest opinion of his loyal subjects; it must be the Jews. The crown prince, who later campaigned for Hitler, forwarded to the kaiser a proposal written by a retired general and pan-German. The elections, the general wrote, proved Germany was in mortal danger from the cynical materialism of the Jews. To protect itself from its racial enemy, no Jew could be allowed to be a German citizen, own land, or serve in the military or the government. Jews must pay special taxes and be limited to commerce and medicine. Jewish-owned newspapers should be forced to print the Star of David on their mastheads and should be banned from public political discussions. Ultimately Jews should be banished from Germany and forbidden to take their wealth with them, for they had amassed it by exploiting honest Germans. Baptism was irrelevant, race was all; only those with less than one-quarter Jewish blood should even be considered for citizenship. The kaiser agreed, though he did not think it wise to drive the Jews from Germany. It would harm the economy.

New anti-Semitic groups called for a dictator to punish the Jews. A Cartel of the Creative Classes was formed, a play on the alleged parasitical activities of Jewry. In 1912 an Alliance Against the Arrogance of Jewry attacked the "immeasurably damaging and horrifying" danger posed by the Jews: "The Reichstag elections of 1912 have taken place under the sign of German Jewry. . . ." Millions of "confused and naive Germans" had helped Jewry as it "works systematically and in mighty associations in every area of German life to push out or dominate the Germans and to make Jewish influence decisive . . . [in] politics and the economy" and "literature, art, theatre, science, the educational system, the practice of law, and not the least in the workers' and women's movements." Everywhere were the "machinations of Jewry" with "unlimited money." "As Richard Wagner has said: To be German is to do a thing for its own sake . . . to be Jewish is to make a business out of everything." Germans must have "the will to vanquish."[9]

After 1912 strikes increased and Theodor Fritsch cultivated connections with wealthy industrialists. Like Hitler, Fritsch believed power could be won if anti-Semitism was manipulated so as to unite upper-class and lower-class racists. In 1913 the Conservative party chose as its propaganda chief "Cudgel" Kuenze, so called because of his violent anti-Semitism. In 1912 Heinrich Class, president of the Pan-Germans, published a virulent anti-Semitic pamphlet, *If I Were Kaiser*—three editions sold out in the first year. (Class used a pseudonym; his views were not officially those of Pan-Germans until 1917.) Declaring the elections a "mass poisoning of German voters" and the "work of the Jews," and democracy a "swindle," Class added that Jewish "half-breeds" had "introduced Jewish spirit and attitudes—the natural consequences of Jewish blood—into the highest strata of our people."[10] He called for the rule of aristocrats and the kaiser, not the parties of the Jews. Jewish-owned newspapers, or those with Jews on their staffs, must be required to print the Star of David on their mastheads. Forbid Jews to vote, teach, hold public office, join the military, or participate in banking, journalism, theatre, or culture; require them to pay double taxes; forbid them to own land or hold mortgages. They polluted Germany with their filth. Expel those who were not citizens and make life so uncomfortable for the rest they would voluntarily leave. Let them follow the Zionists to Palestine or force them out.

Class called for an imperialist war against Russia; one can assume he would not have tolerated the presence of millions of Jews in a German empire in the east. As he wrote, there might be a few innocent Jews, but they must suffer because of the guilt of "their tribal comrades," otherwise "the entire German people [will] perish from their poison." Germans must overcome their natural human sympathy: *"Never before in history has a great, gifted, virtuous people come as quickly and defensively under the influence and the intellectual leadership of a totally alien race as have the Germans under the Jews."* They might have to be "wholly eliminated. . . ." "*It is a question of saving the soul of the German people.*"[11] This is the language of the death camps.

By 1914 significant numbers of upper- and lower-class conservatives welcomed the ideas we call Nazi ideology, and they did so even though

Germany had not suffered the traumas of a lost war, inflation, or depression. By the time of the Great War, German Jews, trapped in a struggle they were powerless to influence, were certain to be victims of the victory of any rightist movement gaining power. Although no legislation had yet been passed against them, they were more isolated and vulnerable than they had been since Napoleon blasted open the ghettos. Anti-Semitism was an explosion waiting to happen; the Nazis would be the beneficiaries, the Holocaust the consequence. By 1910 the man who would forge the anti-Semitic alliance between upper- and lower-class rightists had already absorbed the passionate racial hatreds dominating the Germans of the multiethnic Hapsburg Empire.

11: CATHOLIC ANTI-SEMITISM IN THE AUSTRIAN EMPIRE

The Jew should no longer be our master. Christ must once again become our master. That is the only moral and Catholic anti-Semitism.
— Baron Karl von Vogelsang, founder, Christian Social Party

RACIAL hatreds dominated politics in the Hapsburg Empire, where both Hitler and Adolf Eichmann spent their formative years. From 1882 through 1914 constant demonstrations and riots were mounted by ethnic groups fighting for power within the multinational Austrian state. Already in 1848 Catholic anti-Semitism flourished among Austro-Germans, ultimately led by Mayor Karl Lueger of Vienna, head of the Christian Social party and after Emperor Franz Josef the most important politician in the empire. With millions of voters, Lueger's party was the most powerful anti-Semitic movement in Europe before Hitler. In 1911, the last election before 1914, two-thirds of all Austro-Germans voted for anti-Semites. It is not surprising that Austro-German participation in the Holocaust was higher than that of Germans in general.

Enlightenment ideas had almost no effect in the Austrian Empire. Feudal and agrarian, eighteenth-century Austria offered no significant middle-class constituencies for the new ideas. Empress Maria Theresa was constrained from throwing the Jews out of Vienna, as her predecessor Ferdinand I had done, only because her advisers insisted it would cause economic disaster. Oddly enough, her son, Joseph II, was a model enlightened prince, the exception proving the rule. He tried to free the serfs, recruit civil servants by merit, suppress the monasteries, and seize church properties. Proclaiming freedom of worship, in 1782 his Edict of Toleration allowed Jews to become naturalized subjects, but he required them to live in special neighborhoods, stay out of some occupations, and send their children to secular schools. After his death in 1790, aristocrats and clergy easily reversed his reforms, and Austria joined Prussia to invade France to defeat the revolution. Beaten by Robespierre and Napoleon, in

1809 the new emperor called on Prince Klemens von Metternich to rule. A bitter enemy of a revolution whose forces had seized his estates, Metternich was the perfect diplomat. Cautious, cynical, without a shred of idealism, he maneuvered cautiously to hold together the ramshackle collection of ethnic groups as his emperor directed: "Rule and change nothing."

Friedrich Gentz, Metternich's aide, subsidized young Catholic intellectuals to publicize the counterrevolutionary ideology of the "Holy Alliance of Christian Europe"—of emperor and tsar. His publicists, like Metternich, denounced the Protestant Reformation as the source of an arrogant spirit of individualism which, after it once attacked the holy church, was bound to end in the profanities of the Enlightenment and the Terror of Robespierre. Courtiers eagerly read the work of the German romantic Novalis, who in *Christianity or Europe* (1799) glowingly praised the "splendid days" when Europe was one vast spiritual empire under the Vatican, before the cold uncertainties of secularism and science threatened man's redemption, making him an outcast in a Newtonian clockwork universe that mocked faith and offered no solace for his sufferings. Metternich's publicists reproached Europeans for deserting their medieval faith and sense of feudal duties, thus clearing the way for the corrosive spirit of Protestant individualism, middle-class liberalism, and "Jewish" materialism. To buttress the old regime, they gave public lectures to audiences of princes, aristocrats, and diplomats. Gentz set the theme: "Intelligence—that is the mortal sin of the Jews. . . ." The "heretical and diseased spirit of 1789" appealed to these "born representatives of atheism, Jacobinism, enlightenment; no Jew has yet seriously believed in God. . . . All the misfortune of the modern world, if it is traced to its furthest roots, comes manifestly from the Jews; they alone made Bonaparte Emperor."[1]

Yet demands for reform still plagued the empire, exploding in 1848 when thousands of Viennese students and professionals took to the streets to demand an end to aristocratic privilege and the powers of the church, and called for the liberties associated with 1789, including the liberation of the Jews. Unable to persuade the frightened emperor to crush them, Metternich fled as Czechs, Hungarians, and Italians also rose in revolt. The minority peoples not only wanted reform, they also demanded autonomy. The imperial family fled to Innsbruck, there to organize a counterrevolution among the pious and loyal peasants of the Tyrol. Imperial troops finally defeated the Czechs and Italians; the revolution in Hungary was drowned in blood, but only after a humiliated emperor was forced to appeal for help from the tsar. The end came with a brutal massacre of Viennese students by barbaric Croatian and Russian troops.

1848 was the first time Jews played a significant role in European pol-

itics as Jewish students joined the battle against despotism, and two were
among its leaders. The tiny Jewish community of Vienna supported the
revolution at first, though they withdrew when it became violent. Jewish
participation gave the Austrian Catholic leadership the explanation it preferred. Unwilling to admit that the vast majority of revolutionaries were
Catholics, like the ultraroyalists of France they insisted the revolutions
were caused by "arrogant, insolent Jews . . . impudent hatemongers and
agitators." Catholic publications castigated revolutionary anticlericalism
as a mix of "Jewish disbelief with poisonous hatred against Christian doctrine and Catholic practice. . . ."[2] The Hapsburg government fined the
Jewish community, holding it responsible for 1848, though only two hundred Jewish families were allowed to live in Vienna at the time.

More than any Western nation, Austria, "the favorite daughter of the
church," was dominated by Catholic anti-Semitism. As Arthur May has
written, "In Austrian clerical circles, antipathy toward the Jew was relentless, for he belonged to an alien, accursed folk, the denier of the
Christian savior, the veritable offspring of the devil."[3] In 1848 Father Sebastian Brunner published a popular brochure claiming that Jews still
practiced ritual murder and promoted "all that was evil and destructive
in modern society."[4] Brunner was no maverick but the chaplain of the
University of Vienna and founder of the *Vienna Church Times*, official
publication of the clergy. There and elsewhere he savagely attacked the
Jews, their liberation, and all reforms. Such abuse was more extreme in
Austria than among the Prussian clergy, for the Austrian church had far
more secular power and privileges at risk.

After victory, the imperial bureaucracy, army, aristocracy, and clergy
halted all reforms for two decades. An imperial constitution, granted in
1848 to pacify the revolution, was replaced by authoritarianism. Opponents of the regime were exiled, jailed, or executed; violence quelled the
minorities. In 1855 Emperor Franz Josef signed a concordat with Pope
Pius IX granting the church near medieval powers. Anti-Judaism was
prominent in a new church-dictated curriculum. In the famous saying,
"The empire was ruled by a standing army of soldiers, a sitting army of
bureaucrats, and a kneeling army of priests."

None of this ended decline. In 1859 the Italians and French defeated
the Hapsburg occupying forces and created the United Kingdom of Italy.
In 1867 came the final humiliation: Prussia routed Austria in a few weeks.
The former arbiter of Europe was now a second-rate power. Most ominous of all, the Germans of the empire did not share Franz Josef's hope
that the French would defeat the Prussians in 1870. He thought of the
balance of power, but they admired the prowess of their ethnic brothers
and took to the streets in wild jubilation at the Germanic victory over the
Latin foe. Austrian police were forced to ban demonstrations calling for

unity with the new united Germany—the debut of Anschluss (annexation). But economic power was needed if the empire was to survive, and this meant appeasing liberal Germans. They demanded the reforms Bismarck's Reichstag had passed, and the emperor reluctantly complied; Austrian Germans were the most advanced people of the empire, and he needed them. Defeat in war forced the Austrian reaction to grant those rights it had not yielded to revolution.

By 1870 the empire had a liberal constitution and a parliament in Vienna. As in Germany, the emperor's ministers were appointed by and responsible to him alone, and he could dissolve parliament at will. In a multinational empire with increasing ethnic unrest, it would have been fatal to grant universal suffrage. Instead, rigid ethnic quotas and high property qualifications assured the primacy of wealthy Germans, clerics, and aristocrats. Working with the German upper middle classes, the government reduced some guild monopolies, removed restrictions on capital, and granted civic equality to Jews and Slavs. Electoral limits and the shock of defeat brought victory to the German Liberal party in the parliamentary elections of 1867. Certain the future was theirs, they demanded separation of church and state. Appalled, Catholic leaders declared that Robespierre's Terror had come to sacred Austria; German liberals preferred to recall the memory of Joseph II. Pope Pius IX was outraged. Once a reformer, Pius became a bitter reactionary when revolutionaries drove him from Rome in 1848 and Italian liberals, bent on unifying Italy, held elections in the Papal States. Denouncing the elections as sacrilege, the pope returned to power with the aid of French troops.

Fighting back, Pius IX consolidated his own autocratic power. The modern veneration of the pope dates from him—"When the pope meditates, God thinks in him." Liberal Catholicism was declared heresy, and in his famous encyclical of 1864, The Syllabus of Errors, the pope condemned liberalism, science, and modernism. He made no attempt to persuade; absolute truth from a divine source need only be declared. Religious toleration, secular education, and the separation of church and state were condemned. Declaring himself the final authority in disputes with political leaders, he claimed his power over marriage, divorce, and censorship came from Christ himself and was not to be shared with civil authorities. Above, all, he insisted, the pope would never "reconcile himself to and agree with progress, liberalism, and contemporary civilization." In 1870 the dogma of papal infallibility in faith and morals was announced. Pius IX removed the old limits to papal power even as Europe became more liberal. Angry, but deferring to the emperor's extreme piety, liberals spread their legislation over some years. Even so it was a page out of 1789: civil marriage was legalized, education secularized, freethinking tolerated. To the horror of the clergy, Jews were granted equality before the law.

Catholic dignitaries withdrew from this "Chamber of Infidels." Pius IX declared the legislation "unholy, destructive, abominable, and damnable . . . and null and void."[5] To obey these laws, Austrian bishops declared, was to insult God, but crowds of jubilant Germans roamed the streets of Vienna and the liberal press was ecstatic. Among rural folk, however, fury raged at the victory of "Jewish liberalism," and the local Catholic press constantly reviled the Jews. Representing the peasants of the isolated mountain villages of German Austria, a priest wrote, "Never again shall we entrust the protection of our liberties to a parliament sitting under the guns of the Jewish press. . . ."[6] Artisans and peasants denounced the un-fettered power of "immoral and anti-Christian Jewish" capital. As in Germany in 1873, Austria suffered an economic crash when liberal re-forms released capital from traditional restraints, bringing a wave of spec-ulation, reckless investment, and fraud. Hundreds of new joint-stock companies were formed, railroads were financed, new banks founded. The shares of firms sometimes rose to ridiculous heights. Small investors reveled in their paper profits but soon banks, companies, and ventures failed, and thousands were ruined. Capitalism had arrived. Parliamentary investigations revealed that liberal politicians had enriched themselves in shady deals, and the (very few) Jews who were deputies were instantly suspect, as was the liberal press. Jews were overwhelmingly predominant among newspaper owners and editors, and some had participated in fi-nancial scandals even as their papers offered glowing reports of the wealth to be made by speculation. Many Jewish investors were also ruined, and Christians were heavily involved in frauds, but there was no chance the economic crisis would fail to be seen as the work of "the Jews." The Jew-ish community could do nothing to avoid blame. The Austrian Roth-schilds had avoided wild speculation and suspect dealings but were condemned because they emerged intact at the end of the storm. Some-how, rumor had it, they must have profited from secret knowledge. And the liberalism of the German-Jewish electorate was seen as proof of its complicity in fraud.

In the 1870s Albert Wiesinger, Father Brunner's replacement as editor of the *Vienna Church Times*, gathered a group of Catholic intellectuals and, using medieval sources and German racist literature, published pam-phlets holding "the Jews" responsible for the crisis of unregulated capi-talism, ignoring the heavy Christian involvement. Catholic faith became the bulwark for a racist ideological offensive against liberalism and its mar-ket system. Catholicism offered, as Lutheranism did not, a social counter-vision, one that eventually became the intellectual foundation for the amazingly popular Christian Social party of Lueger. Baron Karl von Vogelsang became the intellectual founder of Lueger's party.

In a personal search for the ritual and mystical grandeur of the medieval church, Vogelsang, a Prussian and Lutheran, converted to Catholicism in romantic reaction against the wintry harshness of north German Protestantism. He left for Vienna, the home of Catholic piety, the baroque symbols of transcending faith, and the most traditionalist social system in Europe. There Vogelsang became tutor and friend to the daughter of Prince Metternich and Prince Alois Liechtenstein, a member of the second highest-ranking family of Austria. In 1875 Vogelsang was named editor-in-chief of the prestigious daily paper *Das Vaterland*, the official voice of the Catholic hierarchy. The masthead read, "Our Battle Is Against the Spirit of 1789." Here Vogelsang and his Catholic intellectuals propagated a now-forgotten ideology of Catholic social reform, using idealized notions of medieval times to criticize and, they hoped, correct the errors of modern society. To them, commercial and urban society was institutionalized sin, created by atheistic philosophes and materialistic Jews blinded by ambition and the desire for profit. Together they had destroyed the hallowed Christian limits to greed with fictions about the alleged natural laws of economics. Spiritually empty, prizing economic growth above all, they had sacrificed social stability, traditional values, and communal responsibility to ruthless competition, elevating aggrandizement to high principle. 1789 did not bring freedom, Vogelsang wrote, for "Freedom is the right to conform to the moral order."

When German romantics traveled south, they also traveled back in time: the Hapsburg Empire was still a peasant and artisan society. As late as 1890 more than 80 percent of all employed were peasants, farm laborers, artisans, or foresters. Their numbers made Christian anti-Semitism more popular than in Germany. In rural areas, Christian attitudes were medieval, the old myths still alive, and the local priest was the sole source of ideas. Like Islamic fundamentalists today, Catholic thinkers believed it heresy to separate religious precepts from state law. Vogelsang also took up the usual rural complaints against Jewish moneylenders, land speculators, and middlemen. Close to God and nature, the peasant was the most vital part of a Christian order. Peasant instincts were rooted in faith and the past, Vogelsang argued, and the peasants were aware, as city dwellers were not, of the limits nature and God placed on man's endless desires. If the urban mentality penetrated the countryside and industrialism drew peasants from the land, faith would be replaced by greed and the Jewish belief that land was simply an object for exploitation and profit. Vogelsang's illusions were typical of his fellow intellectuals; peasant life is not ideal to those who live it. (Nazi leaders would be frustrated when, despite all their efforts, rural folk flocked to the cities.) But Vogelsang wanted to believe that morality was Christian and rested on the village community, and that its disappearance would destroy values created over generations of closely knit personal relationships between village elders, peasants, rustic artisans, and parish priests. The new "Jewish" economy would create a nation of alienated urban masses, denizens of vast cities bereft of the piety of those who daily lived between nature and God. He and Stoecker agreed that as piety and priestly authority swiftly waned among urban workers, atheistic socialism was the inevitable result.

Vogelsang's Vienna was not simply the city of aristocrats, Strauss, coffeehouses, and the opera, as we imagine it. It was a city of artisans and small businessmen, a far higher proportion of the population than in any other major European city. Like those who hated the "dark satanic mills," Vogelsang idealized skilled craftsmen and decried the replacement of their ancient skills by technology and the loss to free enterprise of guild control over prices, wages, and quality. Citing Thomas Aquinas, he demanded a fair price and a just wage, not the miserable wages set by a market economy. He praised the life of the apprentice who worked and lived with the master's family, contrasting it to the miserable fate of anonymous wage slaves in vast factories. His ideology and ignorance of guild realities, however, blinded him to the exploitation of journeymen, apprentices, and consumers by the masters, Christians all. Should the factory prevail, he feared, Austria would be overwhelmed by millions of propertyless, ill-paid, desperate workers, bereft of the fruits of their labor, paid only what was needed to drag them day after miserable day to the factory gate, haunted by the specter of being thrust into the great army of the unemployed. Spiritually empty, dwelling in anonymous urban conglomerations, family and moral life destroyed, the proletariat would be seduced by the atheistic agitators of the radical left. Workers would become the victims, in Vogelsang's words, of "Gin and the Jewish press, that is to say, drunken stupor and obscenities [which] kill the remaining memories of a Christian past in these unfortunate victims."⁷ There was already a violent anarchist movement, led mainly by Jews, he noted. In the future it might destroy everyone.

Believing, as does the Christian right, that sin and heresy is the ultimate explanation for social ills, Vogelsang projected an apocalyptic vision. The atheist Robespierre had liberated greed with the same logic he had liberated the enemies of Christ—usurers, speculators, and parasites "always and everywhere on the side of ecclesiastical and political revolution."⁸ The crash of 1873 resulted from the seduction of spiritually weak Austrians by the temptations of an immoral orgy of profit-seeking speculation. Jewish stockbrokers and commodity speculators gained huge profits from products and crops produced by others; ungodly Jewish liberals and politicians profited from the resulting misery. Even the slogans of commercial society betrayed them: "Let the buyer beware!" Commerce corrupted as it spread beyond village and town into an international network of "Jewish financiers" who, with loyalty to no nation, sought only profitable deals, bringing ruin to millions of peasants and artisans by importing cheap food and goods from exploited foreign workers. Bankers like the Rothschilds seized a monopoly of liquid capital, the product of nature's gifts and human labor; at great profit they sold it back to the people with their usurious loans. Catholic Austria, the last bastion of the faith, had reached a point where those who had hated Christians for centuries now dictated where money would be invested, and therefore which social needs would be met or ignored.

> The Christian social order is being dissolved by Jewry. Workers and craftsmen drift into the factories, landed property into the hands, houses into the possession, and the wealth of the people into the pockets of the Jews. Through their electoral laws they dominate elections, politics, parliament, legislation and the ministries; a few years more of such "progress" and Vienna will be called New Jerusalem and old Austria—Palestine.[9]

Vogelsang's vision recalls the Crusades. His fantasies, incomprehensible to us, were more believable if no less false in the Vienna of 1880. There the contrast between Christian and Jew was far stronger than in Berlin or Paris, where Jews reminiscent of the ghetto past were relatively absent. The Jews who arrived daily in Vienna from the eastern empire seemed medieval, however, and there were far more of them. From 1860 to 1880 the Jewish population of Vienna rose from 2 to 10 percent. The majority were impoverished Galicians, Orthodox, Yiddish-speaking, in ritual, dress, and comportment like the Jews of Christian myth, mysterious and repelling to Christians and even to some secular Jews. Hitler wrote that in Vienna he first saw the Jews as they really were, stripped of the veneer of Christian civilization. His was a reaction common to the thousands of bumpkins from the German provinces who poured into Vienna around 1900. And many Viennese Jews, following ghetto vocations, competed with unskilled Christians for scarce jobs. Impoverished and driven by the need to succeed, the migrants were heavily involved in the house-to-house peddling of secondhand goods, assuring the hatred of the guilds.

Like German racists, however, Vogelsang most feared assimilated Jews, not the Orthodox, for only the secular, successful Jew served as a surrogate for the forces transforming the empire: "The weapons which Jewry uses to reach its sole object, domination of the Christian world, are its money, its commerce, and its newspapers." With these "Jewry has in its power almost all princes, all governments and all peoples." All laws standing in the way of its "speculative and usurious tendencies" had to "be repealed, [and] all barriers protecting Christianity torn down; the craft guilds dissolved, freedom of enterprise introduced, the partition of landed estates legally permitted; the usury laws declared null and void."[10]

Because of their small numbers, the power of the Jews had to be fantastically magnified and labeled almost occult by those seeking religious explanations for dramatic social change. Facing the undeniable fact of overwhelming Christian participation in the new economy, Vogelsang used the metaphor that begged the question, bolstered racist paranoia, and called for expulsion or worse: Christians "have been infected with the Jewish spirit."[11] He and other Catholic intellectuals needed conspiracy theories that joined Jews, Freemasons, and atheist revolutionaries in secret machinations against non-Jews and the old ways. Secular explanations would not do. As Bishop Keppler, famed for his Catholic social views and Christian charity—and an avid admirer of Langbehn—put it: "[The Jews] are a thorn in the flesh of Christian peoples, suck their blood, enslave them with chains of gold and with the tin sceptre of poisoned pens, and contaminate the public fountains of culture and morality."[12] Tragically, Vogelsang and his fellow Catholic ideologists transformed an otherwise legitimate ideological conflict into a deadly racial attack. Like the German nationalists, they brought ideas that have nothing to do with race and ethnicity into the twentieth century carrying a powerful potential for ethnic conflict and racial violence.

Vogelsang's ideas were translated into politics by Karl Lueger, head of the Christian Social party, by 1895 the most powerful anti-Semitic party in Europe. Born in Vienna in 1844 to a building superintendent and a pious artisan's daughter, Lueger graduated from law school in 1870 and found clients among the small businessmen and artisans of Vienna. A Catholic activist, he joined the Liberal party, then the only choice for a German. He resented the "plutocrats" and anticlericals of its leadership, and in the beer gardens he mingled easily with ordinary Viennese, denouncing wealthy liberals and corrupt municipal officials, and praising the sacrifices of the little man. The vote still heavily favored the wealthy, and in 1876 Lueger lost his campaign for the city council. But in 1878 financial scandals forced the mayor and leader of the Liberals to resign, and Lueger was elected to the council. Younger radical members formed a populist faction within the Liberal party, and Lueger joined immediately. The populists were led by the Jewish Dr. Ignaz Mandl. Many younger Jews supported reform, giving the lie to charges that "the Jews" were a united force of plutocrats. Mandl and Lueger, then allies, agitated for universal suffrage to help their populist and reformist cause.

Lueger's activities revealed to him the intense anti-Semitism of artisans and small businessmen, far more virulent than in Berlin even during the glory days of Stoecker. Lueger also met his future rival for the leadership of anti-Semitism, Georg Ritter von Schoenerer, who also hoped to overthrow the Liberal leadership. Schoenerer held no brief for either Catholicism or the empire. Leader of the Austrian pan-German movement, a racist pure and simple, supporter of *Anschluss* and an enemy to the death of both Slavs and Jews, he would become Hitler's ideological model. Schoenerer, educated in Prussia, admired the Hohenzollerns and held a typical Prussian contempt for the casual Austro-Germans. Trained in agriculture, he became estate manager for Prince Schwarzenberg in a rural district of Austria close to the Hungarian and Czech borders. The peasants shared Schoenerer's hatred for Slavs and Jews, and he organized them against Jewish moneylenders and middlemen. He urged the peasants to buy beer and thus boycott a Jew who had bought the right to collect the wine tax. The successful campaign won him a seat in parliament in 1873. A Christian bought the right to collect the tax; it remained as high as before.

In Vienna, Schoenerer made contact with the artisan movement. In 1880 thousands of Viennese artisans and small businessmen organized to fight "Jewish liberal plutocrats" who, they claimed, sacrificed their rights at the behest of Jewish speculators. The artisans also denounced Jewish migrants from the east who competed with them, working harder for less money. The Society for the Protection of Artisans held its first meeting in 1882, demanding laws against the immigration of Jews and house-to-house peddling. "Who are these peddlers? Polish Jews, Hungarian Jews, Russian Jews—fugitives from a justly angered nation; look at these people and tell me if they have ever learned an honest trade or have done any honest manual labor?"[13] Schoenerer harangued the artisans in words so inflammatory they could not be published. His associate, Robert Pattai, held free enterprise responsible for the "dumbfounding rise to prosperity of the Jews" who had reached "almost hegemony in the economic sphere." If reform failed, "discriminatory laws . . . demanded from so many sides, will become necessary."[14] The artisan Franz Holubek went further: "The Jews are no longer our fellow citizens" but "our masters, oppressors, and tormentors." In their own capital city, "Christians are weakened, annihilated, defamed. . . . Judge if such a people has a right to existence in civilized society."[15]

As in Germany, petitions, boycotts, and demonstrations occurred under the slogan, "Do not buy from Jews." In Dresden in 1882, Austrian pan-Germans and artisans met with Stoecker and other European anti-Semites in the first meeting of an International Anti-Semitic League. calling upon all Gentiles to unite to stop the Jewish drive for world domination. Racist leaflets were distributed in Jewish districts and in the lobby of the Royal Opera House, symbol of Viennese culture and its sophisticated, largely German or German Jewish public. In 1881 Tsar Alexander II was assassinated, and a wave of government-supported pogroms spread devastation. The new tsar declared Jews enemies of the people and passed further anti-Semitic legislation. In Vienna and Berlin petitions circulated calling for similar laws and demanding that fleeing Russian Jews be forbidden to enter German territory. In 1882 in Hungary a priest accused Hasidic Jews of murdering a Gentile girl on the sabbath before Passover in order to use her blood for religious rites. A trial ensued, the defendants were acquitted, rioters rampaged. When liberals denounced the riots, Father Sebastian Brunner replied, "We are but defending ourselves against the shameless, destructive, and unbearable volk-destroying activities of Jewish domination."[16]

In 1883 the second annual Congress of Artisans and Small Businessmen drew some three thousand Austro-Germans. By then "virtually the whole handicraft-worker class had been converted to the idea that anti-Semitism was the answer to all its problems."[17] Proposals were made: Jews must pay extra taxes, be kept out of trades, and forbidden to hire Christian servants, marry, or reside without special permission. Some wanted them back in the ghettos or driven out of Austria. One, Franz Schneider, wanted them drowned. A guild reform law was passed in 1883, but it offered little. To restore full guild powers would have kept the empire weak and consumer costs high, and ended the promise of new technologies and the railway system.

The rising popularity of anti-Semitism left only suffrage limits to protect the Liberals, for only about 3 percent of the people were wealthy enough to qualify for the vote—upper bourgeoisie, aristocrats, and part of the Jewish community. In 1879 and 1882 qualifications were lowered, doubling the votes of the Viennese. It was apparent that soon many candidates would lose to racists. In Berlin, democracy brought the victory of liberalism and reformist socialism; in underdeveloped Austria it threatened reaction and racism. Even so, the majority of the Liberal party remained true to its principles, condemning anti-Semitism in 1886 though its leaders knew this would cost votes. The party also asked Franz Josef to protest the tsar's pogroms, but he would not. The request was used as further proof that the Liberals were Jewish tools. In the party, Schoenerer formed a group to overthrow the leaders, and delegates organized caucuses excluding Germans of Jewish origin. Eclipsed by Schoenerer, Lueger needed racist credentials. His chance came with the famous Nordbahn affair.

In 1836 the government had granted a concession to Solomon Rothschild to raise the vast amounts of capital needed to build railroads vital to the empire. As a reward for amassing the money, much from Jewish sources, and for other services, the five Rothschild brothers had been given the title of barons. Over a million kilometers of track were built; after heavy losses, the railroad, called the Nordbahn, proved highly profitable. The government began negotiating terms for renewing the concession in 1884. A storm of protest ensued. Shipping costs and shareholders' profits were too high, it was claimed; railroad profits should be used to cut the rates for food shipped to Vienna. Others believed the good faith and credit of the imperial government would be at risk if the concession terms were violated, and Austria needed much foreign investment. Like all social issues entangled in racial antagonisms, the dispute could have been resolved by negotiated agreement; it was a straightforward conflict between populists and liberals, not Germans and Jews. Indeed, many Jewish deputies wanted rates cut. But a Rothschild enterprise could do nothing to please anti-Semites. To argue for the concession was to subject oneself to virulent racist attacks. After all, "everyone knew" international finance was Jewish, and the lucrative concession was but another example of their enormous power over the dynasty at the expense of ordinary citizens. Vienna's citizens were now the easiest in Europe to persuade that mundane economic conflicts were actually battles in a racial war.

Schoenerer led the outcry. As parliamentary deliberations dragged on in 1885, mass demonstrations in front of the Vienna town hall protested the railroad monopoly, and Schoenerer, rounding up petitions in record numbers, declared the issue simply "The Jews versus the people." The liberal press called him a socialist for attacking shareholders' profits. Infuriated, he replied that "the Jewish and Judaized press, bribed like whores, were the lying representatives of international and Jewish capital."[18] Freedom of the press was a Jewish invention, he added, parliament a tool of the Nordbahn Jews. In fact, majority opinion in parliament wanted lowered shipping costs at shareholder expense, but this was not enough for Schoenerer's people. During the debates the public galleries rang with "Down with parliament, down with Nordbahn Jews, Heil Schoenerer."[19]

Pan-Germans and artisans castigated the "conspiracy" of Jews and Hungarian cattle and grain barons to raise food prices. Schoenerer declared that in Hungary, freedom meant the right to murder Christians, a non sequitur referring to the current ritual murder trial. Thousands of petitions attacked parliament and the "Jewish-bribed" press. Cartoons depicted Rothschild as a vampire consuming the lifeblood of the Viennese. Germans were urged by pan-Germans to join the Hohenzollerns, for unlike Franz Josef they were not dominated by the Jews. In 1885 the prime minister, supported by Liberals, compromised, and shareholders surrendered some profits. Although he was not obliged to, Solomon Rothschild signed the agreements, with quiet dignity voluntarily sacrificing his financial rights for the good of the dynasty. At great personal profit, he could have legally forced the government to purchase the railroad. Franz Josef let his gratitude be known, but by the mid-1880s anti-Semitism had reached a high point.

Schoenerer now became the idol of German shopkeepers, artisans, and clerks, his photo displayed in countless shops, his paper available for reading in nearly every pub. A brisk business was done in watch chains with images of hanged Jews, and in pipes, beer steins, cigarette holders, and other objets d'art with stereotyped caricatures of Jews. Sixty thousand anti-Semitic posters were displayed in the city, and an anti-Semitic reading room was opened.[20] In Vienna, Jews and Jewish shops were attacked. Defaming an ethnic group was against imperial law, but juries acquitted the accused, and mobs lionized them. In 1885 Schoenerer formed the German Nationalists, adopting the usual program: Jewish financiers must be curbed, interest rates restricted, and subsidies offered to the peasantry, the "lifeblood of the Germanic race." Jewish participation in the economy must be restricted; they must not be teachers, and no Russian or east Austrian Jews must be allowed into the western empire. In 1887 the tribune of the people declared in parliament that the Jewish race was more "arrogant, hardhearted, vicious, and exploitative" than ever before—"There is no place we do not see them in battle with the established order; everywhere they are in league with the forces of revolution." Even rich Jews supported revolution; for them race, not class, was the first priority. An Asiatic race, they hated all that was German. "Every loyal son of his nation must see in anti-Semitism the greatest national progress of this century."[21]

Until the escalation of anti-Semitism in the 1880s, many German Jews in the Austrian Liberal party had hoped to extend the vote, protect ordinary citizens from economic burdens, and wrest control of the party from the wealthy. Their colleagues now drove them out, along with some Gentiles unwilling to adopt racism. As one such prominent German reformer remarked, "Anti-Semitism is the socialism of fools." Now Jewish reformers had even less choice than German Jews, for only the Austrian socialists wanted them. Lueger could not support pan-Germans, disloyal to empire and church, but he harangued demonstrations against "Nordbahn Jews" and purged Jewish allies, viciously denouncing his former friend Mandl.

To outbid Schoenerer, Lueger moved closer to Vogelsang's people. Vogelsang, along with priests and Catholic laymen, now founded the Christian Social party. Among them were two future cardinals, the editor of the first Austrian anti-Semitic paper and its patrons, the Archduchess Maria Theresa, and the Countess de Chambord of the French royal family. French royalists and international anti-Semites had long been allies, remaining so down to 1945. Endorsed by ecclesiastical authorities, the founding meeting of the party was held in a church in 1890. The party program was depressingly familiar: Jews must not teach or serve in the army or the civil service, and there should be quotas in law and medicine. Jewish participation in some retail trades must end, society must be "de-Jewified," and the activities of all those "infected" by "Jewish liberalism" must be curbed. Artisans and peasants must be protected and Jews kept out of the empire; those already there were to be treated as aliens with special legal and tax burdens.

The Christian Socials needed a leader. Vogelsang, no politician, was ill; Lueger, popular defender of church and empire, gave further proof of his anti-Semitism. Supporting a bill to keep pogrom victims out of the empire, he declared they deserved their sufferings. Jews ought to be curbed in Austria as well. When liberals objected, Lueger said they were contaminated by Jewish gold. He also supported a bill forbidding Jews to change their names, because they did this only to exploit under a cloak of anonymity. "Whenever a state has allowed the Jews to become powerful," Lueger said, "that state has soon collapsed. . . ."[22] Invited by the Christian Socials to honor a leading Hungarian dignitary in 1887, and impressed by the jubilant response of the audience to the Hungarian's claim that the Jews had destroyed the public morals of Hungary, Lueger declared that in the struggle against corruption, "we come up against the Jews at every step. . . ." People must be protected "against the harmful domination" of this small group. Lueger accused the Jews of trying to expropriate the property of impoverished priests in order to enrich themselves. He was now much in demand at religious meetings and led a popular Anti-Semitic Citizens Club, his support eagerly sought by racists running for election. Vogelsang introduced him to aristocrats, higher clergy, and academics, and Lueger gave a toast to "the final victory of Christianity over its enemies" at a dinner in honor of Pope Leo XIII. Shortly afterward Vogelsang announced, "Lueger must be our leader!"[23]

In 1891 Prince Alois Liechtenstein presented the Christian Social platform to parliament. Commencing with the famous slogan of Otto Glagau, "The social question is the Jewish question," he added, "Where the laws of liberalism are established, there the Jews unite themselves for exploitation." Along with the party program he called for the restoration of guild rights, the enforcement of fair prices and just wages, and Christian banks, seemingly unaware they differed not a whit from Jewish-owned banks in their financial activities and interest rates. Above all, the prince wanted the "sacred" land of peasants protected from Jewish speculation: "Where evil social conditions lead to the overwhelming profit of the Jewish people, then we must take powerful measures to protect ourselves." The Jews "cannot take credit for the least contribution to the Fa-

therland"; they were simply "specialists at the accumulation of the property of their neighbors."²⁴ The prince would no doubt have been mortally
offended to be told that few Austrians were as parasitic as one who inherited huge estates and a life of extravagant ceremonial idleness, paid
for by the labor of his peasants.

Austrian scholars glide over the racism of the most popular politician
Vienna ever produced, claiming Lueger was an opportunist, not "really"
an anti-Semite. One cannot know the inner beliefs of a politician, of
course, but it is irrelevant. When one supports racism, the damage is
done. Lueger even defended ritual murder charges in the Vienna parliament. In 1871 August Rohling, a priest and professor of Hebrew literature
at the University of Prague, published *The Talmud Jew*, a compendium
of medieval Christian assertions that the sacred texts of Judaism commanded Jews to cheat, rob, and murder Christians. Rohling's book, extremely popular in pious Austria, was distributed by Christian religious
societies. Schoenerer's followers echoed his charges. From 1870 through
1914 the empire witnessed some twelve ritual murder trials. When the defendants were acquitted, thousands, including Lueger and Schoenerer,
charged prosecutors and judges with accepting Jewish gold. At the artisans' meeting of 1882, Franz Holubek shouted in anger, "Their Talmud
describes you as a herd of pigs, dogs, and asses."²⁵ Holubek, tried for in-
citing religious antagonisms, was defended by Schoenerer's second in
command, and acquitted when Rohling's book was used as evidence for
the defense.

Canon Rohling testified at a ritual murder trial that Jewish texts required Jews to use Christian blood for their rituals. Rabbi Samuel Bloch
accused Rohling of linguistic ignorance and perjury; Bloch's charges were
true, and Rohling backed down. Liberals supported Bloch; the turmoil
was the talk of Vienna. In a famous speech to parliament in 1890, Lueger
insisted Rabbi Bloch's demonstration that the laws of Moses did not call
for ritual murder was irrelevant, for were not the Jews of the Old Testament famed for disobeying those laws, as their own prophets related?
What could not be doubted, Lueger added, was "the unbelievable, fanatical hate and the never-ending desire for revenge which consumes the
Jews when they persecute their presumed or actual enemies."²⁶ The official spokesman of a party sanctioned by the church, Lueger could not
adopt the racism of a Schoenerer. He resolved the difficulty by declaring
that Jews could not become Germans through baptism alone, for centuries of cultural conditioning were also needed.

In parliament Lueger asked whether it was the fault of Christians that
one found mainly Jews on the stock exchange? And if Christian aristocrats also manipulated the stock exchange, they should be held in even
more contempt "as they sin against their own people" while the Jew de-

stroyed Christians to "defend his folk, his faith, and his race." Was it the fault of Christians and artisans that the grain trade, the factories, the export trade, and peddling were "exclusively in the hands of the Jews?" It was said that Jews succeeded because of superior skills, but in truth it was "their lack of business ethics" that gave advantage. "Taking it all together, these activities must and have created anti-Semitism."[27] When Christianity dominated Europe, Lueger informed the deputies, nails were pounded into the ears of grain speculators; now the state protected the Jewish commodity broker and even prosecuted honest men who exposed Jewish corruption.

The Austrian elites were far less willing than their Prussian counterparts to use anti-Semitism as a political weapon. They could hardly pride themselves on their warrior ethic, given the defeats of the empire, and in any event Jews were strongly represented in the Austrian army. Schoenerer threatened empire and church, and Lueger's populism, like that of Boeckel's, was also suspect. But with far more support than Boeckel, Lueger could afford to offend those aristocrats who defended the imperial government and acted, in his words, as "servants of this Jewish-liberal state" by refusing to free Christians from the "shameful chains of Jewish serfdom." They should help ensure that the "old Christian Austrian Empire is not destroyed and replaced by a new Palestine."[28] Lueger warned that the Jews had been responsible for the Paris Commune of 1870 (by now a firm rightist myth, though in fact Jewish participation was nil), and he reminded the hierarchy that the communards had shot clerical hostages, including an archbishop. See to it, he called out, that if there were another revolution it would be Jews and not archbishops who were shot. "It is not the Jews that have been martyred by the Germans, but the Germans who have been martyred by the Jews." If exposing this made one an anti-Semite, "then I am an anti-Semite."[29] Though constantly employing the image of the wealthy Jew, Lueger knew Vienna had multitudes of poor Jews, and that the vast majority of Austrian Jews lived in misery in Bukovina and Galicia. Thousands of them starved to death each year.

In 1890 Lueger led the United Christian Anti-Semites—Christian Socials and German Nationalists—to victory in close to one-third of the seats of the Vienna city council. In the imperial parliament at Vienna they took over one-third of the German vote as well. The Liberals, though still ahead, lost one-fourth of their seats. With the approval of Franz Josef, the prime minister and several bishops asked Pope Leo XIII for a pastoral letter reprimanding Lueger and his priests for using anti-Semitism. The pope refused. He admired Lueger's social views and would not hinder the party's revitalization of Catholic political influence at a time when the church faced defeat throughout Europe. Franz Josef, personally wounded, was insulted when the Christian Social party published the pope's personal blessing of Lueger and noted that Lueger's portrait stood on the pope's desk. The Catholic establishment rallied to Lueger's cause, led by the papal nuncio and the Metternich family. The young priest who would become Cardinal of Vienna in 1913 and live to welcome Hitler's armies in 1938 was a Lueger supporter as well. Meanwhile, a new and even more dangerous wave of racist anti-Semitism swept the Germans of the Hapsburg Empire as the conflict between Germans and Slavs intensified.

12: RACIAL NATIONALISM IN AUSTRIA

In Vienna you find a Bohemian theatre, an Italian opera, French and Hungarian singers, Polish clubs; in the bus nobody speaks German, in some cafés there are Hungarian, Czech, Polish, Italian journals and not a single German newspaper. You may be a German of pure breed, but your wife will be a Galician or Pole, your cook a Bohemian, your nurse a Bosnian, your valet a Serb, your coachman a Slovene, your barber a Magyar, your banker a Jew, and your tutor a Frenchman. No, Vienna is not a German town.

—Anonymous, 1878

BY 1900 Catholic anti-Semitism and secular racism had made the Austro-Germans the most anti-Semitic people in Western Europe. Schoenerer had hundreds of thousands of admirers; millions voted for Lueger's Christian Social party. Near-revolutionary conflicts between Germans and Slavs broke out, accompanied by virulent anger against "Jewish" liberalism and socialism by Germans who believed both were pro-Slav. As a popular saying went, "The Hapsburgs betray German blood for Slavic votes and Jewish wealth." By 1911 two-thirds of Austro-Germans were voting for anti-Semites. In 1938 Hitler's troops were greeted by Austrians with wild enthusiasm while mobs spontaneously attacked Jews. The percentage of Austrians who joined the Nazis was twice that of the Germans. Only 8 percent of the population of the Third Reich, Austrians formed 14 percent of the SS, 40 percent of the staff of the death camps, and 70 percent of Eichmann's staff.

Industrial might and nationalism—the ability to tap the loyalty of an ethnically united people—created the power of European nations. But industrialism and nationalism only weakened the Hapsburg Empire by escalating conflicts between Slavs and Germans. Excluding Hungary, one-third of the population of the empire was German, many of them sharing territories with Czechs, Poles, Ruthenians, Slovenes, Serbs, Croats, Bosnians, or Italians. Germans dominated the economy, the bu-

173

reaucracy, and the army; only the Slavic aristocracy and the higher clergy shared power. But new railroads, industrial jobs, and markets made Slavic peasants aware of entrepreneurial opportunities while literacy and education made them conscious of their unique culture and traditions, assiduously cultivated by intellectuals and politicians. Moving from village to city, trading kinship and local loyalties for ethnic identity, former peasants became painfully aware of German domination of the jobs and professions they hoped for. Ethnic chauvinism and demands for autonomy were inevitable.

The Hapsburg Empire was not created by war. In the famous saying, "Let others make war, thou, happy Austria, marry." The elites, neither militaristic nor nationalistic, did not embrace the militant racism of the Hohenzollern kaiser and his court. Franz Josef and his ministers had to walk a tightrope stretched taut by ethnic tensions. Ethnic minorities had to be pacified by concessions if the empire were to be sustained. Yet each concession—affirmative action on a grand scale—raised demands among more and embittered Germans whose careers, power, and status were put at risk by "inferior" Slavs. The Jews were the most threatened, for ethnic chauvinists regarded them as aliens. Unlike other peoples, the Jews had no territory of their own. Their only hope was less ethnic conflict in a liberal empire. Thus Jewish liberals supported concessions to the Slavic minorities, earning the emperor's gratitude but intensifying anti-Semitism.

Defeat in war in 1870 revealed Austrian vulnerability. Prussian agents had encouraged nationalistic movements before the war in order to weaken the empire; pan-Slav Russians, happy to break German power, were always at work. Hungarians, inflamed by proud memories of bloody battles for independence, gained control of their own internal affairs in 1867. To pacify other nationalities, the emperor granted each province its own assembly, seventeen in all, and a measure of autonomy, concessions to gain support for future wars. In a first rush of enthusiasm, the German Liberal party supported constitutional provisions granting the "inalienable right" to equality of each nationality. The imperial bureaucracy was required to use the majority language of the local population, and each could receive education in its own language. But the provisions were never carried out, for the Germans soon realized the threat to their power. Suffrage limits alone kept the propertied German minority dominant in provinces with German communities. Liberals had too easily assumed that subject nationalities would prefer German culture and language and that high property qualifications would continue to favor them. But by 1870 democracy seemed a mortal threat.

Urban, educated, ambitious Slavs, without the fatalism of their peasant ancestors, demanded linguistic rights and equal access to imperial posts. Because Bohemia, the province of Czechs and Germans, was the most industrialized area of the empire, the Czechs were the first to feel nationalistic impulses. Educated Czechs had formed an independent Slav Congress in 1848, but they were brutally crushed by imperial forces. Ominously, German liberals in both Reichs applauded the victory. The unity and independence they wanted for themselves they would not grant to others. Spurred on by the defeat of the empire and concessions to Hungarians, Czech nationalist movements proliferated. Responding, the large German minority in Bohemia was the first to forsake liberalism and embrace racism.

The propertied, professional classes of Bohemia were largely German but were outnumbered and fearful when "inferior" Czechs, a generation removed from peasantry, challenged their right to rule. At the first Bohemian Assembly in 1871, composed of Czechs and Germans, Czech economic progress had given them enough votes to gain the majority. Franz Josef infuriated Germans by asking the Czech leaders what concessions they wanted, and the Czechs, hardly believing their good fortune, immediately demanded a guaranteed permanent majority in the Bohemian Diet, the right to participate in military decisions, foreign affairs, and finance, and control of all local public matters. Adding insult to injury, they delightedly informed German deputies that of course they would guarantee German educational and linguistic rights.

The Germans stalked out of the assembly, their anger echoed by pan-Germans, nationalist leagues in Germany, and many Viennese liberals. Bismarck's government also denounced demands for Slavic equality. To make matters worse, an anti-German rebellion broke out among south Slavs. Franz Josef withdrew his offer to the Czechs. Infuriated, a radical group of "Young Czechs" demanded a Czech republic, hinted at armed struggle, and suggested they might appeal to France or even to pan-Slav Russians, bitter enemy of Austrian ambitions. Passive resistance to German rule followed, and Bohemia had to be governed by martial law. In 1873 the Czechs walked out of the parliament at Vienna. Schoenerer demanded that force be used: "One hears talk of equality between Germans and Slavs. It is as if one compared a lion to a louse because both are animals."[1] Even the famous Czech historian Francis Palacky, once a Hapsburg supporter, predicted revolution, adding prophetically: "We Slavs existed before Austria; we shall continue to exist after Austria disappears."[2] The ethnic conflict that would destroy Austro-German liberalism and the empire itself had commenced.

In 1879 Franz Josef dismissed the Liberal prime minister who had ushered in the liberal constitution, because the Liberals, unwilling to bring yet more Slavs into the empire, opposed his budget for military expansion into Bosnia-Herzegovina. Count Edward Taafe was appointed prime minister. Personally loyal to Franz Josef, not to any national group, he sought to regain Slavic support, forming a ministry composed largely of Poles and Czechs. It was promptly dubbed the "Iron Ring" by Germans— a Slavic "ring" threatening to strangle them. But the Slavs in the ministry were older conservatives hoping to rule by conciliation. Czech deputies ended their twelve-year boycott of the parliament, and new elections were scheduled. To appease the Czechs, they were given more votes. Although badly split, the German Liberals remained the largest party in the parliament, but now Slavic politicians as well as Schoenerer and Lueger challenged them.

In 1880 Taafe's cabinet ignited a firestorm of ethnic rage by directing all administrative and judicial officials in Bohemia to use the language of those who petitioned the bureaucracy and defendants. It was a stunning victory for the Czechs, for almost all educated Czechs were bilingual. Germans despised the immensely difficult Czech language. What civilized person bothers to learn Czech, they asked, and where is Czech literature taken seriously? Czechs flocked into the civil service positions, and by the 1880s Bohemia and Moravia were battlegrounds. Even the German Liberal party announced, "We protest against all attempts to convert Austria into a Slav state."[3] Younger Germans moved to Schoenerer and Lueger, for the Liberals still hoped that a federation of nationalities was the solution, and were called traitors to German blood. In the uproar, Czechs demanded their language be given equality at the University of Prague, where lectures were traditionally given in German. Taafe obliged—lectures and exams would be permitted in Czech. Outraged when the lecture halls of the venerable seat of German learning echoed a crude peasant language, German students brawled with Czechs. Hate literature was distributed by both sides, with talk of massacres to come. Czechs wanted those who did not speak Czech barred from office in Bohemia; in Prague, where Germans had been a majority in the 1850s, Czechs now outnumbered Germans and founded schools using their own language. "Young Czechs" appealed to republican France, traditional enemy of German domination in the east. Sudeten Germans, who had lived in this Bohemian region for centuries, swiftly adopted Schoenerer's Nazi-like racism.

Racism now swept university students. More secular than most and swayed by racial doctrines taught by their professors, they had less interest in Catholic anti-Semitism. Flocking to the pan-Germans, they agitated for the suppression of the Slavs and *Anschluss* with the "virile" German Reich, denouncing "Jewish" doctrines of racial equality as threats to the blood of the *Volk*. Like Prussian students, they admired Turnvater Jahn, the "first storm trooper" of the Germanic warrior stock. By the 1880s tens of thousands of students had signed petitions for a customs union with Germany, a step toward unity. Partly students were motivated by fear. Until 1862 Jews had been excluded from medicine by law, but the Liberals opened up all professions. By 1881, 60 percent of physicians in Vienna and 30 percent of undergraduates were Jewish, with the highest numbers in law and medicine, competing with non-Jewish students for scarce positions. In 1884 nearly half of all students were Jewish. The assimilation Germans had once demanded as the price of liberation was now replaced by calls for quotas on Jewish students. If Jews wished to assimilate, German students argued, they should become artisans and peasants. It was a demand few university students, Jew or Gentile, rushed to meet, then or now.

In 1881 the German anti-Semitic petition circulated in Vienna to even greater effect. By 1878 German students at Prague had thrown Jews out of their associations, and by 1883 Austrian students had banned all Jews from their fraternities. As one dueling fraternity announced, "Jews cannot be regarded as Germans even when they are baptized." In 1896 the fraternities declared that no German should duel with a Jew because of the "deep moral and psychic differences between Aryans and Jews" and Jewish "lack of honor and character."[4] Scorned as a merchant race, Jewish undergraduates formed their own dueling fraternities. *Judenrein* gymnastic-paramilitary units provided an elite "storm trooper" bodyguard for Schoenerer. Wagner's overtures were now used as pan-German themes, and students joined Wagner's racist cult, substituting the traditional student greeting of *"Grussgott"* (God's Greetings) with *"Heil,"* and *"Deutschland, Deutschland ueber Alles"* for the words of the Austrian national anthem: "God protect and God preserve our Kaiser and our Land." By the late 1880s student violence against Jews was common.

Austrians of Jewish origin identified with German culture and nationalism, hoping to be regarded as Germans of Jewish faith, not a separate nationality. Franz Josef once called them his only loyal citizens. But no matter what they did, stereotypes intensified, especially because so many Jews remained loyal to the original constitutional hope of religious and ethnic toleration and to the Liberal party. Supporting ethnic reconciliation and symbolizing the threats of secular modernization as well, the Jews of Austria were isolated and trapped, even more hated than the Jews of Germany. Theodore Herzl, future leader of Zionism, illustrates the dilemma. The son of a wealthy investment broker in Budapest and a student at the University of Vienna, Herzl joined a German dueling fraternity in 1881, gaining the scars required as evidence of Germanic virility and sharing student admiration for the Prussian military and their contempt for trade—including his father's business. Bismarck was Herzl's hero, and he was anti-Slav. Not in the least religious, he proposed that Jews convert en masse or be baptized at birth to rid themselves of the pointless difference. Indeed, Viennese Jews had a higher rate of conversion than any European Jewish community. Herzl believed anti-Semitism was a fading holdover of primitive Christianity and the Jewish personality a distortion produced by the ghetto experience. In time, assimilation would correct both. But in 1883 Herzl's dueling fraternity took part in mass anti-Semitic memorial rites for Richard Wagner, and shortly thereafter all Jews were forced out. Herzl resigned with a dignified protest. The doubts that led him to Zionism began.

In 1888 a Viennese newspaper announced the death of Kaiser William I of Germany a day before it occurred, a "scoop" withdrawn in a second edition the same day. Schoenerer, calling the paper "Jewish filth" and insisting the story was a deliberate show of contempt for the Hohenzollerns, led a group to the paper's editorial offices demanding that the staff of "Jewish devils" bow down in shame. They refused, a fight broke out, and Schoenerer's people were beaten. As the aggressor in a criminal act, he lost his parliamentary immunity and title and was sentenced to four months' prison. As one follower said, if they wanted to defeat the "Jew liberals" they must join Lueger. Hundreds of prominent Viennese, Lueger included, showed their moral support for Schoenerer by leaving their calling cards at his prison. Lueger endeared himself to his rival's supporters when, after parliament took away Schoenerer's right to be a deputy for five years, Lueger, weeping crocodile tears, denounced "these Christians who, like Judas Iscariot, betray their blood brothers."[5] In 1889 the imperial government refused to grant the artisan leader Schneider a meeting with the emperor because he had publicly proposed the murder of the Jews. Lueger denounced the decision, and Schneider promptly led his artisans into Lueger's camp.

In 1895, when Lueger led the United Christian Anti-Semites in winning almost one-third of the seats in the municipal council and the German vote for parliament, young radical Czechs won elections to the Bohemian Assembly. The dialectic of racial hatred continued: fists and inkwells flew between Czech and German; Hungarians repressed their Slovaks, Ruthenians, Rumanians, and Serbs; Poles oppressed the national aspirations of "upstart" Ukrainians and Ruthenians; Slovenes battled Italians in Trieste. In parliament, anti-Semites booed the Liberals and their "Jewish friends" who would not use force against Slavs; Jews, Germans, and Czechs exchanged insults and blows in the streets. The Jews, Lueger told parliament, supported the Slavs not out of tolerance but because they hated the Germans: "For the Jews there is no Fatherland, only the international rule of capital." Vogelsang added, "Judaism rejoices over the strife of Germans and Slavs."[6] Anti-Semitism increased among the minority peoples. The trap was closing.

By 1891 the imperial parliament, consumed by endless demands for translations by Slavs too proud to allow German to be the official language, was plagued by walkouts, boycotts, fisticuffs, hurled chairs, and exploding bombs. Lawsuits and judicial proceedings were a babel; interpreters prospered as minorities demanded to use their own language. Justice and education ground to a halt. Each group busily calculated how changes in the complicated electoral system gave ethnic advantage. Taafe, now seen as pro-German by Czechs, lost their support. He could no longer govern without the Germans he had so mightily offended. It was all too much. Count Taafe once boasted that he governed "by keeping all the nationalities in a state of uniform and nicely tempered discontent."⁷ Nicely tempered discontent now belonged to the Hapsburg past. In 1893, bereft of allies, Taafe resigned over a conflict about extending the vote.

Both racists and liberals now faced a powerful new threat: socialism. Three million Austrian industrial workers were working unbelievably long hours for miserable wages. In the 1880s anarchists had used terror and arson against the factories and their owners. Taafe had outlawed them, placed industrial centers under martial law, and suppressed their press. Like Bismarck, Taafe had passed modest welfare measures in 1887, hoping to use the proletariat as a counterweight to ethnic chauvinists. Torn by doctrinal disputes, the Austrian Social Democrats were unified in 1888 by Viktor Adler, a moderate Marxist who ended the party's flirtation with anarchism and committed it to peaceful change, though it rejected Taafe's reforms as inadequate. Austrian socialists were more feared than their German colleagues, for they broke racial taboos when, in the name of the international brotherhood of the proletariat, they recruited thousands of Slavic workers and supported concessions to Slavs. Moreover, they demanded universal male suffrage, a mortal threat to German domination. Adler wanted the empire preserved but believed it could last only if Germans ceased dominating Slavs. This "racial treason" was compounded by the socialists' open contempt for political anti-Semitism. A socialist leader presented the official party position in 1887: "The struggle between the so-called Aryan and Jewish races leaves us cold. It is all one to us if we are exploited by an Aryan or a Semite. As long as there are a quite sufficient number of Aryan exploiters, these men have no right to counter protests against exploitation by blaming the Jews."⁸

Catholic conservatives pointed out that Adler was Jewish. Schoenerites noted that he was baptized, living proof that conversion did not end Jewish treason. Fear escalated when in 1890, on the first proletarian May Day, hundreds of thousands of workers marched in Vienna, their voices raised in the dreaded "Marseillaise." In 1894 even more jammed the streets of Vienna and other cities to demand universal suffrage. The pious Germans of rural village and isolated Alpine regions violently opposed "red" atheism and were shocked at the threat to religion and property. As in Germany, the high percentage of intellectuals of Jewish origin among socialist leaders gave the right a chance to avoid real issues and speak instead of Jewish subversion. For the first time Lueger needed bodyguards when campaigning in workers' districts, confronting hecklers hurling beer bottles. "The Social Democrats [are] the shock troops of the Jews," Lueger declared. "The Jews Marx and Lassalle founded your party, if you keep fighting for them, you will not get your precious revolution, you will get the rule of the Jews."[9] They were the enemies of Christian workers: "Who pays them? The powerful Jews. Can you not see that the socialists attack everything and everyone but the Jews? That in itself shows you who runs the Social Democrats."[10]

The rise of socialism moved hundreds of priests into the Christian Social party, motivated, like Stoecker, by the apathy and hostility they experienced in proletarian parishes. The most charismatic "volks preacher" of the day, the internationally famed Jesuit priest Heinrich Abel, spoke in Vienna in 1891: "We know very well who leads and marches in the movement against Christianity and Christians," he declaimed. "It is the Jew and the secret societies, and they started this agitation in 1789."[11] Priests founded a large Catholic Youth Movement, in effect a branch of the Christian Social party. In spite of all the talk of the Jew-dominated press, the Catholic right controlled most provincial papers, and anti-Semitic attitudes were common in them down to 1945.

Lueger's campaigns were supported by Schoenerer's followers, still leaderless and ostracized in most districts. The Austrian hierarchy disapproved of Schoenerer's attacks against the dynasty and millions of Catholic Slavs. But the pan-Germans did well in Bohemia, for the near civil war between Germans and Czechs fueled German racism there as nowhere else. Lueger's campaign themes were as before: protect small businessmen from Jewish department stores and power over credit, and restore the power of the guilds. Above all, liberalism and socialism, the twin plagues of 1789, must be defeated. "We are friendly toward all Christian classes and nationalities; we only do battle with one nation, the Jews, not because of the religion of this tribe, but because the Jew seizes with thieving hands all we hold sacred—Fatherland, nationality, and finally even our property. Anti-Semitism is a purely ethical movement."[12]

When in the city council elections of 1895, the Christian Social party defeated the Liberals under the slogan "Anti-Semites unite," racists gained an absolute majority of votes in Vienna, something that never happened in any major German city, even later during Nazi campaigns. In the elections of 1896 the United Anti-Semites, as Lueger's coalition called itself, took ninety-six seats to the Liberals' forty-two. "Beautiful Karl" was dubbed the "King of Vienna." Pictures of him sprouted in pubs; photos, paintings, medallions, and walking sticks with his likeness were distributed by the hundreds of thousands. There was a brisk trade in anti-Semitica. Schoenerer was eclipsed; pan-Germans could no longer win elections without Lueger. The city council elected the mayor of Vienna from among its membership, and in 1895 chose Lueger. "Lueger is at the gates," Liberals cried, and the stock market plunged to a new low. Four times the council voted Lueger mayor, but Franz Josef refused to appoint him, as was his right. He feared the economic effects if Jews were to leave. Above all, he knew Lueger's rule could destroy the delicate ethnic balance of the empire. Lueger complicated matters by attacking the Hungarian regime in the midst of delicate negotiations, calling them pro-Jewish and attacking "Judapest," a ridiculous charge given the force of Hungarian anti-Semitism.

While the emperor assured the Jewish community he would not appoint Lueger, the mayor-elect's supporters roamed the streets beating Jews and Czechs. Commodity dealers on the exchange were assaulted, forcing the exchange to move to Budapest. The prime minister, the Polish Count Kasimir Badeni, was shouted down in parliament and followed in the streets with cries of "polack Jew lover"; the emperor was labeled the "Judenkaiser." In March 1897 Austrians voted for parliament under a new electoral law adding more lower-middle-class Germans. Votes were still weighted to favor title and property, but the Christian Socials gained 117,000 votes to the Liberals' 10,000. Austrian liberalism was dead. The pope and the papal nuncio supported Lueger publicly and pressured the emperor, though Slavic church leaders advised against it. In April 1897 the emperor gave in. Lueger replaced Mayor Grubl, the target of vicious attacks because he was a Freemason with a Jewish wife. Delirious crowds celebrated the night through in Vienna and other German cities. Outside city hall, crowds chanted, "Dr. Lueger shall rule, and the Jews shall be destroyed." Racists of all nations, including Stoecker and Ahlwardt, made pilgrimages to Vienna, returning envious and inspired.

Sigmund Freud, a close follower of Viennese politics, said that in 1895 he first looked into the horrifying abyss of the id. Theodore Herzl, in Vienna during the uproar over Lueger, had already covered the trial of France's leading anti-Semite, the royalist Eduoard Drumont, sued for accusing the deputy prime minister of France of accepting Jewish bribes. Herzl heard crowds in Paris shouting "Death to the Jews!" then and during the famous Panama Canal scandal of 1892, even though there were no Jews among the directors of the Panama Company. The Dreyfus case of the mid-nineties, which he also covered, was the final cruel blow. If these outbreaks could occur in France, the land of 1789, it was time for Jews to leave Europe. In Paris in 1897 Herzl wrote The Jewish State and convened the first Zionist Congress at Basel. In 1903 the pogrom at

Kishinev occurred, when forty-nine Russian Jews were murdered with the complicity of church, tsar, and police. In the 1890s, 500,000 Jews left Europe for England and America.

Welcoming the first Zionist Congress as an opportunity to begin ridding Europe of Jews, the *Kreuzzeitung* denounced the rabbis who opposed it. How could one trust a people that refused to build a Fatherland for its own religion? Who but Jews would arrogantly retain an anti-Christian religion and yet demand equal treatment in a Christian state? Wilhelm Marr's periodical insisted that Jewish anti-Zionists knew Jews were incapable of working the land or defending a nation, and feared Zionism would destroy Jewish wealth and power by attracting all Jews to Palestine. Marr and Schoenerer demanded forced emigration, but some voiced the same fear Hitler would: a Jewish state in Palestine would only exploit Arabs and become a base for international Jewry's conquest of the West. There must be a truly final solution.

Although Lueger had crushed the Liberals in 1897, in the same elections the Social Democrats had received almost two-thirds as many votes as the United Anti-Semites, votes from the new industrial suburbs of Vienna. Lueger's party was now the major defense against socialism; Austrian conservatives, once suspicious of his mass appeal, flocked to join. Christian Social party organizers worked in rural provinces, using the same anti-Semitic tirades Boeckel was then using to vilify Jewish moneylenders and grain and cattle dealers. Lueger, aided by priests and the lay organization Catholic Action, had much more support than Boeckel, partly because Jewish middlemen were far more prominent in rural Austria than Germany. Suffering from a long agrarian depression, the peasantry was unable to adapt to competition from the long-distance shipping of grain and farm products. Many relied on Jewish moneylenders who often charged double the normal rate of the banks, themselves Jewish-owned and unwilling to make such risky loans to poor peasants.

It was renewed Slavic unrest in almost all provinces that had caused Franz Josef to appoint Count Badeni prime minister in 1895. To Germans it was bad enough he was a Pole, even worse that as governor of Galicia he had cultivated good relationships with the Jewish community. Bypassing the Germans, Badeni put together a ministry of Poles, Czechs, and upper clergy. In 1896 and again in 1897 his regime was put to the test when Germans in a mixed German-Slovene region rioted when a Slovene Congress called for autonomy. Contemptuous of Slovene language and culture, German rightists demanded that Slovenes be driven out. Czechs also called for greater self-rule. To appease them, Badeni ended martial law in Prague, released Czech radicals from prison, and fired the governor of Bohemia, an opponent of the Czechs.

In April 1897 Badeni touched off an explosion of racial violence with decrees providing that by 1901 government employees in Bohemia and Moravia must speak and write Czech as well as German. The German middle classes erupted. Violence raged in Vienna and other cities, cherry bombs exploded in parliament, and the police ejected obstreperous delegates. German restaurants refused to serve Czechs and vice versa, and Czechs kept their children out of German schools. Badeni fought a duel with a Schoenerite, and mass protests were held in German communities throughout the empire. Students led anti-Hapsburg demonstrations in every university. In an inflammatory speech on the steps of city hall, Mayor Lueger called the ordinances a Judas payment to the Czechs for their support of Badeni. When his speech provoked a riot, he had the effrontery to tell the emperor he could not guarantee peace in the city. Vienna was an armed camp, and many remaining Liberals lost their moderation: Theodore Mommsen, supporter of revolution in 1848, said it was time to crack Czech skulls. Some Germans did so, and some Czechs replied in kind. Jews were attacked by both sides; to the Czechs they were Germans, to the Germans, Jews. Provincial assemblies closed, taxes went uncollected, parliament was paralyzed by riots, and Badeni's efforts to discipline rioting deputies brought a general walkout. Racist anti-Czech cartoons flooded the press, violently attacking Czechs who had become successful and middle class, living refutations of the stereotype of the brutish and stupid Czech peasant. More than half the Germans of the empire were involved in disturbances, led by the Sudetenland, Vienna, Prague, and Graz. Five imperial governments fell.

Schoenerer emerged from political limbo more dangerous than before. Imperial government employees, once the backbone of a neutral Hapsburg administration, were now among his most zealous supporters. Pan-Germanism raged unchecked in Bohemia and Moravia. Schoenerer raised tens of thousands of petitions against the Badeni ordinances while those who called for moderation and negotiations, socialists and Liberals, were reviled as never before. Jews were attacked whatever they said. To the fury of the conservatives, socialists did not oppose the Badeni ordinances, and denounced racism. At the party conference in 1899 the Social Democrats called for national equality and a federal state of nationalities with cultural and political autonomy. Of course the socialists sought Czech votes, but the international fraternity of the workers was a Marxist principle. Even so, many Czech proletarians complained of German and Jewish domination in the party.

Pamphlets attacked Social Democrats as Jewish-led defenders of "subhuman" Slavs. Some suggested "concentrating" Czechs and Jews in camps in order to stop their mouths, others wanted them thrown out. At the turn of the century, as George Mosse has noted, "Every year tens of thousands of anti-Semitic pamphlets [were] sent free to all officials of the state and members of the upper ten thousand. . . ."[13] There was nothing remotely equivalent in any Western nation, including Germany. "Throw out the Jews!" and "Death to the Jews" were rallying cries at pan-German and some Christian Social demonstrations. Even if a Jew spoke German, Schoenerer wrote, he was no more German than a black African. Signs appeared on taverns and restaurants: No Czechs, Jews, or dogs. Anti-Semitic bills proliferated in provincial assemblies. Pan-German literature was passed out by schoolboys, including young Adolf, the most famous schoolboy of all.

In Vienna, crowds larger and more agitated than in 1848 demanded, "Badeni must go." Franz Josef capitulated but thereby agitated every nationality even more. Martial law was needed to restore order in many towns as triumphant Germans heralded the appointment as prime minister of a German—who promptly released German extremists from prison. Now Czechs rioted, boycotted German businesses, reviled the Hapsburgs, refused to serve Germans in Czech restaurants, and raised public toasts to France, to liberty, to independence, to pan-Slavism—even to Russia. Speaking at a mass gathering of European Slavic delegates in 1898, a Russian general brought down the house when he reminded all that a coalition of Slavs had defeated the Teutonic Knights in 1410 at Tannenberg. Forget Slavic differences, he urged, and unite against the Germans of both Reichs. Germans called Prague little Moscow; in Germany, conservatives waxed indignant at "Slavic arrogance" and demanded war against Russia.

In Vienna, Czechs organized their own schools. When Lueger's government refused to certify them, Czechs sent their children to Bohemia for education. The Bohemian Assembly was paralyzed again as Germans walked out. The universities of Linz, Graz, and Innsbruck were closed because of violence. Schoenerer's following, encouraged by many faculty, attacked Jews as pro-Slav without bothering to inquire first. Peasants revolted in Galicia, threatening to kill all Jews. In the imperial army, Czechs refused to obey orders given in German, the official language of the military. Street battles flourished, local governments ground to a halt. Government by emergency decree prevailed as ethnic antagonisms tore apart the institutions of the empire. It was a racial revolution, the prelude to the German-Slav conflict that exploded in 1914.

Baron Paul von Gautsch, the new German prime minister, could not form a government, for minorities everywhere demanded separate institutions. Gautsch resigned and a living compromise, Count Francis von Thun, replaced him. Thun was a Czech who preferred to be German and spoke Czech badly and as little as possible. He too failed, replaced in 1899 by a liberal German whose compromises were blasted in parliament to the sound of fireworks and fisticuffs. Once again a weary Franz Josef sent parliament home, calling for elections for January 1901 and hinting these were the last. If he could not rule with the constitution, he would rule without it.

Lueger was on the defensive, his anti-Slavism inhibited because the church was dedicated to the empire and the salvation of the Slavs. Accused of being too soft, Lueger watched as Schoenerer became the idol of millions of Germans, excluding the left. In the 1901 elections, Schoenerer's nationalists quadrupled their seats, equaling Lueger's party. Entering parliament in triumph, Schoenerer and his supporters sang the German national anthem and cried out, "*Hoch und Heil* to the Hohenzollerns" and "God save the Hohenzollern kaiser!" A new anti-Semitic German People's party gained as many votes as Lueger, and the Social Democrats paid for their "philosemitism and pro-Slavism" with four of their fourteen seats. Overall, more than half of Austro-German voters voted for candidates who wanted legislation to limit the civil rights of Jews. The Liberal party was confined to those districts containing more than half the Jews of Vienna. If voting had not depended on high property qualifications, there would have been no Liberals at all. The self-fulfilling prophecy had come to pass: liberalism was indeed now Jewish.

The 1901 elections showed that as many as 80 percent of Austro-Germans admired Schoenerer. In his exultancy, he made a fatal mistake. He had always despised the Catholic church for its internationalism and its millions of Slavic faithful. The only religion fit for true Germans, he thought, was Lutheranism, the spiritual embodiment of Prussian autocracy and German racial instincts. At the height of his appeal in 1900, Schoenerer started his famous "Away from Rome" movement, personally converting to Lutheranism and ultimately winning some fifty thousand to ninety thousand converts with the slogan, "Without Juda, without Rome, we will build Germania's dome." Aided by some two hundred Lutheran pastors from Germany, Stoecker's League for the Protection of German Protestant Interests, and Lutheran lay societies, the movement offered conversions at meetings where pan-German lyrics were set to traditional Lutheran hymns. Half the converts were from the embattled German communities of Bohemia. Although Schoenerer hoped conversion would unite the German *Volk* of both Reichs, he personally preferred pre-Christian Germanic tribal religions. "The Jew Bible is not a moral and religious work" he wrote. "The founder of Christianity was not an Aryan." After his conversion he said, "I am and remain a pagan."[14] But Schoenerer's "missionaries," his anti-Catholicism and demand for *Anschluss*, and his dictatorial arrogance alienated the bulk of the Austro-Germans.

Lueger seized the day. The Christian Social party held great demonstrations denouncing Schoenerer's treason; Franz Josef, the heir apparent Franz Ferdinand, the higher clergy, and the papal nuncio lent their support. Local priests denounced Schoenerer. The faith of rural Austria was at stake, and all were reminded of Bismarck's onslaughts against Catholic rights. Schoenerer lost his chance. Many of his supporters later joined the Austrian Nazis, and the split between the two fascisms, clerical and volkist, remained until, in 1938, Hitler realized von Schoenerer's dream, and the Austrian Nazis lorded it over the clerical fascists of Christian Socialism.

As mayor, Lueger could pass no racist legislation. Germans could neither control parliament nor alter the constitution; no decrees could be issued without the approval of Franz Josef. In his inauguration speech, however, Lueger promised to curb Jewish influence by ending "Jewish" stockholder control over municipal utilities, thus lowering costs and improving service for the ordinary customer. But the public utilities of Vienna—lighting, gas, streetcars, waterworks, and a slaughterhouse—were actually owned by British, French, and non-Jewish stockholders as well as Jews, and of course the rates charged had nothing to do with the ethnicity or religion of stockholders. Nevertheless, Lueger boasted of his "Aryan" victories over Jewish international finance as the city purchased the municipal gasworks and the slaughterhouse, lowered utility rates, and built schools and hospitals. City banks extended cheap credit to small businessmen and shifted some city contracts to artisans. Homes for wandering journeymen were established, and conditions in orphanages and shelters for homeless adults were improved. The Rothschild family had long preceded the Christian Socials in such charities, and Ignaz Mandl, Lueger's former Jewish ally, had proposed these reforms in the 1870s. Indeed, many Liberals had supported them. Ignorant of the workings of the international financial system, Lueger's artisans, clerks, and shopkeepers were easily persuaded that somehow mainly Jews, not Christians, invested for profit. Other European cities carried out similar reforms, but only in Vienna were they tied to the alleged machinations of the Jews. And Lueger gave the best services to districts loyal to him, neglecting socialist districts.

For peasants, the true *Volk* as Lueger called them, the Christian Social party established cheap credit and insurance against natural disasters and tried to support agrarian prices. As usual, however, the rural depression of the 1890s was blamed by the party on Jewish commodity brokers, land speculators, moneylenders, and rural middlemen, rather than the inability of many Austrian peasants to adapt to new markets and competition. Small farms had failed at a high rate since 1880, and Jewish middlemen usually handled the sales, but the buyers were almost always Christians—German landlords, well-off peasants, or wealthy industrialists—and the prices, of course, were determined by the market. Nevertheless, small and middle-sized landholders moved to Lueger. Rural anti-Semitism was more useful than ever before now that socialism threatened Vienna and other cities.

Lueger deserves credit for reforms but dishonor for increasing the false connection between race and social ills. Anti-Semites of all nations singled him out as the man who had best shown how conservatives might defeat liberals and socialists. In a visit to Rumania, then and until 1945 the home of the most vicious and mystical Christian racism of all, Lueger was hailed as "King of the Anti-Semites." Simply put, and in spite of the denials of Austrian historians, Lueger was a fascist. At large ceremonial mass meetings, Lueger, hailed as "Fuehrer," presided over parades of paramilitary auxiliaries uniting "quasi-religious [and] quasi-military ceremonial" with "anti-Semitic and anti-socialist" ideology.[15] The party organized a Women's League to combat the "Jewish and socialist" moral decay threatening church, home, and family. Like similar Nazi organizations, the Women's League denounced the ungodly notion of equal rights for women, calling feminism Jewish and socialist. With some twenty thousand members organized along paramilitary lines, the Women's League had its own press to teach housewives they must protect racial purity, warn Christian girls not to work for Jews, prevent Jews from teaching, and provide constant warnings against the Jewish menace. The Women's League published lists of Jewish merchants to be boycotted by Christian shoppers, especially at Christmastime. The Nazis did the same in the 1920s. Lueger's people organized an anti-Semitic Christian teachers' association as well as paramilitary youth groups, a kind of Lueger Jugund. The city government distributed an anti-Semitic children's magazine in schools.[16]

The Christian Social party and its supporters despised the new cultural movements of fin de siècle Vienna, seeing them, correctly, as an affront to their traditional piety. Party ideologists defended traditional Christian Germanic culture against what they termed a flood of Jewish "moral nihilism," contrasting the decadence of "mongrel art" with the piety of medieval art, denouncing even Offenbach's light opera as "lewd and Jewish." To church and party, Christian morality was mortally threatened by the sensuality of Klimt's painting, the sophisticated decadence of Schnitzler's stories, Ibsen's social criticism, Schoenberg's atonal music, and Strindberg's dramas of sexual horrors. If these artists were not Jewish, party ideologists insisted, Jewish critics had made them famous. Demanding censorship, the party formed anti-Semitic writers' and theater groups to publish and produce only good Aryan art. Lueger encouraged one of his followers to call for a police watch over the Jews at Eastertime to prevent them from committing ritual murders. Vogelsang believed Jewish merchants and stockbrokers met with their Gentile mistresses in beer gardens in order to mock Easter.

In 1907 Lueger, complaining that education was morally polluted by Jews, demanded an investigation to find out how many of Austria's university faculty were in fact converted Jews peddling subversion. To Catholic leaders he said, "We have still another great task to perform, the conquest of the universities."[17] Like some fascist parties later, the Christian Socials organized racist paramilitary movements to prepare for the day when it would be necessary to fight socialists and Jews. In a famous outburst in 1898, one party leader called for a law offering a bounty to those who shot Jews. In 1902 another announced in the city council, to loud applause, "Yes, we want to annihilate the Jews." Their program was "the elimination of Jewry."[18] Lueger himself publicly called for the murder of Jews in 1894. Without the power to pass racist laws, however, the Christian Social party had to be content with purging Jews from teaching and city jobs and boycotting Jewish merchants.

By 1901 the battle for the German vote was between "blacks" and "reds," Christian Socials and Social Democrats. Lueger tried to organize Christian trade unions but with little success, for he could offer only the sparse consolations of Leo XIII's 1891 encyclical *Rerum Novarum*. Although the pope condemned capitalist exploitation, he forbade strikes and socialism. One must work humbly in the faith that one's employer's Christian conscience would bring fair treatment. Leo XIII, directly influenced by Vogelsang, insisted that social problems could be resolved by a revival of the Christian spirit of mutual sacrifice, and for that revival it was essential that the moral, legal, and educational powers of the church be restored.

Yet socialism continued to grow. In 1905 Viktor Adler was elected to parliament, and the Social Democrats had some fifty newspapers, all attacking the influence of the church in politics and offering proposals for a federation of nationalities that would grant equal rights to all ethnic groups. The Social Democrats also made concessions to the different nationalities within the party, forming seven affiliated national organizations: German, Czech, Croatian, Slovene, Italian, Polish, and Ruthenian. And they organized their own counterculture to rival Catholic cultural organizations, establishing socialist feast and festival days, youth groups, workers' classes, and feminist women's groups. Thus the Austro-Germans were split into two cultures. The collapse of the liberal center deprived the Jewish community of any real choice, and nationalism among the minorities made the Jews the target of anti-Semitism throughout the empire.

In 1906 the Social Democrats mounted great demonstrations for universal suffrage, and Lueger, after demanding safeguards for the German vote, was willing to compromise. Schoenerer complained bitterly that Lueger was aiding a rotten dynasty by giving more votes to subhuman Slavs, joining with Jews and socialists to betray German blood without a fight. Ignored, he quit politics after defeat by a socialist in the 1907 elections, retiring to his castle to sulk and leave the remnants of his movement to others. His fame and ideas still lived on in the border areas, however, and would rise again with a vengeance when the Germans of the Sudetenland were given to the new state of Czechoslovakia in 1919.

In 1907 the emperor consented to a "leap in the dark": practically all males twenty-four years or over could vote for representatives of their nationality, though the Germans were protected with extra seats. With Lueger ill, Prince Alois Liechtenstein led the campaign, insisting "God demands" a vote for the Christian Socials.[19] The party, allied with elite conservatives, gained the largest single bloc in parliament. Lueger still held Vienna and made a solid showing in rural Austria. "Beautiful Karl" was now the first choice of the ill-fated Franz Ferdinand, heir to the throne, for prime minister. Even Franz Josef joined Lueger's admirers. Understandably, for the first time five Zionists were elected to parliament.

But the great shock of the elections of 1907 was the victory of the left, suddenly the second largest party in parliament. The panic on the right was comparable to that which swept Germany's right when the Social Democrats scored their great victory of 1912. The upper classes moved to Lueger. From 1907 to 1914 nationality conflicts and foreign policy dominated Hapsburg politics as never before. Czechs, Germans, and nearly all minorities demonstrated and rioted, and the intense nationalism further isolated the Jews. Nazi-like ideologies proliferated. Those Slavs who wished to save the empire wished to save it only for themselves. Even the Social Democrats were split as Czech, Polish, and Ukrainian socialists declared independence. Generals called for preventive war against Slavs, and terrorist groups sprang up among the minorities.

Extremely ill, Lueger confined his activities to receiving well-known international anti-Semites seeking his blessings, entertaining them with his famous collection of anti-Semitica. Financial scandals arose in the government, but Lueger kept silent; he could no longer credibly blame the Jews. In 1911 a Czech school in Vienna was closed, parliament was picketed, and once again fights broke out between Germans and Czechs. Lives were lost and martial law proclaimed; the government fell and new elections were held. The Christian Social party received 37 percent of the vote of the German electorate. The German Nationalists, Schoenerer's heirs, received 31 percent, and the Social Democrats 32 percent. In this, the last election of the Hapsburg Empire, more than two-thirds of all Austro-Germans voted for extreme anti-Semites, the fruit of pan-German and Christian Social efforts to make all issues racial issues.

But Vienna, like Berlin, was now a socialist stronghold, with the "blacks" confined to middle- and upper-class districts and rural and provincial Germans. Lueger no longer spoke of reform; that was now a socialist monopoly.

Lueger did not live to see his beloved Vienna repudiate him. He died on March 10, 1910. A million Viennese attended his funeral, staged in grand Viennese fashion, with long parades of mourners from mountain-village and provincial town, clad in ancient costumes and following black carriages pulled by black horses accompanied by muffled drums and Chopin's funeral march, culminating in High Mass and a Mozart Requiem in the great Cathedral of Saint Stephan. Processions lasted all day, with dignitaries of church and state attending from all Europe. Young Hitler stood in the vast crowd of mourners. The conservative press in Germany and Europe praised Lueger as a mighty fortress in their common battle.

Schoenerer died in 1921. In his last speech he called for the fall of the empire and unity with Germany, closing with a *"Heil"* to the future "savior of the Germans and molder of pan-Germania!"[20] As defeat loomed in 1917, the new emperor, Karl I, granted amnesty to Czech nationalists in order to gain Allied favor, and, in the balancing tradition of Franz Josef, restored Schoenerer's title to the aging recluse. Schoenerer lived to see the hated empire fall but not to witness the rise of Germany's savior to take up his fallen sword, unite Germany and Austria, conquer the Slavs, and destroy the Jews.

13: HITLER IN AUSTRIA

> Take away the Nordic Aryans and nothing remains but the dance of apes.
>
> —Adolf Hitler

GIVEN the racism of Austro-Germans, Hitler's anti-Semitism was scarcely unique. He was not even the most extreme racist among the Nazis, many of whom complained as late as 1937 that he was too easy on the Jews. Born in 1889, Hitler spent his formative years in the sizable provincial town of Linz, as did Eichmann. There and in Vienna Hitler witnessed the most extreme racist turmoil in Europe and adopted political attitudes similar to those of a majority of middle-class Austrians. By 1919 there were hundreds of similar German and Austrian activists leading dozens of Nazi-like movements, with millions ready to follow any effort that attained national prominence.

Hitler's father, an illegitimate, ill-educated son of peasants, by hard work achieved a rank equivalent to that of captain in the semimilitary organization of the Imperial Customs Service, and was thus a member of the salaried middle class. His struggles made him rigid and harsh, with the self-righteous dogmatism and regard for status of those who achieve against great odds by extreme self-discipline. Alois Hitler shared the racial nationalism of his vocation as a customs official on the Bohemian border where conflict between Czechs and Germans focused on the distribution of posts in the bureaucracy. During Hitler's schooldays in Linz, Germans demonstrated against Czech agitators and against Jews. Linz also had a large contingent of Social Democrats who infuriated middle-class Germans by attacking private property and defending Slavic rights. Young Adolf must have heard much loud and angry talk about inferior Slavs and traitorous Jewish liberals. His hard-drinking father was not a quiet man.

Adolf spent summers among the peasants of the district of his maternal ancestors, where Schoenerer had started his political career. Hitler's peasant mother probably shared their anti-Semitism. Racist disturbances were common, and young Hitler may well have witnessed some. Moreover, pan-Germans were well organized in Linz, with their own press and frequent demonstrations against Jews, liberals, and Slavs. Hitler later boasted about distributing pan-German literature as a boy. The only teacher he admired was a pan-German historian and local politician. Hitler was ten to thirteen years old when the riots over the Badeni ordinances rocked the community, infuriated civil servants, and revitalized Schoenerer. Just south of Linz the Slovenes rioted for autonomy, and the most extreme German riots occurred just when Adolf suffered a series of personal humiliations and failures.

In elementary school his father's status enabled him to browbeat the sons of peasants and artisans in his class, boys not expected to harbor ambitions beyond their station. But in secondary school Hitler grew withdrawn, isolated, and friendless. Facing superior competition, he failed to live up to the expectations of his teachers, his relatives, and above all his unforgiving father, who insisted he aim for a career in the imperial bureaucracy. Adolf failed or did poorly in all but drawing and physical education; without improvement, he would wind up an artisan. Fourteen percent of the students at his school were Jewish, but there were only about a thousand Jews in Linz. Hitler must have been deeply humiliated to fail in their presence. Confrontations between Jewish and Gentile schoolboys were normal everywhere, but in Austria they were sanctioned by the majority of the respectable middle class in a poisoned atmosphere of hate.

His father constantly harassed Adolf and evidently beat him often; his older brother fled home because of the father's irrational furies. With Adolf now the eldest, the pressure was immense, and there was no appeal. His mother, though affectionate, had been raised above peasant status by marriage. Her childlike humility and the patriarchy of the time made it unlikely she would oppose her husband's will. Later Hitler would say that he respected but did not love his father, a conventional disguise for deep hostility, perhaps accompanied by the guilt of relief when the old man died suddenly in 1904, when Adolf was fifteen. His mother reinforced his sense of failure by holding up the memory of Hitler's dead father to semiworship. The constant reminders of his father's success against far greater odds must have been bitter gall indeed until Adolf himself became the highest civil servant of all.

Hitler could have repeated failed courses, but instead he graduated with an unsatisfactory record in 1905, living in idleness for two years on his mother's widow's pension. He revealed his self-contempt years later to his closest advisers, relating that when he finally received his inferior graduation certificate he got drunk and used it "mistakenly" for toilet paper. The discarded certificate was found and returned to the director of the school, who confronted and humiliated the boy. Taking solace in fantasy, the sixteen-year-old withdrew from most human contacts. He claimed to have resisted his father's will by declaring his artistic ambitions, but one doubts that even he had the psychic power to go up against such a man, especially given the patriarchal absolutism of the time. Hitler's resistance was internal, a secret belief that art would compensate for his youthful failures. Only after his father died, one suspects, did he begin to boast to his compliant mother that artistic genius raised him above the mundane world of bureaucrats and the pressure of relatives. We can assume this fantasy, based on no more than good marks in drawing, was both necessary and fragile, for he protected himself from exposure: he attended no art school nor did he associate himself with the small community of youthful bohemians in Linz. Rather than master the realities of his purported career, he found a disciple to impress, his only friend, August Kubizek, who called himself Adolf's "silent listener," a boy who could not remind Hitler of his failures, for they met after Hitler had finished school.

Hitler's battered ego also found comfort in his favorite reading—popular and violent myths of the conquering power of the Aryan gods and goddesses, blood of his blood, acts larger than life, achievements potentially his own. Kubizek tells of attending with Hitler a local performance of Wagner's *Rienzi*, the tale of a dictator who fought to unite Italy, conquer an empire, and regenerate the world. After the performance, Hitler rushed Kubizek to the top of a hill and declaimed in a strange ecstatic voice his divine mission to be the future savior of the Germans in the eternal war against Jews and Slavs. The dammed-up passion and power drives of the unsuccessful adolescent found release and sanction in the soaring, unresolved chords of Wagner, raising Hitler beyond failure, allowing him to partake of the ecstatic realm of the violent Aryan ideal made manifest in art, as it surely must be in his own blood. Kubizek writes that thirty years later, as the conductor of a provincial orchestra, he was invited by the Fuehrer himself to the sacred altar of Bayreuth, there to repeat the story of the initial *Rienzi* performance to Wagner's daughter, Hitler's devoted admirer. Afterward, Hitler turned to her and said, "In that hour it all began."

Even Hitler's adolescent sexual fantasies were dominated by his obsession with Wagner. In the most significant experience of his young life, Hitler fell in love with a young woman named Stephanie, but, timid and fearful of adult relationships, he refused to introduce himself. Teased by his friend Kubizek, but fearing rejection, the repressed romantic adolescent saved his masculine image by escaping into a fantasy world of secret power and future fulfillment. By intuition, he told Kubizek, he knew he and Stephanie were soul mates, but he could meet her and ask her hand in marriage only as a successful artist. He even asked his friend to inform her of his future intentions. Stephanie, he told Kubizek, would be Brunhild to his Siegfried—the god without fear and Stephanie the blond Nordic ideal, to be rescued through a ring of fire as Siegfried does in Wagner's Ring cycle, or perhaps a Valkyrie in Valhalla attending to Hitler's Wotan, god of war, learning, poetry, and magic, creator of earth, sky, and life. Woman, in short, was anything but simply human—either the threatening dark source of life or the pure focus of the guilty longings of the adolescent imagination. Only an idol worshiped from afar allowed him to avoid failure and dwell on his potential for glory. Avoiding Stephanie, Hitler sketched villas for their idyllic life to be.

Hitler's mother, a passive "cleaning animal" (as the Austrians say) for the males in her life, allowed him to live at her expense. In 1907 she was operated on for cancer. After helping to nurse her, Hitler went to Vienna to take the admissions examination at the Academy of Art. His mother died in a few weeks. Now there was nothing left for him in Linz but carping relatives and witnesses to his defeat. In Vienna he would forge his career. But he failed his test for the academy. On a second try his sample drawings were judged too unworthy to allow him even to take the exam. A committed young artist would have scorned the judgment of conservative academicians and found companions among the young artistic radicals of Vienna, but Hitler hated the new art. Rigid, authoritarian, fearing to let go, he needed the exact perspective and literal reproduction of the colors and shapes seen by the common eye. The few people he drew seem like puppets. He could not draw on subjective inner resources for self-expression; he never explored his own emotions and never would. For the new artists of his generation, a blank canvas made all possible, but Hitler drew solid chunks of architectural reality, as rigid and painstaking as if done on a drafting board, without emotive content. They were good picture postcards, nothing more. The academy judges recommended that he study architecture, but, perhaps sensing another failure, he protected his illusions by drawing vast structures in his lonely room. During hours wandering through Linz, the city of his defeats, Hitler had described to his friend how he would raze it all one day and replace it with buildings he would design—a fantasy he returned to, his secretary writes, in the last days in his bunker in Berlin, facing his ultimate failure.

Like Lueger's cultural commissars, Hitler could not abide the moral ambiguity of Viennese culture. Erotic degeneration shined forth from the purple-yellow skin of the lush bodies and angled distortions of the canvases of Klimt and Schiele. Schnitzler's sophisticated cynicism, sentimental decadence, and tales of casual sex offended conservatives; his *Lieutenant Gustl*, depicting the cowardice of a soldier, drew the disapproval of court and emperor. The atonal music of Schoenberg, Webern, and Berg was greeted by near riots. Hitler hated expressionism, as he would later hate Weimar culture. His need for the certainties of traditional art reflected the attitude of millions at a time when culture still had power to offend. Even if Hitler had studied architecture, he would have been scorned by the avant-garde, for he admired the massive structures of Vienna they mocked as overdecorated and pompous remnants of the past. Like pan-Germans and Christian Socials, Hitler dismissed modern culture as "Jewish" moral decay, views echoed in his favorite *German People's Paper*, a vulgar racist tabloid. There he found release for his humiliations: modern art was degenerate, Jewish, mongrel art. The Jews, Hitler wrote, created nine-tenths of all "unclean products" in "artistic life": "literary filth," "artistic trash," and "theatrical idiocy."[1] In these views he was not unique. Before the Nazis, their aesthetic norms were held by countless anti-Semites and found echoes in the bourgeoisie, offended by works that disturbed their calm parade through the fortress-museums of the classics. Racists insisted that Nordic art, realistic and heroic, was scorned because Germany was dominated by French taste and Jewish critics. Thus Hitler's rejection by the academy was most painful, for it came from men of status who defended the classical standards he admired. It destroyed his last defense against failure: if he was not an artist, he was nothing. Only a belief in racial superiority could erect a final and absolute defense for his ego.

Kubizek joined Hitler in Vienna in lodgings in a poor district. More blows fell: his passive admirer was admitted to the academy as a viola student. Hitler, unable to confess his humiliation, told Kubizek he too had been accepted. In fact he spent his time at the opera or drawing new buildings for Vienna, stage settings for Wagnerian operas, even whole cities. He also designed sets based on Teutonic myths, panoramic scenes of violent fury, and planned to finish Wagner's "Wieland the Smith," a sadistic tale of revenge, rape, and murder. Evenings found him pacing his room, ranting to his friend of his destiny as savior of the *Volk*. When Kubizek realized that Hitler was not attending the academy and questioned him about it, Hitler unleashed violent diatribes against crass civil servants with no artistic insight, men who accepted even women for study.

Kubizek was invited to play in the academy orchestra and soon had students of his own. When he brought women home for lessons, Hitler's sexual jealously must have raged. Hitler also attended a ceremony at the end of Kubizek's first year of studies; not only was a composition of Kubizek's played by the orchestra, but the director of the school congratulated Kubizek on his high grades and encouraged him to apply to the Vienna Symphony Orchestra. It was all too much. When Kubizek returned from summer recess, Hitler did not meet him as promised, and he left no forwarding address. Now the ultimate loner, he wandered the streets filled with fierce longings, sensing his power but with nothing to show for it, needing more than ever to believe that, as he would write, "The value of a man is determined by his inner racial virtues." Millions believed the same, but for failures like Hitler it was a final hope. The most avid racists, and Nazis, tended to be low achievers needing enemies to blame for their failures. Vienna attracted the youth of the provinces, but for most it was merely another place to fail. The population soared, far more so than in Paris or London. Terrible housing conditions and un-employment were rife. The police constantly ordered newcomers back to their villages. Radical rightists everywhere were often migrants from provinces to big cities where, unprepared for the shock of urban life and the open contempt for traditional beliefs preached by anarchists and the socialist press, many joined fascist movements that preserved in symbol and myth the attitudes they had left behind. They erected a racial wall between themselves and the aliens whose success was all too visible.

In *Mein Kampf* Hitler tells the fictional tale of a boy who comes to the big city from a rural town in search of employment, there to be lost to the *Volk* by poverty, moral corruption, and the heartless cynicism of the city. Hitler detested Vienna, the second city of his failures. He would always hate large cities. Later, in his racial empire in the east, they were to be razed. Hitler was not the type to enjoy the free and easy ways of many Viennese, superficially at least a city of wine, dance, light opera, and sophisticated distance from rabid enthusiasms, a culture designed to shock the rigid provincial puritan. He never engaged in sophisticated con-versation or ironic wit and was uncomfortable in the presence of those who did.

Hitler sold his drawings to tourists to supplement his orphan's allot-ment and a small inheritance. It may be that he had a dispute with a Jewish merchant ending in court, but such encounters are too often used to explain too much. Like all racists, Hitler needed no direct personal ex-perience to become an anti-Semite. Indeed, the Jew as symbol is best left unmodified by the complexities of the Jew as ordinary human. Hitler was forced to become a resident in a charity men's home, an institution fi-nanced partly by the generosity of the Rothschilds and all the more hated for that. Hitler also frequented soup kitchens, struggling to sell his post-cards in districts inhabited by poor and recently arrived Slavs and Or-thodox Jews from the east. His certainty of superior blood must have been all that kept him from total despair. In these districts he first encountered the eastern Jews whose Orthodox dress, religion, and Yiddish symbolized the racial threat feared by so many Viennese. Many were lowly peddlers, but to Hitler's mortification so was he, and with far less cause. Hitler claimed, falsely, that he first became an anti-Semite when he saw Or-thodox Jews in Vienna. These "caftan wearers" were unclean, repulsive, unheroic; wherever one cut into the "abscess of filth and profligacy," he declared, "one found, like a maggot in a rotting corpse, often dazzled by the sudden light—a kike!"[2] Anti-Semites need stereotypes; corrupt blood must be revealed by corrupt physiognomy. But the successful Jew was the most uncomfortable reminder of personal failure. Nothing created violent urges in the unachieving anti-Semite more than the sight of the successful Jew, living refutation of Aryan superiority. Hitler insisted that no Jew had ever created anything of value; whatever they achieved must necessarily be the result of an international conspiracy of deceit. His struggles increased his will to violence and fantasies of messianic superiority. If the Jews were not what he supposed them to be, then he was nothing, with no one to blame but himself.

Racists starkly distinguish between good and evil in order to avoid the uncertainties and doubts of complex judgments. Hitler's preferred tabloid, under the slogan "Buy Only from Christians," carried racist soap operas, unverified stories of Jewish merchants, bankers, lawyers, and physicians cheating Aryans. Taafe's police confiscated the more violent issues and barred its sale in state shops, but it was readily available for free perusal in hundreds of pubs and restauraunts. Fantasies about the sexual pollution of Aryan blood also abounded in Hitler's favorite reading—pornography legitimated by ideology. The Liberal party had legalized prostitution in 1873 in order to regulate it for health reasons, but the racist press pounced on this as evidence of the corruption of "Jewish" liberalism. Kubizek tells us that Hitler often took him for walks through redlight districts, holding forth on the need to keep one's blood pure until marriage. Homosexuality was also feared and hated, portrayed as a result of "Jewish blood." When the Social Democrats defended the rights of homosexuals, anti-Semites took this as evidence it was indeed a Jewish disease. Long before the Nazis murdered homosexuals, rightist gangs in Vienna and Berlin beat gays, not only for money and "kicks," as was common throughout the West, but for the noble cause of protecting racial purity. The anti-Semitic press also reviled the "Jewish" press for advertisements featuring scantily clad women. Even installment buying was evidence of the immorality of Jewish retailers, luring Gentiles into debt.

When he ran for office in the 1920s, Hitler silenced the volkists among the Nazis: they hindered his search for votes among respectable Christians. But in Vienna he sought the confirming grace of racial superiority in its most extreme forms, avidly reading the writings of Liebenfels, ex-monk, zealous fan of Schoenerer, and devotee of the communal cult of golden, supple-bodied Aryan warriors. Liebenfels named his magazine *Ostara* after the Teutonic goddess of spring, published it under the swastika, and in it demanded the extermination of inferior races. *Ostara* had a circulation of 100,000 and was also readily available for free reading in pubs. "Tormented by visions of the sexual impotence of Aryan males," Liebenfels feared the female sexuality that he believed drew Aryan women to racial inferiors.[3] Eva Braun, later Hitler's mistress and finally his wife, indicated Hitler was not much of a sexual being, yet there has been much speculation about his possible sexual eccentricities. But Hitler's sex life, as oddly interesting as it may or may not have been, is unimportant. Sexual practices alone tell us nothing about fascist proclivities; it is the sexual politics of race that does the damage. Hitler's Wagnerian "Stephanie" fantasies were buttressed by the pornography of race, where blond Nordic women, lured by Jewish brothel owners, are threatened by the dark forces of the inferior races. His favorite tabloid "revealed" that "Jewish" pimps, brothel owners, and white slavers seduced Aryan virgins in order to pollute their blood. For Hitler and those like him, pornography alone did not suffice. Interracial sex must have conspiratorial purpose. In *Ostara*, inferior races used sex to destroy superior blood, protected by Jews who preached toleration and assimilation, which led, in Hitler's obscene words, to "the seduction of thousands of girls by bowlegged, repulsive Jewish bastards," a deliberate move in the race war.[4]

Ostara may have shaken Hitler's belief in his own racial credentials, for it published a chart enabling readers to compare their physiognomy with the Aryan ideal. If Hitler used the chart—and who could resist?— Robert Waite has shown he would have scored only marginally Aryan.[5] The shock would have made it all the more necessary to conform to the most extreme Aryan behavior. Later the Nazi party ordered local officials to stop harping on the blond and blue-eyed, and declared Hitler the highest Aryan type. It is even possible Hitler feared he had Jewish ancestors, though it has been proven he did not. But if he did fear contamination, he would have been even more anxious to prove the opposite. Worry about the purity of his own blood may have been the origin of his lifelong avoidance of contamination of his bodily fluids by alcohol, tobacco, and meat. Fritsch and the volkists did the same. Given the history of intermixing through the ages, few Europeans could be sure they had no Jewish ancestor. Hitler knew no race was pure, but he assumed Aryans were relatively so and hoped to restore purity by destroying the source of contamination.

Desperate to reveal his greatness, among the homeless Hitler exhibited his one great skill, his famous oratory. His endless harangues almost got him thrown out of the men's home. So compelling was his oratory that some historians mistakenly consider it a potent cause of his rise to power. But Hitler's simple worldview was the source of his dramatic speaking power. The voice of reason is tentative and reflective, that of the consensus politician calm and noncommittal. But the stark and angry simplicities of the demagogue are explosively charismatic because they slash through the complexities of reality, blaring simple slogans. The harsh, dramatic cadences we see in old newsreels were common on the radical right (and left): Boeckel, Ahlwardt, and Lenin are said to have possessed the gift, if such it be; Streicher and Goebbels certainly did, and for that matter Father Coughlin and Gerald L. K. Smith in the United States were among the best. These "terrible simplifiers" release hatreds in themselves and in their audiences, who respond with the ecstasy of a religious revival meeting. Like them, Hitler inspired only those who shared his angers; roars of "*Sieg Heil*" came because he avoided all that was new, complex, or thoughtful, repeating ideas his audience had already absorbed from a culture of racism extending over decades. During his public speeches in the 1920s, the socialists in the beer halls did not listen in silent rapture or "*Heil.*" They interrupted him with insults, flying beer bottles, and hurtling chairs. Only after storm troopers cleared the hall did Hitler gain unanimous approval.

Aside from racist trash, Hitler was no reader; his political attitudes were forged by experience. Arriving in Vienna at the high point of racial confrontation and political paralysis, ignorant of Western parliamentary practice, he knew only the parliament at Vienna, visiting it often during the years when it was paralyzed by ethnic confrontations. Allotted by race, the delegates were expected to put the demands of their ethnic group above imperial interests. Pragmatic accommodation was racial treason. Hitler easily concluded that politics was a war between the races, democracy a mortal threat to German blood, racial loyalty the highest virtue. Along with hundreds of thousands of Austro-Germans he believed that "The highest aim of human existence is not the preservation of a state, let alone a government, but the preservation of the species."[6] Germans must destroy the "parliamentary principle of majority rule" that "sins against the basic aristocratic principle of nature." Trust your racial instincts, he advised, "think with your blood."[7] Racial war was the core of Nazi belief, and in Austria ethnic differences were intimately tied to job, status, and income. Kubizek writes that after visiting parliament, Hitler loosed violent diatribes against the Hapsburg betrayal of German blood. For failures like Hitler, Hapsburg concessions to minorities threatened their meager prospects and opened deep psychic wounds.

To anti-Semites in Germany, the Jews were symbols of liberalism. When Hitler reached Vienna, symbolism was unnecessary, for almost all liberal votes came from Jewish districts, and liberalism was finished. Socialism was the great threat. In Linz, Social Democrats were already the majority party. During Hitler's Vienna years, socialists gained one-fourth of the votes in the empire and one-third in Germany. To ingratiate himself with proletarians, Hitler falsely claimed to have been a construction worker who had shared their struggle and learned that socialism was a

Jewish fraud. If Hitler did speak to workers, they were probably fellow
supplicants in the homeless shelter. As Hitler wrote:

> These men rejected everything: to them the nation was an invention
> of the "capitalists" (how often was I forced to hear this single word!);
> the Fatherland an instrument of the bourgeoisie for exploiting the work-
> ing class; the authority of law a means for oppressing the proletariat;
> the school an institution for breeding slaves and slaveholders; religion
> a means for stultifying the people and making them easier to exploit;
> morality a stupid, sheeplike patience, etc. Absolutely nothing was not
> drawn through mud of terrifying depth.[8]

Unlike Stoecker and Lueger, Hitler had no complaints about capitalism except to call for racial reform: a woman worker must be treated with
special care, "at least during the months when she bore the future national comrade under her heart."[9] The child of the race must be protected. Hitler claimed his "discovery" that Jews led socialism was the great
transformation of his life, caused when he saw Jewish names on socialist
writings. But his tabloids told him all he knew, and he found it pointless
to refute Marxism, a poison created by racial enemies who themselves did
not take it at face value. During his Vienna years the Social Democrats
won the votes of a half-million Slavs, uniting the class and blood enemies
of Germans with the slogan "The proletariat has no Fatherland." Hitler
countered, "Only a knowledge of the Jews" revealed "the real aims of Social Democracy."[10] Echoing Luther, he claimed it was useless to debate
Jews, "devils" who aimed for the "collapse of human civilization and the
devastation of the world." Better to drive the "pestilential whores" from
the face of the earth.[11] Also like Luther, Lueger, and Schoenerer, Hitler
believed no amount of persuasion could change Jews' "diabolical crafti-
ness." To protect their "luckless victims," these "seducers and corrupters"
should be shot.[12] "If, with the help of this Marxist creed, the Jew is victorious over the other peoples of the world, his crown will be the funeral
wreath of humanity and this planet will, as it did thousands of years ago,
move through the ether devoid of men."[13]

As we know, violent ethnic conflicts breed brutal, deadly, and non-
negotiable distinctions between friend and foe. More than most anti-
Semites, pan-Germans allowed for no exceptions: whatever Jews
supported, whatever they said, whatever their social role, their goal was
to destroy the Germanic peoples. Already in Vienna, Hitler and thousands like him believed all Jews to be part of a unified racial plot: Jewish international financiers exploited the worker so that Jewish socialists
could spur revolution; Jewish democrats attacked military autocracy in
order to conquer the strong; Jewish intellectuals derided Christian values
in order to sap the racial strength of their foe; Jewish international fi-

nanciers plunged the global economy into depression, revolution, and war for the good of their race. To Hitler, a Jew could never be anything but a mortal enemy of civilization. If Germans were blind to this it was because the Jew had the ability, cultivated through long centuries of half-hearted Christian oppression, to survive by hiding his true motives and using his enemy's strength to his own advantage.

It would be a grievous distortion to think that an Austrian *had* to lead the Nazis, but Hitler's youthful experience was an advantage, and he knew it. It is not too much to say that he adopted Schoenerer's ideology and Lueger's strategy, adjusting both, of course, to the circumstances of Germany in 1919. Rarely one to credit others, he praised both. Schoenerer's pan-Germans revealed Austria's willingness to pander to a worthless collection of multiethnic degenerates and "released the glorious concept of love of Fatherland from the embrace of this sorry dynasty."[14] Schoenerer welcomed the "collapse of this impossible state . . . and with it the hour of freedom for my German Austrian people." Only so "could *Anschluss* with the old motherland be restored."[15] Referring to his pan-German school days, Hitler wrote, "Did we not know, even as little boys, the Austrian state had and could have no love for the Germans?"[16] Schoenerer knew the "poignant emotion" of those who "long for the hour that will permit them to return to the heart of their faithful mother."[17] Hitler also believed the pan-Germans had wasted their energies in a doomed parliament of political amateurs. Consequently the masses never understood the pan-Germans, for the Jewish press distorted their ideas, and Schoenerer never took to the streets with his fiery rhetoric: "Only a storm of hot passion can turn the destinies of peoples."[18] Nor should Schoenerer have reviled Catholicism: "For the political leader the religious doctrines and institutions of his people must always remain inviolable."[19] Hitler ordered his Nazis never to attack Christianity, though many shared a pan-German hatred of Catholicism.

Lueger, Hitler believed, was more politically astute. He worked with the religious sensibilities of the masses, thereby gaining the support of the church, otherwise a Hapsburg weapon. Lueger never offended traditional elites. And Lueger knew that "All great movements are popular movements, volcanic eruptions of human passions" stirred by calamities and lit by the "firebrand of the word."[20] Compromises with parliamentarians were fatal; go to the masses. Unlike Schoenerer, Lueger did not neglect the economic needs of the middle class. He "understood the importance of the social question."[21] Lueger also built upon the power of Christian anti-Semitism, but in this there was a fatal if unavoidable flaw. Dependence on the church forced him to accept the idea that faith transcended race, giving the Jew a chance to save himself by "a simple splash of baptismal water."[22] Christian Social racism was too "halfhearted"; the Jews were secure and they knew it. Circumstances forced Lueger to sacrifice the truth of race. Committed to saving the dying multinational empire, he could not turn with true Teutonic fury on the Slavs. At Lueger's funeral, Hitler wrote, he was "profoundly moved" but knew his work was doomed. "If Dr. Karl Lueger had lived in Germany, he would have ranked among the great minds of our people; that he lived and worked in this impossible state was the misfortune of his work and of himself."[23] Above all, Lueger's success resulted from his belief that hatreds must be focused on the real enemy, the Jew. From him, Hitler learned the most important and fateful lesson of all: "The art of all truly great national leaders at all times consists . . . not in dividing the attention of a people, but in concentrating it upon a single foe."[24]

Lueger was the "last great German" of Austria, Hitler wrote, "a statesman greater than all the so-called diplomats of that period put together."[25] But the destiny of the Germanic *Volk* was a task for the German Reich. The tactics of Hitler's foreign policy depended on the consequences of World War I, but he learned his strategy in Vienna. Germany's primary goal must be unity and a racial war of territorial conquest against the Slavs. In this too he was hardly unique. For him, as for millions of middle- and upper-class Austro-Germans, 1914–1918 was the inevitable racial confrontation between Teuton and Slav, a conviction overwhelmingly reinforced by the conflict between Serbs and Germans as they careened into war.

With Russian help, the kingdom of Serbia had won independence from the Turks in 1878, but inside the Austro-Hungarian Empire there were still some 400,000 Serbs. By 1903 Serbia hoped to liberate them by war and unite with them in a South Slav state. If the Hapsburgs allowed this, the empire would be inundated with independence movements. Franz Josef preferred concessions to war; for Hitler and most nonsocialist Germans, this was a betrayal of German blood to pacify a barbaric tribe of pig herders, "racial mistakes" lucky to be ruled by Germans. In 1909 Austria annexed Bosnia-Herzegovina and its Serbs; in return, Russian agents stirred all Slavs against Austria. Serbs and Germans rioted in Sarejevo and Vienna, Serbia mobilized, and Austrian soldiers massed on the Serb border. Russia backed down when Germany threatened to fight if Russia interfered. Angry and humiliated, Russian pan-Slavs organized a great meeting in Saint Petersburg to denounce the Austrians.

Uproar inflamed the minorities of the Austrian Empire as they shouted "Long live Serbia" and "Down with Austria." Germans and Czechs rioted in the streets and in parliament. In Prague, roving bands rioted, shouting "Kill the Germans." Many were wounded, and martial law was declared. In Vienna, Slavs attacked the Opera House during a performance of Wagner, an act of unprecedented sacrilege. Jews were denounced by

Slavs as pro-German, by Germans as pro-Slav. Once more Franz Josef disbanded parliament; deputies marched out singing national anthems and calling for war. Everywhere Slavs called for independence. The Slovenes attacked Germans and their property when Franz Josef refused to appoint a pan-Slav mayor in a Slovenian town. Infantry had to quell thousands of anti-German protesters. Traveling to Trieste to assert Hapsburg claims, the archduke Franz Ferdinand was shouted down by Italian nationalists, and terrorists tried to blow up his train. Even the Poles, favored by imperial authorities, roared approval when Paderewski, making his political debut, spoke of independence for the Polish Fatherland. Ruthenians requested Russian aid as did the Czechs, who also organized their own economic and political institutions and paramilitary groups and called for a huge Slavic state under Russian rule. The tsar's ministers attended a banquet in honor of Slavic unity. For millions, not just Hitler, it was a racial war to the death.

By 1910 governing was impossible. Hitler, the pan-Germans, and Slavic militants all reveled in the chaos. Regional assemblies and the parliament at Vienna were paralyzed, and Austria was ruled by imperial decree. Only the Social Democrats called for peace and an end to warlike provocations. German nationalists insisted that socialists and Jewish press lords were conspiring to cut military budgets, leaving Germans at the mercy of Slavs. Such ideas thrived in the nationalist papers of Berlin and Vienna. In Vienna, Germans rioted against celebrating Serbs when the Serbs invaded and defeated Albania after the first Balkan War in 1912. Flushed with success, the Serb prime minister announced: "The first round is won; now we must prepare for the second, against Austria."[26] In Berlin, General von Moltke announced in a council of war, "I hold war to be inevitable, and the sooner the better." He was one of those angered by the election of a "Jewish" Reichstag in 1912. Now millions were ready for racial war.

In October 1913 the Austrians told the Serbs to leave Albania or be thrown out. Kaiser William declared his full support should Franz Josef decide to invade Serbia. Russia backed down yet again. As Serb troops left Albania, pan-Slavs denounced the tsar. German publicists crowed; had not Slavic inferiority already been demonstrated in 1904 when the lowly Japanese defeated Russia? Austrian military chiefs regarded it as a defeat even to allow the Serbs to back down; Serbia must be wiped out. The east must be German.

Grotesque cartoons portraying "subhuman" Slavs now became a staple in Vienna and Berlin. Tsarist agents encouraged the Serbs, and Viennese journalists wrote editorials about the Russian peril. Russian leaders spoke of the just demands of their Slavic comrades. Germany declared that Russian intervention would unsheath the German sword. The kaiser's generals called for a "defensive" war against Russia, and recruits flocked to Serb terrorists. By spring 1914 the Austrian government had decided that one more aggressive act by Serbia would mean war. Excluding the Social Democrats and a few remaining liberals, the Austro-German community ached to teach the Slavs a final lesson. Calls for "racial war" abounded; vicious hostility toward Jews and socialists was the norm. Hitler's call in Mein Kampf for racial war against Slavs reflected a prewar consensus among nonleftist Austro-Germans as well as German conservatives, pan-Germans, and nationalist anti-Semites.

Franz Ferdinand's trip to Sarajevo in 1914 was a provocation; to send the heir to the Hapsburg throne to the capital of Bosnia-Herzegovina on the very day when Serbs mourned their defeat by the Turks in 1389 was to ask for trouble. Franz Ferdinand, who had been a fan of Lueger, hoped to thwart the drive for a "Greater Serbia" by creating a German-dominated South Slav entity. With his assassination the iron wheel began to roll. German nationalists believed they must dominate the Hapsburg Empire, which Bismarck had once called a "living corpse," in order to unite the isolated communities of Germans extending to the borders of Russia and beyond—the last Germans excluded from the Reich. Patriotic leagues and bunds were unwilling to leave these islands of ethnic Germans at the mercy of Russian-backed Slavic nationalists.

As war approached, Hitler was ecstatic. In 1909 he had not registered for the draft in Austria. He would not fight for the Hapsburgs; instead he would fight for Germany. In 1913 he left for Munich. In Mein Kampf he claimed that as the bells tolled for the dead Mayor Lueger, he already recognized that the "little flames in the Balkans" meant that "Nothing could save this state of racial desecration; I knew then the Empire could not last. Only its downfall could bring the redemption of the Germans." War was a glorious opportunity to redeem failure and free the suppressed virile racial instincts he had felt in himself since boyhood. "In the hour when war came, I fell down on my knees, tears streaming from my eyes; at last I had been released from the pains and suffering of my youth."[27] There is a famous photograph of his joyful face among the vast crowd in the Odeon Platz in Munich as the outbreak of war was announced. He promptly joined up. Europeans, excluding many socialists, greeted war calmly; nationalists were enthusiastic. In Central Europe millions welcomed a racial conflict for domination of the Continent. Most thought it would be brief, but by 1915 the machine gun, rapid-fire artillery, and trench warfare had destroyed the chivalry of old. Among civilians, even an expressed hint that there might be some good in the foe was treason. Deaths mounted, reason and compassion became casualties, vulgar banality and crude simplicity destroyed rational discussion and subtle ambivalence. Encouraged by government propaganda everywhere, the war intensified national and ethnic hatreds.

Hitler loved war's dreadful and stark distinction between friend and foe. A "runner" carrying messages in the heat of battle, Hitler was still a comrade to no one, but no longer was he a purposeless drifter. He had embraced the noblest and most popular of causes. Although highly decorated for valor in combat, he was not the kind of man who could be promoted; he would never be a good intermediary. War reinforced his belief in a world conspiracy against Germans. From the front he wrote that each soldier had but one thought, to defeat the external enemy, then square accounts with the Jews at home. Later he wrote that the Germans might have won if they had gassed "twelve or fifteen thousand of these Hebrew corrupters of the people." The next time, before "foreign enemies are conquered, the enemies within must be annihilated."[28]

After the defeat of 1918, the beliefs and hatreds of Hitler's adolescence were commonplace among millions of embittered Germans. The failed youth, now a wounded and decorated hero, became, along with hundreds of thousands in Austria and Germany, a dedicated warrior in the struggle against the Weimar Republic, that creature of vengeful Allies and international Jewry. The Austro-Hungarian Empire was gone, replaced by Slavic nations. Russia was Bolshevik, "Jewish" socialists ran Weimar, communism threatened. Millions were receptive to the ideas of a Hitler and thousands of others like him. As Hitler wrote, in Vienna he had learned that when disasters hit, the German middle classes would know whom to follow and whom to destroy. Nazi ideology was scarcely the creation of a near psychotic and a few henchmen. It was an extreme version of ideas long familiar to millions. The tragedy is not that an obsessed fanatic somehow gained power, but that his bellicose racial hatreds were shared by legions of his fellow Germans and Austrians.

14: THE GREAT WAR AND RACISM

> Although my hatred of the enemy . . . is as hot as ever, so is my anger
> and resentment at those German power-politicians who, by their pre-
> sumption and stupidity, have dragged us down into this abyss. Re-
> peatedly in the course of the war, we could have had a peace by
> agreement, if it had not been that the boundless demands of the
> Pan-German-militarist-conservative alliance made it impossible.
> —Friedrich Meinecke, preeminent German historian

ALTHOUGH decisively repudiated by the electorate in 1912, the autocracy,
protected in undemocratic Prussia, still controlled the only weapon left
to halt democracy and social reform—foreign policy. Pressing for war,
often without informing the Foreign Office, the military pushed Austria
to be more aggressive. Chancellor Bethmann-Hollweg had the unenvi-
able task of persuading Europe that Germany was not the aggressor. He
pushed the largest military budget in German history through the Reichstag in 1913, but court circles nonetheless denounced him as weak. To his
associates Bethmann complained that Germany had antagonized France,
Russia, and England with an irresponsible foreign policy meant to
weaken the domestic left. When the kaiser wanted the Social Democrats
outlawed, Bethmann objected and was immediately labeled the "Jewish
chancellor," though the dutiful bureaucrat remained the creature of the
elites. Reichstag leaders were never told of his foreign policies; one could
not share state secrets with civilians and socialists, and the right knew that
an informed Reichstag would press for conciliation. Germany's implicit
demands were impossible to meet: there would be no war if the Russians
gave up their Balkan ambitions, if the French were content to become a
second-rate power, and if the British would allow Germany to dominate
the Continent and share naval superiority. No realist could expect any of
this to happen, and none did.

International belligerence was not a German monopoly, but only in
Austria, Germany, and Russia was bellicosity a substitute for reform. The

French republic and the British government were not at risk, but without war Austria-Hungary faced dissolution, and German and Austrian elites the erosion of their power and privileges by the increasing power of the left. Moreover, German nationalists and Russian pan-Slavs believed war necessary for racial dominance. There was no war guilt in any simple sense; war was the honored profession of the aristocracy, and few foresaw that a modern conflict would consume the youth of Europe in bloody horror.

As the western front stalemated in blood, nationalism and ethnic hatreds burst out in every warring nation. Uncertainty became unbearable and racial stereotypes the norm, encouraged by government propaganda. Because they fought on all sides and yet were still considered one people, the Jews were in the greatest danger. Allied publicists accused them of betraying their liberal principles to fight for autocracy; German publicists accused them of secretly favoring the Allies because they were liberals. In fact, Jewish communities supported the war efforts of their separate nations, though Russian Jews naturally mustered little enthusiasm. German Jews hoped sacrifice in war would convince all of their patriotism, and indeed, in the name of national unity, German anti-Semitism was muted at first. As the war ground on and the wholesale slaughter of drafted civilians commenced, all governments rallied their peoples with high-minded pronouncements of moral purpose. The Allies, in spite of Russian autocracy, prated about making the world safe for democracy. Germany had no universal message but spoke of defending a uniquely superior Germanic *Kultur*. Ethnicity and the identification of Jews with Western liberalism excluded them.

Soon German racism surpassed even prewar intensity, encouraged by the German army. When Jews were accused of slacking, the general staff requested the Ministry of War to conduct a count of Jews at the front. The results were never made public, for they showed the proportion of Jews who fell in battle was the same as in the German urban population and only slightly less than the population in general; peasants suffered the most. Adjusted to reflect the numbers of those with educational and professional skills needed for tasks behind the lines, there were more Jewish casualties than should have been expected. And almost half the German Jews who served were decorated. In an army famous for treating Jewish soldiers with contempt, the medals must have been doubly earned. Anti-Semitism was so strong at the front that German Jewish officers were often amazed when their orders were obeyed.

In the Reichstag only socialists and Progressives protested the military's treatment of Jewish soldiers, charges dismissed as leftist philo-Semitism. No evidence of Jewish bravery in battle could be allowed to contradict the cherished myth of the supremacy of the Germanic Prussian warrior,

208   IDEOLOGY OF DEATH

for upon this myth rested the elite's historical claim to special privilege. Jewish groups said discrimination should end in order to reward the Jewish community for its patriotism. If Jews fought, others declared, it was not for love of Germany but to punish a justly anti-Semitic Russia. Naturally, Zionism became popular among Jewish soldiers.[1]

Jewish businessmen used their talents for the German war effort. The most famous, Walther Rathenau, warned the high command in 1914 that they would lose if they did not collect raw materials on a grand scale. He knew, as most generals did not, that industrial might would be decisive. Rathenau was given the task of organizing Germany's industrial production. But the symbolism of the Jew as traitor prevailed, and nothing Jews could do would change it. In 1916 even Mathias Erzberger, a moderate and leader of the Catholic Center, demanded the government count the number of Jews at work in the various economic ministries in order to respond to rumors they were harming the nation. Rathenau, director of War Materiel Collection, was accused of enriching his fellow Jews. The Agrarian Bund and conservatives supported Erzberger; Social Democrats responded by requesting a report of those in the upper classes who avoided wartime sacrifice. The head of the League for the Prevention of Anti-Semitism noted that if Jews had been allowed to be reserve officers, they would have had more than economic skills to place at Germany's service. Walther Rathenau had not been allowed a reserve commission in the peacetime army. No overrepresentation of Jews in government positions was found, hardly surprising given prewar exclusionary policies. No one counted shirking aristocrats or Gentiles. After the war Rathenau and Jewish business leaders were labeled the "organizers of defeat," yet historians agree that without Rathenau's work Germany could not have held out nearly as long as it did.

As the war dragged on and casualties mounted, anti-Semitic publications grew more vitriolic than ever before, and the Ministry of War was deluged by unsubstantiated stories of Jewish slackers, black marketers, and subversives. The prestigious *Prussian Yearbook* insisted that international Jewry "holds the world in its hands"; all nations should fight the real enemy, the Judaization of peoples by Jewry.[2] In 1916 Theodore Fritsch and Alfred Roth, representing anti-Semitic groups, sent a memo to the kaiser complaining that Jews were war-profiteering by cornering the market in vital supplies. Pan-Germans loudly complained that Jewish profiteering, not just the British blockade, caused food shortages and industrial shortfalls, willfully ignoring the vast war profits piled up by pan-German industrialists and the doubtful patriotism of some—like the "ultrapatriot" Krupp, who early in the war had to be bribed with higher prices to stop selling steel for munitions to France. When the British issued the Balfour Declaration promising a Jewish home in Palestine, Jews were accused of bribing the Allies and secretly supporting them. By late 1917, a time of hunger, the German volkist symbol, the swastika, sprouted up among new and ever more militant racist organizations.

German military leaders, industrialists, aristocrats, and academics demanded that a victorious Germany annex parts of Belgium, Holland, France, Eastern Europe, western Russia, and overseas territories. Excluding the Social Democrats, all parties favored some annexations. Grandiose war aims were not exclusively German, but the aims of the pan-Germans, the Agrarian Bundists, and patriotic organizations were more extreme and were paired with attacks against "international Jewry" and the demand for "living space." Through Alfred Hugenberg, industrialist, war profiteer, and leader in the Conservative party, industrialists established a variety of hidden accounts containing millions of marks subsidizing magazines and papers favoring extreme war aims. Germany's rulers feared the populace would not long endure its sacrifices without the promise of great territorial gains to counter the Allies' appeal to democracy, less hypocritical after Russia's withdrawal and the entry of the United States.

In 1916 Bethmann-Hollweg sent out tentative peace feelers, but he was forced to withdraw them when Generals Ludendorff and Hindenburg, Germany's most famed warriors, threatened to resign. That same year the left wing of the Social Democrats broke with the majority to agitate for peace without annexations. By now it was clear that a humane and just resolution of the bloody stalemate would outweigh any possible gains for any nation involved. The breakaway leftists, the Independent Socialists, were roundly denounced as "Jewish traitors" who ought to be shot. Bethmann-Hollweg and the successor to Franz Josef, Emperor Karl, also interested in peace, were accused of doing the work of the Jews. In the summer of 1917 the Catholic Center proposed a peace resolution with no forced annexations or reparations. Speaking for high command and kaiser, Ludendorff angrily rejected the proposal. Russia was close to defeat, and Ludendorff was planning an empire in the east. Peace without annexations, he insisted, would mean that Progressives and Social Democrats would rule postwar Germany.

Pan-Germans, Agrarian Bundists, veterans' groups, Conservative party members, and anti-Semitic groups organized a furious campaign against the peace resolution. Led by Admiral Alfred von Tirpitz, advocate of all-out submarine warfare, a Fatherland's party was organized to oppose the resolution and demand vast annexations. By 1918 it had tens of thousands of members. Heavy industry contributed huge funds. At Verdun, unprecedented slaughter demoralized even some on the general staff, yet military leaders issued stern warnings of the consequences to morale if the army were "stabbed in the back" by the resolution. Nevertheless, in

July 1917 the resolution passed, supported by the Social Democrats, the Catholic Center, and the Progressives, opposed by National Liberals and Conservatives. Pan-Germans despaired: "The Reichstag of the Jewish vote will make a Jewish peace!"[3]

In all European nations, those who called for a negotiated peace were reviled by the press and often jailed for "aiding the enemy." But only in Germany was so much done to convince millions that the call for peace was yet another example of collective Jewish, Catholic, and socialist treason in the hour of approaching triumph. Bethmann-Hollweg was increasingly reviled as a tool of the Jews by pan-Germans, assorted patriotic leagues, H. S. Chamberlain, and Fritsch because of his tentative support for the peace resolution and his resistance to unrestricted submarine warfare. When the generals forced Bethmann to resign, replacing him with a plodding errand boy for the military, Germany became a military dictatorship. The generals ignored the peace resolution, but they never forgot it. During Weimar, racists insisted it had passed because the Reichstag, bought by Jewish gold in 1912, was determined to sabotage the Reich.

By late 1917 pan-German literature declared that the war was really between Germans and Jewry, and warned Jews they would soon have to "commence a battle for their very lives."[4] Military and political leaders received from Professor Hans von Liebig, pan-German publicist, a memorandum about the subversion of Jewish soldiers, calling Bethmann-Hollweg "the Chancellor of Jewry."[5] By the winter of 1917–1918, talk of the "Jewish Reichstag" was commonplace in the highest circles, especially after the kaiser was forced to promise democratic reforms after victory in order to stiffen German morale. If Germany were defeated, pan-Germans insisted, the Jewish Reichstag would make a Jewish peace and force Germany to pay heavy reparations. The Jewish-dominated Social Democrats, who always fought army budgets, would rule. Had not the Jews Rosa Luxemburg and Karl Liebknecht, German socialist leaders, said in 1914 that the proletariat should not support this "capitalist" war? When Lenin called for peace without annexations, the German right exulted: it was certain proof of the "Jewish-Bolshevik" world conspiracy. Jewish periodicals reported a sharp renewal of anti-Semitism; even Jews in other nations expressed unease about growing German racism.

In 1917 the Bolsheviks seized power, and peace negotiations soon began. In March 1918 the German generals (politicians had no say) demonstrated what the West might expect if Germany won. The Treaty of Brest-Litovsk gave Germany one-third of Russia's population and cultivated land, half her heavy industry, and almost all her coal mines. Only the Social Democrats opposed the draconian terms. Moreover, the German general staff immediately began to organize a satellite empire in Poland, the Ukraine, and Russia, an empire intended to reach into the Caucasus. The drive for *lebensraum* was never just a Nazi goal. Ludendorff and his fellow officers tied down forty divisions to pacify the east, damaging the overall war effort. The use of foreign and Jewish slave labor was also no Nazi invention. In response to requests from industrialists, the army forcibly deported 66,000 Belgian workers to Germany. Some 30,000 eastern Jews, fleeing pogroms, were forced to work in war industries.

For the right, bolshevism was a front for international Jewry. Anti-Semites everywhere believed the same, but the attitude prevailed in the highest circles in Germany. Ludendorff's adviser, Colonel Bauer, liaison officer to the government and pan-German representative to the high command, noted, "The negotiations with the Jews at Brest-Litovsk gave us a great opportunity to unveil through the arrogant loudmouth Jew Trotsky the goals of these secret international societies" who "arrogated to themselves the right to stir up international revolutions and intervene in the destinies of peoples." It was the Germans' "holy duty to do battle with them even beyond our borders"; all monarchists must unite to destroy "Judeo-Bolshevism."[6] Exulted by Russia's collapse, pan-Germans declared that Germany was on the threshold of global power, but only if the "red-gold Internationale" was broken.

In the spring of 1918 Ludendorff's last offensive failed, American troops were arriving, and the morale of the army was crumbling. On August 14 Ludendorff told a shocked Reichstag that Germany must have an armistice and a republican government to please the Allies; in September a stunned public was informed. Until the very end, military censors had allowed only reports of victories; even the Reichstag was kept in the dark. Defeat seemed unreal: Russia had surrendered, no German territory had been invaded, and the troops marched home intact and disciplined. No politician dared speak of defeat. Even socialist leaders officially welcomed the troops as victors. Already the famous "stab-in-the-back" myth spread: German soldiers had been betrayed by the collapse of the home front. "Jewish" slackers, war profiteers, and socialist strikers were blamed, not the elites whose policies had led to the disaster. In fact, France and Britain had experienced more strikes than Germany, and Gentile industrialists had profited most. The public was not told that in the summer of 1918 many German units refused to fight and jeered those who did. Tragically, racism was used to vent mass frustration and hate as well as protect the old rulers. Many leftists played into the hands of the autocracy, insulting and beating officers on the streets. In November 1918 the army advised its officers not to wear uniforms in public.

Ludendorff had hoped to regroup for further battles. When the illusion failed he insisted the armistice accord with Wilson's Fourteen Points, terms he had ridiculed when victory seemed near. When he told the kaiser he must abdicate, the All Highest scornfully replied, "I have not the least intention of resigning because of the machinations of a few hundred Jews and their proletarian followers."[7] Before the war Ludendorff had believed that Jewish socialists and the Catholic Center sabotaged Germany's preparation for "inevitable" war by cutting army budgets—the culprits were Jews and others who had been turned into "artificial Jews." The Weimar Republic was their doing. In 1919, plunged into depression and perhaps hoping to lay to rest the ghosts of those who had died, Ludendorff needed conspiracies more than most: "Gradually I recognized the pernicious forces that had caused the collapse of a people, and in them the real enemies of the freedom of the German race . . . the secret supranational forces, namely: the Jewish people and Rome."[8]

In 1919 Ludendorff devoted himself to destroying the "internationalist, pacifist, defeatist" Jews and the Vatican, people who "systematically destroyed" our "racial inheritance and national character."[9] With his wife he turned out numerous pamphlets denouncing the global plot; one sold half a million copies. German historians rarely mention Ludendorff's obsessions, or dismiss them as the ravings of a demented man. But Ludendorff worked with thousands who thought the same, and he used his high prestige to raise extensive funds from army and business acquaintances for the radical right, including the Nazis. Formally announcing his partnership with Hitler in 1923, he joined in the famous Munich putsch attempt and was elected a Nazi deputy to the Reichstag in 1924. For him and Hitler, 1914–1918 was but the first battle. In his book Total War, Ludendorff exhorted Germany to use dictatorship to mobilize all resources for the next conflict. First, he insisted, Germany must be Judenrein. After 1934 Ludendorff complained that Hitler was too easy on the Jews, as did many Nazis in the early years.

Stunned by the seemingly overnight reversal of the war, the German public too was ready for conspiracy theories. The Pan-German League set up a Jewish Affairs Committee to "take advantage of the situation to issue smashing attacks against Jewry, and thus utilize the Jews as lightning rods for all injustices." Their leader, Heinrich Class, quoted Heinrich von Kleist, the German dramatist of the wars of Napoleon, who had said of the French: "Kill them, kill them all, the world tribunal will not demand of you your reasons!"[10] The translator of Peer Gynt and a close friend of Hitler, Dietrich Eckart, wrote in December 1918: "What, did we die for the benefit of loan sharks?"[11] In a popular pamphlet of 1919, the pan-German publicist Liebig insisted that international Jewry had wanted the war in order to profit from the death of millions. Later, with Nazi-like sincerity, the pan-Germans, upon discovering that Liebig's family was descended from a converted Jew of the eighteenth century, threw him out. Even Himmler was willing to forgive so old an ancestral slip-up for SS members.

As blow followed blow in the war's aftermath, racism gathered momentum. All that conservatives had feared since 1871 came to pass: the kaiser was replaced by a democratic republic controlled by socialists; the Austro-Hungarian Empire dissolved; aided by vengeful allies, inferior Slavs ruled where once Germans were masters; imperial Vienna was now the capital of a tiny, insignificant republic forbidden to unite with Germany and ruled by socialists. The Bolsheviks had Russia, and red revolutionaries roamed Berlin, Vienna, Munich, and Budapest. Hungary was a Soviet republic under Bela Kun, of Jewish origin, sent by Lenin from a Russian prisoner-of-war camp. Councils of leftist workers and soldiers sprang up throughout Germany. A communist revolution broke out in Berlin in January 1919, and in February a Soviet republic was declared in Munich. Numbed by defeat, revolution, and an Allied blockade threatening starvation, Germany became a pariah nation through a draconian treaty forced upon her in the name of war guilt.

Millions feared communism would sweep Germany. Unprecedented and unpredicted, bolshevism was the first powerful challenge to the West, a break with the past that even Marxists had not expected. Explanations were sorely required; to those ignorant of the immense differences between Russia and the West, Bolshevik victories seemed possible anywhere. Since 1789 reactionaries, unable to accept mass rejection, believed revolutions were caused by atheists, Freemasons, and Jews. Hysteria about the contagion of "Jewish bolshevism" was no German monopoly. The Protocols of Zion were published worldwide—a document forged by the tsarist secret police purporting to record a secret meeting of medieval rabbis to plan the conquest of Christian civilization through economic disasters, wars, and revolutions.

In the United States, for example, the radical right used the Protocols to explain Bolshevik success, and the State Department was flooded by rumors that German Jews had used Marxism to drive Russia out of the war. Methodist and Baptist ministers, former missionaries in Russia, "described" the spread of Jewish communism. Some briefed congressional committees. German "experts" in "Jewish affairs" helped write the notorious anti-Semitic articles of Henry Ford's Dearborn Independent, distributed by Ford dealers in the early 1920s. Powerful anti-Semitic organizations, including the Ku Klux Klan, Father Coughlin's Social Justice movement, and Reverend Gerald L. K. Smith's Christian Committee, insisted communism was Jewish. It made no difference that in 1923 almost half the members of the Communist party in the United States were of Finnish origin; the fact did not fit the ideological needs of the Christian right. Nevertheless, the American radical right remained relatively ineffective, a lower-class movement unable to form political alliances with the powerful.

But in Germany and Austria hundreds of thousands of the elite believed in the threat of "Judeo-bolshevism," especially because their new governments were run by socialists always assumed to be a Jewish front. Had not the Bolsheviks followed hard upon the socialist Kerensky in Russia? But in Russia revolution resulted from rural famine, land hunger, endless bloody defeats in war, and the collapse of a backward economy with no liberal tradition. German peasants were committed to private property, German socialists to democracy, and hunger was an urban and temporary postwar phenomenon. Looking back, historians see no potential for communism in Germany, but scholarly assessments after the fact do not affect the anxieties of those who cannot know how it will all turn out.

Inflamed by a flood of pamphlets highlighting the Russian Jews among the Bolshevik leadership, the public did not know that only some 7 percent were of Jewish origin, though Jews composed some 12 percent of the populations from which Bolshevik leaders were drawn. Tsar Nicholas II ruled his subject minorities harshly, hence almost all were overrepresented among revolutionaries. With no democratic or even safe way to protest, they could only submit to tsarist autocracy, secretly agitate for drastic change, or leave. From 1900 to 1920 more Russian Jews fled the country than ever chose revolution. In 1920 the highest proportion of minority peoples in the Bolshevik leadership were in fact Russians of German origin; Jews, Georgians, and Armenians came next. The information fit no racial stereotype. Because revolutionaries often changed names to avoid the secret police, it was easy to claim that a given Bolshevik was Jewish. Alfred Rosenberg, the leading Nazi expert on the communists, insisted that Lenin was the only non-Jew among the Bolshevik leaders. He claimed that world Jewry had paid for the revolution, that Russian workers were their slaves, and that Jewish Bolsheviks had destroyed the old Germanic elites and exterminated whole villages. Today *Pamyat*, the pro-tsarist movement, blames the Jews for 1917 and insists Lenin's mother was Jewish.

Most Russian Jews welcomed the abdication of the tsar, but so did most minorities, liberals, and the Allies, who were pleased to be no longer linked with a tyranny. Before Lenin, the Kerensky government had promised liberal reforms and an end to religious and minority oppression. The vast majority of politically active Russian Jews never supported the Bolsheviks. Even Marxist Jews favored the Mensheviks, who rejected Bolshevik dictatorship and worked for a democratic Russia. The German Social Democrats, including the most radical, Rosa Luxemburg, also feared

Bolshevik success. Only during the civil war in the Soviet Union, when the choice was either Lenin or the tsarists, did large numbers of young Jews choose the Bolsheviks—and they were atheists, a requirement for joining. Such realities did not fit the dogmas of racial determinists and were ignored. But when the Bolsheviks campaigned against anti-Semitism with millions of posters reading: "Anti-Semitism is counterrevolutionary; anti-Semitism is our class enemy," millions of racists took this to be proof that bolshevism was Jewish.[12] Indeed, in the civil war Jewish communities in the path of the white armies or Ukrainian nationalists were massacred; by 1921 more than 100,000 Jewish civilians had been slaughtered in Russia and Poland.

In Munich in November 1918, Kurt Eisner, a Jewish Social Democrat imprisoned for opposing the war, declared Bavaria a republic. Supported by councils of workers and soldiers, he formed a socialist government and held elections for a constituent assembly. In rural districts armed counterorganizations attracted hundreds of thousands under such slogans as "Israel is King of Bavaria!" Eisner was also denounced as a "Jewish traitor" when he published official documents indicating that Germany shared blame for the outbreak of the war. In the elections of January 1919, Eisner was handily defeated. Upholding parliamentary principles, he was about to resign when he was shot by an aristocrat, a member of Fritsch's anti-Semitic Thule Society. A few anarchists then declared a Bavarian Soviet dictatorship, and three Russians, one Lenin's press chief, two of them of Jewish origin, recruited a small "red army," closed banks, and printed money. The vast majority of Bavarians, including the Jewish community and the socialists, rejected them, but it did not help. Army units and thousands of rightists streamed into Munich to crush the dictatorship. The communists shot twenty hostages, but the rightists massacred hundreds, including unarmed "suspects," many Jewish. As memoirs testify, only socialist workers helped protect arrested Jews. In hospital recovering from wounds when he heard of the defeat, Hitler plunged into a deep depression that culminated in an hysterical outburst about his mission as the future savior of the Fatherland. Cured, he too left for Munich to take up arms against the Bavarian Soviet. After the volunteers and the army bloodily repressed the left, Hitler was hired by the army as a political "expert" on the Jewish-Bolshevik menace. An eager witness for the army at drumhead courts, he testified against suspected leftists who were then shot. Hitler was now a paid undercover agent of the most prestigious institution in Germany, fighting, like them, to reverse the consequences of a lost war. It was his first foray into politics.

The call for a republic resounded through Germany in November 1918. The kaiser's resignation brought great crowds into the Berlin streets, many singing the "Internationale" and demanding Soviet rule. Fearing revolution, Friedrich Ebert, acting head of government (who would have preferred a constitutional monarchy) called for an elected constituent assembly to create a democratic republic. As he said, "I hate [revolution] like I hate sin."[13] Ebert then made the most fateful decision of his career. The high command was represented by General Wilhelm Groener, and without consulting his colleagues, Ebert established a secret telephone line with him and asked the army to support the republic. Groener promised to do so, but only if the government would not purge the officer corps or create a citizens' militia, as the workers' councils wanted. Groener also said, "The officer corps expects that the government will fight against bolshevism, and places itself at the disposal of the government for such a purpose." Overjoyed at army support, Ebert agreed. The army, enemy of democracy, was allowed to arrogate to itself the government's role of deciding whom it would fight, and, as it turned out, who was a Bolshevik. Fear of radicalism and disorder led Ebert to override the traditions of his Social Democratic party that had always fought for civilian control over the military. Groener now demanded that Ebert and Gustav Noske (his defense minister) disband the soldiers' councils. They complied. Yet the councils were not revolutionary; they favored a democratic republic. Now the government could not hope to purge its enemies. But there was in any event little enthusiasm for a purge. In the midst of defeat, occupation, and a British blockade, a purge would have made it seem that the left was in fact a tool of an international conspiracy against Germany. Ebert and the Allies wanted the old rulers intact in order to halt communism.

Unlike Western armies, the German army was a powerful political institution, the political representative of the elites. In spite of the terrible losses and the dramatic influx of officers outside the nobility, 22 percent of the officer corps were nobles in 1920, out of a population in which only about one-tenth of 1 percent were aristocrats. Paradoxically, restrictions on the size of the army by the Versailles Treaty made it easier to build what in effect was an autocratic state within a state: by 1927, 80 percent of the cadet officer class were sons of the elites, and 44 percent of these sons of officers were on active duty; only 5 percent came from classes unacceptable before 1914. Naturally, the officers hoped one day to overthrow the republic. Higher officers were loyal to the Conservative party, now renamed the German National People's party, or DNVP. It was even more anti-Semitic than in prewar days. (I shall continue to refer to it as the Conservative party, as is customary.) Younger officers preferred the radical right. In 1919 some army units diverted funds and arms to radical right organizations and cooperated with them in actions against communists, socialists, and trade unionists. Hitler was an army agent when he first visited the headquarters of the National Socialist movement to see if it was worthy of support. Army funds probably helped the group purchase what became the official Nazi newspaper, the *Voelkische Beobachter.*

In the fall of 1918 the high command did not even reveal the imminent danger of a complete rout to its junior officers, nor tell them that the general staff, not politicians, had demanded the armistice. Frightened by the growing disobedience of front-line troops in the summer of 1918, the generals would not publicly admit their impotence. With radical discontent rising at home and socialist workers' councils proliferating, the high command released only divisions they knew would resist the left. Aware the Allies would not allow the use of force by the army, military authorities encouraged officers to form irregular units, armed and often uniformed, into what was called the Freikorps. Recruiting civilians, Freikorps units, many virulently anti-Semitic, fought pitched battles and guerrilla warfare to maintain German control over Poland and the Baltic states and hold off the Bolsheviks during the Russo-Polish War. After the agreement between Ebert and Groener, the army moved swiftly with Freikorps units to "restore order" in various parts of Germany itself.

If Ebert and Noske had ever thought to tame the army or use workers to fight for the republic, they dropped the idea when communist "Sparticists" in Berlin attempted to overthrow the government. Rosa Luxemburg and Karl Liebknecht, leaders of the Sparticists, had broken with the majority Social Democrats before the war, scorning their bureaucratic pragmatism and bitter over the party's support for the war. During hostilities, their courageous public antiwar speeches had won them jail sentences and death threats. Because both were of Jewish origin, the right used them as more evidence of the "Jewish Bolshevik" conspiracy. It did not matter that both were atheists with an overwhelmingly Gentile following, or that the vast majority of Jews were appalled by their revolutionary ideas. Although the workers' councils resoundingly rejected them, the Sparticists rose in armed uprising in Berlin in January 1919. Luxemburg believed they would fail, but she refused to desert them. Ebert used army units and volunteers recruited by the army to fight the left. They shot down workers, armed or unarmed, and captured and murdered Luxemburg and Liebknecht. The left was irrevocably split. The new German Communist party took its orders from Moscow; Lenin denounced the Social Democrats as betrayers of the revolution.

Four days after the Sparticist revolt ended, elections were held for the assembly to draft a new constitution. The Social Democrats received a record 38 percent of the vote; the former Progressives, now the German Democratic party (DDP), received 20 percent, as did the Catholic Center. All agreed to join the "Weimar coalition" government. For the first time a majority, and a large one, supported a democratic republic. The old rulers were still safe, for even if the socialists wished to purge them and pass socialist reforms, their coalition partners would not have agreed. Nevertheless, the right was on the defensive, their powers and privileges threatened. The Conservative party had received the fewest votes in its history, a humiliating 8 percent. Following their mandate, the new assembly met in the city of Weimar and created a model of democratic liberalism in the new constitution. Drafted under the leadership of Germany's leading expert on constitutional law, Hugo Pruess, it was put into effect in August 1919. Pruess had been kept from an academic career before 1914 because he was Jewish. Now the right complained that the republic was the creature of Jewish socialism with a constitution drafted by a Jew.

Ebert, now president of the republic, was detested by conservatives as a former saddle-maker and trade union boss. He was moderate to an excess, but to conservatives, democratic liberalism was the revolution incarnate. For the first time ministers and governments were responsible to political parties and the electorate, not autocratic fiat. The pall of defeat hung over the right, their old prestige forgotten, their fears reinforced when the new government ended discrimination in the civil service, bringing liberals, socialists, and Jews into the formerly private preserve of the right. More shocking still, the socialist Paul Hirsch, of Jewish origin, held Bismarck's hallowed post of minister president of Prussia. Hans von Seeckt, the most important political general in Germany until Hitler gained power, declared Hirsch "unsuitable because he is a Jew." What he and his peers said in private can only be imagined. Prussia was now a democratic stronghold. The inner sanctum of the old guard and the last strongpoint for counterrevolution seemed lost.

But the new republic would have neither the time nor the stability necessary to create a liberal Germany. The first blow fell in May 1919 when the harsh terms of the Versailles Treaty were dictated. Germany was to admit war guilt and pay unprecedented reparations of 132 billion gold marks. Germany had barely 2.4 billion gold marks in reserve, and her gross national product in 1913 had been only about 50 million marks. Some payments in kind were allowed, but manufacturers in other nations did not wish to open their markets to a flood of German goods. Yet Germany was required to allow trading rights to the Allies with no similar rights in return. The army was reduced to 100,000 men, bereft of tanks, offensive weapons, and officer training schools. The air force was abolished and the navy reduced to insignificance and deprived of submarines. The merchant fleet was to be confiscated. German colonies and overseas investments were seized. Some 13 percent of German territory was taken from her. Danzig, predominantly German, was given to Poland, the rich Saarland to France, with provisions for a plebiscite in fifteen years to allow the inhabitants to choose the nation they preferred. Allied troops were to occupy the Rhineland for a minimum of fifteen years, and Germany was refused entry into the League of Nations, which became, in effect, an international body for enforcing the terms of the settlement treaties. The Allied powers demanded the right to try hundreds of leaders as war criminals, the kaiser included, and Allied commissions were to inspect German compliance with the treaty.

Judging from the Brest-Litovsk Treaty and its own war aims, a victorious Germany would have imposed equal or worse terms. Such an unprecedented war allowed for no mercy to the defeated, while France, upon whose territory the war was fought, needed the treaty if Germany was not to emerge the stronger power in spite of defeat. Eventually Germany received far more in loans than she ever paid in reparations. But all this was irrelevant to a public virtually united in hatred.

At first the government refused to accept the treaty, but the Allies threatened to renew hostilities. There was talk of armed resistance, but army and government rightly feared the dismemberment of Germany by France, and local officials reported that the population was sick of war and would not cooperate. Many younger army officers wished to resist, and Ebert told Groener that the government would do whatever the army wanted. Groener privately informed Ebert he could not defend Germany should the Allies renew the war; Hindenburg preserved his reputation by avoiding the discussions altogether. The army hoped the republic would bear the burden of public fury. The majority of the Social Democratic Reichstag delegation initially voted to refuse to sign the treaty; even so, they, not the army, were most often attacked for "betraying" Germany. Forced to sign, the government extracted a guarantee from its opponents that they would not blame the government for Germany's dishonor. This agreement was violated almost immediately. Germany's first democratic republic paid the price for the lost war, while those responsible for hostilities were immeasurably strengthened by the harsh treaty; it was a positive godsend to the radical right. Hitler and hundreds of ultranationalists ranted against the traitorous "November criminals" and "Jewish socialists" who had betrayed Germany.

Austria inevitably suffered even more. The empire lost three-quarters of its territories, including the German Sudetenland. Socialist Karl Renner signed the treaty, and Otto Bauer, also a socialist, was foreign minister at the conference. Ineffective in war, shattered and dismembered, Austria could not even think of resisting Allied demands. Yet the "stab-in-the-back" theory was even more widespread there, partly because in early 1918 a million workers went on strike. Moreover, a larger proportion of the Jewish electorate voted socialist than in Germany; they had no other significant democratic choice. A leading Christian Social, now head

of a popular anti-Semitic bund, charged, "The debilitating disintegration
of the German people by Jewish poison is solely responsible for the Allied victory in the war."[14] Christian Socials and pan-Germans violently denounced "Jewish reds" for the defeat, and Jews were often physically
attacked in Vienna even before the war ended. For the first time the imperial government did not punish such crimes—an ominous portent. All
was exacerbated when thousands of eastern Jews, escaping massacres by
Russian anti-Bolsheviks and Ukrainian nationalists, fled to Germany and
Austria. Only the Social Democrats offered aid; all other parties turned
even more anti-Semitic.

Freikorps leaders hoped Seeckt and the army would lead them in war
against the republic, but Seeckt knew the Freikorps were no match for
Allied troops. In February 1920 the notorious Erhardt Brigade and other
Freikorps units hoped to conquer Poland and the Baltic states and create a
strongpoint for overthrowing Weimar and "purifying" Germany of socialists and Jews. As the Bolshevik danger in the east receded in 1921,
however, the Allies forced Weimar to recall the Freikorps. General
Walther von Luettwitz, furious, confronted Ebert, demanding the orders
be revoked. When Ebert refused, Luettwitz asked Colonel Hermann Erhardt, who swore he would never fight for the "Jewish" flag of the republic, to lead his brigade into Berlin. Having lived up to their agreement
with the high command, Ebert and Noske asked the generals to fulfill their
part of the bargain and protect the republic. To their consternation, the
chief of staff, Seeckt, gave his famous answer: "Troops do not fire
on troops." This was not true, for the army often fired on uniformed
soldiers in the workers' councils. But the army would not fight the ultraright, uniformed or not. The Weimar government fled, and Wolfgang
Kapp, former Prussian civil servant, friend of Ludendorff, and member of
anti-Semitic groups, led the *putsch*. The high command was unwilling
to fight for Kapp, for they knew the French would love an excuse to invade. The generals waited to see if the *putsch* would succeed. The Berlin
police openly supported Kapp.

Now Ebert and Noske needed the aid of the militant workers they once
feared, the only sizable group willing to defend the republic. Calling for
a general strike, the government opened its arsenals. Berlin and the Reich
were paralyzed. Kapp's government gave orders to shoot down all strikers
but backtracked as the army and its civilian supporters realized this would
bring leftist revolution and French troops. The *putsch* collapsed in a
week. Kapp's second-in-command declared, "Within our circle, there is
no enthusiasm left for anything except anti-Semitic agitation."[15] Only thirteen of the officers who supported Kapp were punished, and with laugh-
able sentences, a pattern followed by the judiciary until Hitler's success
gave them a state they believed worth defending.

Thousands of army and navy officers rooted for Kapp from the sidelines. Many donned the swastika worn by the Erhardt Brigade. Being pro-Kapp helped one's promotion, and those not deemed enthusiastic enough were purged. Officer cadets routinely attacked Jews; the army, pompously insisting it was nonpolitical, nevertheless "conducted intense anti-Semitic propaganda."[16] During the *putsch*, as the leading scholar of German industry, Henry A. Turner, has written, "Leading men of big business . . . maintained a posture they characterized as 'neutrality' which amounted to according the new government parity with the old."[17] In short, the Conservative party and business leaders supported violent and armed anti-Semitic rightist revolutionaries, albeit only if they were successful, and this before the ravages of inflation and the Great Depression brought millions of votes to the Nazis—the events, we are so often told, that finally persuaded German industrialists to support Hitler.

Independent socialists detested Ebert's cooperation with the old rulers and demanded the army be held responsible to elected representatives as the constitution specified. Ebert refused, and the electoral split within socialism widened. The first Reichstag elections were held in June 1920. With the terms of the Versailles Treaty known and the Spartacists crushed, the right revived, while the Social Democrats lost many supporters because of their failure to carry out sweeping reforms when the right had been powerless. Fliers illustrated with grotesque Jewish stereotypes informed voters that if they did not vote for the Conservative party, "Germany would become a slave of Judah."[18] In the elections the Social Democrats lost nearly half their seats, the Democrats (DDP) lost more than half, and the Catholic Center party lost one-third, its greatest loss since its founding. The Conservatives doubled their votes. There was no longer a clear majority for the republic, and conservatives still held their vital power bases in the army, the civil service, and the economy. In their campaign for the destruction of the republic, racism would be a major weapon. Starting in 1920, an unprecedented wave of anti-Semitism swept Germany.

15: THE SEEDBED: THE POST-WAR WAVE OF ANTI-SEMITISM

The DNVP [German Conservative Party] opposes every un-German degenerative influence, particularly the disrupting influence of Jewry which has made itself more and more strongly felt in recent decades to the detriment of our people. The Party objects to foreign elements grabbing leadership and leading the state to its downfall.
     —Resolution of the Conservative Party (DNVP), 1919

THOSE who study the Nazis often see them as unique, not understanding that their anti-Semitism was a symptom as well as the cause of the forces that would destroy the Jews. The Nazis were but a small part of a powerful wave of reaction and racism flooding Germany after the war. In 1919, for example, Conservatives, the party of the elites, merged with volkists to declare unity in battle against the "rule of the Jews." The party journal noted, "The flames of anti-Semitism flared high in [our] work."[1] By 1924 Conservative campaign literature was as racist as that of the Nazis, and volkists dominated local chapters. As George Mosse tells us, party leaders believed the "wave of anti-Semitism" helped them in elections, and the party adopted the volkist stereotype of Jews in its campaign literature. As Mosse writes, "While respectable [leaders] played at parliamentary politics, their aides were on street corners disseminating racist propaganda." Vast quantities of anti-Semitic literature poured forth from their presses. In 1922 Count Kuno von Westarp, the party chief, remarked that when speaking to conservative constituencies,

From my experience, the cry of "Jew" would come from the audience at almost all political meetings when criticism was expressed of political circumstances. Moreover, I often noticed that a sleepy meeting would wake up and the house applaud as soon as I started on the subject of the Jews. . . . For the success of the meeting the Jewish question could not be omitted.[2]

Yet many scholars still claim that conservatives found Nazi racism distasteful.

In 1919 the Pan-German League also fully embraced Nazi-like ideas, and the Agrarian Bund, now the Reichslandbund, intensified its anti-Semitism; given its past, this meant hysteria. Led by landowners, aristocrats, and military officers, and under the sign of the swastika, the Bund declared war against "the oppressive and degenerating influence of Jewry."[3] In 1919 a German Racist League for Defense and Attack boasted more than a quarter of a million dues-paying members to fight the "pernicious and destructive influence of Jewry." In 1920 alone the league distributed more than seven million racist fliers of "the most violent and scurrilous anti-Semitic propaganda."[4] Ultimately some twenty million were distributed. One branch declared, "It is absolutely necessary to kill the Jews . . . !"[5] Bund members included tens of thousands of white-collar workers and as many thousands of Freikorps. Peasant groups and the Catholic press had also grown more racist than before the war. If the libel laws of the republic had not made calls for genocide illegal, few today would think that only Hitler and a few Nazis wanted the "Final Solution."

Most nonsocialist Austrians were viciously hostile toward Jews migrating from the east, people who were trying to avoid the discrimination of new nations that were forging their identities at the expense of minorities. Many Christian Social party members forsook the old Christian limits of Lueger to embrace the racism of blood. The most prestigious Catholic magazine in Austria regularly attacked the Jews; "anti-Semitic articles and editorials" were "commonplace" in "countless" "Catholic or Christian Social newspapers and journals."[6] Leopold Kunshak, a leader of the Christian Socials, demanded that Jews be driven back to the ghettos or into special camps. Through 1921 socialists dominated the municipal council of Vienna, but voters restored the Christian Social party to power, and it proceeded to limit Jewish participation in public life. Even greater restrictions would have been enacted, but Austria depended on foreign loans, and the Allies demanded that minority rights be protected. Nevertheless, tens of thousands demonstrated against Jews, who were attacked in street and university. Austrian Nazis, under the leadership of Walter Riehl, fought pitched battles with socialists and Jews, smashing and bombing Jewish stores. Along with hundreds of thousands of Austrians, the Christian Social mayor of Vienna called for Jews who had migrated from the east to be thrown out. Some wanted "concentration camps." Zionists, Jewish war veterans, and socialists fought back, though the police hindered them.

In Germany a racist Fatherland's party enrolled Kapp, Ludendorff, von Tirpitz, and Colonel Bauer, and counted more members in 1919 than the

Social Democrats, as well as secret army funds. The Thule Society, under the swastika, recruited thousands of new members dedicated to the literal "destruction" of the race that had lost the war and caused the Weimar revolution. The Stahlhelm, whose one million members formed the most influential veterans' organization, published a literature replete with tales of German front-line heroism and home-front betrayal by Jews and leftists. The official program of 1919 referred to "this republic of Jewish traitors" and added, "The Stahlhelm fights for the renewal of the Germanic Volk and therefore of the Germanic race; it fights . . . so that foreign racial influences will be eliminated from the nation."[7] For many veterans, the war was the high point of their lives, a sacrificial crusade by warriors bonded in blood sacrifice for the Volk. Veterans' organizations in the West were also usually conservative, but they were not racial revolutionaries trying to compensate for defeat by blaming traitors at home. Stahlhelm activists, however, dreamed of the day they could take up arms against the Judenrepublik and the Allies, retrieve the past, and redeem their comrades' sacrifices. Jewish combat veterans formed their own organizations to defend Jews from physical attacks, and socialist workers often stood with them.

By 1920 there were about 300,000 Freikorps irregulars fighting in the east and against leftists and strikers at home. Robert Waite writes that many "practiced a doctrine in no way essentially different from that political and social cannibalism which was to call itself National Socialism."[8] The army funded and organized the Freikorps, and secret government monies were also available. Army leaders saw the Freikorps as the nucleus of a new Wehrmacht (armed forces), and regular troops often marched with them. Unarmed opponents were often shot; Jews were always at risk. Industrialists and landowners often contributed to Freikorps units, and landed aristocrats provided rest havens on their estates for the warriors, who in return disciplined radical farm workers.

The conflict to regain the Baltic lands formerly ruled by German aristocrats was savage. Battling indigenous peoples and Bolshevik irregulars, clad in death's-head insignia and swastikas, Freikorps units shot, strangled, beat, or hacked prisoners to death, including unarmed suspects and often innocent bystanders, regardless of sex or age. They raped and murdered captured nurses and shot their patients. Villages were destroyed if they were suspected of aiding those who resisted German domination. The atrocities were no secret; Freikorps members sometimes boasted of their deeds in memoirs. The Young German Order fought in Poland, modeling itself on the Teutonic Knights and using medieval symbols in banner and insignia, as the Nazis later would. Allied to the Conservative party, the Order had about 200,000 members; its anti-Semitism was volkist and violent. Many Freikorps volunteers were university students trying to live up to the impossibly heroic caricatures of brothers and fathers who had died in the war. Many came from prewar volkist groups, which also helped army officers select, train, and indoctrinate recruits. When the Allies forced the Weimar government to recall the Freikorps, a wild fury was unleashed against the *Judenrepublik* for doing the bidding of Germany's enemies. As the Freikorps withdrew, they burned and murdered indiscriminately.

As one expert wrote, "Millions of ordinary middle-class Germans had either participated in or supported antisocialist paramilitary activity" before the Nazis were important. "This helps to explain why so many 'respectable' Germans overlooked, tolerated, or openly applauded the brutal actions of the National Socialists during the rise to power" and "willingly acquiesced" to the Nazi regime's "violence, terror, and murder."[9] The supreme commander of Freikorps forces in the Baltic, General Graf Rudiger von der Goltz, campaigned for Hitler, attracted by the promise to conquer *lebensraum*. Hess and Ernst Roehm's right-hand man fought in the Freikorps, as did Wilhelm Weiss, who marched in Hitler's *putsch* of 1923 and became editor of the *Voelkische Beobachter*. Himmler's adjutant, General Karl Wolff, who personally sent hundreds of thousands of Jews to die in the Holocaust, fought with the Freikorps. Colonel Erhardt, head of the most famous Freikorps unit, became a high SS officer on Hitler's personal recommendation, and was a member of the first Nazi Reichstag delegation.

Racism also increased among the clergy. Today liberal Christians, embarrassed because the church did little to protest Nazi terror, assume that organized religion has a humanistic moral thrust. But in Germany then, those who opposed the racist right were usually, though not exclusively, secular-minded progressives and atheistic leftists. The dignitaries of the Lutheran church, wedded to autocracy, remained close to the Conservative party, and denunciations of liberals, leftists, and Jews abounded in Weimar sermons. Their anticommunism, often cited, is no excuse; the Weimar government was never communist or even nearly so. Fear of liberal pluralism and greed motivated many clergy. In 1919 the Social Democratic minister of culture, Adolf Hoffman, abolished state subsidies for the Evangelicals, ended compulsory religious education, and gave Judaism and Catholicism equality with Protestantism. Ministers and the parish press thereupon attacked "atheistic Jewish socialists," and Pastor Stoecker's name was revived. Some rural clergy supported paramilitary organizations. When the Social Democrats lost their majority in 1920, Hoffman's reforms were emasculated.

The ideological career of Pastor Martin Niemoeller, famed after the war for his anti-Nazi stance, is instructive. Although jailed by Hitler in the 1930s for opposing the Nazi takeover of the church, in the 1920s,

Niemoeller was pro-Nazi. Released from the submarine corps in 1919, he organized his fellow seminary students to support the Kapp *putsch*. He voted for Hitler in 1924 and 1933, welcomed the attendance of uniformed SA members in his church, and preached with swastikas decorating the altar. That his change of heart in the 1930s has been held up by many as an example of church resistance to the Nazis is a devastating comment on the paucity of examples. In any event, Niemoeller did nothing for the Jews. In other lands the church was neither reactionary nor racist. In Scandinavia the Lutheran church was liberal. Protestant Calvinist clergy in France, themselves targets of discrimination, often protected Nazi victims during the Vichy regime and at great personal risk.

Naturally the Weimar Republic was constantly attacked from university podiums. Franz Neumann, the famous Marxist scholar, a student at four German universities in 1918–1919, heard professors demand the most extreme annexationist war aims and denounce Weimar, democracy, and Jews as anti-German. Neumann also protected a newly appointed Social Democratic instructor from physical attack by students and found it necessary to "organize students to combat [the] anti-Semitism openly preached by university professors."[10] When the government opened academic positions to merit regardless of ethnicity or political belief, its efforts were foiled by the rigidities of tenure and self-serving statements about academic freedom by those who had never extended it to Jews or nonconservatives. Many former *Wandervogel* of the Youth Movement, their idealism shattered in the mud and death of the trenches, joined racist paramilitaries. Most undergraduates, many of them veterans, supported the radical right; all national student organizations outlawed Jewish membership. Catholic student groups, once wary of attacks against Jews because they feared feeding Protestant intolerance, now felt they had proved their loyalty in the war. Catholic authorities had to forbid them from discriminating against Catholics of Jewish origin, but most organizations banned them anyway, and the hierarchy did not stop them.

Upper-class students tended to remain loyal to the Conservative party of their elders, but lower-middle- and middle-class students moved further right. Postwar economic traumas made a university degree no longer enough to guarantee employment, and the republic had opened the civil service to Jews and Social Democrats. Thus competition increased as the number of undergraduates rose dramatically, leading to widespread verbal and physical attacks against democrats, socialists, and Jews. A special anger was reserved for those few professors who held Germany partly responsible for the war or dared to compare Versailles favorably with the Treaty of Brest-Litovsk; to do so implied that Germans were no better than Slavs. Jewish faculty were attacked no matter what they said. Most faculty either supported rightist student activists, drawing the line only at violence, or claimed to be "apolitical" and withdrew into academic specialization. As assaults against Jews and liberal academics rose, the government threatened to withdraw subsidies from the universities. In 1927 a Social Democratic minister of culture suspended government recognition of *Burschenschaften* (students' associations).

As Bruce F. Pauley has noted, "No other group in Austria was so racially, passionately, and violently anti-Semitic as students of university age." Thirty percent of university students there were Jewish, and competition for scarce jobs after graduation was intense. Veterans frequently attacked Jewish students; "anti-Semitism was so common that it was almost taken for granted."[11] Pan-Germans and Catholics cooperated, and fraternities outdid each other with endless racist declarations. In 1923, honoring Hitler's *putsch* attempt, Austrian Nazis beat Jewish students as the police stood by. Often faculty joined students in demands to remove Jews from Austrian life, and faculty and students cosponsored lectures on the "Jewish problem." Campus violence exceeded that of Germany while delegations of Austrian students tried to persuade their German colleagues to be more racist!

German student associations applauded the murder of Mathias Erzberger, finance minister of the republic, leader of the Catholic Center, and sponsor of the peace resolution of 1917. Erzberger had also led the delegation forced to accept the Versailles Treaty. For these "crimes" he was viciously attacked as a puppet of the Jews, even by those who knew there was no alternative once the army refused to fight. Erzberger had no choice but to meet most Allied demands and try to negotiate easier terms. He was also hated because before the war he had opposed imperialism and revealed corrupt financial deals between colonial companies and the government and the murder of indigenous Africans. It did not help when, in order to pay reparations, he tried to secure a levy on capital and a progressive income tax rather than squeeze the ordinary consumer or print more banknotes. Viciously denounced, and embroiled in a trial for libel in which the judges upheld some of the absurd charges against him, he resigned to be shot down by assassins in 1921. The right rejoiced, but in Heidelberg the socialists went on an angry rampage, even though they had opposed this famed supporter of capitalism.

Walther Rathenau, foreign minister of the republic, was assassinated in October 1922 by a "death squad" called Organization Consul. The Conservative party, led by Karl Helfferich, had viciously denounced Rathenau in the Reichstag on the very day he was shot, accusing him of doing the bidding of the Allies and the Bolsheviks, even though he had helped the German army secretly train and rearm illegally in the Soviet Union. But once again the long history of the Jew as enemy meant that nothing a Rathenau could do would protect him from the fury of the right. A common Freikorps slogan went: "Shoot down Walther Rathenau, the god-damned dirty Jew." Pan-Germans despised him for denouncing war prof-iteering without raising the false issue of "Jewish" profits, and they were furious when he called for heavy taxes on inherited wealth and a high income tax to pay reparations. Ludendorff joined in, denouncing the "Jewish traitor and defeatist," declaring that his assassins had freed Ger-many from "vermin." Rathenau was antisocialist, but huge workers' pro-cessions in Berlin mourned his death to demonstrate support for the republic. Ironically, the Conservative party itself had to compromise with the Allies when it joined the government in 1924; it too was promptly re-viled as a tool of the Jews.

The heaviest economic burdens of the war were borne by those classes already strongly anti-Semitic. Munitions contracts went to big business, harming artisans and small businessmen who lost business and access to raw materials and credit, and blamed this on Rathenau. Proletarians, vital to the war effort, were relatively well paid. By 1917 one-third of all hand-icraft shops had closed, and retailers lost trade because of shortages, ra-tioning, and black-market bartering. By 1920 the anti-Semitic Fatherland's party had mustered more than a million small retailers and clerks. Farm-ers suffered when wartime governments set price controls on food to curb inflation and hunger. Shortages of fertilizer, fuel, and equipment also hurt, as did the postwar agrarian depression caused by the global glut of production for war. By the mid-1920s small landholders constantly com-plained that "Jewish" socialist authorities sided with consumers and "Jew-ish" commodity brokers while the "Jewish" Reichstag enforced state socialism at the cost of Christian country folk. Civil servants and pen-sioners suffered terribly from wartime inflation that reduced the value of the German mark by half. When Jews were given equal access to the civil service, hostility was all the more rancorous.

The great inflation of 1921–1923 devastated the middle classes. In Jan-uary 1921 the mark stood at 65 to the dollar; soaring beyond belief, it climbed to 350,000 by July 1923 and was literally worthless at the end of that summer. Because exchange quotations came at noon, prices on lunch menus increased while one ate. Savings that ensured a college ed-ucation in 1920 purchased nothing at all in 1923; pensioners and those on fixed incomes were wiped out. It was cheaper to burn marks than coal. People left work at lunch hour to shop because prices more than dou-bled by evening, and baskets of groceries often weighed less than the money to pay for them. To eat, many went to the farmers to trade jew-elry and other valuables for food; soon there was nothing left to trade. Not everyone suffered, of course. Land and factory owners did well, and some amassed great fortunes borrowing funds to purchase real assets and pay the debts off later with far less valuable currency. Important businessmen could arrange loans, buy up smaller firms, and pay all off with inflated marks. Exporters of industrial products also thrived as the mark fell. It was commonly charged that Jewish currency speculators fueled inflation by dumping billions of marks on the international market, but Gentile industrialists did the same. Bankers and creditors, many Jewish, were often victims. The connections of important businessmen gave them the power to borrow from the Reichsbank, the state bank, which allowed them to use public money to buy real assets cheaply. Many businessmen "evaded a meaningful share of taxation" and increased their wealth "at the expense of social groups less able to take advantage of the opportunities offered by rapid currency depreciation."[12]

For the victims of inflation, suddenly the traditional rules of respectable and prudent economic conduct were reversed. What was once reckless behavior became the only way to survive. Had one been profligate and neglected to save? Good. Had one carelessly piled up huge debts? Excellent. Had one planned for the future by working hard, saving, and putting away funds for one's children or one's old age? A mistake. Did one live on a fixed pension or a lifetime's savings? Careless. To play the game by the time-honored rules of the middle class was to court ruin. Prudence was absurd, reasonable calculation betrayed. Deferred consumption meant no consumption. Even the old fairy tales made no sense: now the busy thrifty ant was a fool, the spendthrift grasshopper triumphant. A penny saved was a penny lost. "Waste not, want not" was a bitter joke.

Raised on the work ethic and a belief in thrift, saving, and planning for the future, the middle class not only faced ruin but also the erosion of personal identity, pride, and its sense of the meaning of life and work. Millions saw their vaunted self-reliance as a joke, their fate now controlled by mysterious and seemingly irrational forces. By 1924 the Weimar Republic halted the inflation, but many were already ruined—victims now in search of victims. The economy favored speculators, debtors, and owners, often manipulators of the fruits of others' labor. Decades of anti-Semitism had given the German middle classes the delusion they knew exactly who these manipulators were. The potential for violence was explosive; decades of racism provided the target.

The worst years of the Weimar inflation coincided with the greatest Allied demands for German reparations. In crisis, the popular mind makes simple connections, and in Germany the old myths were ready to hand: the Jews dominated international currency speculation, credit markets, and the stock exchanges of the West, while international bankers set the reparations terms. Over decades, racist explanations for social ills had become the norm, and victims ignored the simple truth that Jews suffered or gained according to their economic position, no more, no less than others. The vast majority of Jews suffered because of the collapse of retail trade, losses to creditors, and low Jewish participation in industries that profited heavily. War profiteers like Hugenberg and Class harped on the alleged depredations of Jewry as they counted their huge profits from the misery of others. The republic did not help the victims, rightists insisted, because it did the bidding of international Jewry and vengeful Allies. Embittered, the lower middle classes could not grasp that Jews did not dominate international finance; international financiers dominated international finance, and its rules had nothing to do with ethnicity.

Popular publicists avoided analyses of the defects of the system, for such talk only aided the left. Middle-class victims refused to listen to the arguments of the Social Democrats they had for decades defined as traitors. In every Western nation, of course, millions denounced "Jewish international finance," but in Germany and Austria the suffering was so immense and racism so ingrained that the accusation carried far more deadly intent. In 1925 Fritsch translated Henry Ford's *International Jew,* the famous collection of racist articles from Ford's *Dearborn Independent.* Distributed by his European representatives, Ford's pamphlet, actually written by an expatriate Prussian, was admired by Hitler because of the industrialist's prestige. In a footnote, however, Fritsch declared that Ford was not racist enough, for he had suggested there were some good Jews. Germans knew better, Fritsch declared.

The need to blame international enemies was immeasurably enhanced when, on the pretext of a minor default in reparations payments, the French invaded the Ruhr in January 1923. The German government, unable to tax at the necessary rates if it wished to stay in power, had printed vast amounts of currency to pay reparations with inflated marks. Raymond Poincaré, premier and foreign minister of France, had resigned office in 1920 because he found the treaty terms too lenient, and his constant demands to punish the Germans and keep them weak reflected majority French opinion. Now French troops tried to build a satellite state in the Rhineland, and Polish troops, urged on by the French, seized German areas of Silesia. At a time when pacification was needed for the safety of France, Poincaré and the French right in effect aided militant German radicals by enraging all Germans.

By the summer of 1923 invasion and inflation had stilled the voices of moderation. The Weimar government ordered passive resistance to the French—strikes, slowdowns, and demonstrations—and printed more banknotes to keep the economy moving. Resistance brought reprisals; thousands of Germans were driven from home and job by the French. Their sons often joined militant rightist groups promising revenge. Unions called for a general strike, but factory and mine owners continued deliveries of coal and other goods to France, to the advantage of both occupiers and owners. If the owners were right to compromise, consistency demanded they cease their attacks on the Weimar Republic for its compromises, but they did not. Moreover, though most who resisted the French were leftist workers, the press preferred to praise rightist resisters. The symbol of the resistance, Leo Schlageter, Kapp putschist and Nazi, was shot by the French in May 1923 for blowing up a railway bridge. He became an instant legend in a press which gave far less attention to socialist and communist workers shot down for resistance. The Nazis made the most of the heroic Schlageter, of course, but, as Hitler pointed out, though the French must be resisted, "the really deadly enemy of the German people, lurk within the walls of the nation"—Jews and republicans.[13]

In the midst of the crisis, General von Seeckt met secretly with leaders of paramilitary groups to discuss a dictatorship or the return of the Hohenzollerns. Seeckt feared that Gustav Stresemann, now chancellor, would concede too much to the French. Seeckt also wished to control the paramilitaries. If hotheads attacked the French, he knew the French and Poles would defeat them and the army, should it intervene. In collusion with the government, industrialists, and landowners, the army organized a secret "Black Reichswehr" out of Freikorps veterans. Only the Independent Socialists protested. Seeckt briefly considered combining in himself the offices of chancellor and president, with army, Black Reichswehr, paramilitary, and conservative support. Germany was ripe for a putsch in 1923, but Seeckt dropped the effort when Stresemann gave him full power for the duration of the emergency.

Racial nationalists, sure their day had arrived, wanted guerrilla war against the republic as well as the French. Millions of Germans hoped Weimar would fall to a dictatorship. As Henry A. Turner tells us, "The executive board of the national organization of iron and steel manufacturers" proclaimed in October 1923: "The parliamentary system of government has failed to work. Only men of strong will with clear goals who are supported by the trust of the people can help us surmount the current emergency."[14] Before Hitler's putsch, Freikorps commander Major Ernst Buchrucker attempted one with twenty thousand men, but after a tense confrontation Seeckt arrested him and disarmed his men. Singing the old army songs, they marched off to the landed estates of semifeudal Mecklenburg to await the day when they would be needed to smash the "Jewish-Republic." After four years in prison, Buchrucker promptly joined the Nazis. By then another putschist had taken the lead.

After the destruction of the Bavarian Soviet, Munich was a haven for the radical right. As a popular saying had it, "A republican in Bavaria is either a tourist, insane, or a Jew." States with Social Democratic governments banned paramilitary activities, but with the Kapp putsch Gustav von Kahr became, in effect, the dictator of Bavaria, backed by Bavarian units of the German army and the paramilitaries. Kahr was head of the Catholic Bavarian People's party, the largest party in Bavaria. In 1920 he replaced the legally elected Social Democrats of Bavaria with bundists and reactionary businessmen, encouraging a multitude of Bavarian ultra-rightists. The Nazis, neither the largest nor the most extreme of them, were still a small group of obscure plotters. Hundreds of thousands of Germans and Austrians, often led by veterans, armed and mobilized under anti-Semitic and anti-Bolshevik slogans in a wide variety of volkist groups, home defense leagues, farmer protection leagues, Bunds, gymnastic societies, and even mountain-climbing and "tourist" organizations. Orgesch, active in Bavaria in 1919 and with ties to similar Austrian groups, had 300,000 members. A "power in the land," it possessed 2.5 million rifles, 100,000 machine guns, 3,000 pieces of artillery, and 30 aircraft. Rudolph Kanzler, second in command, said in 1920:

> ... Paid Jewish villains stabbed the army in the back....Jewish charlatans made the revolution; they promised us bread, work, and order; none of the promises have been kept. On the contrary, bribery, corruption, and black marketing have spread....We must do everything to put a stop to the Jew government, that is, the international Jewish black marketeers....We must unite on a racial basis and eliminate the international Jewish rabble which is sucking the last drop of blood from our veins. The Bolsheviks are advancing against us from all sides so as to unite with the misled brethren of our own race, who are paid by Jewish money and impose upon us their well-known salvation.[15]

The Bavarian government and army units cooperated with Orgesch, the Nazis, and other paramilitaries. Indeed, Kahr and his ally, Otto von Lossow, hoped to lead a united military force against Weimar. The Munich police chief, asked by a reporter what he would do if the workers mounted a general strike against Kahr as they had against Kapp, declared he would shoot them one at a time until the strike ended. The popularity of the radical right among younger officers caused Stresemann to fear the army would not defend the republic. Some younger officers believed Stresemann's government, though in fact moderately conservative and probusiness, was a "fully Judaized red Spartakist regime."[16] To Stresemann, Kahr was a far greater threat than Kapp had ever been, for he had a government and regular troops behind him.

Hitler was still on the payroll of the army Propaganda and Press Division, one of a number of agents who spoke in public about the inequities of Versailles, the evils of Weimar "socialism," and the need to cleanse Germany of the Jews. Investigating political groups, Hitler came across the tiny German Workers' party. Founded in 1919 by Anton Drexler and a small group of artisans, bank tellers, and shopkeepers, it was a perfect political movement for Hitler: small and insignificant, it had room for a dynamic leader as larger groups might not. Seizing his chance for personal supremacy, Hitler began intensive fund-raising and beer-hall haranguing in Munich, drawing sizable crowds, especially when posters announced that the Jews would be his theme.

Unfortunately, party records were destroyed after the 1923 *putsch*, so it is impossible to know exactly who contributed to the early Nazis. Considerable sums came from Hitler's audiences and from party members who were subject to membership dues, rally fees, and special levies—one paid for the privilege of being a Nazi. Some wealthy Munich families contributed, including the Wagners and Bechsteins, members of the Bavarian royal house, and other princes. Hitler received a great boost when General Ludendorff publicly endorsed and joined him, bringing more army and business funds. Many small businessmen also contributed. Racist reactionaries routinely received sums from retired army officers, estate owners, and Russian emigrés, including the heir to the tsarist throne—certain that Jewish Bolsheviks had stolen his heritage. Germans dispossessed by the treaty settlements also contributed, including aristocrats from the lost Hapsburg territories, bitter at the transfer of their lands to the hated Slavs, happy to aid anyone who might restore them by force.

Anonymous donations and contributions through dummy organizations protected some contributors to the Nazis; a shopkeeper, brewery owner, or innkeeper might fear losing customers among anti-Nazis. In 1923 Hitler boasted privately that Heinrich Class and the pan-Germans had offered him a million marks to unite forces. Even if Class did so, Hitler did not care to alienate his supporters or reduce his own importance by making the Nazis just another part of the upper-class reaction. Some Nazis already complained of Hitler's penchant for the wealthy, fearing he might sell out to the old crowd.

From the start Hitler stressed only those parts of the party program, written before he joined, that were acceptable to potential backers. The German Workers' party, as it had been called, denounced Gentile industrialists as well as Jewish financiers; Hitler ended this. Jewish international finance was the only capitalism Hitler ever denounced. He renamed the party National Socialist because, like Stoecker before him, he did not want the word "worker" to predominate. National Socialism implied a nonleftist collaboration between all classes for the common good, not Marxist class warfare and internationalism. Above all, Hitler concentrated on the single foe, as he had learned from Lueger. In his popular speeches in Munich, Jews were his constant target. SA members were instructed to attend meetings of other groups and demand that the speakers discuss the Jews. But Hitler was still only one agitator among hundreds; his organization, numbering 47,000 by 1922, was but one of many similar groups, some larger: Orgesch, the Thule Society, the Teutonic Order, Bund Oberland, Reichsflagge, Bund Wiking, Bund Bluecher, the Rossbach Battalion, the Erhardt Brigade, and more. Organization Consul was the most sinister. Implicated in Rathenau's assassination and protected by the Bavarian police, it considered the other groups effete. It assassinated leftists and hoped to stimulate a revolution so that the army and paramilitaries would crush the left and bring dictatorship.

Paramilitary associations were illegal, but Kahr's police chief, asked by journalists if he knew there were many such groups in Bavaria, replied he wished there were more. Asked if he knew death squads assassinated leftists, he answered, "Yes, yes, but not enough!"[1] He marched with Hitler in the 1923 *putsch*. Kahr's government helped the paramilitaries, restraining them only when they broke laws too publicly or denounced Kahr himself. His police often warned paramilitaries of opponents and activities against them and harassed their enemies. The government motor pool was available for demonstrations. Army units trained and armed the paramilitaries, and allowed them to draw weapons from military stores during crises.

Hitler's speeches reflected not just his personal views. He gave voice to the violent impulses of hundreds of thousands of irregulars, members of the regular army, Bavarian government officials, and many civilians. Every one of his vile denunciations of the Jews was common parlance among millions in Germany and Austria. In 1923, with the French in the Ruhr and the mark destroyed, vociferous demands were raised to throw the Jews out of Germany. Many wanted them shot. In Vienna thousands marched under placards demanding their murder. The Nazi press called for special "collection" camps and hinted darkly of a "Final Goal," the ruthless elimination of Jews from German life. Hitler's themes were well known before he ever spoke: Jews had caused the 1918 defeat, bolshevism, and the republic; they had dictated the treaty, ran the black market, and caused the inflation. A race loyal only to its own, they eroded the moral character of Germans with licentious attacks on Christian morality. The real masters of Germany, they led the Social Democrats and cooperated with the Allies. Hitler's oratory was controlled rage; the will to murder was obvious to those who heard him. A reporter who covered Nazi meetings in the 1920s noted how the audience repeatedly punctuated Hitler's harangue with calls of "Death to the Jews." This is Hitler speaking in 1920, though it could have been any of hundreds of now forgotten demagogues: "Don't think you can battle a disease without killing the virus. . . . Jewish influence will never disappear and the poisoning of the people will not end as long as the virus, the Jew, has not been removed from our midst."[18]

Hitler's audiences were not ignorant rowdies. Reporters noted that their dress and comportment indicated mostly solid bourgeoisie. In Berlin in 1921, Hitler addressed the prestigious businessmen of the National Club. When asked how he would solve the Marxist and Jewish "questions," he replied that the Nazis would put Jews and leftists into concentration camps.[19] In Munich, Hitler spoke of the eventual conquest of Eastern Europe, noting that Russia's "subhuman" Judeo-Bolsheviks held resources better used by German industrialists and Aryan settlers. Like millions of Germans and Austrians, Hitler derided Czechoslovakia as a trumped-up collection of real estate, neither a nation nor a people, land that was German by right and would be again.

Hitler hoped to unite all of Munich's paramilitary groups, but the competition was stiff and included Kahr himself. By the end of 1923, however, Hitler had some 55,000 supporters. Inspired by Mussolini's 1922 March on Rome, which had been encouraged by the Italian police and army, Hitler hoped to lead all paramilitary organizations in a *putsch*. With Kahr and others, he helped build a "Fighting Bund" of the united right. On the anniversary of the founding of the Second Reich, September 2, 1923, the groups were to march in Nuremberg, a strong pro-Nazi town well organized by the popular ultraracist Julius Streicher. But Kahr persuaded the prestigious Erhardt Brigade of Kapp *putsch* fame to join him and others who preferred to march with an established political leader seemingly backed by the army and elites.

Other opportunities soon came. Buchrucker's attempted *putsch*, the emerging power of Seeckt, and the threat from the Bavarian right motivated socialists and Communists in Saxony and Thuringia to unite in coalition governments. Unlike Kahr's, these governments were legally elected. Kahr assumed full dictatorial powers and mobilized his forces to overthrow the two governments. Stresemann, aware that the ultimate goal was Berlin, nevertheless refused to move against the Bavarians, deciding it was wiser to pacify the right by disbanding the governments of Saxony and Thuringia. The Communists wanted to fight, the socialists to strike; as they argued, the army marched in. The Social Democrats in Stresemann's cabinet insisted that the illegal government of Bavaria also be disbanded. Stresemann refused, fearing the army would disobey and the businessmen of his party unseat him. The Social Democrats resigned. The message was clear: the radical right might rule illegally, but a legal government including Communists would be suppressed. In October 1923 Bavarian units of the army actually swore loyalty to Kahr's government, and General von Lossow stated publicly that he would obey Kahr, not

Weimar, threatening a march on Berlin as well. Given Lossow's treason, Hitler could gain the loyalty of the paramilitaries only if he swiftly seized the initiative from Kahr and Lossow, especially because Ludendorff was trying to persuade Seeckt to unite army and Freikorps and take Berlin himself.

On September 24, 1923, Stresemann called off passive resistance to the French, and currency reform soon ended the inflation. On November 6, Seeckt, fearing French intervention, ordered the Bavarians not to march and fired the insubordinate Lossow, who simply refused to go. The *Voelkische Beobachter* declared that Seeckt held back because he was married to a Jew with friends in the Jewish press who dictated his decisions: "When Seeckt-Stresemann take action against racists and Communists, one may assume this happens on the orders of Jews and Social Democrats."[20] Berlin ordered Lossow and Kahr to suppress the paper; they refused and went unpunished. Seeckt did not want Bavarian rabble-rousers or a Catholic Bavarian party to lead Germany's revival; the eventual dictatorship should be composed of the "best" people—monarchists and militarists, preferably Prussian. Moreover, Stresemann now did his bidding, and it undoubtedly occurred to Seeckt that he himself might well be the eventual savior. Consequently Kahr was told that if he marched or let others do so, the army would attack. Like Seeckt, Kahr had a powerful position to lose if he moved precipitously—he had just been appointed general state commissioner by the Weimar government, his dictatorship legalized to enlist his aid to counter the threat from his own paramilitaries! The paradox is not so much a measure of the ineptness of Weimar as it is of its justified fear of the right. Kahr called a meeting for November 8, 1923, intending to tell his followers they could not succeed against the will of the German army.

Unlike Kahr, Lossow, or Seeckt, Hitler's future was at stake. He had to act or be replaced by other charismatic militants, of whom there was no shortage. His potential followers demanded action. Hitler had planned a *putsch* in May 1923 but had backed down at the last minute. Afterward many derided him as just another loudmouthed windbag, afraid to put his life on the line. He had to move. Even Austrian Nazis, though blessed with an anti-Semitic government, had taken to the streets. Before Kahr called his meeting, Hitler planned a *putsch* for November 11, the anniversary of the Armistice. Kampfbund leaders could provide as many as 150,000 armed supporters. Kahr was caught between losing his support or taking on the army. Hitler feared Kahr would move first by announcing a *putsch* at his November 8 meeting, three days before Hitler's move. But Kahr had everything to lose if he failed, Hitler everything to win, successful or not. National fame and the leadership of the armed reaction awaited the one who was willing to throw the iron dice. If Hitler did nothing he would fall back into the obscure impotence of his youth.

So it was that Hitler, Goering, and SA leaders burst into Kahr's meeting in the famous Burgerbraukeller on November 8, 1923. Firing his pistol into the ceiling, Hitler declared that the "national revolution has begun." The Nazis had formed a provisional government, he cried, and the army and police were with them. Neither was true, but none could be sure. Goering declared that the action was not directed against Kahr, police, or army. "It is directed solely against the Berlin government of the Jews."[21] Roehm, Himmler, and armed SA units took over the Ministry of War; socialist headquarters were seized and their presses destroyed. At pistol point, Hitler forced Kahr and Lossow into a side room and announced he would be Germany's dictator and Ludendorff the army chief. Kahr and Lossow would be shot if they did not join him. Ludendorff advised them to join, and they probably did indicate support, if only to stay alive. Hitler announced their support to the crowd. Later they denied it, losing a chance to join the Nazi honor roll. Streicher, surrounded by his armed men, was asked what would be the policies of a Nazi government. As the "party of Christian Germans against that of the Jewish bloodsuckers," he replied, we "will hang the Jewish profiteers from the lampposts."[22] He could hardly have been more clear.

Most Bavarians probably favored a *putsch*, but many grumbled. After all, General von Seekt was already in charge, and it was common knowledge that in a civil war the French would seize the Rhineland and set up a separate state. Seekt would not deliver Germany to hotheads he could not control. Lossow received telegraphed orders: stop the *putsch* or the army will. By the morning of November 9 the Kampfbund was breaking up on Kahr's instructions, and troops confronted Captain Roehm's forces in stalemate at the Ministry of Defense. No shots were exchanged—"army does not fire on army." Hitler then made the most important decision of his life: he would march. Joined by at most three thousand supporters, he approached army headquarters. Someone fired a shot, the police fired a volley, and Hitler was dragged to the ground by a dead comrade with whom he had locked arms. Ludendorff marched through the line without a scratch—police do not fire on generals. Some police did not wish to fire on Hitler either, and others, as well as army people in mufti, marched with him. Indicative of the social composition of the early movement, the sixteen "martyrs" killed in the march included four merchants, three bank officials, two engineers, a student, an officer of the Bavarian supreme court, a retired military officer, a servant, and a headwaiter.

The *putsch* failed, but Hitler succeeded. The little-known leader gained national and international press coverage. Now he was the focal point for all who believed that the Weimar Republic had sold them out to the Allies and the Jews. Hitler's movement did not grow to millions simply because of personal charisma or a unique program. It grew because his daring gamble of 1923 gave him the chance to lead the hundreds of thousands of racial nationalists who were anxious to throw in their lot with any revolutionary and racist reactionary willing to risk his life for the cause. Now Hitler had to form the necessary alliances and exploit to maximum advantage the traumas and fears of lower- and upper-class conservatives. The counterrevolution had found its leader.

16: THE BATTLE FOR CULTURE

The metropolis began its race-annihilating work. . . . A race chaos of Germans, Jews, and anti-natural street races was abroad. The result was mongrel art.

—Alfred Rosenberg, Nazi ideologist

LIKE politics, Weimar culture was a battleground between right and left. To most of the avant-garde, art was a weapon against the German bourgeoisie and the establishment, consequently both fury and fanatic support greeted the new work. For some it was an insult flung in the face of Germany, nothing less than Jewish "cultural bolshevism"; to others it was a final break with the stultifying pieties of the Second Reich. Although a great many European artists sought liberation from traditional cultural norms, in Germany the shock of defeat and its traumatic aftermath produced the most intensely creative break with the past. It is difficult to imagine a time when theatre, film, and even music and dance had such revolutionary implications.

The new cultural attitudes originated before 1914, but the shock of war gave them new relevance and broad public awareness. The prewar avant-garde had found no place in the kaiser's museums. "His" artists were expected to uphold tradition, respect Christian pieties, and cling to the old norms: in music, Wagner or the classics; in theatre, the well-made play. Ibsen and Strindberg were considered enemies of society, and those whose images defamed the establishment or received morality were subject to libel suits or suppression. The accepted art of the Second Reich valued sentimental realism, pastoral beauty, and the glorified images of the status quo. An apprentice artist might begin his training by reproducing the various poses of the Prussian military or depicting idealized rural scenes. For conservatives, art, like politics, must be realistic, nationalistic, Germanic, and Christian. In 1919 the Social Democratic minister of culture promoted artistic freedom, though republican politicians were wary of the revolutionary manifestos of artists and their belief that the republic was too cowardly to fight the reaction. Unwilling to censor artistic expression, however, the government was accused of "cultural bol-

shevism" by the right, even after Communist leaders lost their enthusiasm for radical art and Moscow denounced such "flights of anarchistic
nihilism."

In 1919 George Grosz took part in a Dadaist "Happening." A sewing
machine operator worked at top speed and produced nothing, racing
against a typist furiously banging away nonsense, all beneath a hanged
pig in Prussian military uniform. Reviled as disgusting and unpatriotic, it
was, of course, a parody of the meaningless sacrifices in the trenches
brought about by those who used the latest technology of death for no
rational goal. The war seemed a bloody theatre of the absurd that no artistic imagination could hope to match. Dadaism, invented by German
refugees in Switzerland in 1916, deliberately cultivated the absurd, and
some declared the warmongers of the ruling elites to be the first Dadaists.
As one artist remarked, the truest Dadaist act would be to shoot a revolver
at random into a crowd of strangers. Were not the rotting corpses of the
front the final refutation of all sanitized sensibilities, patriotic platitudes,
and reason itself? We must, Dadaists declared, destroy the false idealism
of art just as the war destroyed the old heroic myths. After all, who first
blasted civilized norms if not the bemedaled men of honor, duty, and
glory?

Rational thought could comprehend neither the war nor Dadaism.
Why not abuse the canvas with accidental smudges, streaks, dripped
paint, rips, and pierced objects? Beautiful art was a lie; ugliness was truth.
The famous toilet of Marcel Duchamp, painted with perfect realism,
shocked a public who preferred to deny excremental realities when contemplating works of the spirit. Yet had Duchamp painted the filth of
trenches, as did Otto Dix, a social realist, he would have offended far
more. Tristan Tzara once said, "Dada signifies nothing"; but the accidental act, the collage of unrelated objects and automatic writing, signi-
fied the meaninglessness of a civilization that claimed millions of victims
for empty platitudes. "Dada is German bolshevism," said one artist. Conservatives agreed, and many noted that the leading publisher of Dadaist
art and communist books was a Jewish firm, Malik Verlag.

Exploring the symbols, images, and metaphors of the drives that made
man destructive and society irrational led many to Sigmund Freud, who
introduced his concepts of the id, the ego, and the superego to a Berlin
congress in 1922. In 1916 he wrote that the slaughter showed that civilization had not eliminated the destructive urges threatening communal
life, only repressed them. Psychic awareness and cautious progress could
be achieved only by breaking through the rational structures people built
to disguise the truths they feared. Comforting illusions must be exorcised,
inner horrors must be controlled. Artists translated such ideas into attempts to penetrate below the surface seen by the common eye, to find

symbols adequate to the hidden psyche that, they believed, exploded with such fury in war. Salvador Dali found the psyche in free association undistorted by rational clarification, painting his private obsessions and "dream images." Marc Chagall allowed memories of his *stetl* childhood to emerge without reference to rational assumptions about space, time, and gravity. The inwardly turned surfaces of Giorgio de Chirico's deserted, windowless buildings created an apprehensive, foreboding sense of the unknown evil around and inside men and women. To postwar European artists, loneliness, alienation, and fear were reasonable; optimism and progress were illusions. Traditional art could never illustrate the traumas of war, revolution, and economic collapse which had overwhelmed a generation. If you sought artistic truth, go to the insane asylum, go to the infant, seek out primitive societies. Find the id.

To the right, Freudianism and its derivatives were the latest examples of a "Jewish science" propagating obscene fictions about infant sexuality, incestuous desires, and murderous oedipal feelings—the ultimate aggression against Nordic family values. Atheist and radical Jews, having deserted their own faith, now dismissed religion as an infantile longing to uphold the illusion of a comforting universe, and claimed that life was nothing but a meaningless struggle fraught with injustice and terminated by death. One furious conservative scholar declared, "What else do we need to know about Freudianism than that it was invented by a Jew?" In the radical right's pantheon of hatred, the Jew Freud joined the Jew Marx. Conservative psychologists much preferred Jung's archetypal racial myths of mankind, and in 1934 Jung attacked Freud's "Jewish attitudes," insisting that Freud had never understood the Nordic subconscious or the unique Germanic idealism that created National Socialism. The Aryan soul, unlike those Freud described, was "anything but a garbage bin of untrustworthy infantile desires and unresolved family resentments."[1] The Berlin Psychoanalytic Institute, founded in 1920, was vilified as a Jewish-Marxist attempt to destroy faith in traditional values, just as Marx believed morality was simply a defense of class interests. Conservatives ignored the official communist dogma that held Freudianism to be the ultimate parody of bourgeois individualism, whereas Pavlovian behavior modification would produce the collective personality of Soviet man. The Nazis were more crass: Freudianism was an attack on Aryans by those obsessed with the sex urges of "primitive peoples, such as Jews." Psychoanalysis was just another Jewish "business enterprise" thriving "on a clientele of rich hysterics."[2]

For some artists, Dada and Freud were too inaccessible to use in a revolutionary attack against the evils of the ruling class: "Your brushes and pens should be weapons, but they are empty blades of straw."[3] With this, Grosz left Dada to draw and paint unforgettably acidic, brutal caricatures of the elites. The icons of the right, Ludendorff and Hindenburg, he depicted as bloated "vampires of humanity," hired killers, "pimps of death" for industrialists needing fresh sacrifices for future wars. Officers were depraved murderers, their brute pig heads hiding behind the scarecrow of the republic. Instead of war heroes, Grosz portrayed limbless veterans, stumps naked, ignored like so much leftover garbage, sitting on platform rollers and holding up tin cups as past them walk fat grotesque bourgeoisie and skull-faced generals clutching whores and money bags. Monocled aristocrats, decorated officers, and fat industrialists, genitalia exposed, dangle naked whores on their knees—brutes fornicating with animals—speaking of Fatherland and honor amidst the reek of blood, whiskey, and sex. A hoglike party of wealthy dine under a crucifix, surrounded by wines, cognacs, and maimed veterans they lament—"The war wounded are becoming a veritable national nuisance."

Businessmen, profiteers, and stock exchange manipulators were portrayed by Grosz as swinish exploiters, blotched-skin parasites whose corruption glares out in line and color. He doubly infuriated his audience by stereotyping Aryans, not Jews, as depraved symbols of corruption and greed. His "Toad of Possession" was not the usual distorted Jewish puppetmaster but a huge, flat-nosed, brutal Nordic industrialist, cannons under his arms, sitting on his vast holdings and factories surrounded by piles of moldering corpses: "The hell with the reparations debt, I am not the one who pays for it." Another Nordic, swilling a huge meal, thanks God the French occupation has not ruined his appetite, for the workers pay the costs. Stinnes, inflation profiteer extraordinaire, sits next to his puppet President Ebert: "This is the Orgesch Stinnes loves." In the background a hatchet-faced, monocled civil servant demands, "Throw the Jews out."

Grosz took the social ills that conservatives blamed on Jews and ascribed them to the bourgeoisie and the old rulers. In "We go to pray before God the Just," vicious industrialists and officers are shown with a lascivious, leering priest whose altar is surrounded by bags of money with feet as he intones, "Be fruitful and multiply"; angels float under a sign, "Religion must be preserved for the people." In another drawing, a crucified, mutilated soldier hangs from the cross, and priestly blessings are given to dead soldiers as bloody-handed officers and politicians look on with knowing cynical approval. With Grosz, moral decay was a solid Aryan-Christian responsibility. In striking images that outraged more than words could, Germany's rulers were portrayed as drunken murderers with corpselike faces flushed with barnyard sex. Even Wagner was not spared: the Rhine maidens are drawn fingering their genitals—cultural bolshevism and sacrilege combined. Grosz offended all the more because his deceptively cartoonlike work reached the public in hundreds of thousands of reproductions. Conservatives grew apoplectic, militants issued death threats. The government brought Grosz before the bar three times for blasphemy and defaming public morality.

Berlin was now the theatre capital of the world, its experimental and revolutionary plays bludgeoning traditionalism. In 1896 an editor had spent four months in prison for simply printing a play praising the Revolution of 1789. In 1919 Erwin Piscator's proletarian theatre was dedicated to arousing a revolutionary proletarian class consciousness. Discarding individualism and personal emotions, the new theatre presented nameless characters, universal symbols of man's plight, preaching revolutionary slogans in the midst of symbols of an imagined utopian future. As one playwright said, "Is not reality a capitalist concept?" Old classics were rewritten with revolutionary texts, further antagonizing a theatre public brought up to admire the noble works of the canon, now parodied and turned against them. The audience was even brought into the action on the stage as if participating in revolution; productions sometimes ended with calls for world revolution and rousing renditions of the communist "Internationale." Piscator's theatre was debated and denounced in the Reichstag itself.

In Austria in 1920, students rioted when the satirist Karl Kraus read passages from his work ridiculing the kaiser and his generals. Arthur Schnitzler's play *La Ronde* aroused howls of outrage in Vienna in 1920 with its portrayal of a circle of sexual intimacies connecting individuals of all classes in a dance of decadence, the last authentic relationship between the alienated groups of a dying culture. Equally upsetting were plays about alcoholism, illicit sex, abortion, poverty, the diseased, and the insane. Uproars, demonstrations, and small riots at performances were not uncommon. Paramilitaries, including the Nazis, sometimes climbed onto the stage during performances to smash scenery and punch actors. The extremely high participation of Jews as producers, playwrights, directors, actors, and critics allowed conservatives to denounce the new theatre as yet another Jewish outrage. In 1925 Rosenberg, chief Nazi ideologist, decried the bastardized theatre of trash, "helpless before the drive and activity of the Jewish instinct for decay."[4]

Their long-winded declamations and impersonality prevented Expressionist works from lasting, but Bertolt Brecht's parodies of bourgeois values, far more subtle and bitterly amusing, are still with us. Like Grosz, Brecht wanted to reach large audiences, and his popular *Threepenny Opera* and *The Rise and Fall of the City of Mahagonny* did so. Satirical and witty, the entertaining *Threepenny* opened in 1928. The biting darkness of the German performances, their punchy jazz and mordant lyrics, mocked middle-class pretensions. Even Kurt Weill's music offended—the

Negermusik detested by rightists and Nazis. Captain Macheath, the lead in *Threepenny*, is a thief, rapist, and killer, not a stage villain in a musical intended mainly to amuse, as he is too often presented in the West. He and his comrade in crime, the chief of police, embody the legal criminality of the establishment; both began as soldiers of imperialism, rendering inferior races into "beefsteak tartar." In a later version of *Threepenny*, Brecht made Macheath a bank director, for "It is better to own a bank than to rob one." Those who uphold the law and those who break it are one and the same, dominated by the same entrepreneurial spirit, criminals all. Brecht neither preaches nor waxes indignant, but seems to admire the adept way the ruling classes educate the little man in the noble principles of justice while robbing him blind. And the bosses know best: "First comes eating, then comes morality." Brecht's humorous dismissal of the idealized frauds of the pillars of society angered his opponents more than Expressionist dogmas ever could. As his famous song goes: Just how does one prosper in our time? By robbing, torturing, throttling, and devouring one's fellow man.

The contrast between ideals and reality was brilliantly mocked in Brecht's *The Seven Deadly Sins*. Here it was "conclusively demonstrated" that the deadliest sins of all were committed by those who followed all the received moral precepts. Ruin deservedly awaited those who sought justice from the police, married for love not money, did honest work expecting honest pay, devoted their lives to serious art, and refused to cheat, steal, or betray to get ahead. Such naive idealism was the truly deadly sin, for it left its practitioners trembling in nothingness outside the portals of those who knew how to gain the pleasures of the world: "Why be good when you can be a success?" As the narrator sings in *Threepenny*, most of us are bad, but few are evil enough to do really well. As the beggar king announces: Even those few who want to do good fail, for unfortunately, "social conditions do not permit this/ the world is poor, and man is evil."

In *Mahagonny*, Brecht's view is darker. By 1930, the year of its production, Nazi popularity had soared. "We are one with the beasts/ we live in ruined cities/ below us are sewers/ above us is smoke/ in us is nothing." The most pious Christian is mired in lust, greed, and whoredom; all, noble or ignoble, ends as garbage in a grave. If by some mischance peace and harmony appear on earth, mankind will surely destroy them: "Bad is the hurricane/ worse is the typhoon/ but worst of all is man." The worst sin of all is to be too broke to pay one's bar bill. Otherwise do what you will—life's purpose is to eat, drink, fornicate, and fight, "for we are one with the beasts, and afterward comes nothing." When God threatens to condemn the sinners of Mahagonny to hell, they rise indignantly in chorus, insisting that he cannot do it: they are already in hell, they have always been in hell. *Mahagonny* ends with a giant protest procession to a chorus of majestic hymnal music. Professional beggars march with placards pronouncing "For the just distribution of other worldy goods," and "For the unjust distribution of worldly goods," while a stark and moving last judgment on Germany is intoned to a crescendo of funereal tones: "You can do a lot with a dead man/ you can put a shirt on him/ you can also leave him naked/ you can talk of his golden age/ you can forget about his golden age/ you can speak kindly to him/ you can also rage at him/ you can give him money, you can also leave him broke; but one thing you cannot do, you cannot help a dead man. . . . We cannot help ourselves, or you, or anyone." Brecht's mocking smile hovers above the bacilli festering in the petri dish, coolly rendering what others declaimed in manifestos and slogans, without the music.

Mahagonny was greeted by a crowd of angry rightists in the worst riot ever. Boos, cheers, and fights in the aisles reached their climax in the famous last scene, as rioting spread onto the stage itself. The city council let the production run only with a theatre filled with police. Brecht rejoiced. At least in the theatre the revolutionary masses confronted the forces of order; it would be best of all if the rioting spilled into the streets of every city of the rotten republic. Many opera houses canceled performances of *Mahagonny* or refused to schedule it, though a full house was always guaranteed. By 1932 the Nazis and their conservative allies, already governing Thuringia, suppressed Brecht's work.

Germany now produced more films than all of Europe. Most were popular trash, but some brilliantly explored new techniques and subjects intended to startle or offend. Criminals and crime were glorified, and the horror film came into its own. Scientists were no longer heroes but as diabolical as the technology of slaughter they had created in 1914–1918. Many films were fascinated with sex murders and serial killers, strikingly portrayed in Fritz Lang's movie *M*. The child killer is brought to justice not by the police but by criminal organizations, for he damages their work and reputation. *The Cabinet of Dr. Caligari* shows the passionless murder of the innocent by a mindlessly obedient humanoid in a world which is in fact a mental institution run by the inmates; a happier ending was duly provided for theatre managers in need of profits. Raging inflation and the traumas of the depression made it seem that everyone was inexorably caught in the mortal grip of irrational and destructive dark powers. *Nosferatu* and a spate of vampire movies dwelt on death lust, murderous parasites, and the eroticism of blood purity. In *The Last Laugh* the loss of middle-class status in postwar Germany is brilliantly portrayed in the downfall of one who ends up as an attendant in a men's toilet. In

246 IDEOLOGY OF DEATH

the most famous film of all, *The Blue Angel*, a nightclub singer seduces
and humiliates a tormented schoolteacher, supreme symbol of middle-
class respectability and stiff-collar virtue, who is driven by erotic dependency to babbling insanity.

Films revealed the alleged secrets of the respectable—incest, sadism,
sexual diseases; prostitutes and drugs were glorified, puritanism scoffed.
In 1919 Conrad Veidt portrayed an upper-class and eminently respectable
homosexual victimized by blackmail. The film concluded with a brief
speech by the famous Dr. Magnus Hirschfield, in real life the founder
of the Institute for Sexual Science, who told of a future day when such
suffering would not be allowed. The outraged conservative press pointed
out that Hirschfield was a Jew and a socialist whose Social Democratic
colleagues in the Reichstag had long supported homosexual rights.
Widely picketed, the film provoked riots; Hirschfield was severely beaten
by thugs to the rapturous praise of the Nazi press. In a public lecture in
1921 in Vienna, Hirschfield and the audience were set upon by Nazis firing pistols, hurling stink bombs and anti-Semitic curses. Homosexuality
was labeled the Jewish disease, Himmler began collecting his files of homosexuals, and the rightist press made much ado about the famous American killers Leopold and Loeb. Elsewhere religious conservatives called
for "blue laws" against permissiveness, but morality in Germany and Austria was, as before, an ideological-racial issue. Alfred Rosenberg declared
that the film industry was dominated by the Jewish commercial spirit,
with profits gained by vilifying the morality of the *Volk*. Blue laws were
not enough; there must be a "final, relentless excision of the Jewish-
Syrian influence."[5]

Pacifist antimilitarism affronted most Germans. The leading journal of
cultural criticism, the *World Stage*, published the army's secret violations
of the disarmament clauses of the Versailles Treaty. Many Jews worked
on the journal's staff, and "anti-Semitic critics made the most of it."[6] Erich
Maria Remarque's *All Quiet on the Western Front* was despised by the
right not only because it was a best-seller, but because Remarque had
fought in the trenches. Millions could not live with the idea that the sacrifice of sons, brothers, and fathers resulted from the manipulation of idealism by hypocritical upper-class cynics. For the titled representatives of
the Prussian warrior elite, the book was cultural bolshevism at its worst,
and Remarque's portrayal of the loss of patriotic idealism was treason deserving death. When the film of the novel premiered in 1930, Joseph
Goebbels led the way as storm troopers released mice and exploded stink
bombs in the audience. The film provoked riots and picketing so widespread that fearful bureaucrats had it banned.

Kurt Tucholsky, leftist satirist, announced, "There is no secret of the

German army I would not hand over readily to a foreign power." In "Visiting Verdun," the holy soil where 700,000 had died, he wrote:

> Sin, Penance, Absolution? Is there a newspaper that even now confesses: "We were wrong! We allowed ourselves to be lied to!" It is the least they could do. Was there even one among those who year after year, with mindless and unconditional obedience, flooded their readers with their filthy enthusiasm for death, who tried instead to drum into us the true history of the war? "But we couldn't let ourselves be confiscated." But after the war? When the censor was gone? What could you have done then? Have you even once, just once, described the full, naked blood-sucking vermin-ridden truth? The newspapers want news. Everybody wants news. Nobody wants the truth.[8]

In the visual arts, the average museumgoer clung to sentimental realism as if seeking refuge from incomprehensible horrors. New art forms confounded those who clung to assurance offered by the recognizably real. Vasily Kandinsky's abstractions deprived the onlooker of his bearings. To most, it was the work of children or lunatics. It took fifty years for abstract art to become simply decoration for corporate offices, without hint of revolutionary anarchy. Klee, Kokoschka, Beckmann, Kirchner, Barlach, Feininger, Marc, Dix—all were accused of degeneracy, incompetence, or both. Museums had to protect canvases from being spat upon, slashed, or rubbed with dog feces. Emil Nolde, who found it possible to be a modern artist and a Nazi, was famous for his triptych of a distorted, grotesque, and acidic life of Christ. The government withdrew it from a traveling art show; the Nazis later forbade Nolde from exhibiting his work. Some Nazis saw in German expressionism an art consistent with their values, but they were overruled. And many non-Nazi conservative curators and artists agreed with the Nazi definition of "degenerate art." It could only be the "artistic bolshevism" of "young Jews." Although there were no prominent Jewish visual artists, Rosenberg declared that "the ideal beauty" of Nordic art was being destroyed by "democratic, race corrupting precepts" and the "carefully planned decomposing activities of the Jews."[9]

Similarly, Arnold Schoenberg's atonal music shocked the vast majority of concertgoers everywhere, but German rightists, aware Schoenberg was a converted Jew, recalled Wagner's warning against racial corruption of the arts. Most of Schoenberg's disciples were Gentiles, though it made no difference. When the republic gave him a position in the Prussian Academy of Fine Arts, incensed conservatives howled at the crime. Rosenberg insisted that Weimar promoted atonality because it "contradicts the rhythm of blood and soul of the German people...."[10]

The new architecture was also denounced. With the slogan "Form follows function," the Bauhaus group united crafts and architecture in a community devoted to building appropriate to technology, discarding the old way of selecting from a pastiche of old styles for mere decoration. Bauhaus leaders shunned ideology, but their communal work groups were labeled Leninist. They were forced out of Thuringia, pro-Nazi in 1930, because local artisans feared competition. Bauhaus was labeled a Jewish degradation of traditional style, arrogantly creating churches to look like movie palaces or even synagogues.

In the famous cabarets of Weimar there ruled an ironic, sarcastic, and bitter wit. Nothing was sacred to the comic patter and campy humor of entertainers who played off the hypocrisies of the establishment. Cabaret wit exposed the self-protective frauds of Germany's well-off rulers as they "led" the nation through the disasters of inflation and depression, counseling austerity. (Hollywood and Broadway catch none of this. In their versions of Cabaret the claws are drawn and the patter timid; America is not Weimar.) Outraged conservatives, hard put to counter the brilliant verbal pyrotechnics of the "artistes," instead muttered angrily, and correctly, that most of the lyrics and scripts of the satirical chansons and dialogues were written by Jews.

It is precisely the alienated and sophisticated victim of discrimination who sees the contradictions between public rhetoric and real practice and the true motives hidden behind the respectable façades of public figures. As liberated outsiders, Jewish youth were naturally skeptical about those who postured about traditional verities as misery spread. They could even find amusement and comic caricature in their own predicament and that of the Jewish community itself, often to its embarrassment. The Jewish comic and the Jewish radical both stand at a distance from accepted cultural and social attitudes, leavened by ambivalence about one's place in society, in the minds of others, and even among one's own people. Supporters of the status quo are always uncomfortable in their presence. Cabaret wit would naturally be most prominent in postwar Germany, where social conflicts were strongest and the nation the most polarized. The raspy voices of Claire Waldorf, Kurt Tucholsky, and numerous others gained a bitter edge from their own vulnerability and the power of those who threatened them and civilized life as well. Tucholsky, the most biting of all Weimar critics, disavowed his Jewish origins; he knew this would not help—the right needed Jewish opponents. By the late 1920s Nazis attended cabarets in order to bust them up, rather than try to counter the scintillating play of corrosive wit. The ironic and comic mind could have no place in the Third Reich.

The sexual freedom of Weimar offended traditionalists everywhere, but many Germans decried sex shows, sadomasochistic displays, and transvestite and homosexual balls as Jewish, and rightist toughs often waited outside to beat those leaving the festivities. Social Democrats were also blamed, for they had long campaigned to strike down the paragraph in the penal code forbidding homosexual acts. The liberated women of Vienna and Berlin—short skirts, bobbed hair, confined breasts, and cigarettes—were the target of sexual and puritanical aggression. Women's equality was guaranteed by the Weimar constitution, praised by socialists, and reinforced by the wartime use of women in factories and clerical positions. When high unemployment shook the traditional male self-image, millions demanded a return to patriarchal ways, and rightist intellectuals provided the usual biological justifications. In the kaiser's days, Social Democrats and progressives had supported easier divorce, free access to professions, and legalized abortions. The right had always insisted, as an Austrian Nazi put it, that "Jewry is conducting a systematic, tenacious fight against the morally upright German people. Everywhere sexual revolutionaries preach Jewish morality and succeed, at least among a portion of the subhumans who have been benumbed by Marxism."[11]

By 1930 reactionaries regarded Weimar culture as simply Jewish culture. Certainly, as Walter Laqueur has noted:

> Without the Jews there would have been no "Weimar culture." . . . They were in the forefront of every new, daring, revolutionary movement. They were prominent among Expressionist poets, among the novelists of the 1920s, among the theatrical producers, and, for a while, among the leading figures of the cinema. They owned the leading liberal newspapers . . . and many editors were Jews too. Many leading liberal and avant-garde publishing houses were in Jewish hands. . . . Many leading theater critics were Jews, and they dominated light entertainment.[12]

But the high proportion of Jews in the avant-garde cannot justify racism. Weimar culture, in Peter Gay's famous phrase, was the culture of the "outsider as insider." To be Jewish in Germany meant to belong to a culture within a culture, to know both but to accept and be accepted by neither. Jewish artists and intellectuals knew their work was not taken at face value but was dismissed as an expression of racial proclivity. Jewish participation in the avant-garde was a result of Jews' marginal position in German society. Racism allowed traditionalists to dismiss the uncomfortable truth: the most creative cultural forces of the time were aimed at everything they believed in.

The powerful influence of the Weimar avant-garde has led us to miss the significance of the far more popular culture of those years, one that relied on traditional aesthetics and prefigured much of Nazi artistic style. Experimental works and forbidden topics were vastly outnumbered by

traditional and familiar films, literature, and art. There one still found
Germany's standard heroes—the Prussian officer class, the aristocracy,
Frederick the Great, and Bismarck; war was still glorified, and soldiers
fought with idealistic commitment. In Vienna the Christian Social party
founded a *Judenrein* theatre, as their predecessors had in 1890. As Laqueur
has written, avant-garde writers were far outsold by novels with Germanic
and religious themes, tales of the personal search for God, quasi-
Wagnerian quests for the Holy Grail, nonexperimental works void of social criticism. Provincial authors and some very famous best-sellers
avoided Berlin and depicted a past peopled by Germans free of Weimar
cynicism, their roots planted in a provincial "Homeland," as the genre
was called. Stories of sentimental nostalgia for the fading virtues of rural
Germany and the peasant abounded, and, as before, Jewish land speculators and moneylenders were not rare characters among them. Some
wrote about young men who, consumed by passionate longing for the
ideal, were battered by fate as they sought a world adequate to their intense spirituality. German romanticism was revived, as were the works of
Kleist, the literary voice of the wars against Napoleon. Kleist was especially popular among those who, having missed the war, idealized the sacrifices of their fathers and elder brothers, despised the "unmanly" pacifism
of the left, and detested the material concerns of commerce and the political compromises of the republic. More than one scholar insisted that
no Jew could understand the soul of a Kleist.

Arthur Dinter's *The Sin Against Blood* (1921), a phenomenal best-seller,
depicts a rich Jew who violates an innocent Aryan, polluting her blood. A
volkist, Dinter believed intercourse with a Jew destroyed the capacity of
Aryan woman to reproduce anything but racially polluted offspring, a
metaphor for the rape of the Motherland by the republic. Dinter also
wrote popular books calling for a new Luther. Like the great reformer, he
was convinced the Jews were the reincarnation of the devil. A Nazi leader
in Thuringia, Dinter was forced out of the party for attacking Catholicism
when the party needed Catholic votes. The Christian right also had its
ideological soft porn: one famous poster shows a scantily clad blond
woman hanging from a cross, a knife-carrying Jew leering at her crucified
body—erotic fantasy disguised as ideology to justify the puritan voyeur.

In his fine study, Peter Gay tells of the "chief spokesmen" of the German academy who saw a world "filled with enemies: the dehumanizing
machine, capitalist materialism, godless rationalism, rootless society, cosmopolitan Jews, and that great all-devouring monster, the city."[13] Theologians, historians, philosophers, and professors of law and literature,
living with the bitterness of defeat and reduced status, despised all the
more "Jewish" liberalism, blaming it for cultural mediocrity, democratic
leveling, and the radicalism of an ignorant working class in need of au-

tocratic discipline. The scholar Eckart Kehr ruined his career by demonstrating how German industrialists and aristocrats, seeking profits and a united front against the democratic left, pressed for the international aggression that brought 1914. Social Democrats and Jewish scholars gained a foothold in the academy only through the efforts of republican officials. The Ministry of Culture funded independent research institutes to employ those unacceptable to the tenured specialists of the academy. The German emigré scholars famed for their contributions to American academic life were usually Social Democrats, progressives, or Jews forced to flee from these institutes, not from university faculty. But professors were still the kaiser's men. By 1931 academic support for the Nazis was muted only by contempt for the vulgarity of his lower-middle-class following.

The racist Ludwig Klages was one of many intellectuals who called for a regeneration of the Germanic beast of prey and a violent pagan-Teutonic aristocracy to descend upon the new Germany. Not all intellectuals were pleased when it happened. Faculty and students in Austria had fewer qualms. By the late 1920s the Austrian Nazis were the most important political influence in student associations, the Protocols of Zion were popular, racist posters and anti-Semitic lectures abounded, and Nazi students called for the murder of prominent Jews and often brutally beat Jewish students. The New York Times reported that the University of Vienna was practically a battlefield. In the name of academic freedom, the faculty and administration allowed no interference. And the university's president was a Nazi supporter.

By 1929 reactionaries dominated German university life. Hermann Hesse resigned from the Prussian Academy of Literature in 1931, protesting that it betrayed democratic and educational ideals. Martin Heidegger, Germany's most famous philosopher, denounced the "dehumanizing cosmopolitanism" of liberal idealism, insisting that the highest ethical imperative was to join those great movements, like National Socialism, that expressed the historical mandate of the spirit and sacred mission of the Volk. He joined the Nazis in 1933, and, as head of the University of Freiburg, purged liberals and Jews from the faculty, including his own mentor. Heidegger organized student paramilitary camps, telling them they must discard reason and intellect as the West understood them, and suggesting that others could not be expected to comprehend the students' hatred of Weimar. "The Fuehrer himself, and he alone, is the German reality of today, and of the future, and of its law."[14] A Nazi through 1945, Heidegger never denounced their crimes even after the war, when it was safe. One must assume he did not consider them crimes. Professor Konrad Lorenz, the famous student of animal behavior, hated industrial-urban society and joined the Austrian Nazis in 1938. In 1940 he defended the Nazi euthanasia policy of killing the mentally ill and unfit. He was pleased that the "racial idea" was the base of the state and hoped selection would be used to breed only the useful and the strong. Misguided humanitarianism, he wrote, had left Germany saddled with "socially inferior material" and "domestication-induced degeneracy." Lorenz also converted his students to the Nazis, but, less sincere than Heidegger, he tried to hide evidence of his activities after the war.

Werner Sombart, Germany's famed economist, accepted the volkist image of Jewry and translated it into economic principles. A rootless urban people, hostile to nature, unproductive and driven by limitless acquisitive drives, the Jews were dominated by an unnatural rationality, Sombart wrote. They were "born representatives of the liberal worldview of the abstract citizen."[15] Germans were inventors and heroic entrepreneurs; Jews saw the world only as a vast market to be exploited. Jewish control of finance, banking, commodity markets, and currency speculation strangled technological civilization, as the inflation and depression demonstrated. Root out the Jewish spirit, Sombart insisted, and let the German economy be managed by producers and engineers in the spirit of "national socialism," a term he used to mean managing the economy for the good of the racial community rather than the crass search for ever more consumer goods for individuals. He too joined the Nazis.

With his writings Oswald Spengler inspired a cult following among young rightist intellectuals. The absurd creations of the Weimar avant-garde, he declared, showed that the days of true culture were behind, the twentieth century would belong to the engineer, the imperialist, the soldier, and the dictator. Like Nazi ideologists, Spengler rejected both finance capitalism and Marxism, and demanded autocratic control over the economy and politics in order to end labor militancy and create military power. Above all, Spengler wrote, a new elite must unify and inspire the masses with the sacrificial idealism needed to pursue an imperial destiny, and each must carry out the duties appropriate to his station in life, without complaint. Spengler believed Weimar was a business corporation, not a state, lacking the will and idealism to follow the iron imperatives of the future. Germany would go under, he insisted, if it did not cultivate industry and technology, defeat the "Jewish" merchant spirit, and restore its old loyalty to blood and race in a Faustian spirit of conquest over unproductive Jewry and the restraints of Christian morality. Nazis objected only to his belief that orientals, not Aryans, would dominate the future.

Weimar culture aroused the ire of traditionalists in all Western nations, but only in Germany was the cultural counterattack associated with the belief that constitutional democracy must be destroyed, the left outlawed, and the Jews punished. To this a great many conservative German intellectuals added a call for a "Fuehrer" to rule in the spirit of blood and race in order to save the *Kultur* of a racial community. Hans Grimm, in his very popular *Volk Without Space* (1926), demanded that Germany conquer living space in the east in order to provide for the increase of the race, and personally informed Hitler of his loyalty. The works of Chamberlain, Treitschke, Langbehn, Lagarde, and volkists were revived. A few racial communes were begun, with body worship, Teutonic rituals, and the belief that Nordics must breed and breed again in order to save their racial genius. Himmler, by profession a breeder of hybrid chickens, and Rudolph Hoess, veteran Freikorps fighter and future commander of Auschwitz, may have belonged to the same commune. Conservative educators established special trade schools in the 1920s to teach useful trades to city youth, introduce them to the agrarian ways of their forebears, and instill in them contempt for the "moral decay" of Jews and socialists— ideas later absorbed into the Nazi educational system. Communal groups staged folk dances and folk "costume and culture" displays in public schools; like the Nazis, they believed ballroom dancing was thinly disguised eroticism and jazz the degenerate music of "subhuman" blacks. In 1927 a Combat Bund for German Culture was formed by conservative establishment leaders who denounced almost all forms of Weimar culture. The Nazis, in "Herbert Lons Evenings"—he was the poet of the peasantry of the harsh Lueneberg Heath region—celebrated Germanic "Volk and Homeland" authors. Regional centers displaying local costumes, crafts, and folk songs were given a new ideological significance. Ponderously staged spectacles illustrated the Teutonic past, with massed choirs dressed in the ancient costumes, dancing, chanting, and intoning hymns of praise to ancient Germanic nature gods, not the stations of the cross of a martyred Jewish God.

Nazi artists and critics rejected the perspectival relativism of cubism, the subjectivism of expressionism, and all art of inner experience—as Hitler labeled it, the "degenerate, Negroid, Jewish art of mongrelized and Marxist Paris." Rosenberg insisted that all great art reflected racial beauty. From the Greeks onward, art had used the Semitic or the "hairy-negroid-eastern racial type" only to depict demons, satyrs, or criminals; no true artist had ever embodied his ideal of beauty, heroism, or honor in the face or body of the Jewish race. Jewish critics—spiritual syphilitics and bastardized mongrels—were responsible for the success of Weimar culture. Drive them out, he demanded, for they had put culture, like press and economy, at the service of the Jews. In 1937 the Nazis held their famous exhibition of degenerate art, with slogans reading "Art does not wallow in filth for filth's sake, or paint the human being in a state of putrefaction, draw cretins as symbols of motherhood, or use deformed idiots as representatives of manly strength. This is not art, it is the revelation of the Jewish Racial Soul."

Nazi ideology and culture were extreme and vulgar caricatures of sophisticated themes found in the writings of a variety of conservative intellectuals. When they achieved power, the Nazis proscribed the avant-garde, of course, and Goebbels strove for a unified aesthetic based on traditional art forms readily understandable to millions. Experimentation and social criticism were purged and troubling themes deleted, replaced by pop realism, martial themes, and volkist images, all comforting to lower-middle-class taste. The symbols of a racially revived Germany were presented in monumental and heroic forms. Peasant Venuses, Aryan warriors and nudes, and idealized peasants flooded canvases and sculpture studios. Films were variations of "Hearth and Homeland" themes, with a few sophisticated propaganda films as well, such as the documentaries of Leni Riefenstahl or the famous *Jud Suess* and *The Eternal Jew*. Albert Speer resurrected traditional neoclassical styles of architecture, endless marching rows of columns built on a scale meant to dwarf the individual human spirit, as in his choreographed massive outdoor rallies, the elaborately staged theatre of Nazi ritual, immersing the individual in vast saluting multitudes.

The Nazis allowed no room for the free play of intellect. Constant propaganda reached into home and workplace to replace the individual experience that fosters independent judgment. Private and class identities, crucial to Weimar culture, were drowned in public ceremonies by the terse, repetitive, and sloganizing speechmaking of party officials, Hitler's clones, the mood set by the massed banners, torchlight parades, drums and trumpets of armed legions marching in massed columns to martial or Wagnerian music. Vast marble monoliths, altars to martial glory and death, were intended to overawe and inspire the individual to mindless self-sacrifice for a mythical tribal community. Above all, citizens must become masses. It was not enough to destroy Weimar culture or punish discontent; Nazi culture must manufacture approval.

In 1933 the literature of the avant-garde was consigned to the flames. Amidst a vast exodus of creative talent, Grosz lost his citizenship in 1933, Tucholsky in 1934, Brecht in 1935. Austrian Jews were eased out of cultural life by the Christian Social government; by 1937 the press, publishing, and the theatre were *Judenrein*. As the management of Vienna's most prestigious theatre announced, "The day has arrived when the stage of the Burgtheater can be cleansed of the Jewish filth dumped there by Schnitzler and his ilk." German and Austrian culture have never recovered. None of this was lamented by the right, of course. In the words of one writer of the right, Friedrich Hussong:

> A miracle has taken place. They are no longer here. . . . They claimed
> they were the German Spirit, German culture, the German present

and future. They represented Germany to the world, they spoke in its name. . . . Everything else was mistaken, inferior, regrettable kitsch, odious philistinism. . . . They awarded knighthoods of the spirit and of Europeanism. What they did not permit did not exist. . . . They "made" themselves and others. Whoever served them was sure to succeed. He appeared on their stages, wrote in their journals, was advertised all over the world; his commodity was recommended whether it was cheese or relativity, face powder or contemporary theater, patent medicines or human rights, democracy or bolshevism, propaganda for abortion or against the legal system, rotten Negro music or dancing in the nude. In brief, there was never a more shameless dictatorship than that of the democratic intelligentsia and their uncreative effete esthetes.[16]

17: ORGANIZING THE NAZIS, 1924–1930

We will seize power by any means necessary, even legal.
—Charles Maurras, French royalist and racist

AFTER his failed *putsch* Hitler was front-page news throughout Europe. In Munich in February 1924, reporters jammed the courtroom at his trial for treason. The prosecutor was on the defensive throughout. The judges, considered a bad joke by the foreign press, allowed Hitler to give hour-long propaganda speeches and refer to the republic as a "Jew government" of "November criminals." The leaders of the republic, he insisted, were the real traitors. He was a revolutionary patriot who had done what millions of others wanted to but dared not. Although he was bitter that the army had not joined him, Hitler said nothing about this; he would need the military to gain power. Instead he told of his joy that police, not soldiers, had fired on him: "The hour will come when the army will stand at our side."[1] He knew they shared the same views. As Colonel Werner von Fritsch, future chief of the army high command, said, they must not surrender to "Ebert, pacifists, Jews, democrats . . . and the French, all one and the same, the people who want to destroy Germany."[2] In his final speech, illegal but permitted, Hitler declared that history would judge him and Ludendorff "as Germans who wanted only the good of their own people and their Fatherland. . . ." The court might condemn them but "the eternal court of history . . . acquits us."[3]

The court president was barely able to persuade his fellow judges that Hitler must be found guilty if only because he had confessed, but they agreed to the lightest possible sentence. Announcing the verdict, the chief judge reported, "The court is convinced the motives of the defendants were genuinely patriotic, noble, and selfless." They believed "they had to act to save the Fatherland" because of the "treason of 1918."[4] Hitler was given the minimum sentence of five years. By law he should have served all five, and, as an Austrian, be deported. Instead he was free in five months, deportation waived because he had proven to be too good a German for citizenship to be relevant. In "prison," surrounded by admiring guards and companions, flooded with gifts, he enjoyed every comfort as he wrote *Mein Kampf.*

Hitler's judges detested the republic; the presiding judge was an outright fan of Hitler. Since Bismarck, judges had been famous for partial decisions against Progressives and Social Democrats. Lifetime civil servants, they had more control over trials and decisions than judges elsewhere, and they believed their task was to fight the "enemy within." During Weimar, German extremists on the right, including assassins, received ridiculously light sentences because of their "noble motives." Thus all the leaders of the revolutionary left in Bavaria received harsh sentences, but only one man was sentenced for the Kapp *putsch.* Although it was illegal to call for the death of government leaders or voice racist slanders, judges not only permitted it, they often made anti-Semitic remarks in their own written opinions. During Hitler's trial the delegates of the Conservative party met, and they shouted a rousing *"Heil"* when Ludendorff's acquittal was announced and cries of anger when Hitler was found guilty. The *Kreuzzeitung* praised Hitler's attempt to free Germany from international Jewry, adding that between themselves and him, "we cannot find any fundamental difference in outlooks." The conservative press was favorable to Hitler and Ludendorff; so too was the Berlin stock exchange paper, belying its alleged domination by Jews.[5]

In May 1924 the government fell when the Social Democrats refused to surrender the eight-hour day they had won for workers. Held in the midst of inflation and the French occupation, the elections gave the Conservative party its greatest success ever. For the first time it was second only to the Social Democrats. The Independent Socialists, more leftist than the Social Democrats and the second largest party in 1920, were wiped out. The moderate parties were drastically reduced as well. From prison, Hitler chose Julius Streicher to lead the Nazis, who organized a "racial bloc" and won some thirty-two seats, outpolling even the once-strong member of the Weimar coalition, the German Democratic party. Streicher, Ludendorff, and Erhardt were seated as Nazi delegates. In 1919 about 90 percent of the electorate had voted for parties favorable to the republic; in 1924 only about half did so. Ominously, close to a third of the electorate voted for parties that employed anti-Semitism in the campaign. The elections demonstrated that in time of social trauma great numbers of voters were available to anyone who could unite the racist right. Had it not been certain that the French would crush any military uprising, it is doubtful the republic would have survived the storms of 1923–1924.

In the Bavarian state elections of 1924, the racial bloc received 17 percent of the vote to 33 percent for the dominant Bavarian People's party

(BVP), even though Ludendorff and Streicher were well-known anti-Catholics. The bloc was now the second largest political organization in Bavaria, and the BVP, supported by the clergy, was itself anti-Semitic, though less so than the Nazis. In December, Hitler was free. The Bavarian state police director believed him dangerous because "he is the soul" of the "nationalist-racist movement," able to convert "great masses of people."[6] Because they supported him, however, the Ministry of the Interior released him.

Militants now moved to the Nazis and the brown-shirted storm troopers, the SA. These were not merely brutes, they were brutes with an ideology. The experience of early SA joiners is revealing. They could scarcely expect immediate rewards and were therefore more highly motivated and ideologically committed than later members. Proletarians did not join the SA in great numbers; if unemployed, they joined the Communists, otherwise remaining loyal to the socialists. Catholics disliked the anti-Catholicism of some Nazis. Peasants rarely joined at first. The Nazis were unorganized in the countryside, and local peasant groups, reactionary and anti-Semitic, had prior claims. The lower middle classes were heavily overrepresented in the Nazi rank and file. Contrary to received opinion, the upper classes were especially strong in the party leadership, and from the very beginning. In 1924 some 12 percent of all Nazis were from the upper classes, though they composed only 3 percent of the population. Six percent were university students.

Among early Nazis a sense of national humiliation and personal frustration animated the sons of aristocrats, officers, or higher civil servants. Four percent of Nazis were female, and came usually from military-aristocratic families where women's rights were seen as the subversion of patriarchal strength by leftist "Hebrew women." Many early Nazis came from middle- or upper-class families broken by war casualties and inflation, and forced to become shipping clerks, taxi drivers, or manual laborers. The symbols and mission of the SA revived their lost sense of high status. The sons of military families often joined because professional army careers were cut off by the Versailles Treaty, and the SA offered paramilitary training and a chance to destroy the treaty one day. But the majority of early Nazis were sons of artisans, shopkeepers, lesser civil servants, and small businessmen, groups most threatened by inflation and the power of big business and big labor—the same types who tended to be most racist in the late nineteenth century. Many SA members, unemployed provincials, moved from job to job, often forced to work side by side with the despised enemy, exposed, as Hitler was in Vienna, to Marxist scorn for the traditional beliefs of their rural origins. Migrants to big cities were common in the SA and fascist movements throughout Europe. In the cities, rightist movements revivified their lost past with mythologies of blood and soil glorifying peasant and artisan. The myth of blood supremacy comforted those who were deprived of former social status or who had never possessed much: semiskilled manual laborers, servants, store clerks, petty bureaucrats, butchers, bakers, and so forth. In uniform and ritual, the SA reinforced a sense of superiority. Prevented, like their fallen nation, from asserting themselves by the machinations of Jews and leftists, their Nazi ideology defused the contradiction between their faith in their inner power and the facts of their dreary lives. Violence in word and deed confirms the worth of the warrior. In marching uniformed columns bedecked with Germanic symbols and swastikas, veterans, especially unemployed noncommissioned officers, relived the old battles and the male bonding of the front, convinced the stolen victory could be redeemed by destroying the enemy at home. As with Hitler, so with them, politics was war by other means.

Many early SA came from occupied areas where the arrogant enemy was a constant reminder of defeat. In the Ruhr their sons were caught resisting the French, and some five thousand families lost home and job. For them, Germany's liberation was an intense personal goal. Ludendorff and Hitler, general and corporal, symbolized the unity of the upper and lower classes in common desire for revenge. Among the most violent and determined members of the SA and paramilitaries, especially Austrian, were those whose families had lost homes, status, and jobs because of the vast changes in ethnic borders and exchange of peoples in 1919. An important part of all Nazi meetings was the solemn roll call of lost territories, the sacred lands where Germans had once ruled and Slavs now reigned. Ethnic hatreds had always been strongest where Germans or Austrians faced Slavs. Joining the SA meant keeping the faith that they would return, weapon in hand, to finish the Freikorps's attempt to redeem ancestral land. Ethnic Germans from Russia or the Baltic states where they once ruled, driven out by Bolsheviks or indigenous peoples, eagerly joined.

Throughout Eastern Europe, fascist movements proliferated among tens of thousands who had suffered similar fates. Some two-thirds of the Hungarian Empire was lost in 1918. Forced from home, land, or business, Hungarians shouted as one their famous phrase against postwar treaties: "No, no, never!" Displaced Magyars were plentiful among the White terrorists of Horthy who cleansed "sinful" Budapest and slaughtered Jews when Bela Kun was defeated. Yet even he had fought to regain lost territories. Germans from the Sudetenland, Schoenerer's old stronghold, joined the SA or the even more violent Sudeten Nazis, desperate to throw off Czech rule. Bitterness among Austro-Germans led to proportionally more of them than Germans joining militant groups, including the Austrian Nazis. Some SA also came from the lost German colonies, where,

as in imperialism everywhere, racism was reinforced by the everyday oppression of the defeated and the pleasant life gained at their expense. Joining the SA meant a start at restoring one's personal worth, private loss,
and Germany's empire.

As SA membership soared, Hitler organized the SS, an elite bodyguard
dedicated to him alone. Many SA members hoped to replace the elites;
the SA anthem spoke of marching against "reds *and* reactionaries." Hitler
had to compromise with the upper classes to gain power, and some SA
members even issued public manifestos against him. SS officers were
more reliable. Recruited from the middle or upper classes, they would
happily stifle any radical tendencies in the party. Although the Waffen SS
accepted draftees near the end of the war, two-thirds joined before Hitler
gained power, when ideology, not opportunism, played the largest role.
And as late as 1938 only one-quarter of the SS were paid. Often SS members had served in the elite "shock" troops at the front, or been raised by
extreme nationalist families with great respect for authority, an allegiance
easily transferred to Hitler. SS officers chose wives by racial criteria and
submitted documents proving there had been no Jewish blood in the family since 1750. Because "racial purification" policies were an SS specialty,
they were less threatening to the elites than the populist-tainted SA, and
consequently attracted more of their sons. After all, since 1893 racism had
been used by the Conservative party to battle reform, and populism had
been regarded as a danger since Stoecker's day.

Among the most brutal SS were the fifty commandants and some forty
thousand who later made up the staffs of the death camps, though not
all were SS or German. Camp guards tended to be failed artisans or farmers, small shopkeepers, sons of lesser civil servants or police officers. From
village or small town, most had done poorly at school and work and had
trouble with the authorities. Over one-third of the SA and SS expressed
a belief in God, including most camp commandants. It was "bad form"
to be an atheist; atheism was associated with Judeo-bolshevism. The SA
had chaplains. For some, like Rudolf Hoess, commandant of Auschwitz,
killing followed a lifetime of racial reaction. Born to a long line of military officers, at fourteen Hoess tried to enlist. Sent home, he later joined
and became the youngest sergeant in the army, much decorated. In 1919
Hoess joined the Freikorps, fought in the east, and then joined the Kapp
putsch. Imprisoned for five years for murdering the schoolteacher who
betrayed Schlageter, Nazi martyr of the French occupation, upon his release Hoess joined a volkist commune on an aristocrat's estate, where he
may have met Himmler. As Auschwitz commandant he managed what
was in effect a hellish version of the volkist communes of 1890.

The SA and SS offered a return to the comradeship and blood brotherhood of the trenches for those who had found no civilian substitute for

the high drama that gave their young lives meaning, as with Hitler. To younger nonveterans, the Nazis offered a surrogate for the heroic experience of the fathers and brothers, dramatically recreated in Nazi icons, rituals, torchlight parades, and the formal intoning of names of dead comrades at party rallies. Sadistic and ignorant brutes were drawn to the movement, of course, but such creatures can be recruited anywhere; it was the institutionalization and mobilization of violence behind an ideology of death that made the crucial difference. The cult of race and blood encouraged Nazis to believe they were revolutionaries, not mere killers, idealists who had taken on the hard but necessary task of destroying the enemies of Germany and of all Nordic humanity, a theme Himmler often reiterated when speaking to his murderers in the field.

In order to gain power, however, Hitler had to restrain his most militant followers and curb the populism of the SA. What was most singular about Hitler was not his will to destroy the Jews but the political skills that enabled him to hold the loyalties of his radical followers even as he persuaded the traditional ruling classes to accept him as *Fuehrer.* Immediately after his release, Hitler assured the new Bavarian president that the *putsch* had been a terrible mistake. Elite conservatives would need to know they could entrust their interests to him. As he remarked, "We shall have to play the rotten political game. . . . Instead of working to take power by an armed coup, we shall have to hold our noses and enter the Reichstag against the Catholic and Marxist deputies. If outvoting them takes longer than outshooting them, at least the results will be guaranteed by their own constitution."[7] Millions of votes would make him needed by conservatives, and Hitler risked alienating those who suspected he was selling out. Putschists had to be converted to mere campaign workers so they could conduct recruiting drives, peddle propaganda, fund-raise, and solicit votes—the endless drudgery necessary for elections. They even had to contribute to party expenses. Until power was won, their only emotional release would come from occasionally busting up leftist meetings and beating up Jews.

From 1924 to 1928 Nazi and radical right successes were few. Inflation ended, German reparations were renegotiated, French troops began to withdraw. The Social Democrats were no longer in the government, and Germany was allowed in the League of Nations. The inflation had been ended on terms favoring big business. Over Social Democratic objections, longer hours of work were legislated and new tax laws favored the wealthy. Handsome subsidies were given to those firms required to send raw materials or manufactured goods to pay reparations, but the damaging currency speculation of business firms was restricted. These measures, plus short-term loans from American and British banks, stimulated productivity and trade, increased wages and salaries, and cut bankruptcy rates and unemployment. Economic stability and some political moderation followed.

But in Austria, anti-Semitic radicalism never waned. Huge demonstrations ringing with cries of "Death to the Jews" were held in Vienna in 1925 when Zionists met, and racism flourished in Alpine touring and gymnastic clubs and associations of physicians and lawyers. The Heimwehr (Home Defense) with 400,000 members was at the height of its popularity in the late 1920s. Led by Prince Ernst von Starhemberg, its following was heaviest among Catholic peasants. The popular Anti-Semitic Bund united many groups, and the Greater German People's party was even more extreme than the Nazis. The ruling Christian Social party remained anti-Semitic, and the influx of eastern Jews made racism even more overwhelming among middle- and upper-class Germans. Lacking any liberal alternative, 75 percent of Jewish voters in Austria supported socialism, reinforcing middle-class fears.

Hitler needed time to transform the party into a political organization, and he was hindered because he had been banned from public speaking for two years. Recruiting went on, however, and membership grew from 27,000 in 1925 to 75,000 by 1927; before the depression it reached about 125,000. At first, time and energy were wasted trying to gain votes from the proletariat. But in 1927 the Nazis began serious campaigning in rural areas, and there they were rewarded with immediate success. They also benefited from the reparations clauses of the new settlement, the Dawes Plan, which were still drastic. When the plan was ratified in August 1924, Reichstag sessions exploded as Nazis, Conservatives, and Communists shouted defiance. In effect the terms of the Dawes Plan, set by international financial experts, returned reparations payments and more to Germany as loans, and businessmen thought this a reasonable deal, providing needed capital. But Germany had to guarantee payments with mortgages taken out on her railroads and revenues from import and excise taxes harmful to consumers. The vast majority of Germans hated any reparations whatsoever, and even Allied concessions underlined German impotence. Ludendorff, a Nazi deputy, shouted in the Reichstag: "This is a disgrace to Germany! Ten years ago I won the battle of Tannenberg. Today you have made a Jewish Tannenberg."[8]

The radical right was incensed when, after campaigning against the Dawes Plan as a creature of Jewish international finance, the majority of the Conservative party delegation, swayed by businessmen eager for the loans, voted for it. Worse, in 1924 the Conservatives joined a coalition government for the first time. Nazis and rightists reacted bitterly to this "sellout" to the "Jewish Republic," but the second elections of 1924 showed renewed if ambivalent support for the republic. Social Democrats scored significantly, but Conservatives reached a new high. The Nazi racial bloc was reduced from thirty-two to fourteen seats, though smaller racist parties, especially a new Economics party appealing to the victims of inflation, made up the difference.

In 1925 elections for a new president were called: Ebert had succumbed to the stress of endless libel cases before prejudiced judges who believed the ridiculous accusation that he was responsible for the "stab-in-the-back" strikes of 1918. Hindenburg was elected president. Conservatives rejoiced, believing the avowed monarchist would preside over the demise of the republic and the return of autocracy. They were correct, but it took until 1933. For in the elections of 1928 the republic received a powerful vote of confidence. The issue was a Reichstag vote to build a pocket battleship, the first of four, and legal under the Versailles Treaty. The Social Democrats campaigned with the slogan "Food for children before battleships." The Conservative party suffered a loss of nearly one-third of its seats and won only 14 percent of the vote; the Social Democrats gained 30 percent of the vote, the strongest party by far. The Communists received 11 percent of the vote. The right assumed, or pretended to, that communism was scarcely different from democratic socialism, and voiced fears of a left coalition. In fact the two parties were bitter antagonists. Stalin insisted that socialists merely preserved capitalism and betrayed the proletariat. He instructed Communists to reject the "Social Fascists" of the SPD, and they obeyed.

The leftist surge drove all parties further right, creating an atmosphere in which the Nazis were more acceptable. Once the buttress of republican coalitions, the Catholic Center was now led by an antirepublican priest, Father Kaas, who idealized Karl Lueger. Kaas hailed Mussolini's "corporate state" as the embodiment of Catholic social ideas, agreeing with the Vatican that the old alliance of the Center with "atheistic socialists" was contrary to Christian principles—as many local party branches had always said. Most of the moderate businessmen of Stresemann's German People's party (DVP) were moving to support the racists and reactionaries. A purge of DVP moderates followed a strike settled in favor of the workers by government arbitration courts. When the owners broke the law with a lockout, the workers, benefiting from unemployment insurance, held out long enough for their lawyers to win in the courts. Industrialists attacked unemployment insurance and the compulsory wage agreements of the Social Democrats as "cold socialism." Many looked to a German Mussolini, for it was clear that the economic policies of Il Duce were dictated by industrialists. Stresemann angrily but vainly denounced his colleagues for using the racist slogans of the radical right. Even the German Democratic party, former mainstay of Weimar and once referred to as the "Jewish" party because of its liberal-'sm, now denounced the "charity politics" of Weimar, turned its back on democracy, and negotiated an alliance with representatives of the Young German Order, the paramilitary Freikorps unit which had thrived under the iron cross of the Teutonic Knights. Contrary to accepted views, many business leaders looked favorably on the radical right before the depression.

The shock of the elections brought home to the Conservative party the need for more public support. Stung by charges that it had betrayed Germany by voting for reparations, the party returned to a policy of no compromise. Count von Westarp, the party leader, resigned. Although he was regarded as a moderate, a responsible Jewish journal had spoken of his "anti-Semitic ravings."[9] The Conservatives were losing support from their core constituencies. Police reports indicated that many army officers, aristocrats, and civil servants were attending Nazi meetings. Agrarian and industrial reactionaries chose the leader of their right wing, Alfred Hugenberg, as new chairman. A former high-ranking official in the Prussian Ministry of Finance, Hugenberg had moved into banking and become chairman of the board of Krupp Armaments; then he gained the greatest honor his industrialist friends could confer, being named director of the politically powerful Coal and Steel Syndicate of Rhineland and Westphalia. During the war Hugenberg had demanded maximum German expansion and had worked with Ludendorff after Russia's defeat to plan the economic exploitation of a German empire in the east.

In 1918, determined to fight on, Hugenberg had been entrusted by industrialists with huge sums to donate to a "vast number of counterrevolutionary organizations."[10] How much he gave to the Nazis is not known, but all paramilitary groups shared similar aims. Using his immense war profits, Hugenberg bought a media empire of newspapers, magazines, newsreels, a wire service, and the biggest film company in Germany, and used them to promote rightist causes. Although he praised Hitler's *putsch*, he preferred a counterrevolution led by the old rulers, not a populist seizure of power from below. He had political ambitions, but as a representative of the reactionary elites he could not appeal to lower-middle-class resentment against the upper classes. He wanted alliances with the extreme right to prepare for an autocratic, probusiness regime and smash the socialists; he even denounced Bismarck's minimal welfare policies. The low Nazi vote indicated that Conservatives would dominate any alliance, but there were other signs. The Nazis were beginning to do well in local elections. In their first outright victory, in June 1929 they won the town council in Coburg, Bavaria, outpolling the Conservative party. Significantly, the main issue was the fate of a Nazi government official dismissed for his violently "anti-Semitic speeches."[11]

Hugenberg courted the radical right with the reparations issue. Germany could not meet the payments of the Dawes Plan, and the Allies reduced reparations with the Young Plan of 1929, which ended controls over banking and railroads. The French agreed to remove all occupation troops by June 1930. To accountants, bankers, and consensus politicians, these were reasonable solutions to practical differences; for the German public the sacrifices of the dead could never be resolved by compromise. By bringing reparations to the fore, Hugenberg reopened deep psychic wounds. Goaded by a new spate of Allied "war guilt" accusations, the public was shocked to learn that the rescheduled payments would not end until 1988. The sins of the fathers were to be visited upon the great-grandsons! Now the right had yet another opportunity to mobilize discontent.

In July 1929 Hugenberg formed an alliance to protest the Young Plan before the Reichstag ratified it. Among those who joined him and the Conservatives were Heinrich Class and the pan-Germans, Hitler and the Nazis, Seldte and the Stahlhelm, Admiral von Tirpitz, Fritz Thysen of the powerful Reichsverband of German Industry, four hundred representatives of various nationalist and racist groups, and an assortment of princes and aristocrats. Some industrialists joined as well, but most accepted the new plan. A petition insisted that the Reichstag pass a law against the "enslavement of the German people," denounce the war guilt clause, refuse to pay any reparations ever, and demand the immediate evacuation of foreign troops. Moreover, any officials who made Germany liable for future payments should be punished as traitors—a clause that would have made Germany ungovernable. Close to 6 million Germans voted for these demands, but 21 million were needed to make it law; the Young Plan passed in August 1930.

Hitler profited immensely from the campaign. His speeches were carried by Hugenberg's media empire, and, allied with the most prestigious elites, he gained access to people of wealth and influence. And Hitler had accomplished this with only an insignificant number of votes, and without making any concessions, thus furthering his reputation as a man of principle. Given the public record of his speeches and the violent slogans of his rallies, no conservative could plead ignorance of his intent to do violence to the Jews. No matter, since 1893 conservatives themselves had hoped to reverse Jewish civil rights.

To remain stable, Weimar needed a long period of relative well-being and the rise of a generation for whom the war and postwar traumas faded as jobs proliferated, careers were made, and Allied demands reduced. But 1930 brought the first effects of the worldwide depression. Western nations with long-established constitutional traditions would survive, but Weimar, the unwanted and despised result of defeat, had millions of enemies even in good times. Coming so soon after the lost war and the inflation, the economic collapse was the culmination of disasters suffered by no other democracy. Before public suffering could be relieved, it was too late. By September 1930 the Nazis were the second largest party in Germany; by the summer of 1932 they gained the largest percentage of votes of any party in German history.

Until the slow beginnings of recovery, democracy and capitalism seemed bankrupt everywhere. Economic experts, business leaders, and most politicians agreed that the depression could only be alleviated by following the precepts of classical economics, the sacrosanct practices assumed to have brought prosperity to Europe. Politicians almost always defined their main task as one of assuring a good climate for business, and the precepts of laissez-faire held that the business cycle would restore prosperity in the long run. Already in the 1920s sales were too low to keep economies growing at their prewar rate. A worldwide glut severely depressed raw material prices, and industrial production was too low to take up the slack. Raw material producers and their workers thus saw a fall in purchasing power, and by 1929 mass purchasing power too was well behind advances in productivity; rising unemployment cut it further. Sales, profits, and wages fell, and unemployment grew. By late 1930 investors were ruined and farm earnings drastically reduced. Purchasing power, the key to recovery, collapsed. Politicians had never concerned themselves with stimulating the economy by deficit spending, and during the first three years of the depression most of them endlessly repeated inherited wisdom and corporate views: recovery would occur if austerity policies were followed. Bankers, financiers, and investors would extend the credit necessary to restore growth only if budgets were balanced. Given shrinking tax revenues, "fiscal responsibility" dictated that civil servants and workers be fired and salaries, wages, and unemployment benefits slashed. Such measures reduced purchasing power still more, worsening the depression.

Economic experts advised cutting wages and salaries to enable cheaper exports to win markets. But as nations protected their home markets with tariffs, international markets shrank. During the crucial years of Hitler's rise to power, living standards declined precipitously and unemployment soared. In all nations the public was increasingly frustrated, angry, and anticapitalist. Civil servants were embittered by salary cuts and layoffs; workers protested cuts in wages and unemployment benefits; small shopkeepers and white-collar workers saw their jobs and security destroyed by the drastic plunge in purchasing. Politicians seemed irrelevant, classical economics a trap. Austerity measures brought intense social discontent, yet failure to follow them cost the confidence of the bankers, financiers, and currency speculators who could damage recovery. Capitalism seemed bankrupt, even irrational; extremists of left and right thrived.

There were possible solutions. In Sweden and Scandinavia, well-established social democratic parties provided social insurance, kept prices low, aided producer and consumer coops, and used public housing to stimulate growth. Governments gave public assistance to indigent families, the sick, and the unemployed. By 1939 Sweden had enjoyed a greater rise in real wages in the twentieth century than any other nation. Failing the will to violate orthodox norms, other governments could only avoid cutbacks, maintain unemployment benefits, and fund public works through higher taxes or borrowing. Taxpayer resistance and the refusal of international investment firms like J. P. Morgan to lend unless austerity measures were in place, forced further austerity measures. Without them the national currency would be dumped by currency speculators. In 1928, when the Social Democratic government of Germany requested loans from the American firm of Dillon, Reed, it was told no austerity, no loans—something socialists could not possibly support. In France a socialist and communist Popular Front under Léon Blum gained power in 1936, and investors and speculators immediately sold francs for gold, fearing the higher wages and unemployment benefits to come. The franc lost value, industrialists and currency speculators dumped it, and decline accelerated. When the government tried to prevent French capitalists from taking their money out of France, a howl went up from wealthy "patriots," and the franc declined even further. Blum was able to raise wages some 15 percent, but it was too low to restart the economy. The first socialist and the first Jewish prime minister, Léon Blum was despised by the French right. Among upper-class Frenchmen the slogan circulated, "Better Hitler than Blum."

Everywhere social movements arose offering ways to increase purchasing power by guaranteed pensions, incomes, or cash allotments. Sir Oswald Mosley of England, a potential prime minister, called for massive deficit spending, public works, increased pensions, and a guaranteed living wage to restart the economy. Import and export regulations and other controls would defend the currency from speculators, protecting industry and the public. Economists rejected his violation of dogma; leftists decried this strengthening of "state capitalism." Rejected by his fellow Tories, Mosley joined Labour. When they spurned him, he blamed the collapse of capitalism on the machinations of "Jewish" international financiers and speculators, praised Mussolini and Hitler, and united with small but violent British fascist movements. His alliance with anti-Semites led to a riotous rally in London by his British Union of Fascists, and his influence was ended by government and an outraged public.

Given the power of anti-Semitism in Germany, there would be no such reaction. By 1932 the misery, despair, and anger of the German middle classes far surpassed that of other nations. A lost war and inflation had destroyed the savings, pensions, salaries, fixed incomes, and self-esteem of millions. Almost half the capital of the middle classes was gone in 1924; six years later the depression took even more. In the 1920s more than half a million small businessmen and professional people were forced to find factory or manual labor—if they could. In the early 1930s hundreds of thousands of small businesses and farms were wiped out, forty thousand small businesses in 1930 alone. In record numbers, shopkeepers lost customers, sales plummeted, salaries fell, banks collapsed, investors were ruined, and farm mortgages were foreclosed. Hundreds of thousands of salespeople, white-collar workers, and civil servants were fired, including forty thousand teachers. More than a third of those trained to be physicians had to take clerical jobs. By 1930 there were three university graduates for every job. It was only the beginning, and it was already too late.

Middle-class anger raged against Social Democratic labor unions and communist workers. Small businessmen added big business to the list. Unemployment soared from 9 to 25 percent between 1928 and 1932. Those with jobs had their wages cut, and one-third were employed only part-time. The figures do not include failed first-time job-seekers, who did not qualify for unemployment benefits. These benefits, once given for six months, were now cut to six weeks. Militant action seemed the only hope for unemployed workers, and Communist membership escalated. From 1930 through 1933 millions were trapped in endless personal tragedies by forces they could not understand, and orthodox politicians worsened their plight. Nazi votes soared.

In other Western nations the radical right faced powerful liberal traditions, but in Germany, by 1932, 14 percent of the vote was Communist and 37 percent Nazi. Race hatred overwhelmed the voices of despised politicians and their economic "experts," pompously sermonizing about the need for more sacrifice in order to gain the confidence of international bankers and financiers. When the short-term loans of American and British investors were suddenly withdrawn after the stock market crash, the myth of a coalition of Allies and "Jewish" international bankers out to destroy Germany reached monstrous dimensions. In Austria, Jews were terrorized, their stores boycotted, smashed, and bombed. Walter Riehl, head of the Austrian Nazis, demanded concentration camps for eastern Jews and castration for those who had had sex with an Aryan woman. Only weakness and total dependence on Allied loans kept the Christian Social government from allowing even more anti-Semitic outrages. Christian Social priests now gave racist as well as religious reasons for hating the Jews. As Bruce Pauley tells us, "With the very important exception of the *Anschluss* question, it is doubtful whether any other single issue in Austria . . . appealed to so large a cross section of the Austrian population as anti-Semitism."[12]

In Germany, democratic government collapsed in 1930, replaced with rule by emergency decree. In 1929, under the socialist Chancellor Heinrich Mueller, the Social Democrats (SDP) shared power with the Center party and the DVP. To alleviate suffering, Mueller hoped to maintain unemployment benefits at the levels established by earlier legislation. But contributions from government, workers, and employers did not provide sufficient funds for the dramatic new levels of unemployment. The SDP sought to increase taxes and payments from both workers and employers, but, rocked by a storm of protests from industrialists, the DVP and the Center party blocked this move. The protests were orchestrated by Hugenberg and Hjalmar Schacht. President of the Reichsbank and Hitler's finance minister, Schacht wanted to slash relief payments and the number eligible for them, and he used his Reichsbank post to sabotage relief of the unemployed and recruit businessmen for Hitler. Industrialists demanded lower wages and fewer taxes on capital, insisting that recovery would come from funds thus released for investment, though there was no effective unmet demand. The SDP fought back. By February 1930 the government was paralyzed. No compromise could be negotiated, mainly because Hindenburg and his military advisers, and the DVP and Center party were overjoyed at the prospect of driving the socialists out of the government. Business and military leaders clamored for harsher austerity measures—though not for themselves, of course. Political leaders elsewhere at least tried to relieve suffering, but German leaders successfully sabotaged the attempt to keep even smaller unemployment benefits than before the depression.

From 1929 until Hitler's appointment in 1933, no chancellor held a parliamentary majority. In March 1930 Heinrich Bruening, protégé of Father Kaas, became chancellor. Militarist and antisocialist, Bruening wanted a government "above party politics," but he meant one supported by the Conservative party and the DVP. Though the socialists were by far the most popular German party, Hindenburg granted Bruening the power to rule by emergency decree, a power he had never granted Mueller. Bruening immediately declared he would ruthlessly enforce even harsher austerity measures, and, if thwarted, would hold new elections. Bruening's austerity program did not apply to all: he fired government workers, increased taxes on lower-income groups, cut taxes on business and capital, and used government powers to side with industrialists in the arbitration of industrial wage disputes. He did increase business contributions to the unemployment insurance fund, but the rest of his program was exactly what the business community wanted. Ordinary Germans referred to Bruening as the "Hunger Chancellor." When Bruening did not get the parliamentary majority needed to approve his decrees, instead of resigning he called for new elections for September 1930.

The postponement allowed Bruening to prepare even more drastic austerity decrees, which he was able to enact when the Reichstag was not in session. Given the popularity of the Social Democrats, Bruening could not expect a majority in the new elections; perhaps he hoped Hindenburg would allow authoritarian rule. But popular anger, frustration, and racism raged, and seemingly out of nowhere the Nazis became the second largest party in Germany, soaring from 12 seats to an amazing 107. Conservative party votes dropped dramatically; even the Communists outpolled them. The Social Democrats remained the largest party with 143 seats. Less than two years later, in July 1932, the Nazis scored the greatest electoral triumph in German history by winning 230 seats; Conservative votes fell further. Millions of upper- and lower-class Conservatives had moved to Hitler. The depression provided the final blow to the republic. And for the first time in European history, the adroit use of anti-Semitism enabled a single party to mobilize the social discontent of millions. It is true that without the war and its traumatic consequences there would have been no Nazi seizure of power; but it is also true that without the function and power of anti-Semitism in the German past there would have been no Nazi movement capable of seizing power.

18: ANTI-SEMITISM AND THE NAZI VOTE

> When we have the power of the state in our hands [we] will thoroughly annihilate this international racial parasite.
> —Nazi election leaflet, 1927–1929

IT seems obvious: a vote for the Nazis was a vote to harm the Jews. Yet scholars tell us that most Nazi voters were motivated by other issues, and only some 10 percent supported the party because of its anti-Semitism. Were this true, the causes of the Holocaust would indeed be a mystery, and the intensity and function of racism in German history irrelevant. But it is not true. In pluralistic, pragmatic societies, voters tend to separate issues, hence it is appropriate to measure the relative appeal of each. But convinced racists make no such separation; for them nearly all issues are racial issues. For millions of German rightists, race explained a wide variety of social ills. For example, though we are told that many supported Hitler because of his anticommunism, we should remember that Nazi voters believed communism was Jewish. The single-minded vision of racists informs the most common racist cartoon of the nineteenth century: a stereotyped Jew is shown as a monster puppeteer or giant octopus, his head with its evil, grinning face, hook-nosed and thick-lipped, mounted on a vast body, gross bejeweled fingers clutching stocks, currency, and a Star of David. Supported by parliamentarians, socialists, and revolutionaries, the beast pulls the strings of puppets or clutches his victims: aristocrats, military officers, industrialists, emperors, kings, workers, and bourgeoisie.

Nazi ideology is often dismissed as a collection of inconsistent and contradictory ideas, sheer opportunism. In fact, the key to Nazi electoral power was their ability to connect anti-Semitic myths to the practical dilemmas of millions of Germans, something not possible in other Western societies. As Hitler said, "There is only one possible kind of revolution. It is not economic or political or social, but racial."[1] Reformulating old stereotypes, the Nazis united constituencies otherwise divided by conflicting interests, and by insisting that Jewish behavior was the source of all the sufferings of the *Volk*, raised a resounding echo in millions already historically predisposed to anti-Semitism and ignorant of the social complexities that traumatized them. As Goebbels wrote in a 1930 campaign pamphlet, "The Jew is responsible for our misery, and he thrives on it!"[2] A Nazi leaflet of 1922 accused the Jews of causing the war and the revolution against kaiser and Fatherland and creating a liberal republic controlled by Jewish socialists. German Jews led the Sparticists; bolshevism was the tool of Russian Jews. Reaping immense war profits, the leaflet declared, the Jews sabotaged the Fatherland. Now they ran the black market while their puppets overtaxed honest citizens and saved the Jews from the consequences of their crimes. Jewish Social Democrats cooperated with their racial brethren in Allied lands, using reparations to deliver German wealth to Jewish international finance while Jewish bankers and middlemen mercilessly exploited workers, farmers, and small businessmen.

To the nonracist it seems irrational to believe that the Jews were the power behind both bolshevism and international finance. But extreme anti-Semites believe that Jews are united regardless of class, using their varied powers to destroy Gentile civilization. Jewish financiers bring economic ruin, Jewish Bolsheviks exploit the resulting misery, Jewish liberals preach tolerance and allow the enemy within the gates. As Hitler said, even if the Protocols of Zion was a forgery, it told the essential truth. Those blinded by liberal humanitarianism and "Jewish-Marxist" fictions of class struggle would never see the unity, deviousness, and malignant power of the Jew, a unity transcending all social differences, the unity of a race at war.

The peasants of Protestant north Germany gave the Nazis their first significant success outside Bavaria. Here the Nazis blended traditional rural anti-Semitism and practical peasant needs with the volkist ideology of blood and soil, creating a politics of race. Alfred Rosenberg and Heinrich Himmler believed the peasant to be the "fountain of youth of the *Volk*." As Walther Darré, Nazi agricultural expert, wrote, "Our nation's only true possession is its good blood. . . . All eugenic progress can begin only by eliminating inferior . . . blood."[3] No Nazi ideologist, including Hitler, believed that being Aryan guaranteed pure blood. Racial purity was a goal, and the peasant, isolated for centuries, was the reservoir of Germanic blood, the source for the selective breeding needed to purify the race. If Jewish speculators and mortgage holders continued to drive the peasant from the land, the chance to save the *Volk* would be forever lost. One way or another the Jews must be stopped. What, among nineteenth-century reactionaries had been a will to suppress, with the Nazis became a will to destroy.

Peasants found the new Germany alien to all they had respected in the old. Bearing the brunt of war casualties, less sophisticated than urbanites, they readily accepted the faked optimism of the high command and the "stab-in-the-back" myth. Since 1850 peasant attitudes had been determined by the local clergy, teachers, and press, staunch defenders of kaiser, army, and aristocracy, hostile to cities, liberals, leftists, and Jews. There was little rural support for the democratic values limiting racist extremism in Western Europe and large or industrial German cities. Rural anti-Semitism was still fueled by religious fundamentalism and the fear of the new market system. The Social Democrats, with little rural support, met the needs of their own constituencies. In 1919–1920 they kept wartime ceilings on food prices to protect consumers and workers. As Marxists, they would not protect peasants from the import of cheap food. Already in 1919 one rural political leader declared, "Don't vote for urban party hacks and Jews who take no interest in our homeland, and would abandon it to our internal and foreign enemies!"[4] By 1923 businessmen set Weimar economic policies, and they too would do nothing to protect the most backward sector of the economy, arguing that free trade would make farmers more efficient and avoid the trade wars that would weaken industrial exports. Unprotected, the small farmer was often forced to dump his produce at low prices because of the postwar international glut of agrarian products. His fate determined by shifting land values and choices made in distant markets, the peasant faced changes he could not influence no matter how hard he worked. It was easy to persuade him that he was in the grip of hostile international forces and their puppets in the Weimar government.

The inflation enabled farmers to pay back their debts with cheap marks, but in 1924 the new mark was issued just after the harvest was sold for worthless old marks. New equipment and seed for spring planting had to be bought with valuable new marks. Rural associations cried treason; the *Judenrepublik* was sacrificing them for international Jewish financiers who benefited from reparations. By 1923 the Conservative party's most popular rural speakers were those who ranted against the Jews. A Conservative election manifesto warned: Vote for us or the "Jewish consumer viewpoint wins the upper hand and leads to the ruin of agriculture."[5] In 1924 Conservatives doubled their votes, and the Nazis, though hardly organized yet, gained close to 40 percent of the vote in two rural districts. Even more forcefully than in prewar days, political anti-Semitism showed its electoral potential in rural Germany.

When the Nazis began serious campaigning in rural districts, meat and dairy prices were collapsing and taxes, debt, and interest on farm loans were soaring. Imports of cheap food rose dramatically, and farms went under at record rates. In the 1928 elections, three small farmers' parties gained a total of twenty-one seats. Ten were held by the Landvolk of Schleswig-Holstein, allied with a violent unit of the Stahlhelm that spewed forth a "vitriolic flood of anti-Semitic and anti-republican propaganda essentially indistinguishable from that of the Nazis."[6] But peasant parties blamed not only the Jews for their troubles, they also denounced consumers who demanded low food prices, big landowners who ignored their needs, tax collectors who confiscated the property of tax-delinquent farmers, and big business groups who had resolved the inflation at the expense of the "little man."

The Nazis' national ambitions forbade supporting only peasant interests. Power would come only if a variety of constituencies could be united around a cause transcending class. Himmler, propaganda chief in 1926, addressed the peasants in an essay, *Farmer Wake Up!* When you benefited from the inflation you did not listen to us, he wrote, and now you blame your fellow Germans for your bitter fate. But your racial comrades are not your enemies. You are the victims of the "fertilizer Jew," the "grain Jew," and the "Jewish" dealers and commodity traders who sell you products at high prices, purchase your grain and livestock cheaply, and then sell them at high prices to city folk.[7] A barrage of leaflets told farmers that "bank Jews," "stock exchange Jews," and "commodity trading Jews" held them in thrall. Jewish moneylenders charged farmers usury, enabling Jewish speculators—who controlled mortgages but did not till the soil—to gain German land at the expense of ruined peasants. "Mortgage Jews" would soon own the bulk of German land. A poster declared, "But it is never too late!" Peasants could still protect "the most holy possession of a people, the lands and fields which God has Given Us. Vote National Socialist!"[8]

American Jews, a leaflet declared, ruined the peasant by exporting cheap meat to Germany for huge profits: "Two thousand oxen are led to slaughter every hour in American frozen meat factories."[9] The peasant could not know the frozen meat business was not Jewish nor only American, or that it followed the laws of the market, not ethnic plots. A leaflet, "The Last Cow," shows the beast being dragged from a peasant's barn while a stereotyped Jew oversees the seizure of his new property—the "result of Young politics!" (the latest reparations compromise). International Jewry extorted immense reparations, and Weimar traitors paid them off by borrowing foreign capital at usurious rates; thus German labor and wealth was transferred to the Jewish financiers who negotiated reparations in the first place. Of course, neither Young nor Dawes was Jewish. "Germans," you will be "driven from hearth and home while international money and Jewish capital take possession of the land!" Only the Nazis had the iron will to end this charade and destroy the "Jewish world financial monopoly."[10]

Himmler declared the government "totally Jew ridden . . . German in name only."[11] Jewish politicians protected the Jewish wholesalers. Anti-Semitism enabled the Nazis to defuse the farmers' antagonism toward the elite that nineteenth-century conservatives had feared since Boeckel's movement in the 1890s. Sweep away the diabolical racial enemy, the Nazis urged, the Jew who benefited when German fought German. Only a united Germany free of class antagonisms, a Nazi poster insisted, could break "the insatiable Jewish race lust and fanaticism . . . the driving forces behind the satanic attempt to break Germany's backbone through the annihilation of the German farming community."[12] Strike your enemies hard, Himmler demanded, but not your fellow Germans. With single-minded and brutal calls for racial vengeance, Himmler, Hitler, and countless Nazis insisted that the small landowner must join their united front against the Jews and the left.

The Nazis were the only national party to offer farmers protection from high costs, low prices, cheap imports, and high interest, but such reforms would require sacrifices from other citizens. By converting the need for reform into a call for racist violence, the Nazis bypassed the need for sacrifice. Higher prices for farm products need not burden consumers, if caused, as Nazi leaflets declared, by the "usurious" profits of "Jews." Higher land values were assured if Jews were forbidden to hold mortgages or speculate in land, and if "Jewish" usury were replaced with cheap credit. Farmers paid a fixed rate of taxes on their holdings, causing great hardship in years of low crop yields. The Nazis promised rates proportional to yields, an end to high taxes levied by "Jewish" politicians, and tariffs to protect against Jewish food importers.

Thousands of Nazi orators, memorizing set speeches in the Speakers' School of the party, enabled their audiences to release their frustrations on the ancient enemy. Like Boeckel, and with some of his old supporters, they visited pubs and attended county fairs, cattle shows, and village festivals, discussing crops, weather, prices, and the evils of the Jews. Uniformed SA were conspicuous at the dedication of war memorials, especially effective in village squares with their horrifying lists of the dead. Unlike traditional orators, they avoided long-winded rhetoric and used stark racist slogans to bypass practical solutions that would cost votes. Indebted or bankrupt, the peasant could ignore his own mismanagement or the results of a flawed economic system dominated in fact by Gentiles. Roaring approval in near revivalist fervor, he listened to speakers aping Hitler and Goebbels, harsh voices rising in contorted violence to encourage the farmer to vent frustrations, avoid self-blame, and reduce complex economic relationships to malevolent conspiracies.

Nazi activism made it the most effective party in the countryside, gaining unique credibility among villagers who distrusted urban politicians.

Unlike other parties, the Nazis helped organize demonstrations and blockades, sometimes violent, protesting the heartbreaking auctions of the possessions of the bankrupt. Uniformed party members in village squares conspicuously collected funds to aid the distressed. With local associations and militants, they hindered police and officials protecting auctioneers, shouting, "Why do you do the work of your Jewish masters?" They bombed tax offices or rioted as sheriffs seized farm property. As tax revolts swept parts of Germany, Nazis often went to jail with local protesters, or picketed courts and jails where farmers were tried or imprisoned for refusing to pay taxes and debts or for resisting property seizures. Embattled peasants soon believed that, unlike other politicians, the Nazis meant what they said. Soon the Nazis had local organizations unmatched by any other party, recruiting peasants who spoke the local dialect and had been active in farmers' associations—crucial supporters in isolated communities that trusted only their own.

Other political parties solicited votes at election time, but thousands of SA marches, torchlight parades, ritual ceremonies to the war dead, and patriotic songfests attracted crowds throughout the year. It was a form of political theatre foreign to urban politicians, popular as a kind of organized entertainment in the bleak, cloud-covered German hinterland. Often with the approval of local Protestant clergy, SA members marched to worship in swastika-draped churches, impressing the locals with their piety. Party literature urged all Christians to join in order to conclude the age-old Christian crusade against the ancient enemy. Catholic and Protestant politicians had failed the people, they declared, by joining government coalitions with secular liberals and atheistic reds. In Germany, posters proclaimed, Jews complained about religious discrimination, but in Russia, Jewish reds slaughtered Christian peasants to build a nation of atheists. Naturally, Nazi campaigners did not mention the Soviet war against Judaism.

The Nazis fared best among tightly knit communities of Protestant smallholders, the most isolated, fundamentalist, and backward, those who suffered most, or feared they would, from the modern market system as well as the "moral decay" of "sinful, socialist, and Jewish Berlin." By word and deed, the Nazis demonstrated they were not simply cynical politicians but an uncompromising Germanic *Volk* movement from below, true defenders of the *Volk* soul and the old ways. Moreover, the Nazis told them, though their associations were well intentioned, the peasants were helpless unless they joined the Nazis' truly national organization with its urban votes. Although they gained only 7 percent of the national vote in 1924, in some rural districts the Nazis received from 12 to 15 percent. By 1929 they outpolled the Conservative party—the party, Nazis noted, that had helped resolve inflation at peasant expense, had denounced Jews but introduced no legislation against them, and had done nothing to aid the peasant smallholder. From 1926 on the Nazis gained the support and membership of a variety of farmers' leagues and protective associations. By 1930 they had millions of supporters, attracting local peasant groups because they were the most activist, nationalist, and violent. Younger male peasants, impatient with older organizations and fearing the loss of ancestral lands, eagerly joined the racial revolution.

But rural Catholics remained loyal to the Center party or the Catholic BVP. Parish priests spoke against the Nazis, and the hierarchy forbade Catholics to join. The bishop of Mainz even refused the sacrament to Nazis. None of this indicates sympathy for the Jews, however, for the local Catholic press and the hierarchy were now more racist than before the war. In 1919 Catholics, often supported or led by priests, formed numerous anti-Semitic paramilitary Bunds in Germany and Austria. But the Center party feared the historic Protestant ties of the right and its attacks against the "Black International," and Streicher and Ludendorff's virulent anti-Catholicism frightened them. Hitler rebuked Ludendorff: "I need, for the building of a great political movement, the Catholics of Bavaria just as much as I need the Protestants of Prussia."[13] Purging anti-Catholics, Hitler publicly demonstrated his Catholicism. His campaigners insisted they opposed the Center not because it was Catholic but because its leaders allied themselves with atheistic socialists and cooperated with Allied demands. The church may have denounced the Jews for centuries, but the Center never legislated against them: "The real test of a party's Christianity is its stance on the Jewish question."[14]

Christian unity was essential, Catholic farmers were told, for "Jewish socialism" hoped to steal their land just as the "Judeo-Bolsheviks" of Russia, after promising land to the peasants to rouse them against the tsar, seized their crops at bayonet point. Later, in Nazi campaign literature, Stalin's murderous forced collectivization of land was blamed on the Jews—"You too are destined to become a colonial possession of world Jewry." As Hitler wrote, "In Russian bolshevism we must see the attempt of the Jews in the twentieth century to achieve world domination."[15] A widely read leaflet said, "Do you want your beloved priest to be murdered by the Jews?" "Do you want to lose control over your own harvest to the Jew in the Bolshevik Party Office?" Jewish Bolsheviks were "men who want to rule without God. As Christ said, 'The devil is their Father.' "[16] As the depression plunged Catholic peasants into misery, they voted Nazi, and by 1932 they almost equaled the voting percentage of rural Protestants. Among all Catholics, however, the Nazis did not as well. In Bavaria they received 33 percent of the vote in 1932 when their national average was just over 37 percent. But the Catholic hierarchy's hesitation ceased, and in March 1933 the difference between Catholic and Protestant Nazi votes was less than 1 percent.

The Nazis easily captured the allegiance of artisans and small businessmen, the backbone of anti-Semitic movements since the 1880s. The dramatic rise of industry and the growth of Jewish-owned department stores and large retail outlets frustrated artisans and small businessmen, already damaged by war and inflation. No Weimar government wanted to try to preserve them against the power of corporations and mass retailers. Department stores, 75 percent of them Jewish owned, undercut artisans by establishing in-house shops. After the war, rural migrants and veterans started a flood of small businesses, the most bankrupt prone of all enterprises. Inflation drove the cost of new stock beyond the price retailers could charge for old goods, and the settlement of 1924 pushed credit rates higher. In 1924 there were more bankruptcies than in all the years since the war combined. Artisans, often suppliers to small retailers, saw their production cut by half; from 1928 to 1932 sales fell 40 percent, and the bankruptcy rates of shopkeepers and artisans soared. Merchant and artisan protective associations blamed the "usury" demanded by the "worldwide network of Jews," their socialist unions, and the *Judenrepublik* for allegedly favoring large Jewish retail outlets and overtaxing small businesses to pay for the "cold socialism" of the welfare state. Membership in the retailers' association, the DHV, racist for decades, rose from a quarter-million to a half-million from 1924 to 1932. From their publishing houses poured a flood of racist and anti-Weimar literature. As retailers and shop clerks organized for political action, the Nazis recruited them with no difficulty. One remarked: "A member of the DHV is already an anti-Semite."[17] Clerks in private and government bureaucracies also moved swiftly to the radical right, threatened by fear of joblessness or a decline into the hated proletariat.

Unable to reject values conditioned by a lifetime, artisans, retailers, and clerks suffered near-mortal blows to their faith in accepted norms and guarantees of individual success. Like the peasants, they too seemed trapped by irrational forces they could neither understand nor change. Anti-Semitism offered explanations and enemies to blame, allowing them to maintain their self-esteem and traditionalism. It became more necessary than ever to delude oneself that, rid of Jews and the left, they could regain all they had lost. In Munich, small businessmen were the earliest supporters of paramilitaries, providing funds or trucks needed to carry the SA to anti-Semitic demonstrations and battle stations in the *putsch*. Artisans, more physical, were often the shock troops.

Nuremberg, the most pro-Nazi town in Germany and the location for the annual rites of "Party Days," was a city of artisans and shopkeepers, and almost all town officials were merchants or small businessmen.

Close to half its citizens voted for Hitler over Hindenburg in the 1932 presidential campaign. Julius Streicher, who dominated Nuremberg, was seen as a hero for spending so much time in jail for libeling Jews. Elected to the Bavarian Landtag in 1925, Streicher was the most popular party speaker and fund-raiser when, in 1926–1927, Hitler was forbidden to speak in public. Streicher's vulgar and sadistic racism spoke to the ordinary person through his popular paper, Der Stuermer, which presented endless stories "collected from anonymous sources" of Jewish creditors cheating and hounding to death Aryan war widows with the help of Jewish lawyers and the Jew-ridden republic, and (illustrated) accounts of Gentile maidens forced to surrender to the lusts of race-defiling Jewish bosses. Lurid tales of Jewish white-slavery rings, always in distant lands, stood alongside stories of Jews who cheated honest folk of their savings, businessmen of their customers, and peasants of their land. Ancient tales of kosher butchers selling diseased meats to unwary goyim were revived, as well as accounts of the false advertising, phony bargains, and shoddy goods of Jewish retailers.

Small merchants and artisans belonged to many different organizations, but Hitler offered them an uncompromising national party uncontaminated by cooperation with the republic. And of course the Nazis concentrated on the "single foe." When small businessmen and artisan associations denounced big business, Nazi leaflets insisted that blaming one's fellow Germans was a "Jewish-Marxist" sham; only the "Jews are the beneficiaries of our misery," the "November criminals" who taxed retailers on behalf of the "war guilt" and "reparations Jews," and laughed "at the stupidity of those who divide themselves into different parties led by Jews or dependent upon international Jewish finance capital."[18] Echoing old guild myths, the Nazis explained that the swift expansion of Jewish department stores resulted from "un-Christian" methods, harming Germanic-Christian retailers too honest to stoop to "Jewish" tricks. Low department store prices resulted from the import of shoddy goods by Jewish brokers. Department stores, Streicher observed, could sell cheap Russian goods because Jewish Bolsheviks exploited Christian workers to benefit German Jews, a fantasy difficult to disprove and appealing to Nuremberg retailers, who were already racist and facing ruin. The Nazis ignored the fact that all department stores, Jewish or not, profited from large turnover and low profits per unit. To admit this would have been to declare that the small merchant must adopt modern methods or go under.

Such fictions protected the pride of the failing shopkeeper, enabling him to blame failure on Jewish immorality and scorn for Christian retailers, men dignified in dress and speech, who sold quality products of German workmanship at fair prices and enjoyed a close relationship with their customers, wisely guiding them in selecting appropriate products. One widely distributed poster depicted a giant hook-nosed octopus perched on a department store, its tentacles reaching out to crush small retail shops. The preferred image sublimated the hypocrisy of all sales relationships. In fact, the small retailer had been outcompeted by sales pioneers who simply followed the logic of the market, driven by the need to pioneer or go under by Christian oppression. The Nazi message was preferred: Jewish black marketers undermined your profits and your patriotism during the war; Jewish currency speculators ruined you in the inflation; Jewish international financiers stole from you through reparations; Marxist consumer coops drove you to the wall while Jewish department stores "spring up all around you" and doubled their profits every year.

"Businessmen! Artisans!" a leaflet exhorted, there were twelve hundred bankruptcies per month, suicides were common, uncounted numbers of honorable German families lived in helpless misery in a depression brought on by international Jewry and its German accomplices, the owners of "huge capitalist department stores," "chain stores," and the "single-price stores" (five-and-dimes). "Smash the department store slaughter houses!" "Destroy the cooperative parasites!" In the 1932 presidential campaign, the Nazi press warned that though artisans and merchants were "on the edge of their graves," the press supporting Hindenburg displayed ads for Jewish department stores. "Do not allow the parties which have annihilated the *Mittelstand* to hide behind the honorable figure of the Field Marshall because they fear a day of reckoning! VOTE HITLER!"[19] No mention was made of corporate advertising that appeared in the Nazi press.

European conservatives had long denounced the mindless consumerism of changing seasonal fashions as the wasteful creation of dissatisfaction by psychological manipulation of the consumer's frail self-image. In Germany the accusations were couched in racist terms. Treitschke likened department stores to "pestilential" oriental bazaars run by Polish Jews. Others attacked fashion houses for their eroticism and sabotage of the good sense of the stolid German frau with her sensible clothes, her taste not yet undermined by Parisian prostitutes hired by French homosexuals working for Jewish clothing dealers. Nowadays we see fashion as an expression of individuality, oddly enough, and it is difficult for us to understand the resonance that conservative attitudes found among a people brought up in a culture where most rural folk still wore the costumes of their forefathers, reflecting provincial tradition instead of the suspect international world of glamour, sensuality, and waste. Fichte would have understood.

Again the Nazis gave active proof of their concern. Whenever a new department store was opened, Nazi counterdemonstrations greeted it. Julius Streicher led a mass meeting denouncing the establishment of a Jewish-owned department store in Nuremberg, savaging local socialists who officially welcomed the enterprise. The Jews would offer low prices only until they ruined other merchants and could gouge the people at will, he declared. The Nazis formed a Fighting Bund to Protect the Small Merchant. They mounted a "Buy Not from Jews" campaign against socialist consumer coops and department stores including Woolworth's five-and-dimes. The ominous SA trooper stood outside, arms folded, truncheon at the ready, intimidation at the service of the Aryan retailer. Join the "Fighting Bund," Nazi leaflets urged, for "We declare open war on department stores and consumer coops." Especially active at Christmastime, like the Christian Socials in pre- and postwar Vienna, the Nazis distributed drawings of Christ on the cross, declaring, "Christmas is a Christian festival!" Yet the Christian merchant suffered though his prices were reasonable: "Germans, gain joy from knowing you have bought and will only buy from Christians."[20] The Nazis drew up lists of approved Christian merchants and penalized party members whose wives were caught patronizing Jewish stores. They petitioned and picketed town councils to oppose permits for department stores, activities that Hitler had observed in Lueger's Vienna. Their Reichstag delegation introduced bills demanding cheap credit for small retailers and tax penalties for department stores. "We demand the creation and preservation of a sound healthy German Mittelstand." If given power, "We will limit free competition, and thus promote the quality work of the German artisan and remove mass-produced trash," award government contracts to small businesses, and support small traders. Jewish department stores would be confiscated and rented cheaply to Aryan merchants. Nazis would correct the inequities of the tax office which "is simply the bailiff of the international stock exchange princes."[21] Swiftly, retailers' organizations joined the Nazis, led by activists recruited from merchants' sons for whom the old associations were too passive. These were young men trying to save themselves as thousands of family firms went under.

The investors, savers, and pensioners who suffered so terribly from inflation increasingly voted Nazi. In 1924, when Schacht established the new mark, he sealed the destruction of small investors and protected industrialists and wealthy owners of real property by nearly wiping out the obligations of borrowers to creditors. Betrayed by the elites they had admired, many inflation victims joined movements campaigning for a new inflation settlement. Blaming international Jewish finance for their plight, they also denounced big business, so obviously favored at their expense. The Nazis took up their cause, as did the Economics party, inspired by Fritsch and also anti-Semitic; both demanded compensation for inflation

losses. The Economics party did better than the Nazis in the elections of
the 1920s, perhaps because Fritsch insisted that even the upper classes
were tools of the Jews. Avoiding all taint of class struggle, the Nazis
blamed instead the "Marxist-Jewish swindle" of financiers and their
"pimps, the Marxist bosses. Ask them for your money back!"[22] Even war
bonds were not repaid; lenders found their patriotism rewarded by betrayal. But they blamed the republic, not the wartime government that
had oversubscribed and planned to pay the huge debt at the expense of
a defeated enemy. Only Bolsheviks, Nazis complained, canceled legally
contracted obligations.

Swindlers govern us, a nation is robbed, yet no one is behind bars,
Nazi leaflets declared. Savers, pensioners—their pain was the result of a
conspiracy of world Jewry and their Weimar puppets. Ignoring progressive income tax proposals, the Nazis offered another solution: make the
Jews pay. "The total fortunes of bank and stock exchange Princes, the
eastern Jews who have moved into Germany since 1914, and other foreign elements, together with their families and hangers on, and moreover
their profits gained from war, revolution, inflation, and deflation, will be
expropriated without compensation for the benefit of the community."[23]
Jewish wealth would be used for the unemployed, war invalids, war widows, old-age pensioners, victims of inflation, and farm workers who would
settle the expropriated land. By enormously magnifying the wealth of German Jewry, the Nazis avoided alienating those who did not share the ordinary German's misery. Such was the power of reactionary racism that
by 1930 the Nazis had absorbed the constituency of the Economics party.

In 1930–1933 white-collar workers voted by the millions for the Nazis.
They were the largest group in their Reichstag delegation and were highly
overrepresented in the party. Lesser civil servants also supported the Nazis
far out of proportion to their numbers; their savings, investments, and
pensions, ravaged by inflation, were followed by the austerity measures of
the depression, costing a million of them their jobs and slashing the
salaries of the rest. As conservatives, civil servants detested the republic;
racism had been the norm among them for decades. The Nazis organized
civil service defense groups, promising to dismiss all Jews, one of the goals
of the Conservative party program of 1893. In rallies and posters, Nazis
demanded the restoration of the pay and powers of the civil service in a
government no longer ruled by professional politicians, "pimps for votes,"
and lackeys of Jewish capital. In addition, schoolteachers, who were pan-
German racists before 1914, suffered drastic salary cuts and mass firings
and became extremely active Nazis. By 1931 the Nazis had attracted
masses of middle-class women formerly loyal to conservative or Catholic
parties. But only in 1932 and in Protestant districts did women vote for
Nazis in greater proportion than men, in spite of Hitler's supposed sex-

ual charisma and the crowds of cheering females in old newsreels. Liberation threatened traditionalist women, and they reacted strongly against the easy divorce, homosexuality, and abortion associated with Weimar and socialism. A popular Nazi poster proclaimed sex crimes and diseases the result of the "many years during which our people, and in particular our youth, have been exposed to a flood of muck and filth, in word and print, in the theatre and the cinema."[24]

Like anti-Semitic movements before them, the Nazis tried but failed to divert proletarian discontent by using racism. As George Mosse has written, volkist ideas "never penetrated below the ranks of white-collar employees."[25] Committed to democratic, reformist, and urban values, socialist workers were scarcely nostalgic for the Second Reich that had outlawed their party and imprisoned their leaders. Whatever its defects, the republic was the culmination of decades of social democratic hopes. Even during the revolution of 1918 that established Weimar, German workers' councils overwhelmingly rejected communism in favor of parliamentary democracy. Like their predecessors, the Nazis could not appeal directly to workers' interests without alienating their core constituencies. Instead they somewhat halfheartedly tried to insist that workers' wages were low because of Jewish control of credit and reparations, "a capitalistic undertaking of the American bank and stock exchange Jews."[26] In order to maintain the myth of race and the belief in the inner unity of the *Volk* soul, Nazis, like anti-Semites before them, had to maintain that millions of workers were duped by "Jewish financial hyenas" and "Jewish democrats" in collusion with socialist leaders paid by "the Jew [who] controls them all."[27] "Jewish stock exchange dealers," not industrialists, caused unemployment; the so-called class struggle was "nonsense." The "Jew slyly" supported efforts to destroy German racial unity. "Marxism is a tool of the international stock exchange and its personification, the World-Jew." "Red bosses" feared the Nazis not because they opposed workers but because they "fight against this pestilence," the Jew, and would continue "until we have annihilated its destructive influence upon culture and the economy."[28] As Goebbels wrote in *Why Are We Socialists?*, an election pamphlet in 1930: "Because we see in socialism the only possibility of maintaining our racial existence!"[29] Anton Drexler, Nazi founder, had insisted that a few hundred financiers, bankers, and press lords, "almost all members of the Chosen People" sought to establish a dictatorship of money over work: "Comrades, do you want to become slaves of the Jews?"[30] But he also denounced exploiting industrialists. Hitler never did. As he said, his revolution was racial, not Marxist.

But no amount of racism could counter the worker's experience of the disparity between industrial profits and his wages, and the industrialists' attempts to destroy unions and cut unemployment benefits. Ethnicity re-

mained irrelevant to the left. Consequently the Nazis fared poorly in industrial areas. Those few workers who supported them were usually sons
of the middle classes, bitter at being forced into the detested proletariat.
Some came from public service unions, utilities, and the like, and felt
themselves part of the *Mittelstand*. Some foremen joined; these were
workers who had been promoted on the factory floor to leadership positions but remained suspended between management and ordinary
worker, accepted by neither, isolated by both, enforcing work rules opposed by leftist shop stewards. Amazingly, no worker loyal to the Nazis
was ever elected to workers' councils by his mates. Workers never deserted
the left. From 1924 through 1932 the combined votes of the Social Democrats and Communists averaged roughly 36 percent. Even in the great
Nazi sweep of 1932, the left gained almost as many seats as in its high
point of 1928, and its electoral percentage was close to the Nazis, though
irrevocably split. Indeed, the steady electoral power of the left helped
push frightened upper- and middle-class voters into Nazi ranks. The
Nazis "remained largely a middle-class movement in character and outlook," and they knew it.[31] A famous poster shows a proletarian street
fighter protecting a Jewish financier sitting on a bag of gold labeled "War,
revolution, inflation profits of eastern Jews." The poster asks, "Is this your
battle against capitalism, Marxist?"[32] It is an attack, not an appeal. Nazi
campaign literature ostensibly aimed at the proletariat seemed really
meant to assure the upper and middle classes that socialism and trade
unionism, Jewish tools, would be destroyed in a Nazi regime.

Until recently historians believed that the upper classes did not vote
for the Nazis, but as Thomas Childers writes, "By 1930 the NSDAP [Nazi
party] had begun to transcend its lower-middle-class origins, establishing
itself on an electoral terrain traditionally occupied by the conservative
right."[33] Excellent work by Richard F. Hamilton shows a steady shift of
upper-class votes from wealthy neighborhoods to Hitler from 1930 on, and
favorable treatment by the bourgeois press. When Hitler and Hindenburg
stood against each other in the presidential runoff elections of 1932,
upper-class voters tended to prefer Hitler, and in the 1932 Reichstag elections the Nazis enjoyed "a surprisingly large following in more established
social circles."[34] It helped that the Hohenzollern Prince August William,
who joined the party in 1929, toured the country campaigning for Hitler,
and he and his older brother, the crown prince, both publicly supported
Hitler against Hindenburg. Ultimately a general in the SA and already a
member, Prince August represented the party in the Prussian parliament
and then in the Reichstag in 1932–1933. From 1928 through 1932 the elites
began to desert their conservative parties as the numbers of voters selecting the upper-class parties, DVP or Conservative, sank from 23 to less
than 10 percent. Their votes did not go to the left.

Those who remained loyal to the Conservative party did not necessarily object to Nazi racism, for their own party now modeled its campaign propaganda on that of the Nazis. A widely distributed Conservative party poster of 1932 depicts vicious Jewish stereotypes with the caption: "Such men have guarded the beauty and dignity of the Republic."[35] An analysis of German conservative newspapers shows a continuous use of anti-Semitism throughout interwar days, especially intense after 1929. But one crucial point still kept conservatives wary of the Nazis: the old fear from the 1890s that their interests would be threatened by lower-middle-class constituencies. Well educated and relatively protected from economic chaos, the elites who moved to Hitler were hardly driven by social despair or lack of sophistication. Nor was it impatient and youthful new voters who flocked to the Nazis, as used to be thought. Indeed, they gained their "greatest support among groups composed of older voters."[36] It is time to discard the commonly accepted idea that conservatives only accepted Hitler believing his extremism could be tamed and his racism was just a vote-getting device. Conservatives were already racist, and were content to support Hitler for chancellor once they were assured he would restore autocracy and protect their interests.

It is not surprising that the middle classes moved to the Nazis after losing land, business, savings, and self-respect. Unlike unemployed proletarians and rural workers, the middle classes had a stake in the system, however small, and the Nazis guaranteed it. Moreover, they identified with the elites they imitated and rarely blamed their fate on them. Given their traditional outlook and historical experience, the German middle classes sought revolutionaries who would sanction and protect—with force if need be—their status, salaries, pensions, investments, or property. They needed powerful authoritarians who would restore all they had lost, crush their enemies on the left, sanction their social views, and restore national greatness. Mere pragmatic adjustments had no appeal; the system itself seemed bankrupt. Like the Italian middle classes before them, they sought revolutionaries of the right, not the left, a Mussolini or a Hitler, not a Lenin. But in Germany this allegiance meant a conscious commitment to the most extreme racist movement in modern history.

Their endless attacks on the Jews brought the Nazis the highest percentage of votes in modern German history, a mandate for violence. From the earliest years, no Nazi campaign appeal, if only indirectly, failed to hold the Jews responsible for all of Germany's problems. Inventing nothing new, the Nazis' secret was their ability to integrate traditional racism with the practical demands of traditional lower-middle- and upper-class conservatives, and thereby coopt the constituencies of numerous rival movements that spoke only to a single class. In the elections of 1930, small anti-Semitic parties, middle-class or peasant, won more than fifty seats in the Reichstag; in 1932 they were wiped out—their voters had moved to Hitler. In the Sudetenland, Henlein's Sudeten German party, even more anti-Semitic than the Nazis, won 60 percent of the vote in 1934. There is no longer any reason to doubt the crucial role racism played in Nazi victories. Any German who could read or hear knew that for the Nazis, all issues were racial issues. And their campaign literature bristled with metaphors of death: the Jews were a virus, a cancer, a plague infecting every social organ. Germany's miseries were the symptoms, the Jews were the disease. There could be no cure as long as the Jews remained. In spite of laws against it, some posters called for death: "Annihilate the gravediggers of the *Mittelstand!*"[37] "Our day of reckoning with the Jews . . . [will come] when we have the power of the state in our hands to carry out a thorough annihilation of this international racial parasite."[38] By 1930 one could not live in Berlin, Munich, Vienna, or the smallest village without knowing the Nazis would take revenge on the Jews, a promise trumpeted again and again in thousands of rallies and millions of leaflets and posters. "Death to the Jews" was a common chant at Nazi rallies; *Juda verrecke!* was *the* Nazi slogan, a crude phrase referring to the slaughter of beasts. The very reason for choosing the Nazis rather than older reactionaries was their activism and violence, evidence of their sincerity. Some may not have believed them, and none could predict the scale of the Final Solution because it depended on success in war. But no German could be ignorant of the Nazis' promise to destroy the Jews. It was never a secret.

Those who later protested that they supported the Nazis without suspecting how far they might go presume on our liberal consciousness, which finds it impossible to imagine the deliberate murder of millions of innocents. Those Germans—and there were millions, including Jews and socialists—who shared liberal values and an inability to imagine such a horror, never supported the Nazis. For the others, it was not difficult to imagine the probable fate of the Jews. The Nazis said it again and again: Jews would not own land, banks, or businesses, they would be driven from commerce, government service, teaching, law, and medicine, their citizenship would be taken from them, their young would not be educated, their wealth and property would be expropriated; if they left Germany, they would leave penniless.

Did Nazi voters, who must have thought all reasonable people were anti-Semites, really imagine the world would welcome masses of penniless Jewish refugees? What did Nazi supporters think would happen to the Jews? Forced emigration, prison camps, or death were the only alternatives. And even forced emigration only added to the power of "world Jewry," as Hitler and Eichmann declared when saddled with millions of Jews in the east. Given Nazi campaign literature and rhetoric, their voters, we can safely assume, voted for a racial revolution that meant physical harm to the Jews. To these voters, without such a revolution no German problem could be resolved. Anti-Semitism was never just one issue among many; indeed, it would be less of a distortion to say there were no other issues. And with that issue, by 1932 Hitler became the most popular leader of the most popular party modern Germany had ever seen. It is time to stop believing that "without Hitler, no Holocaust." Many older Germans and Austrians welcome such declarations of their innocence, of course, but most will take a defensive silence with them to the grave. They remember how they voted, and they know what it meant.

19: HITLER AND THE ELITES

In 1932/33 the German elites backed Hitler in order to preserve and strengthen their own anachronistic privileges and power behind a smokescreen of chauvinism and spurious appeals to national honor.
—Peter Stachura

To be appointed chancellor, Hitler needed the approval of Hindenburg and his advisers—generals, aristocrats, and businessmen. Most were sympathetic. With Nazi support the republic could be legally replaced by an authoritarian, antisocialist, and popular regime. As the leading student of party membership, Michael H. Kater, has written, "One of the more startling findings . . . has been the consistency of elite overrepresentation in the Nazi Party from 1919 to 1945."[1] But many still feared their interests might be sacrificed to Nazi populism. Consequently in 1930 Hugenberg urged Hitler to break with economic unorthodoxy, adding that Conservatives agreed with him on all else, including "our attitude toward Jewry."[2] Hitler had always tried to reassure the elites without antagonizing the party faithful. At the Bamberg party conference of 1926 there was a minor revolt when Hitler, fearing radical proposals circulating among the members, refused to allow any changes in the party program. As Goebbels wrote, "What is Hitler? A reactionary?"[3] Some Nazis would have been content to be well-paid lackeys of the old regime, but most wanted power and position for themselves. Carefully balancing their demands with the interests of the elites, Hitler demonstrated great political skill. The only principle he never compromised was anti-Semitism, for it was the principle that enabled him to unite both groups.

The power of the army and its role as the representative of the embattled elites made it indispensable. A state within a state, after 1929 no one could be chancellor without its approval. The high command was well aware that SA hotheads saw them as tired reactionaries, frightened of the French and the republic, men who should be replaced to make way for the new revolutionary wave from below. But Hitler wanted no such split. Just after his victory in 1930, he reassured the high command as he had in his trial of 1924. The circumstance was the trial of three lieutenants accused of trying to persuade their colleagues not to fight the Nazis if they rose. It was illegal for an officer to agitate openly. The judges called upon Hitler to testify, and he betrayed his young zealots, telling the court the SA was a political organization not intended to compete with the army. "I have always held the view that every attempt to disintegrate the army was madness."[4] The Nazis pursued power legally, and when they had it they would give the strongest support to the army. The young officers quit the party in disgust, and many SA members grumbled about Hitler's groveling before reactionary generals.

But the high command was now convinced, and it trained SA volunteers to protect the eastern borders of Germany and thus evade the restrictions of Versailles. The army hoped for Nazi victories to rid them of the Social Democrats, enemies of their budgets and now rulers of Prussia, the historic source of the Germanic warrior. In the summer of 1931 General Kurt von Schleicher, the most important political general and Hindenburg's liaison to Chancellor Bruening, secretly spoke to SA chief Roehm about Nazi participation in the government. Although he thought them not quite respectable, he said, "If the Nazis did not exist, it would be necessary to invent them." By 1932 the army was arming the SA, training its recruits, and welcoming Nazis into its ranks. For the first time, soldiers were permitted to attend Nazi meetings. Hitler met with General Kurt von Hammerstein, chief of the army command, and Francis L. Carsten tells us that Hammerstein believed the army wanted the same things as the Nazis, if not as quickly.[5] Hitler's appointment as chancellor in 1933 was a victory for the army, and enthusiastically greeted as such. In the summer of 1934, after Hitler had ordered the killing of Roehm and SA dissidents in the "night of the long knives," the army allowed Hitler to combine the office of president and chancellor, took half its recruits from the SA, and gave preference to SA commanders over former army officers.

The upper civil service resented their loss of status and power under Weimar. In the Second Reich a civil servant was a man of semimilitary rank who treated mere politicians as he did the public, with bureaucratic arrogance. Even the least of civil servants felt part of the ruling class and was convinced that bureaucratic experts, not politicians, should govern. But after 1919 democratically elected politicians dictated policy, and the civil service was opened to socialists and Jews. Worst of all, in Prussia, some three-fifths of Germany and the last bastion of the right, civil servants took their orders from Social Democrats and a Jewish minister president. Thus the majority of the civil service welcomed both the Kapp and Hitler *putsches* and longed for the return of autocracy.

Early on, wealthy princes supported the Nazis, hoping Hitler would restore the monarchy and protect their extensive properties, constantly under threat from the socialists. In 1925 some Nazi Reichstag delegates wanted to support a socialist bill to expropriate the wealth of princes. Hitler was furious. Business leaders would not countenance confiscation of property, and aristocrats were outraged by such a denial of their prerogatives. Denouncing the bill as a "Jewish-Marxist swindle," Hitler withdrew party support. Pro-Nazi sentiment among princes, officers, aristocrats, and civil servants also rose when the son of the exiled kaiser, Prince August, joined the SA in solemn ceremony and toured with Goering in 1930, praising Hitler's "superhuman powers" as the "instrument of a higher power."[6] The exiled kaiser's pro-Nazi views were well known.

Since the 1890s the Conservative party had supported only those anti-Semites who directed discontent away from them. But the Nazi party program of 1920, written without Hitler's guiding hand, not only called for land reform but even for "expropriation without compensation." In an abrupt switch at the height of the 1930 campaign, the Nazis made the only change they would ever make in the program. The new "Official Party Statement" declared there would be no land reform and no limit to the size of landed estates. Land would be expropriated only if it were totally misused or "not owned by German folk comrades."[7] Only Jewish land would be seized. The importance of the change was stressed by publishing it in the *Voelkische Beobachter*, signed by Hitler with much publicity. Police reports indicated local notables and estate owners were now more evident at Nazi meetings.

Henry Turner has demolished the old Marxist theory that the Nazis were simply puppets of the industrial elites.[8] But Hitler did finally gain business support, and he started working for it in 1921, dropping Nazi proposals to abolish credit, establish worker profit-sharing, and nationalize cartels. Only Jewish finance capital was to be the target of Nazi wrath. From 1919 to 1923 many industrialists supported paramilitary units, but after 1924 governments were usually probusiness, and business leaders were not subject to the irrational angers that economic disasters created in the lower middle classes. Denunciations of "Jewish international finance" did not impress them, for they knew they all obeyed the same rules of the game. Thus until 1930 industrialists would not waste money on a party with only twelve seats in the Reichstag. Those businessmen who did support Hitler tended to be men of small-business mentality, angry at their dependence on financiers and enamored of reactionary values, men like Otto Kirdorf, Fritz Thysen, Herman Siemens, Ernst Borsig, and Hjalmar Schacht, all of whom recruited for the Nazis. Hugo Stinnes, industrialist and inflation profiteer extraordinaire, gave much to the Nazis; undoubtedly others also did. But until the Nazi victory of 1930, most contributions came from small firms whose owners resented both big business and big labor.

Both large and small business leaders were unhappy with the republic, especially because the Social Democrats were a constant threat. Although inflation was ended in their favor in 1924, industrialists were angry because the republic sided with the trade unions in labor disputes and pressed for unemployment benefits, shorter working hours, and welfare benefits. Bruening, named chancellor in 1930, shaped austerity policies to please businessmen. But the Nazis were still useful because they deflected hostility aimed at big business. In the Reichstag session of 1924, both the Nazi delegation and the left demanded compensation for creditors victimized by the currency exchange that ended the inflation. The left, ignoring racist irrelevancies, blamed business influence over Stresemann, demanding that corporations pay higher taxes to compensate the abandoned creditors. After Hitler silenced a few who supported the bill, the Nazi delegates blamed the *Judenrepublik* for bilking citizens to please international Jewish financiers, and demanded compensation from the "vast profits" the Jewish community had allegedly gained from war, inflation, reparations, and depression. Additionally, in 1926 Hitler fought off attempts to establish Nazi trade unions, and in May 1930 he confronted Nazis who broke the party line by supporting strikers. Otto Strasser, their leader and editor of the Berlin party journal, insisted that reforms be promised to the proletariat. Hitler refused. When Strasser accused him of "strangling the social revolution," a furious Hitler shouted: "There are no revolutions but racial revolutions!" When Strasser spoke of nationalizing some industries, including Krupp, Hitler exploded, "Do you think I would be so mad as to destroy the German economy?"[9] Rebuffed, Strasser quit the party, asking all true National Socialists to join him in a Black Front; almost none did, and he left Germany. But Strasser was no leftist in the Western sense. He believed workers were hostile to Germany because they were exploited, but he added that "these millions were left to the Jew Marx . . . who intended only to destroy the German nation with the strength of these millions and make it a colony of world capital."[10]

The elections of 1930 radically altered matters. Hitler was now a viable alternative. But more than one-third of the electorate still voted left, and the weakness of the People's party (DVP) and the Conservative party, as well as Bruening's isolation, caused businessmen to look to the Nazis. They could not offer the Nazis many votes, of course, and financial support, though important, was not crucial. Hitler really needed their help to persuade Hindenburg to appoint him chancellor, and for that he must show them the party was probusiness, would crush socialism and its unions, and would rearm Germany in order to stimulate industrial expansion. Many Nazi voters would have been alienated by probusiness campaign literature, hence most assurances were given by Hitler and other leading Nazis in private. In August 1931 the rapprochement gained momentum when the Conservative party and the DVP joined with Hitler to try to bring down the socialist government of Prussia by referendum; businessmen contributed heavily. Hugenberg's slush fund was large, and his presses helped print Nazi publications. Thirty percent of Prussians voted for the referendum. It was not enough to win, but it showed the potential power of such an alliance.

In October 1931 the Nazis joined in a highly publicized formal ceremony to cement the Nazi-Conservative alliance, the famous meeting of the Harzburg Front. Significantly, it met in Brunswick, governed by a coalition of Nazis and the DVP, a state that harassed the Jews and had passed a law against kosher butchering. A brilliant array of luminaries attended the Harzburg Front: Hugenberg and Conservative party leaders, Hitler himself, General von Seekt, Theodore Duesterberg and Franz Seldte (leaders of the Stahlhelm), the Hohenzollern crown prince, the president of the Agrarian Bund, and the chiefs of the Fatherland League. Business representatives included the chairman of the association of Ruhr coal owners, the managing director of the leading organization of Ruhr industrialists, the former president of the Imperial Bank, Schacht, the managing director of the Northwest Employers' Association, and the leading public relations officer for heavy industry, their personal liaison with the Nazis. Hitler, vulnerable to dissident SAs, kept a low profile, well aware the Conservatives hoped to keep the Nazis a junior partner in the coming destruction of the republic. A week later Hitler demonstrated his independence, holding his own meeting as 100,000 SA marched past in salute. A few weeks later, at a meeting of "staff officials of regional industrial associations in Berlin," the "political agents of big business" agreed to try to influence the Nazis "not with money but with men and ideas."[11] They advised their representatives they might join the Harzburg Front provided "Hitler and his economic staff are actually firmly resolved to leave the core of the private enterprise system unmolested. . . ."[12] No objections were raised to Nazi racism. In November 1931, however, when the Nazis gained some 40 percent of the seats in the parliament of Hesse, the new government, probably to Hitler's dismay, immediately proposed a large increase in unemployment benefits. Businessmen were still wary.

In a famous public speech to the members of the Industry Club in Duesseldorf in early 1932, Hitler informed the assembled worthies that they were "God-Gifted geniuses" whose superior talents enabled them to amass wealth through economic struggle and build the nation. Among the best of the race, they should not have to submit to the interference of a mediocre democracy of the weak and untalented; in politics as in economics, prosperity meant submission to the capable few. Without a strong and united political will, Hitler insisted, even a great economic power could come to naught, as Germany had learned in 1918. Germany must end its party divisions; it could not survive if half the nation thought property was theft. Labor costs must be reduced, but workers must believe there would be future rewards for present sacrifices—though Hitler asked none of his audience. Industry and Germany could prosper if they fulfilled their destiny and gained access to foreign markets, and for this they must have a strong military and an aggressive foreign policy. Military, not just economic, power would determine the outcome of the struggle for markets. As all could see, Hitler declared, everywhere the "white race" dominated the globe. The racial qualities of the Germans guaranteed that properly governed, they too would excel. Hinting at the riches of the Slavic east, he insisted that above all, Marxism must be torn from the face of the earth. Gentlemen, Hitler concluded, you should be grateful to my SA for their sacrifices to protect you from the left. The speech was warmly received.

By 1931 big business contributions to the Nazis increased, although the amounts and sources cannot be known with certainty. "Expenditures for the Nazi Party were hardly ever reflected in a firm's business records"; entrepreneurs "often preferred to make clandestine financial contributions . . . in order to avoid harming their businesses."[13] Many feared offending their regular parties or suffering socialist boycotts. Most business support for the Nazis came from iron, steel, and coal magnates, those who depended most on low wages, were least competitive internationally, and needed arms contracts. Hitler made it quite clear he would arm Germany to the teeth. Less support came from the electrical and chemical industries, which were more competitive and had lower wage costs. Nazi economic support from the "middle reaches of industry, commerce, and finance" steadily increased in 1931. But "during the spring and early summer of 1932 more money than ever before flowed from the business community to various Nazis."[14] Among the contributors were Flick enterprises, I. G. Farben, Royal Dutch Shell, the employees association of the iron and steel works of the Ruhr, the chairman of the Mining Association, and other Ruhr magnates. The pan-Germans, once an industrialist bastion, lost out to the Nazis by 1932. Unrecorded donations were received by individual party members. Money laundering is not a recent invention: dummy organizations were set up to channel funds from those who did not wish the government, their customers or stockholders, or tax collectors to know; tax-free gifts to worthy causes might be all that appeared in the accounts. Sanitizing the books was a major industry in 1945. The national financial records of the Nazi party and all but one regional organization were destroyed, along with meticulous accounts kept by the treasurer of the party, Franz Schwarz. Many prominent Germans must have breathed a sigh of relief when Schwarz died in 1946, the result, we are told, of a brutal interrogation by American occupation forces.

The increasing influence of the SS was another sign of Nazi acceptance by the elites. The SS attracted the children of the elite from the start. As Hitler once said, the way to appeal to the reaction was through its children. During the war, "One in every three members of the leadership corps of the SS had received higher education...."[15] This figure is startling because there were only 120,000 undergraduates in all of Germany in 1920. There were honorary upper-class SS members as well, including industrialists noted for personal contributions to the SS. Far from being hesitant about Hitler's anti-Semitism, many from the upper classes were strong supporters of the group most responsible for the Holocaust. The 10,000 or so SS in 1931 knew their main task was to enforce racial purity and train the future ruling elites. Himmler and Heydrich, SS chiefs, unlike the hotheads of the SA, harbored no radical social ideas. For them race was all; racial cleansing and the murder of the Jews was their special task.

The rise of the SS, Hitler's collaboration with conservatives, and his choice of Reichstag candidates acceptable to them caused trouble in the SA. SA leaflets labeled the SS an agent of the reaction and accused Hitler of selling out. One leaflet asked if the leadership needed the sons of the elite to protect them against their own following. Where were these over-educated youths in the heroic days of the beer-hall brawls and the *putsch*? Another leaflet accused Hitler of betraying the movement: "Party Comrades! SA Comrades! National Socialists! It is not a question of Roehm, Goebbels, or even Hitler! It is a question of our movement! Protect our old ideals!" The party bosses had betrayed them. "Hitler and his comrades have made the party a cesspool of dried-up bankrupts." Another leaflet predicted that Nazi parliamentary leaders would soon "crawl on their knees" to Bruening and say, "Dear Reichschancellor, forgive us for we knew not what we did. It was the fault of our stupid SA comrades! We will dissolve the SA at once! In the future we shall be legal and good!"[16] In 1930 an open revolt in Berlin was led by SA Fuehrer Walter Stennes. Hitler rushed to the scene, rallied loyal SA men in street battles, threw Stennes out of the party, and replaced him with Ernst Roehm. To calm the fears of business leaders, in March 1931 the *Voelkische Beobachter* announced: "The abolition of the capitalist system has been for centuries nothing more than an empty slogan."[17] Dissidents were purged. Geobbels was put in charge of propaganda to prevent publication of unauthorized material. Many defected when Hitler forbade the SA to use unsanctioned violence, but potential allies among the respectable were reassured.

Party membership increased sevenfold from 1930 until Hitler's appointment as chancellor; fully 50 percent of new members came from the upper classes. Even the most respectable began to support Hitler. By 1930 the Nazis had a "substantial following" among Protestant clergy.[18] Bishop Otto Dibelius, the leading Evangelical official, wrote to his pastors on Easter 1928: "I have always regarded myself as an anti-Semite. The fact cannot be concealed that the Jews have played a leading part in all the symptoms of disintegration in modern civilization. . . ."[19] By 1930 there was a long list of local pastors who helped preside over Nazi ceremonies. In 1932 a small movement led by clergy called itself the German Christians and declared Hitler "the redeemer in the history of the Germans . . . the window through which light fell on Christianity."[20] To this the second son of the kaiser added his voice: "It is about time . . . that the churches open their doors wide and plant the Swastika on the Cross of Golgotha—then German freedom will quickly be achieved."[21] By 1931 one-third of all church committees, elected by parishioners, were pro-Nazi, as were the majority of seminary students, the future clergy.

The Catholic hierarchy was more reluctant. Under the republic, the church received state subsidies for the first time, and its seminaries, monasteries, priesthood, and youth movements expanded far more than did Protestant organizations. Although many bishops had condemned the establishment of a republic in 1919, the Catholic Center supported it and provided the majority of its chancellors. Cardinal Bertram held the Nazis guilty of "overglorifying race," though denunciations of Jewish international finance and of leftists were commonplace in the local Catholic press. In Austria anti-Semitism was rife in virtually all Catholic publications. In Germany the Center party and its offshoot, the Bavarian People's party, major political forces, were unwilling to support a movement that included virulent anti-Catholics. Indeed, until Hitler silenced them, some Nazi ideologies insisted the party intended to create a Germanic Christianity free of Jewish influences. Some openly scorned Jesus as a "Jewish coward" who, by counseling men to turn the other cheek, was hardly a model for Aryan warriors.

As Hitler silenced anti-Catholics and millions of their parishioners moved to the Nazis, however, the hierarchy reconsidered. After the 1930 elections, Father Kaas spoke with the Nazis about forming a coalition government. After all, the Bavarian People's party had allied itself with racist groups since 1918, and had used anti-Semitism in political campaigns. Provided they did not attack the church, the Nazis received a good press in Catholic publications. In the 1932 Bavarian state elections, the BVP promised not to attack Hitler if the Nazis did not attack the church. Appropriate assurances were given. The Nazis promptly increased their percentage of the votes from 6 to 32, equaling the BVP for the first time and taking half the Conservative party vote as well. After the 1932 elections the Catholic hierarchy, with Vatican support, no longer opposed Hitler. Rome had never liked Center participation with socialists in governments. Catholic anti-Semitic groups and voters moved into Hitler's camp.

The future leaders of the nation joined in: about half of all organized students were Nazi, most of the rest were conservative. In 1932 Nazis won majorities in elections to the most important German student association. Here too the Nazis were adept at fusing anti-Semitism with practical interests, demonstrating for lower student fees, higher government subsidies, and the exclusion of Jews from the professions, civil service, and teaching. Between 1929 and 1933 student organizations and fraternities throughout Germany and Austria held anti-Semitic demonstrations, often ending in riots or brutal attacks against Jewish students. Students were sometimes openly encouraged by faculty, and, once the Social Democrats were out of power, there was no serious government pressure to punish rioters; academic freedom and university autonomy were invoked against it. Several universities dismissed Jewish faculty before Hitler came to power. The situation was such that the Jewish press had to list the few schools where Jewish students might attend unmolested.

Intense, often hopeless, competition for professional positions during the depression helps explain the rapid increase in Nazi popularity among physicians and lawyers. One-third of SS officers with higher degrees were lawyers. Many physicians were angry because of the new competition from thousands of refugee Jewish physicians from the east. As before the war, Jewish physicians were active in groups offering cheaper medical care to the poor. Respected German medical journals continued to complain about too many Jewish physicians. In the end, about half of all German physicians joined the Nazi Physicians League; the party never demanded it, and refusal did not end one's private practice. But mundane reasons alone do not explain strong Nazi support among physicians, geneticists, biologists, and psychiatrists. The belief in eugenics and euthanasia as a means to "racial purity" for the superior Nordics was now even more influential than it had been in the 1890s. Many complained that the social welfare policies of the republic preserved inferior racial stock, and they denounced socialist efforts to liberate homosexuals for the same reason. In pamphlets and posters, biologists and Nazis insisted that women in the professions damaged the race by producing less than the "inferior" poor. Vicious cartoons portraying Jewish physicians offering abortions to Aryan women were staples of Nazi propaganda. Before the Nazis, calls for an end to intermarriage between Aryan and Jew were not uncommon. When the Association of Socialist Physicians insisted that social and environmental factors formed human character, some biologists denounced them as "Jews, Freemasons, and Bolsheviks," because the Soviets had denounced racism as bad science and fascist terrorism.

From the German medical and biological community, a "racial hygiene" movement was formed, and "the forces on the right held sway in the movement's leading journals, publishing houses, and professional societies."[22] In 1922 the Prussian Council for Racial Hygiene recommended the establishment of a Reich Institute for Human Genetics and Population Science to fight the degeneration of the *Volk*. The Kaiser Wilhelm Institute for Anthropology, Human Genetics, and Eugenics, established in 1927, was dominated by genetic determinists. Alfred Ploetz helped form a Nordic supremacist society in the 1920s with Fritz Lenz, an even more prominent geneticist. In Ploetz's learned journal, *The Archive for Race and Social Order*, he wrote that Aryan blood was precious and must be preserved, hence the ethnic Germans in the east should be incorporated into the Reich. The racial hygiene movement later became a Nazi institution.

In 1917 Lenz praised the "German *Volk*, the last bastion of the Nordic race ...."[23] The first professor of racial hygiene, Lenz was appointed to the University of Munich by Kahr's dictatorship in 1923. As Robert N. Proctor tells us, Lenz, with Eugene Fischer and Erwin Bauer, wrote the "most important textbook on genetics" during Weimar.[24] In the book the authors insisted that mental and moral qualities were hereditary by race, and Jews, recognizable by physical type, carried uniquely "Jewish" ideas, a talent for commerce, and an inbred ability to adapt to different cultures and dominate them by manipulating others. (Women, Lenz added, were by heredity best fit for nursing and homemaking roles.) Ignoring the heavy Jewish casualties in 1914–1918, Lenz argued that Jews survived better than Nordics because they were unwilling to enlist and hence were killed only half as often as Nordic soldiers. Jewish scientists, Lenz continued, were tainted by Marxism and believed in the inheritance of acquired characteristics only because they hoped in vain that Jews would become truly Germanic by exposure to a German environment. Lenz and his coauthors attributed the usual qualities to Nordic man—industry, intelligence, obedience, and idealism; they loved danger and had a natural predilection for Protestantism. Lenz, Bauer, and Fischer's textbook was highly praised in Germany, and by the late 1920s Ploetz was "a darling of the Nazi cause."[25] In 1931 Lenz spoke for many of his colleagues when he wrote that the Nazis strove for a healthy race, and "The question of the quality of our hereditary endowment is a hundred times more important than the dispute over capitalism and socialism."[26]

Lenz's coauthor, Professor Eugene Fischer, had provided the racial research for legislation outlawing interracial marriages in German Southwest Africa in 1908. He had studied the offspring of mixed marriages and found them mentally and physically inferior. A nonracist, of course, would have looked at the disabling effects of racial discrimination and cultural differences. Fischer, a Conservative, believed racial superiority justified German rule over inferior peoples, and wrote that the indigenous peoples and offspring of racial mixing in Africa should be allowed to live only as long as they were capable of useful work—slave labor, in short. In the 1920s he tried to persuade Mussolini that the racial heredity of Italians must be purified. Later he would help organize the death camps. Fischer was appointed director of the Kaiser Wilhelm Institute for Anthropology in 1927.

The Kaiser Wilhelm Society for the Advancement of Science, the most prestigious German scientific institution and a leader in German genetics, rejected research projects associated with the belief that culture and society, not blood and race, determined social attitudes. The institute believed that Nazi ideologists were amateurs in need of scientific guidance. Scientists created racist biology, Robert Proctor suggests, and the party simply coopted them. Irritated by a Nazi speaker who claimed euthanasia as a Nazi invention, Fischer once shouted out: "Your Party has not been in existence nearly as long as our eugenics movement!"[27] Before Hitler gained power, "racial hygiene had become a scientific orthodoxy in the German medical community." As Lenz said in 1933, Hitler was "the first politician of truly great import who has taken racial hygiene as a serious element of state policy," and other prestigious academics applauded the "new age of racial-biological revolution."[28] Social Democratic physicians' associations rejected racism; like Germany itself, the medical-biological community was split along ideological lines, but here too the right swept the boards. Fischer and his colleagues, former Freikorps and Kapp putschist Dr. Otmar von Verschuer, would one day, with Lenz, aid Nazi racial murder programs. Dr. Josef Mengele was Fischer's graduate student.

As the elites moved to the Nazis, the depression hit with full force. In 1931 Bruening cut more civil servants, public services, salaries, and benefits. Businessmen demanded more wage cuts and reductions in unemployment benefits, as well as lower business taxes and subsidies for industries losing overseas markets. Some staunch anticommunists even wanted government credits extended to the Bolsheviks so they could purchase German steel! Bruening did almost all they demanded, and also ended the compulsory arbitration of labor disputes. But he did not cut the army budget or halt heavy state subsidies to the estate owners of East Prussia; Hindenburg and the high command forbade this. Deficit spending was retained for the well-off. Grain and bread prices were more than double those of the world market. To divert attention, Bruening tried to rearm and join Austria in a customs union, violating Versailles. The French promptly withdrew their loans from Austria, and the economy collapsed, accompanied by a wave of vicious anti-Semitic acts. In Germany, frightened by growing Nazi strength, Social Democrats and some businessmen in light industry explored compromises. But Hindenburg, the army, civil servants, estate owners, and heavy industry wanted no compromises now that they had the Social Democrats on the run. They lobbied to bring Hitler into the government.

In 1932, with 30 percent unemployed and government by emergency decree the rule, only the Social Democrats were still committed to parliamentary democracy. Pompous, well-fed businessmen, politicians, and economic "experts" prated about sacrifices for Germany, though making none themselves. The Nazis did better than ever in local elections. More workers moved to the Communists. As Hindenburg's term as president neared its end in 1932, Bruening tried to persuade Hitler not to run against him, promising that the rapidly aging Hindenburg would soon step down and Hitler could replace him. Gleefully, Hitler declared: "Now I have them in my pocket. They have recognized me as a partner in their negotiations!"[29] But he ran against Hindenburg.

Hindenburg was the only national figure with the stature to counter Hitler. The Conservatives supported a Stahlhelm leader, Duesterberg; the Communists nominated Ernst Thaelmann. In a sacrifice to stop the anti-Hitler vote from being split, the Social Democrats and the Center supported Hindenburg. If Hitler entered a runoff with more votes than Hindenburg, they knew the old autocrat would drop out of the race; as president, Hitler would then control emergency powers. To save what was left of the republic, one had to vote for a monarchist general who conspired against it! As Hindenburg complained, "The wrong people are voting for me!" Duesterberg was finished when the Nazis gleefully revealed that his grandfather had been Jewish. Hindenburg outpolled Hitler but did not win a majority. A runoff was held. The Conservative party urged its voters to switch to Hitler, another blow to the notion that they supported the Nazis only reluctantly. Hindenburg was the very symbol of traditional German conservatism. In the runoff he received 53 to Hitler's 37 percent. As Richard Hamilton's research shows, in some cities and resorts, including Hindenburg's district, the wealthy supported Hitler.

Pleased with the high Nazi vote, the army high command connived to effect Bruening's dismissal and bring Hitler into a new government. Hindenburg would have dismissed Bruening had he not been offended by Nazi attacks against his chancellor in the campaign. Meanwhile the SA, now 300,000 strong, roamed the streets seeking confrontations with communists, who were happy to oblige. As violence escalated, the socialist minister president of Prussia, Braun, offered to join forces with the republic in order to restore order. Schleicher was furious; he did not want the SPD upholding social stability just as he and other power brokers hoped to smash the left. Bruening's support vanished. As a representative of big business put it, "The democratic parliamentary system of Weimar is the last root of many evils. It is to be rejected as unsuited for Germany."[30] State elections were held in Prussia. As Henry Turner notes, most of Germany's business corporations had headquarters in Berlin, and Ruhr executives believed the Nazis would do very well: "Most viewed that likelihood in a positive light. . . ."[31] To avoid violence, Bruening forbade the SA and the SS to march or wear uniforms during the campaign. Hindenburg reluctantly vetoed high command objections that this would weaken army frontier units with Nazis in their ranks. Aided by significant financial contributions from landowners and industry, the Conservative party deserted Bruening and joined the Nazis in the campaign. The Nazis went from 6 to an amazing 162 seats, to become the single largest party in Prussia. The socialists dropped from 136 to 94 seats but were able to form a government with the Center. The SA wanted a *putsch*, but Hitler waited. In state elections where the anti-Semitic parties of the 1890s had done well, the Nazis were getting voting percentages in the mid-forties; in Bavaria they equaled the BVP for the first time. Hitler was winning the "rotten political game."

The army was angry when Bruening refused to increase its budget; businessmen were upset when he threatened to lower prices; estate owners were furious when he tried to foreclose mortgages on state-subsidized bankrupt estates and settle unemployed on the land. Landowners denounced his "communism," and Hindenburg joined them—he had been presented with an estate by the Junkers in 1927. In May 1932 Hindenburg dismissed Bruening; he who had sacrificed so many to protect the old rulers was deserted when he tried to impose a measure of austerity on them. The same day, the Nazis won 48 percent of the vote and a majority of seats in Oldenburg. But Schleicher and Hindenburg were not ready for Hitler. Franz von Papen was appointed chancellor. The very model of aristocratic idiocy, Papen was a perfect choice for the old guard. An aristocrat, monarchist, and former general staff officer (cavalry, naturally), he had married into a wealthy industrialist family, was on the extreme right of the Center party, and avidly admired Karl Lueger. As a member of the Prussian parliament, he routinely supported the reaction.

Schleicher gave Papen little leeway, selecting his cabinet members for him—a "cabinet of Barons," as it has been labeled, ministers ridiculed for their feudal obtuseness. It included seven nobles and two corporation heads. Schleicher was minister of defense. Papen's stupidity was irrelevant. Schleicher declared, because he would not be allowed to make important decisions. Papen did as he was told, increasing taxes on those with lower incomes, cutting wages, ending collective bargaining, slashing unemployment and health benefits yet again, and proposing to subsidize business firms in trouble. Purging republicans from the government, he sought to rearm Germany, and he lifted the ban on SA and SS rallies. In Prussia this led to some 140 deaths when the Nazis descended on communist districts and the workers fought back. In an amazing and illegal non sequitur, Papen used Nazi and communist violence as the reason to suppress the Social Democratic and Center government of Prussia! He declared himself Reichs commissioner for Prussia in what was in reality a government *putsch*. Many socialists wished to fight, but party elders believed, correctly, that the army would be pleased to join the Nazis and crush the socialists once and for all in the bloodbath the military had hoped for since 1890.

In a deal with the Nazis, Papen called for new elections. Even the international press knew this would increase Hitler's votes. Now the most powerful party in all state parliaments except Bavaria, the Nazis were supported during the 1932 campaign by a variety of upper-class notables. The kaiser's son, Prince August, demonstrated his mastery of the linguistic subtlety of his father: "You too my people shall arise like a phoenix from your own ashes. And other peoples shall bow mutely before your Holy Third Reich."[32] Princes made large financial contributions. Some six thousand Nazi speakers led endless rallies, and marches abounded. Anti-Semitism was not moderated to satisfy allegedly reluctant conservatives. In Charlottenburg, the wealthy bourgeois district in Berlin, a Nazi spoke of the Jews as insects who ought to be exterminated and was greeted with great enthusiasm. Catholics who attacked Nazi paganism were told it was the Center that consorted with atheistic Marxists and thus helped "German Christian culture" to be "poisoned by Jewish pestilence."[33] Everywhere calls resounded for a Hitler dictatorship. In July 1932 came the astounding surge of the Nazis to 230 seats, nearly twice as many as their nearest rivals, the socialists. The Nazis had achieved what no political party ever had in Germany, and it was anti-Semitism that enabled them to unite Germans from all segments of society but the left. Had it not been for proportional representation, they would have had an outright Reichstag majority from those who for decades had blamed the Jews for the ills of industrial society, the traumas of 1918–1930, and the threats to their interests posed by a liberal republic.

Hindenburg and his advisers still wanted assurances that Hitler would be fiscally responsible, because the Nazis had campaigned on the misery of the middle classes and against conservatives. As chancellor, Hitler would not be easy to dismiss. More popular than any German politician ever, he also commanded a military force of about 400,000 SA. Only the army could stop him if he held power, and it seemed likely it would not. When Hitler demanded the chancellorship and the Prussian presidency, Papen and Schleicher rejected him, offering instead the vice-chancellorship: the tail wanted to wag the dog. The Nazis were far too dynamic and popular to play the role of mere enforcers for the bankrupt old guard. Hitler was no Franco or Mussolini, nor did he have the least intention of becoming just another Weimar chancellor who, forced to balance conflicting interests through compromise, would end by sacrificing popularity and power.

Faced with an uncooperative, contemptuous Reichstag, Papen nonetheless held on and again called for new elections, evidently hoping to weaken Hitler and make him more pliable. Businessmen were shaken when the Nazis supported a transport workers' strike in Berlin. Hitler had opposed this but countered that it was not a socialist union. In November 1932 the Nazis lost thirty-four seats, but the non-Nazi right almost disappeared. The Conservative party won only a miserable fifteen seats and the businessman's DVP but four. Moreover, the Communists won a record one hundred seats. The Nazis had stumbled, but for that very reason Hitler was more necessary to the elites than ever before, and they knew it. If the Nazis collapsed, their hope for a popular, autocratic, and legal regime would be dashed. The republic and the left would survive.

Hindenburg hesitated, angered that Nazis had attacked him as the candidate of Jewish socialists during the presidential campaign. Nor did he trust a man from below. Hindenburg and Papen considered suspending the constitution to create a dictatorship of the "right people." Schleicher warned them off: to thwart the will of the public might mean civil war. To influence the decision, the high command held war games based on the absurd notion that if Hitler were denied power, communists and Nazis would join forces in revolution as Poles invaded and socialists held a general strike! The German army lost. Senior officers wanted Hitler as dictator, provided only that he assure them the SA would integrate into the army, not replace it. Papen was unable to form a new government. Schleicher, angry with the attempt of the puppet to pull his own strings, had him dropped. On November 23, 1932, at a meeting of the famous and influential industrialists of the Langnamverein, with some fifteen hundred members, "One observer reported that most of the industrialists he had talked with favored Hitler's appointment as chancellor."[34] In the same month, agrarian landowners and important figures in "banking, finance, retailing, and export industries" wrote a joint letter to Hindenburg asking that Hitler be brought into the government. Necessary sacrifices "will only be made willingly if the largest element of the national movement takes a leading part in the government."[35] The signees did not expect to be the sacrificial offering. Prominent business figures—Siemens, Bosch, Schacht, Thyssen, Krupp, and others—pressed Hindenburg, writing that the Nazis, "through the overcoming of class contrasts, create the essential basis for a rebirth of the German economy."[36]

To coopt the Nazis, Schleicher persuaded Hindenburg to allow him to form a government and offer the vice-chancellorship and the minister presidency of Prussia to Gregor Strasser, thought to be Hitler's main party rival. When Strasser considered accepting, a furious Hitler forced him out of the party. He left quietly, without support. Schleicher now tried to steal Hitler's voters. On December 15, now chancellor, he announced on the radio to a startled audience, "I am a social general," and declared the army would not protect "outdated economic forms or indefensible distributions of property." Pragmatism was needed to mitigate social misery and restart the economy, he announced, asking the Reichsbank for credits for a public works program to stimulate demand and employment. He proposed using the army to train the unemployed for a new labor service. Schleicher also spoke of concessions to workers and preventing employers from reducing wages—wages so low, he noted, that the economy suffered from lack of purchasing power. He even indicated he would offer the Social Democrats cabinet seats, and he proposed to end state subsidies to East Elbian landowners and seize a million acres from bankrupt estates to resettle the landless poor. He would also cut import quotas that were driving up the price of bread. He capped all this by asking that the Communist and Nazi parties be dissolved. In effect, Schleicher offered a new deal and an end to the extremes of left and right.

The "Red General" was immediately denounced by big landowners for his "agrarian bolshevism" and his threat to publicize a report of their corrupt misuse of government subsidies. (Hitler would later quietly drop the report, and he undoubtedly let this be known during the negotiations for his appointment.) The Reichsbank refused to grant Schleicher sufficient emergency credits for his public works. Businessmen protested any rise in wages and were "horrified by Schleicher's commitment to some form of revolutionary collaboration with labor. . . ."[37] Conservatives rejected the renegade; Social Democrats refused to trust one who had always desired their extinction. When Schleicher asked Hindenburg to let him rule by emergency decree, Hindenburg refused, and Schleicher was out. Only the Nazis took Schleicher seriously, for his program might well have slashed their votes. Two years later, in 1934, Hitler ordered Schleicher's murder. No army leaders showed up at his funeral. Even now historians do not see the significance of his proposals. He had glimpsed a reasonable path to rebuild Germany, but it was too threatening to his peers and, coming from him, too unbelievable to any who might wish to support it.

The Reichstag was to meet on January 31, 1933. During January, Papen and Hitler met, probably to discuss the allocation of cabinet positions. It was assumed the Nazis and Conservatives would form a coalition government under Hitler. A meeting was held at the home of the banker Kurt von Schroeder; Papen and Hitler also met at the home of the Bechsteins, the wealthy piano manufacturers close to Hitler since Munich days. Hitler consulted with the chief of the army command, General von Hammerstein, a crucial supporter. Some industrialists, fearing Hitler might be another Schleicher, preferred Papen. Princes and aristocrats lobbied for Hitler, led by Prince August: "There where a Hitler leads, a Hohenzollern may with confidence join the ranks."[38] On January 15 the Nazis campaigned in Hindenburg's state and won some 38 percent of the vote at Conservative expense. Many allegedly reluctant members of the upper class voted for Hitler.

Hindenburg's staff met with Hitler and Joachim von Ribbentrop. Letters of support came from influential notables. General Werner von Blomberg and his staff "were enthusiastic about Hitler." Senior officers warned that were Hitler refused, soldiers would not fight the SA, "because the younger generation strongly sympathizes with their national convictions." The president's son, Oscar, worked avidly for Hitler, and General Hammerstein and Schleicher "were both convinced that only Hitler was possible as the future chancellor."[39] "The church . . . almost unanimously welcomed the Hitler regime, with real confidence, indeed, with highest hopes," according to Karl Barth, the leading Protestant theologian. An historian of religion tells of a "wave of enthusiasm in [both] the churches" for Hitler.[40] The "best people" wanted him. As Peter Stachura wrote, "The Nazis ultimately came to power as the spearhead of a counter-revolutionary, anti-modernist groundswell of opinion which aimed to turn the clock back to attitudes associated with the Wilhelmian Reich."[41] On January 30, 1933, Adolf Hitler became the last chancellor of the Weimar Republic. Wild enthusiasm broke out in the army and the civil service, champagne celebrations lit up the homes of estate owners, all-night celebrations exploded at every university. The SA terrorized leftists, looted and burned Jewish stores and synagogues, desecrated Jewish cemeteries, stormed through department stores, and dragged Jews out of cafés and shops and beat them. Posters demanded death. As the Nazi deputies marched to the Reichstag, they chanted the familiar cry: "Germany awake. Death to the Jews!"

Only two Nazis were named to the cabinet: Goering, state commissioner of Prussia, and Frick, minister of the interior. Papen was vice-chancellor and Hugenberg minister of economics and agriculture—presumably they would protect the economy from radicalism. Franz Seldte, Stahlhelm leader, was minister of labor. The allocation of cabinet portfolios pleased Conservatives: they would control economic policy while Hitler took care of the Social Democrats and the Jews. It was not quite that simple, but nearly so. The stock market remained calm. It is commonly assumed the elites believed they could control Hitler; it is more accurate to say they supported his policies. All cabinet members belonged to a political party that for decades had campaigned to harm the

Jews. The majority of the political establishment voluntarily cooperated with Hitler's purge of the Jews. Thousands collaborated in the horror of the death camps. With Hitler's selection, the iron logic that led to the Holocaust was set in motion. No significant opposition to it would come from those who voted for Hitler or used their influence or wealth to help put him in power.

20: HITLER IN POWER

> The German establishment not only knew and tolerated what was being done, provided it was done out of their sight and hearing, but had prepared the grounds and provided the means for it.
>
> —Hugh Trevor-Roper

HITLER had no intention of being at the mercy of his Conservative allies or of Hindenburg, nor of foundering in the morass of coalition politics. Instead he planned a final election to gain a parliamentary majority and become the undisputed master of Germany. In order to raise funds, in February 1933 he met with Krupp and leading industrialists, and he and Goering gave the usual assurances: they would support private property and the profit system and would crush the left and rearm. Moreover, this would be the last election for five years, perhaps a century. Speaking for the businessmen, Krupp guaranteed Hitler their support. No objections were voiced to Nazi terror. The Jews were not mentioned. The industrialists soon delivered some three million marks to the Nazis.

On February 27 the Reichstag burned down. Blaming the communists, Hitler issued a Decree to Protect the German People and the State. But the decree suspended the civil rights of all citizens, not just communists, and ended the powers of state governments as well, though none were pro-communist. The decree also gave the Nazis full power to terrorize anyone designated an enemy. Before the elections, union leaders, leftists, and Jews were terrorized. Goering, head of the Prussian police, replaced republican officials with SA and encouraged violence. Hindenburg and the cabinet approved these acts; indeed, Hugenberg and Papen had hoped to establish authoritarian rule well before Hitler's appointment. On March 5, 1933, the electorate also approved, giving the Nazis 45 percent of the vote and the Conservatives 8. For the first time Germany had a parliamentary majority of the racist right.

To open the new Reichstag, a "Day of National Awakening" was held at the garrison church in Potsdam where lay the remains of Frederick the Great. The crown prince, Hindenburg, and Hitler paid homage at the tomb as SS, SA, and Stahlhelm marched by, the old order sanctioning the new. Bishop Otto Dibelius blessed the proceedings. Hitler then requested an Enabling Act to give him full power for four years. Hindenburg and his cabinet approved. Otto Wels, leader of the Social Democrats, was the only deputy to speak out against it, and his party voted accordingly. Communists were unrepresented. All other parties unanimously approved Hitler's dictatorship, and the bill passed in March. On April 1 the regime announced a boycott of Jewish businesses and professions, and celebrated by placarding cities with anti-Semitic posters as the SA beat Jews and leftists. Everywhere spontaneous anti-Semitic meetings and institutional purges occurred. Where conservatives dominated, it was unnecessary for the Nazis to move first. The so-called Jew Republic was dismantled, though in fact less than one-sixth of 1 percent of government posts were held by Jews. Of the 250 cabinet ministers who had served under Weimar, six were of Jewish origin.

Conservatives swiftly deserted their party. So many government officials, aristocrats, university graduates, academics, and professionals rushed to join the Nazis that in April a temporary moratorium was imposed on new applications. Four hundred thousand strong in January 1933, the SA soared to two million by December. Some 15 percent of the SS were aristocrats, though they composed less than 1 percent of the population. Opportunism was a powerful motive, but ideological affinity played a significant role. No government members protested the terror against the Jews, for they were anti-Semites. Paul Bang, economics expert and a top official in the Economics Ministry, had written a book titled *Jewish Crimes*, calling for the protection of German blood and military expansion in order to free Germany from international Jewry.[1] He was part of the mainstream of the Conservative party.

In July 1933 the Nazis declared themselves the only legal party. The Reichstag, it was said, was now the most expensive glee club in the world. State governments were in effect abolished, trade unions replaced by a Nazi Labor Front, and small business and agrarian economic organizations coopted. Only the powerful organizations of heavy industry retained their autonomy, for they were vital to the regime's aggressive foreign policy. Many executive officers of corporations joined the party or the honorary SS. Corporations contributed lavishly to the "Hitler Fund" and the private account of Himmler. Friedrich Flick, strongly pro-Nazi before 1930 and later rewarded with stolen Jewish property, was a regular contributor to Himmler and the SS as were representatives of Siemens and I. G. Farben, among others.

By July more than 25,000 socialists, communists, and Jews were in concentration camps or prisons. Neither an opportunist nor in danger, Hindenburg not only signed the decree giving Hitler full power, he used his influence to get it passed, voluntarily destroying the power of his office.

When Hitler abolished trade unions and political parties, Hindenburg congratulated him; when told of inhumane conditions in the prison camps, he was silent. When Jews were purged from government, Hindenburg's only request was that war veterans be exempted. It was done; Hitler could wait. As Hindenburg's biographer notes, "The fact is that he had made his peace with Hitler."[2] In February he signed an unprecedented law allowing Nazi symbols on army uniforms. When Papen gave a speech casting mild doubts on Nazi terror, Hindenburg agreed that Papen must be dismissed.

As for the army, in 1933 War Minister General von Blomberg declared, "There remains only one thing to do: to serve the National Socialists with complete devotion."[3] But the army still feared Hitler might replace them with the SA. Ernst Roehm publicly complained that the revolution was being betrayed to "reactionary plutocrats," latecomers who should be replaced by his "old fighters." In the famous purge of June 1934, Hitler, with army logistical support, proved his reliability. Roehm and hundreds of his SA and others whose existence had become inconvenient were slaughtered. Hindenburg congratulated Hitler. When he died in August, his son broadcast a radio appeal in support of Hitler's desire to combine in himself the offices of chancellor and president. The high command granted approval and required its troops to swear an unprecedented loyalty oath to Hitler, not to Germany, giving him the full backing of the most prestigious of German institutions.

Before required to, municipal governments fired Jews and broke contracts with Jewish firms. Universities purged Jewish faculty. Some fifteen hundred Jewish attorneys lost the right to practice. The judiciary needed no purge and, along with civil servants, took a personal oath to Hitler in 1934. Many judges and lawyers even requested anti-Semitic laws before the 1935 passage of the infamous Nuremberg Laws. Law professors insisted that racially mixed marriages, still legal, violated the national need of "cultivating German blood and maintaining its purity." A conference of law professors demanded racist laws in 1933. Before the Nuremberg Laws forbade marriages between Germans and Jews, eminent jurists published articles against blood mixing, and civil officials prevented mixed marriages. The court of appeals in Karlsruhe gave the following opinion: "The Jewish race differs considerably from the Aryan race with regard to blood, character, personality, and view of life." Mixed marriages were "undesirable, injurious," and "unnatural." In 1934 a medical conference on racial hygiene demanded action against "Jewish racial poisoning" and "contamination by Jewish blood."[4] Frick, Nazi interior minister and one of Hitler's oldest and most determined Nazi comrades, had to tell the zealots to wait until racial laws were actually passed.

The laws soon came. The Nuremberg Laws of 1935 defined a Jew as one who descended from three Jewish grandparents. All civil rights were denied, and sexual relations between Jew and Gentile were forbidden, as was the hiring of Gentile maidservants by Jews. The German Medical Association assured the regime it would find a test for Jewish blood; naturally it failed. The Nazis had to be content with religious distinctions: a Jewish grandparent was defined as one who belonged to the Jewish religious community, even if by conversion.

The Nuremberg Laws also granted the judiciary powers it had long sought. Defendants' rights were slashed and the prosecution's power increased, and judges became the final authority. Defense attorneys could not demand proof of charges, and there was no right of appeal. With no fear their decisions would be overturned, the courts routinely violated their own rules of evidence in order to punish suspected enemies of the regime. They allowed the torture of prisoners and even regulated how much was allowable and with what instruments. They were also encouraged to act on their old belief that defendants with long criminal records were hereditary "criminal types," deserving of extra punishment. Jews were routinely punished without real proof of their alleged crimes. As the right had long held, a Jew was by nature an enemy of Germany. Thus courts often refused to allow Jews to testify or to be represented by defense counsel, and the word of a Gentile against a Jew was usually accepted without corroboration. Nothing was covert. A court decision in 1933 was "positively dripping with anti-Semitism," according to Ingo Mueller. Even the supreme court demonstrated an "obsessive determination to prosecute all Jews."[5] The judiciary was often more extreme than the party, at times ordering the death penalty even when Nazi law did not require it.

But Hitler's conservative allies, though they did not otherwise object, wanted the punishment of the Jews to be legal. Even the moderate Schacht "never opposed anti-Jewish decrees; to the contrary, he welcomed them and was impatient when they were not issued quickly enough."[6] But Schacht, Papen, and Hitler's conservative allies did object to SA initiatives, partly because the old guard itself was sometimes threatened by Nazi hotheads. Thus the great silence when Roehm's SA radicals were murdered in June 1934—Hitler's guarantee that the regime would punish even its own if they violated the law. For he too wanted the "Jewish question" solved legally and without unsanctioned violence. The party must be the sole source of all law. Even some SA members were imprisoned and beaten by SS troopers for unsanctioned actions. Hitler also knew that millions of Germans opposed anti-Semitism. During the April boycott, some workers made "a point of buying" at Jewish shops, as did a few of all classes.[7] And thousands of leftists and proletarians and hundreds of young Jews were attempting to resist. But above all,

Hitler despised the pogrom mentality. Transient emotional outbursts settled nothing, he wrote. The "ultimate goal" of a "rational anti-Semitism" . . . "must unalterably be the elimination of the Jews altogether."[8]

But "ultimate goals" would have to wait. Schacht, Funk, and officials of the Foreign Office argued that counterboycotts would harm German business interests abroad, and in fact markets and contracts were lost when foreign businessmen canceled agreements in response to Nazi actions. Until Germany was strong enough to ignore international opinion and trade, Hitler wished to be thought of as a more or less normal German politician, striving only to correct the wrongs of the Versailles Treaty. Local leaders were told that violent initiatives would not be tolerated. Interviewed by the foreign press, Hitler insisted he would renegotiate Versailles peacefully and denounced the "libels" of international Jewry, but he denied imprisoning innocent Jews. Goering and Hitler did not wish to offend nations that held German assets while the Nazis needed foreign currency and trade. Foreign Minister Constantin von Neurath wanted it known that racial legislation was directed only against Jews, for some of Germany's overseas trading partners asked about the fate of the nationals under laws against "non-Aryans." The Foreign Office, men of aristocratic connections, also wanted the punishment of the Jews to be by legislation. Nevertheless, as Christopher R. Browning has told us, by May 1933, "on their own initiative, the highest echelons of the Foreign Office approved the official dissemination throughout the world of the crudest kind of anti-Semitic propaganda. . . ."[9] As the representative of Germany to the Netherlands, Otto von Pfeffer, told a British official, if war came, Germany could not afford a hostile minority in its midst and would be forced to expel or kill the Jews of Germany, Poland, Hungary, and the Ukraine.[10]

By 1936 hundreds of thousands of Jews had been fired with little need for Nazi prodding. Civil servants withheld pensions, universities purged Jews, school directors fired Jewish teachers. Physicians' and lawyers' groups welcomed restrictions on Jewish professionals. Bankers, manufacturers, retailers, and artisans benefited from seized Jewish property. By 1938 seventy thousand Jewish businesses had been expropriated or ruined; only firms essential to the war effort remained. Banks prevented Jews from transferring money abroad, businessmen cut Jewish salaries, bureaucrats levied special taxes and lowered food rations.

Austria did not lag behind. The Christian Social heirs of Karl Lueger ran the government and established the "clerical fascism" of the "Fatherland Front" before the invasion by Hitler. Upheld by Catholic journals and newspapers, the Front abolished democracy and buttressed its rule with the militia of the brown-shirted Heimwehr of Prince Starhemberg. The Social Democratic party was outlawed, and army troops fought bloody battles against Viennese Marxists. Jews were purged from the civil service, hospitals, state theatres, medicine, banking, law, businesses, and sports. Jewish businesses were boycotted, and Jews were segregated in schools. Although Catholic, the government allowed divorce for "racial incompatibility." The church did not object. Austrian towns and villages posted signs declaring Jewish tourists unwelcome, and anti-Jewish riots were worse than any in Germany.

By 1939 the Jewish communities of Germany and Austria lived in ghetto conditions, but the laws against them were not uniquely Nazi. Almost all had been demanded by Stoecker's Christian Social party and the petition campaigners of the 1880s, the anti-Semitic parties and the German Conservative party in the 1890s, the Agrarian Bund, Lueger's Christian Socials, and Schoenerer's Pan-Germans. Millions had long hoped to ban Jews from government, education, professions, and institutions; many had agitated for decades to prevent them from owning land, subject them to special taxes, or remove them from Germany. Before Hitler became chancellor, Papen's government had drafted laws that would have purged Jews from the civil service and deprived them of citizenship, and the Prussian Ministry of the Interior had drafted a decree preventing Jews from changing names because, it insisted, they did this only to deceive the non-Jewish population.

Voluntary cooperation was also offered by thousands of physicians, psychologists, biologists, "racial hygienists," and scientists who helped "purify" the race. Well over half of Germany's Gentile physicians joined the Nazi Physicians' League. After all, Nazi ideology was simply a vulgarized version of ideas held for decades by prominent German anthropologists, geneticists, and physicians. Some had long demanded harsh measures against racial contamination, and some psychologists sought to detect the "racial psychology" of Jews just as medical researchers sought the physical characteristics of "Jewish blood." As one physician wrote, if the research succeeded, "then neither deception, nor baptism, nor name change, nor citizenship, and not even nasal surgery could help. One cannot change one's blood."[11] Academic experts certified those who were unfit, useless, or carriers of hereditary diseases and should be sterilized or killed. Medical experts sterilized the "racially contaminated" children left behind by the African occupation troops of the French army after the Ruhr occupation. As Robert N. Proctor tells us in his excellent study, Germans to be sterilized were selected by special courts whose records are still secret. This may be because they not only reveal the complicity of scientists but also show that such decisions were often made on the basis of race alone. When Eugene Fischer, acknowledged "expert" on the Jews, was appointed president of the University of Berlin in 1933, in his inaugural address he praised Nazi attempts to "safeguard" Germany's "hereditary endowment." He set up a course for SS officers at the Institute for Anthropology, and he and his colleagues trained SS medical personnel and thousands of physicians and "racial experts" as SS consultants. "Physicians," Proctor tells us, "played an active role both in the theory and practice of each phase of the Nazi program of racial hygiene and racial destruction."[12]

Perhaps the most telling indication of the historical force of racism in Germany was the support for Nazi anti-Semitic laws given by the German church leadership. In April 1933, when Hitler announced the boycott and the SA attacked Jews in the streets, Christian leaders in other lands protested, and some supported a counterboycott. In a radio broadcast to the United States, Bishop Otto Dibelius, general superintendent of the Evangelical church, blamed world Jewry for starting the agitation by boycotting Germany, and expressed "the widely held opinion among Evangelical Churchmen that the measures against the Jews were perfectly justified. . . ."[13] The central organ of the Church Federation raised no outcry against Hitler's treatment of the Jews then or ever.

In 1934 the Evangelical church insisted the Nazis must be "welcomed by Lutheranism," and thanked "the Lord God" for giving the Germans a "pious and trusty overlord." A prominent Lutheran declared Hitler's advent in 1933 "a divine gift and miracle."[14] A Protestant bishop wrote to his clergy, "He has been sent to us by God."[15] The majority of Protestant theologians in conference praised Hitler as "the last bulwark against communism."[16] Yet every government of the Weimar Republic had been anticommunist; it was the secular liberalism of Weimar the clergy detested. The Catholic church tried to restrict the worship of converted Jews when important Nazis were present to see the despised yellow star, but official Protestantism declared "racially Jewish Christians had no place and no rights in a German Evangelical Church."[17] The overwhelming majority of Evangelical pastors took the loyalty oath to Hitler, though there was no retaliation against those who did not. Citing the "racial consciousness" of the nation, churchmen were told by the hierarchy "to ensure that baptized non-Aryans had no part in Church activities. . . ."[18] In so doing, the church denied the power and grace of Christ and baptism. In 1933 the theologian Gerhard Kittel, famed as a leading expert on Judaism, declared that the Jew corrupted the Volk and should be excluded from citizenship and profession. Considering solutions to the "Jewish problem," he ruled out extermination as impractical. Joining the Nazis in 1933, he wrote anti-Semitic articles for Goebbels even after he knew about the death camps. After the war he denied he had done anything wrong, and by his lights he had not.[19]

In July 1933 more than 70 percent of church committee members, lay parishioners, voted for Nazi "German Christian" candidates to lead the church, men influenced by H. S. Chamberlain and Lagarde, and demanded the church drop "Rabbi Paul" and the Old Testament and drive out converted Jews. In response, about one-third of Evangelical pastors formed a "Confessing Church" to protect the church. Led by Pastor Martin Niemoeller, they decried attempts to drive out baptized Jews—yet even he said of Jewry in 1935, "Whatever it takes up changes into poison," and Jews carried "the unforgiven blood guilt of their fathers."[20] Famed for his anti-Nazi stance after the war, Niemoeller was jailed by Hitler in the 1930s for opposing the Nazi takeover of the church. Yet he had been pro-Nazi in the 1920s, and in 1939, though overage and a daily witness of the fate of Nazi opponents, he volunteered to enlist. He was refused. That his change of heart at the end of the war has been used to exemplify church resistance is a devastating comment.

The Confessing Church never attempted to protect Jews but only Jews who had converted to Christianity, that is, only Christians. Most Evangelical clergy did not even do this. Even after the killings and synagogue burnings of Kristallnacht in 1938, and even in the Confessing Church, the "majority did not oppose Hitler."[21] The German Methodist church attacked world Jewry for its "lying propaganda" and agreed with Bishop Dibelius that Hitler had saved Germany from an imminent Bolshevik revolution, bringing peace and stability, in happy contrast to the "bloody revolution" that had established the Weimar Republic.[22] The Mormon church advised its faithful that opposing Hitler was a violation of Mormon law. When a Mormon youth spoke against the Nazis during the war, he was promptly executed. In 1976 a play was written in the United States by a Mormon to honor the martyr; it was suppressed by the president of Brigham Young University.[23]

As a group, only the Jehovah's Witnesses resisted the Nazis. Of some twenty thousand of them, only five thousand survived the war, yet any Witness sent to a concentration camp could have been released simply by signing a paper renouncing his or her faith. Founded in the United States in the nineteenth century, the Witnesses were free of German racial nationalism and had not brooded for centuries over the failure of the Jews to convert. The Witnesses still held to the original, if patronizing, Christian belief of the need to persuade all potential converts to Christ. Believing, as the early Christian had, that the Second Coming was near, they gave sinners a chance to repent. For them, all governments were the work of Satan. They would not salute the flag, bear arms, participate in politics, or cooperate in any way with the Nazis. Some 97 percent were persecuted; one-third died in the camps, and many were beheaded for refusing military service. Their example illustrates the uniquely stubborn and heroic power early Christianity had before institutionalization and commitments to the social order overwhelmed the desire to live an uncompromising life. As a Protestant pastor wrote of them, "Not the great churches, but these slandered and scoffed-at people were the ones who stood up first against the rage of the Nazi demon, and who dared to make opposition according to their faith."[24]

In sharp contrast, the German Catholic hierarchy approved the Enabling Act and encouraged the Center party to vote for it, thereby destroying the organization that had protected Catholic rights since the 1870s. Negotiating with the Vatican for a concordat, Hitler reminded the bishops he was a Catholic and that his Jewish policies were those the church had advocated for centuries. He also promised to protect Catholic rights and state subsidies. Cardinals Bertram and Faulhaber and the German bishops supported him. The papal nuncio, Cardinal Pacelli, later Pius XII, signed the famous concordat with Hitler in July 1933. Hitler was overjoyed; he had not expected such swift recognition of the legitimacy of his government by the Vatican. To the dismay of many Catholics in the West, it was the first significant international recognition of the Nazi dictatorship. As Hitler told his cabinet, they were immensely helped in "the urgent fight against the international Jews." The *Voelkische Beobachter* added that the concordat "signifies a tremendous moral strengthening of the National Socialist government. . . ."[25] The Catholic press in Germany boasted its loyalty. As Cardinal Faulhaber said in a sermon of 1937: "At a time when the heads of the major nations in the world faced a new Germany with cool reserve and considerable suspicion, the Catholic Church, the greatest moral power on earth, through the Concordat, expressed her confidence in the new German government. This was a deed of immeasurable significance for the reputation of the new government abroad."[26] Catholics were told it was a sacred duty to obey the new state, a duty never withdrawn even after the full horrors in the east were known to the clergy. The moral power of the German hierarchy and the Holy See stood against any German Catholics who might have opposed the regime, and caused immense anguish to millions of Catholics elsewhere.

Why the unseemly haste to recognize the Nazis? The Nazis granted no rights to the church not already given by the Weimar constitution. And the Nazis were given a veto over candidates for bishop, who also had to swear an oath of loyalty to the Third Reich. Moreover, the concordat was violated by the Nazis even before the Vatican ratified it in September 1934, and several prominent Catholic leaders were murdered in the purge of June 1934, including the head of Catholic Action. It seems apparent that, however much the bishops may have feared a loss of church rights, they supported racism because they were conditioned by German history and culture. Thus in an official handbook for priests, Archbishop Groeber wrote: "Foreign blood will always represent a risk. . . . Hence no people may be denied the right to maintain undisturbed their previous racial stock and to enact safeguards for this purpose." Cardinal Faulhaber announced that the church had no objection to keeping the "characteristics of a people . . . pure and unadulterated" and preserving the "common ties of blood which unite" the *Volk*. Cardinal Faulhaber also insisted that the Old Testament could not be the result of the Jewish spirit because it was morally superior. The official publication of the Bavarian priests' association instructed its teachers to inform their students that the "sacred books of the Old Testament were not only beyond the Jewish mentality, but in direct conflict with it." Indeed, "The greatest miracle of the Bible is that true religion could hold its own and maintain itself against the voice of Semitic blood." One bishop wrote that though Jesus was Jewish, Christianity had not been "influenced by their racial characteristics."[27] A church-approved work explained that Pontius Pilate was an Aryan who had hoped to free Jesus. The church even supplied birth records to the Nazis to help them decide who was not Aryan, and helped track down Jehovah's Witnesses for persecution, publicly boasting of its services to the regime. Some priests encouraged youths to join the party. One-fourth of the SS were practicing Catholics, yet none were so much as denied communion for their bloody deeds. Simply put, the Catholic hierarchies in Germany and Austria did not regard the Jews as an innocent people.

Yet Pius XI rejected racism: "Anti-Semitism is a movement which is repulsive. . . . It is not possible for Christians to be a part of it. Anti-Semitism is not permitted. We are spiritually Jews through Christ. . . ."[28] He also publicly supported Cardinal Mundelein of Chicago when he bitterly denounced Hitler in 1937, and he attacked Mussolini in 1938 when Il Duce supported anti-Semitic policies. As the Nazis harassed Catholic schools and held show trials with fake evidence to "prove" that monasteries and convents were hotbeds of sexual perversities, Catholics begged Pius XI to speak out. In 1937 he issued his famous encyclical "With Burning Sorrow," protesting the violations of the concordat and declaring a belief in God inconsistent with the "deification of earthly values such as race, people, or the state." He also forced Cardinal Innitzer of Vienna to retract the joyous public statement with which he greeted the German armies in 1938. Catholic clerics in other nations counseled the pope to repudiate the concordat, and the Nazis feared he might. But he did not. Just before he died in 1939, Pius XI was about to issue an encyclical against the Nazis. Pius XII suppressed it.

In 1939 the greatest moral test for the church and the elites was yet to come. Until Hitler was ready to march, the worst the regime could do was to make life so difficult for the Jews that they would emigrate. Hitler assumed other nations would vigorously protest his plans for a truly "final solution." Like the radical right everywhere, he really believed the Jews were a powerful international force. But when the slaughter began, tens of thousands of the German elites would cooperate in the destruction of the Jews. It is time to question the accepted idea that Hitler deceived Germany's old rulers into thinking his extremism would be curbed by power or their influence. The more we learn about the Holocaust, the more it seems that the anti-Semitism of tens of thousands of upper-class Germans was not all that different from that of the Nazis themselves.

21: TOWARD A RACIAL EMPIRE

> We demand land and territory for nourishing our people and settling
> our surplus population.
>
> —Nazi Party Program, 1930

> The aim of German foreign policy must be to conquer land in the
> east for the German *Volk.*
>
> —Hitler, *Mein Kampf*

IN 1930 an addition to the party program revealed the ultimate meaning
of the ideology of blood and soil: "The creation of space on a large scale
for food production and settlement by the growing German people is the
necessary task of German foreign policy."[1] Dictatorship, rearmament, and
the exploitation of slave labor and raw materials in the east would end
German vulnerability in a collapsing liberal-capitalist world. A vast racial
empire would stretch to the Urals, enslaving or murdering the indigenous
peoples. As Walter Darré, Nazi agrarian specialist, wrote in 1931: "The
German *Volk* cannot avoid a life-and-death struggle with the advancing
East. . . . In this struggle there can only be one solution for us: absolute
victory!"[2] German peasant-warriors would settle the former lands of Jews
and Slavs. All Germans would benefit, and the massive social discontent
that had brought Hitler to power would end. With the conquest of the
USSR, "Judeo-Bolshevism" would be torn out by its roots. As Hitler wrote,
"The end of Jewish rule in Russia will be the end of Russia as a state."[3]

Racism was never simply a way to unite Germans in the search for
votes; it was the vital ingredient of Nazi social and foreign policy. In spite
of the myths of the anti-Semites, the German economy would not have
been significantly different had there never been a German Jewish community. Removing them would not improve the lot of Germans. Economic well-being started with a drastic rearmament program yielding
temporary economic growth and social stability through deficit financing.
When the arms were used, the twin "final solutions," *lebensraum* and
genocide, would bring a permanent resolution. United, armed, and free
of their mortal enemy, the Jews, Nordic Germany would permanently

317

prosper. The war in the east and the Holocaust were inextricably connected in the Nazi mentality.

Until 1937–1938 German rearmament depended heavily upon raw material imports and foreign exchange. Allied suspicions must be lulled and appeasement encouraged. Consequently, until 1937 Hitler compromised. Many Germans, not just SA, were angry that Jews were still among them, some allowed to carry on business as usual. Until the conquest of new land and labor, Hitler's basic constituencies would not benefit. A society of artisans, small businessmen, and peasants could not conquer Russia. Peasants were a drag on the economy; land reform, proposed by Schleicher, Bruening, and the socialists, would alienate the elites. Thus East Elbian landowners still received the largest share of agrarian subsidies and high prices for their grain. Cheap credit, subsidized prices, and technological modernization were offered to small farmers. In recognition of their superior blood, the noble title of *Bauer* was given to those of impeccably Aryan ancestry, their farms declared *Erbhoefe*—land protected from speculators, indebtedness, and high taxes. Nevertheless, throughout the 1930s rural income lagged significantly behind urban wages and salaries, rural indebtedness increased, and farm profits fell. Prices could be raised only by hurting consumers, who were already spending a larger percentage of their income on food than under Weimar. In spite of Conservative and Nazi idealization of rural life, hardship fueled the migration of youth to the cities. The leadership was alarmed; urban life would dilute the life-source of Germanic blood. But more protection for the small, inefficient farmer would perpetuate backwardness, raise food prices, and threaten economic stagnation. As big landowners prospered, dangerous rumblings were heard from the small farmers so crucial to Nazi support. Conquest and free land in the east would eventually still the critics, but they could not be indefinitely postponed.

Nazi policies favored big business from the start. Some 300,000 small businesses collapsed during the 1930s. Small businessmen and artisans, Hitler's loyal voters, were still plagued by competition from large industries and retail outlets, and they complained vociferously. In response, their taxes were reduced, and the government offered grants, subsidies, and orders for goods. Government officials and party members were forbidden to buy in department stores. In 1933 a Law for the Protection of Retail Trade levied special taxes on department stores, forbade them from competing with independent artisans, and prohibited the creation or expansion of department and chain stores. Socialist consumer coops were banned or turned over to the Nazis. Artisan controls and examinations were reestablished. But it was not enough. Artisans protested this sellout of the faithful, but preserving inefficient small businessmen would damage consumers. Party officials impatiently reminded small retailers that consumers were also part of the *Volk*. To his extreme annoyance, Hitler even had to authorize a Reichsbank loan to the very symbol of Jewish department store ownership, the Tietz family, which, nearly bankrupt, had fourteen thousand Gentile employees at risk. Department stores suffered, but their growth rate was only decreased, not halted, and their turnover actually increased. Small retailers were infuriated, grumbling about the failure of the leadership to make good its campaign promises to end "unfair Jewish competition." The regime mollified critics by "Aryanizing" Jewish enterprises, but racial extortion and looting could only favor a few thousand recipients of stolen Jewish property, not enough to preserve the bulk of small retailers from the consequences of economic modernization. Efficiency and mobilization for war, the permanent solution, took priority.

Contrary to racial myths, any immediate or drastic moves against the Jews inevitably hurt Gentiles. Jewish firms had non-Jewish stockholders, supplied Gentile wholesalers, and had thousands of non-Jewish employees as well. The larger the Jewish firm, the more difficult it was to force it out of business without harming non-Jews. Moreover, rearmament required large imports of raw materials, and even foreign Gentiles indifferent to Jews were wary of trading or investing in a nation that willfully canceled the rights of private property. When local party zealots organized unauthorized boycotts, Rudolf Hess admonished them; Jewish businesses could not be abolished outright, and boycotts worsened the already severe shortage of foreign exchange. When the SA boycotted Woolworth stores, for example, Woolworth announced it would no longer import German products. Other firms threatened similar actions.

Many German Jews and non-Jews, too humane and liberal to imagine otherwise, assumed the regime would be rational and abandon the goal of a *Judenrein* Germany. Instead the Nazi leadership merely postponed matters until war freed it from the restraints of international opinion. As Goering said in 1939, "The war provides us with possibilities not available in peace." Until then, Jews were only gradually forced out of the economy. Even then there were complaints: what was the use of kicking out Jewish retail owners if the Gentiles who purchased them still competed on unfair terms? As Boeckel's followers discovered in the 1890s, Christian middlemen behaved no differently than Jews. A few impatient party economic experts pointed out that retailers and artisans would have to accommodate themselves to a modern economy and could not expect to be permanent beneficiaries of state subsidies and artificial regulations. In early 1939 the *Voelkische Beobachter* lectured the *Mittelstand* that they must sacrifice for the good of the *Volk*. Undoubtedly this shocked those who had been told for fifty years they were the *Volk* incarnate, the victims of Jewish machinations and not their own failure to adapt. In the end, the Jews and Slavs of the east would pay for the contradiction between Nazi campaign promises, economic facts, and anti-Semitic myths.

The Nazis silenced the proletariat and destroyed their unions. Industrial profits far outstripped both wages and *Mittelstand* salaries, and workers' wages remained well below even those of the depression. Income distribution favored the well off. The salaried middle class did somewhat better than before, but consumption declined among workers' families. Worker discontent could do little against the army, police, and SS. Yet the Nazis could not create a war machine with millions of German workers permanently opposed, or in a mood to shirk or sabotage. The party needed the proletariat. Rearmament and jobs helped. By 1936 there was a shortage of labor in construction, metal trades, and mining, and the drive for economic self-sufficiency had driven up the demand for labor. The regime prevented workers from forcing wages up, but skilled workers in arms industries were well rewarded. The party also glorified the worker in song and ceremony as an equal comrade in a classless society. The head of the Nazi Labor Front, Robert Ley, declared that once the Jews were removed, all Germans, from corporate head to lowly assembler, would be seen as equal producers for the *Volk*. But the leaders of the Nazi Labor Front were middle class and responsible to party and corporation, not workers. In a less publicized remark, Ley told industrialists, "When the worker knows his employer is a comrade, you can demand anything of him."

Unlike Bruening and Papen, the Nazis would not return to bankrupt liberal economic policies. Hitler feared the potential military power generated by the Bolsheviks' forced industrialization of Russia and believed time was on Stalin's side. Private property and the profit system remained in effect in Germany, of course, but government planning for rebuilding and rearmament was extensive. From 1933 to 1938, heavy industry expanded by about 200 percent while consumer production lagged far behind. Ultimately the wealth and labor of the east would end the disparity. Meanwhile, heavy industry enjoyed the largest profit increases of any sector of the economy, but in return it had to accept Nazi regulation. Under Schacht, bankers, businessmen, and the regime controlled investment, dividends, trade, and export, all to make sure there would be extensive reinvestment and expansion in war-related industries. Consumption was held down, but not so low as to intensify discontent. Controls and tax policies stimulated the growth of heavy industry, the construction of infrastructure, and the manufacture of synthetics for war. Wages, prices, and trade were manipulated to assure war production. By limiting shareholders' dividends, the government forced the reinvestment of undistributed profits into industrial expansion. State funds funneled into growth were steadily increased, providing most of the investment and costs for the arms industry and the production of synthetics. I. G. Farben received vast amounts of labor, steel, and subsidies for its synthetic oil and aviation gas research, Money poured into arms, engines for tanks and trucks, road building, and construction, and special "Mefo Bills" were issued to government contractors to pay for what was needed. Large-scale government investment and deficit financing to stimulate import substitution, synthetic production, and rearmament were keys to economic recovery.

But sooner or later such policies would have to be abandoned or end in war. Like businessmen in consumer and export industries, by 1937 Schacht believed arms production had run its course as a stimulant for the economy. Germany should lessen arms production, end subsidies to inefficient small producers, and produce more consumer goods for the domestic market and products for competitive international export. Hitler abruptly rejected him; he would not return to bankrupt policies in the midst of a global depression, policies that had plunged Germany into chaos in the first place. Accepting Schacht's resignation as economics minister, Hitler allegedly remarked that he had always suspected Schacht was not a real Nazi. Schacht did not understand that arms production was designed to culminate in the conquest of wealth. Declaring "the economy must be converted for war," Goering took over, inaugurating a four-year plan for even greater arms production.

By 1938 German economic growth was well above even 1913. Some 17 percent of Germany's gross national product was used for direct military expenditures, with further vast amounts spent for the production of synthetics and war-related products. In 1933 the budget of the Wehrmacht had been 23 percent of public expenditures; the Nazis immediately doubled it. By 1938 it commanded over 74 percent of a budget itself seven times higher than in 1933. By 1938 the government was the largest investor and consumer in Germany. General Georg Thomas, head of the armed forces economic staff, estimated that 70 percent of the labor force worked on military orders, and that military spending had increased 2,000 percent. In 1938 the turning point was reached. Thomas reported that more arms production would siphon too many workers from the overly restricted civilian economy. Furthermore, assured of government contracts, industrialists were becoming inefficient and wasteful. And the shortage of consumer goods threatened inflation; only wage and price controls prevented it.

A return to economic orthodoxy was out of the question, even if Nazi ideology was not based on war. All sectors of the economy would suffer if exposed to the imperatives of a world market. Worker discontent, especially feared by Hitler, would intensify if competition for international markets led, as it must, to unemployment and lower wages. Extensive arms production and the highly expensive production of synthetics had forced consumption and purchasing power down and created the potential for depression or inflation. And this time there would be no Jews or treaties to blame. By 1938 it was apparent that without war Hitler would have to be another "Hunger Chancellor," like Bruening, or a Franco, using tyranny to protect a small elite in a declining economy. All this would mock the ideological dynamism of the party and force Hitler to crush the true Nazis in his ranks. It was no more possible for the Nazis to return to the economic policies of Weimar than for the Bolsheviks to return to those of the tsar. The Nazi belief in racist and military solutions to social discontent and economic collapse was at stake. Nazism without war was a contradiction in terms. It was time to march.

Unlike Western leaders and most Germans, Hitler was not obsessed by fear of a rerun of 1914–1918 and the murderous stalemate of trench warfare. Instead he promoted the ideas of young officers like Erich von Manstein and Heinz Guiderian. *Blitzkrieg* called for quick breaks in enemy lines by aircraft and shock troop strikes on enemy weak points, followed by swiftly moving armored columns breaking through to sweep into open country without digging in for static defense. The tank would end the superiority of the defense, product of the machine gun and rapid-fire artillery, and total economic mobilization and millions of casualties over years of home-front suffering would not be required. *Blitzkrieg* embraced the Nazi emphasis on will and daring, and would yield the swift conquest of the raw materials and productive facilities of the east.

In November 1937, at a secret meeting with Foreign Minister Constantin von Neurath, War Minister Werner von Blomberg, and the chiefs of the army, navy, and air force, Hitler announced that the regime would enlarge the racial community by conquest in the east. The current economic boom, he added, was based on arms production and could not last; food production could not be increased, and it would be folly to enter into international commercial competition during a time of world depression and high tariffs. The future of Germany depended on conquest of raw materials and land in the east, where there was already a strong Germanic racial core to bind the whole together. The conquest of Austria and Czechoslovakia alone would mean food and supplies for twelve new divisions—if, he added ominously, Germany drove three million people out. The necessary equipment for the armed services was nearly complete; any long delay would render it obsolete and allow Germany's enemies to catch up. The leadership, not just a few Nazis, knew that such a permanent solution to Germany's economic difficulties would require the "removal" of millions of Jews and Slavs to make room for Germans, and the extensive use of slave labor. No objections were raised. Without war, all Nazi efforts, campaign promises, and ideological views made no sense. The violent racism of the Nazi movement was not mere rhetoric on the road to power, nor would Hitler betray his supporters. The primary social policy of the Third Reich was racial war. There would be no more need to return to the unfruitful tinkering of Weimar or the subversion of leftist reforms.

None of this could be revealed prematurely, and indeed until the breakup of Czechoslovakia in the spring of 1939, Western leaders could still assume that Hitler merely wished to correct the inequities of Versailles. In order to mollify them, Hitler kept public silence and ignored what he had written in *Mein Kampf*. But the volkist ideal of racially pure communal settlements for the cultivation of the peasant-warrior were, for Nazi leaders, models for the future. In the vast lands of the conquered east, the great cities would be razed and replaced by SS centers governing networks of Germanic-peasant villages and those Slavic subhumans whose lives would be spared for slave labor. As Himmler said, these "human animals" would live only "in so far as we need them as slaves." Beyond the moral precepts of a dying Judeo-Christian world would emerge a Germanic community of blood commanding a vast reservoir of recruits, raw materials, and foodstuffs for an imperial power second to none.

In 1937 Hitler was ready to pursue the Austrian pan-German vision of his youth to its bloody extreme—the vengeance of the Austro-Germans on the hated Slavs. The iron logic of the ideology of death would complete what the monastic crusading order of the Teutonic Knights had begun. As Hitler had said to Strasser, "Ours is a racial revolution." The Bolsheviks would be destroyed before they could finish equipping themselves with their imitations of the technology of war created by the Germanic peoples. When the east was won, Hitler declared, the blood of the conquerors must not be diluted—the mistake the Spanish had made in their empire. Obviously, the millions of Jews in the east would not survive in a Germanic racial empire. In the event, the murder of the Jews and the leaders of the Slavic peoples, including priests, would come first, then the Judeo-Bolsheviks of the Soviet Union. The "human animals" would be worked to death, shot, or simply starved. There would be no rival nations in the east, no written language but German, and no attempt to Germanize the Slavs.

On March 10, 1938, exactly twenty-eight years after Karl Lueger's death, Hitler ordered the invasion of Austria. Except for the left and the Jews, the Austrians greeted him with great enthusiasm, led by no less a figure than the Cardinal of Vienna, who as a young priest had been a member of the Christian Social movement. We can still see and hear Hitler speaking to his Austrian audience on old newsreels, and his speech, unlike others, reveals in voice and gesture a personal moment of great feeling. Gone are the calculated theatrical poses of the consummate charismatic campaigner. At one point he almost cannot speak because he is overcome by emotion. It is the closest we will ever come to a vision of the man overwhelmed by the passions of the adolescent youth who had finally found his mission. In Linz, the city of his youth, Hitler declared the unity of Germany and Austria.

Freed from the restraints of foreign opinion, Hitler could finally settle accounts with the Jews. Thus the bureaucratic preparations for elimination began. In January 1939 the Jews were required to adopt "Jewish" names. In March the legal status of all Jewish community groups was ended, Jewish property had to be registered, and the police drew up lists of Jews in their precincts and prepared to seize all remaining Jewish property. The Gestapo, Hitler's secret police, prepared lists for mass arrests. In June the great synagogue at Munich, an abomination to the right and the Nazis, was destroyed. Other synagogues went up in flames, and about two thousand Jews were arbitrarily arrested as the SA destroyed Jewish shops. Posters and placards showing dead and tortured Jews were hung throughout Germany and in the new Austrian province of the Reich. In the pogroms of November 1938, including *Kristallnacht*, hundreds of Jewish businesses and synagogues were burnt, Jews were beaten and killed, and somewhere between twenty thousand and thirty thousand Jewish men were sent to concentration camps. It was the beginning of the Final Solution.

22: THE IDEOLOGY OF DEATH

> Look, you can see for yourself. They are not like you and me. They
> do not behave like human beings. They are here to die.
> —Rudolf Hoess, commandant of Auschwitz
>
> I don't feel the slightest stir of pity. That's how it is. . . .
> —Sergeant Felix Landau,
> after helping to shoot hundreds of Jews

THE Holocaust was not simply a consequence of the war. For the Nazis, the destruction of the Jews was itself a war aim of the highest priority. Just as the Nazi revolution was a racial revolution, so also the war was a racial war. In a war to secure the future of the Germanic race, the Jews, symbol of all the humane values the Nazis opposed, could not be allowed to live. The SS began to organize special killing units in 1938, and with army help they killed Jewish and Polish civilians in the first weeks of the war, hanging them in public squares for all to see. As Martin Gilbert has pointed out in his excellent work on the Holocaust, within two weeks noncombatant Jews as well as Poles were murdered in "a hundred towns and villages." Within eight weeks "five thousand Jews were murdered behind the lines."[1] In October 1939 Hitler decreed that Jewish property be distributed among ethnic Germans. As Hans Frank, governor general of eastern Poland, said to his officials in December 1941: "We cannot shoot 2,500,000 Jews, neither can we poison them. We will have to take steps, however, designed to extirpate them in some way—and this will be done."[2] Crematorium ovens were ordered in 1940.

The murder of the Jews could not wait. Despite their small numbers, they had survived centuries of persecution and subverted whole civilizations. Millions of Slavs would also die, but one could safely work them to death and allow millions to live as slave laborers, bereft of independence, literacy, leaders, and cultural memory. By November 1939 the Racial Political Office had plans for the destruction of all Poles except slave laborers and children of Aryan physical type, whom Himmler planned to place in German homes to be reared. To tolerate the pres-

325

ence of any Jews, however, was to risk their ultimate victory. Communists might cease to be communists, homosexuals might quit their behavior, but Jewish blood could never change. In October 1940 the German government of occupied Poland forbade exit visas to Polish Jews, insisting that if they emigrated overseas they would simply have another base from which to subvert Germany.

Even when the Germans were losing the war, materials, transport, and energies were diverted from the front to complete the slaughter of the eternal enemy. In the last two weeks of the war, on the very eve of the surrender of May 8, 1945, Hitler was dead, many army units had surrendered, and all knew the war was lost, yet thousands of Jews were shot, burned to death, or sent on forced death marches to avoid Allied liberators. Truly, as has been said, the Holocaust was the greatest single battle of the war. The day Hitler killed himself, in the final sentence of his Last Testament he wrote: "Above all I charge the leaders of the nation . . . to uphold at all costs the racial laws and the merciless resistance against the world poisoners of all peoples, international Jewry." That was the army the Nazis feared the most.

Racial purification was as necessary to the regime as the conquest of land. As one academic enthusiast exclaimed, the new regime was "biology in action." Even some Germans had to be killed, those deemed "useless mouths" or threats to the racial stock—the mentally ill, carriers of hereditary illnesses, and "asocial types." Homosexuals were high on the list. Himmler called homosexuality "an error of degenerate individualism that is contrary to nature."[3] In 1939 he demanded extermination. An Office for Combating Abortion and Homosexuality was established, but only for Aryans. Lesser peoples should be encouraged to decrease their numbers. If not already named in police or SS files, it was possible for a German homosexual to survive by abstaining or avoiding denunciation.

The Nazi attack on the gay community (though lesbianism was never listed as a crime) was, like all Nazi policies, an extreme version of older attitudes. In the eighteenth century, Prussia had more punitive laws against homosexuals than any Western nation. Long before the Nazis, anti-Semites routinely insisted that homosexuality was the result of degenerate Jewish blood, the "Jewish disease." The penal code of the Second Reich mandated jail for "criminally indecent acts" between males, and only the Social Democrats consistently supported petitions and Reichstag motions to revoke these laws. Marxists believed homosexuality was socially conditioned and should not be penalized. Racial nationalists claimed socialists really wanted to protect the carriers of the "Jewish" disease, though they were embarrassed by some spectacular homosexual scandals at the Hohenzollern and Hapsburg courts. Conservatives noted that the French revolutionaries of 1789 not only liberated Jews but also removed homosexuality as a crime from the French penal code, and the Bolsheviks had abolished tsarist laws against homosexuals. As noted earlier, the most prominent advocate of gay rights in Germany, Dr. Magnus Hirschfield, was severely beaten because he was a defender of homosexuals, a socialist, and a Jew. In May 1933 Hirschfield's Institute for Sexual Research was stormed by the SA; from then on homosexuals were routinely arrested.

Nazi ideologists held that "Jewish" socialists supported homosexual rights in order to destroy the reproductive ability and warrior spirit of the Germanic peoples. Believing the still common notion that homosexuals make bad soldiers, Goebbels argued they were a threat to Germanic blood. The shameless result of promiscuous Weimar culture and its corruption of all sexual norms, homosexuals must be banished or hung. Himmler believed that homosexuality was unknown in rural areas because there German blood was most pure—an idea not based on experience. In the early 1930s he collected the names of "socio-sexual criminals" to be killed because they were a threat to the *Volk*. "We must exterminate these people root and branch."[4] He noted approvingly that the ancient Teutons had drowned homosexuals in bogs.

Since 1945 the myth that homosexuality was common among the Nazis has often been repeated. Hitler unwittingly encouraged the idea by claiming the SA leadership shot in 1934 was riddled with homosexuals, but this was his bid for public approval. There is no evidence that homosexuals were overrepresented in the movement. In accord with a 1933 Law for the Protection of Hereditary Health, the Nazis persecuted, silenced, or imprisoned homosexuals, including those among their party, declaring they "must be entirely eliminated." In 1934 Himmler announced a return to the "Nordic principle that degenerates should be exterminated" for "Germany stands or falls with the purity of its race."[5] If they were caught attempting seduction more than once, death in the camps was the usual outcome. Richard Plant estimates that more than fifty thousand gay men were arrested and convicted, and between five thousand and fifteen thousand perished in the camps. No one was ever punished for these murders, and until very recently no one outside the gay community was concerned about them. After 1945 the German establishment did not consider it worth discussion, and in this it had widespread support among Germans—and, one suspects, not only them.

Gypsies have always been subject to hostile myths and persecuted by both Christians and Moslems. In medieval Europe they were thought to be a race formed by the intermarriage of Jews and non-Jewish vagabonds, a mongrel people sharing responsibility for the death of Christ. Like Jews, Gypsies were shunned as homeless wanderers and possessors of satanic and occult powers. In modern times Gypsies were thought to be racially impure, unnatural kidnapers and disease-carriers, even cannibals. Hunted like game in Eastern Europe, they were often hanged simply because they were Gypsies. But because most were usually poor metal workers, blacksmiths, or producers of costume jewelry, they never attracted the complex of ideological antagonisms used to explain away Jewish success in the modern world.

The Nazis believed that Gypsies would introduce contaminated blood into Aryan racial stock. The Nuremberg Laws state, "In Europe only Jews and Gypsies are of foreign blood." Consequently Gypsies were sterilized in 1934, and in 1939 Heydrich sent Gypsies to Poland. In the occupied territories of the east, the army and local civilian administrators, non-Nazi as well as Nazi, killed Gypsies almost casually, though some of the more "correct" bureaucrats petitioned for permission. Polish Gypsies were shot in the first weeks of the war; the notorious killing squads (*Einsatzgruppen*) and German army units slaughtered them with or without orders, knowing their superiors would approve. Gypsies were killed at Babi Yar and used for medical experiments and slave labor at Auschwitz. By 1942 death was the penalty for anyone known to have Gypsy blood, and even some found serving in the army were sent to the death camps. The policy was approved and supervised by the academics and physicians of the Reich Department of Health. The title of Himmler's office reveals the attitude—Central Office for Fighting the Gypsy Nuisance. Ukrainians, Rumanians, and Croatian fascists (Ustashi) slaughtered Gypsies wholesale, and a well-known Hungarian slogan read, "After the Jews, the Gypsies." In 1942 German diplomats and bureaucrats were told that Himmler had ordered all Gypsies killed; there are no recorded objections. Perhaps a half-million Gypsies died in the Holocaust. No one was ever tried for the murders until 1991. No reparations to Gypsies have ever been paid. No serious international concern has been shown for the Gypsies; they are still persecuted in Rumania, Slovakia, Austria, and Hungary, discriminated against in Germany, and unwelcome everywhere.

In 1933 Jews comprised fewer than 1 percent of the German population, slightly more than a half-million in a nation of just over sixty million. Although 30 percent were in commerce, Jewish bankers and stockbrokers comprised only 2 percent of the total, while 16 percent were lawyers, 10 percent physicians, and 5 percent journalists and writers. Given these numbers, it is obvious they could dominate nothing even if they agreed to try. Such statistics did not deter anti-Semites, of course, who refused to believe them or spoke of the mysterious power of so few Jews to control so much.

Once the Nazis were in power, the rest followed from the logic of their ideology and their victories in the east. There is no need to look for a specific time of decision for the Holocaust, nor to write as if all depended on Hitler. Until 1938 the officially stated policy of the Nazis was forced emigration without property, but the regime knew no nation would accept hundreds of thousands of impoverished Jews, let alone millions of eastern Jews. The regime did not want the West to know of its ultimate plans for the "resolution" of the Jewish problem, anymore than it wished to discuss publicly the true goals of its foreign policy. To do either endangered both. The German Foreign Office, not the Nazis, first proposed shipping the Jews to Madagascar, then a French colony off the coast of Africa. Madagascar was to be turned over to Himmler and the SS for this purpose after the defeat of France. But first England would have to be defeated, because during wartime the British fleet would likely prevent any huge resettlement by stopping German ships. Hence the plan was forgotten when the invasion of England was postponed and the east was available. Some assume the Madagascar proposal indicates the Nazis did not at first plan mass murder, but there is no reason to assume the SS would have behaved any differently in Madagascar than in the death camps. Moreover, the Madagascar plan was a familiar idea to nineteenth-century anti-Semites, who had suggested that European Jewry be shipped there and pay for the privilege. Once there, according to pre-Nazi anti-Semites, they were to be surrounded with naval forces to prevent escape; some suggested that any Jews found in Europe afterward be shot; others wanted yellow fever introduced to hasten their demise. In a news conference in February 1939, Rosenberg suggested the Jews be sent there, and in a news conference that summer, not secret, said that in the "wild island" with its "deadly climate" . . . "the obnoxious Jewish race will find itself isolated in a reservation . . . from where there is but one exit—death."[6]

Too much has been made of the Nazi encouragement of Zionists during the prewar years. Hitler never desired an independent Israel; he did not want international Jewry to have a national base. The Nazis, like prewar anti-Semites, held that in Palestine the Jews would exploit the Arabs, and, incapable of building a nation, would continue their international commercial domination and subversion. Eichmann worked with Zionists for a brief time, but, as he said, "The policy of the Reich is . . . to hinder the development of a Jewish state in Palestine."[7] In 1937 Eichmann declared it wrong to place Jews in nations abroad, although until 1940 German and Austrian Jews were pressured to emigrate. But as Hitler said to the mufti of Jerusalem in November 1941, "The objectives of my fight are clear. Primarily I am fighting the Jews without respite, and this fight includes the fight against the so-called Jewish home in Palestine."[8]

Hitler's moves toward war and his Jewish policies were inextricably connected. In 1936 he made economic sabotage a war crime punishable by death and held the Jewish community collectively responsible for such crimes. After rearmament and his march into the Rhineland, Hitler knew that Western leaders would not risk war over actions seemingly meant only to redress what was generally regarded as a vengeful treaty. The French huddled behind the Maginot Line, making it clear they would not fight to save their allies in the east. In November 1937 Hitler instructed his military and foreign policy officials to plan for the conquest of *lebensraum*. When Hitler invaded Austria in March 1938, the League of Nations did not even meet to consider condemning Germany. Austrians brutalized the Jews of Vienna to such an extent that the occupying Germans had to restrain mobs of civilians. Although Austrian leftists and many older Catholics did not wish to merge with Germany, Hitler did not invade a free Austria, he invaded a fascist Austria ruled by the heirs of Lueger and threatened by those of Schoenerer. The government of the Christian Social party was as anti-Semitic as the Nazis. Lueger's Catholic anti-Semitism seems to have had the same terrible potential as the secular racism of the Nazis. As the Bishop of Linz wrote in a pastoral letter about "degenerate Judaism" in 1932: "It is not only the undisputed right, but the strict and conscientious duty of every devout Christian to fight the harmful influence of Judaism, and it is much to be desired that the dangers and damages arising from the Jewish spirit should be ever more strongly combated by the Aryan and Christian side."[9] Austria was far too weak to conquer the Slavs and murder the Jews of the east, but given the chance, thousands eagerly helped to do both.

Step by step, the war against the Jews accompanied military aggression. Two weeks after Austria was invaded, the government made it clear there would be no Jewish community in Germany. Eighty percent of the forty thousand Jewish businesses still existing, once deemed necessary for re-armament or essential services, were liquidated. After July 1938 no credit was extended to Jewish businessmen. Gentiles and bankers eagerly competed to buy out Jewish enterprises at extortionate rates, often blackmailing Jewish businessmen with the threat of outright expropriation. Jewish welfare agencies were shut down, and many Jews arrested for minor offenses, even traffic violations, were sent to prison or the camps. Goering and Martin Bormann, chief of staff to deputy *Fuehrer* Rudolf Hess, assured their impatient followers that the regime was about to "settle accounts with the Jews," and many were publicly taunted with their forthcoming fate. "Perish Judah" rang throughout Germany and Austria.

In May 1938 Hitler told his generals he would soon smash Czechoslovakia. As he had predicted, in September at Munich the West showed him they would not try to save the Czechs. In the same year the West also showed it would do nothing to save the Jews. The terrible scenes of the beating and humiliation of Jews in Vienna had been widely reported in the international press and in newsreels. William L. Shirer had described Vienna at *Anschluss* as an anti-Semitic "orgy of sadism" worse than anything he had seen in Berlin. Consequently President Franklin Roosevelt called for the Evian Conference to discuss ways to help the Jews. Although he was annoyed at this interference, Hitler offered "his" Jews to the international community. He knew the offer would be refused. Before the conference, as Hitler was aware, the U.S. State Department, with the approval of Congress, failed to follow even existing U.S. law and approve sufficient visa applicants to fill the already established quota for Germany. Moreover, assurances had been given by the United States to the other powers that they would not be forced to accept tens of thousands of Jews. In fact, FDR called the conference as a substitute for action. He feared he would risk his popularity if he accepted Jewish refugees. He was probably right. At Evian the Germans duly offered the Jews to the assembled thirty-two nations; only the Dominican Republic and later Costa Rica increased their quotas. International opinion smirked at the hypocritical posturing of the Anglo-Americans. Goebbels exulted. Had he not known all along that no civilized nation would accept the accursed race? Indeed, Poland, Hungary, and Rumania requested they too be relieved of their Jews! As a German newspaper commented, "One likes to pity the Jews as long as one can use this pity for a wicked agitation against Germany, but no state is prepared" to accept "a few thousand Jews. Thus the conference serves to justify Germany's policy against Jewry." [10] Jewish property could be stolen; Jews could be beaten and killed. There would be little but talk, and not much of that.

By early 1938 Hitler forced the resignation of Generals Fritsch and Blomberg to assure Nazi control of the army. In March he demanded the Sudetenland from the Czechs. Ready to march, he allowed the SA to escalate violence against the Jewish community. In the summer of 1938 synagogues were burned and more Jews were beaten and killed. Two thousand Jews were sent to the camps. In July a Belgian newspaper reported, "What is going on now in Greater Germany is the systematic extinction of a given race, a sort of biological war of extermination. . . ." [11] But the Nazi leaders and their conservative allies were still wary of unsanctioned violence. Goering told the SA to hold back; stronger measures were being prepared.

On November 9 a Jewish youth, Herschel Grynszpan, bitter at the cruel treatment of his parents when the government drove out Polish Jews residing in Germany, assassinated a German official in Paris. November 9 was the anniversary of the Munich *putsch*; it was an opportunity not to be ignored. Goebbels and Hitler agreed there should be a short, violent attack on the Jewish community. On the night of November 9, 1938, *Kristallnacht*, the night of broken glass—so called because of the shards of glass from Jewish shop windows lying in the streets—close to 200 synagogues and 7,000 Jewish businesses were destroyed, and some 200 Jews were murdered. The SS arrested about 35,000 Jews and sent them to concentration camps, where about a thousand died within three months. Although presented as a spontaneous outburst of ordinary Germans outraged at the assassination, *Kristallnacht* was party controlled. There was extensive looting by civilians but no attempt to create mass rioting. The Nazis and their conservative allies still wanted the punishment of the Jews to be legal, orderly, and final. In Hitler's words:

> Anti-Semitism based on purely emotional grounds will always find its ultimate expression in the form of pogroms. A rational anti-Semitism, however, must lead to the systematic legal fight against and the elimination of the prerogatives which he alone possesses in contradistinction to all other aliens living among us. . . . Its ultimate goal, however, must unalterably be the elimination of the Jews altogether.[12]

Two days later, top Nazi leaders and representatives of different ministries met to consider the next steps. Ribbentrop and Minister of Economics Walter Funk feared an international boycott. Goering believed the American government, which he assumed to be Jewish-dominated, would seize German assets, and he was upset that German overseas investments were not withdrawn before the pogrom. He was also angry with the destruction of property, shouting at Reinhard Heydrich, chief of the security service (SD), "I wish you had killed two hundred Jews instead of destroying such valuables!" Heydrich replied apologetically (and with an underestimate), "Well, there were thirty-five killed."[13] Goering complained that *Kristallnacht* would cost valuable foreign exchange because the insurance companies had reinsured abroad. Ironically, the insurers had to inform Goering that most of the damaged businesses were Aryan-owned and only rented by Jews. Moreover, German insurance companies would have to pay the Belgian glass industry for half its total yearly production just to pay for the broken windows. And most of the looted or destroyed goods were not Jewish-owned but had been taken on consignment from Gentile suppliers. Insurers were obligated to pay for these as well. The government also stood to lose many thousands of marks in taxes by business loss write-offs. Goering plaintively asked if there were some way to retrieve the looted goods for the government, but there was none. Evidently only the government, the banks, and selected German businessmen should be allowed to loot the Jews, not ordinary Germans. Goering sought a legal way to enable the insurance companies to avoid compensating Jews. Insurance companies, though they wanted the money extorted from Jews, would have to pay Gentiles, but they would not have to compensate Jews. The Jews themselves would have to make good the damage, paying an "atonement fine" of one billion marks, about a fifth of all German Jewish holdings.

Kristallnacht solved nothing. The leadership wanted a legal and truly "final solution" to solve the "Jewish Question" once and for all time. At the post-*Kristallnacht* meeting, Goering announced that Hitler had written a letter stating, "From now on the Jewish question must be treated . . . with a view to a final resolution." Goebbels ordered an end to pogroms: "The final reply to the Jewish outrage in Paris will be given by legal means, i.e., by decree."[14] Three days later Bormann chaired a committee of representatives of the Foreign Office, the Economics Ministry, and party leaders to decide how to remove the Jews from the economy by legislation. The committee decided to speed up the Aryanization of Jewish property, block Jewish capital from moving abroad, and complete the takeover of all Jewish businesses and investments. No Jew should be a member of a business corporation. Once again, the Austrians were ahead. They already had a plan, they merely requested a decree. All necessary decrees were issued the same day, including one forbidding Jews to claim any damages from pogroms. All measures were to take effect January 1, 1939. In Hitler's mind this was the year hostilities would commence.

Step by step the logic of the Ideology of Death unfolded. In their meeting after *Kristallnacht*, Goering, Goebbels, Heydrich, and various non-Nazi bureaucrats considered the fate of the Jews: How can we continue to allow Jews to attend schools or enjoy public parks and places alongside Germans? Why are Jews allowed to own cars, take up space on public transport, or inhabit dwellings with Aryans? Should we not ban the Jews from major cities, deny them valuable hospital space, bar them from good neighborhoods, spas, theatres, film houses, art exhibitions, parks, or restaurants? Why should any Jew live as well as the poorest Aryan, let alone have a better-paying job? Someone suggested limiting Jews to subsistence wages; naturally, forced labor was mentioned; and again, quite naturally, the discussion turned to the creation of ghettos or camps. After all, concentration camps already held thousands of Jews, and eastern territories would soon be available. Mass murder was the obvious, indeed the only "final solution." Many leaders and scientists were already discussing the means to do so, including gassing, as Colonel Victor Brack of the SS, who helped supervise concentration camps, testified after the war.

Shortly thereafter, Jews were excluded from schools and universities, concerts, public baths, theatres, restaurants, sports facilities, and museums, and forbidden to own telephones, radios, automobiles, or precious metals. They were forced to move into special "Jewish houses." Ominously, murdering a Jew was in itself no longer a serious crime. After

Kristallnacht, SA members were punished for theft, a violation of their personal code of honor, and rape was punished as a violation of the laws against interracial intercourse. One man was punished for killing two Jews when ordered not to; another was lightly punished for killing after Hitler had ordered the action halted. But twenty-four SA members who had killed Jews were only reprimanded, and the court itself requested of Hitler that no further action be taken.

In 1927 Hitler had called for the death of "unhealthy racial elements," and in 1933 the Ministry of Justice had proposed death for incurable patients. The regime had dropped the ministry's proposal because of church objections. As a temporary substitute, some 375,000 persons were sterilized. The victims included the feebleminded and mentally ill, carriers of "hereditary" diseases, alcoholics, rapists, homosexuals, tuberculosis patients, dwarfs, epileptics, and even delinquents and others guilty of "antisocial behavior." Sterilization at the time was public policy in fourteen of the United States, and ultimately claimed some sixty thousand victims from the mentally ill, the feebleminded, and criminals. But only in Germany was the phrase "the racially undesirable" used to describe potential victims. Moreover, in Germany there was never a distinction between the sterilization and euthanasia programs. For the regime and the thousands of participating judges, physicians, psychiatrists, health workers, and university-trained "racial hygienists" who worked to remove "useless mouths" and "diseased grafts" from the racial stock, sterilization was a prelude to euthanasia, euthanasia a prelude to genocide. In September 1939 war ended compromise; "useless mouths" and "social and racial undesirables" were slated for death by euthanasia.

Since 1937 German physicians and psychiatrists had prepared for euthanasia. With the invasion of Poland and the start of the war in September 1939, Hitler ordered the murders to start. By December 1939 murders were carried out in asylums, hospitals, and nursing homes. Schoolchildren were given cost-benefit problems to analyze the price of keeping alive those who were a social burden. Never simply "mercy killings," as the West understands euthanasia, the program was meant to purify the race of undesirable "blood" regardless of the disease or will of the victims. To facilitate matters, in October 1939 physicians filled out forms describing the mental and physical disabilities of each of their patients residing in long-term care facilities. Most significant, the form asked the patient's race as well.[15] The way was open for killing Jews regardless of their mental or physical health. By the summer of 1940 Jewish psychiatric patients were being gassed; "in early 1941" the Ministry of the Interior ordered all hospitalized Jews to be killed, "not because they met the criteria for euthanasia but because they were Jews."[16]

In May 1939 a program to kill retarded or disabled infants was established, and the killings began one month before the war. Physicians and midwives made the selections. Five thousand children were eventually murdered. Dr. Hermann Pfannmueller, one of the killers, "did not hide the fact that among the children murdered . . . were also children who were not mentally ill, namely children of Jewish parents."[17] After all, the most respected German genetics textbook of the 1920s repeated the old notion that certain crimes were the result of inherited Jewish traits, and distorted statistics "proved" the criminal rate highest among Jews. Consequently, "To be Jewish was to be both sick and criminal; Nazi medical science and policy united to help 'solve' this problem."[18] The judiciary cooperated.

In the fall of 1939 six special killing centers were prepared in Germany. At first medical personnel gave fatal injections. The first collective gassing, by carbon monoxide, occurred in December 1939 at the Brandenburg Killing Center. Bottled gas was used, and contracts were let for the development of gas vans. The bodies were cremated. Showers were used to prevent "difficulties." Gassing patients was called the "definitive solution." The euphemism did not fool the public, who soon knew of the killings, but it enabled health personnel to pretend they were not simply murderers. After the invasion of Poland, the children of Polish, Jewish, and Gypsy slave laborers in Germany were routinely killed, as well as healthy Jewish children. By 1940 some hospitals and long-term care institutions in Germany accepted only Aryans as patients, sending Jewish patients on to the killing centers without worrying about disabilities. Soon healthy Jewish and Gypsy children were routinely killed, as were orphans and inmates of juvenile homes. By August 1941 the program was allegedly ended, though "some 1,200 Jewish slave laborers" were certified insane and gassed at a euthanasia institute near Berlin.[19] By then perhaps 70,000 to 90,000 German hospital patients, among them an undetermined number of Jews, had been shot, fatally injected, or gassed, though some estimate the total victims of euthanasia as high as 275,000. The statistics mean little, for all murders of innocents were seen by the regime as hygienic measures to purify the race or, as Himmler put it, to dispose of "human garbage." As the death camps opened in the east, hundreds of health personnel from the euthanasia program were sent to give technical advice, another sign that few saw any great distinction between the two programs. Dr. Walter Gross, head of the Race Policy Bureau, who had wanted Jews sterilized and had avidly supported euthanasia before the war, publicly announced in March 1941: The definitive solution must comprise the "removal of Jews from Europe."[20] By then he was helping to organize the bureaucracy for mass murder in the camps.

After 1937 Hitler's military and civilian elite knew the war in the east would be a race war "without mercy." Given the killing centers in Germany and their selection methods, it seems inconceivable that anyone should have thought the millions of Jews who dwelled in lands destined for the purified Germanic *Volk* would be allowed to live. And all knew after Evian that foreign governments would never accept millions of impoverished eastern Jews, even if the Nazis wanted them to. Hence the move to war and the Holocaust continued on parallel tracks. Dismantling Czechoslovakia in March 1939, Hitler demonstrated conclusively that he sought an empire in the east, not simply the redress of Versailles. With the Nazi-Soviet pact in August 1939, the road to the east was open. War and the destruction of the Jews were both dictated by the logic of Nazi ideology, and both were consistently implemented from the mid-1930s on. Halfway measures would not resolve economic or racial "problems." Long before Hitler, millions had blamed the Jews for the social ills of Germany; once their racism brought them victory, the Nazis could regard the destruction of the Jews as an historic mandate.

By 1939 there were some 300,000 Jews left in Germany, unemployed and destitute; millions waited in the east. In the midst of a savage war for a racial empire, how could those believed to be the most dangerous racial enemy be allowed to survive? On January 30, 1939, Hitler made his famous, public, internationally publicized, and crystal-clear prophecy: "If international finance Jewry inside and outside of Europe should succeed once more in plunging nations into another world war, the consequence will not be the Bolshevization of the earth and thereby the victory of Jewry, but the annihilation of the Jewish race in Europe." Almost every book and film on the Nazis repeats these words, yet many still do not believe the decision to destroy the Jews was made long before the summer of 1941.

With the invasion of Poland, Goering ordered the exploitation of the eastern territories, and plans were drawn for the seizure of Polish and Jewish properties for resettled Germans. In September 1939 resettlement, concentration camps, and the killing squads were put under Himmler's authority, as Reichs commissar for the "Strengthening of the Germanic Volk." In the same month his deputy Heydrich and General Otto Wagener of the high command agreed that Polish Jews, clergy, intelligentsia, and nobles must be destroyed. Heydrich told the commanders of several operational groups in Poland that the first killings were simply the beginning of the total destruction of Jewry. Shortly thereafter, some of the equipment and personnel of the killing centers of Germany were readied for transfer to the future death camps. The notorious *Einsatzgruppen*, units that eventually shot some two million Jews, were being organized; one was trained before the invasion of Poland. In the first five months of the war, thousands of Jews were murdered and their property confiscated, as were thousands of Polish leaders and intellectuals, and hundreds of Polish priests who together might lead a revived Poland. All knew the Polish Catholic church was an historical ally of Polish national liberation movements. Ethnic Germans, the advance guard of the expected millions of settlers, helped kill and loot. The army and the SS discussed mass killing techniques, and half the area of German-conquered Poland was designated as the place for the Final Solution. By then at least thirty thousand Polish Jews had been murdered.

In the fall of 1939 appropriate personnel were told of the decision to move the Jews of Poland into ghettos; in winter the earliest ghettos appeared. In November 1939 expulsions began, and in December the first trains rolled. The ghettos were not to be permanent; they were holding stations until the camps were ready. The Jews of Poland were doomed even if the Soviet Union had never been invaded. The administrator in charge of organizing ghettos in the part of Poland including Lodz said in December 1939: "The creation of the ghetto is, of course, only a transition measure. . . . In any event the final goal must be that we ceaselessly burn out this plague boil."[21]

In February 1940 a German newspaper wrote that the ghettoization of European Jewry was the "purest *temporary* solution to the Jewish question anywhere in Europe."[22] Until the death camps were ready, hunger, disease, and murder in the ghettos and the mass shootings of the *Einsatzgruppen* continued. In 1940 Jews in Poland were worked to death in local camps. In the spring of that year the first ghetto, Lodz, was sealed. Jews worked and died there while ever larger numbers were sent to overburdened death camps whose commandants complained of a lack of sufficient facilities. In 1939 Jewish children were starving to death in the ghettos. By the end of 1939 there were 50 to 70 deaths per day in the Warsaw Ghetto, and by March 1942 some 5,000 people a month died there. Before the invasion of Yugoslavia in April 1941, *Einsatzgruppen* were organized to kill all Germany's enemies; Jews were included whether they acted like enemies or not. In 1941 thousands of Jewish men in Serbia were shot; in the spring of 1942 gas vans killed their women and children. SS and some army units murdered Jews in the Baltic states and White Russia as soon as they found them; by October 1941 some 120,000 Jews had been murdered there. More than 230,000 were murdered in Lithuania between July and November 1941, and at least 20,000 in Russia. In December 1941 gassing began in Chelmno, Poland; soon the police in the village were saying, "One day / one thousand."[23] In the spring of 1941 mass deportations commenced from Austria; in the fall, from Germany. In October 1941 Hitler said the ultimate purpose of sending the Jews east was to exterminate them as punishment for their crimes. In December, Hans Frank, governor general of Poland, declared that "we must annihilate the Jews wherever we encounter them." By October 1941 all the Jews of Estonia were dead, as were all male Jews in Serbia.

In the Berlin suburb of Wannsee, a conference was held in January 1942. Heydrich wished to clarify bureaucratic arrangements for the destruction of the Jews, and to make sure the attending bureaucrats and ministers knew that he and Himmler were in charge of the Final Solution. The Foreign Office representative at the conference, who aggressively helped plan the murder of the Jews, proudly boasted that the "Jewish problem" in Serbia was the first to be solved. An officer of a Baltic killing unit replied that Estonia was actually the first nation to have that honor. Heydrich told attending officials that no Jews who survived forced labor in the east could live, because they "represent a natural selection . . . of the toughest" and would become the "germ cell of a new Jewish reconstruction." The eventual murder of eleven million Jews was discussed, a number including those from all areas to be conquered, England as well. No voices were raised against the plan, but there was disagreement about how much "Jewish blood" qualified one for death.

Millions of propaganda leaflets were dropped by the German air force on the Baltic nations and the western USSR to encourage local support for the killings. Germans, the leaflets read, attacked the "Jewish-Communist government" and the "criminal machinations of the Jewish clique," and hoped to "liberate all the peoples of the Soviet Union from the Communist yoke, the cursed Jew . . ." and "Jewish Communism." Many Soviets needed no encouragement: thousands of Jews were killed by Estonians, Latvians, Lithuanians, Croatians, Hungarians, Ukrainians, White Russians, and Rumanians. As soon as the Germans crossed the border into the Soviet Union, Rumanians shot, bayoneted, tortured, or starved and worked thousands of Rumanian Jews to death, and Rumanian and Hungarian troops, part of the invading force, also killed "Judeo-Bolsheviks."

In Odessa the Rumanians tortured and raped Jews before murdering them, and it has been said even the SS was shocked. But it seems unlikely. Himmler often insisted the Germans sought the most humane way to destroy the Jews, and we are told the death camps were needed in part because the morale of the killers suffered from direct killing in the field. But in fact there is no imaginable horror that was not committed by the SS or the regular army: Jews were drowned in urine, strangled in pools of excrement, forced to dance and then shot. Soldiers competed to see who could throw infants the farthest; children were burned to death and killed in front of their mothers; women were tortured before they were killed, and untold thousands were deliberately buried alive. In one instance German soldiers castrated men and then beat them to death. The German war gave many violent anti-Semites of Eastern Europe the opportunity to massacre the Jews, though millions of them, like millions of Germans, disapproved of the killings. Perhaps the only difference between the German and Eastern European killers was that fewer of the latter saw any world historical significance to their vicious activities, and stopped the murders, as the Germans did not, when they realized the war was lost.

Nevertheless, mass gassing in the camps was supposed to be a legal, systematic, and controlled action, removed from individual brutality, a function and extension of the ideology of race and the consummation of the war. Such high-minded ideological distance was violated more often than not, of course, but it did exist; paradoxically, it was the ultimate denial of humanity, a sickening parody of moral values. Many have commented on the perversity of Himmler for punishing SS troopers who stole the personal effects of those they murdered. But Himmler's attitude was consistent with the myths of the anti-Semites. The Jews, evil by blood, must be disposed of by legal and bureaucratic measures, so that this necessary and noble historical cause would not be sullied by mere selfishness and personal vengeance. Consequently, any SS man caught stealing anything but life from his victims risked punishment. As Himmler said, "We have the right to annihilate this people which wanted to annihilate us," but "We don't want in the end, just because we exterminated a germ, to be infected. . . ."[24]

By law, all Jewish property was to be sent to the Reichsbank or other bureaucratic or private institutions for legal disposal by judges, bankers, and lawyers. Camp personnel were taught that the destruction of the Jews was an historical imperative to destroy a race which, down to the last infant, was the blood enemy of the Germanic peoples and of all civilization. SS guards felt inferior to front-line troops but were constantly reminded of their high ideological purpose by Nazi intellectuals, academics, and "racial experts" who provided appropriate lectures and readings. Streicher's *Der Stuermer* was posted in the living quarters of camp guards, and they were repeatedly told they were valuable soldiers, not common murderers, in the crusade against Germany's most dangerous enemy. Visiting the *Einsatzgruppen*, Himmler told them any guilt they felt was because their conscience had been distorted by centuries of Judeo-Christian ethics, but future generations would praise their great sacrifice in cleansing Europe of this plague. If, as is said, Himmler vomited when he witnessed some shootings, and was splattered with brains, that too is consistent. Some of the worst of the bureaucratic SS and army commanders who killed often thought themselves to be "good family men," above personal viciousness. Undoubtedly many were. For that very reason they were corrupt to the core, terrible evidence of the historical power of the ideology of death among the Germans.

As the war turned against them, Nazi propagandists added new charges to the litany of anti-Semitism. International Jewry was held responsible for the Allied "terror raids." If Germany loses, the public was told, the Jews will annihilate us. They have always known they are in a racial war to the death, and now they have the armed might of the Jew-dominated Allies on their side. Everywhere the valiant German troops have fought, the Jews act as partisans, spies, saboteurs, and assassins behind the lines, enemies to the death of the Reich and all public order. Goebbels told the public that Russian troops were followed by Jewish death squads ready to slaughter all Germans. That was why, army officers declared, it was perfectly appropriate to shoot any Jew as hostage, whether caught in specific anti-German activities or not. Soldiers were told not to give way to the temptation of "Jewish humanitarianism," for the Jews themselves were the original historical murderers of innocents—"ritual murder" materials were sent to SS and army officers and distributed to the troops. To kill any Jew, armed or unarmed, man, woman, or child, was a hygienic measure, a necessary defense of all higher life, a blow at the eternal racial enemy of Christian-Germanic civilization. With some notable exceptions—black Allied troops in the west, many Russians in the east—the Germans allowed enemy soldiers to surrender, for they were not racial enemies. But not even a Jewish infant could be allowed this privilege; by definition no Jew at any age could be innocent. Their guilt was in their blood.

Paradoxically, a sincere anti-Semite frustrates the moral judgment of the liberal and humane mind. We still find it impossible to believe such deeds can be done with a clear conscience, and we seek arcane psychological explanations rather than accept the power of historical anti-Semitism among the Germans. Yet their very sincerity justifies the most extreme punishment for those who murdered in the service of anti-Semitic myths. Precisely because they are not monsters, murderers of good conscience are worse than those who slaughter from some grisly psychological drive. Nor will it do to think of the SS as psychotic killers. The vast majority of psychotics are harmless to others, less violent as a group than the normal population; their demons are within them, their victims are usually themselves. In our disgust at the work of the Nazis and the millions of Germans who believed them, we cannot even discount the youthful idealism often invested in the Nazi movement. Many have noted with puzzled horror the oft-found combination of murder and bourgeois morality, yet it is exactly what one would expect given the dreadful force of anti-Semitic myths among the Germans.

As the Red army approached Hungary in the summer of 1944, the Germans rushed to transport and kill all Hungarian Jews. This "waste" of German military resources has persuaded many that the Nazis were irrational. For the Nazis, however, the resources were not wasted. Either the Germans or the Jews would survive the war, not both. If the Jews survived, the war was truly lost and Germany doomed; if the Jews were destroyed and Germany defeated, Germany might rise again. The Jew and the armed enemy were one and the same. In 1944 the propaganda ministry spoke of Jewish plutocrats driving on the armies in the west while Jewish Bolsheviks smashed in from the east. Miklós Horthy, a vicious anti-Semite who had ordered the killing of innocent Jewish civilians in the counterrevolution of 1919, tried to prevent his German ally from killing Hungarian Jews when he knew the war was lost, hoping to curry favor with the Allies. Even the Rumanian sadists and killers changed sides as the Russians approached.

But German units kept on killing to the end, as Martin Gilbert has pointed out in his thorough history of the war. As American forces approached Mauthausen on May 5, 1945, three days before the formal German surrender, thirty thousand prisoners were ordered into a tunnel at Ebensee to be murdered with explosives. They refused, and the guards, fearing retribution, gave way. The Gestapo ordered the blowing up of Buchenwald and its inmates, but the guards had fled. An inmate answered the phone and reported it had already been done. A thousand Jews from Buchenwald were shot on April 27, 1945, at Marienbad. On May 3 Hitler Youth and German marines shot five hundred Jews who were trying to get ashore from a boat in Luebeck harbor. On April 5 more than five thousand Jews from Auschwitz were burned to death by Hitler Youth and ordinary police from the town of Gardelegen, who forced them into a barn, poured on gasoline, and watched as they screamed in the raging inferno. Those who ran out were shot.[25] As Lucy Dawidowicz has said, it *was* a war against the Jews.

Hans Huetig, former commandant at Buchenwald, told an interviewer from his comfortable retirement in 1986: "Today it seems so cruel, inhuman, and immoral. It did not seem immoral to me then: I knew very well what I was going to do in the SS. We all knew. It was something in the soul, not the mind. We all knew what we were going to do in the SS. When it comes down to it, it is a very simple story. I was a Nazi."[26]

23: COMPLICITIES

In the future they will say: As characterless as a German official, as
Godless as a Protestant minister, as unprincipled as a Prussian officer.

—Ewald von Kleist-Schmenzin

THE murder of millions in five years needed the voluntary complicity of
tens of thousands. Public and private institutions participated directly
or indirectly in the oppression and killings: army, police, civil service, Foreign Office, railroads, postal services, utilities, bureaucrats, corporations,
bankers, lawyers, judges, physicians, and scientists. Careerism, fear, and
traditional obedience were motives, but it is wrong to ignore a simple
truth: the culture of anti-Semitism that thrust the Nazis to power also encouraged voluntary cooperation in the destruction of the Jews.

Elsewhere, powerful countervailing forces held anti-Semitism in check.
In France, support for the republican tradition was strong; only defeat
propelled the reactionary racists of Vichy to power. In Italy, despite fascism, comparatively few freely cooperated with the German killers. The
land of Renaissance humanism and commerce could scarcely regard Jews
as a corrupt symbol of urbanism and commerce. Having escaped the Reformation and religious wars, Italy's historic greatness resided in the multiethnic Roman Empire, not a mythical volkist past. And Italy was united
by liberals, not rightest militarists. Thus the Italian right included Jewish
intellectuals and politicians, and Jews held important positions in the
army and in the early fascist movement. Mussolini regarded anti-Semitism as the "German disease," though he cooperated with the Nazis in
1938. Some 80 percent of Italy's Jews survived, and none were handed
over while Italy was still sovereign; Vichy France did so voluntarily. In
their occupation zones in France and the Balkans, Italian bureaucrats
and army officers protected thousands of Jews, even against orders from
Mussolini.

In contrast, thousands of senior and junior German army officers cooperated with or took part in racial murder, many from ideological conviction. The commander in chief, Walter von Brauchitsch, insisted in

342

1939 that the army must not be "surpassed by anyone in the purity and conviction of its National Socialist *Weltanschauung*."¹ As German troops stormed toward Warsaw, General Wagener declared there must be a "cleanup once and for all" of "Jews, intelligentsia, clergy, nobility."² Army and SS units killed Jewish civilians in Poland from the start. In his study *The Eastern Front*, Omer Bartov shows that many officers murdered Jewish noncombatants on their own initiative. In 1939 a high command leaflet to all officers called the war a "struggle against World Judaism," to be fought like a "poisonous parasite."³ In 1940 it notified the troops, "Everything in the world which is Jewish . . . is identified by its hatred of Greater Germany"; the war was the "decisive battle between the totalitarian, racially defined *Weltanschauungen* and the aspirations of the Jewish World-democracy."⁴ In the summer of 1941, commanders of the *Einsatzkommandos*, who ultimately murdered about two million Jews, reported they were "pleasantly surprised" that the military went out of its way to help.⁵ There were, of course, officers who detested the Nazis, but they rarely intervened and were too few to influence events. Describing Bolsheviks, the high command sounded no different from the Nazis: "We would insult the animals if we were to describe these men, who are mostly Jewish, as beasts. They are the embodiment of a satanic and insane hatred against the whole of noble humanity."⁶

In Yugoslavia armed resistance began with the invasion of April 1941; hostages were massacred and villages destroyed with little regard to guilt or innocence. General Boehme demanded ruthless countermeasures against civilians, including women and children, whether they were resisters or not. An Austrian, he justified this by referring to the Serb "betrayal" of Germans in 1914. His army units shot suspected communists and nationalists as hostages, and included all Jews regardless of political allegiance. When some soldiers even shot friendly Serbs, the high command ordered that only "known enemies" of the regime be shot, defining "known enemies" as democrats, communists, Serb nationalists, and "all Jews."⁷ When the army ran out of Jews, they shot Gypsies. The SS, German occupation police, and local fascists carried out most of the mobile van killings by gas, but army units helped.

Wherever the German armies went, their officers recruited local anti-Semites to help them kill. On the eve of the invasion of Russia, the high command ordered ruthless measures against "Judeo-bolshevism." Anti-Semitic slogans were circulated throughout the army. In 1942 all officers were instructed that:

> Every officer must be filled with the conviction that it is first of all the influence of the Jews which hinders the German people from realizing its claims for living space and status in the world and forces our

people for the second time to turn against a world of enemies with the blood of our best sons. Therefore the officer must have an unambiguous, completely uncompromising position regarding the Jewish question. There is no difference between so-called decent Jews and others.[8]

Such ideas were spread among the troops with films, radio talks, pamphlets, traveling libraries, and lectures from officers and academics. In November 1941 General Erich von Manstein issued an order of the day: the German soldier must understand "the necessity of a severe but just revenge on sub-human Jewry." Thousands of Jews were slaughtered by army units in the next weeks.[9] As Field Marshal Walther von Reichenau said, "The soldier in the east . . . is the carrier of an inexorable racial concept, and the avenger of all the bestialities inflicted upon the Germans. . . ."[10] He ordered extermination, and 25,000 Jews were burned or shot to death by German and Rumanian soldiers in Odessa. Bartov writes that soldiers in need of morale-boosting after severe battle stress were told the Russians fought with such barbaric intensity because they were driven by a "conscious Jewish-Marxist intelligentsia drunk with hatred and a desire for destruction," who aimed to end all civilized life.[11]

At first many Ukrainians and Belorussians welcomed the Germans. But soon the behavior of the German army convinced even those who detested Bolshevik rule to fight, and this in spite of searing memories of Stalin's murderous terror, purges, and enforced famines. The German army burned villages simply because they were located in partisan areas. Men were killed outright, women and children were either shot or, their clothing and food stolen, driven toward Russian lines to hide attacking Germans. Soviets were sometimes used as helpers; Jews were used for running over mine fields. Even Stalin never treated German prisoners of war as badly as the German army treated captured Soviets. Of some five million Soviet prisoners, three million died. As the German army staggered from defeat to defeat in the winter of 1943, German officers wanted to form an army of disaffected Soviets to help stem the tide. But so bad was the German terror that only some fifty thousand Soviets joined the Nazi forces. The average Soviet soldier was convinced it was better to die than be taken prisoner.

As they retreated in 1944–1945, driven by fury, the Germans killed indiscriminately, shooting women and children, blasting villages, and dumping corpses in the wells to poison them. Some units, not all SS, descended on unsuspecting villagers, raping, looting, then murdering everyone, often by cruel methods, usually keeping some women for a few days of sexual violence before killing them. After all, their superiors had ordered them to burn any village on the slightest suspicion that it harbored partisans and to shoot the inhabitants as they ran out. The Germans left behind a land of misery, famine, and death. Some seven million civilians died, and about seventeen hundred towns and seventy thousand villages were destroyed. The vision of race and death of the nineteenth-century volkists was made manifest in the east; the Teutonic Knights had returned, equipped with modern weapons of mass destruction, but this time with no desire to convert.

But the officer corps of the German army was not composed of Teutonic barbarians. These were the highly educated children of the elite and the middle classes. In the highest ranks the landed aristocracy was heavily represented. Many felt superior to the Nazis and would not cooperate with the murder of civilians, but they were exceptions. Most behaved consistently with their past support for the party or their Freikorps experience. Field Marshals Manstein and Reichenau, and Generals Brauchitsch, Rundstedt, Hoth, Keitel, and Jodl, to name only the most prestigious, all spoke at one time or another to the troops or signed orders calling for death to "Judeo-Bolsheviks," or simply to Jews. Manstein said they must "exterminate Judeo-Bolshevism once and for all." It was not necessary to be a Nazi leader to believe in and voluntarily help in the murder of European Jewry.

About one-third of the officers of the professional killers of the *Einsatzgruppen* held university degrees, many in law, and regular and Nazi officers were recruited chiefly from the educated and social elite. Although most junior officers were educated under the Nazis, in 1930 the great majority of younger officers supported the Nazis without benefit of a Nazi education. Few officers came from working-class families, of course, and former Social Democrats were rarely to be found and generally suspect. Junior officers, like the SS killers, came mainly from the middle class. Decades of racism had done its work. After the war most Germans were incensed when the Allies accused the officer class of having lost its honor; in truth, with some notable exceptions, there was little to be lost.

Next to the army and the SS, the civil service was the most heavily implicated in Nazi terror, often anticipating Nazi commands. Ninety percent of bureaucrats kept their jobs; they needed no purge. The Finance Ministry and Reichsbank collected the stolen valuables of Jewish families and "Aryanized" property. The Ministry of Justice made agreements with the SS against Jews, Gypsies, and "asocial" Germans, violated criminal law, and aided the extermination program. When the killings began, the Ministry of the Interior asked to participate. In May 1941 the heads of various ministries agreed that German troops must live off the land, and "Consequently doubtless millions of humans will starve to death." They added that ten million Russians in the northern regions alone were superfluous.[12] The chief of the civil administration in Serbia, Staatsrat

Turner, explained to army commanders that shooting the Jews helped resolve the Jewish question, "and besides, they have to disappear." After all,
"It is the Jewish intellect that has brought this war and must be annihilated."[13] Most Gestapo personnel were recruited from the ranks of the
civil police. Racial nationalists, they were happy to punish leftists and
Jews.

Many officials of the Foreign Office also believed the war was a necessary crusade against "Judeo-bolshevism" and cooperated fully. By September 1940 the Foreign Office viewed forced emigration as undesirable
"in view of the doubtless imminent final solution of the Jewish question."
As Germans marched into Poland, the head of Jewish affairs in the Foreign Office noted in an official memo the two purposes of the war: "the
securing of political, military, and economic space for Germany as a
world power; . . . [and the] liberation of the world from the chains of
Jewry and Freemasonry." When deportations to the east began in 1941,
the Foreign Office played a major role. When the killing began, some of
the "nazified civil servants" of the Foreign office "carried out the most
horrendous of all Nazi policies."[14] Some organized the shooting of eight
thousand Jews in Serbia in 1941. Felix Bendler, in charge of foreign affairs in Serbia, established a camp to "concentrate" Jewish civilians in
Belgrade. At first officials wanted to deport the Jews to camps elsewhere,
but the camps were too full and mass gassing had not yet been perfected.
The aptly named Martin Luther, head of Jewish affairs in the Foreign Office, drew up a memo for State Secretary Ernst von Weizsaecker, urging
that the military commander in Serbia "take care of the immediate elimination of these 8,000 Jews"; the army had already killed "considerably
greater numbers of Jews without even mentioning it."[15] Weizsaecker, an
honorary SS member, did not object. Another Foreign Office official insisted the Jews were the enemy, and it was common knowledge they
would not survive the war. By 1942 all Jews in Serbia were dead.

In the fall of 1941 *Einsatzgruppen* reports listing those murdered by
nation and ethnicity were routinely sent to the Foreign Office. In spite
of the alleged secrecy, a chilling memorandum circulated urging that
world Jewry be informed that in the east "many a Jew no longer lives."
That would make the Jews think twice about reprisals against Germans
overseas.[16] German diplomats aggressively pressed other nations, Allied or
occupied, to surrender their Jews. Prince Otto von Bismarck, diplomat at
Rome, urged the Italians to let the SS round up Croatian Jews for the
camps. The Italian general in charge insisted that such measures were
"incompatible with the honor of the Italian army."[17] State Secretary
Weizsaecker pressured reluctant Italian officials to surrender Jews to the
SS and tried to stop the Swedish government from offering haven to Nor-
wegian Jews. Others tried to stop the Danes from helping Jews make their

escape to Sweden. Foreign Office officials, told that Germany's Jewish policy was unacceptable to the Finnish people and violated their constitution, replied: "In the same way as the defense against bolshevism is a vital question for Finland, so for Europe the ruthless destruction of Jewish political and economic power represents the unalterable precondition for the freedom and the future of the Continent."[18]

Even when it was obvious that Germany faced defeat, the Foreign Office pursued the killing of the Jews. When Germany's ally Hungary tried to halt deportations as the Red army neared in the summer of 1944, Foreign Office officials urged the dispatch of more railroad cars in order to ship all Hungarian Jews to Auschwitz quickly. As an official spokesman of the Foreign Office had said in 1943, "Jewry is to be combated wherever it is found, because it is a political infectant, the ferment of disintegration and death of every national organization."[19] To consider such complicity as mere careerism is to beg the question, for one must still explain how it was that German culture could produce civilized and sophisticated people from the very "best families" who willingly participated in the mass murder of innocents, even when defeat loomed and identification with the Nazis would invite retribution. Nor was this the work of lesser officials; all anti-Jewish documents were signed by the appropriate bureaucrats, though no doubt some did so with distaste. As Christopher Browning notes, they "were not coerced by any external threat to behave the way they did."[20] In short, they volunteered their services to Himmler.

Ingo Mueller has written in his fine book about the judiciary, *Hitler's Justice*, "The overwhelming majority . . . shared responsibility for the terror."[21] Nor were these gentlemen simply party hacks, much to the annoyance of the "old fighters" of the party who coveted their posts. Ninety-five percent of judges voluntarily joined the party, the highest proportion of any profession, and quite consistent with their views during the Second Reich and Weimar. A judge of the infamous Nazi People's Court, Wilhelm Weiss, SA officer and editor of the *Voelkische Beobachter*, was one of those who believed the court's purpose was to "exterminate the enemies of the Third Reich . . . to the last man."[22] In 1939 the judiciary demanded death sentences for the slightest violation even remotely considered to hinder war morale. In the first days of the war, special courts were established to legalize the looting of Jewish and Polish property and order the execution of any who tried to defend their holdings. Poles and Jews were condemned to death with abandon. By 1940 the courts were doing with a brief ceremony what the SS killers did with none. In April 1941, when the decree forming ghettos in Poland was issued, the courts enforced the death penalty for those who tried to leave and sanctioned the shooting of innocent hostages. By 1944 there were some ten million foreign workers in Germany, and prosecutors demanded and received death sentences for the most minor of their infractions. In short, the judiciary legalized Nazi terror and racism with enthusiasm. A judge might refuse and not be imprisoned. Yet Mueller could find only one, and his punishment was early retirement. The willingness to enforce fascist law was unique to the German judiciary; Mueller estimates that German judges handed out some eighty thousand death sentences for wartime offenses, Italian fascist tribunals about twenty-nine.[23]

The actions of corporate executives demonstrate the falsity of the accepted view that they found Nazi anti-Semitism abhorrent. The record is replete with the uncoerced cooperation of important business, banking, and industrial firms in robbing, enslaving, and even killing. Bankers eagerly competed to confiscate Jewish property, banks, securities, investments, and diamonds. Trailing the army into conquered lands, German corporations blackmailed Jewish firms in order to extort their property on the cheap. There is no evidence of reluctance; indeed, corporations and banks requested the right to steal Jewish property, and banks gained huge profits buying and reselling Jewish businesses, keeping choice shares and properties for themselves. Some German businessmen simply looted, seizing even private coin and stamp collections.

As Benjamin J. Ferencz has shown in his remarkable book *Less Than Slaves*, businessmen were not pressured to use slave labor, they competed for it. Corporate executives of numerous firms met with Himmler and SS officers just after the invasion of Poland to request slave labor. Rudolf Hoess, commandant of Auschwitz, testified that camp prisoners were continually requested, and he was constantly importuned by industrialists for more. When some firms were refused because they were inefficient, they begged to have such judgments reconsidered. Albert Speer was in charge of the requisition of slave labor, though sometimes firms wrote directly to camp commandants. Speer and his rocket scientists, Wernher von Braun and Arthur Rudolph, enthusiastically requested thousands of slave laborers, who were forced to work under conditions that brought early death to thousands. Companies built factories in or near the camps in order to take advantage of cheap, disposable "subhumans." Krupp, Siemens, and I. G. Farben built plants near Auschwitz-Birkenau and Buchenwald. Profits were the goal, racism was the ideology. Alfred Krupp ingratiated himself with the SS so that he might manufacture at Auschwitz with inmate labor. As he wrote to a high-ranking SS officer in 1943: "A very close cooperation exists between this office and Auschwitz. . . ."[24] In February 1941 Farben added I. G. Auschwitz to its vast holdings, later expanding synthetic production with Buchenwald prisoners. An I. G. Farben chairman wrote to Himmler in 1943 that he was pleased prisoners would be available. Krupp, Siemens, and others built vast complexes covering many kilometers at Auschwitz. Krupp employed some 100,000 slaves in scores of different plants and work projects; Siemens, AEG, Flick, Telefunken, Daimler-Benz, and Rheinmetall all used slave laborers from Dachau, Buchenwald, and Mauthausen; thousands also slaved for Messerschmidt, Junkers, Heinkel, Brabag, and a variety of German and Austrian construction firms. A dozen firms had their own plants in the camps, and sixteen major corporations used Jewish slave labor. The Bayer Pharmaceutical Company paid seven hundred marks each for females from Auschwitz to use for medical experiments.[25] In all there were some sixteen hundred slave labor camps and thousands of special projects, bridges, military installations, roadworks, and such contracted out to private firms using forced labor. By 1945 there were about a million slave laborers, including Jews and citizens of conquered nations.

Jewish workers in unheated barracks were beaten for the slightest infraction of the rules, and their rations were rarely better than camp fare. I. G. Farben provided camp fare plus the infamous "buna soup," a thin mixture of the water in which the guards' potato peelings had been boiled. Disease was allowed to take its toll; to become ill or injured on the job often meant swift execution. Beatings and torture by corporation supervisors of their "work police" were commonplace. In the Nuremberg trials, Krupp foremen were repeatedly cited for beating Jews to death. I. G. Farben, Flick, Siemens, Telefunken, Daimler-Benz, construction firms, and aircraft and rocket manufacturers did the same. Business managers were not pressured to treat their workers so badly; indeed, they sometimes personally requested the SS to punish "lazy" workers. Jewish workers who fell behind were regularly taunted with the crematoria ovens, and many were handed over to the SS to be sent to the gas chambers. In the I. G. Farben plant at Auschwitz, thirty thousand laborers died in three years; some 20 percent of those engaged in heavy labor for various firms perished each month. Visiting executives of I. G. Farben once complained of the "Jewish swine," "If they can't work, let them perish in the gas chamber."[26] Workers had a life expectancy of two to three months.

As the Allies neared and Nazi rule collapsed, it was easy to free laborers and let them fend for themselves. Yet as American troops approached Essen, and the city government fled, Alfred Krupp, president of Krupp works, personally approved sending hundreds of his Jewish women laborers back to Buchenwald.[27] Like the worst criminal, Krupp wanted to kill the innocent victims of his crimes to prevent them from testifying. He was no ordinary criminal; to make his vicious choice he had to have the mentality of an Eichmann.

One could have treated workers with some decency, even protected them, though it would have been unreasonable to expect many to risk it. Oscar Schindler owned a small factory in Cracow employing some five hundred Jews producing war materials. He protected them and their relatives from SS attempts to deport them to camps, hiring their relatives at his own expense, though he did not need them, and transferring workers to protect them when the Germans were in retreat, saving more than one thousand Jews. He died in 1974 and would have died poor if Jewish groups had not aided him. Germans never did. Flick, Krupp, and the like died rich. Schindler's actions show what a small entrepreneur without influence could do, but heroism aside, any industrialist could have asked permission in the name of the war effort to use a small portion of profits to improve conditions. It was not done.

Of all the complicities, the moral support given the regime by the German churches is the most surprising. Most Christian leaders elsewhere were appalled by Nazi terror, but the anti-Semitism of the German and Austrian church had never been countered by liberal influences. Consequently the church leaders utterly failed to protest the greatest moral infamy of our time and stifled any potential popular revulsion among ordinary German Christians. But it was not a failure of Christianity in general. Although the French Catholic hierarchy was historically close to French racists, many French clergy took grave risks, publicly denouncing the Nazi deportation of Jews and shielding Jewish children on church grounds. French Protestant clergy, possibly because of their own past oppression, were even more notable for their help to victims. Church leaders often spoke against the Nazis in Holland and Scandinavia, and in Denmark, Lutheran clergy denounced German authorities from the pulpit and helped Jews to flee the roundup for the death camps. Scandinavian Lutheranism had always been influenced by the liberal societies in which it flourished. Even in fascist Italy, many ordinary priests and nuns protected Jews at the risk of their own lives and without Vatican support.

Protest was possible. Indeed, as hospitals, asylums, nursing homes, and sanitariums emptied out, the public demonstrated and the press editorialized. After all, the victims were their relatives, suffering a fate they might one day share. Even General Wilhelm Keitel, famous for ordering the massacre of innocents, complained. His soldiers feared that if wounded, they too might end up in the killing centers, as some did. After these public and popular protests, Cardinals Bertram, Faulhaber, and the Lutheran Bishop Wurm also complained. In 1941 the Catholic Bishop Galen declared that euthanasia violated divine law, and he demanded punishment for the "criminals and murderers." "No one has the right to kill innocent persons," he said. Soon, "nobody will be safe. . . ."[28] Copies of Galen's sermon were sent to church and military dignitaries, and thousands were dropped among soldiers at the Russian front by the Royal Air Force. Hitler ended the program, though it was resumed covertly. Many nursing homes and long-term care facilities were church-owned and operated, and euthanasia was an offense calling for excommunication—but no one ever was.

In stark contrast, at no time did the German church hierarchy say anything publicly about the Jews and Poles, including priests, slaughtered in the east. Like Bishop Galen, a former Freikorps fighter, many of the clergy evidently agreed that Germany had a right to lebensraum at the expense of "Judeo-bolshevism." The official church handbook, written by Archbishop Groeber, called bolshevism a despotism "in the service of a group of terrorists led by Jews." Some Catholic bishops made a few vague pronouncements against the killing of innocents of another race or language, but they never mentioned the Jews by name or spoke of the killing of those of another religion, although Bishop Preysing, the outstanding exception, tried to get them to do so. It is no excuse to say that the church opposed communist atheism or feared hindering the war effort; those were not the issues. The issue was the murder of millions of noncombatants. The bishops did appeal for better conditions in the camps, but they specifically referred only to Christian priests and prisoners. Certainly the hierarchy knew of the fate of the Jews. In 1944, fearing a proposed measure that would define Christians of partial Jewish ancestry as Jews, Cardinal Bertram warned the government that Christians would "be deeply hurt if these fellow Christians would have to meet a fate similar to the Jews," that is, "segregation" which "threatens extermination."[29] To the end of the war, Catholic bishops called for victory in the east, though they knew that each day the Germans resisted meant the death of thousands of Jews. One-quarter of the SS were Catholic and could have been refused the sacraments as is done to abortionists. But no camp guard, killing squad member, or Catholic Nazi leader, including Hitler, Himmler, and Goebbels, was ever threatened with church penalties, even though many Catholics pleaded with the pope to excommunicate Hitler.

It is said the church feared losing millions of Catholics. This one cannot know, but if it is necessary to keep silent about the mass murder of millions in order to hold on to the faithful, then the faith is dead. Nor could German bishops assume they would be killed if they protested, provided they did so as a group and objected on the grounds of Christian theology. The Nazis feared antagonizing any significant number of Aryan Germans while the war was on. The church even helped the regime keep the public in line: clergy chastised conscientious objectors, and the bishops issued a joint public declaration insisting that Catholic soldiers must do their duty and obey Hitler, making no exception for SS killers or guards in the death camps. Gordon Zahn is correct: German Catholic bishops (and most Evangelical leaders) called for the martyrdom of Christians not against the murder of innocents but to serve Nazi ideals.[30]

There were martyrs. A Catholic provost in Berlin, Bernhard Lichten-

352 IDEOLOGY OF DEATH

berg, gave a sermon the day after *Kristallnacht* to protest the burning of synagogues. Lichtenberg also publicly prayed for the Jews on the eve of their deportation; when arrested, he asked to accompany them to the east. In his home, police found a sermon denying that the Jews were the enemy of the Germans. Sentenced to two years in prison, when released he was sent to Dachau and died of illness on the way. His fellow bishops did not help him. The papal nuncio, an object of ridicule among the Nazis because of frequent requests not to be told embarrassing facts, asked only that proceedings against Lichtenberg be swift.

As might be expected from their long ties to the Prussian right, Protestant clergy were even less inclined to protest. Even the most anti-Nazi of the clergy, those of the Confessing Church, did nothing to help unconverted Jews, though some offered clandestine help. Bishop Marahrens of the Confessing Church publicly supported the Nazis and the persecution of the Jews. Protestant leaders also blessed the war even when they knew exactly what it meant for the Jews. In 1943 the Evangelical church sent Hitler a telegram stating that it "loyally pledges to use all its power to conquer victory."[31] In July 1944, when thousands of soldiers and civilians were dying in a lost cause, the official Evangelical church paper gave thanks to the Almighty that Hitler's life had been spared from the "infamous criminals" of the resistance.[32] The Evangelicals did not even support their own martyrs; indeed, on occasion they publicly disavowed them. When Pastor J. von Jan protested the burning of the synagogues on *Kristallnacht*, no one supported him. He was beaten and imprisoned. Pastor Gruber protested the deportation of the Jews; sent to Dachau, he was released in 1943, broken and isolated. Dietrich Bonhoeffer bravely returned from exile to engage in resistance; he was hanged at the end of the war, a lone hero. The official publication of the Evangelical church passed its judgment after the war:

> The Confessing Church resisted . . . the separation of Jewish Christians out of the Evangelical church of Germany, but against anti-Semitism they uttered no word, and even at the time of Jewish persecutions and of their extermination it could not bring itself to stand up against these acts of terrorism in the Third Reich. The official church in general approved openly or secretly the Jewish policy and accepted the measures of the National Socialist regime both in and without the church.[33]

Hitler said that if he kept the clergy on the public payroll, they would stay in line. But he was too crass. The clergy failed to condemn Nazi terror because, as part of German and Austrian culture, they were not influenced by liberal and enlightened opposition to centuries of Christian anti-Semitism. Thus in spite of our naive belief that religious faith brings moral courage, those most opposed to Nazi terror were the least religious: Progressives, Social Democrats, and communists.

The great tragedy of modern Catholicism was the selection of the pro-Nazi Cardinal Pacelli as Pope Pius XII. Given his record, Pius XI would have issued strong public condemnations against the murder of the Jews. But Pacelli had spent twelve years in service in Germany and was enamored with German conservative nationalism and the views of Karl Lueger, attitudes reinforced when the Bavarian Soviet Republic almost had him shot on the steps of the Munich cathedral in 1919. Pius XII warned German bishops not to speak out against the regime. As a mark of his special favor, Hitler was the first head of state he notified of his selection as pope, and he instructed L'Osservatore Romano, the official Vatican paper, to cease its anti-German statements. He did not even publicly protest the Nazis' numerous violations of the concordat he himself helped conclude with such unseemly haste. The complicity of the Vatican, duly noted by the Nazis, was greeted with amused contempt mixed with the occasional fear that, after all, the pope just might attempt to rally Catholic opinion against them.

Pius XII was silent on the Nazis' euthanasia. He protested the invasion of Belgium and Holland but assured the German Foreign Office that he had to protest because these were Catholic nations. He did not commiserate with the sufferings of invaded Norway; as L'Osservatore Romano pointed out, there were very few Catholic Norwegians.[34] Yet the pope was pleased when Catholic France was invaded. Like any German nationalist, he detested French republicanism and was glad to see it replaced with a Catholic, reactionary, and racist regime. In an encyclical of October 1939, the pope expressed sympathy for the suffering of the Poles, again assuring the German ambassador that he did not intend to offend Germany. In the spring of 1940 the Vatican was informed that Polish priests were being executed: more than two hundred were murdered and about a thousand were sent to concentration camps in the first four months of the war. By March 1941 the Vatican knew that some seven hundred Polish priests had been sent to concentration camps, and many Catholics begged the pope to denounce the Nazis. He did not. Eighteen percent of all Polish priests were killed in the war.[35] In short, Pius XII supported the Nazis' bid for lebensraum in Catholic, noncommunist Poland even if it meant the murder of priests, let alone Jews.

In August 1942 the Brazilian ambassador to the Holy See, a Catholic, attempted to persuade the pope to denounce the atrocities in occupied territories. He was supported by the Belgian ambassador, U.S. Secretary of State Cordell Hull and Under Secretary Sumner Welles, and the British ambassador to Washington. Poland, Uruguay, and Great Britain also sent notes urging a statement of concern. Representing the American government, Myron C. Taylor delivered an official letter in September 1942 decrying the massacre of tens of thousands in Poland, the killings in the Warsaw Ghetto, and mass executions in the camps. Such was the "butchering" of civilians, he wrote, that there "is not one Jew left in the entire district east of Poland, including occupied Russia," adding that all Jews in the control of the Germans in the east were being shot. Taylor asked if the pope could help prevent such "barbarities." In his Christmas message of 1942–1943 the pope responded, but managed not to condemn the Nazis or mention Jews. Instead, in a twenty-six-page message, he said only that "humanity" must vow to create a society that would assure the well-being of all, including the "hundreds of thousands of people who, through no fault of their own and solely because of their nation or their race, have been condemned to death or progressive extinction."[36] It was as though "humanity," not the Nazis, was the problem. The German government did not deem the pope's comment worthy of protest. Nor did the pope protest when, in October 1943, the Germans took the Jews of Rome under the very eyes of the Vatican. The German Foreign Office feared the pope would protest, but to their relief he said nothing. Pius XII did shelter a few dozen or a few hundred Jews in the Vatican, the number is uncertain.[37] But hundreds of ordinary Italians, secular and religious, rescued some 8,000 Jews, and priests, communists, and democrats helped. The pope also did nothing for the 265 Catholic and 70 Jewish civilians murdered as hostages in the Adreatine caves in March 1944, despite appeals from his own priests.

Pius XII was pro-Nazi to the end. In 1944 he hoped the Allies would not invade Europe and prevent the defeat of the USSR. Like the Nazis and their generals, the pope saw the war as a battle to the death against Judeo-bolshevism. This was not simply zealous antibolshevism, for the pope could have supported a German victory in Russia and still denounced the Holocaust. And after Mussolini fell, the pope believed the new pro-Allied Italian government of Pietro Badoglio was a front for "Masonic and Jewish circles." Like the embattled *fascisti*, the pope feared a German evacuation of Italy. He who did not aid his dead Polish priests, appealed to the Badoglio government to protect Mussolini and his fascists from Allied and Italian revenge. Saul Friedlander asks how it was that in 1943 "the Pope and the highest dignitaries of the church were still wishing for victorious resistance in the east" when they must have known this meant the continued operation of the "entire Nazi extermination machine." The answer seems clear. They were pro-Nazi.[38]

After the war the pope and his apologists argued that he had not wished to bring millions of Catholic German soldiers into conflicts of conscience, but one does not ignore evil to avoid conflicts of conscience among its perpetrators. It was said he feared that many more would suf-

fer Nazi wrath if he spoke out, something he could not know. It is just
as easy to say he might have stayed the Nazis' hand long enough for more
to be saved. The Nazi leadership always feared his moral authority, and
many ordinary German Catholics were upset at his silence. It was said
he feared the German people would blame him if they lost the war—an
irrelevancy, for he was not asked to take sides, only to oppose the massacre of innocents; even German judges after the war recognized the difference. It was said he could not speak out because he feared losing thirty
million German Catholics, thus assuming German Catholics would leave
a church that condemned genocide—a devastating comment, but perhaps as a twelve-year veteran of German politics he believed he was right.
In the end, Pius commiserated with the German victims of Allied bombing and prisoners in Russia more than he ever did with the victims of the
Nazis.

In none of this did Pius XII represent Catholicism. Most ordinary
Catholics and many dignitaries begged him to speak out. The archbishop
of Toulouse protested the deportation of the Jews, as did the nuncio of
Bratislava. The nuncio in Budapest demanded that the Hungarian government end "its war against the Jews" and avoid acts the "conscience of
the entire Christian world" would feel obliged to protest." But the pope
made only private complaints to Horthy and then only after Horthy himself opposed the deportations, had no influence left, and most Hungarian Jews were on their way to death. Pius XII endangered the church and
the loyalty of his flock by his silence. The French church was offended,
American Catholics lost confidence in him, and Catholic resistance fighters and those who suffered under the Nazi occupation were bitterly dis-
appointed, above all the millions of Catholic victims in the ravaged
church in Poland. His failure gave the communists of Eastern Europe
fuel for their brutal suppression of the church, especially when the pope
received some well-known Eastern European pro-Nazis after the war. He
was as blinded by his sympathy with much of the Nazi cause as were the
bishops of Germany, and with less excuse. When all is said and done,
Pius XII was a disaster to his office and to Catholicism. Even the popes
of the Crusades protested the murder of Jews, as they were theologically
bound to. But Pius XII violated Catholic doctrine and seriously damaged
the reputation of the church. The Vatican has never regained the moral
authority he squandered, but the church has recognized the errors of Pius
XII, if only indirectly. Monsignor Roncalli, the future Pope John XXIII,
during the war "spared no effort to succor the Jews of Central Europe
and the Balkans."[39] It is no accident that he brought the freedoms of Vatican Two and pressed for the statement of 1965: "True, authorities of the
Jews and those who followed their lead pressed for the death of Christ;
still, what happened in His Passion cannot be blamed upon all the Jews

then living, without distinction, nor upon the Jews of today." It was helpful, if too little and too late.

Thousands of German physicians and eugenicists, including Fischer,
Verschuer, and Lenz, cooperated in the murder of "undesirables." When
the sterilization program was replaced by outright murder in 1939, it was
no surprise to the medical community. As Erwin Bauer, coauthor of
Lenz's famous textbook on genetics and director of the Kaiser Wilhelm
Institute for Biology, had said in 1933, "No one approves of the new sterilization laws more than I, but I must repeat over and over again, that
they constitute only a beginning."[40] Psychiatrists, physicians, anthropologists, nurses, and midwives selected and killed the mentally ill, those with
allegedly inheritable diseases, the disabled, the "antisocial," and the
racially "undesirable." As Robert Proctor writes, "For Nazi physicians, no
sharp line divided the destruction of the racially inferior and the mentally or physically defective."[41] Academics and anthropologists lectured
about the racial dangers of Gypsies and homosexuals and filled out reports affirming who was of Jewish ancestry, the necessary prelude to murder. Teams of physicians and psychiatrists planned the murder of mental
patients, selecting thousands of Polish mental patients to be shot.

No one was forced to participate in these killings; indeed, some chiefs
of clinics requested permission to kill their patients. Nor were the murders secret. Many of the physicians in the euthanasia program lost private patients who feared their own fate. In 1940, when the public
campaign against euthanasia commenced, the chairmen of departments
of psychiatry in German universities were asked to join the widespread
(and safe) public protests; all refused. Only one psychiatrist publicly
protested; he was himself disabled. Support for euthanasia was widespread
among hospital administrators, physicians, and medical technicians, so
much so that months after the war ended, the American occupation
forces discovered patients, including children, still being killed in hospitals and institutions "all over Germany."[42] By then it could hardly have
been careerism; evidently they approved of murder for racial purification.
Ironically, had there been euthanasia in the nineteenth century, the
Kaiser Wilhelm Institute would probably have recommended the murder
of its namesake, and Goebbels would not have survived.

As "guardians of the genetic constitution," medical students were required to study racial science. Professor Othmar von Verschuer and others conducted research on the racial nature of disease. The head of the
Physicians League described the Jews as a virus among peoples, a "diseased race," even "disease incarnate," an old myth. In 1938 the specialists
of the Office of Racial Policy labeled homosexuals as unreliable and incapable of contributing anything of value to society, "enemies of the state

to be eliminated." Medical researchers tried to detect homosexual and Gypsy blood so they could be found and eliminated; in 1938 a medical journal demanded a "final solution of the Gypsy question."[43] In June 1939 Professor Fischer, lecturing to the coal barons of the Ruhr, declared of the Jews that a people "must reject alien racial elements" and "eliminate them." In a published lecture delivered in occupied Paris, probably in 1941, Fischer declared the "Bolshevik Jews" to be of "monstrous mentality . . . beings of another species." His connections with the SS and his friendship with Rosenberg, noted for his open discussion of supposedly secret Nazi policies, made him quite knowledgeable about the mass murders in the east. In November 1936 the German Association for Scientific Research funded an investigation into the racial origins of the Gypsies. Dr. Robert Ritter, professor of medicine and an administrator of racial policies, participated in one of their conferences in the winter of 1941. The conference considered a plan to drown thirty thousand German Gypsies by sending them out into the Mediterranean Sea on ships and then bombing the ships.[44] Ritter, a specialist in the physiognomy of "criminal types," helped choose tens of thousands for death. Already in 1938 and 1939 German physicians, meeting with their colleagues, discussed the need for a "final solution" to the Jewish problem.[45]

In March 1941 Rosenberg spoke at the founding meeting of an institute for the Investigation of the Jewish Question. In his audience were the rectors of many universities, important academics, and two honored guests, Professors Hans Guenther and Fischer. Guenther, professor at the University of Berlin, had been an anti-Semite before 1914 and a leader in the sterilization and euthanasia programs. Head of the Institute of Race Science, he was also involved in the "resettlement" programs in the east. At the conference, Rosenberg announced the "total solution of the Jewish question" and spoke of a "cleansing biological revolution." Professor Walther Seraphim, after the war a respected professor at the University of Munich, agreed that the "volkstod" (genocide) of the Jews was the "ultimate aim" of the "total solution." Lectures were given about methods to be used. Seraphim suggested pauperizing the Jews and resettling them in the east, but this would not cause the immediate "physical disappearance of Jewry, for the death of a people is never a swift death. . . ." The conference was not secret, for its proceedings were published, as was a report on the conference in a well-known medical journal. As Professor Benno Mueller-Hill rightly remarks, "Those who had heard or read the lectures could come to only one logical conclusion: the 'necessary and total solution' was to be achieved more quickly by violent killing."[46]

Before the use of Zyklon B in the death camps, discussions of better methods had been going on for some time. A Dr. Ernst Grawitz is supposed to have been the first to suggest the use of the pesticide, but there were undoubtedly others who, had the Nazis won, would have claimed the prize. Academics suggested various poisons and were kept informed about killing methods. A professor in the Interior Ministry suggested burning the corpses rather than burying them, in order to destroy the evidence if the Allies won. Many scientists and academics, helping to select Jews, Gypsies, and homosexuals for the labor and death camps, were staff for the SS Office for Race and Resettlement, prestige positions for which one had to compete. Anthropologists, physicians, psychiatrists, and "racial hygienists" were prominent among those who decided who should live and who should die. Verschuer helped select candidates for death; other academics suggested compiling a register of social misfits to be killed after the war. In December 1941, when the first mass gassings began, traveling medical boards helped select those who could work or be killed immediately. A few of the physicians were overeager; the SS men had to tell them not to condemn too many, for someone had to do the work.

Physician-researchers kept trying to isolate the properties of Jewish blood in medical experiments on camp victims until the very end of the war. Many also did research on Gypsies who were about to be murdered. Physicians and researchers who performed experiments on live prisoners were themselves murderers, of course, often using horribly painful tortures in the name of science, and killing or mutilating thousands. More than five hundred such experiments were carried on at Dachau alone, and reports of them were regularly sent to universities. The experimenters were not under duress, nor were they limited to a search for survival methods to help the armed forces. Right down to 1945, some camp victims were used by research personnel and physicians for experiments designed to test even more efficient ways to murder the "excess" millions of the east.

Research departments of universities requested corpses and body parts from death camp commanders. Some of the research was used in scientific papers as late as the 1970s. One professor had a collection of Jewish skeletons. Body parts were collected at universities, and technicians were sent to the camps to supervise the dissection, preservation, and shipping of the gruesome materials—too often the SS bungled the job. Professors attended scholarly talks given by researchers explaining the significance of their work. Verschuer, head of the Kaiser Wilhelm Institute of Anthropology, successfully applied, along with others, for funds to do research on the different types of victims available at Auschwitz. Professor Kurt Hallervorden, head of the Brain Institute at the Kaiser Wilhelm Institute, received for research the brains of children killed in the camps. He provided materials for packing and preserving, and personally extracted the brains. When questioned by Allied interrogators in 1946, he said he told the SS, "Look here now boys, if you are going to kill all these people anyway at least take the brains out, so that the material can be utilized."[47] It was all quite normal. Professor Auguste Hirt, surgeon and head of the Anatomy Institute at the University of Strasbourg, wrote to Himmler in February 1942: "By procuring the skulls of the Jewish-Bolshevik Commissars, who represent the prototype of the repulsive but characteristic subhuman, one has the chance to obtain palpable scientific data. . . . Following [the] induced death of the Jew, the head, which should not be damaged, should be separated from the body and sent in a hermetically sealed tin filled with preservative fluid."[48]

As Verschuer wrote in 1939, Hitler was the "first statesman" who made "hereditary biology and eugenics a directing principle of state policy."[49] In 1944 Verschuer noted that though the danger of the Jews and Gypsies to Germany was nearly over, "racial-political policies" should continue to be carried out throughout Europe.[50] His famous colleague Lenz, who helped design the racial test given to potential SS brides, agreed that drastic measures must be taken to purify the race for the future. Another department head at the Kaiser Wilhelm Institute and professor at the University of Berlin, Dr. Wolfgang Abel, wrote that after victory one must protect the Aryan future by either Germanizing those Russians who were Nordic or simply exterminating them all. Early in the war Lenz requested an appointment in the east from the Office of Race and Settlement so that he might help to "restructure" the region racially. Resettlement, he wrote, was now the most important topic: "It will determine the racial character of the population in this area for centuries to come." As Proctor concludes, "There is little evidence that physicians ever refused to participate in Nazi programs; those few who did . . . do not seem to have suffered for their refusal."[51] Ideological conviction stifled guilt, careerism added impetus, and personal innocence was assumed. Many of the academic participants were surprised in 1945 at Allied revulsion.

In light of the widespread complicity of the scientific community, it is obvious that the notorious Dr. Josef Mengele has too often—one hesitates to say unfairly—been singled out as an aberrant and singular monster. Mengele was not satanic or an unsophisticated devotee of Nazi ideology. He was a scientist, a racial researcher, and an assistant professor at the Kaiser Wilhelm Institute for Genetics. In that capacity he selected victims for death at Auschwitz, and did research under the sponsorship of Professors Fischer and Verschuer when he became a camp physician in May 1943, selecting those deemed useful for experimentation. As difficult as it may be to accept, Mengele was a respected scientist conducting inquiries sponsored by the Institute for the Advancement of Science. While doing graduate work under Verschuer, he collected blood samples from different racial groups at Auschwitz for Verschuer's laboratory. Mengele's special interest was the study of twins—the perennial fascination of geneticists—and he sent back to the institute the bodies, organs, and blood of murdered Gypsy and Jewish children in pursuit of his research. The institute administrations always thanked Mengele profusely when learned papers were composed or published with his cooperation, and academic colleagues evidently listened with respect to his and other scholars' papers based on similar research.

It bears repeating: if, in the name of racial purity, the regime's collaborators could construct killing centers to murder German Christians because they were retarded, mentally ill, wounded veterans, "useless mouths," or "asocials," it could hardly have been a moral problem for them to destroy Jews, the blood enemies of the Volk. It was all part of the academic routine. Our own intellectual predispositions, the consequence of our liberal tradition, make it extremely difficult for us to understand how scientists, physicians, and health-care workers could destroy human life in the name of racial purity. This difficulty has led to a proliferation of psychological speculation about the general origins of human evil, speculation fed by the belief that somehow we are all capable of such acts. We would do better to turn to the unique history of Germany for explanations. We need not assume such men were monsters. They were normal human beings but part of a scientific ethos which over decades had sanctioned violence in the name of racial purity.

As the murder of the Jews in the east neared its end in June 1944, the regime planned to celebrate with a grandoise anti-Semitic congress in Cracow, Poland. Alfred Rosenberg was to give the major address, and Professor Fischer was invited to be chairman of one of the sections. His theme was to be the necessity of the defense of European civilization against Jewry. "I am delighted to accept your invitation," he wrote. Furtwaengler was to conduct Fidelio to celebrate the liberation of Germany from Jewry, and an Aryan brothel was to be provided for the delegates.[52] By June 1944 the Red army rendered Cracow unavailable; the congress was never held. But like the killings, the research continued.

It has been argued that even if the German elites supported Hitler before 1939, they could not have known his full intentions. But after 1941 the argument is not valid. Their guilt was not simply one of silence born of fear, apathy, or indifference; it stemmed from the voluntary and active cooperation of so many of them with the killers. So much was done by way of cooperation, so many vicious acts could have been avoided with impunity—one must conclude that the power and political function of anti-Semitism in German history was so intense that collaborators did not see such acts as immoral, as their meticulous record-keeping shows.

When the war ended and they met Allied outrage, most were honestly surprised. Swiftly they tried to hide their past and distort the historical record, and in this they had the support of the bulk of the German middle classes.

24: RESISTANCE, PUBLIC OPINION, KNOWLEDGE

Without social cooperation of various kinds . . . the anti-Semitic policies would have remained so many idle fantasies.
—Robert Gellately

MILLIONS of Germans detested the Nazis, thousands resisted, but the popularity and brutality of the regime prevailed. Until 1944 active anti-Nazis were most often communists or socialists; most other Germans shared Nazi antagonisms toward them. By July 1933, 26,000 enemies of the regime, most of them leftists, were in camps or prison, hundreds were dead. Even so, the left distributed tens of thousands of leaflets protesting *Kristallnacht*, millions of other anti-Nazi leaflets, and even some newspapers. Red flags flew defiantly over factories, posters attacked the regime, and shelter was offered to some pursued by the Gestapo. Hitler was the target of four assassination plots in the 1930s, two by German Jews. A socialist, Georg Elser, planted a bomb in the Buergerbrau in Munich in November 1939, when Hitler spoke on the anniversary of his *putsch*. Eight Nazis were killed, but Hitler had left early. He was greeted by a wave of public sympathy. During the war an anti-Nazi paper was distributed in socialist strongholds, and many small groups of Progressives, some Jewish, distributed leaflets as late as 1943. As Detlev Peukert tells us, youth gangs composed of "young working-class people," one calling itself the Proletarian Troops, painted anti-Nazi graffiti and regularly beat up members of the Hitler Youth.[1] Even in 1944 foreign workers, escaped prisoners, camp refugees, and proletarians fought pitched battles against Nazis in the bombed-out rubble.

With the help of many ordinary citizens, the Gestapo inflicted appalling losses on opponents of the regime. Thousands of public or secret trials were held in the thirties, the vast majority of them involving workers and leftists. Torture, executions, exile, and prison destroyed the left. Some thirty thousand political opponents may have died in the camps; hundreds more were simply executed. The SS, aided by police and firemen, sealed off workers' districts, capturing thousands. The famous "White Rose" group—fourteen students led by Hans and Sophie Scholl—distributed thousands of leaflets before being caught and beheaded. In the camps were about three million political prisoners.

Even so, the proletariat still showed a "sullen refusal" to make peace with the regime.[2] Industrialists reported thousands of examples of slowdowns, stoppages, or sabotage, as well as a few strikes and mass protest meetings. During the war, Krupp alone reported to the Gestapo some five thousand examples of such "treason." Most work stoppages, the Nazis believed, were used as a safe way to protest their rule. In the first and only elections for factory delegates to the Labor Front, Nazi candidates were overwhelmingly defeated, and Nazi-appointed workers' "representatives" were scorned. Propaganda meetings were sparsely attended, the Hitler greeting ignored. Workers supporting the regime were often harassed or beaten, and antiwar slogans and songs were distributed. In other classes, prosperity stifled discontent, but even when workers were fully employed, thousands were arrested and punished. Ian Kershaw suggests that, based on reports of the Nazi Security Service, most workers remained opposed to the Nazis.[3]

Barring a few prominent individuals, and undoubtedly many who have gone unrecorded, the military, aristocratic, and industrial leaders complained least. The small circle of military officers and aristocrats who attempted to assassinate Hitler in 1944 were brave men and women, but their resistance cannot compare with that of the left. They did not attempt to rouse the public with underground leaflets, preferring lengthy discussions about Germany after Hitler with others of their class. In 1938–1939, fearing defeat in a two-front war, a few military men asked the Allies to stand firm, but as victory crowded upon victory, they stopped objecting. Carl Goerdeler, the proposed new chancellor of the opposition, a former Conservative party and Bruening cabinet member, had advised Hindenburg to give Hitler dictatorial powers in 1933. He was rewarded with a high position in Hitler's government and Nazi support in his successful campaign for mayor of Leipzig in 1936. Goerdeler's first protest had been against Hitler's nonaggression pact with Poland in 1934; he feared it would end Germany's claims to Polish territory! It was a protest Hitler could live with.

Goerdeler and most leaders of the resistance wanted Germany to be predominant in Eastern Europe and the Balkans after the war, and believed that Czechoslovakia ought to be a German protectorate. General Ludwig Beck, Goerdeler, and Claus von Stauffenberg, the most important resistance figures, wanted the Allies to guarantee that, with Hitler gone, Germany would be allowed to retain the Sudentenland, Austria, and parts of Poland. A few were so blind as to hope Germany would be allowed to hold on to Alsace-Lorraine as well. As late as 1943, the prominent resistance figure Adam von Trott hoped that a new Germany would not have to surrender territory, pay reparations, or suffer postwar occupation, and that the punishment of Nazi crimes would be left to the very German judges who enforced Nazi terror. Only a few resisters, among them the courageous idealists Dietrich Bonhoeffer and Helmut von Moltke, believed opposition was an act of repentance. Moltke hoped for Germany's defeat and occupation, willing to accept the loss of territory, including his own estates in Silesia, because of Nazi crimes and the complicity of so many. Otherwise, it is not surprising that the Allies saw little difference between most conservative oppositionists and the Nazis.

Hitler's conservative opponents were hamstrung because they shared many of the goals and values that brought him to power, if without his brutal vulgarity. They rejected liberal democracy, preferring autocracy. Stauffenberg, who courageously placed the bomb that almost killed Hitler, wanted no strong labor unions or leftist political parties. Goerdeler wrote, "We need the stabilizing ballast of state leadership unhampered by elections."[4] Others wanted a monarch or *Fuehrer* able to overrule parliament and, of course, prevent the rise of a social democratic movement. Many wanted to keep the Nazi Labor Front, and most agreed that Speer, director of slave labor in the camps, should be part of the new government. Goerdeler even toyed with the idea of replacing Hitler with Goering. Gerhard Ritter, a conservative German scholar and sympathetic biographer of Goerdeler, saw their various plans for Germany's future as little short of absolutism. Hans Mommsen wrote that Goerdeler's proposals "would have resulted quite unintentionally in a somewhat dubious replica of the National Socialist state party."[5] But it was not unintentional. Like their earlier support for the Nazis, their proposals were consistent with values they had upheld for decades.

Stauffenberg, Goerdeler, Johannes Popitz, Trott, and others repeated traditional conservative ideas: Germans should remain close to the soil, happy in the class God had assigned them in a state based on conservative Christian values, uncorrupted by secularism, individualism, liberalism, and materialism. Still blind to the consequences of their own actions, they blamed democracy and the "proletarianized millions" for the rise of the Nazis. Count Werner von Shulenburg, a courageous opponent of Hitler, believed there was no need to rebuild Germany's shattered cities, the center of unhealthy industrial life—and, one might add, Social Democratic votes. The Kreisau Circle, the most idealistic of the conspirators, believed Germany had lost its way because of the erosion of Christian values, and wanted restrictions on cultural freedom in teaching, the arts, science, and the press. In the future, they held, one must show a true German respect for the "nation's spiritual and moral tradition."[6] One historian commented that they wanted "the *voelkische Fuehrer* State without Hitler."[7] Ernst Wolf wrote, "A successful coup on the part of conspirators drawn exclusively from the military and aristocracy would have meant the replacement of the National Socialist regime by one that was conservative, reactionary, and nationalistic."[8]

The record on opponents of anti-Semitism is clouded. Of the two hundred arrested for resistance activities, some twenty told their Gestapo interrogators they had been motivated by the murder of the Jews. Goerdeler, as mayor of Leipzig, had protected Jewish businessmen against the outburst of the SA. Yet there is an elusive and darker subtext. Many of the resisters, the most anti-Nazi of their class, still coupled traditionalist ideas with the evil influence of the Jews. In their many plans, there is no mention of the death camps, though undoubtedly they were personally appalled. Nevertheless, Goerdeler, held to be too "leftist" by many of his fellow conspirators, wrote: "The Jewish people belong to a different race.... The world can only come to rest if the Jewish people are given a realistic opportunity to found and maintain their own state." He suggested Canada or South America, insisting the great powers should help end the "Jewish problem." As a "citizen of his Jewish state," he would have "the same right to engage in trade and commerce as any other alien in Germany." But he could not be a German citizen or "a public servant, nor can he be elected to serve in popular representative assemblies or vote in such elections" unless he had served in 1914–1918 or was a citizen before 1914.[9] Popitz also wanted Jews removed from Germany, and Trott, slated for an important role in a new government, argued as well for international help in solving the Jewish question. Their attitude is ominously still that of the Conservative party program of the 1890s, and at a time when they knew the fate of the Jews.

Many of Goerdeler's supporters approved the racist legislation of the 1930s. Implying the Jews were to blame for Germany's plight, while on a visit to the United States Trott arrogantly told Justice Felix Frankfurter that American Jews should not complain so much. American officials were puzzled at his claim to oppose the Nazis, especially since he held high office under them and seemed similar in attitude. Many assumed he was a Nazi informant. It was not true, but it was easy to believe. Even the most moderate resisters believed there was a "Jewish problem," by which they meant that Jews had held too many prominent positions during Weimar. To call Jewish overrepresentation in education, commerce, law, and medicine a problem, one had to believe they were a bad influence. Stauffenberg wanted no physical cruelty used against them but believed they were a "foreign race" of baleful influence who ought not share in the rights and freedoms of a German citizen. Even after they had seen or heard of the murders in the east, few of the aristocratic and military leaders who opposed Hitler shook off the racism that had made them amenable to Nazi appeals in the first place. As late as 1944 Popitz declared that in the future Germany would need a strong, united state to combat the "internationalism and Judaization of the Weimar regime."[10] Much honored for his service to the regime by Hitler himself, Popitz proposed Himmler as Hitler's successor and carried on clandestine negotiations with the SS leader to that end. If Popitz, slated to be part of the new cabinet once Hitler was gone, could accept Himmler as head of state, one shudders to imagine the attitudes of those of his class who opposed the resistance. But there were brave and noble exceptions. Moltke opposed the Nazis from the start, and as a lawyer worked publicly and at great risk to protect Jews from Nazi persecution. Admiral Wilhelm Canaris and Hans Oster helped Jews to flee.

For the vast majority of army officers, the words of General Johannes Blaskowitz are correct. Witnessing atrocities in the east and failing to persuade other officers to offer even verbal opposition, he wrote in despair, "No one has the humanity to stand up for those subjected to unjust persecution."[11] Field Marshal Brauchitsch, directly responsible for the death of tens of thousands of Jews, expressed the common belief: it was treason to have contacts with the enemy when winning, and he added the chilling and revealing phrase: "This is not a struggle between governments; we are concerned here with a contest of ideologies"; Hitler's removal would "accomplish nothing."[12] He was right: killing Hitler and a few Nazi leaders would not alter the old elites' belief in most Nazi ideas. They could be expected to fight for Hitler until they knew the war was lost, as they did.

Even Stauffenberg, in early 1944, still believed the army should first win the war and then turn against the Nazis, a postponement certain to guarantee the end of the Jews, as he must have known. It was also sheer fantasy. The army would never resist a Hitler enjoying a conqueror's prestige. Significantly, the aristocratic-military opposition did not wish to move until the massive Red army offensive of June 1944 drove the Nazis back three hundred miles, inflicting 350,000 casualties in six weeks, and Runstedt faced twenty-five divisions and overwhelming air superiority in Normandy. He had already advised Hitler to make peace. To gain support, Stauffenberg stressed that Germany faced defeat, Bolshevik rule, and more senseless slaughter—not of Jews but of German soldiers and civilians. Even so, few were moved. Stauffenberg's allies were sunk in "helpless passivity," and he was almost the lone driving force behind the attempt to kill Hitler.[13] Some of his supporters hoped that, with Hitler dead, they would be able to negotiate an armistice in the west or the east to concentrate on one foe. Others hoped the Allies would support a

"Christian crusade" to defend the West from bolshevism. They had little idea of the horror with which the West would react to the Holocaust.

On July 20, 1944, Stauffenberg, scheduled to report in person to Hitler in his East Prussian headquarters, brought a time-delayed bomb in a brief-case, placing it near the *Fuehrer*. After Stauffenberg left the room on a pretext, the bomb exploded. Four people died of their wounds, but Hitler was spared. Believing Hitler dead, Stauffenberg flew to Berlin to lead the coup. The journey took two hours. He found almost nothing had been started in spite of promises. His hope that many officers would join the coup on their own was in vain. Even in those few hours when it seemed Hitler was dead, they did little. The war was lost, tens of thousands were falling victim to Allied bombs and Russian troops, the army leaders had weapons, and their courage was proven under fire. But they could not imagine a real alternative to the Nazis. Bound to them by shared values, implicated in the slaughter in the east, army officers did not rise. Para-doxically, the fate of the aristocratic resistance serves mainly to show how close traditional conservatives were to the Nazis in outlook and aim. Long after the war, when all knew the fate of the Jews, the majority of Ger-man adults who had lived in the Nazi era still believed Stauffenberg was a traitor, as he, knowing them well, predicted they would.

Contrary to older views, Kershaw writes, there was in Nazi Germany "remarkably free expression of great discontent."[14] And it throws a harsh light on the lack of protest about the fate of the Jews. Discontent arose from the Nazis' failure to live up to their campaign promises. Peasants complained about the lack of cheap credit, low prices for their products, high costs for farm machinery and fertilizer, heavy indebtedness, and price controls on food. The drain of farm labor into the factories brought harder work and less income. Some farmers held back produce from the market, and some even clashed with the Nazis. By 1938 the Jews could no longer be blamed, and some discovered that Gentiles charged more with the Jews gone. Some Bavarian peasants declared they would sabo-tage the regime's economy if their neglect continued. As war production replaced farm machinery, peasants clamored for foreign labor, and it soon came. Throughout the protests, however, Gestapo and civilian informers assured the regime that the disturbances were economic, not the result of ideological antagonisms.

The Nazis were surprised by Protestants who complained when "Ger-man Christians" who rejected the Old Testament replaced their old priests. When Hitler ended this blasphemy, however, peasants and clergy alike declared their loyalty to the regime. Rural Catholics in Bavaria were far more upset when, in 1941, overzealous Gauleiters removed crucifixes from schools. Rising spontaneously to demonstrate, Bavarians demanded

to know why Germans suffered the "atheistic bolshevism" of their own
leaders even as their sons were sent to die in Russia. Thousands rallied
with "rapturous ovations" for bishops opposing the Nazification of the
church. Nazi offices were trashed, and protests were read from the pulpit. Before "unrest in the entire province," the Nazis retreated.[15] But barring further errors, the regime was aware they would enjoy the loyalty of
the faithful. After the war, Christianity could be eradicated from a new
generation.

Contrary to the alleged absolute power of the Nazis, civil disobedience
and militant action could change their policies. Ordinary citizens were
the first to protest the shipping of patients from hospitals to be gassed in
the killing centers, and Himmler was forced to close one down. The
Nazis feared Gentile unrest in time of war and were reluctant to suppress
it if enough dissidents—not of the left—were involved. But church leaders of both faiths supported only denunciations of euthanasia and blatant
anti-Christian activities. As Kershaw notes, their protests contrast "starkly
and depressingly with the absence of strong feeling on the Jewish question."[16] The invasion of Russia occurred in the midst of the euthanasia
program, and the church hierarchies, in spite of their new insight into
the dreadful meaning of Nazi racial purification, agreed with Bishop
Michael Rackel, who declared the war "truly a crusade, a holy war for
homeland and people, for faith and Church, for Christ and his most holy
Cross."[17] Nazis must have been amused by such blessings, but pleased by
their effect.

With the left gone, public grumbling did not threaten Nazi rule.
Craftsmen and small businessmen complained when the Nazis favored
large businesses over small and did not ban department stores and consumer coops. But battlefield successes and the removal of the Jews helped
still the grievances of craftsmen and small businessmen doing well in the
booming economy. Lesser civil servants complained when their salaries
suffered or party officials browbeat them. Teachers were upset because,
overworked and underpaid, and true to their pan-German convictions,
they contributed much extra time to voluntary work in Nazi organizations, like the Hitler Youth, but received little in return. They were no
threat. In short, the grousings of the *Mittelstand* were the frustrations of
loyalists, and the Nazis could count on them as they prepared for the victory that would end all Aryan grievances. Nazi agents reported that none
of the complaints of the lower middle classes implied an alternative to
Nazi rule. As Detlev Peukert says, for all its criticism the *Mittelstand*
continued to "show an especially high degree of loyalty."[18]

Upper-middle-class groups often complained about some of the practices of the regime. Peukert tells of a "swing youth" of well-off middle-
class children, who, aping British upper-class style and disdainful of Nazi

enthusiasms, danced and caroused in the style of the "flapper era" to American jazz, even though censors roundly condemned the degenerate Benny "Gutmann" and his "Neger musik." Most middle-class complaints were aimed at party corruption, low salaries, high prices, and taxes. But as a Nazi report notes, the complainers were "not judging National Socialism a system of corruption and barbarism," or objecting to terror.[19] Most approved of the oppression of the left and the killing of Roehm and his radicals. Some hoped Hitler would conduct another "purge" of the "old fighters" who lived like petty feudal lords at public expense. Their dissatisfaction merely reflected what Kershaw calls a "broad basic consensus" in favor of Nazi values in the middle class.[20]

Among all the complaints, one is lacking: Gestapo and Security Service reported no significant disapproval of anti-Jewish legislation. In fact the Nuremberg Laws were popular. Peukert tells us that "The public labeling of Jews with the yellow star, the deportation to the east, and the exterminations in the gas chambers left no great mark in the public-opinion reports."[21] Only 1 percent of the court cases for dissent dealt with citizens making pro-Jewish statements. Nor was the German public simply indifferent or apathetic. Indeed, the Gestapo received such a "flood of denunciations" about Jews or Gentiles violating anti-Semitic regulations that it complained about the time and work needed to check them.[22] Robert Gellately, always careful in his judgments, tells us that "Without social cooperation of various kinds . . . the anti-Semitic policies would have remained so many idle fantasies."[23] There could hardly be a stronger indictment.

Gellately notes that though the Gestapo was "heavily dependent on public participation in the enforcement process" and employed paid informants, it received a "relative paucity" of reports of complaints about anti-Semitic policies. Peukert says such complaints in Gestapo files were "astonishingly rare." From 1933 through 1944 in all Munich, a grand total of sixty-seven Gentiles were tried for complaining about racial legislation, and half the cases were dropped for lack of evidence. Certainly many held their tongues from fear, but even so, Gellately says that "negative remarks" about the Jewish policies "must be termed so small as to be almost insignificant."[24] In contrast, German farmers made many protests against the harsh Nazi treatment of Polish slave laborers.

When Mussolini declared the Jews enemies of the regime in 1938 and ordered them handed over to the Germans, his bureaucrats sabotaged him with a confusion of technical difficulties, and he received little public cooperation. Four of five Italian Jews survived the war; one in a hundred German Jews managed to. And many of those Italian Jews who were arrested had been denounced by paid agents or Italians coerced by the SS after Italy's surrender. In Vichy France, however, there were thousands

of voluntary denunciations. The royalist and racist right had long hoped
to harm the Jews; the Germans gave it the chance it never had the popularity or electoral mandate to gain on its own.

Some argue that Germans who betrayed the Jews may not have acted
from racist motives, for their denunciations had practical advantages. One
might gain Jewish property, remove a rival in romance or business, advance one's career or cancel a debt. Personal jealousy, envy, greed, or ambition might indeed have been the motive. But practical motives cannot
be separated from anti-Semitism even if denunciations convey advantage.
All motives are mixed; here they coincided, as during the Crusades when
Christian anti-Semitism justified the seizure of Jewish property. Certainly
Nazi rule gave anti-Semites a unique chance to gain practical advantages
from the persecution of innocents, but a population relatively free of extreme racial hostility would not have seized this advantage in such great
numbers, especially because denouncing a Jew was tantamount to sending him or her to prison or death in a concentration camp. Bound by
no legal rules, the Gestapo rarely believed the victim. To accuse a Gentile of friendly relationships with Jews, especially "racial defilement,"
might bring the beating, torture, or incarceration of the accused; the Jew
would die.

By 1938 tens of thousands of German citizens were imprisoned or dead,
facts that were circulated in order to intimidate enemies of the regime.
Can we not assume, consequently, that the man who coveted an elderly
Jewish woman's apartment and falsely accused her of violating racial regulations to get it was an anti-Semite? And what of those who made accusations to get rid of a business competitor, divorce a wife, or gain
property? Or those who denounced Gentiles for consorting with Jews because they hoped to avoid paying a debt, rid themselves of a business
partner, or punish a hated teacher? Private advantage and racial hatred
merged, and guilt was erased because the action was both sanctioned by
the authorities and coincided with a personal belief in the "Jewish menace." There are those in every society who would use any means to advance, but we are not speaking of criminals. Indeed, some of the most
immoral and irresponsible accusers may have been the least racist. If I
accuse you of sleeping with a Jew only because you refused to sleep with
me, I may not be a racist; if I am sexually uninterested in you but accuse
you because I think you actually did sleep with a Jew, I certainly am.

In any event, many of the recorded denunciations have no practical
motive but were made simply to punish traitors to the *Volk*. Reliable estimates show that something like one-quarter to one-half of all accusers
received only the psychic reward of punishing Jew or Gentile "enemies"
of the people. Countless private citizens voluntarily complained to local
party headquarters. Some denounced those who hid a Jew, accused a Jew-

ish boss of sexually harassing an employee, denounced a Gentile for sleeping with a Jew or a prostitute for having Jewish customers, or a businessman for overpaying a Jew in a transaction or selling a scarce item to a Jew. Some even accused party members of being friendly with Jews, a dangerous act if the Gestapo decided that the accuser had lied. Accusations were also leveled against Gentiles who complained about anti-Semitic legislation, or were seen dining, visiting, presenting a gift to a Jew, or simply shaking hands in a friendly way with someone who was or "looked" Jewish. Wealthy Jews might be denounced because the accuser wished to humble the high and mighty member of an "inferior race" and felt the Nazis were lax in their duties not to have already done so. Roughly 60 percent of all denunciations came from private citizens, but an unknown number were rejected out of hand as patently false or ridiculous. There were even denunciations of Gentiles for having had relationships with Jews before World War I, though Goering put a stop to such retroactive zealotry. For the first time in German history, a regime acted upon the accusations of anti-Semites. Hence the public response is an indication of the depth of racism among the Germans. Gestapo records are incomplete, and the destruction of many security files allows for no accurate percentages, but this much is certain: without overwhelming public cooperation, the Gestapo would have been unable to isolate, deport, and kill almost all the Jews of Germany.

The denouncers, naturally, tended to come from the same groups that voted strongly for the Nazis: Protestants were more zealous than Catholics. "Old liberals and democrats were especially sympathetic to the Jews, while one-time 'reactionaries,' such as members of the Pan-German League, agreed with the measures."[25] Dov Kulka argues persuasively that among those "openly critical" on "ideological, religious, social, or economic grounds" were Communists, Social Democrats, liberal intelligentsia, and some businessmen.[26] Most of the protests against anti-Semitic legislation came from Berlin and the industrial cities of the Ruhr, socialist strongholds, or Hamburg, the most liberal German city, a center of international commerce with strong English connections, historically famed for its disdain of nationalist extremism, a city where intermarriage among Jewish and German commercial families was the most frequent in Germany.

"The smaller the town, the larger the Nazi vote"—the old guide indicates the major source of popular anti-Semitism. (In the 1950s neo-Nazis received most of their votes from rural areas.) In the 1930s many rural towns and villages, including tourist haunts with income to lose, had to be restrained from putting up signs threatening violence to Jews; they were allowed only to raise signs banning Jews. Before *Kristallnacht*, Austrian villages were physically dangerous for Jews. By 1937 Jews still in

372IDEOLOGY OF DEATH

small towns in Germany fled to big cities to escape hostility. Neither socialists nor liberal intelligentsia, of course, were to be found in any great numbers in rural Germany. By and large, security and police reports indicate that rural Germans were pleased to see the Jews leave during the expulsions of 1941. Local newspapers happily reported their town was *Judenrein* and hoped all Germany would be soon. International reports of German reactions against the persecutions usually originated from big cities that had voted socialist or Progressive; reporters rarely knew the activities of small-town Germany. This has led to an overestimation of words and actions friendly to Jews. But even in the largest cities, hundreds of restaurants refused to serve Jews even before the regime marked ration coupons with a "J" so that Jews could not eat in public establishments.

Much has been made of the public distaste for the violence of *Kristallnacht*, but the evidence is uncertain. In Berlin the correspondent for the *London Daily Telegraph* reported that many well-dressed citizens were "screaming with glee" as Jews were beaten and synagogues burned; the *Washington Post* told of large crowds of civilians plundering Jewish stores. The British consul found strong public support for the attacks.[27] Witnesses claimed that many Germans laughed and hurled insults, though it is also reported that many silently disapproved. The Gestapo reported much plundering in villages. In Austria and the Sudetenland, the public reaction was uniquely savage. Some complained of the economic damage done to the *Volk*. They had sacrificed to save scrap metal, property, and food as war loomed, and hooligans were allowed to destroy all—an attitude shared by many highly placed Nazis. Police in rural areas often reported that the "population agreed" with the removal of Jews but disliked property damage. Kershaw tells us that anger at the Jews caused 80 percent of the teachers of Franconia to refuse to teach the Old Testament during religious instruction. Rural Germany, the strongest source of anti-Semitism, was underreported.

Many might have protested property damage because it was safer than defending Jews outright. But the attitude of the clergy indicates otherwise. Barring rare exceptions, they kept silent. If many disapproved, perhaps they knew their attitude would be unpopular with their congregations. Destruction of property, unauthorized murder, and uncontrolled mob action frightened many; without the rule of law, who might be next? A widespread and "uncritical approval of the anti-Semitic decrees of the government" was not incompatible with disapproval of the "gutter elements" of the SA.[28] There is no record of protest against the "legal" arrest and shipment to concentration camps of some forty thousand Jews, nor against the brutal murders reported in the foreign press. But there were many German complaints against the international outcry over the barbarism of *Kristallnacht*. Tragically, when the Holocaust was confirmed in 1942, the international reaction was much weaker.

Kristallnacht aside, "the response to the legal measures of 1938" taken against the Jews was "positive and uncritical."[29] Tens of thousands of Jewish businesses remained, and Berlin city officials complained that the flood of citizens claiming Jewish property was so large their agencies were swamped. Many who had protested about other matters were silent about the Jews. In Franconia the thousands of peasants who had massed to protect their bishop from being replaced by a "German Christian" were historically "a hot bed of vicious popular anti-Semitism."[30] Once the Nazis capitulated on that issue, Franconians remained loyal, as Gestapo agents reported. Taking the crucifixes out of Bavarian schools aroused violent protests; taking the Jews out of Bavarian towns aroused nothing much, one suspects, but approval.

In Vienna, civilians needed no prompting. They ransacked Jewish homes and stores, threw Jews out of cafés and trolleys, and beat them in the streets. In rural Austria racism was stronger than in Vienna, but there were few Jews to torment. As Bruce Pauley tells us, "Three months after the *Anschluss*, Jews had already been more thoroughly purged from [the] public life of Austria than in the five years following Hitler's takeover of power in Germany."[31] Austrian Nazis even complained that the public supported them only because of their anti-Semitism and not the rest of their program. Socialists in the resistance were shocked to discover that many Austrian workers approved the seizing of Jewish wealth, though they took no part in the atrocities. Some five thousand Berlin Jews survived the war, but only seven hundred Viennese Jews. And the Jewish population of Vienna in 1938 had been more than twice that of Berlin.

Significant public protests, supported by a united clergy and conservative elites, might have saved the Jews of Germany, but the assumption that protests were stifled by fear of Nazi terror is untested. The anti-euthanasia actions indicate that when confronted by significant nonleft and Gentile opposition, the regime backed down. One incident is illustrative. Until January 1943 Jews married to Aryans and involved in war work were not normally sent to camps. But the regime decided to clear Berlin of Jews and surrounded the factories and workers' homes, arresting some ten thousand Jews who were to be shipped to Auschwitz. Many had Gentile wives who, joined by other workers, demonstrated day and night for about a week in front of Gestapo headquarters, demanding their husbands be freed. They did not desist even when threatened with machine guns. As the crowd grew, Goebbels decided to release some of the prisoners. Thus two thousand Jews were saved from extermination by the demonstrations of hundreds of Gentiles, and the protesters were unharmed.

The regime also ordered all Jews in Auschwitz related to living Ayrans released or transferred to work camps. One may at least wonder if, given
enough Gentile protests, the murder of at least the German Jews might
have been postponed until the war was won, as were other extreme Nazi
goals. As Nathan Stoltzfus has written, "Apparently the exemption of a
Jew from Nazi genocide depended on whether an Aryan somewhere in
German society was likely to make problems for the Nazi regime. . . ."[32]

Public anti-Semitism was often too powerful for even a decent silence.
When Jews were cruelly driven from Hanover into Poland in October
1938, for example, "The streets were black with people shouting, 'Jews
out to Palestine.' "[33] When Jews were dragged from their homes by force
in 1941, some reports say they were jeered, others say some Gentiles
were sympathetic, but satisfaction or indifference seems the main reaction. The police did not move secretly; Jews were often held in illumi-
nated areas for two days before being marched off to the trains. The
police were forced to seal the doors of the homes and businesses of de-
parting Jews to prevent looting. Kershaw says "probably most" Germans
were "opposed to the Jews" and "welcomed their exclusion from economy and society. . . ."[34]

We cannot know exactly how many Germans knew the Jews were being
murdered as it was happening, but a reasonable estimate is possible and
important, for it highlights the extent of anti-Semitism. Evidence indicates millions knew that masses of Jews were being killed, whatever they
knew about methods and pace. After all, Hitler constantly promised their
destruction. In his first political statement in 1919 he declared the "ultimate goal" of anti-Semitism must "unalterably be the elimination of the
Jews altogether." In Mein Kampf he declared Jews should have been
gassed in 1914; in 1924 he said death was the answer to "Juda, the world
plague."[35] In 1936 he told a Conservative supporter he would exterminate
whole races. In January 1939 he informed the Czech foreign minister,
"We are going to destroy the Jews."[36] On January 30, 1939, he declared to
the world that war would bring the annihilation of the Jews in Europe.
Reichstag deputies applauded this loud, long, and on camera. In 1942
Hitler told the Reichstag that Germany was engaged in a war of humanity
against the Jews who were supported by Western plutocrats and Jewish
Bolsheviks. In January 1942, ten days after the supposedly secret decision
of the Wannsee Conference confirmed the regime's determination to
murder all Jews within reach, Hitler announced the policy in a broadcast rally before thousands of spectators at the Sportspalast in Berlin,
knowing full well his words would be picked up by the Allies:

> The war can only end with the extermination of the Aryan peoples or
> the disappearance of the Jews from Europe. . . . The war will not end

as the Jews imagine it will, namely with the uprooting of the Aryans, but the result of this war will be the complete annihilation of the Jews. . . . The hour will come when the most evil universal enemy of all time will be finished. . . .³⁷

Hitler reminded the public again in September 1942, as he once prophesied, "If Jewry should plot another world war in order to exterminate the Aryan peoples of Europe, it would not be the Aryan peoples who would be exterminated, but Jewry."³⁸

To listen to Hitler's broadcasts was a public duty; work stopped, all were assembled, and the press gave extensive coverage. In short, Hitler told the Germans of the regime's determination to kill the Jews of Europe, and he repeated it with utter clarity on several ceremonious and solemn public occasions. Other Nazis did the same. In November 1941 Rosenberg told journalists about the resettlements in the east, saying: "There are still about six million Jews living in Russia, and the problem can only be solved by a biological elimination of the entire Jewish population of Europe."³⁹ In the same month Goebbels wrote in the newspaper *Das Reich* that Hitler's prophecy "concerning the extermination of the Jewish race in Europe was now coming true." As the Bolsheviks advanced in the east, he added, "Jewish liquidation commandos" accompanied them; the threat would be met by "the complete and radical extermination and elimination of Jewry."⁴⁰ The war against the Jews was never a secret war.

Westerners think such remarks too horrible to be believed, just as their humanistic values still fail them when confronted with "ethnic cleansing." Given the information published about Nazi terror in Germany by 1941, however, those who shared the regime's anti-Semitism could easily imagine the fate of the Jews in the maelstrom of horror in the east. But millions of Germans, including the Jews, were too progressive and humanistic to believe the Jews were really being exterminated to the last child. Even so, in Vienna and Berlin the suicide rate among Jews soared when deportations began, and officials assumed the Jews knew what awaited. In June 1942 very reliable authorities in Europe reported that 700,000 Jews had already been killed and that all were doomed. Jewish leaders in the United States could not believe it. The editors of the *Jewish Frontier*, progressive and humane, did not publish the report for weeks. Later, apologizing profusely, they confessed they had held back because they believed the report must be "the macabre fantasy of a lunatic sadist."⁴¹ Long after the war, Westerners believed Speer's fantastic claim that he did not know of the killings though he "should have known" but somehow "did not want to know." He avoided such psychobabble in the German edition of his memoir. He must have known it would bring amusement and contempt from his peers, aware he had visited Mau-

thausen, an extermination camp, in search of slave labor. Once in Mauthausen he recommended that inmates be worked harder; a kinder-
hearted SS officer protested that Speer did not realize the "tremendous
rise in mortality" that would be caused by the more "primitive working
methods" he wanted.[42]

The murders in the killing centers of Germany were public knowledge.
The physicians, nurses, attendants, and bureaucrats evidently spoke of it
publicly, children in the streets knew of it, jokes circulated: "Keep acting
that way and you too will end up in the baking ovens!" The stench of
the crematoria was detectable for miles, and the transport vans carrying
victims were known everywhere because tens of thousands were transferred to the centers on the roads. Many of the victims knew what would
happen to them in the "showers," and there were horrible scenes. If public knowledge about the murder of so many disabled German Christians
for "racial purification" was widespread, it seems evident that millions of
Nazi supporters would have known that the Jews were not sent east simply to become farmers.

Before the invasion of Russia, the high command agreed to help kill
Russian prisoners, civilians, and Jews, and with little secrecy. The *New
York Post* of October 23, 1941, reported: "German Troops Massacre Thousands of Jews in the Ukraine.... Corpses Floating in the Dniester
River."[43] Hundreds of thousands of soldiers in the east must have participated in, witnessed, or heard about the massacres. Why assume they kept
silent when on leave? Non-Jewish slave laborers on German farms had
many horror stories to tell, as did the personal slaves sent home by German officers. Thousands of ethnic Germans in the east knew about the
massacres, and many helped kill; a leader of an *Einsatzkommando* group
testified that even he was frightened by their thirst for blood. They too
traveled freely in Germany. A recent book tells of thousands who voluntarily helped kill, and has "documented accounts of soldiers and officers
who refused to kill Jews and did not suffer serious consequences."[44] Thousands of German occupation officials in the east knew from reports, documents, or their own acts what occurred. Local police guarded the trains,
worked with the SS, shot Jewish hostages, or spoke with those who did.
Christopher Browning tells of a unit that killed more than eighty thousand Polish Jews. Only a small minority of the killers were Nazis or SS,
and they included small businessmen, waiters, teachers, druggists, dock-
workers, truck drivers, and construction workers. Some refused to kill and
were not punished. It has never been shown that Nazi killers acted under
duress.[45]

In 1942 the Nazi party had about six million members, perhaps 200,000
SS, and more in affiliated organizations. It seems highly improbable that
they, the SA, the 52,000-man Gestapo, and other security forces were un-

aware of the killings. The murderers also needed a "supporting cast of diplomats, bureaucrats, and military officers."[46] In the camps were thousands of guards, mechanics for the gassing facilities, construction workers, electricians, civilian personnel for the SS, industrial managers, accountants, stenographers, suppliers, and so on. Auschwitz was a major railway junction, not a rural backwater, and police and city officials in nearby towns and along the railway lines in Germany and Austria tracked escaped prisoners. In 1941 Himmler gave permission to a local official to kill the 100,000 Jews in his district, just one example of local initiative. In November 1941 police officials and camp commandants reported that in transfer many prisoners died on the march, and it was impossible to keep the public ignorant of such matters. Rumors of the killings circulated in Germany in 1941; when they were brought to Hitler's attention, he said, "It's not a bad idea . . . that public rumor attributes to us a plan to exterminate the Jews. Terror is a salutary thing."[47] Often no attempt was made to hide the murders. When an order from General Manstein brought death to thousands of Jews in Russia, hundreds witnessed. In Serbia mobile gas vans were used to kill thousands of Jewish women and children in 1942: "Clearly if the Germans could drive a gas van through downtown Belgrade day after day while its passengers screamed and pounded on the back door in their death agony, secrecy was not the highest priority at the time, except in regard to the unsuspecting victims still in the camp."[48]

As Raul Hilberg remarks, it was possible to kill without seeing the victims. Thousands of professionals—lawyers, judges, financial experts, physicians, clerks of all sorts—managed the bureaucratic intricacies of the removal and death of the Jews. These "desk murderers" worked in many government agencies. Heydrich and Ernst Kaltenbrunner distributed weekly extermination reports. *Einsatzgruppen* regularly reported in writing the number and ethnicity of their victims to various officials and agencies. In the Foreign Office, reports were freely circulated in hundreds of copies, and more than fifty bureaucratic agencies or officials in Berlin received reports. Undoubtedly thousands of office workers involved in the bureaucratic niceties of mass murder saw these reports. Eichmann's people coordinated some twenty separate railway centers to transport Jews; hundreds of clerks were involved, and tens of thousands of Germans and Ukrainians worked on the railroads in the east. The Reichsbahn, which did the transporting, employed a half-million civil servants and close to a million workers. The travel plans of the death-camp trains were handled by the same people who handled regular railway traffic. Hilberg relates that in one transport office the papers were not stamped "secret"; presumably they were lying around for all to peruse. Business executives knew what was happening in the death camps because they helped request and process slave labor in Germany and the east. Accountants, supervisors, and other employees were involved, and the high death rate of slave laborers was a matter of company record. Companies freely competed for contracts to produce the gas, crematoria, and other death-camp needs, and their technicians often visited the sites. Some corporation employees helped select those fit to work; SS men stood by to send the unfit to the gas chambers.

Some 46,000 physicians joined the Nazi party, and thousands of them, along with scientists and "racial hygienists," ran the racial programs, including the killing centers in Germany. They knew Jews were often killed simply because they were Jews, not because they met the criteria for disabled Gentiles. In 1941 hospitals helped exterminate all Jewish patients. Physicians and "racial hygienists" helped select death-camp victims and also trained SS men. Physicians were informed about racial policies in a special newsletter. As early as 1939 the need for a "final solution" of the Jewish, homosexual, and Gypsy "problems" was discussed at physicians' meetings. Academics attending conferences where the "findings" of people like Dr. Mengele were reported in scholarly papers knew who were the subjects of the experiments. When universities and institutes received the human organs and skeletons they requested from the camps, forensic knowledge alone would have ruled out natural death.

Germans to be resettled in the east were told they would encounter no Jews. Ethnic Germans who witnessed or participated in the killings corresponded with and visited relatives in the west. Soldiers may well have told their relatives and friends of the "secret." The White Rose resistance group included a veteran who told his fellow students of the atrocities. In August 1941 Helmut von Moltke wrote in a letter: "Again and again one hears reports that in transporting . . . Jews only twenty percent arrive."[49] As we know, those who set up the ghettos of Poland in 1939 knew "the final goal" was to "burn out this plague boil"; in February 1940 a newspaper called ghettos only a "temporary solution to the Jewish question." In June 1942 the international service of the BBC broadcast that 700,000 Jews had been killed, and many Germans listened to these trusted broadcasts, though it was a crime. Clergy knew of the murders in the east from their colleagues, who were chaplains there. Soldiers sent letters from the front asking their priests to speak out, in vain. Bishop Wurm sent a letter to the regime in 1943: "We Christians consider the . . . extermination of the Jews as a grave injustice and of fatal consequences for the German people."[50] Cardinal Bertram wrote in 1944 that German Christians would be upset if Christians of Jewish origin met "a fate similar to the Jews" . . . "extermination."[51] Both assumed—and they would know—that their flock was quite aware of the killings.

In 1942 the government noted a fear among the population that German prisoners in Allied hands "might be executed in the same way as were the deported Jews by the SS." Similar reports told of a German anxiety of paying with their own lives for the murder of the Jews. True anti-Semites, many assumed the immense power of "international Jewry" was certain to bring harsh revenge. When the Allied bombing raids began, some suggested that the West be warned that ten Jews would be shot for each German killed, evidently assuming this would stop the raids. "Similar sentiments also found expression in the files of unbelievably inhumane letters sent to Goebbels from all over Germany."[52] Given Hitler's and Goebbels's public statements, it seems the regime cared little if foreign governments knew of the killings. In any event, the Germans could not control the many leaks of information from occupied nations or those allied with them whose officials or peoples had witnessed or heard of the actions. Whatever the regime kept secret, its aim was to hide the policy from the Jews, in order to avoid riots and resistance. The Jews must not know, for they alone would cause trouble. There was no reason to fear the general public once Progressives and leftists had been silenced.

Nazi terror was neither hidden nor concealed. Evidence indicates strong public approval provided the acts were legal and directed against the left, the Slavs, and above all the Jews. Indeed, the arrest of political suspects, homosexuals, Gypsies, and Jews seems to have been plainly popular among the millions who had voted for or otherwise supported the Nazis. Given the historical belief that the Jews were the primary enemies of Germany, and the benefits that would have accrued to the average German if the Nazis conquered their racial empire, it is hard to imagine there would have been much protest by Germans about the Holocaust. We cannot be certain, but insights may be gained by analyzing the reaction of Germans to former Nazis and war criminals after the war.

25: AFTERMATH: JUDGMENT AND INNOCENCE

EICHMANN: "I had nothing to do with killing the Jews. I never killed a Jew ... and I never ordered anybody to kill a Jew."

INTERROGATOR: "You say you had nothing to do with the killing?"

EICHMANN: "That's right."

— Trial of Adolf Eichmann, 1962

IN 1945 the German establishment stood accused of massive complicity with the Nazis. As their power returned, however, they were able to clear themselves. And they were able to persuade most scholars that though conservatives helped pave the way for Hitler, they did so only because they naively assumed they could control his excesses and did not imagine he would harm the Jews. De-Nazification proceedings, war crimes trials in German courts, countless memoirs protesting innocence, and the writings of German academics, themselves appointed or approved during the Nazi era, soon made these the accepted views: Only Hitler, Himmler, and a few other Nazis were guilty of the Holocaust; the Nazis had no roots in German history. They were criminals, even psychopaths, who, in a time of trauma and despair, took power by historical accident. The acceptance of these ideas constitutes the final success of the pre-Weimar ruling class.

Ernst Kaltenbrunner, leader of the Austrian SS in 1938, supervised the death camps and personally ordered the killing of many Sephardic Jews previously exempted because "racial experts" believed they were not blood-related to the Ashkenazim. Sentenced to hang by the Allies in 1946, he declared: "I do not feel guilty of any war crimes. I have only done my duty. ... I refuse to serve as a substitute for Hitler."[1] His attitude became the preferred stance of the elites and was supported by the German judiciary itself. Ingo Mueller, author of the invaluable *Hitler's Justice* — upon which I heavily depend — found that the names of many former Nazi judges had been crossed out or omitted from documents implicating them in Nazi crimes. He discovered them only by going through old newspapers. A law student in Germany in the 1960s, Mueller recalls how he and others interested in the Nazi past of their teachers "would often discuss our misgivings in private. But in classes it was taboo. Our careers would have been harmed."[2] In 1946 one of Erzberger's assassins was re-tried because a public prosecutor wanted to reverse the amnesty awarded the killer by Hitler. But the court dropped all charges, repeating the old phrases: the murderers were simply "overzealous" . . . "with patriotic mo-tives."[3] In 1939 a would-be assassin of Hitler had been executed; when his relatives sought exoneration and reopened the case in 1955, the judges not only confirmed the original sentence but added new symbolic posthu-mous punishments.

After the Nuremberg War Crimes Trials, West German courts set the standards for guilt and innocence. But more than 80 percent of the ju-diciary were themselves the former instruments of Nazi terror. Some had even served sentences as war criminals in former occupied territories. Ob-jectors were punished: a judge who exposed the Nazi past of another judge who supported killing "inferior beings" was himself disciplined for "failing to show the proper respect to his superior." The judiciary adopted the view "that a judge could be found guilty of murder, manslaughter, or false imprisonment only if it could be proved that he had knowingly broken the law."[4] But the terror of the regime was legal, as the conserva-tive allies of Hitler had wanted it to be, and now the courts could acquit colleagues claiming they only followed the law. Judges who had sen-tenced Jewish prisoners to be worked to death, regardless of any crime, were acquitted because, though they may "possibly" have acted unjustly, their decisions were not technically illegal. Even obedience to law was not enough. One judge was acquitted though he had exceeded Nazi laws. The court ruled that his overzealous loyalty to Nazism was insufficient grounds for punishment, for "he could have been such for thoroughly understandable and laudable reasons." Precisely. For the court, Nazi ide-ology was laudable.

Even the supreme court, nearly all ex-Nazis, was determined to hand down decisions that would "acquit Third Reich judges of responsibility to the last man." The courts freed the most murderous judges, those of the infamous People's Court, Hitler's special tribunal for punishing pre-sumed enemies of the regime. In 1944 the notorious ultra-Nazi Roland Freisler of the People's Court ordered the hanging of defendants on mere suspicion of plotting against Hitler, allowing no contrary testimony and cursing defendants who spoke up. Although the films of the trial show the proceedings to be on a par with Stalin's purge trials, the courts nonetheless insisted there was no real proof that legal procedures had been violated. Like millions, the judiciary regarded Stauffenberg and his associates as traitors, and disguised judicial murder with legal obfuscation. Judges who had handed out illegal sentences were not guilty, because as "fanatic Nazis" they may have been blinded by "political delusions."[5] Such reasoning would have acquitted Hitler and Himmler themselves. Outraged Social Democrats introduced legislation to condemn such actions, but they were stalled by Christian Democrats until, in most cases, the senility or illness of the few survivors could be used as an excuse to keep them from trial. A host of legalisms cleared the judiciary of almost all the decisions that had upheld Nazi terror. As Mueller has written, to convict even one judge would have led to an "avalanche" engulfing "the majority of postwar West German judges." When a judge was acquitted of murder by a series of absurd technicalities, another scholar noted that the tribunal knew that to convict the murderer "would have meant that the West German judicial system had been established by murderers in the hundreds."[6] Indeed. No judge was ever convicted of anything; no court ever nullified any Nazi law.

As earlier noted, lawyers were highly overrepresented among those who administered the Final Solution and commanded the killing units. Now, after 1945, most were back in practice in courts all over the Federal Republic. Often, therefore, former Nazis judged former Nazis defended by former Nazis. If, as nearly all judges claimed to the Allies, they were appalled by Nazi atrocities, a wave of convictions would have flooded Germany. Instead, having cleared themselves, the judiciary proceeded to clear others. The Bundestag helped by blocking the extradition of war criminals, refusing to recognize the decisions of foreign courts. Men who had killed tens of thousands in other nations and now lived in Germany (some of them already tried in absentia and found guilty) got off scot-free. When the West German judiciary was asked to help collect evidence for East German courts in order to try some three thousand prominent Nazis and war criminals, the jurists found technical reasons to declare such proceedings illegal. They would not help a court that would undoubtedly have found many of the three thousand guilty. The judges refused not only the communist courts but prosecutors in democratic nations. Army leaders declared they would refuse to participate in the defense of Europe unless pardons were given to their colleagues charged with murders in the east. The courts then ruled that Jewish hostages were actually partisan fighters deserving of execution. Some officers declared that all Jews were known enemies of the regime, and killing them was a normal wartime duty. The courts agreed. The same arguments would have justified the killing of all unarmed prisoners of war and, if available, their relatives and the civilians of any conquered nation, whether they resisted or not. By manipulating legal concepts shrouded in jargon and shot through with contradictions, the guilt of hundreds of many of the worst war criminals was concealed, forgiven, or punished with embarrassingly mild sentences. Law triumphed over justice, as, supported by the majority of Christian Democratic politicians, the courts exonerated or slapped on the wrist those who had slaughtered Jews, Gypsies, Poles, and homosexuals.

A startling example of the perversion of justice is the case of SS General Karl Wolff, no less a personage than Himmler's personal adjutant and liaison to Hitler. In 1943 he wrote to a subordinate: "It gave me great pleasure to learn that for the last fourteen days, a train leaves daily with five thousand passengers of the Chosen People to Treblinka; and we are even in a position to complete this mass movement of people at an accelerated rate." Undeniable evidence forced the supreme court to admit that Wolff not only supervised the transfer of thousands of Jews to the death camps but believed their murder "necessary and correct." Nevertheless, the judges ruled there was "no proof that he acted on his own convictions." True, the court admitted, he had aided Himmler and shared his views, but it could not be proven that Wolff would have committed these acts or had acted on his own initiative because of his personal beliefs: he only "wanted to help Himmler carry out his task." Thus he was not a murderer but an accomplice to murder, and this, of course, carried a far lighter sentence.

In 1958 ten members of SS annihilation units which had murdered some four thousand Jews were tried. The court held that the actual "originators of these deeds" were "Hitler, Himmler, Heydrich, and their immediate circle," and decided that though the murderers had not acted under duress or orders but "of their own free will," one could not prove they were "personally motivated to commit the murders." They had merely supported "the deeds of the chief perpetrators." As accomplices they were given sentences "averaging two days for each proven murder." As Mueller writes, such sentences mocked the dead. Courts continued to rule that Hitler, Himmler, Heydrich, and perhaps Kaltenbrunner were the "real perpetrators," and manslaughter charges led to acquittal or brief sentences.[8] In 1960 the parties of the right in the Bundestag passed a statute of limitations on manslaughter. The Social Democrats tried to stop them but were outvoted and suffered at elections; millions of voters hated the phrase "war criminal," and some politicians demanded it be dropped.

To be punished for murder, one had to be guilty according to Nazi law; none of these laws was repealed, and the Nazis had legalized murder in service of the state. Thus one had to be found guilty not of killing, but of killing for pleasure or from "base motives" or with "malicious intent."[9] If one merely obeyed orders, or believed one was defending the state from its enemies, the charge was manslaughter. One could have

killed, helped kill, or ordered the killing of thousands, but if "base motives" or "malicious intent" could not be proven, one had not murdered.
Worse, some defendants who admitted they had sincerely believed in
racial murder were freed or received reduced sentences—sincere belief
was held to cancel out "malicious intent." It was permissible to kill even
a Jewish infant if one believed he or she would become a mortal threat
to Germany and one had no "base motives." In short, a truly sincere Nazi
killer was not a murderer.

Contradictions abounded. A killer was excused because he acted out
of a "frenzy of anti-Semitism," hence was not responsible for his acts—
another plea that would have exonerated Himmler and Hitler. "Sometimes the participation in the mass murders in the east was even regarded
as 'service in war' " and excusable under military law.[10] Some defendants
were freed because they argued they lacked the character to refuse the
regime, others because, motivated by "patriotic considerations," they
killed those who denounced Germany or were communists. Corroborat-
ing witnesses were not demanded. Those freed for obeying orders did not
have to prove they would have been punished for refusing to kill noncombatant civilians. One could believe in racial murder, or admit killing
others solely because of race or religion, and still be acquitted.

Some were acquitted because their crimes were committed for state security during wartime. The judges simply accepted, without saying so,
the Nazi definition of state security, which included, of course, the murder of noncombatant Jews. The Holocaust was unique precisely because
the Jews were not and never had been a menace to Germany, except in
anti-Semitic mythology. Obviously, many judges accepted these myths.
During the war, for example, the Nazis executed a submarine captain for
deriding the idea that Germany was threatened by "world Jewry," and for
declaring that Hitler, not the Jews, had caused the war. After the war his
relatives appealed for his rehabilitation, but the court ruled that his statements had in fact been "demoralizing . . . reprehensible, and irresponsible."[11] In effect, the judges accepted Hitler's claim as written in his Last
Testament: "It is not true that I or anyone else in Germany wanted war
in 1939. It was willed and prepared exclusively by those statesmen who
were either of Jewish origins or worked for Jewish interests." Most judges
viewed participation in the Holocaust as manslaughter at worst; it is fortunate indeed that they did not have the chance to try Eichmann.

It took the revolutionary 1960s to arouse interest in the Holocaust and
bring strong international pressure against German war criminals. In the
famous "Auschwitz trial" of 1963–1965, twenty-one of the SS officers in
charge of extermination at Auschwitz were tried; eight were university
graduates. Only five of the twenty-one were found guilty of murder and
received life sentences; the others received an average of six years for

"complicity." Three were acquitted, and one was excused because of poor health. And this in a trial attracting world attention because of the dread symbolism of Auschwitz. When there was less international attention, outcomes differed. In 1964 a former Nazi who had organized and helped kill some ninety thousand victims was acquitted, and the federal supreme court upheld the acquittal on appeal.

Even without Nazi duress, the civil service supported their own. When the Allies fired Nazis from the civil service, the German legal profession and the civil service rose in near unanimity to protest. Most also scorned de-Nazification proceedings and denounced Germans who helped locate war criminals. In the 1950s, when Germans could hire without Allied interference, practically all those dismissed by the Allies were returned to public service. Hans Globke, coauthor of the Nuremberg racial laws, supporter of anti-Semitic measures before 1933, and part-time concentration camp inspector, not only got his government job back but, defended by Adenauer and the Christian Democrats, became the most influential civil servant in Germany. Franz Massfeller, who had helped plan the Final Solution from the Ministry of Justice, was rehired, recommended by the "old boys" network of former Nazis. But those the Nazis had purged were prevented from regaining their old positions. Social Democrats protested, but they were in the minority.

The bureaucrats who had planned and organized mass murder were far less likely to be prosecuted than those with blood on their hands. Consequently, most people thought Nazi crimes were committed only by brutes and sadists, not Germans of education and status. Unlike the Allies, German courts accepted the plea of those who said they stayed in high positions only because they feared being replaced by someone worse. Hans Frank, the "butcher of Poland," had so argued at Nuremberg; he was convicted and hanged. Under Secretary Franz Schlegelberger, the most important member of the Ministry of Justice to survive the war, was convicted by the Allies because of his participation in the atrocities in the east. He too insisted he cooperated only because he feared someone worse would replace him. As Mueller says, everyone ever tried could have said that, "leaving Hitler as the sole culprit."[12] Schlegelberger received a life sentence. German courts, however, released the highest civil servants on such pleas, pleas impossible to prove or disprove, which should have been ruled irrelevant. Yet another way had been found to remove the guilt for the Holocaust from everyone but dead Nazi leaders.

Death-camp guards and SS camp personnel, including one who helped kill some 26,000, were freed, judged to have been engaged in the "normal duties" of soldiers in wartime. A federal court decided that an SS "Death's Head" regiment from Dachau had performed "service similar to that of the regular army," and released them.[13] Such judgments could have been rendered only by men with beliefs like the Nazi academics, "racial experts," and education officers who, during the war, had told the guards their work was as much a war service as front-line combat. Thousands of staff members of the death camps were released. Still today, camp guards who helped murder Jews are not held accountable unless they committed voluntary and excessive acts of cruelty above and beyond the call of duty.

Of 180 Gestapo members in Frankfurt who sent victims to death camps, only 7 were briefly jailed. The courts decided they would not necessarily have known that death awaited their victims![14] High-ranking officials of the Ministry of Justice who had ordered thousands of prison inmates, including Jews with minor offenses, to be sent to camps were acquitted as "unwitting tools" of "Hitler, Himmler, and minister of justice Thiereck." Although they had frequently referred in writing to the "annihilation" of those they sentenced, the court judged this insufficient to conclude that the officials "knew or suspected the killings were taking place." The word "eliminate" was also held insufficient, because it might be interpreted to mean simply "move, put away," or "render harmless."[15]

By the late 1960s hundreds of accused mass murderers, against whom cases had been painstakingly prepared with thousands of witnesses, had been let off by the statute of limitations, legal obfuscations, and the awareness of prosecutors that the judiciary would invent fantastic legalisms to free them. More and more of the accused pleaded ill health. A medical certificate indicating unfitness for trial would do, and thousands of former Nazi physicians were pleased to help. A man accused of participating in the death of one million avoided trial because it might increase his already high blood pressure. When international pressure did force life sentences, as with the Auschwitz killers, legal maneuvers gained early release for the criminals after the international press moved on to other concerns. Aside from Social Democrats and Jewish groups, prosecutors had little support. Cases were simply dropped, and thousands of killers, including those from the "special units," were safe, their honor unstained and their pensions intact.

Many of the same judges ruled on compensation claims for survivors, and naturally found many applicants "unworthy of reparations." Gypsies were refused because it was held they had been murdered for antisocial and criminal tendencies, though the Nazis had classified them as a degenerate race, an acknowledgment that would have required compensation. Only in 1991 was the first German, a former SS officer, indicted for killing Gypsies. No reparations were made for homosexuals because, until 1970, the courts regarded Nazi laws against them as valid. The murders of Jehovah's Witnesses were not held to be crimes because, as conscientious objectors, they were held to have been justly punished. Relatives of euthanasia victims were refused compensation; one court declared the victims were "people below the level of ciphers."[16] One court refused to punish those who acted in the euthanasia program because euthanasia had had its supporters before the Nazi era, and therefore the act was not punishable as a specifically Nazi crime. Yet most Nazi ideas predated Hitler. No judge could admit that, for it would be tantamount to sanctioning the close connection between Nazi ideology and the German past.

In Austria, war criminals were even more fortunate. Officially classified as an invaded and liberated nation, Austria did not face Allied pressure for trials, though Austrians may have been responsible for as many as half of all war crimes. Amnesty was granted in the 1950s to SS and Gestapo members. The sentences of those tried were even less proportional to their crimes than in Germany. Hermine Braunsteiner, supervising warden at Maidanek, a death camp, was tried and convicted in 1949 for murder; convicted, she was sentenced to three years. Only four Austrians were executed for murders related to the Holocaust. Even Austrian Social Democrats, once staunch antifascists, did not press for prosecutions. Like all Austrian politicians, they knew that most of their fellow citizens did not regard the Nazis as criminals and voted against those who did. "The Austrian press almost unanimously opposed the negotiations over reparations. . . ."[17] Most prosecutions took place only because of the constant and careful work of Simon Wiesenthal and his Documentation Center of the Society of Nazi Victims.

By blaming a handful of dead leaders, the judiciary and civil service enabled Germans to ignore the force of anti-Semitism among millions and over decades. Outrage is the justifiable reaction of Westerners and many of the new generation of Germans, but moral turpitude in the ordinary sense seems beside the mark. The judges and civil servants who committed and forgave Nazi crimes were part of an historical culture sanctioning racist violence, and they willingly helped carry out the dreadful logic of their own beliefs. Had they been repelled by Nazi terror, they would have salvaged the honor of Germany by punishing those who had sullied it. But that they could not do, and not just because they too bore responsibility for the Holocaust. As demonstrated by the legal gyrations they used to spin out their tales of innocence, most of them believed the Holocaust was a legitimate act of state in time of war, because they believed, like the Nazis, that the Jews were in fact Germany's racial enemies.

As amnesties, pardons, and "not guilty" verdicts piled up after 1945, the Allies lost interest. Both sides in the cold war wanted German support, and they knew they would not receive it if they pressed the issue. The

Soviet puppet government of East Germany insisted that as communist anti-Nazis during Weimar, they need pay no reparations, ignoring the fact that they ruled over a population once heavily pro-Nazi. Still, Eastern Europeans tried and punished thousands more war criminals than the West, even though most war criminals fled to the west as the Red Army approached. The Soviets at first simply shot ex-Nazis after perfunctory one-day trials; later they used many in the new government. American security services busily "laundered" the murderous records of those scientists they needed for rocket and biological research. General Reinhard Gehlen, former Nazi spymaster, handed over for American use his eastern anti-Bolshevik agents, many of whom were heavily implicated in the murder of the Jews. Ukrainian nationalists recruited by the United States in the "Nightingale" program to be anticommunist spies behind the iron curtain, had worked for the Nazis during the war and had massacred thousands of Jews, and their new employers knew it. In the end the Allies granted pardons or amnestied almost as many war criminals as they convicted. John J. McCloy, U.S. High Commissioner for Germany, freed or lowered the sentences of more than half of the twenty SS *Einsatzkommando* killers convicted by the Allies, not because he doubted their guilt but because he needed to placate the German government and public. McCloy freed many the Allies had convicted of war crimes. If occupation and State Department officials felt impelled to free convicted mass murderers to please the German public, we can sense how popular the killers were thought to be among those in the best position to know.

In the 1950s increasing public pressure in Germany brought amnesties for convicted criminals. Of the fourteen bureaucrats and party officials who had attended the Wannsee Conference, twelve survived the war; only one was tried, and he was released early. The vast majority of the "special unit" and ordinary killers were not hunted down, let alone prosecuted. The army was never purged. The German clergy exerted far more pressure calling for mercy for the criminals than it ever did for compensating their surviving victims. General Alfred Jodl, chief of the operations branch of the German army and Hitler's most loyal disciple, was executed for war crimes at Nuremberg; he was posthumously pardoned and rehabilitated in 1953. SS General Gottlob Berger, who, in his instructional booklet "The Subhuman," called the people of Russia the "afterbirth of humanity" and had slaughtered accordingly, was condemned to twenty-five years by the Allies. He was released in 1951 after serving three. Much of the German press and public denounced the hanging of four *Einsatzgruppen* leaders, and this when Hitler was no longer there to hypnotize them or the Gestapo to punish them, and no one could claim not to know exactly what the killers had done and to whom. De-Nazification proceedings sentenced some 9,600; within four years only 300 were still in prison. No legal claims for damages were made for the estates of the dead victims. As Raul Hilberg remarks, had the Germans killed all the Jews "there would have been no claims whatsoever." After the war a German court tried a Foreign Office official accused of aiding the massacre of Bulgarian Jews. The court decided that though a terrible crime had probably occurred, without survivors, and with all witnesses dead, "no proof existed that a crime had been committed."[18]

In 1993 the German government recognized the claims to medals and pensions of the survivors of a Latvian SS division of murderers. When questioned, the Christian Democratic attorney general declared them not guilty of any crimes. In 1965 Kurt Franz, deputy commander of Treblinka, where 900,000 Jews died, was sentenced to life for complicity and for his personal murder of 193 Jews, many of whom he shot in the genitals. He was freed in 1993 because German law says those whose guilt is not deemed "of particular gravity" may be released. As Daniel Goldhagen asked, would he have been released if his victims had been German, or "would virtual silence have greeted his freedom?"[19] The silence reveals more than do the public and general expressions of sorrow of German leaders about the Holocaust.

At the Nuremberg Trials the myth of Hitler's hypnotic charisma was used by defendants to avoid responsibility. For them the popular and odd phrase "No Hitler, no Holocaust" became a personal declaration of innocence. At their trials or in memoirs, even the most sophisticated spoke of the hypnotic spell Hitler cast rather than admit they approved of much of what he stood for. Even today we are told by otherwise sophisticated realists, not all German, that Hitler's dominating presence was irresistible. But before television, oratorical charisma was a common and well-cultivated rhetorical skill among a host of radical demagogues, left and right. The most powerful speakers cannot convert those who are not already prepared to believe; demagogic rhetoric does not persuade, it confirms. That Hitler could "mesmerize" so many is testimony to the strength of his ideas among them, not his ecstatic posturing. The thousands of university graduates who administered the Holocaust were hardly susceptible to high-decibel rhetoric. But it is no surprise that they used the excuse. What is surprising is that many scholars have taken Hitler's supposedly overwhelming charisma to be a major source of his appeal and have embalmed the notion in textbooks, thereby avoiding the real issues raised by the relationship of fascist ideology to the historical power of anti-Semitic myths among the Germans.

Self-"de-Nazification" after 1945 swiftly cleared the way for business as usual in church, industry, science, medicine, and the universities. Important members of the Catholic and Protestant hierarchies, once Nazi supporters, continued to advance within the church. Bishop Wilhelm

Berning, a virulent anti-Semite and a member of Goering's state council
to the end, was made an archbishop in 1949. Pro-Nazi clergy carved out
good careers for themselves and retained control of the church. Clerics
notable for their silence or worse from Kristallnacht through 1945, prated
unblushingly about the need for Christian forgiveness when they pressed
for the release of convicted war criminals. Hastily sanitizing their record,
they attacked those who exposed them, held tight to their prerogatives,
and gave official imprimatur to books denying their complicity or magnifying acts of heroic but extremely rare resistance by the Christian martyrs they themselves had opposed during the war.

Some Vatican authorities helped Nazi war criminals flee the wrath of
the Allies, escaping to South America by means of the infamous "mon-
astery" or "rat" line, as it was called by American intelligence officials.
Bishop Alois Hudal, representative of the Nazis in Rome during the war
and a personal friend of Pope Pius XII, helped organize the escapes.[20] He
could have done so only if he believed their acts were not crimes, for the
church gained no advantage. In 1937 Hudal had published The Foundations of National Socialism, dedicating it to Hitler, the "Siegfried of German hope and greatness," and meaning to show that Nazi ideology and
Christian faith were compatible. Cardinal Theodore Innitzer of Vienna,
who welcomed Hitler's troops into the city, admired Hudal's book as did
most Austrian clerics. In 1953 Pius XII excommunicated the communist
states of Hungary, Rumania, and Poland, though he had never so much
as threatened the neopagans of the Third Reich or excommunicated any
leading Catholic mass murderers, ignoring the pleas of Catholics to do
so, Pius XII also officially received Anton Pavelic, the Croat leader who,
with the help of local priests, had directed the murder of thousands of
non-Catholics, including some 30,000 Jews and an estimated 200,000 or
more Orthodox Serbs. The perpetrators were never repudiated by the
pope. Human decency was left to the Italian army, which gave asylum
to Jews trying to escape Croatian Ustashi terror. Silent while some 18 percent of Polish priests were murdered, the pope appealed to the Allies to
commute the death sentences of those condemned at Nuremberg.

The vast majority of those who employed slave labor escaped punishment. Nevertheless, industrialists could have shown they had acted under
duress by paying the wages due the few survivors. The dead made no
claims. Nazi wrath could no longer prevent this penance, but why make
amends when one does not believe one is guilty? No German firm volunteered to reimburse survivors. When the victims persisted, the firms
hired armies of lawyers to keep indemnities low or tie up the courts until
claimants died, meanwhile dissociating themselves from Nazi crimes with
extensive public relations handouts. In the end, the sums paid by industry were insultingly paltry, forced by legal judgments, fear of publicity, or

threatened international boycotts. I. G. Farben destroyed its concentration camp records in 1944, just before the Russians reached Auschwitz. But remaining evidence persuaded Allied judges of the firm's abuse of slave labor, and they concluded that the Auschwitz industrial establishment was in effect "financed and owned by Farben" and the workers' suffering personally known to its board of directors.[21] Even German judges held its management personally responsible for the treatment of slave labor, ruling in effect that such extreme oppression of workers was not demanded by the regime. Dr. Heinrich Buetefisch, Farben's expert in synthetic fuel production, a colonel in the SS and Farben's liaison with Himmler, testified in 1946 that though Farben made significant contributions to Hitler before he gained power, the firm was ignorant of Hitler's plans to outlaw trade unions and socialists or harm the Jews. Topf and Sons, who were awarded the contract for the death camp crematoria, regularly sent a representative to Auschwitz who recommended ways to increase the efficiency of the killing and disposal of the bodies. Friedrich Flick, honorary SS member and close friend of Himmler, personally heard reports by General Ohlendorf, the commander of a killing squad who was later hanged by the Nuremberg tribunal for the murder of ninety thousand Jews. Flick was one of many Germans who protested Ohlendorf's execution. Flick spoke on behalf of all the business defendants in 1947: "Nothing will ever convince us we are war criminals."[22] He was right: nothing ever did, nothing ever could. Nazis saw no crime in working Jews and Slavs to death.

The behavior of industrialists during the Third Reich was not simply the consequence of greed or fear, nor are psychological complexities needed to explain their denials. They simply felt no guilt when faced with the ruined survivors of a people they must have believed less than human. Herman Siemens of industrial fame, a beneficiary of slave labor, was a prominent member of the Society for Racial Hygiene long before the rise of the Nazis. If it is argued that businessmen used slave labor merely for profit or because others were doing it, one still must ask: Is it likely that their counterparts in other civilized Western nations would voluntarily help to enslave and murder millions of innocent civilians in order to advance their careers? Flick was sentenced to serve seven years; McCloy gained his release in four. Alfred Krupp, who employed thousands of slave laborers, was sentenced to twelve years at Nuremberg. In 1951 McCloy released him after two and a half years in prison; he was greeted by a cheering crowd and a champagne breakfast. His property and position were restored, though this contravened the original judgment.

Arms manufacturers, protesters were told, were needed for rearming Germany, but neither the Krupp nor other works depended on the personal attentions of the handful of imprisoned executives. And when Mc-

Cloy, who did much to help them receive amnesty, tried to persuade them it would be good public relations to pay indemnities, he failed. Flick, who had a controlling interest in some three hundred companies, including the producers of Mercedes-Benz, still enjoyed the fruits of large profits and a good conscience at the age of ninety when he finally went to Valhallah. In 1986 a bank bought out Flick's holdings, and, under international pressure, a Flick subsidiary paid $2 million in reparations for fifteen hundred slave laborers. But a spokesman for the Christian Democratic party declared there was "no legal or moral basis" for the claim, adding, "The fact that it comes up now creates the impression that Jews are quick to show up whenever money tinkles in German cash registers."[23] The government disavowed the remark; Shimon Peres of Israel was about to make a state visit. Taxpayers, not the guilty, finally paid millions in indemnities to Israel.

The vast majority of physicians, health-care workers, and scientists in the racial purification programs were never tried. In 1947 an American military tribunal convicted sixteen physicians of war crimes and executed some who had killed prisoners in medical experiments. But those who ran the killing centers were absolved by German courts for "obeying orders" or for conducting "mercy killings." A physician who directed the murder of children in the killing centers was not tried because the court decided he believed his actions had been legal. When they saw the revulsion of their Allied colleagues, physicians and scientists swiftly covered their tracks. All who were asked, including some who had visited the camps, claimed ignorance of the killing of the Jews. One denied he had even heard of the euthanasia program, correcting himself only when he realized that his interviewer knew that all Germany had been aware of it—and as it was happening. Physicians who helped deport and kill Gypsies or homosexuals were not considered criminals by German courts. Soon scientists and academics were busily providing letters of recommendation and declarations of innocence for one another, ostracizing those who broke ranks. Almost no one did. To expose the murderous activities of the profession was to risk one's academic career. Academics and scientists shared what Benno Mueller-Hill calls "a cult of silence." Robert Proctor notes that any "discussion of the recent persecution of Jews, Gypsies, communists, and other 'undesirables' was virtually taboo in medical journals published after the war."[24] Max Weinreich published *Hitler's Professors* in 1946, indicating the extent of academic complicity. In Germany his book was ignored and not translated, and this in a nation that prides itself on its abundance of translations. Proctor writes that of 422 articles published about physicians under the Nazis from 1966 to 1979, only two came from West German authors.

In 1949 a committee of professors at the Kaiser Wilhelm Institute cleared Professor Verschuer of any wrongdoing, though he had demanded the extermination of Jews and Gypsies and had trained their murderers. Unbelievably, the committee then cleared Dr. Mengele, declaring: "We cannot tell, from the evidence available to us, to what extent Dr. Mengele himself was aware of the abominations and murders perpetrated in Auschwitz during the period under discussion. . . ."[25] Had it been up to his colleagues, Mengele would never have fled; only Allied inquiries caused him to leave Europe in haste. By clearing Mengele the scientists were clearing themselves, and testifying that even one of the worst of them was innocent in their eyes.

All but a few Nazi physicians and scientists remained in their posts, and some still taught in the 1970s. Many went on to important positions in genetics. Verschuer, tried and declared a Nazi "fellow traveler," was fined $300 and declared free of responsibility for Nazi crimes. He then became a geneticist at a major university, his new students soon joining his old colleagues at different schools. After the war Verschuer served on the editorial board of an international journal called the *Mankind Quarterly*, still used as a source by those who seek to prove the racial superiority of whites.[26] Fritz Lenz, who had urgently requested a position in the east to help kill in the name of racial purity, continued as an eminent professor, and, upon retirement in the 1970s, was given an honorary dinner by neo-Nazis.

In the opinion of most German and Austrian university students and faculty, Allied de-Nazifiers were in fact revenge-seeking Jews or their tools. Pastor Martin Niemoeller was heckled in 1947 by thousands of students at three universities when he said, "Germany must accept responsibility for what happened in Poland, for the sufferings of Russia, and for the five or six million murdered Jews."[27] In Austria the old professors retained their positions and their views. There was much anger with exiled German scientists and physicians who, upon returning, asked embarrassing questions about the past; they were dismissed as Jews or leftists or both. Proctor writes that a report published by West German physicians under great international pressure to reveal something of their past was informally suppressed, disappearing once the Allies had been obeyed. One German who reviewed it said that only "perverts" would read such trash. Soon it became the standard view that at the very most some three hundred physicians had been involved in racial purification. In fact thousands were. The participation of scientists and academics was also minimized. One had to kill; it was not enough to plan or administer the program, not even enough to have decided who should live and who should die.

In 1929 Hans F. K. Gunther, perhaps the most widely read racial scientist in Germany, published a popular book supporting Nordic supremacy and racial selection by death. A professor at Berlin, Jena, and Freiburg, he wrote after the war that he had never subordinated his science to ideology. Quite possibly he believed this; simply put, he was and remained convinced that racism to the point of murder was scientifically valid and nonideological. His attitude shows the true meaning behind the defensiveness or silence of those whom their Western colleagues regarded as betrayers of science and humanity. One need not assume such men were monsters. They were otherwise normal human beings but part of a scientific and historical ethos that sanctioned racial violence. All vehemently denied they were vulgar anti-Semites. They did not add that their false science assured them that Jews were harmful to the race, and like so many and long before the Nazis, they believed racial purification essential to the future of civilization.

Naturally, such beliefs did not die merely because of defeat. After 1945 the prestigious German Chamber of Physicians elected three former SS doctors as presidents. Complaints were met with silence. In 1978 it was revealed that a prominent and much-honored physician, Dr. Hans-Joachim Sewering, had been a medical killer for the SS. The accusation was ignored. In 1992 he was elected president of the most important world medical body, the World Medical Association. When protests erupted, "the German medical establishment closed ranks in cold defiance as it had against previous efforts to bring the truth to light." But hundreds of younger German physicians, never part of the historical culture of race, joined the international outcry. Sewering was forced to resign.[28]

Scientific validation was invaluable to the Nazi regime, and the leadership recognized it with honors and prestigious appointments. But this does not mean that scientists and academics were simply opportunists or even uniquely vicious. We assume too readily that scientific learning imparts liberal values. But the assumption applies only to those in a culture accepting the values that were integrated with the scientific worldview when it became the intellectual basis for social and political liberalism during the Enlightenment and the liberal era. Those who are part of that tradition will always find it difficult to grasp that many scientists—and not only Germans—rejected the idea that social experience is primary and instead believed that many are "racially defective" and "harmful" permanently and by birth. Consequently it was not difficult for them to distance themselves with cold rationality from any human connection with their victims. Indeed, it is the main reason why the bureaucratic murderers, far from feeling guilty with their work, maintained the thorough and detailed records of the killings that were so useful to the Allies at the Nuremberg Trials. They knew they might lose the war; they did not grasp how the world would view their crimes. Only fear, not guilt, caused so many to hide or remain silent during the few years when the Allies searched for Nazis to punish.

The deep roots of anti-Semitism in Germany are tellingly revealed by the attitudes and activities of the bureaucrats, businessmen, military leaders, scientists, and academics who voluntarily supported and participated in the persecution of the Jews. For too long, the workings of the academic system helped disguise the complicity of the upper classes and academics, many of whose students during the war had written theses about the evils of Jewry. From 1930 to 1945 some 45 percent of those professors who would later hold posts in postwar Germany were selected with Nazi approval. Those who were already tenured in 1933 were overwhelmingly conservative nationalists with Nazi sympathies; if not, they were purged and exiled. As is the way in academia, tenured professors choose their successors, and they were careful not to select young candidates who would explore the history of anti-Semitism among the Germans—as when Ingo Mueller found that his work effectively ended his hopes for an academic career. It was not the victors, therefore, but the defeated who wrote the history of the Third Reich for the German public. Only with the 1970s did nonconservatives gain a foothold in the academy and join with foreign scholars in the work that enables us, with ever greater clarity, to understand the deep relationship between the Nazis and the German past, and the complicity of so many with the regime.

It is misleading to speak, as many do, of the "hidden potential" for racial murder in all of us. All mankind has cruel impulses, of course, but much more significant is the simple fact that German culture and society *were* different from those of other Western nations, and German business leaders, bureaucrats, lawyers, army officers, and civilian personnel who helped in the killings were creatures of a long history that made murderous anti-Semitism respectable and normal among even the educated. The myths of the anti-Semites conditioned the response of millions of Germans to the war crimes trials, though of course there were also self-serving motives.

Had the vast majority of the German people not known about the murders until the Allies revealed them, and had they been outraged by these obscene atrocities committed in their name against innocent civilians, an outburst of patriotic indignation and revulsion and an unstoppable desire to punish the guilty would have been inevitable. The opposite occurred. During the Allied occupation, public opinion researchers found that 37 percent of Germans polled agreed with the statement: "Extermination of the Jews and Poles and other non-Aryans was necessary for the security of the Germans."[29] Polls are unreliable, the question was more awkwardly phrased than my rendering, and other evidence is contradictory. But all in all, 37 percent seems a reasonable figure; it is the same percentage the Nazis received in their triumph of 1932. About half of Austrians polled after the war believed that "although the Nazis had gone too far in the way they dealt with the Jews, something had to be done to place limits on them." After 1945 Austrians agitated against Jewish refugees temporarily housed in Austria for transit, even though they were supported at Allied and American Jewish expense. Leopold Kunschak, a famous Christian Social leader, virulent anti-Semite, and honored cofounder of the Austrian republic, was still making anti-Semitic speeches after the war.[30]

Among the "Nazi generation," anti-Semitism could scarcely be expected to die with defeat. A third or more of those born into this generation in Austria and Germany have gone or will go to their graves denouncing—usually privately—those who try to "come to grips" with the Nazi past by demonstrating the complicity of so many in the Holocaust. Long after the war, old myths about the Jews still circulate at private gatherings or in local pubs. As former Nazi supporters maintained, outsiders never understood the invidious activities of the Jews. Constant talk of the Holocaust is seen as a means for "international Jewry" to gain support for Israel. The denial of the Holocaust is nothing new; it started in 1945.

Sincerity intensifies horror. In his last letter to his wife, Rudolf Hoess, commandant of Auschwitz, wrote that he believed in everything he had done; Eichmann said the same at his trial in Jerusalem. Neither demonstrates the banality of evil, as is still said, but rather a terrible and unshakable personal faith in the ideology of death. In Auschwitz, Mengele was once asked, "When will all this extermination cease?" "Never," he answered. "My friend! It will go on and on and on."[31] He was right. As a learned academic and a specialist in racial purification, neither unique nor uniquely monstrous, Dr. Mengele, holder of degrees in anthropology and medicine, knew that even after the Jews and Gypsies, millions of Slavs and political enemies would remain, and a constant stream of German babies would have to be "selected out" for mental and physical disabilities.

The inevitable continuation of killing in the service of ethnic cleansing reveals the universal significance of the Holocaust. Until the end of World War II, German physicians and research personnel continued their vain quest to isolate the properties of Jewish blood. Research on the "racial souls of the Jews" was funded by German scientific institutes even as the last Jews of Europe were being slaughtered in the death camps. For, as one scientist declared, even if all the Jews were killed, it would still be necessary to detect the continuing spiritual influence of Jewry and destroy it wherever it existed. Sixty years before, the Austrian Catholic anti-Semite Baron Vogelsang had written, "If by some miracle all our

1,400,000 Jews were to be taken from us, it would help us very little, for we ourselves have been infected with the Jewish spirit."[32] In 1934 Werner Sombart declared that the Jewish spirit must be rooted out, for even if "every last Jew and Jewish family is annihilated," their spirit had been institutionalized in the economy.[33] The long history of equating the ills of society with world Jewry meant to racists that if the ills continued after the Jews were gone, then Judaization, as the volkist theorists maintained in the 1890s, was to blame. Mengele was correct, the killing would never stop. The Nazis were defeated, but their spirit did not die.

Racial purification can never end for Nazis, neo-Nazis, and "ethnic cleansers" everywhere, for its intent is ultimately to destroy any person or society where humane instincts and progressive values have overridden the primitive impulses of ethnocentrism and bloody nationalism. Throughout the long dark decades of German anti-Semitism, liberal and progressive values had been for anti-Semites the only consistent guide to who and what was Jewish. Thus "Never again" must not be a cry of pain rising only from the Jewish community as it meets to memorialize the terrible consequences of the ideology of death. It must be the demand of all who strive to strengthen the hard-won, fragile, and always endangered civilized values that a small part of humanity has achieved in the long struggle to create an enlightened, just, and free society.

NOTES

1: THE CHRISTIAN LEGACY

1. Judith Hershcopf Banki, *The Oberammergau Passion Play* (New York, 1980), p. 5.
2. *New York Times*, January 8, 1987.
3. James Parkes, *The Conflict Between Church and Synagogue* (New York, 1974), p. 99.
4. *Ibid.*, p. 158.
5. *Ibid.*, pp. 165, 166.
6. *Ibid.*, p. 167.
7. Leon Poliakov, *The History of Anti-Semitism*, I (New York, 1976), 25.
8. Parkes, *Conflict Between Church and Synagogue*, p. 166.
9. Salo Baron, *A Social and Religious History of the Jews*, IV (New York, 1962–1983), 74.
10. Poliakov, *History of Anti-Semitism*, I, 31.
11. *Ibid.*, p. 48.
12. *Ibid.*, p. 42.
13. *Ibid.*, p. 48.
14. *Ibid.*, p. 47.
15. Baron, *Social and Religious History of the Jews*, p. 6.

2: LUTHER AND THE REFORMATION

Epigram: Poliakov, *History of Anti-Semitism*, I, 223.
1. *Ibid.*, p. 222.
2. *Ibid.*, p. 219.
3. *Ibid.*, p. 218.
4. *Ibid.*, p. 223.
5. John McNeil, *The History and Character of Calvinism* (New York, 1967), p. 210.
6. Poliakov, *History of Anti-Semitism*, I, 198.

3: THE ENLIGHTENMENT

Epigram: John Herman Randall, Jr., *The Career of Philosophy*, I (New York, 1962), 937, 898.
1. *Ibid.*, p. 668.
2. *Ibid.*, p. 864.
3. *Ibid.*, p. 898.
4. Adam Smith, *The Theory of Moral Sentiments* (London, 1853), p. 348.

4: THE LIBERATION OF THE JEWS IN FRANCE

Epigram: The Declaration of the Rights of Man and the Citizen, 1789.
1. Arthur Hertzberg, *The French Enlightenment and the Jews* (New York, 1968), pp. 120, 58.
2. Leon Poliakov, *History of Anti-Semitism*, III (New York, 1968), 151.
3. *Ibid.*, p. 154.
4. *Ibid.*, p. 155.
5. Hertzberg, *French Enlightenment and the Jews*, p. 338.
6. *Ibid.*, pp. 250, 252.
7. Poliakov, *History of Anti-Semitism*, III, 148.
8. Zosa Szajkowski, *Jews and the French Revolution* (New York, 1970), pp. 150ff.

9. *Ibid.*, p. 385.
10. Jacob Katz, *From Prejudice to Destruction* (Cambridge, Mass., 1980), p. 110.
11. Robert B. Holtman, *The Napoleonic Revolution* (New York, 1967), pp. 123–124.
12. Geroge Rudé, *Revolutionary Europe, 1783–1815* (New York, 1964), p. 238.
13. Poliakov, *History of Anti-Semitism*, III, 227.
14. Jacques Soustelle, *The Long March of Israel*, (New York, 1969), p. 24.
15. Katz, *From Prejudice to Destruction*, p. 113.

5: THE NATIONALIST REACTION: GERMANY, 1815–1848

Epigram: Bridges, Dukes, Hargreaves, and Scott, *Nations and Empires* (New York, 1978), p. 23.
1. *Ibid.*
2. Poliakov, *History of Anti-Semitism*, III, 178.
3. *Ibid.*, p. 184.
4. Leon Poliakov, *The Aryan Myth* (New York, 1974), p. 172.
5. Poliakov, *History of Anti-Semitism*, III, 182.
6. J. G. Fichte, *Beitrag zur Berechtigung des Urtheils des Publikums ueber die Franzoesische Revolution*, Collected Works, I (Stuttgart, 1964), 293.
7. Poliakov, *Aryan Myth*, p. 171.
8. John Weiss, *Conservatism in Europe* (New York and London, 1977), p. 30.
9. Poliakov, *History of Anti-Semitism*, III, 237, 204.
10. Katz, *From Prejudice to Destruction*, p. 60.
11. J. G. Fichte, *Reden an die Deutsche Nation* (Berlin, 1807), p. 12.
12. Egmont Zechlin, *Die Deutsche Politik und die Juden im Ersten Weltkrieg* (Goettingen, 1969), pp. 25–26.
13. Poliakov, *History of Anti-Semitism*, III, 301.
14. Zechlin, *Deutsche Politik und die Juden im Ersten Weltkrieg*, p. 23.
15. Poliakov, *History of Anti-Semitism*, III, 381.
16. *Ibid.*, pp. 384, 301, 299.
17. *Ibid.*, p. 301.
18. *Ibid.*, p. 299.

6: ANTI-SEMITISM IN THE BISMARCK ERA

Epigram: Walter Frank, *Hofprediger Adolf Stoecker und die christlichsoziale Bewegung*, 2nd ed. (Hamburg, 1935), p. 79.
1. Rudolph Meyer, *Politische Gruender* (Berlin, 1877), p. 204.
2. Ernest K. Bramsted, *Aristocracy and the Middle Classes in Germany* (New York, 1964), p. 203.
3. Richard S. Levy, *Antisemitism in the Modern World* (New York, 1991), p. 15.
4. *Kreuzzeitung*, no. 189, August 15, 1878.
5. Zechlin, *Deutsche Politik und die Juden im Ersten Weltkrieg*, p. 33.
6. *Ibid.*, p. 32.
7. George L. Mosse, *Germans and Jews* (New York, 1970), p. 63.
8. Katz, *From Prejudice to Destruction*, p. 204.
9. Bramsted, *Aristocracy and the Middle Classes in Germany*, pp. 134–135.
10. Heinrich von Treitschke, *Preussische Jahrbuecher*, 1879, vol. 44, 572ff.
11. *Ibid.*, p. 574.
12. Levy, *Antisemitism in the Modern World*, p. 126.
13. George L. Mosse, *The Crisis of German Ideology* (New York, 1964), p. 193.
14. Frank, *Hofprediger Adolf Stoecker*, p. 19.
15. *Ibid.*, p. 29.
16. Stoecker's speech is reproduced in Paul Massing, *Rehearsal for Destruction* (New York, 1949), pp. 279ff.
17. Frank, *Hofprediger Adolf Stoecker*, p. 94.
18. *Ibid.*, p. 84.

19. Massing, *Rehearsal for Destruction*, p. 214.
20. Frank, *Hofprediger Adolf Stoecker*, pp. 188, 225.

7: THE RISE OF POPULIST ANTI-SEMITISM

Epigram: *The Nazi Primer* (New York and London, 1938), p. 29.
1. Moshe Zimmerman, *Wilhelm Marr: The Patriarch of Anti-Semitism* (New York, 1968), p. 69.
2. *Ibid.*, p. 106.
3. Levy, *Antisemitism in the Modern World*, p. 82.
4. *Ibid.*, p. 91.
5. *Ibid.*, p. 84.
6. *Ibid.*, p. 90.
7. *Ibid.*, p. 93.
8. Anonymous, *The Strangers in Our Land: A Warning to the German Volk from a Citizen of Berlin* (Berlin, 1876), p. 3.
9. Here I rely on the excellent study by Richard S. Levy, *The Downfall of the Anti-Semitic Political Parties in Imperial Germany* (New Haven and London, 1975).
10. *Ibid.*, p. 49.
11. *Ibid.*, p. 52.
12. Hans Rosenberg, *Grosse Depression und Bismarckzeit* (Berlin, 1967), p. 99.
13. Levy, *Downfall of the Anti-Semitic Political Parties in Imperial Germany*, pp. 51, 52.
14. *Ibid.*, p. 43.
15. Peter Pulzer, *The Rise of Political Anti-Semitism in Germany and Austria* (New York, 1964), p. 339.
16. Levy, *Downfall of the Anti-Semitic Political Parties in Imperial Germany*, p. 81.
17. *Ibid.*, p. 95.
18. Zechlin, *Deutsche Politik und die Juden im Ersten Weltkrieg*, p. 42.
19. Raul Hilberg, *The Destruction of the European Jews* (New York, 1985), I, 18–19.
20. Poliakov, *Aryan Myth*, p. 297.
21. Levy, *Downfall of the Anti-Semitic Political Parties in Imperial Germany*, p. 218.
22. Sheila Rowbotham, *Women, Resistance, and Revolution* (New York, 1974), p. 80.
23. Pulzer, *Rise of Political Anti-Semitism in Germany and Austria*, p. 222.
24. Theodore Fritsch, *Antisemiten Katechismus* (Leipzig, 1893), pp. 358ff.
25. *Ibid.*
26. Lanz von Liebenfels, *Ostara*, no. 23, Vienna, 1908.

8: ANTI-SEMITISM AMONG THE ELITES, 1890–1914

Epigram: *Journal of Central European History* XVII, no. 1 (March 1984), 23.
1. Gordon A. Craig, *Germany, 1866–1945* (New York, 1978), p. 175.
2. J. Alden Nichols, *Germany After Bismarck* (Cambridge, Mass., 1958), p. 302.
3. Frank, *Hofprediger Adolf Stoecker*, p. 233.
4. Uriel Tal, *Christians and Jews in Germany* (Ithaca, 1975), p. 259.
5. Levy, *Downfall of the Anti-Semitic Political Parties in Imperial Germany*, p. 72.
6. *Kreuzzeitung*, in Pulzer, *Rise of Political Anti-Semitism in Germany and Austria*, p. 122.
7. Frank, *Hofprediger Adolf Stoecker*, pp. 234, 236.
8. *Ibid.*, p. 233.
9. Mosse, *Crisis of German Ideology*, p. 239.
10. Frank, *Hofprediger Adolf Stoecker*, p. 234.
11. Levy, *Downfall of the Anti-Semitic Political Parties in Imperial Germany*, p. 74.
12. *Ibid.*, p. 88.
13. Mosse, *Crisis of German Ideology*, p. 222.
14. Levy, *Downfall of the Anti-Semitic Political Parties in Imperial Germany*, p. 139.
15. Frank, *Hofprediger Adolf Stoecker*, p. 242–243.
16. Nichols, *Germany After Bismarck*, p. 239.
17. Frank, *Hofprediger Adolf Stoecker*, p. 235.

18. Hilberg, *Destruction of the European Jews*, I, 17–19.
19. Levy, *Downfall of the Anti-Semitic Political Parties in Imperial Germany*, p. 89.
20. *Ibid.*, p. 101.
21. James J. Sheehan, "Conflict and Cohesion Among the German Elites in the Nineteenth Century" in Sheehan, ed., *Imperial Germany* (New York, 1976), p. 71.
22. John C. G. Roehl, "Higher Civil Servants in Germany, 1890–1900," in Sheehan, *Imperial Germany*, p. 139.
23. *Ibid.*, p. 138.
24. Tal, *Christians and Jews in Germany*, p. 218.
25. Craig, *Germany, 1866–1945*, p. 159.
26. *Ibid.*, p. 265.
27. Massing, *Rehearsal for Destruction*, p. 134.
28. Leon Poliakov, *L'Europe suicidaire, 1870–1933* (Paris, 1977), p. 40.
29. *Ibid.*
30. Zechlin, *Deutsche Politik und die Juden im Ersten Weltkrieg*, p. 48.
31. Poliakov, *L'Europe suicidaire*, p. 40.
32. H. S. Chamberlain, *Briefe* (Munich, 1928), I, 136ff.
33. John C. G. Roehl, *The Kaiser and His Court* (New York, 1995), pp. 205, 210.

9: ANTI-SEMITISM, ACADEMICS, AND INTELLECTUALS, 1890–1914

Epigram: Poliakov, *Aryan Myth*, p. 270.
1. *Ibid.*, p. 255.
2. *Ibid.*, pp. 294–295.
3. Mosse, *Crisis of German Ideology*, p. 99.
4. *Ibid.*, p. 101.
5. *Ibid.*, p. 152.
6. Jeffrey Herf, *Reactionary Modernism* (New York, 1986), pp. 141, 139.
7. Frank, *Hofprediger Adolf Stoecker*, p. 219.
8. Eugene Black, ed., *Posture of Europe* (Homewood, Ill., 1964), pp. 249, 251.
9. Roehl, "Higher Civil Servants," p. 138.
10. Poliakov, *Aryan Myth*, p. 317.
11. Fritz Stern, *The Politics of Cultural Despair: A Study in the Rise of the Germanic Ideology* (New York, 1965).
12. *Ibid.*, p. 146.
13. *Ibid.*, p. 109.
14. *Ibid.*, pp. 150, 62.
15. Poliakov, *Aryan Myth*, p. 308.
16. Stern, *Politics of Cultural Despair*, p. 61.
17. *Ibid.*, pp. 62–63.
18. *Ibid.*, pp. 57, 67–68, 142.
19. Werner Angress, "Prussia's Army and the Jewish Reserve Officer Controversy Before World War I," in Sheehan, *Imperial Germany*, p. 114.

10: OPPOSING ANTI-SEMITISM

1. Massing, *Rehearsal for Destruction*, pp. 311–312.
2. Mosse, *Crisis of German Ideology*, p. 9.
3. Pulzer, *Rise of Political Anti-Semitism in Germany and Austria*, p. 345.
4. *Ibid.*, p. 259.
5. Sheehan, "Conflict and Cohesion," p. 82–83.
6. Frank, *Hofprediger Adolf Stoecker*, pp. 250, 268.
7. Zechlin, *Deutsche Politik und die Juden im Ersten Weltkrieg*, p. 45.
8. *Ibid.*, p. 213.
9. Levy, *Antisemitism in the Modern World*, pp. 129–130.
10. *Ibid.*, pp. 130–133.
11. *Ibid.*

11: CATHOLIC ANTI-SEMITISM IN THE AUSTRIAN EMPIRE

Epigram: Rudolf Kuppe, *Karl Lueger und seine Zeit* (Vienna, 1933), p. 177.
1. Poliakov, *History of Anti-Semitism*, III, 297.
2. Pulzer, *Rise of Political Anti-Semitism in Germany and Austria*, p. 130.
3. Arthur J. May, *The Hapsburg Monarchy, 1867–1914* (New York, 1951), p. 179.
4. Katz, *From Prejudice to Destruction*, p. 227.
5. May, *Hapsburg Monarchy*, p. 48.
6. Pulzer, *Rise of Political Anti-Semitism in Germany and Austria*, p. 131.
7. Andrew Whiteside, "Austria," in Hans Rogger and Eugen Weber, eds., *The European Right in Historical Profile* (Berkeley, 1965), p. 322.
8. Pulzer, *Rise of Political Anti-Semitism in Germany and Austria*, p. 131.
9. *Ibid.*, pp. 131–132.
10. *Ibid.*
11. *Ibid.*, p. 133.
12. Stern, *Politics of Cultural Despair*, p. 149.
13. David Bakan, *Sigmund Freud and the Jewish Mystical Tradition* (New York, 1969), p. 26.
14. Pulzer, *Rise of Political Anti-Semitism in Germany and Austria*, p. 146.
15. Bakan, *Sigmund Freud and the Jewish Mystical Tradition*, p. 28.
16. Kuppe, *Karl Lueger und seine Zeit*, p. 98.
17. Andrew Whiteside, *The Socialism of Fools* (Berkeley, 1975), p. 87.
18. *Ibid.*, p. 109.
19. *Ibid.*, p. 110
20. *Ibid.*, p. 87.
21. Eduard Pichl, *Georg Schoenerer* (Oldenburg, 1938), III, 338.
22. Richard S. Geehr, *Karl Lueger: Mayor of Fin de Siècle Vienna* (Detroit, 1990), p. 181. This is an excellent study.
23. Kuppe, *Karl Lueger und seine Zeit*, p. 171.
24. *Ibid.*, pp. 256–258.
25. *Ibid.*, p. 95.
26. *Ibid.*, p. 207.
27. *Ibid.*, p. 211.
28. *Ibid.*, p. 213.
29. *Ibid.*, pp. 215, 209.

12: RACIAL NATIONALISM IN AUSTRIA

1. May, *Hapsburg Monarchy*, p. 211.
2. *Ibid.*, p. 62.
3. *Ibid.*, p. 210.
4. Pulzer, *Rise of Political Anti-Semitism in Germany and Austria*, p. 253.
5. Whiteside, *Socialism of Fools*, p. 133.
6. William Jenks, *Vienna and the Young Hitler* (New York, 1960), p. 134.
7. May, *Hapsburg Monarchy*, p. 487.
8. Kuppe, *Karl Lueger und seine Zeit*, p. 153.
9. *Ibid.*, p. 300.
10. *Ibid.*, p. 302.
11. *Ibid.*, p. 245.
12. *Ibid.*, p. 309.
13. Mosse, *Crisis of German Ideology*, p. 144.
14. Jenks, *Vienna and the Young Hitler*, p. 103.
15. Geehr, *Karl Lueger*, p. 158.
16. *Ibid.*, pp. 227ff, 177.
17. Jenks, *Vienna and the Young Hitler*, p. 130.
18. Levy, *Antisemitism in the Modern World*, pp. 117, 120, and Geehr, *Karl Lueger*, p. 176.
19. Kuppe, *Karl Lueger und seine Zeit*, p. 479.
20. Jenks, *Vienna and the Young Hitler*, p. 110.

13: HITLER IN AUSTRIA

Epigram: Adolf Hitler, *Mein Kampf* (Boston, 1943), p. 12.
1. *Ibid.*, p. 58.
2. *Ibid.*, p. 57.
3. Bradley F. Smith, *Adolf Hitler, His Family, Childhood, and Youth* (Stanford, 1967), p. 124. I am indebted to this excellent book.
4. Hitler, *Mein Kampf*, p. 412.
5. Robert G. L. Waite, *The Psychopathic God: Adolf Hitler* (New York, 1987).
6. Hitler, *Mein Kampf*, p. 97.
7. *Ibid.*, p. 81.
8. *Ibid.*, p. 40.
9. *Ibid.*, p. 45.
10. *Ibid.*, p. 51.
11. *Ibid.*, pp. 63–64, 38.
12. *Ibid.*, p. 63.
13. *Ibid.*, p. 65.
14. *Ibid.*, p. 97.
15. *Ibid.*, p. 38.
16. *Ibid.*, p. 15.
17. *Ibid.*, pp. 97, 124.
18. *Ibid.*, p. 107.
19. *Ibid.*, p. 116.
20. *Ibid.*, p. 107.
21. *Ibid.*, p. 122.
22. *Ibid.*, p. 120.
23. *Ibid.*, p. 121.
24. *Ibid.*, p. 118.
25. *Ibid.*, p. 69.
26. May, *Hapsburg Monarchy*, p. 466.
27. Hitler, *Mein Kampf*, pp. 122, 161.
28. *Ibid.*, pp. 679, 682.

14: THE GREAT WAR AND RACISM

Epigram: Craig, *Germany, 1866–1945*, p. 395.
1. Zechlin, *Deutsche Politik und die Juden im Ersten Weltkrieg*, pp. 413ff.
2. Poliakov, *L'Europe suicidaire*, p. 164.
3. Zechlin, *Deutsche Politik und die Juden im Ersten Weltkrieg*, p. 548.
4. *Ibid.*, p. 549.
5. *Ibid.*, p. 519.
6. *Ibid.*, p. 531.
7. *Ibid.*, p. 559.
8. D. J. Goodspeed, *Ludendorff, Genius of World War One* (New York, 1966), p. 6.
9. Zechlin, *Deutsche Politik und die Juden im Ersten Weltkrieg*, p. 561.
10. *Ibid.*, pp. 558–559.
11. Barbara Miller Lane and Leila J. Rupp, *Nazi Ideology Before 1933* (Austin and London, 1978), p. 7.
12. J. P. Nettl, *The Soviet Achievement* (New York, 1967), p. 63.
13. Robert G. L. Waite, *Vanguard of Nazism: The Free Corps Movement in Postwar Germany, 1918–1923* (New York, 1969), p. 2.
14. Bruce F. Pauley, *From Prejudice to Persecution: A History of Austrian Anti-Semitism* (Chapel Hill, 1992), p. 184. This is an invaluable study.
15. Mosse, *Crisis of German Ideology*, p. 240.
16. Francis L. Carsten, *The Reichswehr and Politics* (Oxford, 1966), p. 85.
17. Henry A. Turner, Jr., *German Big Business and the Rise of Hitler* (New York, 1985), p. 13.
18. Mosse, *Crisis of German Ideology*, p. 242.

15: THE SEEDBED: THE POSTWAR WAVE OF ANTI-SEMITISM

Epigram: Lewis Hertzman, DNVP: Right-wing Opposition in the Weimar Republic: 1918–1924 (Lincoln, Nebr., 1988), p. 127.
1. Zechlin, Deutsche Politik und die Juden im Ersten Weltkrieg, p. 563.
2. Hertzman, DNVP, pp. 127, 129; Mosse, Crisis of German Ideology, p. 224.
3. Zechlin, Deutsche Politik und die Juden im Ersten Weltkrieg, p. 563.
4. Waite, Vanguard of Nazism, pp. 40, 206.
5. Robert Gellately, The Gestapo and German Society (Oxford, 1990), p. 88.
6. Pauley, From Prejudice to Persecution, p. 153.
7. Mosse, Crisis of German Ideology, p. 255.
8. Waite, Vanguard of Nazism, p. 40.
9. James M. Diehl, Paramilitary Politics in Weimar Germany (Bloomington, Ind., 1977), p. 22.
10. Peter Gay, Weimar Culture (New York, 1968), pp. 43–44.
11. Pauley, From Prejudice to Persecution, p. 89.
12. Turner, German Big Business and the Rise of Hitler, p. 33.
13. A. J. Nicholls, Weimar and the Rise of Hitler (New York, 1979), p. 76.
14. Turner, German Big Business and the Rise of Hitler, p. 13.
15. F. L. Carsten, Fascist Movements in Austria (New York, 1977), pp. 46–47.
16. Carsten, Reichswehr and Politics, p. 176.
17. Charles Bracelen Flood, Hitler: The Path to Power (Boston, 1989), p. 159.
18. Ibid., p. 153.
19. Ibid., p. 236.
20. Harold J. Gordon, Jr., The Reichswehr and the German Republic (Port Washington, N.Y., 1957), p. 236.
21. Flood, Hitler: The Path to Power, p. 491.
22. Ibid., p. 538.

16: THE BATTLE FOR CULTURE

Epigram: Robert Pois, ed., Race and Race History and Other Essays (New York, 1974), p. 149.
1. Ernst Jung, "Zur gegenwaertigen Lage der Psychotherapie," Zentralblatt fuer Psychotherapie, VII (1934), 28.
2. Goeffrey Cocks, Psychotherapy in the Third Reich (Princeton, 1985), p. 88.
3. The works described here are to be found in George Grosz, The Face of the Ruling Class, Reckoning, and Ecce Homo.
4. Pois, Race and Race History, p. 169.
5. Ibid., p. 174.
6. Walter Laqueur, Weimar: A Cultural History (New York, 1974), p. 72.
7. Ibid., p. 45.
8. Kurt Tucholsky, Panter, Tiger & Co. (Hamburg, 1955), p. 91.
9. Pois, Race and Race History, pp. 189, 152.
10. Ibid., p. 165.
11. Pauley, From Prejudice to Persecution, p. 199.
12. Laqueur, Weimar: A Cultural History, p. 73.
13. Gay, Weimar Culture, p. 96.
14. Victor Farias, Heidegger and Nazism (Philadelphia, 1989), p. 118.
15. Werner Sombart, Die Juden und das Wirtschaftleben (Berlin, 1911), p. 329.
16. Laqueur, Weimar: A Cultural History, p. 81.

17: ORGANIZING THE NAZIS, 1924–1930

1. Alan Bullock, Hitler: A Study in Tyranny (New York, 1971), p. 63.
2. Carsten, Reichswehr and Politics, p. 203.
3. Joachim Fest, The Face of the Third Reich (New York, 1970), p. 25.

4. Ingo Mueller, *Hitler's Justice* (Cambridge, Mass., 1991), pp. 15, 16. I am greatly indebted to this excellent book.
5. Richard S. Hamilton, *Who Voted for Hitler?* (Princeton, 1982), pp. 520–521, 93.
6. Flood, *Hitler: The Path to Power*, p. 597.
7. *Ibid.*, p. 591.
8. Craig, *Germany, 1866–1945*, pp. 514–515.
9. Mosse, *Crisis of German Ideology*, p. 241.
10. John A. Leopold, *Alfred Hugenberg* (New Haven, 1977), p. 12.
11. Geoffrey Pridham, *Hitler's Rise to Power* (London, 1973), pp. 85–86.
12. Pauley, *From Prejudice to Persecution*, p. 202.

18: ANTI-SEMITISM AND THE NAZI VOTE

Epigram: NSDAP Bayerisches Hauptstaatarchive, Rehse Sammlung, F8.
1. Milan L. Hauner, "A German Racial Revolution?," *Journal of Contemporary History*, XIX (October 1984), 675.
2. Louis L. Snyder, *Encyclopedia of the Third Reich* (New York, 1989), p. 274.
3. Walther Darré, *Das Bauerntum als Lebensquell der Nordischen Rasse* (Munich, 1929), p. 264.
4. Timothy Alan Tilton, *Nazism, Neo-Nazism, and the Peasantry* (Bloomington, Ind., 1975), p. 16.
5. Thomas Childers, *The Nazi Voter: The Social Foundations of Fascism in Germany, 1919–1933* (Chapel Hill, 1983), p. 76.
6. Tilton, *Nazism, Neo-Nazism, and the Peasantry*, p. 64.
7. Heinrich Himmler, "Farmer Wake Up!," in Lane and Rupp, *Nazi Ideology Before 1933*, pp. 95ff.
8. Simon Taylor, *Prelude to Genocide* (New York, 1985), p. 47.
9. *Ibid.*, pp. 47–48.
10. Taylor, *Prelude to Genocide*, p. 62.
11. Himmler, "Farmer Wake Up!", p. 98.
12. Taylor, *Prelude to Genocide*, p. 47.
13. Werner Bruecker, *Die Tragik Ludendorffs* (Oldenburg, 1953), p. 107.
14. Hitler, *Mein Kampf*, p. 563.
15. *Ibid.*, p. 661.
16. Taylor, *Prelude to Genocide*, pp. 74, 65.
17. Jeremy Noakes, *The Nazi Party in Lower Saxony, 1921–1933* (New York, 1971), p. 105.
18. Childers, *Nazi Voter*, p. 68.
19. Taylor, *Prelude to Genocide*, pp. 78, 79, 81, 82.
20. *Ibid.*, p. 73.
21. *Ibid.*, p. 140.
22. *Ibid.*, p. 30.
23. *Ibid.*, pp. 40–41.
24. *Ibid.*, p. 83.
25. Mosse, *Crisis of German Ideology*, p. 262.
26. Noakes, *Nazi Party in Lower Saxony*, p. 102.
27. Taylor, *Prelude to Genocide*, p. 50.
28. *Ibid.*, p. 45.
29. Snyder, *Encyclopedia of the Third Reich*, p. 274.
30. Taylor, *Prelude to Genocide*, pp. 27–28.
31. Pridham, *Hitler's Rise to Power*, p. 195.
32. Taylor, *Prelude to Genocide*, p. 28.
33. Childers, *Nazi Voter*, p. 178.
34. *Ibid.*, p. 264.
35. Mosse, *Crisis of German Ideology*, pp. 242–243.
36. Childers, *Nazi Voter*, p. 265.
37. Taylor, *Prelude to Genocide*, p. 79.
38. NSDAP Bayerisches Hauptstaatarchive, Rehse Sammlung, F8, as reproduced in Taylor, *Prelude to Genocide*, pp. 221–222.

19: HITLER AND THE ELITES

Epigram: Peter D. Stachura, ed., *The Nazi Machtergreifung* (London, 1983), p. 23.

1. Michael H. Kater, *The Nazi Party: A Social Profile of Members and Leaders* (Cambridge, Mass., 1983), p. 237.
2. Leopold, *Alfred Hugenberg*, p. 82.
3. Louis P. Lochner, ed., *The Goebbels Diaries* (New York, 1948), p. 48.
4. Bullock, *Hitler*, p. 85.
5. Carsten, *Reichswehr in Politics*, p. 333.
6. Richard Hamilton, "Who Voted for Hitler?," *Central European History*, XVII, no. 1 (March 1984), 25.
7. Lane and Rupp, *Nazi Ideology Before 1933*, pp. 42, 121.
8. Turner, *German Big Business and the Rise of Hitler*.
9. Bullock, *Hitler*, p. 81.
10. Taylor, *Prelude to Genocide*, p. 90.
11. Turner, *German Big Business and the Rise of Hitler*, p. 189.
12. *Ibid.*, p. 190.
13. Kater, *Nazi Party*, pp. 65, 63.
14. Turner, *German Big Business and the Rise of Hitler*, pp. 191, 253.
15. Detlev J. K. Peukert, *Inside Nazi Germany: Conformity, Opposition, and Racism in Everyday Life* (New Haven, 1982), p. 96.
16. Taylor, *Prelude to Genocide*, pp. 95–96.
17. *Voelkische Beobachter*, March 24, 1931.
18. J. S. Conway, *The Nazi Persecution of the Churches, 1933–45* (New York, 1968), p. 9.
19. *Ibid.*, p. 411.
20. *Ibid.*, p. 11.
21. Hamilton, "Who Voted for Hitler?," pp. 25–26.
22. Robert N. Proctor, *Racial Hygiene: Medicine Under the Nazis* (Cambridge, Mass., and London, 1988), p. 27. I am much indebted to this fine study.
23. *Ibid.*, p. 25.
24. *Ibid.*, p. 48.
25. *Ibid.*, p. 27.
26. Benno Mueller-Hill, *Murderous Science: The Elimination of Jews, Gypsies and the Mentally Ill, Germany, 1933–1945* (Oxford, 1988), p. 9.
27. Mueller-Hill, *Murderous Science*, p. 28.
28. Proctor, *Racial Hygiene*, pp. 47, 48.
29. Bullock, *Hitler*, p. 99.
30. Hamilton, "Who Voted for Hitler?", p. 26.
31. Turner, *German Big Business and the Rise of Hitler*, p. 222.
32. Hamilton, *Who Voted for Hitler?*, p. 340.
33. Childers, *Nazi Voter*, p. 258.
34. Turner, *German Big Business and the Rise of Hitler*, p. 302.
35. Dirk Stegman, "Zum Verhaeltnis von Grossindustrie und Nationalsozialismus," *Archiv fuer Sozialgeschichte*, XIII (1973), 62, 64.
36. Siemens, Bosch, Schacht, Thyssen, Krupp Doc. PS 3901, Nuremberg Trials.
37. Dick Geary, "The Industrial Elite and the Nazis in the Weimar Republic," in Stachura, *Nazi Machtergreifung*, p. 94.
38. Hamilton, *Who Voted for Hitler?*, p. 413.
39. Carsten, *Reichswehr in Politics*, pp. 389, 390, 392.
40. John H. Conway, "National Socialism and the Churches During the Weimar Republic," in Stachura, *Nazi Machtergreifung*, p. 124.
41. Stachura, *Nazi Machtergreifung*, p. 5.

20: HITLER IN POWER

1. Mosse, *Crisis of German Ideology*, p. 247.
2. Andreas Dorpalen, *Hindenburg and the Weimar Republic* (Princeton, 1964), p. 470.
3. Carsten, *Reichswehr in Politics*, p. 397.

4. Mueller, *Hitler's Justice*, pp. xiii, 92, 95, 96.
5. *Ibid.*, pp. 94, 109.
6. Hilberg, *Destruction of the European Jews*, I, 38.
7. Karl A. Schleunes, *The Twisted Road to Auschwitz* (Urbana, Ill., 1970), p. 89.
8. Eberhard Jaeckel, *Hitler's World View* (Cambridge, Mass., 1972), p. 48.
9. Christopher R. Browning, *The Final Solution and the German Foreign Office* (New York and London, 1978), p. 13.
10. David Fisher and Anthony Read, *Kristallnacht: The Nazi Night of Terror* (New York, 1989), pp. 163–164.
11. Proctor, *Racial Hygiene*, p. 79.
12. *Ibid.*, pp. 104, 222.
13. Conway, *Nazi Persecution of the Churches*, p. 32.
14. Hermann Graml, Hans Mommsen, Hans-Joachim Reichhardt, and Ernst Wolf, *The German Resistance to Hitler* (Berkeley, 1970), p. 206.
15. Conway, *Nazi Persecution of the Churches*, p. 94.
16. Pridham, *Hitler's Rise to Power*, p. 170.
17. Hilberg, *Destruction of the European Jews*, I, 179.
18. Graml, et al., *German Resistance to Hitler*, p. 211.
19. Robert P. Ericksen, *Theologians Under Hitler* (New Haven, 1986), p. 55.
20. James Bentley, *Martin Niemoeller* (Oxford, 1984), p. 63.
21. Edwin Robertson, *The Shame and the Sacrifice: The Life and Martyrdom of Dietrich Bonhoeffer* (New York, 1988), p. 118.
22. *Reichsanzeiger*, no. 8, April 6, 1933.
23. *New York Times*, February 15, 1984.
24. *Jehovah's Witnesses: In the Divine Purpose*, International Bible Students Society (Brooklyn, 1972), p. 173.
25. Gunther Lewy, *The Catholic Church and Nazi Germany* (New York, 1965), pp. 78, 86.
26. *Ibid.*, p. 90.
27. *Ibid.*, pp. 275–277.
28. *L'Allemagne Nazie et le Genocide Juif* (Paris, 1985), p. 384.

21: TOWARD A RACIAL EMPIRE

Epigram: Nazi Party Program. Hitler, *Mein Kampf*, p. 652.
1. Lane and Rupp, *Nazi Ideology Before 1933*, p. 121.
2. *Ibid.*, p. 133.
3. Hitler, *Mein Kampf*, p. 655.

22: THE IDEOLOGY OF DEATH

Epigram: Tom Segev, *The Commandants of the Nazi Concentration Camps* (New York, 1987), p. 40.
Martin Gilbert, *The Holocaust: A History of the Jews of Europe During the Second World War* (New York, 1985), p. 171.
1. *Ibid.*, p. 87.
2. *Ibid.*, p. 106.
3. Richard Plant, *The Pink Triangle: The Nazi War Against Homosexuals* (New York, 1986), pp. 88–89.
4. *Ibid.*, p. 99.
5. *Ibid.*, p. 5.
6. Fisher and Read, *Kristallnacht*, p. 226.
7. Schleunes, *Twisted Road to Auschwitz*, p. 211.
8. J. B. Schechtman, *The Mufti and the Fuehrer* (New York, 1961), p. 308.
9. Pulzer, *Rise of Political Anti-Semitism in Germany and Austria*, p. 441.
10. Helen Fine, *Accounting for Genocide* (Chicago, 1979), p. 167.
11. Fisher and Read, *Kristallnacht*, p. 201.
12. Jaeckel, *Hitler's World View*, p. 48.

13. Fisher and Read, *Kristallnacht*, p. 145.
14. Edouard Calic, *Reinhard Heidrich* (New York, 1985), p. 133.
15. Gregory Gallagher, By *Trust Betrayed: Patients, Physicians, and the License to Kill in the Third Reich* (New York, 1990), p. 66.
16. Proctor, *Racial Hygiene*, p. 207.
17. Gallagher, By *Trust Betrayed*, p. 127.
18. Proctor, *Racial Hygiene*, p. 205.
19. Martin Gilbert, *Auschwitz and the Allies* (New York, 1981), p. 16.
20. Proctor, *Racial Hygiene*, p. 211.
21. Hilberg, *Destruction of the European Jews*, I, 222. My translation.
22. Proctor, *Racial Hygiene*, p. 199. Emphasis added.
23. Gilbert, *Holocaust*, p. 287.
24. Hilberg, *Destruction of the European Jews*, III, 1010ff.
25. Martin Gilbert, *The Second World War: A Complete History* (New York, 1989), pp. 687, 661, 663, 684.
26. Segev, *Commandants of the Nazi Concentration Camps*, p. 218.

23: COMPLICITIES

Epigram: Peter Hoffman, *The History of the German Resistance, 1933–1945* (Cambridge, Mass., 1977), p. 19.
1. Omer Bartov, *The Eastern Front, 1941–1945: German Troops and the Barbarization of Warfare* (New York, 1986), p. 74.
2. Hilberg, *Destruction of the European Jews*, I, 191.
3. Bartov, *Eastern Front*, p. 94.
4. *Ibid.*, p. 80.
5. Hilberg, *Destruction of the European Jews*, I, 304, 301.
6. Bartov, *Eastern Front*, p. 83.
7. Christopher Browning, *Fateful Months: Essays on the Emergence of the Final Solution* (New York, 1985), p. 48.
8. Bartov, *Eastern Front*, p. 94.
9. Simon Wiesenthal, *Justice Not Vengeance* (New York, 1989), p. 285.
10. Bartov, *Eastern Front*, p. 84.
11. *Ibid.*, p. 94.
12. *Ibid.*, p. 185.
13. Hilberg, *Destruction of the European Jews*, II, 687, 689.
14. Browning, *Final Solution and the German Foreign Office*, pp. 29, 37, 44.
15. *Ibid.*, p. 59.
16. *Ibid.*, p. 54.
17. Hilberg, *Destruction of the European Jews*, II, 715.
18. Browning, *Final Solution and the German Foreign Office*, p. 153.
19. Hilberg, *Destruction of the European Jews*, II, 739.
20. Browning, *Final Solution and the German Foreign Office*, p. 180.
21. Mueller, *Hitler's Justice*, p. 196.
22. *Ibid.*, pp. 142–143.
23. *Ibid.*, p. 196.
24. Benjamin B. Ferencz, *Less Than Slaves: Jewish Forced Labor and the Quest for Compensation* (Cambridge, Mass., 1979), p. 69.
25. Proctor, *Racial Hygiene*, p. 221.
26. Hilberg, *Destruction of the European Jews*, III, 930.
27. Ferencz, *Less Than Slaves*, p. 95.
28. Gallagher, By *Trust Betrayed*, pp. 294ff., 241.
29. Lewy, *Catholic Church and Nazi Germany*, pp. 277, 291–292.
30. *Ibid.*, p. 236.
31. Conway, *Nazi Persecution of the Churches*, photodocument, pp. 160–161.
32. Robertson, *Shame and the Sacrifice*, p. 261.
33. Ernst Helmreich, *The German Churches Under Hitler* (Detroit, 1979), p. 332.

34. Saul Friedlander, *Pius XII and the Third Reich: A Documentation* (New York, 1966), pp. 51–52.
35. Bruno Shatyn, *A Private War* (Detroit, 1986).
36. Friedlander, *Pius XII and the Third Reich*, pp. 119–121, 131, 145.
37. Leon Poliakov, "The Vatican and the Jewish Question," *Commentary*, November 1950, pp. 439–449.
38. Friedlander, *Pius XII and the Third Reich*, pp. 210, 237.
39. *Ibid.*, pp. 218, 222.
40. Proctor, *Racial Hygiene*, p. 131.
41. *Ibid.*, p. 209.
42. Gallagher, *By Trust Betrayed*, p. 250.
43. Proctor, *Racial Hygiene*, pp. 82, 213, 214.
44. Mueller-Hill, *Murderous Science*, pp. 12, 16.
45. Proctor, *Racial Hygiene*, pp. 210–211.
46. Mueller-Hill, *Murderous Science*, pp. 45ff.
47. *Ibid.*, p. 67.
48. Gilbert, *Second World War*, p. 299.
49. Poliakov, *Aryan Myth*, p. 298.
50. Proctor, *Racial Hygiene*, p. 211.
51. *Ibid.*, pp. 350, 220.
52. Mueller-Hill, *Murderous Science*, p. 80.

24: RESISTANCE, PUBLIC OPINION, KNOWLEDGE

Epigram: Gellately, *Gestapo and German Society*, p. 184.
1. Peukert, *Inside Nazi Germany*, p. 155.
2. *Ibid.*, p. 118.
3. Ian Kershaw, *Popular Opinion and Political Dissent in the Third Reich* (Oxford, 1983), p. 303.
4. Graml, et al., *German Resistance to Hitler*, pp. 80, 90.
5. *Ibid.*, p. 140.
6. *Ibid.*, p. 112.
7. *Ibid.*
8. Ernst Wolf, in Graml, et al., *German Resistance to Hitler*, p. 196.
9. Peter Hoffmann, *The History of the German Resistance, 1933–1945* (Boston, 1977), p. 189.
10. Mommsen, in Graml, et al., *German Resistance to Hitler*, p. 113.
11. Hoffmann, *History of the German Resistance*, p. 151.
12. *Ibid.*, p. 167.
13. *Ibid.*, p. 358.
14. Kershaw, *Popular Opinion and Political Dissent in the Third Reich*, p. 64.
15. *Ibid.*, pp. 201, 353.
16. *Ibid.*, p. 357.
17. *Ibid.*, p. 340.
18. Peukert, *Inside Nazi Germany*, p. 89.
19. Kershaw, *Popular Opinion and Political Dissent in the Third Reich*, p. 149.
20. *Ibid.*, p. 154.
21. Peukert, *Inside Nazi Germany*, p. 60.
22. Gellately, *Gestapo and German Society*, p. 34.
23. *Ibid.*, p. 184.
24. *Ibid.*, pp. 16, 206, 214, 207.
25. *Ibid.*, p. 124.
26. *Ibid.*, p. 125.
27. Fisher and Read, *Kristallnacht*, pp. 68–70.
28. Kershaw, *Popular Opinion and Political Dissent in the Third Reich*, p. 269.
29. *Ibid.*, p. 268.
30. *Ibid.*, pp. 176–177.

31. Pauley, *From Prejudice to Persecution*, pp. 283, 299.
32. *The Week in Germany*, March 3, 1992; Nathan Stoltzfuss, "Dissent in Nazi Germany," *Atlantic Monthly*, September 1992.
33. Gilbert, *Holocaust*, p. 67.
34. Kershaw, *Popular Opinion and Political Dissent in the Third Reich*, p. 371.
35. Jaeckel, *Hitler's World View*, pp. 48, 57.
36. Sarah Gordon, *Hitler, Germans, and the Jewish Question* (Princeton, 1984), p. 130.
37. Gilbert, *Holocaust*, p. 285.
38. Hilberg, *Destruction of the European Jews*, II, 407.
39. Mueller-Hill, *Murderous Science*, p. 47.
40. Arno J. Mayer, *Why Did the Heavens Not Darken* (New York, 1988), pp. 242–243.
41. Haskel Lookstein, *Were We Our Brothers' Keepers?* (New York, 1985), p. 107.
42. Hilberg, *Destruction of the European Jews*, III, 932.
43. Browning, *Final Solution and the German Foreign Office*, p. 84.
44. Ernst Klee, Willi Dressen, and Volker Riess, eds., *The Good Old Days: The Holocaust as Seen by Its Perpetrators and Bystanders* (New York, 1992).
45. Christopher Browning, *Ordinary Men: Police Battalion 101 and the Final Solution in Poland* (New York, 1992), p. 170.
46. Browning, *Fateful Months*, p. 83.
47. Gilbert, *The Second World War* (New York, 1989), p. 249.
48. Browning, *Fateful Months*, p. 83.
49. Gordon A. Craig, "The Way to the Wall," *New York Review of Books*, June 28, 1990, p. 30.
50. Gilbert, *Holocaust*, p. 591.
51. Lewy, *Catholic Church and Nazi Germany*, pp. 291–292.
52. Kershaw, *Popular Opinion and Political Dissent in the Third Reich*, p. 369.

25: AFTERMATH: JUDGMENT AND INNOCENCE

Epigram: Eichmann trial transcript, 1962.
1. Snyder, *Encyclopedia of the Third Reich*, p. 190.
2. Mueller interview, New York Times Book Review, April 28, 1991, p. 3.
3. Mueller, *Hitler's Justice*, pp. 240–241.
4. *Ibid.*, pp. 213–214, 276.
5. *Ibid.*, p. 277.
6. *Ibid.*, p. 283.
7. Gilbert, *Second World War*, pp. 351–352.
8. Mueller, *Hitler's Justice*, pp. 254, 250–255.
9. *Ibid.*, pp. 255, 257.
10. *Ibid.*, pp. 256, 257.
11. *Ibid.*, p. 284.
12. *Ibid.*, p. 271.
13. *Ibid.*, p. 207.
14. Adolf Diament, in Gellately, *Gestapo and German Society*, p. 262.
15. Mueller, *Hitler's Justice*, pp. 251, 275.
16. *Ibid.*, p. 287.
17. Pauley, *From Prejudice to Persecution*, pp. 307ff.
18. Hilberg, *Destruction of the European Jews*, III, 1001ff.
19. Daniel Goldhagen, "Treblinka's Other Monster," *New York Times*, August 21, 1993, p. 19.
20. Alois Hudal, as told by Erhard Dabringhaus, American agent who "handled" Klaus Barbie. See Max Ophuls's film *Hotel Terminus*.
21. Ferencz, *Less Than Slaves*, p. 34.
22. *Ibid.*, p. 155.
23. *New York Times*, January 1, 1986, p. 3.
24. Proctor, *Racial Hygiene*, p. 303.
25. Mueller-Hill, *Murderous Science*, p. 83.

26. Charles Lane, "The Tainted Sources of 'The Bell Curve,'" *New York Review of Books*, December 1, 1994.
27. Bentley, *Niemoeller*, p. 177.
28. Jennifer Leaning and H. Jack Geiger, "German Doctors and Their Secrets." *New York Times*, February 2, 1993, Op-ed page.
29. Gordon, *Hitler, Germans, and the Jewish Question*, p. 199; Kershaw, *Popular Opinion and Political Dissent in the Third Reich*, p. 370.
30. Pauley, *From Prejudice to Persecution*, pp. 301–303.
31. Mueller-Hill, *Murderous Science*, p. 104.
32. Pulzer, *Rise of Political Anti-Semitism in Germany and Austria*, p. 133.
33. Herf, *Reactionary Modernism*, p. 149.

INDEX

A NOTE ON THE AUTHOR

John Weiss is professor of history at Lehman College and the Graduate Center of the City University of New York. He was born in Dearborn, Michigan, and grew up in Detroit. After serving in the navy in the Pacific theatre during World War II, he studied at Wayne State University and Columbia University, as well as in Austria and Germany. A former Fulbright scholar, he has written widely on European anti-Semitism and fascism. His other books include *The Fascist Tradition*, *Nazis and Fascists in Europe*, and *Conservatism in Europe, 1770–1945*.